Seventh Edition

A Short History of Western Civilization

Volume 2: Since 1600

John B. Harrison
Late Professor Emeritus of History
Michigan State University

Richard E. Sullivan
Michigan State University

Dennis Sherman
John Jay College of Criminal Justice
City University of New York

McGraw-Hill Publishing Company

New York   St. Louis   San Francisco   Auckland   Bogotá   Caracas   Hamburg
Lisbon   London   Madrid   Mexico   Milan   Montreal   New Delhi
Oklahoma City   Paris   San Juan   São Paulo   Singapore   Sydney   Tokyo   Toronto

to Mary, Vivian, and Pat

The present overwhelms our forgotten selves;
but we are what we were,
with only a frosting of changes
—D.S.

A Short History of Western Civilization
Vol II: Since 1600

1 2 3 4 5 6 7 8 9 0   RMT RMT   8 9 4 3 2 1 0 9

ISBN 0-07-557088-2

This book was set in Palatino by Ruttle Shaw & Wetherill, Inc.
The editors were Christopher J. Rogers and Eleanor Castellano;
the designer was Wanda Siedlecka.
Rand McNally and Company was printer and binder.

Credits for Part Opening Photos
Part Eight: Alinari/Art Resource; *Part Nine:* Historical Pictures Service; *Part Ten:* The Granger Collection; *Part Eleven:* Don McCullin/Magnum; *Part Twelve:* NASA.

Cover Photo Credit
"Turner, Joseph Mallord William (1775–1851). *Rain, Steam and Speed, the Great Western Railway.* National Gallery, London/Bridgeman/Art Resource."

The maps were executed by Jean Paul Tremblay, Francis & Shaw, Inc., Dyno Lowenstein, and Vantage Art, Inc.

Library of Congress Cataloging-in-Publication Data

Harrison, John Baugham.
   A short history of Western civilization / John B. Harrison,
Richard E. Sullivan, Dennis Sherman. — 7th ed.
      p.   cm.
   Includes bibliographies and index.
   Contents: v. 1. To 1776 — v. 2. Since 1600.
   ISBN 0-07-557084-X — ISBN 0-07-557088-2
   1. Civilization, Occidental—History.   I. Sullivan, Richard
Eugene, (date).   II. Sherman, Dennis.   III. Title
CB245.H32   1990
909'.09821—dc20   89-35195

ABOUT THE AUTHORS

John B. Harrison was born in Lawrenceville, Virginia, and grew up in Rich Square, North Carolina. He received his B.A. and M.A. at the University of North Carolina, and his Ph.D. at the University of Wisconsin. He also studied at the Sorbonne. He taught history at Lees Junior College, Jackson, Kentucky, the University of Wisconsin extension, Ohio Northern University, and Michigan State University where he was Professor Emeritus of History. He was Visiting Professor at the University of North Carolina, 1963–1964. Professor Harrison was a member of the American Historical Association and the Society for French Historical Studies. During seven trips to Europe he visited twenty-one countries. He has also traveled in the Far and the Middle East, Africa, and Latin America. He is the author of *This Age of Global Strife* (1952), and of a number of articles and book reviews.

Richard E. Sullivan was born and raised near Doniphan, Nebraska. He received a B.A. degree from the University of Nebraska in 1942, and an M.A. degree and a Ph.D. degree from the University of Illinois in 1947 and 1949 respectively. His doctorate was earned in the field of medieval history. He has taught history at Northeast Missouri State Teachers' College (1949–1954) and at Michigan State University (1954 until his retirement in 1989). While at Michigan State University he has served as chairman of the Department of History (1967–1970), Dean of the College of Arts and Letters (1970–1979), and Associate Provost (1984–1987). Professor Sullivan held a Fulbright Research Fellowship and a John Simon Guggenheim Fellowship to Belgium in 1961–1962. He is the author of *Coronation of Charlemagne* (1959), *Heirs of the Roman Empire* (1960), and *Aix-la-Chapelle in the Age of Charlemagne* (1963). His articles have appeared in many scholarly journals.

Dennis Sherman is Professor of History at John Jay College of Criminal Justice, the City University of New York. He received his B.A. (1962) and J.D. (1965) from the University of California at Berkeley and his Ph.D. (1970) from the University of Michigan. He was Visiting Professor at the University of Paris (1978–1979, and 1985). He received the Ford Foundation Prize Fellowship (1968–1969, 1969–1970), a fellowship from the Council for Research on Economic History (1971–1972), and fellowships from the National Endowment for the Humanities (1973–1976). His publications include *Western Civilization: Images and Interpretations* (1987), a series of introductions in the Garland Library of War and Peace, and several articles and reviews on nineteenth-century French economic and social history in American and European journals.

CONTENTS

Preface   xi

History and the Historian   xiii

Introduction   xvii

PART EIGHT
THE AGE OF ROYAL
ABSOLUTISM, SEVENTEENTH
AND EIGHTEENTH CENTURIES   417

32/ The Dominance of France: The
Age of Louis XIV   419
1. The Rise of France Under Henry IV,
   Richelieu, and Mazarin   420
2. Louis XIV and His Government   422
3. The King and His Court: Versailles   422
4. Colbert and the French Economy   424
5. Absolutism and Religion   424
6. Louis XIV's Wars of Aggression   425
7. The Decline of French Absolutism   426
   Suggested Reading   428

33/ The Challenge to Absolutism:
England and the Dutch Netherlands   429
1. Early Stuart Absolutism   430
2. English Civil War, Commonwealth, and
   Protectorate (1642–1660)   432
3. The English Restoration (1660–1688)   434
4. England's Glorious Revolution and Its
   Consequences   435
5. The Dutch Netherlands   437
   Suggested Reading   440

34/ Eastern European and the Rise of
Prussia and Russia   441
1. The Early Hohenzollerns   442
2. Competition with the Austrian Hapsburgs

and the Emergence of Prussia as a Great
   Power   444
3. Russia Before Peter the Great   445
4. Russia Under Peter the Great,
   1689–1725   447
5. Russia Under Catherine the Great,
   1762–1796   448
6. The Disappearance of Poland and the
   Decline of Sweden and the Ottoman
   Empire   448
   Suggested Reading   451

35/ Overseas Colonization and
Competition for Empire   452
1. The New World: The English, the
   French, and the Dutch   453
2. European Penetration of the Far East and
   Africa   455
3. The Impact of European Expansion: The
   Native Americans   455
4. The Impact of European Expansion: The
   Far East   457
5. The Impact of European Expansion:
   Sub-Saharan Africa   459
6. The Struggle for Overseas Empire   460
   Suggested Reading   463

36/ Society, Faith, and Culture in the
Seventeenth and Eighteenth Centuries   464
1. Society   465
2. Faith: The Growth of Pietism   469
3. Culture   470
   Suggested Reading   476

37/ The Scientific Revolution   477
1. Causes and Spread   478
2. Astronomy and Physics: From
   Copernicus to Newton   479
3. Scientific Methodology   482
4. Other Disciplines   483
   Suggested Reading   485

38/ The Enlightenment   **486**
1. Enlightenment Concepts   487
2. The *Philosophes*   488
3. Women and the Social Context   491
4. Enlightment and Religion   491
5. Political and Economic Aspects of the Enlightenment   491
6. Enlightened Despotism   493
7. Conclusion   494
    Suggested Reading   494
    Retrospect   494

PART NINE
THE AGE OF REVOLUTIONS,
1776–1850   **497**

39/ The American Revolution   **499**
1. American Colonial Society   500
2. The American Revolution: From Salutary Neglect to War   502
3. The American Revolution and the Democratization of American Society   504
4. Launching the New Nation   506
    Suggested Reading   508

40/ The French Revolution, 1789–1799   **510**
1. The Last Days of the Old Regime in France   511
2. The Breakdown of the Old Regime   512
3. The Triumph of the Third Estate   513
4. Making France a Constitutional Monarchy   515
5. Foreign War and the Failure of the Moderate Regime   516
6. The Triumph of the Radicals and the Reign of Terror   518
7. Reaction and the Rise of Napoleon   521
    Suggested Reading   521

41/ The Era of Napoleon, 1799–1815   **523**
1. Napoleon's Rise to Power   524
2. The Consulate—Peace and Reform, 1799–1804   524
3. The Empire—War and Conquest   526
4. Decline and Fall of the Empire   528
5. Overseas Effects: Latin America   530

6. Significance of the French Revolution and Napoleon   530
    Suggested Reading   531

42/ Restoration and Reaction, 1815–1830   **533**
1. The Congress of Vienna (1814–1815)   534
2. The Concert of Europe   536
3. The Bourbon Restoration in France   538
4. Restoration and Repression in the Germanies   539
5. Restoration and Repression in Italy   540
6. Conservatism in Great Britain   540
7. Reaction and Repression in Russia   542
8. Conservatism and the Challenge of Liberalism   542
    Suggested Reading   543

43/ Liberalism and Revolution, 1830–1850   **544**
1. General Nature of Nineteenth-Century Liberalism   545
2. Political and Social Reform in Great Britain   547
3. Liberal Revolutions in Belgium and France   548
4. The Revolution of 1848 in France   550
5. The Revolution of 1848 in Central Europe   550
6. Revolution in Italy   552
7. An Assessment   553
    Suggested Reading   554

44/ The Industrial Revolution   **555**
1. The Course of the Industrial Revolution   556
2. Technology and Transportation   556
3. The Factory System   558
4. Social Changes   558
5. New Economic and Social Thought   563
6. The Arrival of Industrial Society   566
    Suggested Reading   567

45/ Romanticism in Philosophy, Literature, and the Arts   **568**
1. The Nature of Romanticism   569
2. The Philosophy of Idealism   569
3. Romantic Literature   570

4. The Romantic Spirit in the Arts 573
    Suggested Reading 576
    Retrospect 576

PART TEN
NATIONALISM AND
INDUSTRIALIZATION,
1850–1914 579

46/ Nationalism and the Nation-State,
1850–1871 581
1. The Nature of Nationalism 582
2. The Second Empire of Napoleon III 582
3. Cavour and the Making of Italian Unity 585
4. German Unification 587
    Suggested Reading 593

47/ Politics in the Age of Progress,
1871–1914 594
1. Western Europe: The Spread and Reform
    of Democratic Institutions 595
2. Eastern Europe: Conservatism,
    Militarism, and Nationalism 599
    Suggested Reading 604

48/ Democracy, Expansion, Civil War,
and Reform in the United States,
1800–1920 606
1. Democracy and Geographic Expansion,
    1800–1861 607
2. Slavery, Civil War, and Reconstruction,
    1861–1877 609
3. Industrialization and Urbanization,
    1865–1901 611
4. Reform and Progressivism, 1901–1920 613
    Suggested Reading 613

49/ Imperialism 615
1. Causes for the New Imperialism 616
2. The Exploitation and Awakening of
    China 618
3. The Emergence of Japan 620
4. Competition for the Strategic Near and
    Middle East 622
5. The Scramble for Africa 623
6. The British Empire 626

7. The Legacy of Imperialism 627
    Suggested Reading 627

50/ Industrial Society, Social Classes,
and Women 629
1. The Second Industrial Revolution 630
2. The Rise of Working-Class Organizations
    and Ideologies 633
3. The Growth and Movement of
    Population 634
4. Social Classes 636
5. Women's Roles and Experiences 638
    Suggested Reading 639

51/ Science and the Challenge to
Christianity 641
1. The Physical, Biological, and Medical
    Sciences 642
2. The Rise of Social Science 644
3. Challenges to Christianity 645
4. The Christian Response 647
    Suggested Reading 649

52/ Thought and Culture in an Age of
Nationalism and Industrialization 650
1. Popular Education and Journalism 651
2. Currents of Thought: Nationalism and
    Disenchantment 652
3. Realistic Literature 653
4. Impressionist and Modern Painting and
    Sculpture 655
5. Functional Architecture 657
6. Music Old and New 658
    Suggested Reading 658
    Retrospect 659

PART ELEVEN
THE ERA OF THE TWO WORLD
WARS, 1914–1945 661

53/ World War I, 1914–1918 662
1. Origins of the War 663
2. The Fatal Explosion 665
3. Germany's Near Triumph 665
4. The Home Front 666

5. The Entry of the United States and the
   Victory of the Allies — 667
6. The Peace Settlement — 669
7. The Effects of World War I and the Peace
   Settlement — 672
   Suggested Reading — 674

54/ Revolution and Communism in Russia — 675
1. The Russian Revolution of 1917 — 676
2. The Rise of the Bolsheviks — 677
3. The Bolsheviks in Power, 1917–1927 — 677
4. The Five-Year Plans and the Purges — 680
5. Totalitarian Control — 681
6. The Soviet Union and the World — 684
   Suggested Reading — 685

55/ The Rise of Fascism and Authoritarianism — 686
1. Totalitarianism, Fascism, and
   Authoritarianism — 687
2. Mussolini Creates the First Fascist State — 687
3. The Weimar Republic in Germany — 689
4. The Rise of Hitler and National Socialism — 690
5. The Triumph of Hitler — 691
6. Nazi Germany — 694
7. Authoritarian Regimes in Eastern and
   Southern Europe — 695
8. The Triumph of Authoritarianism in
   Japan — 695
   Suggested Reading — 697

56/ Paralysis of the Democratic West — 698
1. Challenges of the 1920s and 1930s — 699
2. The Harassed British Empire — 699
3. Frustrated France — 700
4. Isolationism, Boom, and Bust in the
   United States — 701
5. The Road to War — 703
   Suggested Reading — 707

57/ World War II, 1939–1945 — 708
1. Two Years of Axis Triumph — 709
2. The Nazi Empire — 712
3. The Entry of the United States into the
   War — 712

4. Climax and Turning Point of the War,
   June–August 1942 — 715
5. Victory — 716
   Suggested Reading — 720
   Retrospect — 720

PART TWELVE
GLOBAL INTERDEPENDENCE IN THE CONTEMPORARY WORLD, 1945–PRESENT — 723

58/ The Recovery of Europe and the Superpowers, 1945–Present — 725
1. The Settlement and the Cold War — 726
2. Revival of a Divided Europe and the
   West — 732
3. Integration and International
   Organizations — 742
   Suggested Reading — 743

59/ Decolonization and the Non-Western World, 1945–Present — 744
1. Japan Between East and West — 745
2. The Rise of Communist China — 746
3. The Korean War — 750
4. The Revolt of Southern Asia — 751
5. The Embattled Middle East — 754
6. The Emancipation of Africa — 757
7. Latin America — 760
   Suggested Reading — 763

60/ Culture and Society in the Twentieth Century — 764
1. Western Society in the Twentieth Century — 765
2. Religion and Theology in the Twentieth
   Century — 770
3. Twentieth-Century Science — 771
4. Twentieth-Century Culture — 774
5. Problems of the Present and Future — 779
   Suggested Reading — 781
   Retrospect — 782

Where Historians Disagree
The Origins of the French Revolution — 517
Who Was Napoleon? — 529

The New Imperialism   617
Causes for World War I   673
What Caused Nazism?   693

Maps

Map 32.1 The Growth of France Under
          Louis XIV   427
Map 33.1 The United Provinces, 1609   438
Map 34.1 The Growth of Prussia, 1614–
          1807   443
Map 34.2 The Growth of Russia in the West   446
Map 34.3 Eastern Europe, Sixteenth–
          Eighteenth Centuries   450
Map 35.1 Overseas Possessions, 1763   456
Map 39.1 Revolutionary War Campaigns   505
Map 41.1 Europe, 1810   527
Map 42.1 Europe, 1815   537
Map 43.1 European Revolts, 1820–1831
          and 1848–1849   546

Map 46.1 The Unification of Italy   588
Map 46.2 The Unification of Germany   589
Map 47.1 Language Groups, Austria-
          Hungary   603
Map 48.1 Territorial Expansion of the
          United States, 1783–1853   608
Map 49.1 Imperialism in Asia, 1840–1914   618
Map 49.2 Imperialism in Africa, 1914   624
Map 53.1 World War I   664
Map 53.2 Europe, 1923   670
Map 57.1 Europe, 1942   714
Map 57.2 The Pacific War   717
Map 58.1 Europe During the Cold War   729
Map 59.1 Asia, 1989   748
Map 59.2 Africa, 1989   755
Map 59.3 Africa, 1989   758
Map 59.4 Latin America, 1989   761
Index   783

PREFACE

In this seventh edition of A SHORT HISTORY OF WESTERN CIVILIZATION, we have attempted to achieve the right mix of continuity and change. Those features that made the sixth and previous editions so successful have been retained. We have kept our account brief enough so it offers readers a realistic opportunity to absorb a meaningful overview of the essentials of the history of Western civilization. The scope of the book is not limited to European history; brief treatments of other parts of the world, such as the United States, and non-Western civilizations as they have come to interact with the Western world, are included to put Western civilization into a broader context. The book continues to be organized into sixty chapters, a structure that fits well with most academic calendars. Introductory and retrospective essays at the beginning and the end of each of the twelve units of the book provide a broad summarizing perspective on major historical eras. The interpretative essays featuring points on which historians disagree are designed to encourage readers to develop a healthy skepticism toward accepted generalizations about the past and to learn to ask questions about the meaning of historical investigation. The large number of maps and illustrations highlight and complement the written text. The suggested reading lists offer alternatives for deeper study of topics covered in each chapter. The instructor's manual is a tool available to assist in making full use of this book.

Several important changes have been made in this edition to improve the quality and appeal of the book. There has been an additional infusion of social history and women's history into the text, continuing the changes already made in this direction in the sixth edition. The addition of this material reflects a growing consensus in modern scholarship that such matters need greater attention in order to portray past human experience fully and accurately. Parts of the book have been reorganized, particularly those chapters covering the early modern and modern eras. There have been extensive revisions of the text to include the most recent historical scholarship and, in some cases, new sections have been written. Sixteen pages of color plates have been added, and a large number of illustrations are new to this edition. Most of the maps have been revised and clarified. Five additional "Where Historians Disagree" essays have been added. A new introductory essay on historiography has been written for this edition. The suggested readings have been completely revised and updated.

As in previous editions, our goal is to produce a high-quality, clearly written, useful, and flexible account of Western civilization. We are indebted to numerous teachers and students who have aided us in this effort. We hope this book can serve as the basis for an effective survey of the history of Western civilization, a subject that remains essential for any understanding of who we are and what of significance is happening in the present.

We would like to thank the following reviewers for their many helpful comments and suggestions: Richard L. Bates, Villanova University; Miriam J. Levy, University of Hartford; and David C. Riede, The University of Akron.

RICHARD E. SULLIVAN
DENNIS SHERMAN

HISTORY AND THE HISTORIAN

As our readers undertake to expand their knowledge and understanding of the past, we ask them to reflect for a moment on what history is and on how the historian works. These are perplexing questions. At the heart of the problem is the fact that history has a dual meaning. On the one hand, history is everything that has happened in the past: all that an almost infinite number of humans beings did and thought over the millions of years of human existence. On the other hand, history is the reconstruction of these already completed activities and thoughts undertaken by explorers—called historians—who can only be outsiders trying to discover what happened, to explain why something occurred as it did, and to ascertain why such occurrences are in some way meaningful. The gap between what happened in the past and what historians are able to discover about what actually occurred is immense. Our readers can perhaps sense this gap by comparing all the things that must have happened to each of them with what they can accurately reconstruct about all the events of their own lives. As a consequence of the distance between the two meanings of history, the examination of the past goes on continually, and the reconstruction constantly changes as explorers of the past discover more about what happened and as they change their interpretations of why and how humans acted and thought as they did in the past.

There is no law that dictates that the limitless past should be explored, described, and understood. But people continue to find that exercise irresistible. Many have found and still find the past inherently interesting, just as is gazing at stars or watching birds. Others have been and still are convinced that learning about the past has an important social function. It can inform us about who and what we are as human beings. It can shed light on the contemporary situation, either by providing an understanding of how things came to be what they are or by supplying analogies that help us comprehend our situation and formulate solutions to issues that face our society. Societies have especially prized history as an instrument for socializing their members (particularly the young), that is, for teaching them how to behave and to think in ways that are appropriate to their cultural environment. In writing this book, we have assumed that both of these perspectives are equally valid. We firmly believe that gaining knowledge and insight into the past not only is interesting but also is constructively useful to the collective well-being of any society.

In their explorations of the past historians differ in many ways, but most agree that there is a common, basic methodology suited to the task facing them, that is, reconstructing the past. Fundamental to that methodology is the formulation by the historian of a question or a hypothesis about what happened in the past. Obviously, the range of such questions and hypotheses is infinite; as a consequence, historical studies are richly and unpredictably varied. In many ways the vitality of historical studies depends on the imagination and the ingenuity of historians in formulating the problems they wish to study. Once having defined a "subject," the historian starts searching for sources that will provide information about that subject. Of crucial importance are what historians call primary sources, which are surviving pieces of evidence produced by human beings who were directly involved in the activity under investigation or by those in a position to know what happened. Primary sources exist in many forms. Most important are written documents of a variety of kinds in which observers of past events recorded what happened. But other kinds of primary sources can help the historian find out what happened, including buildings, art works, maps, pottery, tools, clothing, and oral traditions. Primary documents do not necessarily speak to the historian in clear and unmistakable terms. Historians must apply critical techniques to them in order to evaluate them and to extract information from them. That criticism can be external, aimed at such things as uncovering forgeries and errors; or it can be internal, aimed at resolving such matters as the motives that moved someone to produce the source or the meaning intended by the creator. In addition to primary sources, historians must also take into account what are called secondary sources. They are the works of other historians and scholars who have examined the same general subject and the same segment of time. Secondary sources must also be critically evaluated.

When historians have completed their search for sources and have extracted from them whatever information they can relative to the question or hypothesis with which they began, they then must present in comprehensible form the results of their research. This is a formidable task. In oversimplified terms it involves a series of choices: what sources to emphasize; how those sources relate to the problem under investigation; what data is not relevant; how to organize information in order to convey a meaningful explanation of what happened; and what literary devices to use in order to permit others to understand what happened in the past. This process can never be totally objective, for historians inevitably decide these issues in terms of their own perspective and their own values about the human condition. As a consequence, many prefer to call the reconstruction of the past an art rather than a science.

Although it is impossible to provide a neat formulation of how history is finally presented, in a rough way historians tend to reflect one of two perspectives in their treatment of the past. Some, representing a humanistic orientation, see the past in terms of unique actions and events that are studied for their intrinsic value and for the insights they provide about the human situation in a particular historical setting. These historians tend to present the past in narrative form, telling a story that unfolds in a chronological order with each succeeding episode somehow related to and conditioned by what went before. Others, reflecting a social science orientation, look for patterns in human thought and behavior over time. They tend to focus on repetitive commonalities rather than uniqueness, on comparisons rather than chronology, and on the universal relevance of the past rather than the unique, nonrepetitive nature of the past's specific episodes. These historians tend to write history in an analytic style, focusing on explanations, causes, and relationships. In this book, both perspectives will be used.

Given the vastness and the complexity of the past, historians cannot deal with all of history at once. To meet this problem, they have adopted several conventions that permit more effective and meaningful reconstruction. One means is to divide the past into periods, each of which has common features allowing it to be treated as an entity. An example of such a periodization scheme is the one applied to the history of Western civilization. The six-thousand-year span involved in that history is typically divided into four periods: the ancient period; the Middle Ages; the early modern period; and the modern period. As will be illustrated in this book, these larger periods are divided into subperiods. Historians often disagree on periodization schemes, and the boundaries between periods shift considerably. A second way to break up history into manageable segments is to focus attention on topics; sometimes these topics are broad, such as the Reformation, and sometimes they are narrow, such as the consequences of World War I. A third way of segmenting the past is to focus on geographical areas. In this book the area treated is extensive: In geographical terms Western civilization embraces what is today Europe, the Mediterranean basin where Western civilization originated, those areas of the world where offshoots of Western civilization have been established, and areas where there existed non-Western civilizations that were significantly affected by the Western world. Historians often focus on smaller areas: nations, regions or cities. The choice made by historians about how to break up the entire past into manageable units has an important bearing on the way the past is treated.

Historical research and writing are decisively affected by the judgments made by historians as to what aspect of human activity is most important in shaping and explaining the collective destinies of past societies. For example, some argue that political factors are crucial in forming societies, while others insist that economic conditions are decisive. Such formulations have produced several widely recognized categories of history: political history, economic history, social history, intellectual history, religious history, and cultural history. Each of these categories produces its unique version of the past and its unique manner of explaining the historical process. Such categorization also invites some historians to undertake a synthesis that will produce a version of the past embracing all aspects of human activity. The effort to synthesize has played an important part in the writing of this book.

Historians constitute a scholarly community in which knowledge, interpretations, interests, and concepts are shared. As a result, schools of historical thought develop, usually derived from shared assumptions about the fundamental characteristics of human development. An example is one of the best-known schools of thought in the twentieth century, the Marxist school. Proponents of this school argue that modes of economic producton are the determinant force in historical development. Each mode of production serves as a dynamic force creating its own unique political, social, religious, and cultural structures. And each contains within it conflicting class interests that provide the impetus for change and that determine the direction of change. Such schools encourage a collective approach to the past guided by a shared angle of attack and by a common mode of interpretation. They also tend to produce generalized explanations of the past. The constraints implicit in almost any school of historical thought cause most historians to withhold commitment to a particular school. But the existence of such schools often plays a role in shaping the way uncommitted historians approach major historical developments. In this book an effort has been made to represent various interpretations and to emphasize those that seem most useful in explaining a particular situation in the past.

Over the generations there have been numerous changes in what is most challenging both to historians and to their audiences. In recent years three broad developments have been particularly influential. Efforts have been made to integrate some of the results of these developments into this text.

First, there has been a broadening and growing importance of social history. Social historians increasingly emphasize looking at the past "from the bottom up" by studying the everyday experiences and attitudes of "ordinary" people or sub-ordinated groups rather than concentrating on political leaders, elite groups, and great thinkers. To recount the history of these heretofore "silent" people and to assess its significance, social historians have had to ask new questions and to make innovative use of sources often overlooked by traditional historians, such as parish registers, gravestone inscriptions, police reports, manorial records, folk tales, and popular art. Their efforts have greatly enriched our knowledge and understanding of the past in its entirety.

The second development is often termed "the new history" (although, like many elements of social history, its roots go back several decades). The new history has been shaped by the methods and the theoretical constructs formulated by social scientists. For example, historians have applied to the past the methods and the findings of demographers to expand knowledge of changes in population size, age groups, birth rates, age of marriage, fertility rates, family size, and death rates. Other historians have used the methods and findings of modern psychology to expand their understanding of the past. Psychohistorians emphasize emotional factors in explaining individual and group behavior in all kinds of historical situations, including such often-overlooked topics as child rearing, family relations, charismatic leadership, and death. Many historians practicing the new history rely on comparative and quantitative analysis to support their conclusions. Increasingly this approach involves the use of computers and statistical analysis of data pertaining to such things as voting patterns, price fluctuations, and population changes.

A third development has been the growing interest in women's history. Traditionally history has been written from the male perspective and has focused primarily on the thoughts and behavior of men. Women's history attempts to correct this neglect of women in history and the distortions that inevitably result. It focuses on women's experiences and on the roles women played in a large number and variety of historical developments. It also tries to alert us to gender bias in the way historical questions are posed, evidence is evaluated, and history is written.

Perhaps all of these considerations will suggest what is most important: The writing of history involves numerous choices, judgments, and compromises. The history one studies or writes depends on what questions are posed. Historians usually want to know more than only what happened, more than only the facts. They want to know how something of importance happened, why it happened, and why it is significant. They must create some reasoned order out of the chaos of past acts and thoughts. All of these considerations shape how they use historical facts and determine what they make of those facts. It may be true that history defined as all that has happened over the ages is a closed book in which nothing changes. But history defined as reconstructing that past is always in the process of change. Not only are new events happening every day and forgotten events of the past constantly being discovered, but the way we look at and interpret the past also changes as our interests, perspectives, and interpretative modes change. In this book, we have attempted to reflect this dynamic quality of history by making revisions that reflect our changing views and those of our colleagues engaged in exploring the past.

INTRODUCTION

The roots of modern Western civilization were put down long ago, in about 4000 B.C., in the remote river valleys of the Near East. They then spread over an ever-enlarging area, eventually reaching throughout Europe. A brief overview of that background may be helpful in providing a context for the history of Western civilization since the seventeenth century.

THE ANCIENT NEAR EAST, 4000–300 B.C.

During long ages prior to 4000 B.C., the human species slowly evolved the basic cultural patterns that prepared it to master the unique environment of two Near Eastern river valley systems. About 4000 B.C. some of these prehistoric groups, having already perfected the basic techniques of agriculture, learned how to control the floodwaters of the Tigris-Euphrates and the Nile rivers, by means of complex irrigation systems, so as to make full use of the rich valley soil. This involved not only great technical and engineering feats but also, more importantly, the organization of large numbers of people into institutional patterns that promoted planning, disciplined cooperation, and the specialization of labor. It was this complex organization that prompted the leap forward to higher civilization. In both Mesopotamia and Egypt, the focal points of the new order were urban centers where dwelt divinely sanctioned authority figures, the Mesopotamian priest-kings and the Egyptian pharaohs. They wielded the power required to form and sustain large-scale political and economic organizations. In order to exercise absolute power over their subjects, these rulers developed highly sophisticated institutions: bureaucracies, armies, systems of taxation, uniform law codes, courts, priesthoods, and so on. Many of these institutions and techniques served to direct agricultural labor, producing the vast wealth on which

the evolving civilization was to rest. In addition, the rulers organized trade and manufacturing, thus further enriching their economies and material lives.

Having achieved considerable prosperity, the urban centers of Mesopotamia and Egypt became focal points of intensive cultural activity. In both river valley civilizations, writing developed to serve not only the practical ends of government and commerce but also the intellectual aim of expressing ideas. And this cultural activity was shaped mainly by religion—by a belief in powerful nature deities that were thought to control human destiny. In order to praise and please them, huge temples were constructed and elaborately decorated, sculpture was perfected to portray them, myths were recorded to explain their activities as well as those of their earthly servants, and data about a variety of natural phenomena were recorded to help predict their behavior. The result was a splendid art, literature, and science that was to inspire future generations far beyond Mesopotamia and Egypt.

The maturation of these first civilizations occurred over a long period of time—from about 4000 to about 2000 B.C., and these ancient centers remained vital long after the latter date. Shortly after 2000 B.C., however, as the wonders wrought by the Mesopotamians and the Egyptians spread beyond the river valleys, a new chapter of ancient history began. This complex process of diffusion dominated the history of the Near East between about 1750 and 800 B.C. It extended considerably the zone of higher civilization and introduced new peoples to the fruits and burdens of civilized life. Several factors were involved in this process: the outward thrust of the original inventors of higher civilization; imitation of the superior ways of the river valley civilizations by peoples long settled on their fringes; and the intrusion into the Near Eastern scene of new peoples, creating new centers of political power whose leaders were anxious to share the benefits of civilized life. During the early part of this period, between about 1750 and 1200 B.C., the chief agents of diffusion were the Egyptians, who thrust outward into Libya, Nubia, and Syria-Palestine; the Hittites, who brought their civilization to Asia Minor; and the Minoans, who developed a brilliant civilization, based on Crete, that asserted a powerful influence over the entire Aegean world, including the Greek peninsula. After about 1200 B.C., these major agents of diffusion suffered an eclipse, but other peoples—such as the Phoenicians, the Aramaenans, and the Hebrews—continued the process until about 800 B.C.

Of these other peoples the Hebrews deserve special attention, chiefly because of their religious system. Having grown out of historical events during the age of diffusion, this system has not only persisted to the present day but also provided a point of departure for such other religions as Christianity and Islam. During the age of diffusion, the Hebrews overcame numerous hardships to establish an independent kingdom that reached its apogee under the leadership of kings Saul, David, and Solomon (ca. 1020–930 B.C.). Simultaneously, they articulated a revolutionary belief in a single god—an all-powerful, righteous, and caring deity—who entered into a covenant with the Hebrews, his "chosen people." The terms of this covenant made the Hebrews the instruments of the divine plan for humanity, destined to help realize God's will within the framework of history. Thus, in the Hebrews' scheme, human beings (as opposed to gods) were given a much more exalted place than they had in other contemporary religious systems. They were, in fact, created to become godlike, which they could do only by becoming morally perfect—in other words, by obeying God's law. This law stressed the individual's obligation to treat others with righteousness and justice; it also imposed on the community a collective responsibility to act justly and mercifully toward all its members. With its emphasis on a universe ordered by a single, transcendent, just, and merciful deity and on good conduct as the key to pleasing that god, ancient Judaism opened new vistas that challenged the human spirit to create a social and cultural order transcending the concepts that governed the lives and thought of most other Near Eastern societies.

The long period of diffusion of the basic elements of Mesopotamian and Egyptian civilization across the ancient Near East provided large numbers of peoples with common techniques, interdependent economic interests, and shared cultural values. This process invited attempts at political consolidation, and adventuresome leaders were at hand to respond to that opportunity. The result was the creation of vast empires whose histories dominated the era from about 800 to 300 B.C. The most successful empire builders were first the Assyrians and then the Persians, both of whose empires were created by military conquest. The new rulers strove chiefly to create social structures that would assure peace, order, and commonality among various peoples of different ethnic and cultural backgrounds. These efforts helped to bring ancient Near Eastern civilization to its peak, and many of the highest achievements of these societies, especially those of the Persian Empire, were passed along to other peoples yet to establish their place in history.

Yet for all the majesty and power of these empires, they proved extremely fragile, as demonstrated by the ease with which Alexander the Great and his Greek-Macedonian armies toppled the Persian Empire. Alexander's easy victories showed that the ancient Near Eastern world, despite its remarkable accomplishments, was losing its vitality and that other peoples were ready to take the lead in shaping Western destiny. However, these newcomers were to benefit in untold ways from earlier achievements in government, economic life, social organization, art, literature, science, and religion.

GRECO-ROMAN CIVILIZATION, 1200 B.C.–A.D. 200

While the civilizational patterns of the ancient Near East were reaching maturity in the huge Persian Empire, a new civilization was developing to the west, one destined to find its ultimate locus in the Mediterranean basin and its chief creative agents in the Greeks and the Romans.

This new civilization originated in the lands washed by the Aegean—the Greek peninsula, the western coast of Asia Minor, and the islands that dotted the Aegean. Since this was an area of limited resources, its inhabitants were very soon forced to take to the seas to assure their livelihood. Beginning about 2000 B.C., these people—the Greeks—felt powerful cultural influences from the more advanced Near East. Around 1200 B.C., however, forces beyond their control cut them off from these contacts and put them on their own. In subsequent centuries the Greeks developed their own unique pattern of life. Central to that development was the emergence of a particular institution that provided the basic framework within which Greek civilization evolved: the *polis* or city-state. Over time, several hundred city-states emerged in the Aegean basin. Although there was infinite variety in their structure, certain features were common to all. For example, each city-state was small in area and population. In each *polis*, group life focused on an urban center, familiar to all, where were concentrated those political, economic, religious, and cultural activities that bore directly on the lives of the city-state's rural and urban inhabitants. Each made citizenship a distinctive and precious aspect of life involving direct and active participation. Although the constitutional forms of the city-states varied widely, all required each citizen to play a role in making ultimate political decisions. Thus some degree of direct democracy was a common feature of ancient Greek life; it nourished a fierce patriotism in each citizen, making him (only males were citizens) eager to expend his talents in the service of the larger community. Indeed, the intensity of life nourished by the *polis* encouraged an unusual degree of freedom and brought forth remarkable achievements in every sphere of life.

As the many small, inward-looking, independent city-states developed in the crowded Aegean world, a challenge—the problem of intercity relationships—emerged to test the Greek system. In the early stages of Greek development, the numerous city-states found much to share, including a common language, Panhellenic religious ideas, and shared cultural values. These forces tended to minimize intercity conflict. Indeed, at a crucial point in Greek history early in the fifth century B.C., several major city-states managed to join forces to repel a Persian attack and prevent the Persian Empire from absorbing the Greek world. But rivalry was implicit where many proud communities each claimed the absolute right of self-determination. During the fifth and early fourth

centuries B.C., intercity strife became a dominant feature, largely because of the aggressiveness of Athens, one of the great city-states, against some of the others. The mounting rivalry ultimately led to the Peloponnesian Wars (431–404 B.C.), which pitted two great alliances of city-states, respectively led by Athens and Sparta, against each other in a destructive struggle that exhausted most of the participants. Despite Athens' ultimate defeat, which reestablished the independence of other, previously dominated city-states, the senseless rivalry continued. This struggle so weakened the Greeks that they were unable to resist conquest by the Macedonians in 338 B.C., and the peace then imposed compromised the world of the independent *polis*.

Before the Greek world of city-states succumbed to Macedonian domination, the Greeks had made their mark in another way. They shaped a view of the universe that manifested itself in a brilliant art, literature, philosophy, and science—a view that has influenced Western culture ever since. Much deserves to be said about the Greek cultural achievement in detail, but overall it was richer and more advanced than that of the Near Eastern civilizations. Greek culture was intensely humanistic, placing human beings on center stage. It stressed harmony between humans and nature, coexisting in an ordered universe that operated according to laws implicit in its very nature. It exalted the power of reason, which enabled humans to understand the natural world, solve problems through their own intelligence, and strive for absolute good. It emphasized restraint and balance in human conduct as the key to happiness. It celebrated a spirit of inquiry that constantly pushed men and women to learn more about themselves and their world. Inspired by these new concepts, Greek thinkers, artists, and writers greatly expanded their knowledge and understanding of humanity and the natural world. The quest to realize the Greek vision of human potential has inspired the Western world since the golden age of the fifth century B.C.

The conquest of the Greek city-states by the Macedonians opened an era called the Hellenistic age, whose history extended from the early fourth to the late first century B.C. The essential feature of this era was the geographic extension of Greek civilization. The Greek city-states themselves had begun to spread their patterns of life and culture in the Mediterranean Basin as early as the eighth and the seventh centuries B.C., chiefly through colonizing efforts that planted Greek city-states in southern Italy, southern France, and around the Black Sea. Their Macedonian conquerors turned the Greeks to even more aggressive expansion. Under Alexander the Great (ruled 336–323 B.C.), Greeks and Macedonians joined forces to conquer the Persian Empire and establish Greek political, economic, and cultural domination over a large segment of the ancient Near East. In the wake of these conquests, large numbers of Greeks migrated to the Near East, reinforcing Greek domination. The political history of the Hellenistic age centered in three large kingdoms into which Alexander's empire was divided—the Macedonian, the Ptolemaic, and the Seleucid kingdoms—in each of which prevailed a system of monarchy reflecting both Greek and Near Eastern concepts and practices of government. Within these kingdoms, city-states, many newly founded on the model of the ancient Greek *polis*, played an important role as cultural and economic centers, thus sustaining urban life as a focal point of human activity. The Hellenistic age saw the spread of Greek cultural models and concepts over much of the Near East. As time passed, Greek and Near Eastern cultural styles and values mingled to enrich each other. Out of this amalgam emerged new achievements of importance for the future, especially in science and philosophy. While the Greek way of thought and expression tended to dominate cultural life, Near Eastern religious concepts and practices increasingly asserted a powerful influence on thought and conduct.

Even as Greek influences spread eastward and changed society and culture over most of the Near East, the ground was being prepared for the transmission of Greek culture westward and for the unification of the Mediterranean world into a single cultural community. The agents for this development were the Romans, whose history began in a tiny village on the Tiber River in west central Italy. Having been introduced to the existing civilization by the Etruscans, who conquered them during the seventh and sixth centuries B.C., the Romans in 509 B.C. established an independent city-state, called the Roman Republic. It slowly forged an internal political structure dominated by

an aristocracy that acted through the Roman Senate (to which only aristocrats belonged) but permitted to ordinary citizens enough political involvement to make them loyal supporters of the Republic. Between 509 and 265 B.C. the well-led and loyal citizen body conquered most of Italy and effectively organized its population. These efforts gave the Roman state the human and material resources it needed to establish ascendance over the Mediterranean Basin. Beginning in 265 B.C. the Romans proceeded step by step to conquer the major powers in the Mediterranean area: first the maritime empire of Carthage, then the Hellenistic kingdoms in the East, and finally the small principalities of Gaul. By the end of the first century B.C., they were unchallenged masters of the lands and the peoples ringing the Mediterranean Sea, including the old Greek sphere of influence and most of the Hellenistic world.

However, these successes had a price. Expansion engendered a series of problems that, between 133 and 31 B.C., created an internal crisis in Rome—a crisis so severe that the republican political order came to an end. In essence, the political system of the Roman Republic, shaped originally to govern a small city-state, was incapable of handling the governance of a vast empire and coping with the political, economic, and social dislocations accompanying its creation. The resultant tensions, demanding some sort of resolution, called forth ambitious individuals who were prepared to disregard the traditional political processes and to use force in order to acquire the power they needed. The gradual erosion of republican institutions paved the way toward the formation of the Roman Empire and the establishment of the political system that constituted Rome's greatest achievement.

The architect of the new order was Augustus (31 B.C.–A.D. 14), who, having emerged from the bloody power struggles of the late Republic, ended the century of civil strife. He fashioned a political order that concentrated power in the hands of a single ruler—called the *princeps* or emperor—while still respecting the rights of the Senate and of the people as the source of this power. During the first and second centuries A.D., that system was steadily perfected as the prime instrument bringing peace and order across the huge Roman Empire. The authority of the emperor, exercised through a professional army and a well-regulated bureaucracy and guided by a sophisticated legal system, was the decisive factor in establishing the Roman peace. Yet the central government wisely permitted and even encouraged local city-states to play a significant role in shaping local affairs, thus helping to ensure cooperation in the provinces while also sustaining a Greek institution as a focus on civic life. This harmonious arrangement resulted in one of the most stable, humane, and effective political systems ever devised.

The Roman peace and its accompanying economic prosperity, assured by the imperial political system and directed by humane rulers, promoted the spread of a common culture across the Mediterrean world. In its form and content that culture was essentially Greek, for from as early as the third century B.C. the Romans became ardent admirers, imitators, and disseminators of Greek culture. As a consequence of the Roman effort in this realm, Greek culture was not only kept alive but also propagated over a large area in the west that had, until then, hardly been touched by higher civilization. The Romans also made valuable additions to the Greek cultural heritage, especially in literature, engineering, and law.

Greco-Roman civilization reached its height in the second century A.D. Over the long period beginning with the emergence of the Greek city-states, a vast community had been created around the shores of the Mediterranean—a community united by Rome's poltical structures, shared cultural values rooted in the Greek achievement, and common economic ties. That civilization still impresses many as being one of the most magnificent achievements in all human history, especially glorious for the emphasis it placed on human powers and achievements and for the opportunities it offered to gifted individuals, particularly in political, artistic, and intellectual pursuits.

THE FALL OF GRECO-ROMAN CIVILIZATION, A.D. 180–500

Despite its splendor during the second century A.D., Greco-Roman civilization was not destined to last forever. Beginning late in the second century and continuing during the next three centu-

ries, forces of disintegration became dominant. Greco-Roman civilization was irreparably weakened and substantially transformed, so that by A.D. 500 the people of the Greco-Roman world were left with no alternative but to begin anew to construct a basis for civilized life.

The process of change and decline began with dramatic suddenness between A.D. 180 and 285. In contrast with the peaceful second century, the third century was characterized by almost incessant civil war. These destructive struggles—promoted chiefly by elements in the army who were seeking to control the government for the benefit of the soldiery—were products of fundamental flaws within the structure of Roman imperial society. The constitution provided no effective system of succession to the imperial office and no clear definition of the limits on the emperor's power; the defense system could not cope with mounting threats from the outside; the economic system could not cover the expenditures of a profligate society; the social order encouraged an aristocratic elite to oppress those upon whose labor their society depended; and the cultural values failed to satisfy the universal yearning for security in an age of crisis. In short, events of the third century A.D. revealed that Greco-Roman civilization had its limitations.

During this critical period, subtle changes in Greco-Roman civilization began to occur. The emperors became increasingly autocratic, and the imperial government, chiefly in the interests of strengthening the military establishment, moved inexorably toward greater regimentation of society and of economic production. As the central government expanded its powers, the once vital city-state governments declined. Urban life began to decay, and agriculture became more crucial. As a result, imperial society was gradually impoverished. New elites—landowners, army leaders, bureaucrats—asserted greater control at the expense of peasants, artisans, and shopkeepers. Perhaps most ominous of all was the widespread loss of faith in the humanistic, rational values of traditional Greco-Roman civilization and the increasing quest for meaning through religion.

The spiritual searching of this troubled age manifested itself in many ways, but one development was especially significant for the future: the emergence of Christianity. Having originated in the age of Augustus as an offshoot of Judaism, the Christian message won an ever-growing following—especially among the non-Jewish population of the Roman Empire—during the first, second, and third centuries A.D. The essence of the Christian appeal lay in the message proclaimed by Jesus. It called for belief in a single god; for acceptance of Jesus as the incarnate son of that God, sent to redeem humanity; and for a spiritual rebirth involving love for one's neighbor and the cultivation of moral purity. In return for accepting the "good news" proclaimed by Jesus, Christians were promised eternal life—salvation from the evils of this world. To this basic message the early Christian movement added other elements promoting success: a solid organization; a persuasive articulation of the tenets of the new faith, greatly enriched by the adaptation of Greco-Roman philosophical concepts to Christian uses; an appealing set of ritual practices; and a social consciousness that emphasized charity and kindness toward society's unfortunates. By A.D. 300, these forces combined to create a vital community within the Roman state whose members no longer gave their full and final allegiance to the Greco-Roman version of civilized life.

The crisis of the third century A.D. eventually evoked a response aimed at restoring Roman society. The architects of this reform were two able emperors, Diocletian (A.D. 284–305) and Constantine (A.D. 306–337). Their reforms aimed at institutionalizing some of the trends that had emerged in the third century. In seeking to vest total power in their own hands, they reorganized and centralized the machinery of government so as to gain more direct control of political life, and they expanded the governmental bureaucracy in order to assert that control. In addition, these emperors expanded the military establishment and focused the army's job on defense of the frontier. To pay for all this, the emperors began regimenting the work force so as to maximize the production of goods and services. Finally, they sought to channel the newly burgeoning religious forces toward service of the state, a decision that led to Constantine's acceptance of Christianity and the adoption of policies pointing toward the Christianization of the previously pagan Roman Empire.

The vast reorganization of imperial society by Diocletian and Constantine appeared to have saved the empire. The fourth century A.D. was marked by internal peace, economic and social stability, intellectual and artistic vitality (chiefly in the service of Christianity), and a rapid advance toward Christian unity. Yet there were ominous signs of deep-rooted troubles. The cost of autocratic government bore heavily on the populace, causing many to evade their civic responsibilities. The quality of service offered by the bloated bureaucracy deteriorated, giving rise to corruption and oppression. The economy became stagnant. The administrative reorganization effected by Diocletian and Constantine produced divisions within the empire. Finally, Christianity, though victorious, failed to unify the populace, chiefly because the Christian community became bitterly divided over what constituted the true faith and because some Christian leaders balked at subordinating the Christian establishment to the state. All these signs of deteriorating imperial strength were ominous; a crisis was in the making as the fourth century drew to a close. Its source lay beyond Roman control, in the world of the Germanic barbarians of central Europe.

The Romans and the Germans had long faced each other across a fixed frontier created and defended by the Romans since the reign of Augustus. The two sides represented two different cultures, for the Germans had, over the centuries, developed unique political, social, economic, and religious institutions differing markedly from those of their southern neighbors. Prior to A.D. 400, many Germans had entered the Roman Empire to serve as soldiers, farmers, and servants; therefore the Germans knew of Greco-Roman civilization, admired it, and were eager to share its fruits. Nor were the Romans averse to romanizing the Germans as long as they could control the process, and this depended on maintaining their frontier defenses. During the third and fourth centuries, Germanic pressure steadily increased, due in large part to changes in Germanic society that produced larger political groupings, an organized warrior aristocracy, and the need for more agricultural land.

In the last years of the fourth century, when Rome's frontier defenses finally began to break down, the "barbarian invasions" or "Germanic migrations'' began. Throughout the next century, group after group of Germans flocked in and settled on Roman soil, primarily in the western part of the empire. The Roman government was able neither to stop these movements nor to control the Germans once they had come in, so that the newcomers were able to establish a number of independent Germanic kingdoms within the empire. Wherever these states emerged, the Roman imperial government simply vanished—a certain sign that another turning point in history had arrived. In addition, the influx of the Germanic hordes hastened economic decline and cultural stagnation in the west, further undermining the old Greco-Roman civilization but not obliterating it entirely. Those remnants of the old order that remained had a civilizing influence on the Germanic settlers. Especially significant was the energetic Christian establishment, which, during the fourth and fifth centuries, devised means of strengthening its hold on Romans and Germans alike and developed new ways of sustaining its spiritual and intellectual sway.

In assessing the Germanic invasions as a decisive event marking the end of Greco-Roman civilization, it is crucial to remember that the eastern reaches of the Roman Empire were not overrun. There the established patterns persisted with considerable vigor. However, the invasions reduced contacts between east and west, thus ending the cultural, religious, and political unity of the Mediterranean world. By the end of the fifth century, therefore, Greco-Roman civilization had largely passed into history.

THE EARLY MIDDLE AGES, 500–1000: STRUGGLE TOWARD A NEW ORDER

The collapse of their old society brought the peoples of the Mediterranean area the new challenge of rebuilding their civilizational patterns. Despite considerable confusion, they met this challenge with remarkable creativity. Between 500 and 1000, three new cultural communities emerged: Byzantine, Moslem, and Germanic western European. In each of these communities, new institutions and ideas were spawned from powerful vestiges of Greco-Roman civilization as well as the new peoples and especially the newly evolving religions.

Byzantine civilization began as a direct continuation of the Roman imperial order in the eastern provinces of the old Roman Empire. The rulers of this region nourished the fiction that, as successors of the Roman emperors, they were masters of the old Roman Empire in its entirety. However, by the reign of Justinian (527–565), it became clear that they could not assert effective control over most of the German-dominated west. In fact, the very survival of the reduced empire depended on these rulers' ability to defend their territories against attackers from the east and north. Most of Byzantine history from Justinian's reign to 1100 centered on a struggle to fend off a variety of such attackers, who nevertheless pared away crucial territories, ultimately reducing the direct sphere of Byzantine influence to Asia Minor, the Balkan peninsula, and southern Italy.

While their territorial sway was shrinking, however, the Byzantines—chiefly through diplomacy and missionary activity—expanded their cultural and religious influence into the Slavic world of eastern Europe and Russia. This ability of the Byzantine Empire to flourish despite the constant onslaught of invaders stemmed chiefly from the vitality of its institutions, which, increasingly across the early Middle Ages, developed certain unique characteristics. The pillar of Byzantine society was the central government, directed by an emperor who claimed to be God's agent and exercised absolute power through a skilled, devoted bureaucracy and a loyal army and navy. A balanced economy, carefully regulated by the imperial government, provided a solid material base for Byzantine society. Especially vital to Byzantine civilization was its Christian religious establishment, which, during the early Middle Ages, developed distinctive organizational, doctrinal, and liturgical features that set it off from other segments of the Christian world. Particularly characteristic of the Greek Orthodox church was its close alliance with the state, a tie so intimate that the emperor directed it as well as the government. The Byzantine world gradually shaped its own unique artistic, literary, and intellectual patterns, which were basically grounded in ancient Greek culture but also deeply colored by Christian concepts and values.

The Moslem cultural world was created by the nomadic inhabitants of the Arabian Desert. The divided, impoverished Arabs, uninfluential in history before A.D. 600, were suddenly united in the early decades of the seventh century under the banner of a new religion, Islam, founded by Muhammad (ca. 570–632). Claiming to be the last in a long succession of prophets (including the Jewish prophets and Jesus), Muhammad proclaimed that he brought to the world the final revelation of Allah, the single, all-powerful god of the universe. Calling on the Arabs to abandon their false gods, to submit to Allah, and to regulate their lives according to Allah's commands, Muhammad was able, before his death, to rally an important segment of the Arab world to his cause.

During the next century the Arab adherents of Islam performed one of the great military feats in history: They conquered a vast empire stretching east to India and the borders of China and west from Syria and Palestine across north Africa to Spain. These conquests made the Moslem Arabs a major force in world affairs. As this vast empire took shape, its leaders set up a centralized government to secure their rule. This government was strongly influenced by Byzantine and Persian precedents, but its uniqueness rested on the religious role of its leader. That is, the government's head, the caliph, was essentially a religious leader, a deputy of Allah charged with interpreting and applying the law as it was revealed by the Prophet and written down in the *Koran*, the sacred book of Islam. Within the vast caliphate the new religion was widely accepted, most of the converts coming from the ranks of Jews, Christians, and Zoroastrians. As it spread, Islam became a prime bond of unity in the sprawling Moslem Empire, which by the tenth century began to disintegrate politically. Most of the new converts were non-Arabs, so that the Arab founders of the Moslem world eventually lost their power over its destiny.

The political unification achieved by the Arabs stimulated economic growth, giving rise to the Moslem world's considerable prosperity during the early Middle Ages and helping it to develop its distinctive pattern of culture. Although this was based on a synthesis of earlier cultures—Greco-Roman, Persian, Egyptian, Indian, Jewish, and Germanic—it was shaped by the powerful influence of Islamic religion and articulated in Arabic, the language of the *Koran*. Particularly notable were the Moslem achievements in science and philosophy, which were destined to be influential down through history and far beyond the borders of the Moslem Empire.

The third new culture to arise in the immediate postclassical period was that of Germanic western Europe. Its genesis was much more troubled and chaotic than that of either the Byzantine or the Moslem cultures. The boundaries of the several Germanic kingdoms erected on Roman soil during the invasion period were not clearly defined nor were their governments especially strong. As a result, at least down to about 750, the Germanic west suffered from political instability. During the period between 500 and 750, several of these kingdoms disappeared; by 750 only the Frankish, Anglo-Saxon, and Lombard kingdoms remained. After much painful experimentation, certain basic political institutions began to take shape in these kingdoms: a limited form of monarchy bearing a strong Germanic stamp, a powerful warrior-landowner nobility, a system of personal dependency subordinating the weak to that aristocracy, and a customary law defining a wide range of interpersonal relations. Between 500 and 750, there was a marked, progressive decline in the urban-based commerce and industry in what was once the western Roman Empire; in its place, an agricultural economy emerged. A consequence of this development was the gradual impoverishment of the west, especially as compared with the Byzantine and Moslem lands. The social structure became simpler, embracing only two classes: a landowning, power-wielding nobility and a dependent peasantry.

Although the Christian establishment also suffered from the prevailing chaos, the Church remained the most vital institution of the age. It enlarged its membership, chiefly through its efforts to convert the pagan Germans and the rural population; extended and solidified its organization; increased its wealth; and expanded its political and social role. Its biggest challenge was to sustain spiritual life amid violence and ignorance. Of crucial importance for the future was the gradually expanding influence of the bishops of Rome—the popes—who were seen as the source of spiritual guidance and arbiters of right belief for all Christians in Germanic western Europe. Hardly less significant was the spread of monasticism, which created cadres of specially prepared Christians who were expected to serve as models for Christian spiritual perfection. Among the Church's many roles was its nourishing of cultural life. Through its efforts the use of Latin was preserved, as was a heritage of classical and patristic literary models and ideas. Monastic schools provided for the transmission of Latin literacy, the copying and collecting of books from earlier ages, and even the creation of new writings in theology, history, and poetry. At least in rudimentary form, the Germanic world was shaping its own unique cultural life. While this was rooted in a Latin tradition that reached all the way back to ancient Rome, its leading ideas were based on the Christian teachings.

By 750 the reconstruction of Germanic society had progressed far enough to permit a sudden upsurge of activity beyond the sheer struggle for survival. This new development eventually gave the West an expanded awareness of its own civilization while also making it more visible in the larger world. The central force behind all this was a new dynasty of kings, the Carolingians, who ruled over the Frankish kingdom and, with the support of the clergy and some of the nobility, dominated the European scene between 750 and 900. After seizing the Frankish throne in 751 (with the blessing of the papacy), a succession of Carolingian rulers greatly enlarged and consolidated the Frankish kingdom, strengthened its internal political institutions, promoted a vigorous renaissance in education and literary and theological studies, and initiated wide-ranging religious reform guided by Church norms. The Carolingians demonstrated their favor toward the papacy by establishing a papal state in central Italy, thus freeing the popes from their long domination by the Byzantine emperors. The culmination of Carolingian power came in 800, when the great Carolingian ruler Charlemagne was crowned emperor by the pope, renewing in the west an exalted title and concept of governance that Byzantium had monopolized since the late fifth century.

In the long run, the Carolingians were not able to sustain their efforts to unify the west and uplift spiritual and cultural life. After 840, to serve dynastic interests, the unified empire was divided into several small kingdoms. In quest of support, the several competing rulers of these kingdoms greatly weakened central government by ceding lands and political privileges to ambitious aristocrats and religious officials. These mounting political problems were made worse by the periodic attacks of Moslem, Magyar, and Viking marauders. By 900, the Carolingian dynasty was thoroughly discredited and the empire divided beyond repair, setting the stage for a new and difficult age that extended into the eleventh century.

Amid the wreckage of the Carolingian Empire, two institutions emerged to provide the base for the eventual reestablishment of order and prosperity: feudalism and manorialism. Both were products of forces that had been germinating since the fall of the Roman Empire and the Germanic invasions. Feudalism was a form of political organization based on the exercise of political power on the local level. That is, a lord would attach to himself a circle of vassals who pledged to serve him politically and militarily. In return, the lord promised them protection and granted to each something of value (land or an office) called a fief. These private jurisdictions, usually created at the expense of the public authority of feeble royal governments, fragmented the west politically and produced considerable strife. However, it eventually succeeded in restoring order and security on the local level. Manorialism was the economic support of feudal society. In this system, the manor was a self-sufficient unit of agricultural production. Here, a dependent serf population was obligated, by virtue of its social status, to till the soil belonging to a noble seigneur. In return for payments of various kinds, the serf enjoyed hereditary possession of a tenancy, including a plot of land on which his household depended for its food. Each manorial collectivity developed its own customs to regulate peasant life and define peasant relationships with the seigneur, who was usually a member of the feudal aristocracy. Together, feudalism and manorialism helped to create small, closely knit, stable collectivities that had a potential for growth.

The emergence of three new civilizations made the early Middle Ages a decisive era in history. In addition to the creative forces at work in each of these cultures, a new dynamism had appeared—in the form of interactions among them—that was to have a decisive influence on much future history.

THE HIGH MIDDLE AGES, 1000–1300: THE REVIVAL OF EUROPE

By about 1000 the new cultural patterns shaped in the Byzantine, Moslem, and Germanic civilizations were solidly in place. The succeeding three centuries (1000–1300), called the High Middle Ages, were highlighted by a remarkable surge of creative activity in the Germanic regions of western Europe, which had previously been far less developed than the Byzantine or Moslem worlds. The revival in Europe not only brought medieval European society to its full maturity but also elevated western European society to a central position in world affairs.

Two important developments provided the impetus for the achievements of this period: greatly increased material prosperity and the growth of an urban way of life. These changes came up from the bottom—from the toiling peasants, peddler merchants, simple artisans, and modest manorial seigneurs. Pressured by steady population growth, these working people increased agricultural production by clearing new lands, improving agricultural technology, and developing more effective management techniques. Trade picked up, industry grew, villages grew into towns and towns into cities. For the first time, western Europeans developed a thriving international trade, penetrating the richer, more advanced Byzantine and Moslem economies. On the basis of this economic growth and increased wealth, society became more diverse and complex. Especially notable was the appearance of a new class, the bourgeoisie, joining the nobility and the peasantry.

While western Europe's working people were producing new wealth and giving rise to a new middle class, its kings and nobles were building new and more effective political structures which, in many cases, have remained viable down to the present day. Each of the major states created in this period—the Holy Roman Empire, England, France, Castile, Aragon, Portugal, Poland, the Scandinavian kingdoms—had its own unique institutional forms. But central to the development of each was the kings' use of feudal practices to extend their authority; in fact, the emergence of feudal monarchy was the crucial political development of this age. Everywhere, kings used their positions as heads of feudal hierarchies to exercise authority over their vassals. From these efforts emerged effective instruments of central and local government: armies, taxation systems, and legal systems that allowed kings to control large areas and large numbers of people. This process of centralization was resisted by privileged groups, especially the feudal nobles and the Church, but they gradually gave in when it became clear that the emerging monarchies were able to provide a degree of security, justice, and material well-being that was unprecedented in the earlier medieval world. As the feudal monarchies developed, ways were found to protect the "rights" claimed by the feudal interests, the Church, and the towns; that is, representative government and basic laws to which even the rulers were subject gradually evolved.

The economic growth and the political consolidation of western Europe made possible the remarkable geographic expansion that occurred between 1000 and 1300 and greatly extended western Europe's sway at the expense of the Byzantine, Moslem, Slavic, and Scandinavian worlds. Expansion took many forms. Missionaries converted and organized the populations of the western Slavic world, Scandinavia, and Iceland. Noble and peasant colonists occupied extensive lands in central Europe and Spain. Enterprising merchants, especially from Italy and the area of the Baltic and North seas, established their presence in the Byzantine and Moslem empires and gained control over large parts of the Mediterranean Sea. Western European military forces captured most of Spain from the Moslems, southern Italy and Sicily from the Byzantines and the Moslems, and—most dramatically of all—an outpost in Syria and Palestine, this last as a consequence of the Crusades. Of course, western institutions and ideas were also carried to these areas, previously untouched by European influence. This medieval expansion, therefore, marked a major step toward the west's future domination of the world, and it was to continue far beyond the Middle Ages.

During the High Middle Ages there was also a powerful religious "reformation" dictated by corruption and moral laxity within the Church—defects stemming largely from its deep involvement in the politics of the tenth and early eleventh centuries. This reform movement took two main directions: (1) a drive to free the Church from lay control and to strengthen it as an independent community capable of directing its own destiny and (2) an effort to probe more profoundly the spiritual meaning of the Christian message.

The first kind of reform was spearheaded by the papacy. The papal program assumed its basic thrust during the Investiture struggle beginning in the last half of the eleventh century. The papal reformers—deeply committed to the idea that the Church was the primary earthly community, created by God under his vicar, the pope, to assure the salvation of souls—initiated a move to free the Church from the control exercised over its property, personnel, and operations by secular feudal nobles. Having claimed the Church's right to liberty and self-determination, a succession of reforming popes labored during the twelfth and thirteenth centuries to find a way of making the Church the prime directive force in society. They created a powerful organization directed by Rome that not only defined a unified body of doctrine through its theology and a standard code of behavior through its canon law but was also able to assert a decisive influence over European political, economic, and social life.

The popes and the clerical hierarchy of bishops and priests were always concerned with improving the spiritual and moral lives of their flock. However, there was, beyond this, also the medieval reform movement's second major thrust: the search for deeper spiritual meaning in the Christian message. This found its most vital expression in the monastic world and among the laity rather than in the hierarchy. The period 1000 to 1300 was marked by repeated efforts to redefine the monastic structure that would embody the Christian life most perfectly. Each of these experiments produced a new monastic order that came to exercise a powerful influence on spiritual life; each had its unique characteristics and emphases, but they all stressed the need for perfect Christians to involve themselves in the world, to combat its evils, rather than escaping from it. Another common thread was an emphasis on the individual's ability to work actively for God's grace—as opposed to waiting passively for eventual salvation. Various popular religious movements emerged in this questing age, usually stressing poverty, charity, and simplicity of worship. Because they were often critical of the organized Church's increasing wealth, power, and inflexible insistence on conformity in belief and practice, many of these movements were condemned as heretical. But they all repeatedly called for a fuller understanding of the Christian teaching and a better practice of the Christian way of life.

Taken together, these reform movements had a profound effect on western European society during the High Middle Ages, helping to shape the Church as an institution. And it was the Church that provided the integrating and directive values for all elements of society. It encouraged and deepened the spiritual seeking that gave direction to the lives of individuals as well as communities. It unleashed the vital forces of the age and gave life meaning within a universal framework.

The crowning achievement of the High Middle Ages was the culture of the time—its thought, literature, and art—which was of major importance in establishing western preeminence. In the realm of literature and thought, medieval cultural life found expression in two linguistic traditions: Latin and the local venacular languages. The world of Latin literature and thought, nourished chiefly in the constantly evolving educational system (which culminated in the establishment of the first universities), served the interests of both Church and state.

Among the most impressive intellectual products of this era was a body of theological writings inspired by an effort to reconcile Christian revelation with human knowledge (represented chiefly by Greek and Moslem philosophy and science). Other scholarly achievements included a single body of Church (canon) law, compiled by organizing the huge, confused, body of law the Church had developed throughout its history; a massive body of commentary on Roman law as embodied in the Code of Justinian; a systematic body of political theory; an increasing accumulation of knowledge about the natural world derived from both classical sources and the observation of nature; and a large body of Latin belles lettres, including history, geography, political polemics, poetry, and letters.

The literature in the vernacular languages was more uniquely western European and was produced chiefly for the amusement and edification of the feudal nobility, most of whom had been illiterate prior to this period. The vernacular literature took many forms: epics recounting the deeds of warrior heroes; troubador lyrics reflecting on the joys and pains of love; romances celebrating courtly life, where adventure and love combined in the chivalrous life style; *fabliaux* dwelling on the humor of everyday life and the foibles of men and women. Vernacular literature played an important part in defining the world of the nobility and the behavior expected of ladies and gentlemen.

In the visual arts, the High Middle Ages produced two notable styles, Romanesque and Gothic, which are exemplified in splendidly decorated churches throughout Europe.

Inspired by an urge to know and to honor both God and humanity, the art and culture of this era reflected a high level of culture, permitting thinkers, writers, and artists to make many original contributions to western civilization. Most of modern European culture has its roots in this medieval achievement.

THE LATE MIDDLE AGES, 1300–1500

The creative energies that worked so powerfully between 1000 and 1300 began to flag after 1300. Increasingly during the fourteenth and fifteenth centuries, western Europe was plagued by strife and tension, causing dislocation, suffering, disillusionment, and even despair. With the benefit of hindsight, we can see that the Late Middle Ages were building toward a new period of creativity that would further enrich and strengthen European society and extend its preeminence. But to those living in this difficult age the decay and disintegration of the "old" ways seemed overwhelming. In a fundamental way, the difficulties of the Late Middle Ages stemmed from the new problems and new aspirations growing out of earlier achievements, but—at least in the short run—western Europeans were unable to make the needed adjustments.

A major source of difficulty emerged in the political realm. As we have seen, the medieval feudal monarchies were based on a sharing of power between kings and privileged groups on the basis of a well-defined system of mutual obligations. This system, guaranteed by shared rights in land, proved incapable of coping with such problems as large-scale national wars and complex economic problems affecting whole populations. The intrinsic limitations of medieval monarchies in the face of new problems led to declining respect for royal dynasties, disaffection with traditional political processes, and self-seeking by privileged groups, especially the nobility. All over western Europe, kingdoms suffered from civil war, disregard for law, expansion of privileges for the few, and oppression of the many. At one time or another, it seemed that every medieval kingdom might disappear, as did indeed one of the most powerful medieval political entities, the Holy Roman Empire, which embraced Germany and most of Italy. This political instability was aggravated by vigorous assaults from the Mongols and Ottoman Turks, which overpowered western Europe's eastern outposts, destroyed the Byzantine Empire, and left the west open to new attacks.

The feudal monarchies were also faced with crippling economic and social problems. Largely because of limitations inherent in the medieval manorial system and the localized, guild-dominated trading and manufacturing establishments, the prolonged economic growth of the High Middle Ages gradually came to an end. This economic contraction was hastened by a demographic disaster—repeated outbreaks throughout all of western Europe of the deadly bubonic plague. From 1347 onward, its onslaught drastically reduced the population, disrupted the labor supply, altered demand patterns, and disturbed conventional patterns of production. The economic decline put important elements of the nobility, the peasantry, and the urban tradesmen and artisans under stress. Established social relationships were severely disturbed, and the resulting social tensions often flared up into peasant and urban violence.

The religious establishment, too, was seriously disturbed. After 1300 the powerful Church, which had earlier decisively influenced all aspects of life, encountered increasing difficulties in asserting its leadership role. Its teaching, its system of government, and its leaders were subjected to merciless criticism and open defiance. And it failed to discover new means of meeting these assaults. Part of the difficulty stemmed from a failure of leadership at the Church's apex, the papacy. Papal claims to "fullness of power" were effectively challenged by secular rulers, especially the kings of France, as early as 1300. This clash led to the relocation of the papal court from Rome to Avignon, where—in the eyes of many—the popes became agents of the French monarchy rather than servants of all Christendom. Efforts to deal with this problem led to the Great Schism, during which two and even three popes claimed headship of the Church. Important lay and clerical leaders promoted the conciliar movement, which challenged the idea of papal supremacy over religious life by claiming that a representative body of Christians should exercise supreme authority in ecclesiastical affairs. Amid these troubles and challenges, the beleaguered popes gave more attention to increasing the papal resources than to handling pastoral problems. The result was an ever more demanding system of financial exactions managed by an ever more corrupt ecclesiastical bureaucracy, all of which produced bitter criticism, resistance, and open defiance of papal authority. Ineffectively guided from above, the lower clergy grew corrupt and negligent of pastoral duties. Especially afflicted by decadence and corruption was the monastic world, once a major source of spiritual renewal.

Accompanying the disarray in the Church's governmental system was a widespread outcropping of new religious movements. These reflected a search for religious fulfillment outside the formal, rigid patterns of religious life sanctioned by the Church's official theology and canon law. This searching took many forms: mysticism; the founding of brotherhoods and sisterhoods of lay people, based on the sharing of wealth and simple devotional practices; attacks by intellectuals on the papal claims to supremacy and on the sacramental system; a search for religious meaning through a return to Scripture; emotional cults proclaiming the end of the world; morbid rituals associated with death; witch-hunts; and savage anti-Semitism. For the most part, the Church repudiated these movements as heretical while failing to acknowledge its own weaknesses, thereby demonstrating an almost total insensitivity to felt religious needs. All these phenomena pointed to the need for a major reformation of religious life.

Not the least of the Church's problems and another source of disarray in the Late Middle Ages involved subtle shifts in the intellectual world. The majestic efforts of the scholastic theologians and philosophers to reconcile, through reason, Christian revelation and human knowledge into one consistent, complete order of truth failed to satisfy many thinkers. The scholastics continued to work toward this end, but their efforts grew increasingly pedantic and trivial. Several thinkers devised powerful arguments demonstrating that religious knowledge and human knowledge were separate, irreconcilable spheres that required different approaches. They increasingly insisted that the realm of human knowledge must depend on sense perceptions of individual objects in the natural world; in this way, the philosophical groundwork for modern science was laid. Many intellectuals grew weary of the sterile, ivory-tower exercises of the scholastics and turned instead to the Greek and Roman heritage. In the classics they discovered a value system that, in many ways, clashed with the prevailing world view.

Taken together, the diverse trends affecting late-medieval society pointed to the transformation of an old order and the end of an era. In fact, by the late fifteenth century, the stresses of the Late Middle Ages had begun to abate and signs of recovery were appearing everywhere. Included were the restoration of royal authority on new bases; population growth; the stabilization of the agricultural system on the basis of rents; new techniques for the accumulation of capital, permitting the establishment of large-scale trading and manufacturing enterprises; new technological advances; tentative explorations by sea of new frontiers; fresh approaches to knowledge and expression; and new religious insights. All these newly emerging patterns of civilization were rooted in the medieval civilization of western Europe. No catastrophic break such as that which had marked the transition from the Greco-Roman to the medieval era would herald the advent of the "modern" world.

THE BEGINNING OF EARLY MODERN TIMES: THE FIFTEENTH AND SIXTEENTH CENTURIES

During the fourteenth and fifteenth centuries, various tensions and a weakening of social institutions marked the transformation of the medieval world. During the fifteenth and sixteenth centuries, the institutions and developments that would characterize early modern times grew out of the changing medieval system. The five most important developments of the fifteenth and sixteenth centuries were the Renaissance, the rise of national states, the expansion of Europe, the rise of a capitalistic economy, and the Reformation.

The first challenge to the medieval system came in the cities of northern Italy during the fourteenth and fifteenth centuries. There the ideas, values, and culture of the Renaissance arose. Scholars, writers, and artists began looking back to classical Greece and Rome for models instead of accepting medieval scholastic authority. Cultural leaders focused more on individual human beings living in a concrete, material, Christian world rather than medieval theology. Western Europeans of the social and cultural elite were becoming more self-centered, proud, versatile, and materialistic. These Renaissance qualities produced new, vibrant literature and art, making northern Italy the cultural center of the west.

During the fifteenth and sixteenth centuries the Renaissance spread from Italy to northern Europe, particularly to the courts of princes and kings and to university towns. There the Renaissance took on a more piously religious character as northern humanists tried to reconcile Christian and Classical cultures.

In place of the declining feudal monarchies and empires arose the national or territorial state, which became the dominant political institution of the early modern era. The rise of the national states ended the independence of numerous of feudal lords by bringing them under the authority of national monarchs. Talented monarchs such as Ferdinand and Isabella in Spain, Louis XI in France, and Henry VII in England increased their own power and established foundations for the continued growth of national monarchical power. Those areas that did not unify into national states, such as in Germany and Italy, suffered from political weakness.

National monarchs encouraged Europeans to expand into the nonwestern world. Voyages of discovery soon led to commercial trade, spreading Christianity, and political control. During the fifteenth and early sixteenth centuries, Portugal and Spain led in this expansion of Europe. England, France, and the Netherlands soon followed. By the end of the sixteenth century, large parts of the rest of the world, particularly in the Western Hemisphere, southern Asia, and coastal Africa, had come under European economic and political domination.

The expansion of Europe was also stimulated by new economic developments. Europe's medieval economy, characterized by subsistence agriculture, monopolistic guilds, and localism, slowly gave way to capitalistic practices and institutions. Increasing population and rising prices spurred commerce and created social turmoil, with poorer peasants suffering the most. The old landed aristocracy was now threatened by newcomers into the class and by a new middle class of aggressive entrepreneurs, merchants, bankers, and lawyers. It is true that the bourgeoisie sought most of all to enter the ranks of the nobility, and did so whenever possible, and that the nobility held the upper hand politically and socially for two or three more centuries. But by 1600 class lines had become more fluid.

The fifteenth and sixteenth centuries were marked by a deepening concern for religious matters. During the 1500s the western Christian church, which had monopolized religious life and strongly influenced the intellectual, political, and economic life of Europe during the Middle Ages, was split asunder by the Reformation. Great religious leaders such as Martin Luther and John Calvin broke from the Roman church and laid the foundations for the various Protestant churches. Much of northern Europe became Protestant. This stimulated reform efforts already underway within the Roman Catholic church for revitalization or reformation. Catholic doctrine was forcefully affirmed at the Council of Trent, and new religious orders such as the Jesuits reinvigorated the Church.

The religious struggles of the Reformation combined with political forces to give rise to the Wars of Religion. From the middle of the sixteenth to the middle of the seventeenth centuries, much of Europe was struck by war and political turmoil that was connected to religious issues. The most devastating of these wars was the Thirty Years' War, which broke out in Germany in 1618 and was not concluded until 1648 with the Peace of Westphalia. By this time, the developments initiated during the fifteenth and sixteenth centuries were achieving a new maturity. Europe was already entering into the Age of Royal Absolutism.

PART EIGHT

THE AGE OF ROYAL ABSOLUTISM, SEVENTEENTH AND EIGHTEENTH CENTURIES

As we have seen, the fifteenth and sixteenth centuries were a period of change and upheaval. The Renaissance, the Reformation and the Wars of Religion, the rise of the new monarchs, the commercial revolution, and the expansion of Europe marked the period as substantially different from the preceding Middle Ages and as the beginnings of early modern times. The seventeenth and eighteenth centuries constituted a period when the society, culture, and institutions of early modern Europe matured. The mid-seventeenth century to the last decades of the eighteenth century was a period of relative stability. Historians have often referred to this period of European history as *"l'ancien régime,"* the Old Regime before the French Revolution of 1789.

The dominating development of this period was the growing power of central governments, particularly in the form of royal absolutism. The government of France under Louis XIV epitomized this royal absolutism. An important contrasting trend to royal absolutism was constitutionalism, where the king lost the struggle for greater power. The most striking examples of constitutionalism were in England and the Netherlands.

In most other ways the society and culture of the seventeenth and eighteenth centuries evolved only slowly, reflecting the growing power of central governments and their reigning monarchs. Aristocrats remained socially dominant but with some exceptions, such as in England and the Netherlands, were domesticated by royal monarchs or integrated into the service of the crown's central government. Life for most people still took place in the countryside and in traditional villages, which were only starting to evolve as the tentacles of central governments and economic change reached them. Here it was only in the second half of the eighteenth century that the agricultural revolution and the spread of cottage industry quickened economic and social change. Most religious affiliations remained as determined during the course of the Reformation and Wars of Religion, with established churches usually working hand in hand with monarchs and aristocrats. The most important cultural trends—the baroque and the classical styles—reflected royal grandeur and aristocratic tastes.

Intellectually, however, two developments occurred that would eventually undermine this traditional order of early modern Europe and provide a foundation for the modern society of the nineteenth and twentieth centuries: the Scientific Revolution and the Enlightenment. Yet even these intellectual developments took place only among a small elite and within the political and social context of the seventeenth and eighteenth centuries.

This period, then, is best organized around its most dominating and striking development—the rise and maturation of royal absolutism. The first two chapters examine royal absolutism and the challenges to royal absolutism in western Europe. The third chapter traces the rise of royal absolutism in eastern Europe. The next chapter turns to the competition among states for power, colonies, and empire—in many ways another element of the growing power of central governments. Focus then broadens to economic, social, cultural, religious, and intellectual developments of the period, most of which in some ways reflect the rise of and struggle with royal absolutism in the seventeenth and eighteenth centuries.

CHAPTER 32
The Dominance of France: The Age of Louis XIV

FIGURE 32.1. **Pierre Patel the Elder, "Versailles," 1668**   This painting shows Louis XIV's palace and grounds at Versailles in 1668. The scale and order of Versailles reflected the grandeur of the French monarchy at its height. Other European monarchs modeled their palaces after Versailles in an attempt to increase their own prestige. (Lauros-Giraudon/Art Resource)

France was the dominant nation in Europe throughout most of the seventeenth and eighteenth centuries. Under Louis XIV royal absolutism not only reached its peak in France but also served as a model that other monarchs sought to emulate. The well-lighted stage across which the "Sun King" strode was set for him by three able predecessors—Henry IV, Richelieu, and Mazarin.

1. THE RISE OF FRANCE UNDER HENRY IV, RICHELIEU, AND MAZARIN

When Henry IV became king of France in 1589, his country was torn from several decades of bitter religious war. Respect for law and order had broken down. The feudal nobility had in many cases reasserted its own authority. The finances of the central government were in chaos. Roads and bridges were in disrepair. French prestige abroad was at a low ebb; even the city of Paris was garrisoned by the Spanish troops of Philip II.

Henry of Navarre, the first of the Bourbon dynasty to rule France, set out to change all this. The new king, in his prime at the age of thirty-six, was debonair and witty, courageous, generous, and optimistic. His slogan, "A chicken in the pot of every peasant for Sunday dinner," was more than an idle phrase; it is little wonder that *Henri Quatre* became the most popular monarch in French history. The romantic Henry had in the duke of Sully an able, methodical administrator to serve and steady him. The most urgent task was to restore the authority of the central government. This Henry set out to do by vigorously suppressing brigandage and enforcing the law. The lesser nobility was brought to heel directly and quickly. The powerful nobility was dealt with more gingerly, but by the end of Henry's reign real headway had been made toward reducing the nobles to obedience to the central government.

Henry and Sully launched a comprehensive program of economic reconstruction. Agriculture and commerce benefited from the increased security of life and property, from the repair of roads, bridges, and harbors, and from the freeing of internal and external commerce of many obstructions and tariff barriers. Marshes were drained for farming. Better breeding methods were introduced. The peasants' livestock and implements were protected against seizure for debt or taxes. New industries producing glass, porcelain, lace, tapestries, and fine leather and textiles were subsidized and protected by the state. Silk culture, which brought vast wealth to France, was introduced. The building of France's overseas empire began in 1608 when Champlain founded Quebec, the first French colony in the New World.

When Henry IV came to the throne, only about a fourth of the heavy taxes, from which the clergy and the nobility were largely exempted, ever reached the national treasury. The rest went into the pockets of corrupt officials and tax farmers, that is, the collectors who bid a fixed sum for the privilege of collecting the taxes and were permitted to keep anything over and above the contracted amount. Sully was unable to change this vicious system, but by means of careful bookkeeping, efficient administration of expenditures, and elimination of corruption, he was able to show a surplus for the first time in many years.

Another major achievement of Henry's reign was the granting of religious toleration to the Huguenot minority. A *politique,* Henry abjured Protestantism in order to gain acceptance as king of an overwhelmingly Roman Catholic nation. The Edict of Nantes, which Henry IV issued in 1598, granted the Huguenots not only complete freedom of conscience and limited public worship but also civil and political equality. Moreover, they were given military control of some two hundred fortified cities and towns as a guarantee against future oppression.

Having laid the foundations for royal supremacy, economic health, and religious toleration, Henry IV in the last years of his reign devoted an increasing amount of attention to foreign affairs. His goal was to make France first secure and then supreme in Europe by weakening the power of the Spanish and Austrian Hapsburgs. In 1610 he readied his armies for a campaign, but just as he was preparing to join them he was assassinated by a fanatic.

After fourteen years of retrogression under Henry IV's Italian wife, Marie de Médicis, and their young and inept son Louis XIII (1610–1643), Cardinal Richelieu gained active control over the

FIGURE 32.2. Champaigne, "Cardinal Richelieu"
The imperious and ruthless Richelieu played a major role in making the royal power supreme in France and France the supreme power in Europe. Here he poses in church robes befitting his office as a cardinal. (Scala/Art Resource)

government of France (see Figure 32.2). Although technically a mere servant of the fickle Louis XIII, the masterful cardinal made himself so indispensable that for eighteen years (1624–1642) he held firm control over French affairs. Handsome, arrogant, and calculating, Richelieu was a true Machiavellian. His twofold policy, from which he never veered, was similar to that of Henry IV—to make the royal power supreme in France and France supreme in Europe.

Believing the high nobility and the Huguenots to be the chief threats to royal absolutism, Richelieu crushed them both. With the royal army at his disposal, he boldly destroyed the castles of the nobles who remained defiant, disbanded their private armies, and hanged a number of the most recalcitrant. The special military and political privileges that the Huguenots enjoyed under the Edict of Nantes were considered by Richelieu to be intolerable, giving them the status of a state within a state. After a bloody two-year struggle, he stripped the Huguenots of these privileges, although he left their religious and civil liberties intact.

In order to bypass local political influence, which in some provinces was still strong, the dynamic minister divided France into some thirty administrative districts called *généralités*, each of which was placed under the control of an *intendant*,[1] who was an agent of the crown. So absolute was the power of the *intendants* over local affairs, even of the most minute nature, that they came to be called the "thirty tyrants of France." They were chosen from the ranks of the bourgeoisie and were shifted around frequently lest they become too sympathetic with the people over whom they ruled. The royal will was thus extended to every part of France.

Although Richelieu was a cardinal in the Roman Catholic church, he did not hesitate to plunge France into the Thirty Years' War in Germany on the side of the Protestants. His purpose, of course, was to weaken the Hapsburgs, chief rivals of the French Bourbons for European supremacy. When Richelieu died in 1642, he had gone far toward bringing to fruition Henry IV's policies of royal supremacy in France and French supremacy in Europe. Richelieu, however, did not share Henry IV's concern for the common people. Their lot became harder under the imperious and ruthless cardinal, at whose death they rejoiced.

Richelieu was succeeded by his protégé, Cardinal Mazarin. Louis XIII's death in 1643, one year after that of his great minister, left the throne to Louis XIV (1643–1715), a child of five. Mazarin played the same role in the early reign of Louis XIV that Richelieu had played during most of the

---

[1]The *intendants* existed before Richelieu's time, but he greatly increased their power and functions.

reign of Louis XIII. From the death of Richelieu in 1642 until his own death in 1661, Mazarin vigorously pursued the policies of his predecessor. The Thirty Years' War was brought to a successful conclusion. All who challenged the crown's absolute authority were crushed.

The most noteworthy events during his administration were a series of uprisings between 1648 and 1652, known as the *Fronde*. The Fronde was a revolt of the disgruntled nobility and townspeople against the ever-increasing authority of the central government. At times it looked as if the rebels might succeed, but the rebellious factions could not unify. In the end only Mazarin and the monarchy represented order in the face of apparent chaos, and the rebels were defeated. The failure of the Fronde marked the last overt resistance to royal absolutism in France until the French Revolution in 1789. When Cardinal Mazarin died in 1661, he passed along to young Louis XIV a royal power that was at last absolute and a national state that was easily the first power of Europe.

2. LOUIS XIV AND HIS GOVERNMENT

Louis XIV was twenty-three years old when, in 1661, he stepped forth as the principal actor on the world's gaudiest stage. Young Louis was well fitted for the part. He had a sound body and a regal bearing. His lack of intellectual brilliance and of deep learning were more than offset by a large store of common sense, a sharp memory, a sense of responsibility, and a capacity for hard, tedious work. From his Spanish mother, from Mazarin, and from his tutors he had gained the conviction that he was God's appointed deputy for France. In Bishop Bossuet he had the most famous of all theorists and exponents of royal absolutism. Bossuet in numerous writings argued that absolute monarchy is the normal, the most efficient, and the divinely ordained form of government. He contended that, furthermore, the royal monarch, the image of God and directly inspired by God, is above human reproach and accountable to God alone. These ideas as acted out by Louis gained and held the ascendancy throughout the continent

of Europe during the late seventeenth and most of the eighteenth centuries.

Absolute though he might consider himself [the words "*L état, c'est moi*" ("I am the state") are often attributed to him], Louis could not possibly perform all the functions of government personally. Actually, the great bulk of the decisions and details of government were handled by a series of councils and bureaus and were administered locally by the *intendants*. Distrusting nobles, Louis appointed members of the middle class to the important offices of his government. The functions of the chief councils, such as those of state, finances, dispatches, and the privy council, appear on paper to have been overlapping and ill defined. As supervised by the industrious Louis XIV, however, the administrative machinery worked smoothly and efficiently. In fact, it was the envy of his fellow monarchs and probably constituted his most constructive achievement. There was no semblance of popular participation in government. The role of the people was to serve and obey; in return, they enjoyed reflected glory and received such benefits as the monarch might be willing and able to bestow on them. The Estates General was not called once during the seventy-two years of Louis XIV's reign or the fifty-nine-year rule of his successor.

3. THE KING AND HIS COURT: VERSAILLES

In line with Louis XIV's concept of divine right absolutism, he believed that he should have a palace worthy of God's chief deputy on earth. Hating tumultuous Paris, congested and crowded with vulgar tradespeople, he selected Versailles, eleven miles southwest of the city, to be the new seat of government. There as many as thirty-five thousand workmen toiled for thirty years, turning the marshes and sandy wastes into the world's most splendid court. The cost was so staggering that Louis destroyed the records. The greatest artists in the land were employed in the creation of the palace and the grounds. The most costly marbles, glass, tapestries, paintings, and inlaid woods were used in profusion in the ornate baroque style

FIGURE 32.3.   Charles Lebrun, "Chancellor Seguier"   Chancellor Seguier, a patron of the seventeenth-century French artist Lebrun, is shown here as an ambitious courtier to Louis XIV. In formal robes, this member of France's new nobility (*noblesse de robe*) is attended by pages as if he were a monarch. (The Louvre, Paris)

of the period. Hundreds of acres of gardens, parks, walks, canals, and artificial lakes were laid out with mathematical precision. Playing fountains and marble statues formalized the landscape.

Around his court Louis XIV gathered the great nobles of France (see Figure 32.3). Henry IV, Richelieu, and Mazarin had broken their power; Louis XIV turned them into court butterflies. The inevitable jostling for the king's attention, which was the one source of preferment, and the conflicting claims of so much titled rank necessitated the drawing up of an elaborate code of etiquette. The king was dressed and undressed, bathed, and fed by the highest noblemen in the land—all in strict ritual. The household personnel consisted of ten thousand soldiers in brilliant uniforms and four thousand civilians. Nor was the pageant of Versailles mere glitter alone. Louis XIV subsidized or gathered around himself the leading French artists and literary figures.

But there was a reverse side to the coin. Versailles was a showplace, not a comfortable home for the king. It was cold, drafty, and inconvenient. The balls, parades, hunts, and social ritual were not sufficient to absorb the energy of the vivacious and ambitious nobility of France. The court seethed with gossip, scandal, and intrigue. Nor did the hard-toiling, heavily taxed French masses, who were supposed to enjoy the reflected glory of the monarch, always appreciate such extravagant glamour. Indeed, there were increasing expressions of discontent.

4. COLBERT AND THE FRENCH ECONOMY

Louis XIV was fortunate to have at his command during the first half of his reign a prodigious financial manager. Jean Baptiste Colbert (1619–1683) was an inordinately ambitious social climber who realized that, because of his bourgeois origin, his only means of advancement was through indispensable service to the king. An engine of efficiency, he toiled endlessly, supervising the countless details of the French economy.

Colbert's first and probably his most difficult task was to balance the national budget, which had become badly unbalanced under Richelieu and Mazarin. The careful accounting of receipts and expenditures that Sully had inaugurated three-quarters of a century earlier was resumed. Some of the debts that the government had contracted at exorbitant rates of interest were canceled; on others the rates were reduced. Dishonest tax collectors were dismissed and punished.

With Colbert, mercantilism reached its peak. French industries were protected by prohibitive tariffs, while exports and new industries were subsidized. Raw materials, however, were strictly husbanded. Imperial and commercial activities in India and North America were vigorously promoted. To protect this growing empire and the commerce that it generated, a large navy was built. But Colbert did not stop with these traditional mercantilist practices. In order to gain a world-wide reputation for the uniformly high quality of French products, all manufacturing was subjected to the most minute regulation and supervision. So many threads of such and such quality and color must go into every inch of this textile

and that lace. A veritable army of inspectors enforced the regulations. This extreme policy of mercantilism, the economic adjunct to royal absolutism, has come to be called Colbertism. It achieved its immediate end so far as quality and reputation were concerned, but it stifled initiative and retarded future industrial development. That Colbert was able to balance the budget and achieve general economic prosperity in the face of Louis XIV's lavish expenditures, including the building of Versailles, was a remarkable feat. It is well, however, that Colbert died in 1683, for Louis' wars of aggression eventually wrecked most of the great minister's work. Much of Europe copied Colbert's policies and techniques during the latter part of the seventeenth and most of the eighteenth centuries.

5. ABSOLUTISM AND RELIGION

It was virtually inevitable that Louis XIV's concepts of divine right monarchy would have religious repercussions. First, they ran counter to the claims of the pope. All his life Louis considered himself to be devoutly loyal to the Roman Catholic faith, as were the majority of his subjects. But when it came to matters of church administration Louis was not willing to have his royal authority limited, even by Rome. Numerous conflicts between king and pope led to the calling of a great council of the French clergy in 1682. This council, under the domination of Bishop Bossuet, faithful servant of Louis XIV and famed exponent of the theory of royal absolutism, drew up a statement of Gallican Liberties, special privileges or freedoms of the French church from Roman domination. The Gallican Liberties brought the French church to a position close to that of the English church under Henry VIII. They might even have led to eventual separation from Rome had not Louis XIV in later life fallen increasingly under the influence of the Jesuits and the pious Madame de Maintenon, who were able to rekindle his loyalty to the pope.

Louis' absolutism also ran afoul of the Jansenists, so called because they were followers of a Belgian bishop, Cornelis Jansen. This group represented a Puritan movement within the Roman Catholic church. The Jansenists had no intention of breaking away from the Church, to which they considered themselves entirely loyal. It was their wish to return to the teachings and practices of the Church in the days of St. Augustine. They emphasized predestination, inner piety, and the ascetic life. A number of intellectuals and people of means were attracted to their ranks, including the dramatist Racine and the mathematician and philosopher Blaise Pascal. At Port Royal near Versailles a group of prominent Jansenists practiced a communal life and established an excellent school that attracted much favorable attention. Eventually the Jesuits persuaded the pope to declare Jansenism heretical and aroused Louis XIV against the Jansenists. He outlawed the sect and destroyed its buildings.

The chief religious victims of Louis XIV's absolutism were the Huguenots. Although the Huguenots numbered not more than a tenth of the total population in France, many of them were industrious, prosperous, and educated members of the middle class. The Huguenots were subjected to a variety of persecutions. Regular army troops were quartered in Huguenot homes and instructed to cause havoc. Whole Huguenot communities would abjure their faith at the approach of the troops. Finally, in 1685 the Edict of Nantes was revoked and the Protestant religion outlawed. Although Huguenots were forbidden to emigrate, many—probably a quarter million—succeeded in doing so, taking much of their wealth and all their economic knowledge and skills with them. Not only were these industrious citizens lost to France, but they strengthened some of France's rivals and enemies, such as England, the Dutch Netherlands, and Brandenburg, which welcomed them. Forbidden to enter the underpopulated French colonies, many Huguenots helped to people the English colonies in America.

6. LOUIS XIV'S WARS OF AGGRESSION

The Sun King was not content to rule the world's most powerful nation. Louis' immediate and expressed goal was to extend his rule to France's natural frontiers. Since the French boundaries were already delimited by mountains and sea on every side but the northeast, it was in that direction that Louis looked for expansion. He claimed that only the Rhine River would provide France with an adequate natural strategic boundary on that side. An advance to the Rhine would involve France in war with most of Europe. Between the French frontier and the Rhine lay the Spanish Netherlands, much of the Dutch Netherlands, imperial territory belonging to the Austrian Hapsburgs, and many German states. England, too, would be threatened, and the balance of power upset. But Louis felt himself equal to the task of defeating these powers.

Louis' war minister, Louvois, organized France's huge military establishment on a scientific and businesslike basis, replete with supply depots and hospitals. He introduced strict discipline, uniforms, and marching drill. Vauban was one of the great designers of fortifications and of siege operations. It was a common saying that a city defended by Vauban was safe and that a city besieged by Vauban was doomed. Condé was an able and dashing military leader, and Turenne a masterly planner of campaigns and battles.

During the last four decades of his seventy-two-year reign Louis XIV fought four wars of aggression. In 1667 he unceremoniously sent French armies in to conquer the Spanish (Belgian) Netherlands. Spanish power had declined rapidly since the sixteenth century, and Louis' armies captured one fortress city after another. The Dutch, however, took alarm and formed an alliance with England and Sweden to check the French menace. This array of powerful nations along with Spain caused Louis to accept a peace that granted him only a slice of the Spanish Netherlands.

The frustrated Grand Monarch determined to punish the upstart prosperous Dutch. He sent huge French armies into the Netherlands. The cause of the Dutch seemed hopeless, and in desperation they opened their dikes. Large portions of their land were flooded, but the French were held at bay. Meanwhile, the power of France frightened Spain, the Holy Roman emperor, Brandenburg, and several small German states into joining the Dutch in alliance. Louis XIV won many victories over the allies, but when the English Parliament forced Charles II to break his agreement with the French king and join the alliance against him, Louis XIV decided to make peace. Again hapless Spain was the loser, giving up to France the long-coveted Franche-Comté (free county of Burgundy) and another strip of the Spanish Netherlands.

At the end of the Dutch War (1678) Louis XIV stood at the peak of his power (see Map 32.1). He had defeated all the greatest military powers on the western European continent and had gained valuable territories. But the tide was about to turn. Turenne was killed near the end of the Dutch War, and the aged Condé retired at the end of the war. No comparable generals were found to replace them. Colbert's hard-won surplus and balanced budget were now things of the past, and France's economy was suffering. All Europe had become alarmed by the French aggression.

No sooner had the Dutch War ended than Louis began trumping up claims to various territories in Alsace and Lorraine and sending in his armed forces to occupy them. The result was another defensive alliance against Louis composed of the Dutch Netherlands, Spain, Sweden, the Holy Roman emperor, and a number of small German states. The heart of the alliance was William of Orange, stadholder of Holland, and when the redoubtable Dutchman became King William III of England after the Glorious Revolution of 1688, England, too, was brought into alliance against Louis. The alliance was called the League of Augsburg. After nine years of fruitless struggle, Louis accepted a peace giving him only the city of Strasbourg.

But the Sun King was not about to give up. He persuaded the last monarch of the Hapsburg line in Spain just before he died in 1700 to choose one of Louis' grandsons as king. The prospect of Spain and the Spanish Empire joined to the already inordinately powerful French monarchy frightened the other powers of western Europe into once more forming an alliance against France. The ensuing War of the Spanish Succession lasted eleven years (1702–1713). The allies administered to the French and Spanish armies a series of severe defeats. In 1713 Louis XIV, beaten and exhausted, was forced to accept the Treaty of Utrecht. The settlement was complicated, but France had been somewhat humbled. It was beginning to lose ground overseas to Great Britain and in Europe had been halted short of the Rhine. But France was still the most powerful single nation in Europe.

Louis XIV lived only two years after the signing of the Treaty of Utrecht. He had long outlived his popularity. As the body of the grandest of all the absolute monarchs was drawn through the streets of Paris, some of his abused people cursed in the taverns as the coffin passed.

7. THE DECLINE OF FRENCH ABSOLUTISM

The French monarchy never again achieved the power it wielded under Louis XIV. Certainly France remained a first-rank power, with a large army, a centralized bureaucracy, and a growing economy. But between 1715 and 1789 the monarchy slowly declined.

Louis XIV was succeeded in 1715 by his five-year-old great-grandson, Louis XV. Louis XV was never interested in the day-to-day affairs of government like Louis XIV. Most historians consider him a mediocre king, concerned with his own pleasures and willing to leave governmental administration to his ministers, most of whom were of questionable quality. Until 1720 the duke of Orléans ruled as regent. He diminished the prestige of the monarchy by backing the financial schemes of John Law, which resulted in a scandal known as the Mississippi Bubble. The duke of Orléans also opened the door to the crown's greatest competitor—the aristocracy—by strengthening the *parlements*—courts dominated by aristocrats that declared laws or acts of the monarch valid or invalid.

From 1726 to 1743 Cardinal Fleury served as chief minister. The most effective of Louis XV's ministers, Fleury brought relative stability to political affairs and a needed period of peace. But neither he, nor the less effective advisers of Louis XV that followed, nor the monarchy of the indecisive Louis XVI that succeeded in 1774 were able to solve fundamental problems weakening the monarchy.

Map 32.1 **THE GROWTH OF FRANCE UNDER LOUIS XIV** These maps indicate the extensiveness of the wars waged by Louis XIV during his reign and the areas in which he made the most significant gains—along the eastern border of France.

Expensive wars and unreformed taxation policies left the treasury depleted after Louis XIV's death. The clergy and nobility retained most of their immunities from taxation despite efforts of several ministers to break those privileges. The debt grew, and the monarchy was weakened by its inability to reform its finances to lessen the burden of that debt.

Underlying these political and financial problems was a resurgence of the aristocracy. In the decades between 1715 and 1789 the monarchy was faced by an increasingly assertive aristocracy, anxious to recapture some of its old political power. Ambitious aristocrats thwarted the kings' efforts to reform taxes. They set themselves up as centers of aristocratic opposition to the monarchy, above all through their control of the *parlements* (law courts).

Thus by the middle decades of the eighteenth century, the French monarchy had clearly declined from its heights under Louis XIV. When problems came to a head in the 1780s, the king was unable to handle them and the monarchy was toppled by a great revolution.

SUGGESTED READING

General

P. Anderson, *Lineages of the Absolutist State* (1974). A good Marxist analysis.

G. N. Clark, *The Seventeenth Century* (1961). Good brief survey, emphasizing cultural aspects.

R. N. Hatton, *Europe in the Age of Louis XIV* (1979). A well-illustrated survey.

Rise of France Under Henry IV, Richelieu, and Mazarin

L. A. Moote, *The Revolt of the Judges: The Parlement of Paris and the Fronde 1643–1652* (1971). A detailed analysis of the Fronde.

V. L. Tapié, *France in the Age of Louis XIII and Richelieu* (1974). A good survey.

Louis XIV and His Court

W. F. Church, ed., *Louis XIV in Historical Thought* (1978). Conflicting interpretations of Louis XIV.

P. Goubert, *Louis XIV and Twenty Million Frenchmen* (1970). A respected study of French society and politics.

H. Rowen, *The King's State: Proprietary Dynasticism in Early Modern France* (1980). Analyzes the theory of Louis XIV's rule.

A. Trout, *Jean-Baptiste Colbert* (1978). Analyzes his economic policies.

J. B. Wolf, *Louis XIV* (1968). An excellent biography.

The Decline of French Absolutism

A. Cobban, *A History of Modern France, Vol. 1* (1966). A clear, well-written interpretation.

Sources

L. R. Saint-Simon, *The Memoirs of the Duc de Saint-Simon*. A disgruntled courtier's detailed eyewitness account of Versaille under Louis XIV.

Marie de Sévigné, *Letters from Madame la Marquise de Sévigné*, ed. and trans. Violet Hammersley (1956). Well-written eyewitness account of life at Versailles.

CHAPTER 33

The Challenge to Absolutism: England and the Dutch Netherlands

FIGURE 33.1. The English Cabinet This scene shows Robert Walpole, who served as prime minister of England from 1721 to 1742, presiding over a session of the cabinet. Walpole and the other cabinet members shown here all were members of Parliament and belonged to the majority party in that body. In sessions such as this they decided upon the major policies to be followed by the government; their control of Parliament allowed them to enact their decisions. Thus, the cabinet became the effective executive power in Great Britain, a position that it still holds today. The emergence of the cabinet system was one of the major outcomes of the bitter political struggle in seventeenth-century England. (The Bettmann Archive)

While royal absolutism was being perfected in France and elsewhere on the Continent, England and the Dutch Netherlands moved toward a form of government that placed limitations on the authority of the executive and on the power of the state. This constitutional system gave to a representative body the authority to define the law. It also sought to create a balance between the power of the state and the rights and liberties of citizens of the state. The constitutional changes made in England and the Dutch Netherlands during the seventeenth century strongly influenced later struggles against absolutism in many parts of the world.

1. EARLY STUART ABSOLUTISM

The absolutism shaped by the Tudors (see Chapter 28) was subjected to serious challenges during the seventeenth century. "Good Queen Bess" died in 1603 without a direct heir. She was succeeded by a distant cousin, James Stuart (1603–1625), king of Scotland. He was an avowed absolutist, but he was woefully ignorant of the delicate working of the Tudor political system and not suited by temperament for the hard work nor gifted with the political adroitness needed to keep that system working. His political ineptitude led to a progressive breakdown of the Tudor system and to a polarization of political forces.

But not all of the troubles of James I's reign were the making of a king known in his own days as "the wisest fool in Christendom." New problems were facing England that threatened the general satisfaction that most people had felt toward Tudor governance. Major economic changes were in process, creating new opportunities in agriculture, manufacturing, trade, and the professions. Enterprising groups seeking to take advantage of these opportunities were eager to assert greater control over royal policy in order to promote their economic interests. These same changes were adversely affecting other groups, especially rural tenants and laborers, thereby fostering popular discontent. A major realignment of power was taking shape in Europe, marked by the ascendancy of France. This development encouraged the English rulers to seek closer ties with their traditional enemy, Spain, a course that many still basking in the glories of the victory over the Armada viewed as unpatriotic.

The very structure of the Tudor political system lacked key elements conducive to effective absolutism. Too much depended on the personal qualities of the monarch and a narrow circle of royal advisers. There was not a well-developed bureaucracy nor a well-organized military force. The central government had limited control over local government, dominated by a local gentry, the members of which were jealous of their offices and protective of their local interests. The traditional system of common law served to limit arbitrary acts by the royal government. Most serious of all were the limited financial resources of the crown. It could not manage on the traditional sources of revenue—income from royal lands, customs duties, and feudal dues. Additional income could only be derived from taxes, which Parliament had long since established the right to approve. If absolutism was to continue, significant political reforms aimed at increasing the power of the monarch were required. Such changes posed a threat to powerfully entrenched interests in England.

Another increasingly acute source of tension involved religious issues. Many were not satisfied with the Anglican settlement carried out during Elizabeth's reign (see Chapter 31). The major dissenters were the Puritans, who wanted reforms that would make the established religion more "Protestant": simpler ritual, more emphasis on Scripture, less episcopal control over local churches. There also remained many Roman Catholics who hoped to undo the Reformation; their presence was a cause of constant concern for all Protestants.

During James I's reign these issues found their focus in Parliament, especially in the House of Commons, a body theoretically representing the entire English populace but actually dominated by the country gentry, merchants, and lawyers. The king was forced to summon Parliament because of the constant and increasing need for money. Although Parliament usually provided some financial aid, its members constantly raised issues that challenged royal policy. They criticized James I's royal advisers for corruption, favoritism, and incompetence. They questioned his unwavering support of Anglicanism and his lenient policy toward the Catholics. They condemned the alliance he made with Spain early in his reign and his failure to support the Protestant forces when the Thirty Years' War began in 1618. James responded by repeatedly dismissing Parliament. He then tried to utilize other means of raising money, but these efforts were challenged in the courts as contrary to custom and thus illegal. The king answered by dismissing judges, leading to more parliamentary criticism. Throughout this long series of clashes, Parliament proved itself to be an undisciplined, intemperate body. But its confrontations with the king heightened the fear that the royal government was bent on extending its prerogatives to the point where the constitution and the law would be subverted, opening the way to tyranny.

Under James' successor, Charles I (1625–1649), the conflict deepened into civil war. Charles was no less stubborn than James in his insistence on royal absolutism and in his refusal to bend before the claims of Parliament and the courts. The king's major problem continued to be a need for funds, a need made more desperate by a blundering foreign policy that resulted in costly military ventures in France and Spain that produced no victories. Charles was forced to request taxes from Parliament, which responded by challenging royal policy on a variety of issues. Increasingly, the leaders of Parliament began to make specific their definition of what they meant by royal violation of the constitution and the law. Their views found expression in the Petition of Rights submitted to the king in 1628. This bold document demanded that the king desist from various illegal acts: imposing martial law in peacetime, levying taxes without Parliament's approval, imprisoning citizens without trial, and quartering soldiers with private citizens. Desperate for money, Charles accepted the Petition of Rights, thereby admitting that he had acted illegally. But when Parliament in its next session in 1629 insisted that the king respect the petition's provisions on taxation, Charles dismissed Parliament, over the bitter protests of its leaders.

For the next eleven years Charles ruled without Parliament. To do so he was forced to rely on a variety of means of raising funds that pushed royal authority to the limits of legality. Ultimately, it was Charles' religious policy that forced him once again to confront his enemies on their ground—in Parliament. With Charles' support, his chief religious adviser, William Laud, archbishop of Canterbury, initiated a vigorous "reform" aimed at giving greater emphasis in the Church of England to elaborate rituals, episcopal authority over local churches, and the doctrine of free will. To the Puritans Laud's reforms were detestable, the very opposite of the most fundamental precepts of Protestantism. Many of them fled to the New World in search of a setting where they would have the freedom to institute real Protestantism. Laud's policies also alarmed many Anglicans, who sensed that England was on a course that would lead it back to Roman Catholicism. But it was the absolute refusal of the Scotch Presbyterians to accept the "beauty of holiness," as Charles called Laud's reforms, that precipitated a crisis. In 1639 they revolted, posing a military crisis that forced Charles to summon Parliament into session in 1640 in order to raise money to resist the Scotch threat to the kingdom.

The first Parliament of 1640, called the Short Parliament, was dismissed after three weeks because it again challenged royal authority. But the Scots continued to press and Charles was forced to capitulate. He summoned the Long Parliament, so called because it was to sit for twenty years. With an amazing show of unity Parliament proceeded to legislate the end of Stuart absolutism. It forced Charles to sacrifice his chief ministers, including Laud. It abolished the hated extraordinary courts, including the Star Chamber and the Court of High Commission, which had long been tools used by the crown to avoid the common law. An act was passed requiring a meeting of Parliament every three years and curbing the power of the king to dismiss Parliament. Severe limitations were placed on the king's power to tax without parliamentary approval. To all of this Charles acceded, chiefly because he needed money to fight the Scots.

Up to this point Parliament had succeeded brilliantly in legislating what amounted to a bloodless revolution that established limited monarchy. But the parliamentary forces then began to falter over the question of how to use Parliament's power. In general, its leadership was forced in directions that caused alarm in many quarters and drove many back toward support of the king. Charles helped to cause this split by giving every sign that he would resist being a limited monarch. Suspicion of his motives caused parliamentary leaders to remove from his hands control of the administration and the army and to impose taxes that seemed as burdensome as those imposed by Charles earlier. Religious opinion in Parliament moved in the direction of ending Anglicanism "root and branch" in favor of some form of Presbyterianism. This mounting extremism caused many influential leaders to believe that Parliament was setting a course that would upset the established order. The division in the parliamentary ranks emboldened Charles to try to restore his control; he went so far in early 1642 as to attempt to arrest the leaders of Parliament. This action was a call to arms, pitting against each other elements of a ruling class that had lost its community of interest, an interest that had long focused on the monarch.

2. ENGLISH CIVIL WAR, COMMONWEALTH, AND PROTECTORATE (1642–1660)

The opening of armed strife divided England along lines that defy easy definition. The opposing forces did not represent clear-cut economic interests or social classes. A considerable following, soon known as the Cavaliers, rallied around Charles, who represented himself as the champion of the established order against the political and religious radicals in Parliament. The backbone of the Cavalier forces came from the great noble families and their clientele among the country gentry living in the more economically backward areas of northern and western England. Although the opposition, called the Roundheads, had its noble supporters, it drew its main strength from lawyers, the gentry of the south and the east, and the commercial interests; many from these elements were Puritans. This core was soon reinforced by radical elements from the poor and op-

pressed, especially those living in London. In the intricate matter of choosing sides, there figured complex personal factors—family ties, friendships, personal loyalties—much after the fashion of the American Civil War.

The first phase of the civil war lasted through 1646. While neither side was prepared militarily, for a time the Cavaliers seemed to have the upper hand. But the Roundheads had forces working in their favor: support of the navy, domination of the richest part of England, control over the regular administrative system and Parliament, power to vote taxation. In 1643 the Roundhead cause was bolstered by an alliance with the Scots. But ultimately the outcome of the struggle was determined by the success of the Roundheads in creating an effective army. The chief architect of the victorious army was a simple farmer with strong Puritan convictions, Oliver Cromwell. He organized a cavalry regiment of disciplined, deeply religious recruits who proved more than a match for the Cavalier forces they faced. His system was soon applied to the entire Roundhead force to create the New Model Army, made up of selected troops paid and equipped in a businesslike fashion. It quickly proved itself superior to the Cavalier army, so that by 1646 the Cavalier army was crushed and Charles was forced to surrender.

However, with victory in their grasp, the Roundheads were unable to work out an acceptable settlement. After the defeat of the Cavaliers the Roundheads were led by moderates who wished to establish a limited monarchy and a Presbyterian religious order. Charles remained unwilling to accept such a settlement and raised fears of a renewal of the civil war by fleeing his captors and allying himself with the Scots. More ominous was the increasing prominence of Roundhead leaders who demanded a more radical religious reform favoring the independence of local churches and freedom of conscience. These religious Independents were joined by the Levellers, political radicals who advocated the end of monarchy, democratic elections, and the redistribution of wealth. The strength of these religious and political radicals became centered in the New Model Army, where discontent was fed by the fact that pay was considerably in arrears. Fearful that the radicals would seize complete control, the moderate Roundheads ordered the army demobilized. And they turned back to the king, who suddenly expressed considerable enthusiasm for parliamentary control over the monarchy and for Presbyterianism. The Independents, led by Cromwell, would not be denied. They destroyed the hope of Charles and his Scotch army in a single battle in 1648 and, along with it, the cause of the Cavaliers and the moderate Roundheads. Backed by the New Model Army, Cromwell acted decisively to ensure the position of the Independents. He purged the Long Parliament of all members not dedicated to his cause and gave to the so-called Rump Parliament chief authority in the land. It immediately legislated out of existence the Anglican church, the House of Lords, and the monarchy. And at Cromwell's urging it decreed the execution of the king in 1649 on the grounds that he was "a tyrant, traitor, and murderer."

For eleven years after Charles I's death Cromwell's forces sought to rule England without a king. Always in a minority and dependent on the army, their desperate experimentation failed to establish a stable order. England steadily retreated from revolution.

The first experiment sought to create a republican form of government called the Commonwealth. A one-house Parliament was made the supreme authority, with a state council of forty-one members charged with conducting the daily affairs of government. The political and religious extremists in the army were curbed, and considerable toleration was extended to all Protestants. Severe measures were taken to subdue the rebellious Irish and the Scots. An aggressive foreign policy, aimed at promoting English commercial and colonial interests, was undertaken. Navigation acts were passed to ensure that trade within England's emerging empire would be monopolized by England. War was waged on the Dutch, England's chief commercial rival. None of these policies, however, helped to popularize the Commonwealth. The Cromwellians could not shed their image as regicides and Puritan extremists (see Figure 33.2). Resistance to the Commonwealth grew steadily.

Cromwell ultimately blamed the failure of the

Oliver feeking God while the K. is murthered by his order.

FIGURE 33.2. A Satire on Cromwell The deep religious fervor of the Puritans and the taint of regicide that lingered throughout the Commonwealth and the Protectorate are satirized here as Oliver Cromwell is shown at prayer while Charles I is being executed. (NYPL Picture Collection)

Commonwealth on what he considered the self-seeking leaders of the Rump Parliament. Finally, in 1653, he dissolved the Rump by force and tried to replace it with a handpicked body (called the Barebones Parliament, in honor of Praise-God Barebones, the first name on its roll). This body failed to distinguish itself in any way, and it too was dissolved. Finally, the very instrument that had stood against tyranny—Parliament—was gone. The tide of revolution had peaked with Cromwell and his army in control.

In pursuit of what he called a "healing and settling" course for England, Cromwell tried one more experiment, called the Protectorate. A written constitution was drawn up entrusting power to a lord protector (Cromwell), who was advised by a Council of State and guided by a one-house Parliament elected by property holders. From the beginning the lord protector and Parliament clashed on most issues, largely because the elected Parliament represented political and religious positions that ran contrary to the convictions of those who alone could sustain Cromwell in power, the "godly" men of the New Model Army. Despite the constant turmoil the Protectorate achieved some successes. The specter of radical political change was dispelled by the suppression of the Levellers. The central administration was honestly administered. Traditional patterns of local government were restored. A variety of Protestant groups enjoyed considerable independence and freedom of religious choice. Cromwell pursued a firm foreign policy that pacified Ireland and Scotland, extended English overseas colonies, and promoted commercial interests. But never could Cromwell escape the fact that the army, not civilian consent, kept him in power.

As the Protectorate floundered, opinion began to run in favor of the restoration of monarchy. In 1657 Parliament asked Cromwell to become king, an honor he declined, but he did agree to remain lord protector for life. Thus, when he died in 1658, the wheel had come nearly full circle: A man who had led his soldiers to the abolition of monarchy was himself king without title.

At Cromwell's death, his son, Richard, became lord protector. This weak figure was soon swept aside by forces favoring the restoration of monarchy. By 1660 elements in the New Model Army joined with people of property and commerce to end the Protectorate. The Long Parliament voted to dissolve itself. A new Parliament was elected and soon invited Charles Stuart, the son of Charles I, to return from exile and assume the crown in 1660.

3. THE ENGLISH RESTORATION (1660–1688)

The Restoration of the Stuarts by no means resolved the basic problems that had divided England since 1603, particularly those involving the relationship between king and Parliament and the religious establishment. Between 1660 and 1688 these problems continued to disturb society. However, the struggles of the Restoration era were more moderate than had been the case in the preceding two decades.

The reign of Charles II (1660–1685) began in a climate of forgiving compromise. The king and Parliament joined in repealing all the acts of the Commonwealth and the Protectorate. Only a few Cromwellians were punished for their part in killing Charles I. Confiscated property was returned to property owners. The king was assured of a sizable income on a regular basis, but he was deprived of many ancient feudal rights that had allowed his predecessors to exact taxes without approval of Parliament. Not only was control of taxation reserved to Parliament, but the Triennial Act was passed to ensure that it would meet every three years whether or not the king so wished. However, this settlement did not get to the basic political issue: where ultimate authority rested.

Even less satisfactory was the religious settlement embodied in a series of parliamentary acts passed in 1661 and 1662 and known as the Clarendon Code after Charles II's chief adviser, the earl of Clarendon. These acts not only reestablished the Anglican church but also threatened to destroy the Independents and Presbyterians. The Act of Uniformity required all clergy to abide by the Book of Common Prayer. The Corporation Act ruled that all members of city governments worship in the Anglican church. The Conventicle Act made religious meetings other than Anglican illegal, and the Five Mile Act forbade all preachers who were not Anglican to come within five miles of any city. In brief, the Clarendon Code promised to nonconformists (that is, non-Anglicans) little better than criminal status.

These troublesome issues soon began to surface, to divide opinion and generate conflict. They were intensified by a series of disasters that befell England during the early years of Charles' reign.

He involved England in a war with the Dutch that led to a humiliating defeat. In 1665 a plague struck England, to be followed the next year by a fire that destroyed most of London. Many god-fearing English felt that these misfortunes were divine retribution for the immorality of the royal court, where the model of profligacy was set by the king himself.

Parliament again became the center of dissatisfaction. It reacted to public wrath by forcing Clarendon out of office in 1667 and by becoming stingier in approving taxes needed to fund an unsuccessful war and Charles' personal extravagances. Charles paid little heed to the growing opposition, choosing instead to pursue two policies he personally favored: an alliance with France and religious tolerance in England that would permit Roman Catholics to worship freely. In 1670 he signed a treaty with Louis XIV agreeing, in return for a subsidy, to join France in a war on the Dutch and to promote the Catholic cause in England. In 1672 Charles issued a Declaration of Indulgence, which set aside laws restricting the practice of Roman Catholicism. An outraged Parliament forced the king to withdraw the Declaration of Indulgence and passed the Test Act (1673), which excluded Catholics from all public offices. And when Charles joined France in another unsuccessful war against the Dutch in 1672–1674, Parliament forced him to seek peace by refusing financial support.

Although the tensions continued, especially those involving religious issues, Charles showed considerable ingenuity in neutralizing Parliament during the last years of his reign. An improving economy resulted in growing tax returns, minimizing Parliament's power to control the crown by controlling taxation. Louis XIV's subsidies helped ease the financial burden on the king. More significantly, Charles skillfully built a political following—an embryonic "party"—devoted to strong monarchy and Anglicanism. Its members, scornfully dubbed "Tories" (a term used to designate Irish bandits) by the opposition, could often control Parliament in support of the king. An opposing "party," committed to parliamentary supremacy and religious tolerance for all Protestants, was also formed; its members were called "Whigs" (after a term used to designate Scottish horse thieves and murderers). Charles' successes led many to feel that absolutism was returning to England. But one obstacle kept Charles from totally controlling English political life: a rising fear that the king was determined to restore Catholicism.

James II (1685–1688) inherited a strong position from his brother, based in large part on the Tory majority in Parliament, a sound financial position, and general satisfaction with legitimate succession. But he soon dissipated this strength by his open avowal of Catholicism and attempts to improve the position of Catholics in England, which neither Tories nor Whigs would tolerate. When in 1688 a son was born to James and his Catholic wife and baptized in the Catholic faith, ensuring that the Stuart dynasty would be perpetuated by a Catholic successor, Tory and Whig leaders invited James' Protestant daughter, Mary, and her husband, William of Orange, the stadholder of several provinces in the Dutch Netherlands, to assume England's throne. When William invaded England in late 1688, the great majority of the people rallied to his side; James II fled to France. For a second time, the unhappy Stuarts had been forced off England's throne, but this time the revolution was bloodless.

4. ENGLAND'S GLORIOUS REVOLUTION AND ITS CONSEQUENCES

The flight of James II, unlike the execution of Charles I, did not lead to radical political experimentation. Instead, what the English call a Glorious Revolution was carried through in the form of several fundamental legal enactments that pacified England and established the basis for its future political system.

Immediately after the triumph of William and Mary, Parliament declared the throne vacant by reason of James' abdication. It then voted to grant the crown to William and Mary. A Bill of Rights was passed in 1689. This fundamental charter asserted Parliament's authority to depose a king and choose a new one. It assured to the members of Parliament the right of free speech, immunity from prosecution for statements made in debate, and freedom from royal intervention in elections. It forbade a variety of acts that had long been the basis for royal absolutism: taxing without consent of Parliament, dispensing with laws, maintaining a standing army in peacetime, requiring excessive bail, depriving citizens of the right to trial in the regular courts, interfering with jurors, and denying people the right to petition the king. The Bill of Rights implied that government was based on a contract between ruler and ruled, a concept of government increasingly attractive among "enlightened" leaders in western Europe. This theory of government was set forth with special force by John Locke in his *Two Treatises on Civil Government*, published in 1690. Locke argued that a government was the product of a contract entered into by rational people in order to establish an authority capable of protecting rights that belonged to all humans by the laws of nature: the right of life, liberty, and property. Any government that violated these natural rights broke the contract that brought it into existence; in this event its subjects had a right to correct or even overthrow it. For settlement of the long-standing religious issue a Toleration Act was passed, allowing religious freedom to Puritans and Independents but not to non-Protestants. Finally, the Act of Settlement was passed in 1701 to ensure that none but Protestants could inherit the throne.

The initial settlement marking the Glorious Revolution certainly addressed in a positive way fundamental issues that had troubled England for nearly a century. However, there remained problems still to be resolved. The accession of William and Mary resulted in a basic reorientation of England's foreign policy, which called on the nation to commit its resources to a long, burdensome series of wars in many parts of the globe to prevent France from establishing world dominance. We have already seen (Chapter 32) the decisive role that England played in foiling Louis XIV's ambitions. Closer to home Ireland was brought under English control. Early in his reign William led an army into this unhappy land, where discontent had long festered and which now became a center of Stuart intrigue—funded by the French—aimed at recovering the English throne. Having established control by force, William in-

stituted a policy of suppression, reducing Ireland to colonial status, a policy that provided splendid opportunity for English landlords to uproot Irish Catholic landowners and take possession of their property. Scotland enjoyed an easier fate in the face of increasing English power. Early in his reign William began negotiations with the Scots that finally bore fruit after his death. In 1707 Parliament passed the Act of Union, which joined the two kingdoms into a single nation henceforth known as the United Kingdom of Great Britain. The settlement gave the Scots a liberal number of seats in Parliament and guaranteed their Presbyterian religious establishment.

The burdens of global war placed stresses on the political system and led to important changes. As we have already seen, Parliament was actively engaged in defining the settlement after the Glorious Revolution. Its role in political life intensified thereafter, chiefly because its approval was needed for taxes. Annual government expenditures increased threefold between the reign of Charles II and the reign of William and Mary. To meet these expenditures, the monarchs had to call Parliament nearly every year. Frequent sessions of Parliament required that the royal government pay special attention to the election process in search of sufficient votes from qualified voters—chiefly property owners—to secure a majority in Parliament willing to support royal policy. Because Parliament was increasingly important, party strife between Whigs and Tories became a decisive feature of political life. Party leaders played an ever-larger role in counseling the rulers and overseeing public affairs. This ever-increasing identification of Parliament with the management of the nation's affairs probably did more than the noble principles of the Bill of Rights to make secure parliamentary control of public life.

The progress toward parliamentary supremacy following the Glorious Revolution left unresolved one major constitutional issue—that of the exact nature of the executive power responsible for the conduct of the routine affairs of state. For centuries, English kings had relied on powerful ministers to assist them in conducting government affairs and in shaping policy. Until 1688, these ministers had usually been chosen by the king and were responsible to him. After the supremacy of

Parliament was established in 1688–1689, this system began to change with the emergence of the *cabinet system*. Royal ministers were increasingly chosen on the basis of their ability to influence Parliament, especially the House of Commons. Since Commons tended to divide into parties that controlled large blocs of votes, it proved wisest for the rulers to seek out party leaders from that body for appointment as ministers responsible for exercising executive functions.

With the accession of Anne (1702–1714), this trend developed rapidly. Neither she nor the first Hanoverians, George I (1714–1727) and George II (1727–1760), were especially qualified for or interested in the rigorous tasks of administration. As a consequence, the direction of the government and the formulation of policy fell into the hands of royal ministers able to secure from Parliament approval to carry on the affairs of state in the name of the monarch. This *cabinet* of ministers slowly learned to accept mutual responsibility for the total operation of the government, which required that they all be members of the same party and that they use their collective influence in Parliament to ensure approval of their program. If they failed to command a majority in that body, then they had to surrender their positions as ministers in favor of a new cabinet that did have a parliamentary majority. One member of the cabinet, the *prime minister*, came to be recognized as the leader and spokesperson of the whole group; a major qualification for this designation was leadership of the majority party in Commons.

Although Queen Anne relied heavily on John Churchill, duke of Marlborough, to conduct her government, the first real prime minister and architect of the cabinet system was Robert Walpole (see Figure 33.1). A longtime member of Commons, he became George I's chief minister in 1721, primarily because of his leadership of the dominant Whig party in Commons. From then until 1742 he virtually ran England by surrounding himself with fellow ministers who could control votes in Parliament. Not until he lost control of Commons over a foreign policy issue was he forced to relinquish his position as prime minister. However, the king had little choice but to appoint another prime minister and cabinet that could command a majority in Parliament. Henceforth to the present the executive functions of government in Great Britain would be carried out in the name of the monarch by a circle of party leaders who could command a majority in the House of Commons but who were likewise required to render account to that body for their conduct of public affairs.

The Glorious Revolution and the settlement that followed it marked a turning point in Great Britain's history. Two great decisions had been reached. First, royal absolutism had been repudiated in favor of a limited monarchy in which ultimate authority was entrusted to an elected Parliament. Second, religious uniformity had given way to religious toleration for all Protestants. The resolution of these issues restored Great Britain's internal stability and provided a basis for its rapid advance to the status of world power. However, the "revolution" had its limitations: Even as it unfolded, steps were taken to limit eligibility for Parliament to men of wealth, chiefly landowners. Until the nineteenth century these "gentlemen" dominated Great Britain in a fashion that served their collective interests.

5. THE DUTCH NETHERLANDS

Absolutism was also successfully challenged during the seventeenth century by the Dutch. Their success led to the creation of a new nation in which prevailed a political and social environment that allowed the Dutch to forge for themselves a leadership role in European commerce, banking, and intellectual and artistic life. That new nation emerged from the Dutch refusal to accept the absolutist system that Philip II of Spain attempted to force on them (see Chapter 31). Although Philip II was able to impose Spanish rule over the ten southern provinces of the Netherlands (now Belgium; see Map 33.1), the seven northern provinces resisted and by 1609 had established effective independence as the United Provinces of the Netherlands; independence was officially recognized by the Treaty of Westphalia (1648).

The new state adopted a republican form of government. Each province, ruled by an elected executive (called the stadholder) and a provincial representative assembly, retained extensive control over local affairs. Although most of the stad-

Map 33.1   THE UNITED PROVINCES, 1609
This map illustrates how small a territory the Dutch Republic occupied in its golden age—no larger than a corner of England. Yet through the cities of this small area flowed much of the commerce of the seventeenth and eighteenth centuries. With that commerce came a flow of money that made such cities as Amsterdam the financial centers of the world.

holders came from the landed aristocracy, especially from the House of Orange, a powerful family that had played a crucial role in the struggle for independence, the provincial governments were dominated by commercial and financial leaders who resisted the establishment of strong central government. The only truly national political institution was the States General, made up of delegates from each province who acted only on instructions from the provincial governments. It enjoyed limited powers and asserted very little direction over national affairs. The citizens of the Dutch Netherlands enjoyed considerable freedom to pursue their personal and collective interests. Particularly noteworthy was religious freedom. The Reformed church, strongly Calvinist in doctrine and practice, was established by law, but other religious groups, including Roman Catholics and Jews, were tolerated, a fact that attracted religious refugees from other European nations.

The Dutch Netherlands, a nation of only about

one million, made its chief mark on the seventeenth-century world in commerce and finance. That success was based on the seafaring skills of its people and the entrepreneurship of its vigorous bourgeoisie. Those talents, developed over many centuries, allowed the Dutch to become world leaders in commerce. Experienced Dutch sailors plundered Spanish commerce and overseas colonies to reap a rich reward. When Spain temporarily annexed Portugal in 1580, the Dutch seized most of Portugal's lucrative holdings in the East Indies. The Dutch East India Company, set up in 1602 to develop trade with the East Indies, returned huge profits to its stockholders during the entire seventeenth century. The Dutch established a flourishing colony in North America. Dutch traders also took advantage of their favorable geographical position at the mouth of the Rhine and its tributaries and of their excellent harbors along the northern European trade routes to gain a near-monopoly of the carrying trade of Europe. A large

FIGURE 33.3. **Rembrandt, "Syndics of the Cloth Guild"** In the Dutch Netherlands of the seventeenth century, commerce was king. Under the leadership of such men as shown here, the tiny Dutch Netherlands attained a first-rank position in the world of science, philosophy, and trade. Rembrandt, one of the greatest portrait painters of all time, was probably also the greatest of the baroque painters. (Fotocommissie Rijks-museum Amsterdam)

proportion of Europe's ships were built in Dutch shipyards.

The extensive trading activities of the Dutch led to a huge flow of wealth into the hands of Dutch merchants. This capital allowed them to become Europe's leading money lenders, serving princes, merchants, and landowners willing to pay for the use of Dutch capital. The financial activities of the Dutch were institutionalized in the Bank of Amsterdam, set up in 1609. It became a model for national banks later established elsewhere in western Europe. Its location in Amsterdam reflected the fact that that city had become the world's chief commercial and financial center.

The wealth and the freedom of Dutch society generated a vigorous cultural outburst. Some of the chief intellectuals in Europe found refuge in the United Provinces, including the philosophers René Descartes from France, John Locke from England, and Baruch Spinoza, a Jewish refugee from Portugal. Among the notable Dutch intellectuals was Hugo Grotius, whose *On the Law of War and Peace* was the first great treatise on international law and has remained a classic on the subject ever since. Freedom of the press enabled the United Provinces to become the leading European center of book publishing. This was the golden age of Dutch painters. While baroque painters in other countries were glorifying royalty and nobility, Jan Vermeer, Franz Hals, and above all, Rembrandt van Rijn were celebrating the spirit of Dutch society by dignifying—sometimes glamorizing—the middle and lower classes (see Figure 33.3). Dutch scientists played an important role in advancing the Scientific Revolution, including the invention of the telescope and the microscope. All of these activities gave the Dutch an important role in western European literary, intellectual, and artistic life.

As the seventeenth century drew to a close, the Dutch preeminence in commerce and banking began to decline, especially in the face of England's sea power and France's land might. But that decline could not efface the notable contributions of the Dutch to seventeenth-century western European civilization, a contribution due at least in part to the freedom enjoyed by Dutch citizens to assert their talents as they chose.

SUGGESTED READING

General Treatments

J. P. Kenyon, *Stuart England* (1978).
Barry Coward, *The Stuart Age. A History of England 1603–1714* (1980).
Either of these works will provide a fine overview of Stuart England.
Derek Hirst, *Authority and Conflict: England, 1603–1658* (1986).
J. R. Jones, *Country and Court, England, 1658–1714* (1978).
These two volumes, parts of a new general history of England, give a balanced treatment of the period.
Christopher Hill, *A Century of Revolution, 1603–1714,* 2nd ed. (1982). A provocative study from a Marxist perspective.
C. G. A. Clay, *Economic Expansion and Social Change, England, 1500–1700,* 2 vols. (1984). An excellent synthesis, rich in details.

From Civil War to the Glorious Revolution

Robert Ashton, *Reformation and Revolution, 1558–1660* (1985). Helps to establish the background for England's revolutionary age.
Lawrence Stone, *The Causes of the English Revolution, 1529–1642* (1972). Analyzes various interpretations of the causes of the English revolution.
G. E. Aylmer, *Rebellion or Revolution? England, 1640–1660* (1986). A balanced treatment of the civil war and the era of Cromwell.
C. V. Wedgwood, *The King's Peace, 1637–1641* (1955); *The King's War, 1641–1647* (1959); and *A Coffin for King Charles* (1964). Brilliant treatments of the crucial years of the English civil war.
Christopher Hill, *The World Turned Upside Down: Radical Ideas During the English Revolution* (1972). An important work on radicalism.

Patrick Morrah, *Restoration England* (1979). A good social history.
John Miller, *The Glorious Revolution* (1983). A brief, thoughtful description and assessment of the Glorious Revolution.
P. Laslett, *The World We Have Lost,* 2nd ed. (1971). A brilliant evocation of the English society of about 1700.

The Dutch Netherlands

Pieter Geyl, *The Netherlands in the Seventeenth Century,* rev. ed., 2 vols. (1961–1964). An excellent detailed treatment.
Charles Wilson, *The Dutch Republic and the Civilisation of the Seventeenth Century* (1968).
K. H. D. Haley, *The Dutch in the Seventeenth Century* (1972).
Two brief treatments that will help the reader to understand Dutch society in its most glorious age.
C. R. Boxer, *The Dutch Seaborne Empire, 1600–1800* (1965). A good description of the source of much of Dutch wealth.
Simon Schama, *The Embarrassment of Riches. An Interpretation of Dutch Culture in the Golden Age* (1987). A brilliant portrayal of social life.

Biographies

Pauline Gregg, *King Charles I* (1981).
Antonia Fraser, *Cromwell. The Lord Protector* (1973).
Antonia Fraser, *Royal Charles: Charles II and the Restoration* (1979).
S. Baxter, *William III and the Defense of European Liberty, 1650–1702* (1966).

CHAPTER 34

Eastern Europe and the Rise of Prussia and Russia

FIGURE 34.1.   Frederick II Before His Troops   During the seventeenth and eighteenth centuries, the rulers of Brandenburg-Prussia used their armies to build up the state, making it one of the major powers of eastern and central Europe. Here, Frederick II of Prussia is shown in a characteristic military pose, exemplifying the strong alliance of the monarchy and army. (The Mansell Collection)

At the beginning of the seventeenth century eastern Europe exhibited certain characteristics that set it in sharp contrast to western Europe. Economically, the states east of the Elbe River were less commercially developed than those in western Europe. Estate agriculture (large landed estates owned by lords and worked by their serfs) remained the rule. Socially, the landed aristocracy dominated these areas to a greater extent than in western Europe. Indeed, this aristocracy had generally succeeded in reversing medieval trends toward greater freedom for the peasantry and the growth of towns. During the fifteenth, sixteenth, and seventeenth centuries serfdom was reimposed with greater severity than ever, and the landed aristocracy won in its struggle with competing urban centers. Politically, many areas lacked the strong central government found in the western European states. In political struggles the nobility had sometimes gained the upper hand over monarchs. Nowhere was this pattern more marked than in Poland, where there was a corresponding decline in the strength of the state to the point that Poland was literally divided and annexed by outside powers during the eighteenth century. Yet the seventeenth and eighteenth centuries would witness some important changes in eastern Europe, particularly in political affairs.

The most significant political developments in central and eastern Europe during the seventeenth and eighteenth centuries were the rise of Prussia and Russia. At the opening of the seventeenth century, the two chief powers in central and eastern Europe were the Ottoman and Hapsburg empires. Although the Moslem Ottoman Turks had been restrained by Hapsburg military power in the sixteenth century on both land and sea, they were about to renew their effort to conquer Christian Europe. The Austrian Hapsburgs, in addition to disputing the control of southeastern Europe with the Turks, dominated the Holy Roman Empire, which included all the German states. In northeastern Europe, Sweden, Prussia, Poland, and Russia competed for hegemony. Among all these powers, Prussia and Russia had hitherto been the least conspicuous in world affairs. During the seventeenth and eighteenth centuries, Prussia and Russia would become major powers and assume active roles in international politics.

1. THE EARLY HOHENZOLLERNS

The history of Prussia is in large measure the history of the Hohenzollern family. This aggressive and prolific dynasty was first heard of in the tenth century. At that time the Hohenzollerns were obscure counts ruling over the castle of Zollern and a tiny bit of surrounding territory in southwest Germany just north of the Swiss border. In the twelfth century they became burgraves of Nuremberg, an important commercial city in Bavaria. Early in the fifteenth century the Holy Roman emperor, looking for an able ruler for the mark of Brandenburg, a military province near the exposed northeastern border of the empire, chose the head of the house of Hohenzollern. Although its ruler was one of the seven electors of the Holy Roman emperor, Brandenburg was a bleak and thinly populated little province. Yet around this nucleus the Hohenzollerns built the important state of Prussia and, later, the German Empire (see Map 34.1).

From the time the Hohenzollerns became margraves of Brandenburg (1415) until they were finally overthrown at the end of World War I in 1918, they followed a threefold policy: militarism and territorial aggrandizement, paternal despotism, and centralized bureaucracy. The first to take major steps toward making Brandenburg an important power was Frederick William (1640–1688), the Great Elector. One of the ablest of all the Hohenzollerns, he acquired several new territories at the end of the Thirty Years' War. He centralized and administered the governments of his scattered territories with energy and skill. He won in his struggles with the Estates, the representative assemblies of the realm, gaining the crucial power to collect taxes and eliminating the Estates as a functioning institution. He established and strengthened his standing army. He managed an important compromise with the landed aristocracy, allowing them complete control over their serfs but committing them to his government as members of his bureaucracy and his military officer corps. He protected the native industries, improved communications, and aided agriculture. In a most intolerant age he followed a policy of religious toleration. When Louis XIV revoked the Edict of Nantes in 1685, Frederick William wel-

Map 34.1 **THE GROWTH OF PRUSSIA, 1614–1807**
These maps show the growth of Brandenburg-Prussia during the seventeenth and eighteenth centuries. The maps reveal the lack of connections between many of Brandenburg-Prussia's lands; one of Prussia's long-term goals in the eighteenth and nineteenth centuries was to connect those territories it already controlled as well as to expand its holdings.

comed thousands of industrious Huguenots to Brandenburg. At the death of the Great Elector in 1688, Brandenburg was on the road to becoming a great power.

The next Hohenzollern, Frederick I (1688–1713), acquired the title of king for the dynasty. The Hapsburg Holy Roman emperor in 1701 granted Frederick the title in return for aid against Louis XIV in the War of the Spanish Succession. Frederick I chose Prussia rather than Brandenburg for the name of his kingdom, since Prussia was outside the Holy Roman Empire and a free sov-

ereign state. Hence Brandenburg became Prussia.

From 1713 to 1740 Prussia was ruled by a vigorous militaristic autocrat, Frederick William I (since he was the first Frederick William to be king). Unquestioned absolutism, machinelike centralized bureaucratic administration, and, above all, militarism were his obsessions. He built the Prussian army into the most efficient and one of the largest fighting forces in Europe. And yet Frederick William was so efficient and miserly that he was also able to pass along to his talented son, Frederick II, a well-filled treasury.

2. COMPETITION WITH THE AUSTRIAN HAPSBURGS AND THE EMERGENCE OF PRUSSIA AS A GREAT POWER

In the same year that Frederick II became king of Prussia (1740), the beautiful and gracious young Maria Theresa became archduchess of the Austrian Hapsburg dominions. These dominions included, in addition to the Austrian lands, the Kingdom of Hungary and the triune crown of Bohemia, Moravia, and Silesia. After the Thirty Years' War, the Austrian Hapsburgs initiated a long policy of centralizing their power in those lands they directly controlled (rather than the Holy Roman Empire) and expanding to the east. This policy was effectively carried out during the second half of the seventeenth century and the eighteenth century. The monarchy improved its administration, established a powerful standing army, gained at least a fragile allegiance of the nobility, and acquired territories at the expense of the Ottoman Empire and Poland. Maria Theresa's father, Emperor Charles VI, had spent much time in his last years attempting to safeguard his daughter's accession to the Hapsburg throne. He succeeded in obtaining the signatures of virtually every European sovereign, including the king of Prussia, for a document called the Pragmatic Sanction, which guaranteed the integrity of Maria Theresa's crown and territories. Two months after Charles VI died, however, Frederick II, without a declaration of war, marched his troops into and seized Silesia, one of the richest of the Hapsburg provinces. This Machiavellian act of the young Prussian king plunged most of the major European states into a series of wars for the mastery of central Europe.

The War of the Austrian Succession lasted for eight years (1740–1748). Maria Theresa successfully repelled the Bavarians, Saxons, French, and Spaniards, but she was unable to dislodge Frederick II from Silesia. Frederick, on his part, cynically deserted his allies as soon as he had achieved his own purposes. The Treaty of Aix-la-Chapelle in 1748 brought the hostilities to an end. Frederick retained Silesia, and Maria Theresa's husband, Francis of Lorraine, was recognized as Holy Roman emperor. The only real gainer from the war was Frederick II. Silesia, a fertile province inhabited by more than a million German-speaking people, nearly doubled the population and resources of Prussia.

The Hapsburgs, however, had no intention of being thus despoiled of one of their fairest provinces by the upstart Hohenzollerns. Proud rulers over territories many times the size and population of Prussia and for centuries emperors of the Holy Roman Empire, they viewed the Hohenzollerns with condescension. Maria Theresa's able diplomat, Count Kaunitz, was soon at work lining up allies. Saxony, Sweden, Russia, and even France were won over. Spain, now ruled by the Bourbons, later followed France into the alliance. This time, however, Great Britain took the side of Prussia. Great Britain did this in order to oppose its archenemy France, with whom it was already at war in India and North America, and to safeguard Hanover. This double shifting of alliances came to be called the Diplomatic Revolution.

Frederick was not one to wait for his enemies to strike first. As soon as he became aware of their designs, he opened hostilities by overrunning Saxony. Thus began the Seven Years' War (1756–1763). Frederick, with his slender resources, soon found himself at bay; the four greatest military powers on the continent of Europe were closing in on him from all directions. After tenaciously holding his enemies off for six years, defeat appeared to be near. Then in 1762 the Russian Tsarina Elizabeth, one of his bitterest enemies, died and was succeeded by the ineffective Peter III, who was an ardent admirer of Frederick II and who put Russia's forces at the disposal of Prussia. Although Peter III was soon murdered by a group of his own officers and court nobility and Russia withdrew from the war, the remaining allies had no further stomach for the fight. The Peace of Hubertusburg in 1763 left things as they were at the beginning of the war, Prussia retaining the controversial Silesia. In the same year the Treaty of Paris brought to a close the colonial struggle between Great Britain and France in India and North America, leaving Great Britain master of both.

Having so narrowly escaped destruction, Frederick the Great spent the remaining twenty-three years of his life reconstructing his war-ravaged territories. He encouraged agriculture, subsidized and protected industry, and invited immigrants into his well-governed territories. At no time, though, did he neglect his war machine. In 1772 he joined Austria and Russia in the first partition of Poland. Frederick took West Prussia, thus joining East Prussia with the main body of the Prussian state. When Frederick II died in 1786, Prussia had been raised to the status of a great power, sharing equally with Austria the leadership of central Europe. During his reign Prussia's size and population had more than doubled, and its military exploits pointed to a spectacular future.

3. RUSSIA BEFORE PETER THE GREAT

While Prussia was becoming a great power in central Europe, Russia was rising to prominence to the east. The first shaping of some of the Slavic tribes of eastern Europe into what eventually became the Russian national state was begun by Viking invaders in the ninth century. These intrepid seafarers moved out from their Scandinavian homes in all directions—across the Atlantic, into the Mediterranean, and up the rivers of what are now England, France, Germany, and Russia (the word *Russia* is apparently derived from the Swedish word for rower). Their most important commercial and political center in eastern Europe was Kiev, which became Russia's first capital. Eventually the Norse invaders adopted the Slavic culture of their subjects.

In the tenth century Christianity was brought to Russia by missionaries from Constantinople. Through the influence of the Greek Orthodox church, whose headquarters were in Constantinople, Russia became a somewhat Byzantine civilization, differing from the Greco-Roman and Roman Catholic culture common to the countries of central and western Europe.

A second crucial influence on Russian civilization was the Mongol conquest of the thirteenth century. Around the turn of the thirteenth century the Mongol conqueror Genghis Khan (1162–1227) had established a vast empire in eastern Asia. Shortly after his death the Golden Horde, as the

Mongol warriors were called, swept westward into Christian Europe. The thirteenth-century Europeans were no match for the Mongols. Russia was easily overrun, and in 1241 a combined German and Polish army was defeated at Liegnitz in the heart of central Europe. All Christian Europe appeared to be at the mercy of the invaders. At that moment, however, the great khan died in eastern Asia, and the Mongol commander withdrew his forces to Russia and hastened back to seize his share of the spoils. The Golden Horde never resumed its triumphal surge westward, but for two and a half centuries it inundated Russia and there was considerable mixing of cultures.

During the Mongol occupation the grand dukes of Muscovy managed to ingratiate themselves with their Mongol masters and build up their own influence and power. The first of the grand dukes of Muscovy under whom Russia took on the shape of a modern national state was Ivan III (1462–1505). In 1480 Ivan III defeated the rapidly declining Mongols and limited their power in Russia to the southeastern area. Ivan greatly extended his sway both to the north and to the west by military conquest. After his marriage to Sophia Palaeologus, heiress to the now-defunct Byzantine (Eastern Roman) Empire, Ivan declared himself successor to the Eastern Roman Caesars—hence the title Tsar. When he died, the foundations of a Russian national state had been laid (see Map 34.2).

Ivan IV (1533–1584), "the Terrible," added both to the authority of the Russian tsars and to the territories over which they ruled. He destroyed the remaining power of the Mongols in southeastern Russia and annexed most of their territory. The Ottoman Turks, however, seized the strategic Mongol territory north of the Black Sea. Although Ivan IV established trade relations with England by way of the White Sea and the Arctic Ocean, his efforts to gain a foothold on the Baltic were frustrated by Sweden and Poland. It was during Ivan IV's reign that Russia's conquest of Siberia was begun. Half a century later the Russian flag was planted on the shores of the Pacific.

The twenty-nine years following the death of Ivan IV are known as the Time of Troubles (1584–1613). Weak rulers and disputed successions resulted in such anarchy that the Poles were able to

Map 34.2 **THE GROWTH OF RUSSIA IN THE WEST** These maps show the steady expansion of Russia to the west and south, acquiring access on the Baltic Sea and Black Sea under Peter the Great and extending its territories further in the course of the eighteenth century.

capture Moscow and hold it briefly. To end the political chaos, a group of leading nobles in 1613 chose Michael Romanov as tsar.

The early decades of the Romanov dynasty, which was to rule Russia until the Revolution of 1917, were not easy. There were great popular discontent and numerous uprisings between the late 1640s and the early 1670s as the lower classes rebelled against the nobles and the central government, who were making serfdom even more onerous and life for townspeople more difficult. The discontent reached a climax with the revolts led by Stenka Razin in the late 1660s and early 1670s. Razin was finally caught and executed, soon ending that series of threats. During this

same period problems within the Russian Orthodox church broke out as many, known as the Old Believers, rejected liturgical changes initiated by the patriarch of Moscow. The effect of this controversy was to drive the Church into greater dependence on the secular government. Nevertheless by the final decades of the seventeenth century the Romanov tsars had managed to overcome these problems, improve the central administration, and extend their authority. They gradually established commercial and cultural contacts with the West. Increasing numbers of traders, artisans, and adventurers from central and western Europe, particularly Germany, came to Russia to seek their fortunes. Thus the stage was set for Russia to become more fully involved in European affairs. This involvement became especially important during the reign of Peter the Great.

4. RUSSIA UNDER PETER THE GREAT, 1689–1725

Peter I (1689–1725) was an unusually large, vigorous, and ambitious individual (see Figure 34.2). At the age of seventeen he seized the reins of government from his elder sister. For the next thirty-six years he devoted his boundless energy to the twofold policy of strengthening his own authority and his military forces and of gaining access to the west on the Baltic and Black seas.

Peter concluded that one of the best ways to increase his own political and military power was to copy Western practices. He traveled in western Europe and learned much about Western customs and techniques, which he proceeded to introduce into Russia. After crushing a revolt of his bodyguard with a ruthlessness that cowed all potential troublemakers, he adopted the bureaucratic system of western European monarchs in both central and local government to make his authority more absolute. Western technicians were brought to Russia in large numbers and new industries were subsidized and protected by mercantilist policies. Western, particularly French, social customs were introduced to the upper and middle classes of Russian society. Women were brought out of seclusion, and the long beards and flowing Oriental robes of the men were banned. These reforms hardly touched the peasant masses, who were increasingly tied down in a system of serfdom bordering on slavery—a process that had been going on in Russia throughout the sixteenth and seventeenth centuries. When the patriarch of the Russian Orthodox church opposed the tsar's authority and some of his Westernizing policies, Peter abolished the patriarchate. He placed at the head of the church a Holy Synod composed of a committee of bishops and presided over by a lay procurator-general, all appointed by the tsar. Henceforth, the Orthodox church was a powerful instrument of the Russian government. But Peter the Great's chief concern was always his military

FIGURE 34.2. Peter the Great Peter the Great was a physical giant. This portrait gives us a hint of the vigor and forcefulness that he put to use in Westernizing and modernizing Russia, making the nation a military power to be reckoned with. (Culver Pictures)

establishment. He built a navy and patterned his conscript army after that of Prussia. By the end of his reign, Russia had one of the major fighting forces of Europe.

When Peter became tsar, Russia had no warm-water access to the West. Sweden held the coveted shores of the Baltic Sea, and the Ottoman Turks occupied the territory north of the Black Sea. Peter's efforts to dislodge the Ottoman Turks were not very successful, but after an extended, costly war with Sweden, in which Peter lost early battles to his adversary Charles XII, Peter's efforts were rewarded. By the Treaty of Nystad in 1721, Russia received the Swedish Baltic provinces of Livonia, Estonia, Ingria, and Karelia. On the Neva River near the Baltic, Peter built a new modern capital, St. Petersburg, facing the West. At his death in 1725, Russia was a great and growing power ready to play a major role in European affairs.

5. RUSSIA UNDER CATHERINE THE GREAT, 1762–1796

Peter the Great was followed by a succession of weak or mediocre rulers. After an interval of thirty-seven years, Catherine the Great (1762–1796) ascended the Russian throne. Catherine was an obscure princess from one of the little German states. She had been married for political reasons to young Peter III, grandson of Peter the Great, while he was still heir to the Russian crown. After he became tsar, Peter III quickly alienated all classes of his subjects. Less than a year after her husband became tsar, Catherine conspired with a group of aristocratic army officers, who murdered Peter and declared Catherine tsarina of Russia.

The Machiavellian tsarina prided herself on being an enlightened despot, as was fashionable in the late eighteenth century, but few of those enlightened ideas were translated into political or social deeds. Some apparent reforming efforts ended when Russian serfs rose in one of the greatest insurrections in history. In 1773, under the able leadership of a Don Cossack, Pugachev, hundreds of thousands of serfs marched against their masters. The rebellion was put down with difficulty. The cruel repression left Russian serfs almost as slaves to the privileged nobility.

The chief significance of Catherine the Great in political history lies in her aggressive foreign policy (see Figure 34.3). Peter the Great had reached the Baltic by despoiling the Swedes. Catherine reached the Black Sea, the Balkan peninsula, and the heart of Europe by defeating the Turks and destroying Poland. In two major wars between 1768 and 1792 Catherine defeated the Turks and seized all of their territory north of the Black Sea as far west as the Balkan peninsula. Russia also gained a vague protectorate over the Christians in the Ottoman Empire, which provided a standing opportunity to meddle in the internal affairs of the Turks. But Catherine fell short of her real goal, Constantinople. By 1772 Russia, Prussia, and Austria had already seized strips of Poland. In 1793 Russia and Prussia enlarged their holdings, and in 1795 the three powers divided among themselves the remainder of the once huge Poland. Catherine's share, which was about two-thirds of the total, brought Russia's western boundary deep into central Europe. The second and third partitions of Poland and concern over the French Revolution, which began in 1789, absorbed Catherine's energies during the last years of her life. When she finally died in 1796, Russia was a nation ominous in size and power and a major factor in European and world affairs.

6. THE DISAPPEARANCE OF POLAND AND THE DECLINE OF SWEDEN AND THE OTTOMAN EMPIRE

Poland, at the opening of the eighteenth century, was the third largest country in Europe, exceeded in size only by Russia and Sweden. In the sixteenth and seventeenth centuries it had appeared that Poland would become a major power. Taking advantage of Russia's Time of Troubles (1584–1613), the Poles had captured Moscow. In the latter part of the century they had saved Vienna from the Turks.

Actually, however, the Polish nation was far from strong. Sprawling over a large area between Russia and the German states, it enjoyed no natural boundaries either to the east or west. The eastern half of its territory was inhabited by Russian-speaking people. The northern provinces were peopled largely by Latvians, Lithuanians, and Germans. There were also many Germans in the west. Religious cleavages followed the language lines.

Moreover, there was no strong middle class to vitalize Poland's economy. In the late Middle Ages a sizable overland commerce between the Black and Baltic seas had flowed across Poland. But with the shifting of commercial routes and centers to the west in the early sixteenth century, Poland's commerce had withered. Furthermore, the Polish nobility, jealous of its own power and fearful of

FIGURE 34.3.   Catherine the Great   Catherine the Great's territorial ambitions are satirized in this cartoon, which shows her leaping toward her coveted goal, Constantinople, as the pope and other European leaders look on in dismay. (NYPL Picture Collection)

an alliance between the bourgeoisie and the king, deliberately penalized commerce with severe restrictions. The great mass of the people were serfs, tilling the soil of the powerful nobility.

In the face of so many divisive forces, only a strong central government could have made Poland a stable national state. But here lay Poland's greatest weakness. The kingship was elective, and the great nobles who held the elective power saw to it that no strong king ever came to the throne.

During the eighteenth century the kings were all foreigners or puppets of foreign powers. The legislative Diet was completely monopolized by the nobility. So that each noble's rights were safeguarded, unanimity was required for the passage of every measure. Thus any noble could veto any proposed law (*liberum veto*). In addition, any noble could disband ("explode") the Diet and cancel all its acts. This system guaranteed virtual political anarchy. National spirit was weak. The all-pow-

Map 34.3 EASTERN EUROPE, SIXTEENTH–EIGHTEENTH CENTURIES Between the sixteenth and eighteenth centuries, political power in central and eastern Europe shifted fundamentally. The first map shows the Holy Roman Empire, Poland, and the Ottoman Empire in the sixteenth and early seventeenth centuries. The second map shows that by the eighteenth century, these powers had all but been replaced by Prussia, the Russian Empire, and the Austrian Empire.

erful nobles were far more concerned for their own private interests than for the well-being of the nation.

It would have been surprising had such a power vacuum as eighteenth-century Poland not invited the aggression of its ambitious neighbors. In 1772 Catherine the Great and Frederick the Great bargained to take slices of Polish territory. The somewhat less greedy Maria Theresa of Austria, fearful of being outdistanced by Russia and Prussia, joined them. This aggression at long last stirred the Poles to action. Sweeping reforms were passed, improving the condition of the peasants and the bourgeoisie and giving the king and the Diet power to act effectively. But it was too late. Russia and Prussia were determined to prevent the emergence of a vigorous Polish nation. In 1793 they marched in and seized additional slices of territory. The Poles, under the leadership of Thaddeus Kosciusko, now flew to arms, although the arms were often only agricultural implements. They were no match for the professional armies of Russia, Prussia, and Austria, who in 1795 divided the remainder of Poland among themselves.

Poland was not the only victim in eastern Europe of the powerful Russian, Prussian, and Austrian armies. Sweden and the Ottoman Empire declined, both relatively and actually. Sweden had become the dominant military power in northern and eastern Europe under Gustavus Adolphus in the early seventeenth century. At the opening of the eighteenth century Sweden was second only to Russia in size among the nations of Europe, holding large areas east and south of the Baltic in addition to the homeland. However, its population and resources were too small to hold for long such far-flung territories, which were coveted by ambitious and growing Prussia and Russia. Charles XII made a spectacular effort to hold them, but in the end he lost all his trans-Baltic territories except Finland, and he dissipated Sweden's strength in so doing. Sweden has never been a major power since.

The Ottoman Turks, after reaching the gates of Vienna early in the sixteenth century and again late in the seventeenth century, weakened rapidly. The Treaty of Karlowitz in 1699 limited their power in Europe to the Balkan peninsula and a strip of territory north of the Black Sea. Their two serious defeats at the hands of Catherine the Great marked the beginning of the breakup of the Ottoman Empire.

By the end of the eighteenth century, the three dominant powers in central and eastern Europe were the relativeiy static Austrian Hapsburg Em-pire and the two rapidly rising states—Prussia and Russia (see Map 34.3). Each of these states had developed strong central governments with standing armies, large bureaucracies, and organized systems of taxation under the monarch's control.

SUGGESTED READING

General

D. McKay and H. Scott, *The Rise of the Great Powers, 1648–1815* (1983). A good recent survey.

I. Woloch, *Eighteenth-Century Europe: Tradition and Progress 1715–1789* (1982). A recent, thorough introduction.

Rise of Prussia

F. L. Carsten, *The Origins of Prussia* (1954). A solid, brief account of the reign of the great elector, Frederick William.

G. Craig, *The Politics of the Prussian Army, 1640–1945* (1964). A highly respected analysis of the influences of the Prussian Army.

H. Holborn, *A History of Modern Germany 1648–1840* (1966). Best on the subject.

H. C. Johnson, *Frederick the Great and His Officials* (1975). Focuses on Prussian administration.

The Austrian Hapsburgs

R. J. Evans, *The Making of the Hapsburg Empire, 1550–1770* (1979). A solid, recent account.

Rise of Russia

P. Dukes, *The Making of Russian Absolutism: 1613–1801* (1982). A solid survey.

I. de Madariaga, *Russia in the Age of Catherine the Great* (1981). Highly regarded recent study.

B. H. Sumner, *Peter the Great and the Emergence of Russia* (1962). A brief introduction.

A. Yanov, *Origins of Autocracy: Ivan the Terrible in Russian History* (1981). Excellent recent analysis.

Disappearance of Poland and Decline of Sweden and Ottoman Empire

P. Coles, *The Ottoman Impact on Europe, 1350–1699* (1968). A well-written study.

O. Halecki, *A History of Poland* (1961). Sound coverage of the partitions.

R. N. Hatton, *Charles XII of Sweden* (1968). An excellent, thorough biography.

CHAPTER 35

Overseas Colonization and Competition for Empire

FIGURE 35.1. **The Taking of Quebec, 1759** This eighteenth-century engraving shows British forces capturing Quebec from the French in 1759. This victory was a major turning point in the eighteenth-century competition for world empire. (Library of Congress)

During the age of royal absolutism, the European nations intensified their competition for overseas possessions and commerce. They were spurred on in large part by the riches that flowed to Europe from these possessions but also by a conviction that overseas possessions enhanced the power of nations. Whereas Spain and Portugal had led the way beyond the Atlantic frontier during the sixteenth century, England, France, and the Netherlands threw themselves vigorously into colonizing and commercial expansion in various quarters of the globe during the seventeenth and eighteenth centuries. The newcomers indeed outstripped their older rivals and established themselves as the leading European colonial powers. As large as the world beyond western Europe was, the competition for it led to struggles among the leading European powers; the outcome of these struggles decisively affected the power relationships among the competing nations. And while the Europeans colonized, traded, and competed around the globe, European civilization spread with them, impacting with varying results on the native populations encountered by the Europeans. The seventeenth and eighteenth centuries marked a decisive turning point in the establishment of western European domination over much of the world. No less significantly, European expansion laid the basis for a global economy.

1. THE NEW WORLD: THE ENGLISH, THE FRENCH, AND THE DUTCH

One of the areas attracting the English, French, and Dutch was the New World, where all three nations established thriving colonies during the seventeenth century and eventually became embroiled in bitter rivalry for dominance. The northern European nations had their appetites whetted by the fabulous profits reaped from the New World by the Spanish and the Portuguese during the sixteenth century. These two powers retained their vast empires in Central and South America during the seventeenth and eighteenth centuries and continued to earn a rich reward from their enterprises. During the seventeenth century the hauls of gold and silver declined, and the Spanish

and Portuguese turned their energies toward creating large plantations worked by oppressed natives and imported African slaves to produce products marketable in western Europe. Their presence in South and Central America forced the attention of the English, French, and Dutch toward North America and the Caribbean area.

The English were the most successful colonizers in North America. Although some settlers were prompted by political and religious reasons, most were lured by the prospects of available land. Colonizing ventures were organized by joint stock companies chartered by the government to plant settlements in the New World or by individual leaders granted huge tracts of land for the purpose of colonization. Between 1607, when the first colony was planted at Jamestown, Virginia (see Figure 35.2), and 1733, when a colony was founded in Georgia, England established control of the Atlantic seaboard from Maine to the Spanish colony in Florida. In the thirteen colonies a stable order soon emerged that showed considerable potential for agricultural and commercial growth. This growth was promoted by a steady flow of emigrants, not only from England but also from other northern European nations. By the beginning of the eighteenth century the English settlers were beginning to push westward out of the coastal colonies in search of new lands to occupy. English explorers and traders penetrated into the Hudson Bay area in Canada and claimed for England a huge territory, where soon a profitable trade in fur developed. Flourishing English colonies were established in the West Indies, the chief ones being Barbados, Jamaica, and Bermuda. In this area the English concentrated on developing highly profitable sugar plantations, utilizing African slaves as a labor supply.

France also undertook to colonize in the New World, although not as successfully as England. Its first American colony was established by Samuel de Champlain at Quebec on the St. Lawrence River in 1608. Champlain later explored and claimed for France the entire St. Lawrence Valley from the Atlantic to the Great Lakes. Toward the end of the seventeenth century during the reign of Louis XIV the French extended their holdings in North America by claiming a huge territory called Louisiana, stretching down the Mississippi

FIGURE 35.2. The New World Frontier This representation of the first settlement at Jamestown, Virginia, suggests something of the drastic changes that affected those who left European society—symbolized by the great ship standing at anchor—to face the wilds of the New World. (Culver Pictures)

Basin from the Great Lakes to the Gulf of Mexico. The French also established prosperous colonies in the West Indies, especially on Martinique and Guadeloupe, where sugar production was the major economic activity.

Except for the West Indies, settlers were slow to come to France's vast, rich lands in the New World, in part because of governmental policy. France closed its empire to non-Catholics, thus excluding an element so important in populating England's colonies—the religiously dissatisfied. By adopting a policy of land allocation that favored the aristocracy, the French government made it difficult for commoners to obtain land overseas. The opportunities for profits offered by the fur trade discouraged agricultural settlement. When England seized France's American empire in 1763, perhaps no more than eighty thousand settlers lived in New France, compared with the 1.5 million inhabitants of the English colonies. But that sparse population left its marks, especially in the form of Roman Catholicism, the French language, and the imitation of French social practices by

settlers in the St. Lawrence Valley and southern Louisiana—marks that persist to the present to give a distinctive character to society in these areas.

The Dutch also became involved in the colonizing of North America. In 1621 the Dutch West India Company was chartered to undertake colonizing and commerce in the New World. In 1624 a Dutch colony was planted on Manhattan Island, a location made especially attractive because of its potential as a center from which trade could be controlled. Soon other Dutch communities were established in the valleys of the Hudson, Connecticut, and Delaware rivers. However, the Dutch did not push their colonizing effort very seriously. Their interest was chiefly in trading activities, leading them to concentrate their energies on the more profitable East Indies. Their American colonies became a bone of contention in the Anglo-Dutch struggles that preceded the Glorious Revolution in England. In 1664 the English seized New Netherland, ending Dutch colonization in North America.

2. EUROPEAN PENETRATION OF THE FAR EAST AND AFRICA

During the sixteenth century, Portugal had established supremacy in the Far East. In the seventeenth century, however, the Dutch, English, and French aggressively entered into the area (see Map 35.1). The Dutch were the first. In 1602 all the competing Dutch companies interested in Far Eastern trade were joined into a single Dutch East India Company, to which the Dutch government gave almost complete freedom of action. The company soon drove the Portuguese out of the Spice Islands, which became the center of the Dutch trading empire. In 1641 Malacca on the Malay peninsula was seized, giving the Dutch control of the seas around the East Indies. Ceylon and the Celebes were also captured. The English tried to seize a share of this rich area, but they were driven out by the Dutch as early as 1623. To safeguard the sea route to the Indies, the Dutch established a colony at the Cape of Good Hope in South Africa. Its growth was slow, but the Dutch influence was eventually strong enough to influence the history of South Africa to the present. To watch its interests in the Indies, the Dutch East India Company established a governor-general in Java, who in turn set up several other fortified governmental centers in the island empire.

For years after, the Dutch continued to profit from their holdings in the Indies. They demonstrated remarkable skill in utilizing the native agricultural economy to produce commodities such as spices that were in great demand in western Europe. Consequently, their presence disturbed very little the existing patterns of life in the area. The Dutch also made attempts to penetrate China and Japan but enjoyed only limited success, chiefly because neither the Chinese nor the Japanese welcomed them. Both were too strong to permit entrance by force.

The English, although shut out of the East Indies by the Dutch, made rapid progress toward replacing the Portuguese in India. The English East India Company was chartered in 1600 and given a monopoly of English trade in the East. This company concentrated chiefly on India, slowly forcing the Portuguese to let English traders into that rich land. The company founded its own "factories" (trading posts) at key locations—Surat, Madras, Bombay, and Calcutta (see Figure 35.3). For a long time the East India Company was content to exploit the trading opportunities available in these cities; the merchants interfered little with Indian affairs and had little influence on Indian society.

Rather belatedly, the French entered the competition in the Far East. Colbert organized a French East India Company (1664), which soon established a French outpost at Pondicherry in India. From this center the French company built up a prosperous trade that returned large profits.

During the seventeenth and eighteenth centuries, western Europeans made significant crossroads into sub-Saharan Africa. Again the Portuguese had been the early leaders, but they were eventually joined by others. It was the establishment of the plantation system in the New World that sparked a new interest of Europeans in Africa. The plantations needed labor; African slaves could provide that commodity. Portuguese, Dutch, English, French, and North American traders and adventurers, acting with the support of their governments, established a series of trading posts along the West African coast stretching from modern Senegal to Angola chiefly for the purpose of purchasing slaves to be transported to the New World.

3. THE IMPACT OF EUROPEAN EXPANSION: THE NATIVE AMERICANS

The increasing presence of European colonists and traders around the world during the seventeenth and eighteenth centuries had a significant impact on the native populations of the areas to which Europeans went. In many ways these encounters between Europeans and natives set a pattern that was destined to impose a bitter heritage on the modern world.

Of all the non-Europeans who felt the impact of the white man, the native Americans—the American Indians—were perhaps most immediately and drastically affected. Their patterns of life, ranging from the highly sophisticated civilizations of the Incas in Peru and the Aztecs and Mayas in

Mexico and Central America to the simple pastoral and hunting cultures of the North American Indians, were irreparably disrupted by the onslaught of the intruders.

We have already described the destructive impact of the Spanish and Portuguese *conquistadors* on the Aztecs, Mayas, and Incas. During the seventeenth and eighteenth centuries, the dislocation continued. Spanish and Portuguese colonial policies cast the Indians into the role of laborers on the expanding plantation system and in the reviving mining enterprises from which the Europeans drew huge profits. To add to the disruption of native social and economic life, the new masters imported large numbers of black slaves from Africa. Although the foreign Europeans were few in number, they dominated political, economic, and social life with little respect for the established practices of native life.

Despite their indifference to established native American culture, the Europeans in Latin America were never numerous enough to exterminate the native Americans or their cultures. Inexorably, their blood and their culture intermingled with those of the native Americans. As a result, significant elements of native American culture survived, especially in family structure, agricultural techniques, art motifs, and even religion. Although the ancient Indian civilizations of Central and South America were forever disrupted, enough Indian culture survived to give Latin American society a special hybrid character that has survived to this day.

The Indians of North America suffered a dif-

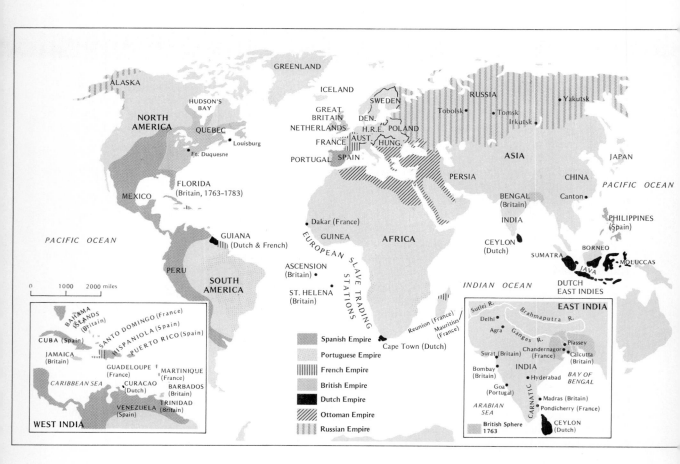

ferent, and perhaps a crueler, fate. In general, the interactions between French settlers and the Indians were not particularly disruptive to Indian society, chiefly because the French were few in number, usually more concerned with trade than land occupation, and interested in the Indians as potential converts to Christianity. The English settlers pursued a more ruthless course. From the beginning they were chiefly interested in occupying and exploiting the land, an intent that demanded the displacement of the natives. Although English-Indian relationships were occasionally marked by friendliness and mutual assistance, the burgeoning seaboard population began to assert inexorable pressure on the Indians. As a consequence, the Indians began to disappear from "new" America; their demise was often accompanied by conniving and brutality on the part of the settlers, who began to perceive themselves as *the* "Americans." In the effort to protect their land, the Indians fought back savagely. Their resistance nourished a feeling among the colonists that the native Americans were inferior savages whose extermination would best serve everyone's interest. The British government struggled from afar to establish an Indian policy aimed at respecting Indian rights to their lands and dealing with them honorably in resolving conflicts. But the westward-bound, land-hungry newcomers paid little heed and proceeded with the grim business of displacing or exterminating the Indians in the vast Indian stronghold lying between the Appalachians and the Mississippi. The resultant dislocations completely undermined the foundations of native American culture and condemned the Indians to a long-standing inferior status in America.

Map 35.1 OVERSEAS POSSESSIONS, 1763 This map shows the extent to which the major European powers had established control over the world by the middle of the eighteenth century. It especially points up the success of England in the quest for overseas possessions. The rich trade flowing to and from Europe to the overseas possessions had become a vital factor in the economies of these nations. Increasing its overseas possessions and trade was of vital importance to every Euorpean state.

4. THE IMPACT OF EUROPEAN EXPANSION: THE FAR EAST

In contrast with the impact of Europeans on the New World, their impact was minimal on the peoples of the Far East. Few Europeans went to that part of the world as colonists. Those few who did isolated themselves in trading depots located in seaboard cities in India and the East Indies, where their contacts with the natives were slight. The limited impact of the Europeans on the world of the Far East resulted also from the fact that the newcomers encountered ancient cultures and solidly established societies.

When the Europeans first began the penetration of India, that ancient land was politically unified for one of the rare moments in its history. Unity had been imposed by Moslem foreigners, the Moguls, a branch of the Mongol horde of Tamerlane. Mogul rule brought prosperity to India's upper classes and a brilliant chapter in India's already rich cultural history. As the seventeenth century progressed, Mogul power began to decline. Political power increasingly fell into the hands of native local princes, a development that proceeded rapidly during the eighteenth century. Because this situation aided the English and the French in establishing their commercial interests in India, the intruders encouraged political localism. Thus, their presence had a significant impact on the political structure of India.

However, Indian society retained its cohesion and its unique identity despite the presence of the foreigners, be they Moslem Asiatics or Christian Europeans. Its primary social institutions—the family, the village, and the caste system—remained intact, fundamentally untouched by the outsiders. Undergirding these ancient social institutions were powerful religious beliefs and practices, embodied above all in Hinduism, which emphasized the acceptance of the existing order as a part of the divine order. Hindu Brahmins, or priests, played a crucial role in sustaining the traditional order. Indian social institutions, religion, and culture combined to incline Indians to accept their situation in the present world because each individual's lot represented a necessary step in the progression toward ultimate fulfillment in another

FIGURE 35.3. A Refuge in a Foreign World. This drawing shows a European factory, or trading settlement, built in seventeenth-century India. Within the confines of such structures were warehouse, places of residence, market facilities, and even a church. The structure illustrates how the Europeans isolated themselves from the native population in the Far East. (The Bettmann Archive)

world. Progress, competition for wealth, and the search for new things did not hold the same attraction for Indians as they did for Europeans. Indians were not impressed by European civilization. They were convinced that they had reflected as deeply on human problems as the foreigners and had arrived at superior answers. Indians could point to a remarkable art and literature as proof of the vitality of their way of life. Little the Europeans could offer to India seemed able to improve on Indian institutions and values. The outsiders found that a few hundred soldiers and a few cannon could not shake the Indians'

confidence in their village and family life, their caste system, their religion, and their culture. Moreover, the continued existence of the basic pattern of Indian civilization in no way impeded the Europeans from reaping huge profits from their commercial enterprise in India. Only slowly and almost imperceptibly did the European way of life make any significant impression on India. And as time passed, Europeans developed a deep respect for some aspects of Indian civilization.

The Dutch presence in the East Indian world likewise had little effect on native society. In fact, the Dutch found it in their interests to sustain the existing order because it lent itself easily to commercial arrangements favorable to the outsiders.

The other major cultural centers in the Far East—China and Japan—were also little affected by the intrusion of Europeans during the period from 1500 to 1800. Again, this was a consequence of the vitality of native civilizations. In China the Manchu dynasty established a strong political regime during the seventeenth century that brought internal peace, prosperity, and a revitalization of Chinese social, religious, and cultural life along traditional patterns. Chinese civilization came to be greatly admired in Europe in the eighteenth century. However, the Manchus carefully controlled the activities of Western traders—called "Ocean Devils" by the Chinese—with the consequence that European influences were barely felt in China. Japan also enjoyed internal stability under the rule of the Tokugawa shoguns, who in the early seventeenth century established firm control over Japan's ancient feudal system and encouraged close adherence to ancient social, cultural, and religious customs and values. The new rulers soon adopted a policy of excluding all Europeans from access to Japan, a policy of isolationism that continued until the nineteenth century and that ensured that European influences would be minimized.

5. THE IMPACT OF EUROPEAN EXPANSION: SUB-SAHARAN AFRICA

European expansion into sub-Saharan Africa during the seventeenth and eighteenth centuries had a decisive effect on the societies existing in that vast territory. The centuries prior to 1500 had witnessed the formation of several prosperous states across a wide belt of territory south of the Sahara from the Atlantic to the Indian oceans and then far southward along that inviting sea. These states—Ghana, Mali, Songhay, the kingdoms of Hausaland, and the Swahili city-states on the east coast of Africa—were strongly influenced by Moslem religion, culture, and technology from North Africa. However, in all of them the imprint of much older native African cultures was also strongly felt, producing an amazingly cosmopoli-

tan culture, especially in the cities that dominated these states. The remarkable affluence of these states depended on a vigorous trans-Saharan and Indian Ocean trade that carried gold, ivory, slaves, and many other products northward to the Moslem world and Europe and eastward to India. In fact, many of these states were brought into existence by enterprising native chieftains who organized extensive realms so as to control more effectively the trading ventures that brought such great riches. Because their existence depended so heavily on trade and because the techniques their rulers borrowed to assert their power had little impact on the great bulk of the native population, these African states tended to be unstable. Nonetheless, their creation and their active intercourse with outside cultures marked an important stage in the development of sub-Saharan Africa and its involvement with the larger world. Farther to the south, beyond the sphere of Moslem influence, the native population continued its agricultural existence according to ancient customs, as yet little touched by developments to the north.

These developments in pre-1500 sub-Saharan Africa created a situation that made Africa particularly susceptible to the onslaught of the western Europeans, chiefly because the destiny of so many African states was tied directly to trade with the outside world. Coming by sea to the coastal areas of sub-Saharan Africa, the Europeans almost instantly caused a redirection of trade routes from the traditional trans-Saharan routes toward the coastal regions that gave access to western Europe and the expanding European empires in the New World and the Far East. The newcomers made little effort to settle in sub-Saharan Africa, partly because the Africans resisted their settlement but more importantly because they could get what they wanted by doing little more than establishing a few trading posts in the coastal cities of Africa. What they wanted were the valuable raw materials of Africa, especially gold, and then before long the Africans themselves—as slaves to perform the arduous labor of creating a rich agricultural establishment in the New World. Throughout the seventeenth and eighteenth centuries massive numbers of black Africans—perhaps as many as 9 or 10 million—were uprooted from their native soil, often as a result of the efforts of their black compatriots, sold into the hands of English, French, Dutch, Portuguese, Spanish, and American slave traders, and distributed under inhuman conditions far and wide to toil as chattels in the service of white landowners intent on exploiting the vast agricultural potential of the New World.

As the Europeans opened slave stations along the coasts of sub-Saharan Africa, significant new political alignments occurred in Africa. African kingdoms along or with access to the Gold Coast flourished as a result of their domination of trade flowing from inland into the hands of European traders. Among the most prominent of these kingdoms were Oyo, Benin, Asante, Kongo, and Ngola. Often the ruling elements of these kingdoms became prime agents in supplying slaves to the Europeans, leading them to intervene among inland tribes to find slaves to sell. Native chiefs living inland likewise became caught up in the slave trade. Armed with deadly weapons from Europe, the native tribes began to wage war on one another as a means of procuring slaves. The Europeans asserted subtle influences on the coastal states in order to enhance their own trading interests, thus promoting a slow deterioration of the capability of the Africans to control their own destiny. As the demand for slaves increased and the prices commanded by the African slave suppliers rose, European traders moved farther and farther south along the west coast of Africa to turn the attention of more and more native Africans toward serving European trading interests, especially slavery, with the same disruptive consequences. European influences, especially Portuguese, on the east coast of Africa were equally disruptive of the brilliant Swahili civilization flourishing there. Only deep in the central part of Africa did the native population remain relatively free of the impact of European intrusion.

On the whole, the development of sub-Saharan Africa was seriously impeded by the encounter of its peoples with the western Europeans during the seventeenth and eighteenth centuries. Africa's human resources were depleted, her natural resources plundered, and her political and social structures disoriented. The Europeans gave little in return, especially when compared with what the Moslems of North Africa had contributed to the enrichment of sub-Saharan Africa prior to

1500. Despite the traumatic consequences of European expansion in this era, the Africans retained many elements of their native tradition, which would later reassert itself as a significant aspect of the liberation of Africa from European domination. And those who were uprooted from Africa in this period took much with them to add important elements to the civilization that was forming in the New World, where they were laboring as slaves.

6. THE STRUGGLE FOR OVERSEAS EMPIRE

In spite of the vast lands to occupy in the New World and rich trading opportunities to exploit in the highly civilized East and in sub-Saharan Africa, the aggressive European nations could not keep out of one another's way in their overseas expansion. As a consequence, the rivalry of European nations became global. The outcome of these struggles began to determine the destinies of peoples only remotely involved in the competition of the European states.

The competition for empire was rooted in two interrelated factors: the essential importance of overseas trade to the expanding economies of the major European nations and the policy of mercantilism practiced by most European powers.

The growing importance of overseas commerce to national economies was abundantly clear. New products from abroad—among others, spices, sugar, tobacco, cotton, silk, tea—were in high demand. So also were some manufactured goods from the Far East, especially cotton textiles and chinaware. Colonists needed the products of European manufacturers. The opportunities to transport these goods stimulated shipbuilding. The need to distribute products from abroad created new opportunities for merchants. The funding of overseas trading and colonizing ventures stimulated the development of banking and credit. The profits garnered from overseas trading activities not only improved the standard of living of those who earned the profits but also became a prime source of capital for investment in agriculture, manufacturing, and commerce. Even governments relied on the gains from overseas trade to provide taxes and loans. In short, Europe's economy had become the focal point for a global system. Control of that economy was vital to the well-being of European nations, even to the point of fighting others for a share of the lucrative overseas trade.

The realities of seventeenth- and eighteenth-century economic life found expression in the widely accepted economic policy of mercantilism, which accentuated the importance of competition for overseas trade and colonies. Mercantilist policy was based on the conviction that the economic well-being of a nation depended on directing the total national economy in a way that would produce a favorable balance of bullion coming into the economy. Among other things, this policy saw colonies as a source of cheap food and raw materials and an outlet for manufactured goods that would return a profit to the mother country. Such a view made the accession and the careful management of the colonies crucial to each nation that aspired to be powerful. Especially important was the need to monopolize trade with a nation's colonies, which placed a premium on developing naval power. Likewise, mercantilism dictated that every effort be made to restrict the colonizing ventures of rival nations and to deprive them of their colonial possessions whenever possible. Thus, every conflict among the major European nations in the seventeenth and eighteenth centuries was extended to their colonies, and every major peace settlement included a redistribution of overseas possessions (see Chapters 32 and 34 for the European aspects of these wars).

The competition for the fruits of overseas empires began in the sixteenth century with the English and Dutch assaults on Spanish and Portuguese trading activities and overseas holdings. By the middle of the seventeenth century competition began to intensify and to become more general. More than any other country, England allied governmental economic policy with private commercial interests, with a view toward promoting national well-being. This approach cast England into a particularly aggressive role in the competition for empire and trade. As early as 1651 England passed its first Navigation Act, providing that all goods coming to and from England and its overseas possessions must be carried in English ships.

This policy posed a challenge to Dutch commercial power, which was especially successful in providing shipping services to other nations. It also encouraged the growth of the English merchant fleet and the navy, badly neglected during the early Stuart period. On three different occasions between 1651 and 1688, England engaged the Dutch in warfare. As a result, Dutch commercial ascendancy began to be undermined while England's commercial power grew; the Dutch also lost their North American colonies.

Toward the end of the seventeenth century the English and the Dutch began to see that France was the chief threat to both. The result was an Anglo-Dutch alliance made by William of Orange when he became king of England in 1689. By that time the Netherlands was no longer the major sea power in Europe. The Dutch were increasingly content to keep their already established holdings in the East Indies, to continue their declining but still profitable carrying trade, and to reap a great profit as the chief bankers and money lenders of Europe.

From 1689 until 1763 England and France fought each other regularly in Europe, and each engagement had its repercussions abroad (see Map 35.1). Several times during the War of the League of Augsburg (1688–1697), the English and the French forces engaged in North America, where the war was called King William's War. Neither in Europe nor in America was the action decisive, and no changes were made in the holdings of either combatant. England had more success during the War of the Spanish Succession (1702–1713). In North America, where the struggle was called Queen Anne's War, England captured Acadia (Nova Scotia) and received recognition of its claims to Newfoundland and Hudson Bay. From France's ally, Spain, England received Gibraltar and Minorca, assuring entrance into the Mediterranean. Spain also granted to England the right to supply Spain's colonies with slaves (the *asiento*) and the privilege of sending one ship a year to the Spanish colonies in America. These concessions ended Spain's long effort to close its empire to outsiders and gave England the advantage over other nations in exploiting trading opportunities provided by the Spanish overseas holdings.

From 1713 to 1740 England and France remained at peace. During this calm neither nation was idle in overseas matters. France, realizing the weakness of its position, was especially active in North America. France tried to protect its holdings from English sea power by building a strong fort at Louisburg at the mouth of the St. Lawrence. France also began constructing and garrisoning a series of forts in its territories west of the Appalachians designed to keep the English colonists pinned to the Atlantic seaboard. England concentrated its efforts on widening the commercial breach it had made in Spain's empire in 1713. A new European war in 1740, the War of the Austrian Succession, led to a sharp conflict between England and France in America (King George's War) and in India. At the end of the war in 1748 each power restored its spoils to the other, England giving up Louisburg and France restoring Madras.

An eight-year truce ensued in Europe, each side preparing desperately for the struggle that everyone knew would soon reopen. In North America, France went back to the policy of building a barrier against the westward expansion of the English colonies. The inevitable clash came in 1755, when the British unsuccessfully tried to stop the French from occupying Fort Duquesne, at the present site of Pittsburgh. The issue was clearly joined; one power must destroy the other in America.

In India a no less dramatic struggle was shaping. France had entered the scene later than England but had made steady progress up to 1740. Between 1740 and 1756 the French and British manipulated the internal chaos in India resulting from the decline of Mogul authority to wring for themselves concessions from India's various princes or political factions. Competition became so vicious that soon an undeclared war was on in India. Thus, at the opening of the Seven Years' War (French and Indian War in America) in 1756, France and England were pitted against each other on three continents. In that war England, led by William Pitt, threw its chief efforts into the naval and colonial war and won a smashing victory. In North America the French held their own until 1757. After that the superior British forces, sup-

ported by the navy, overpowered the French outposts one by one. The decisive blow came in 1759, when the British captured Quebec, opening all Canada to the British (see Figure 35.1). British naval units captured the chief French holdings in the West Indies. In India, Robert Clive, a resourceful agent of the East India Company, gave the British a decisive victory at the battle of Plassey in 1757. Clive added large territories to England's sphere of influence by conquering several native Indian states.

The Seven Years' War ended in 1763 with the Treaty of Paris. France surrendered Canada and all Louisiana east of the Mississippi (except New Orleans) to England. Spain, which had been an ally of France, ceded Florida to England. By a special treaty France compensated Spain for this loss by giving Spain the rest of Louisiana (west of the Mississippi). All French possessions in the West Indies except Guadeloupe and Martinique also fell to England. France's empire in India likewise went to Britain. The French were permitted to enjoy trading privileges in India and to keep Pondicherry, but Britain controlled the chief centers of trade, ending any hope of a French recovery of power there. The Treaty of Paris closed an era in European expansion. Although the Dutch and the Spanish still had extensive holdings abroad, Great Britain had fought its way to supremacy in colonial and commercial affairs. The English could now turn to the exploitation of that empire.

Since Columbus' voyage the Europeans had wrought an important change around the world. Energetic colonizers had planted European civilization on the soil of the New World. Enterprising merchants had begun to tap the wealth of a considerable part of the Far East and of sub-Saharan Africa, creating for the first time a global economy in which the level of prosperity in European nations was directly related to their access to the labor and products of peoples all over the earth. European patterns of civilization had begun to alter the lives of peoples who had developed their own cultures long before the Europeans came. For good or bad, the Europeanization of the world had begun. And European history never again ceased to have a world-wide scope.

SUGGESTED READING

European Expansion

J. H. Parry, *Trade and Dominion: The European Oversea Empires in the Eighteenth Century* (1971).

Holden Furber, *Rival Empires of Trade in the Orient, 1600–1800* (1976).

Either of these studies will provide an excellent account of the building of commercial empires.

The Impact of European Expansion

Bernard Bailyn, *The Peopling of British North America: An Introduction* (1986).

W. J. Eccles, *France in America* (1972).

These two works will help the reader understand the occupation of North America by Europeans.

Wilcomb E. Washburn, *The Indian in America* (1975). A good survey.

Karen Ordahl Kupperman, *Settling with the Indians: The Meeting of English and Indian Cultures in America, 1580–1640* (1980).

James Axtell, *The Invasion Within: The Contest of Cultures in Colonial North America* (1985).

Two excellent studies of the impact of European civilization on native American life.

James Lockhart and Stuart B. Schwartz, *Early Latin America: A History of Colonial Spanish America and Brazil* (1983). A good survey.

Stanley Wolpert, *A New History of India,* 2nd ed. (1982). The appropriate parts of this work will provide a good introduction to Indian society at the time of the European intrusion.

Roland Oliver and Anthony Atmore, *The African Middle Ages, 1400–1800* (1981). A clear treatment of a complex subject.

James A. Rawley, *The Transatlantic Slave Trade. A History* (1981). A balanced account.

Imperial Rivalry

W. L. Dorn, *Competition for Empire, 1740–1763,* rev. ed. (1963). A classic work.

CHAPTER 36

Society, Faith, and Culture in the Seventeenth and Eighteenth Centuries

FIGURE 36.1. Gainsborough, "Miss Catherine Tatton" Although the middle class was growing during the early modern era, the culture of the period was still dominated by the aristocracy. This portrait of an aristocratic lady by Thomas Gainsborough (1727–1788) reflects the luxury and tastes of the eighteenth-century aristocracy, which commissioned many such paintins. (Scala/Art Resource)

For most people the structure of society, the way of life, and the relevant social institutions changed only slowly throughout most of the seventeenth and early eighteenth centuries. More rapid change occurred thereafter, but it was usually concentrated in certain areas and classes. Despite the continued rise of the bourgeoisie and considerable political change, the aristocracy remained socially dominant and governments headed by kings generally continued to centralize their power. Religious faith remained of great importance to most people, but after the middle of the seventeenth century new religious movements such as pietism were no longer the revolutionary force they had been during the previous century. The literature and arts of the period reflected the spirit of royal absolutism and the values of the aristocracy, with their exaltation of kings, princes, and nobility and also their concern for order and form. The classical style prevailed in literature and music and shared dominance with the baroque in painting and architecture.

1. SOCIETY

Population Growth and Social Structure

One of the greatest sources for change in Western society has been population growth. As we have seen (see pp. 388–390), European population grew substantially during the sixteenth century, putting pressures on economic life, adding to social turmoil, and creating changes in the quality of life for different classes of people. This population growth leveled out during the first two decades of the seventeenth century. On the whole, Europe's population was able only to maintain itself or grow slightly during the seventeenth century. In some areas population declined markedly. The typical enemies of population growth were poverty, disease, famine, and war. Most people lived close to the subsistence level. Any disturbance—a poor harvest, a natural catastrophe, a war—quickly used up their meager reserves of food and opened the door to hunger, declining health, disease, and famine. The Thirty Years' War was particularly devastating, leading to a decline in German population of some 40 percent during the first half of the seventeenth century. The relatively late age of marriage—in the late twenties for men, the mid-twenties for women—also helped keep down the number of births in a society in which life expectancy was short and only about half of the babies born would reach maturity.

During the eighteenth century, particularly after the 1730s, European population grew sharply—from approximately 110 million in 1700 to 190 million in 1800. Although the causes are unclear, it seems that an increasing birth rate and declining death rate were achieved by earlier marriages, better and more regular nutrition, fewer plagues, and less devastating wars. Agricultural and commercial prosperity, along with continuing improvements in transportation facilities, diminished the periodic famines in many areas. Historians credit in particular the introduction of the potato from the New World and its widespread cultivation in eighteenth-century Europe with crucially increasing supplies of nutritious food. Certainly medical practices were not one of the causes for population growth. With the exception of developing small pox inoculation, which was little used outside of England until the nineteenth century, eighteenth-century doctors, hospitals, and medicines probably caused more deaths than they prevented.

Seventeenth- and eighteenth-century people viewed their society as divided—into different occupational groups and classes—and hierarchically ordered—the different groups and classes ranked from high to low status by birth, office, wealth, or education. Mobility between these ranked orders of society was viewed as the exception. People considered the social order to be relatively rigid and correct. In fact, however, mobility and change occurred. Wealth, education, and new opportunities for governmental service opened avenues for middle-class merchants, bankers, and professionals to move into the ranks of the aristocracy. Nevertheless, social mobility was never the option for many, as it would become during the nineteenth and twentieth centuries.

Rural Life

Seventeenth- and eighteenth-century Europeans lived predominantly in rural settings. In western

FIGURE 36.2. Louis Le Nain, "The Cart," 1641 In contrast to most seventeenth-century artists, Le Nain shows the life of the French peasantry. This farmyard scene (notice the mixture of ages), so typical of the countryside, contrasts sharply with life for the aristocracy. (The Louvre, Paris)

Europe approximately 80 percent still lived in the countryside; in the less urbanized eastern Europe the percentage was even higher. In rural areas life was centered on the traditional village (see Figure 36.2). There life was communally oriented: villagers knew each other, strangers stood out, and almost all effective authority was local. Community pressures limited what we today would consider the rights of dissent or privacy.

This pattern of life was slowly being altered. The traditional village was experiencing intrusion from the outside, change in its age-old pattern of life, and loss of people to the growing cities. The political isolation of the village was being broken by the increased presence of officials from the growing central governments, by the growing absence of the local nobility (who were attracted to the courts and capital cities), and by the decline of communal political institutions. Above all, economic life was being changed by the agricultural revolution and by the spread of cottage industry—both facilitated by improving means of transportation.

The Agricultural Revolution At the beginning of the seventeenth century, crops and animals

were raised in western Europe much as they had been since the Middle Ages. Most fields were open and divided into various strips of land. Crops were rotated and land allowed to lie fallow (unplanted) one out of every two or three years to keep the soil fertile. Large strips of land were set aside as "commons"—open areas where villagers grazed their animals and gathered food and hay. Decisions about crops, animals, and land use were usually determined by tradition and the practices of the community.

During the seventeenth and eighteenth centuries, changes in agricultural production initiated in Holland spread to England and then to other areas of western Europe. These changes were so important that they have been called an agricultural revolution. New crops such as potatoes, turnips, and clover were introduced. New methods of rotating crops, such as from grains to tubers (potatoes and turnips) to hay (grasses for animal fodder), were developed. Fertilization of the soil was increased by using manure from larger animal herds. These changes enabled farmers to eliminate fallow land. In addition, Dutch innovators developed methods of draining wetlands so that new crops and methods could be introduced easily.

They also experimented with breeding to create new strains of productive cattle.

In the early eighteenth century, the new crops and methods spread to England. Charles "Turnip" Townsend experimented with crop rotation and the use of turnips and clover. His contemporary and compatriot, Jethro Tull, advocated the use of a seed drill, which made planting more efficient and productive. Another Englishman, Robert Bakewell, improved the existing types of sheep and cattle by selective breeding.

These changes were sometimes connected to the enclosure of open fields and commons, particularly in England. The consolidation and enclosure of scattered strips and farms allowed larger landowners the freedom to apply new agricultural methods. Enclosures had been used in Great Britain since the sixteenth century, but the profits that could be made in commercial agriculture employing new crops and methods stimulated numerous landlords to seek enclosures during the eighteenth century. After 1750 Parliament authorized a wave of enclosures that transformed the British countryside. While these enclosures hastened the agricultural revolution, they left large numbers of rural poor unable to survive as small farmers. Many of them were forced into the ranks of rural or urban workers.

Cottage Industry During the seventeenth and eighteenth centuries, "cottage industry," or the "putting-out system," expanded greatly in rural areas. According to this system, a merchant-capitalist provided raw materials (usually for textile production such as wool or linen) and sometimes equipment (such as a handloom or spinning wheel) to peasants. Peasants, working in their cottages, turned these raw materials into finished products—spinning and weaving wool into cloth (see Figure 36.3). The merchant periodically returned, paid for the peasants' labor by the piece, and distributed the finished products to distant markets. The pay was low, lower than that offered in cities, but it was enough to help large numbers of peasants and rural workers to survive. The growth of cottage industry during the eighteenth century, particularly in Great Britain and parts of France and Germany, helps explain how so many people could remain in rural areas.

Urban Life

Cities grew during the seventeenth and eighteenth centuries, but unevenly. Until the middle of the eighteenth century, most of the growth was in the capital and port cities, particularly in northern and western Europe. These cities swelled with the growth of central governments and commerce. After the 1750s new cities arose and small cities grew, reflecting the general population growth and new concentrations of agricultural and industrial activity—particularly in Great Britain.

This urban growth meant greater prosperity for some, but the urban masses were not the beneficiaries. Most continued to live precariously at little more than a subsistence level. Any improvement in the standard of living was enjoyed almost exclusively by the middle and aristocratic classes, particularly those taking advantage of opportunities in commerce and industry and in the expanding governmental bureaucracies. A growing class of urban professionals attended institutions of higher education. In an expanding number of colleges they joined young aristocrats sent by families who felt that more education and culture was appropriate to members of the aristocracy. The middle classes continued to use their wealth to enter the aristocracy through the purchase of titles and offices, the acquisition of large estates, and judicious marriages.

The Family

The family, so central to social life and the socialization of future generations, is usually one of our most conservative institutions, evolving only gradually over time. This pattern of subtle, slow change held true for most of the seventeenth and eighteenth centuries.

The family functioned as both a social and an economic unit. In this household economy (or family economy), everyone who could worked for the good of the household. Husband, wife, children, servants, and apprentices were part of this unit of production and consumption. Even those who earned wages elsewhere usually sent part of their earnings back to the family. Children were often sent away to other households when they could earn more outside their own family.

Child rearing and attitudes toward children

FIGURE 36.3. Cottage Industry Most cottage industry was in textiles. Here the various members of a rural household in Ireland work together, beating and combing flax into linen, which will be spun and woven. (The Mansell Collection)

were strikingly different from those of today. Children were generally not at the center of family life nor of primary concern. Infanticide was not unknown, abandonment was a common practice, and what we would consider neglect was more often the rule than the exception. Much of this behavior may be explained by the high rate of infant mortality, the generally precarious state of the household economy, and simple poverty. Parents usually had to view their children not only as family members, but as assets or liabilities in the survival of the family. With life so precarious for their children, great emotional involvement with them was risky.

It was once thought that most people lived in extended families—more than one married couple and their children in the same household; how-ever, most historians now agree that as a rule people lived in a nuclear family household consisting of one couple and their children. Nevertheless, the typical family household during the sixteenth, seventeenth, and most of the eighteenth centuries was a much more populated, public place than the household of a modern nineteenth- and twentieth-century nuclear family. At various times a variety of relatives lived in or moved through the household, as did domestics and laborers. The household was far more open to members of the community and pressures from the community at large. The father, older children, other relatives, and community adults in general participated with the mother in raising and socializing young children.

Marriages continued to be entered into for primarily economic and social reasons. The land, the wealth, the skills, and the position one held were the most important considerations in contemplating marriage; sentiment, particularly being in love, played a secondary role. Children were the expected product of a successful marriage. Typically, a married woman gave birth to more than five children, though odds were that many of those would fail to reach adulthood or even get beyond the first few years of childhood.

Significant change came during the second half of the eighteenth century. Sentiment was becoming more important as a motivation for marriage; economic and social considerations, while still important, were not quite as dominant as before. Premarital sex and sex outside of marriage were on the increase, as evidenced by the growing number of births registered within a few months of marriage and by rising rates of illegitimacy. People were marrying at an earlier age and moving around more. Child rearing and homemaking were being turned into a woman's profession in middle-class households. Along with the rising likelihood that most babies born would survive came a changing perception of children as more special, precious, and loved—not miniature adults to be used, as they were more often perceived in the sixteenth and seventeenth centuries. Indeed, what was happening during the second half of the eighteenth century was a slow transformation to the modern family, which would come into bloom with the spread of industry and the dominance of the middle class during the nineteenth century.

Women

Women, while continuing to play a subordinate role to men, were central to the economic well-being of the family among the lower classes. Their work started when they were children, helping with the lighter tasks of farming or cottage industry. In her early teens, a girl often left home to work as a servant, trying to gain the skills and money for her future marriage and the establishment of a new household. As a married woman, her tasks as a child bearer and child rearer were important but secondary to her other economic and social functions. In addition to the standard household chores, women were expected to work

as much as possible. Women participated in the collecting and threshing of grain, took primary responsibility for gardening, raised the poultry, supervised and processed dairy production, and shared in the manufacture of household items and products for commerce (particularly spinning) as the putting-out system spread. When women worked in wage-earning occupations, it was generally at less pay and in lower-status positions than men. The line between acceptable "women's work" and "men's work" widened as the emphasis on women's domestic responsibilities grew. Outside a household, women were particularly vulnerable. They lacked many legal rights and were denied most alternatives for independent employment.

Middle- and upper-class women had fewer opportunities for participation in economic life. Respectable careers open to unmarried middle-class women were limited to those of governess or lady-in-waiting. Once married, the middle-class woman was at the center of the family, but for any real economic independence she had to wait for the death of her husband. More than lower-class women, middle-class women were increasingly seen as responsible for upholding standards and supervising the help within the home. Aristocratic women were similarly limited in the economic roles they played, but they could turn to influential social and cultural roles (see Chapter 38).

2. FAITH: THE GROWTH OF PIETISM

After the end of the Wars of Religion in the mid–seventeenth century, a relative status quo existed between Catholicism and Protestantism. While hostility still existed between believers of different Christians faiths, it no longer broke out into the violence and revolution characteristic of the Reformation era. Religious life remained centered in the local parish. In his church, the priest or pastor conducted services and supervised various charitable and educational activities. Although most people retained allegiance to established Catholic or Protestant churches, some new religious movements did arise during the seventeenth and eighteenth centuries. The most important were a number of pietistic sects, which stressed the importance of active faith in leading a religious life.

In Germany Philipp Spener (1635–1705) and Count Zinzendorf (1700–1760) became leaders of pietist movements of considerable dimensions. Spener, a Lutheran pastor, recoiled from the formal officiousness that his church had fallen into after the heated religious strife of the sixteenth and early seventeenth centuries. He minimized dogma and external forms in favor of inner piety and holy living. His largely Lutheran following included some of the leading intellects of Germany. Count Zinzendorf, a well-to-do Saxon noble man, undertook to restore the Bohemian Brethren, the persecuted and scattered followers of the early-fifteenth-century reformer John Huss. He called his group the Moravian Brethren. The Moravians, too, shunned intricate dogma and formal ritual. They set up model communities based on brotherly love, frugal living, hard work, and inner piety.

In Lutheran Sweden, Emanuel Swedenborg (1688–1772), a distinguished scientist, inventor, and public servant, founded a movement somewhat like the Moravian Brethren, based on his visions, which he took to be direct revelations of God. Swedenborg wrote several learned theological works stressing inner and outward piety and individual communion with God.

England, however, was the seat of the most widespread and influential pietistic movements of the seventeenth and eighteenth centuries. The first was the Society of Friends, or the Quakers, as they were generally called, founded by George Fox (1624–1691). Fox, a man of great energy and stubborn independence, detested formalism in religion as well as in society and government. He believed that true Christianity is an individual matter—a matter of plain, pious living and of private communion with God under the guidance of divine "inner light." Opposed to war, to rank, and to intolerance, the Quakers refused military service, the use of titles, and the taking of oaths. In these respects the Quakers were different from most of the other pietists. They were considered dangerous to the established order and were severely persecuted.

A more moderate and popular pietist movement was Methodism. The prime mover in Methodism was John Wesley (1703–1791). John Wesley and his brother, Charles, became converted to a more fervent, evangelical type of Christianity. When the Anglican churches closed their doors to John Wesley, he preached emotional sermons to huge throngs in the streets and fields. George Whitefield, the most eloquent of all the early Methodists, electrified tens of thousands in England and America and converted many to pietistic Christianity. The real founder of Methodism in the American colonies was Francis Asbury (1745–1816), who duplicated in many respects the work of John Wesley in England. In both England and America the Methodists grew rapidly in numbers, mostly among the middle and lower classes.

The various pietist groups were definitely not political revolutionaries. They were intensely interested in social reform—in education, health and sanitation, temperance, penal reform, and abolition of the slave trade. But they hoped to achieve these reforms by private charity rather than political action. They tended to accommodate themselves to political status quo in the belief that spiritual and social conditions could be improved within that framework of government.

3. CULTURE

The cultural styles of the seventeenth and eighteenth centuries reflected the dominance of royal and aristocratic tastes—particularly in the baroque, classical, and rococo styles. The main exceptions came in the Dutch Netherlands and eighteenth-century England, where paintings and literature often reflected the tastes of the ascending middle class.

Literature

The reign of Louis XIV (1643–1715) was the golden age of French literature. The elegance, the sense of order, and the formalism of the court of the Grand Monarch were all reflected in the literature of the period, sometimes called the Augustan or the classical period of French literature. It was in the field of the drama that the French writers attained their greatest success. Corneille wrote elegant tragedies in the style of and often on the same subjects as the ancient Greek tragedies. The struggles of human beings against themselves and against the universe furnish the dramatic conflicts. Corneille's craftsmanship and style are handsomely polished, though often exalted and exaggerated.

Even more exquisitely polished were the perfectly rhymed and metered couplets of Racine's tragedies: *Andromaque* relates the tragic story of Hector's wife after the death of her husband at the hands of Achilles and the ensuing fall of Troy. *Phèdre* is about the wife of the legendary Greek king Theseus who falls in love with her stepson. This story had also been the subject of plays by Euripides, Sophocles, and Seneca.

One of the greatest of all the French dramatists was Molière. In his charming and profound comedies—such as *Tartuffe, Le Misanthrope,* and *Les Femmes Savantes (The Learned Ladies)*—Molière devastatingly portrays and satirizes the false, the stupid, and the pompous: egotists, pedants, social climbers, false priests, quack physicians. The tragic conflicts and the personality types of Corneille, Racine, and Molière are universal and eternal.

Other major French writers of the age of Louis XIV were Blaise Pascal, the scientist and mathematician who also wrote the marvelously styled *Provincial Letters* against the Jesuits and the deeply reflective *Pensées (Thoughts);* Madame de Sévigné, who wrote almost two thousand letters to her daughter, each a work of art; and duke de Saint-Simon, who spent the latter part of his life writing forty volumes of *Mémoires.* Madame de Sévigné and the duke of Saint-Simon, both of whom were eyewitnesses of the court of Louis XIV, constitute two of the most important sources we have for the history and the life of that period.

The common denominator among all these writers is their emphasis on and mastery of elegant and graceful form. In this emphasis they reflect the spirit of royal absolutism at its height. However, the form is valued not merely for its own sake but as an artistic clothing for subtle and critical thought. French literature in the late seventeenth century overshadowed that of all other countries of Europe, much as did French military and political influence. The lucid and graceful French language became the fashionable language of most of the royal courts and courtiers on the European continent.

French literature in the eighteenth century continued for the most part in the classical vein. Voltaire wrote dramas and poems carefully tailored to the dictates of classical formalism. His prose works exalted logic and the ideals of Greece and Rome. Only Rousseau among the major eighteenth-century French writers departed from the classical spirit to anticipate the romanticism of a later era.

Next to France, England produced the most important literature in the seventeenth and early eighteenth centuries, and like the French, the English authors generally wrote in the classical vein. The giant of English letters in the mid–seventeenth century was John Milton (1608–1674). This learned Puritan was steeped in the literature of ancient Greece and Rome. His exquisite lyrics *L'Allegro* and *Il Penseroso* and incomparable elegy *Lycidas* are thickly strewn with references to classical mythology. The conscientious Milton contributed much of his great talent and energy to public affairs. During the Puritan Revolution he went blind while working as pamphleteer for the Puritan cause and as secretary for Oliver Cromwell. The chief literary product of this period of his life is *Areopagitica,* probably the noblest defense of freedom of the press ever penned. Milton's masterpiece is *Paradise Lost,* written in his blindness and after the restoration of the Stuart kings had ruined his public career. *Paradise Lost* is a poem of epic proportions based on the Genesis account of the rebellion of Satan against God and the temptation and fall of human beings. This majestic theme is treated in stately blank verse of formal elegance. Even in this deeply religious work, Holy Writ is interwoven with classical pagan myth.

The two greatest poets to succeed Milton were John Dryden in the late seventeenth century and Alexander Pope in the early eighteenth century. Both were satirists, both displayed a massive knowledge of Greek and Roman lore, and both wrote chiefly in the formal rhymed couplets typical of the classical period. In the precision of their form, as in the sharpness of their satire, their appeal was to reason rather than to emotion.

The eighteenth century in English literature was an age of great prose. Following the upheavals of the seventeenth century, the Puritan and Glorious revolutions, it was a time of political and religious bitterness and bickering. In pungent and incisive prose Jonathan Swift, in his *Gulliver's Travels* and political essays, and Richard Sheridan, in his numerous dramas, pilloried the fops, pedants, bigots, and frauds of the day, much as Molière had done a century earlier across the channel. It was in the eighteenth century that the English novel was born. More than other literary forms, it was aimed at and reflected the tastes of England's rising middle class. Samuel Richardson, in *Clarissa Harlowe,* and Henry Fielding, in *Tom Jones,* used this medium to analyze human personality, emotions, and psychology, just as Corneille and Racine had used the poetic drama in France for the same purpose.

In the eighteenth century several writers—Robert Burns in Great Britain, Rousseau in France, Schiller and Goethe in Germany—anticipated romanticism (see Chapter 45). But the prevailing spirit in eighteenth- as in seventeenth-century literature was classical. Precision, formalism, and ofttimes elegance marked the style. Ancient Greece and Rome furnished the models. The appeal was generally to reason. The royal monarchs and their courts had little to fear from this literature. They could derive comfort from its formal order and laugh with the rest of the world at its satire, which was aimed at humankind in general rather than at ruling regimes.

Painting and Architecture

If the literature of the seventeenth and eighteenth centuries did not offend the absolutist kings and their aristocratic courtiers, the visual arts of the period usually glorified them (see Color Plate 14). The dominant style of painting and architecture during the seventeenth century was the baroque, which used elaborate swirling forms and colors to achieve dramatic, emotional effects. The baroque style was originally associated with the Roman Catholic Reformation and reflected the resurgence of a revitalized Roman Catholic church led by the militant Jesuits. Later its massive and ornamental elegance reflected the wealth and power of the absolutist monarchs and their courts, then at the peak of their affluence.

The most popular of the baroque painters of the early seventeenth century was the Fleming Peter Paul Rubens (1577–1640). After studying the work of the Italian High Renaissance masters, Rubens returned to Antwerp and painted more than two thousand pictures, many of them huge canvases. He operated what amounted to a painting factory, employing dozens of artists who painted in the details designed and sketched by the master. Rubens, a devout Roman Catholic, first painted religious subjects (see Color Plate 15). His later subjects were pagan mythology, court life, and especially voluptuous nude women—all painted in the most brilliant and sensuous colors (see Figure 36.4).

Spain boasted two of the greatest seventeenth-century painters: El Greco and Velásquez. El Greco, whose real name was Domenikos Theotokopoulos, was a native of the Greek island of Crete (hence "The Greek"). After studying the Italian Renaissance masters, he settled down in Toledo and developed a style of his own. By deliberate distortion and exaggeration he achieved sensational effect. *View of Toledo, St. Jerome in His Study,* and *Christ at Gethsemane* illustrate his genius. El Greco's favorite subject was the reinvigorated Church of the Roman Catholic Reformation. Considered to be a madman by his contemporaries, he is now regarded as the forerunner of several schools of nineteenth- and twentieth-century painting. Velásquez was a painter of great versatility. Although much of his earlier work was of a religious nature, he also painted genre subjects (depicting the life of the common people) and, later, portraits. He is considered one of the greatest of portrait painters. As official court painter, he exalted and glorified the Spanish royalty and ruling classes at a time when they had really passed their peak in world affairs.

During the second half of the seventeenth and then the eighteenth century, classicism, with its greater emphasis on control and restraint, gained favor. Good examples of classicism are in the works of the French artists Nicolas Poussin and Claude Lorrain (see Color Plate 16). Poussin spent most of his life in Italy studying the Renaissance masters. Although his biblical and mythological

FIGURE 36.4. Peter Paul Rubens, "Henry IV Receiving the Portrait of Marie de Médicis," 1621–1625 Rubens was commissioned by Marie de Médicis, widow of King Henry IV of France, to paint this allegorical scene showing Henri IV considering a proposed marriage to Marie de Médicis. The swirling lines, dramatic perspective, rich color, and opulence are typically baroque. (The Louvre, Paris)

scenes are more vibrant and pulsating than the Italian Renaissance paintings that inspired them, they are much more serene, subtle, and controlled than the works of Rubens and El Greco.

In eighteenth-century Great Britain, Reynolds, Gainsborough, Romney, and Lawrence vied with each other for commissions to paint the portraits of royalty and aristocracy. The results were plumes, jewels, buckles, silks, brocades, and laces in dripping profusion (see Figure 36.1).

In the Dutch Netherlands painting did not reflect royal and aristocratic tastes. Here in the busy ports and marketplaces commerce was king, and the great Dutch painters of the seventeenth century, notably Frans Hals, Jan Vermeer, and Rembrandt van Rijn, portrayed the bourgeoisie and the common people (see Color Plate 17). Rembrandt is universally recognized as one of the greatest artistic geniuses of all time. As a portrayer of character he has never been surpassed. His mastery of light and shade (*chiaroscuro*) made it seem as if the very souls of his subjects were illumined. *Syndics of the Cloth Guild, Night Watch,* and *Anatomy Lesson of Dr. Tulp* (see p. 439) are among his most powerful portrait studies. These three paintings also vividly depict the commercial prosperity, the festive urban life, and the growing interest in natural science, respectively, in seventeenth-century Dutch Netherlands.

Baroque architecture, like baroque painting, was an elaboration and ornamentation of the Renaissance and a product of the Roman Catholic

FIGURE 36.5. The Baroque Style This photo is of the interior of the basilica St. Andrea della Valle, which was built in the latter part of the seventeenth century. It well illustrates the elaborate, gaudy splendor of the baroque style, the hallmark of the age of royal absolutism and affluence. In this case the royal monarch was the pope, ruler of a Church reinvigorated by the Roman Catholic Reformation. (Alinari/Scala/ Art Resource)

Reformation (see Figure 36.5). In the late sixteenth, the seventeenth, and the eighteenth centuries Jesuit churches sprang up all over the Roman Catholic world. The most important and one of the best examples of the baroque style is the Jesuit parent church, Il Gesù, in Rome. Also, like the painting, baroque architecture was later used to represent the gaudy splendor of the seventeenth- and eighteenth-century absolute monarchs and their courts.

Towering over all other monuments of baroque architecture, much as St. Peter's towered over all

other Renaissance structures, was the Versailles Palace of Louis XIV (see Figure 32.1). The exterior of Versailles is designed in long, horizontal, classic lines. The interior is lavishly decorated with richly colored marbles, mosaics, inlaid woods, gilt, silver, silk, velvet, and brocade. The salons and halls are lighted with ceiling-to-floor windows and mirrors and crystal chandeliers holding thousands of candles. The palace faces hundreds of acres of groves, walks, pools, terraces, fountains, statues, flower beds, and clipped shrubs—all laid out in formal geometric patterns. So dazzling was this symbol of royal absolutism that many European monarchs attempted to copy it. The most successful attempt was Maria Theresa's Schönbrunn Palace in Vienna.

In England Sir Christopher Wren was the greatest architect of the baroque period. The great fire that destroyed most of the heart of London in 1666 provided Wren with an opportunity to build numerous baroque structures. His masterpiece is St. Paul's Cathedral, with its lofty dome and columns.

In the eighteenth century, architecture tended to become less massive, relying heavily on multiple curves and lacy shell-like ornamentation. This style is usually referred to as rococo. One of the best examples of the rococo style is Frederick the Great's Sans Souci Palace at Potsdam. The rococo style, like the baroque, represented an age of royal and aristocratic affluence.

Music

The classical spirit pervaded the music of the seventeenth and eighteenth centuries as it did the literature and the visual arts; and like the literature and the visual arts, the music was an outgrowth of Renaissance developments.[1] The piano and the violin family of instruments, whose forebears appeared in the sixteenth century, developed rapidly in the seventeenth. In the late seventeenth and early eighteenth centuries, three Italian families, the Amati, the Guarneri, and the Stradivari, fashioned the finest violins ever made. The seventeenth century was also marked by the rise of the opera. Alessandro Scarlatti in Italy, Lully in France, and Purcell in England popularized this grandiose combination of music and drama. The eighteenth was the great century of classical music—the age of Bach, Handel, Haydn, and Mozart.

Johann Sebastian Bach (1685–1750) was a member of a German family long distinguished in music. Noted in his own lifetime chiefly as an organist, he composed a vast array of great music for

FIGURE 36.6. Mozart Mozart, shown here as a boy, gained fame as an infant prodigy. Mozart died when he was thirty-five, but this prolific genius composed over six hundred works. (Mozart Museum, Salzburg)

organ, harpsichord, and clavichord (forerunner of the piano), orchestra, and chorus, much of which has been lost. Most of Bach's compositions were religiously inspired, and he holds the same position in Protestant music that the sixteenth-century Palestrina does in music of the Roman Catholic church. Bach was not widely appreciated in his own day. It was not until Felix Mendelssohn in the nineteenth century "discovered" him that he became widely known.

George Frederick Handel (1685–1759) was born in central Germany in the same year as Bach and not many miles distant. He studied Italian opera in Germany and Italy and wrote forty-six operas himself. He became court musician of the elector of Hanover. Later he made his home in England, as did the elector, who became King George I of

---

[1]Some music historians designate the music of the seventeenth and early eighteenth centuries, including that of Bach and Handel, as baroque, which was a forerunner of the classical.

England. Handel wrote an enormous quantity of music, both instrumental and vocal. All of it is marked by dignity, formal elegance, and melodious harmony—fitting for and appreciated in an age of royal splendor. His best-known work is the majestic oratorio *The Messiah,* heard every Christmas season.

Franz Joseph Haydn (1732–1809), unlike Handel, was primarily interested in instrumental music; he was the chief originator of the symphony. During his long career in Vienna, which he helped to make the music capital of the world, he wrote more than a hundred symphonies in addition to scores of compositions of other forms of music, particularly chamber music. It was in his hands that orchestral music really came into its own. All his work is in the formal, classical style. He became a friend and an important source of inspi-

ration for the younger Mozart.

Wolfgang Amadeus Mozart (1756–1791) is regarded by many students as the greatest musical genius of all time. Born in Salzburg, he spent most of his adult life in Vienna. Mozart began composing at the age of five (possibly four), and gave public concerts on the harpsichord at the age of six (see Figure 36.6). At twelve he wrote an opera. Before his untimely death at the age of thirty-five, he wrote more than six hundred compositions in all the known musical forms. Symphonies, chamber music, and piano sonatas and concertos were his favorite forms. His best-known operas are *The Marriage of Figaro, Don Giovanni,* and *The Magic Flute.* In the masterful hands of Mozart the classical style reached the peak of its perfection. Never was music so clear, melodic, elegant, and graceful.

SUGGESTED READING

General

F. Braudel, *The Structures of Everyday Life: The Limits of the Possible* (1982). A massive, highly respected social history.

H. Kamen, *European Society, 1500–1700* (1985). A solid survey.

G. Rudé, *Europe in the Eighteenth Century* (1972). Emphasizes social history.

Society

P. Ariés, *Centuries of Childhood: A Social History of Family Life* (1962). A path-breaking work.

J. Blum, *The End of the Old Order in Rural Europe* (1978). Excellent comparative study.

M. W. Flinn, *The European Demographic System, 1500–1820* (1981). A recent survey.

P. Laslett, *The World We Have Lost* (1965). A classic study of English society during the period.

E. Shorter, *The Making of the Modern Family* (1975). Interpretive, controversial, and well written.

L. Stone, *The Family, Sex and Marriage in England, 1500–1800* (1977). A sophisticated interpretation.

L. Tilly and J. Scott, *Women, Work and Family* (1978). A highly respected work.

J. de Vries, *European Urbanization, 1500–1800* (1984). Broad recent survey.

Faith

A. Armstrong, *The Church of England, the Methodists, and Society 1700–1850* (1973). A broad survey.

G. R. Cragg, *The Church and the Age of Reason* (1961). A solid survey.

Culture

A. Adam, *Grandeur and Illusion: French Literature and Society 1600–1715* (1972). A thorough survey of French literature and its relation to seventeenth-century society.

P. Burke, *Popular Culture in Early Modern Europe* (1978). Focuses on ordinary people.

C. Palisca, *Baroque Music* (1968). Excellent survey.

C. Rosen, *The Classical Style: Haydn, Mozart, Beethoven* (1972). Excellent study.

V. L. Tapié, *The Age of Grandeur: Baroque Art and Architecture* (1960). A solid survey of art history.

I. Watt, *The Rise of the Novel: Studies of Defoe, Richardson, and Fielding* (1957). A good introduction.

CHAPTER 37
The Scientific Revolution

FIGURE 37.1. Isaac Newton   Isaac Newton (1642–1727) became the leading figure of the Scientific Revolution, employing the new methods of science and drawing together discoveries in astronomy and physics to create a systematic explanation of the physical laws of the universe. This portrait suggests his youthful vigor and keenness. He was still in his twenties when he developed some of his greatest theories. (The Bettmann Archive)

Until the seventeenth century even the most learned scholars of Europe agreed with the standard medieval understanding of the physical nature of the earth and the universe. This medieval understanding was based on the views of the fourth-century B.C. Greek, Aristotle, as modified by Ptolemy and medieval Christian scholars. According to this Christian medieval understanding the earth was stationary and at the center of the universe. Around it moved the planets, the sun, the stars, and the heavens in an ascending series of spheres. This universe was finite and and focused on the earthly center of God's concern. "Scientific" investigation generally took the form of making deductions from accepted, authoritative medieval assumptions about the physical universe. The questions asked were usually the more philosophical or theological ones of ultimate causes for an event—guesses on why something occurred.

During the seventeenth century a relatively small number of scholars undermined this medieval understanding of nature and replaced it with a modern scientific view. According to this new scientific view, the earth was a moving body and no longer at the center of the universe. Rather it, along with the planets, moved around the sun in an infinite universe of other similar bodies. Scientific investigations generally took the form of observing, measuring, experimenting, and coming to reasoned conclusions through the use of sophisticated mathematics. Medieval assumptions about the physical universe were viewed with a skeptical eye. The questions asked were usually the more concrete, pragmatic ones of how an event occurred rather than the ultimate reasons for why such an event occurred. The new scientific synthesis was one of a mechanistic universe of forces acting according to mathematically expressible laws and open to human reason and investigation.

Until the eighteenth century the impact of this modern scientific view, known as the Scientific Revolution, was limited. Nevertheless, it was an intellectual revolution of great significance, for with it Western civilization was making a turn from its medieval assumptions and embarking in a direction unique among the cultures of the world. Science would grow to become one of the main factors distinguishing the West and accounting for its power and dynamism.

1. CAUSES AND SPREAD

There were several causes for the development and spread of the Scientific Revolution, some of which extend back to the late Middle Ages and Renaissance. Medieval universities had been growing for some time and included the study of philosophy and other subjects that would be central to the Scientific Revolution, including astronomy, physics, and mathematics. Certainly the emphasis and the greatest prestige was accorded to theology and nonscientific study in these medieval universities, but nevertheless there were places on the faculty for many of the central figures of the Scientific Revolution, such as Galileo and Newton.

The Renaissance involved a search for classical writings. The discovery of Greek authorities who contradicted Aristotle and the growth of Neoplatonism as an alternative to Aristotelian thought in Renaissance Italy encouraged scholars to question medieval scientific assumptions. The Renaissance stimulated interest in analyzing and describing physical reality, a key concern of the Scientific Revolution. The Renaissance was also an age of commercial and geographic expansion in the West, which created a demand for new instruments and precise measurements, particularly for navigation in the open seas. This demand encouraged scientific research, especially in astronomy and mathematics. In turn, the better instruments developed during the Renaissance helped scholars make accurate measurements, something crucial for the new science. During this same period, the printing press was invented, which facilitated the dissemination of the new science, even if initially to only a select few.

The Reformation played a mixed role in the Scientific Revolution. Generally, both Catholics and Protestants criticized the scientific discoveries that so threatened the medieval-Christian view of the universe. During the sixteenth century there was perhaps more room within the Catholic church for scientific research than among Protestants, but by the middle of the seventeenth century this was clearly not the case. By then the Counter-Reformation Catholic church had turned into an enemy of much of the new science, while Protestants began to accept it. This was particularly so in England, where the Puritans encouraged the new science and where science took hold most firmly.

During the seventeenth century, governments gave support to science, in part hoping that scientific inquiry would yield discoveries that would increase the power and prosperity of the state. With governmental support scientific academies were established and played a significant role in the advancement of science. The earliest and most important of these were the Royal Society in England, chartered in 1662 by Charles II, and the Académie des Sciences in France, founded by Colbert four years later. These organizations and others patterned after them furnished laboratories, granted subsidies, brought scientists together to exchange ideas, published their findings, and encouraged scientific achievement generally. They also helped make scientists a more socially acceptable group and contributed to the creation of a new set of values supportive of the new science.

Finally, religious and psychological factors played an important, if difficult to evaluate, role in the development and spread of the Scientific Revolution. Many of the new scientists had strong, though not always traditional, religious motives for their work, particularly a desire to gain insight into the perfection of God's universe.

2. ASTRONOMY AND PHYSICS: FROM COPERNICUS TO NEWTON

The first branches of modern natural science to attract systematic attention were astronomy and physics. Discoveries in these fields would dramatically alter the perception of nature and the earth's place in the universe.

Nicolaus Copernicus

The first steps were taken in the sixteenth century by Nicolaus Copernicus (1473–1543), a Polish cler-

gyman interested in astronomy, astrology, mathematics, and church law. Like so many other northern European scholars in the fifteenth century, he crossed the Alps to study in an Italian university. There he was influenced by the rediscovery of Greek scholarship, particularly Platonic and Pythagorean thought, that differed from the accepted, mathematically complex Aristotelian-Ptolemaic tradition. This rediscovered Greek thought emphasized the importance of a hidden, simpler, mathematically harmonious reality underlying appearances. With a religious, mystical passion, Copernicus sought a simpler mathematical formulation for how the universe operated. This search convinced him that the earth was not the center of the universe but, rather, that the sun was the center. Moreover, the earth was not stationary but moved in perfect divine circles around the sun, as did other bodies in the universe. This change from an earth-centered (geocentric) to a sun-centered (heliocentric) universe has come to be known as the Copernican revolution (see Figures 37.2 and 37.3).

Copernicus worked on his heliocentric model of the universal for almost twenty-five years, but fearing the ridicule of the laity and the ire of the clergy, he did not have it published until 1543, the year of his death. Few knew of his views and even fewer accepted them. Nevertheless, their significance and their threat to the Christian conception of the universe would be recognized and condemned by Catholic and Protestant authorities. They denounced the Copernican system as illogical, unbiblical, and unsettling to the Christian faith. Nevertheless, his views would stimulate other scholars investigating the physical nature of the universe.

Tycho Brahe

After Copernicus, the most important astronomer of the sixteenth century was a Danish aristocrat, Tycho Brahe (1546–1601). He persuaded the king of Denmark to support him, and he built the most advanced astronomy laboratory in Europe. There he gathered unusually accurate, detailed information about the planets and stars (even though the telescope had not yet been invented). Partic-

FIGURE 37.2. **The Medieval View of the Universe** This woodcut (1559) shows the traditional Ptolemaic conception of the universe. At the center is the earth, surrounded by ascending spheres of air, fire, the sun, the planets, the stars ("firmament"), the crystalline ring, and the "primum mobile." (The British Museum)

FIGURE 37.3. **The Copernican conception of the universe (woodcut, 1576).** At the center is the sun, surrounded by the circling planets (one of which is the earth), all bounded by an infinity of stars and the heavens. One of the central developments of the Scientific Revolution was the replacement of the Ptolemaic geocentric by the Copernican heliocentric conception of the universe. (The British Museum)

ularly important were his discoveries of a new star in 1572 and a comet in 1577, both of which undermined the Aristotelian assumptions about a sky of fixed, unalterable stars moving in crystalline spheres. He did not share Copernicus' belief in a heliocentric universe nor did he grasp the sophisticated mathematics of the day. He believed that the earth remained the stationary center of the universe, as argued by Aristotle and Ptolemy, but he concluded that the other planets revolved around the sun, which itself moved around the earth and moon. However, the astronomical observations he gathered would be used by other scholars who became convinced that the earth moved around the sun.

Johann Kepler

Tycho Brahe's assistant, Johann Kepler (1571–1630) built upon Brahe's observations while returning to the Copernican heliocentric theory. A German Lutheran from an aristocratic family, Kepler believed there was an underlying mathematical harmony of mystical significance to the physical universe. He sought such a mathematical harmony that would fit with Brahe's observations. His most important findings were the three laws of planetary motion, proposed between 1609 and 1619: first, that the planets moved in ellipses around the sun; second, that their velocity varied according to the distance from the sun; and third, that there was a physical relationship between the moving planets that could be expressed mathematically. He thus further undermined the Aristotelian universe accepted by medieval thought and provided support for the Copernican revolution. Moreover, he extended the Copernican revolution in ways that would be fully realized by Galileo and Newton.

Galileo Galilei

The Italian astronomer, physicist, and mathematician Galileo Galilei (1564–1642) believed, like Copernicus and Kepler, that there was a hidden harmony to nature. He felt that this harmony could be discovered through experimentation and mathematics. He investigated motion through controlled experiments and demonstrated that motion could be described mathematically. He showed that bodies once set in motion will tend to stay in motion and described mathematically the speed of falling bodies. He thus undermined Aristotelian physics and established rules for experimental physics.

Galileo then moved to astronomy, using a telescope he built in 1609. The telescope revealed to Galileo that the moon had a rough surface not unlike the earth's, that Jupiter had moons, and that the sun had spots. He confirmed the Copernican hypothesis and provided support for the view that other heavenly bodies were like the earth and imperfect. By implication, this finding meant that the natural universe was ordered and uniform, without the hierarchical distinctions of the accepted medieval view.

Galileo aggressively published and defended his views against detractors, most notably in *Dialogue on the Two Chief Systems of the World*, published in Italian in 1632. This text brought him into conflict with conservative forces in the Catholic church, which condemned his theories at an Inquisition in 1633, forcing him to recant.

Isaac Newton

The uphill trail blazed by Copernicus, Brahe, Kepler, and Galileo was continued on to a lofty peak by Isaac Newton (1642–1727). As a student at Cambridge University, he distinguished himself enough in mathematics to be chosen to stay on as professor after his graduation. Starting in his early twenties, Newton came forth with some of the most important discoveries in the history of science—or indeed of the human intellect. He developed calculus and investigated the nature of light. He formulated and described mathematically three laws of motion: inertia, acceleration, and action/reaction. He is probably best known for the laws of universal attraction, or gravitation. The concept matured and was refined in Newton's mind over a period of years. As it finally appeared in 1687 in his *Principia (The Mathematical Principles of Natural Knowledge),* the law is stated with marvelous simplicity and precision: "Every particle of matter in the universe attracts every other particle with a force varying inversely as the square of the distance between them and directly proportional to the product of their masses." This law, so simply expressed, applied equally to the movement of a planet and a berry falling from a bush. The secret of the physical universe appeared to have been solved—a universe of perfect stability and precision.

What Newton had done was to synthesize the new findings in astronomy and physics into a systematic explanation of physical laws that were true for earth as well as for the heavens. This Newtonian universe was uniform, mathematically describable, held together by explainable forces, atomic in nature. The universe was essentially matter in motion.

Newton, like most other figures of the Scientific Revolution, was profoundly religious; he believed in God and a God-centered universe, as well as alchemy. By the later years of the seventeenth century and the beginning of the eighteenth century, the new science was becoming more acceptable than it had been for Newton's predecessors, as is illustrated by his career. He became a member of Parliament and served for many years as director of the Royal Mint. He was knighted by Queen Anne. His acceptance, as contrasted with the ridicule and persecution suffered by Copernicus and Galileo, indicates the progress that had been made by the scientific attitude between the sixteenth and the eighteenth centuries.

3. SCIENTIFIC METHODOLOGY

The scientists who made discoveries in astronomy and physics succeeded in undermining the medieval view of the universe as stable, fixed, and finite, with the earth at its center. They replaced it with a view of the universe as moving and infinite, with the earth merely one of millions of bodies, all subject to the laws of nature. In the process they were also developing and using new methods for discovery, for ascertaining how things worked, and for determining the truth. Indeed, at the heart of the Scientific Revolution was the new methodology of science. According to this new methodology, earlier methods for ascertaining the truth, which primarily involved referring to traditional authorities such as Aristotle, Ptolemy, and the Church and making deductions from their propositions, were unacceptable. The new methodology emphasized systematic skepticism, experimentation, and reasoning based on observed facts and mathematical laws. The two most important philosophers of this new scientific methodology were Francis Bacon and René Descartes.

Francis Bacon

Francis Bacon (1561–1626) was a politician and once was lord chancellor of England under James I. He had a passionate interest in the new science. He rejected reliance on ancient authorities and advocated that scientists should engage in the collection of data without holding preconceived notions. From that information, scientific conclusions could be reached through inductive reasoning—drawing general conclusions on the basis of many particular concrete observations. He thus became a proponent of the empirical method, which was already being used by some of the new scientists. In addition, he argued that true, scientific knowledge would be useful knowledge, as opposed to medieval Scholasticism, which Bacon attacked as too abstract. He had faith that scientific discoveries would be applied to commerce and industry and generally improve the human condition by giving human beings greater power over their environment. He thus became an outstanding propagandist for the new science as well as a

FIGURE 37.4. Title Page of Bacon's *Novum Organum* This title page from Francis Bacon's *Novum Organum* (*New Instrument*), published in 1620, shows a ship of discovery sailing out into the unknown. Below is the quotation, "Many shall venture forth and science shall be increased." (The Bettmann Archive)

proponent of the empirical method (see Figure 37.4). He did not, however, have a good understanding of mathematics and the role it could play in the new science. Descartes did.

René Descartes

René Descartes (1596–1650) was born in France and received training in Scholastic philosophy and mathematics. He spent his most productive years as a mathematician, physicist, and metaphysical philosopher in Holland. In 1619 Descartes perceived connections between geometry and algebra that led him to discover analytic geometry, an important tool for scientists. He expressed his philosophy and scientific methodology in his *Discourse on Method* (1637), a landmark in the rise of the scientific spirit. It was an eloquent defense of the value of abstract reasoning. He would question all authority no matter how venerable—be it Aristotle or the Bible. He tried to remove systematically all assumptions about knowledge to the point where he was left with one experiential fact—that he was thinking. "I think, therefore I am," he believed to be a safe starting point. From this starting point he followed a rigorous process of deductive reasoning to come to a variety of conclusions, including the existence of God and the reality of the physical world. He argued that the universe could be divided into two kinds of reality: mind, or subjective thinking and experiencing; and body, or objective physical substance. According to this philosophy, known as "Cartesian dualism," the objective physical universe could be understood in terms of extension and motion. "Give me extension and motion," said Descartes, "and I will create the universe." Only the mind was exempt from mechanical laws.

Descartes, like Bacon, rejected Scholastic philosophy as not useful (although there were similarities in his deductive method and the reasoning used in Scholastic thought). He emphasized the power of the rigorous, reasoning individual mind to discover truths about nature and turn them to human needs. Unlike Bacon, he emphasized mathematical reasoning, not empirical investigation. By challenging all established authority, by accepting as truth only what could be known by reason, and by assuming a purely mechanical, physical universe, Descartes was in dispute with medieval thought and established an influential philosophy and methodology for the new science.

4. OTHER DISCIPLINES

The individuals who made the great discoveries of the Scientific Revolution all used, to varying degrees, the new scientific methodologies promoted by Bacon and Descartes during the first half of the seventeenth century. Clearly astronomy and

FIGURE 37.5. Modern Anatomy This illustration from an anatomy book published in 1639 by William Harvey shows the circulation of blood. Harvey's empirical, descriptive approach was typical of the new science. (Art Resource)

physics led the way, but important discoveries were made in other sciences as well.

In the sixteenth century Vesalius, a Fleming living in Italy, wrote the first comprehensive textbook on the structure of the human body to be based on careful observation. Because he dissected many human bodies in order to make his observations, he ran into serious opposition from clerical authorities. In disgust he gave up his scientific studies and became the personal physician of Emperor Charles V. In the seventeenth century William Harvey, an Englishman who also studied in Italy, discovered the major principles of the circulatory system, thus making it possible for surgeons to operate on the human body with somewhat less fatal consequences than had previously been the case (see Figure 37.5). Vesalius and Harvey are regarded as the founders of the science of anatomy.

In the seventeenth century, an Irish nobleman, Robert Boyle, laid the foundations for modern chemistry by attacking many assumptions inherited from the ancients and by beginning the systematic search for the basic physical elements. He relied on the experimental method and argued that all matter was composed of atoms. He discovered a law of gases that still bears his name.

The language in which science is expressed is mathematics. In the early seventeenth century a Scotsman, Sir John Napier, invented logarithms, by which the process of multiplying and dividing huge numbers is greatly simplified. Shortly afterward the system was applied to the slide rule. About the same time, René Descartes adopted the symbols now used in algebra and devised analytic geometry, a method of combining and interchanging algebra and geometry. In the latter part of the seventeenth century Newton and the German Wilhelm Leibnitz, working independently, invented calculus, upon which many of the most intricate processes of advanced science and engineering are dependent.

During the seventeenth century some of the basic scientific instruments were invented. Both the telescope and the microscope were products of the Dutch Netherlands. However, it was Galileo who first used the telescope in systematic astronomical observations. Leeuwenhoek, a Dutchman, was the chief pioneer in the use of the microscope. He discovered bacteria two hundred years before Pasteur learned how to combat them; he also observed the cellular structure of plant and animal tissue, the structure of the blood, and its circulation through the capillary system. Another Dutchman, Huygens, invented the pendulum clock, making possible for the first time in history the precise measurement of small intervals of time.

The methods and discoveries of the Scientific Revolution spread to disciplines outside of what are usually considered the sciences. A good example is political theory, with the seminal thought of Thomas Hobbes (1588–1679) and John Locke (1632–1704).

Hobbes gained contact with the new sciences from several quarters. As a young man he served as a secretary to Francis Bacon. While traveling on the continent, he came into contact with René Descartes and Galileo. He studied the writings of William Harvey. Hobbes acquired an expertise in both geometry and optics. Toward the middle of his life Hobbes became involved in the political events of his times and turned his attention to political theory. Dismayed by the civil strife raging during the civil war in England, Hobbes developed a political theory justifying absolutism in the name of law and order. In his *Leviathan* (1651), Hobbes started from a very few principles about human nature and rigorously deduced explanations for the founding and proper functioning of the state. He argued that human beings are most concerned with the preservation of their own lives, the avoidance of pain and the pursuit of pleasure, and the striving for power to protect themselves and get what they want. In the hypothetical state of nature, people are in a continual competitive struggle with each other. Self-interest and reason eventually lead people to exit the state of nature by way of a social contract between themselves. This social contract creates and grants massive powers to a sovereign, who uses those powers as necessary to keep the peace. Hobbes, like other seventeenth-century scientists, assumed a mechanistic, materialistic universe. His reasoning was much like Descartes'—rigorous, mathematical, and deductive. In the end, Hobbes concluded that absolutism was in accordance with natural law, though his method of reasoning pleased neither kings nor aristocrats.

John Locke was also heavily influenced by the new seventeenth-century science. He acquired a medical education at college, read the works of leading scientific thinkers such as Francis Bacon and Isaac Newton, and was a friend of Robert Boyle. Like Hobbes, Locke was involved in some of the political events of his times. Locke also started with human beings in a state of nature, made some basic assumptions about the human condition, and traced the exit from the state of nature by way of a social contract. Yet Locke came to some significantly different conclusions. Assuming that human beings were not quite so self-centered and that things were not so bad in the state of nature, Locke argued that the sovereign had far fewer powers than Hobbes had claimed and that individuals retained the right to revolt under certain circumstances. Applying reasoning similar to that of seventeenth-century scientists, Locke concluded that British constitutionalism was in accordance with natural law.

Thus both Hobbes and Locke extended the Scientific Revolution to new fields. While their conclusions differed, they set a new standard for political theory, becoming two of the most influential political theorists of modern times.

By the end of the seventeenth century, the Aristotelian-medieval world view had been broken and replaced by the Copernican-Newtonian world view. The methodology of modern science was established. Scientists had created the foundations for the modern sciences of astronomy, physics, mathematics, chemistry, and anatomy, and study in other disciplines was underway. Although the new scientists' work had gained considerable acceptance, their ideas were still known to only a few. During the Enlightenment of the eighteenth century, the ideas of the Scientific Revolution spread widely and were applied in new ways.

SUGGESTED READING

General

J. Ben-David, *The Scientist's Role in Society* (1971). A sophisticated social interpretation.

A. R. Hall, *The Scientific Revolution 1500–1800: The Formation of the Modern Scientific Attitude* (1966). A good analysis.

M. Jacob, *The Cultural Meaning of the Scientific Revolution* (1987). A strong interpretation.

A. G. R. Smith, *Science and Society in the Sixteenth and Seventeenth Centuries* (1972).

Astronomy and Physics

Ludovico Geymonat, *Galileo Galilei* (1965). A solid biography.

T. S. Kuhn, *The Copernican Revolution* (1957). An excellent analysis.

F. Manuel, *A Portrait of Isaac Newton* (1968). Uses a psychoanalytic perspective.

R. S. Westfall, *Never at Rest: A Biography of Isaac Newton* (1981). An excelient new biography.

Scientific Methodology

T. S. Kuhn, *The Structure of Scientific Revolutions* (1962). An important, influential interpretation of the Scientific Revolution.

Other Disciplines

P. Laslett, *Locke's Two Treatises of Government* (1970). Includes an introductory analysis with the texts.

C. B. MacPherson, *The Political Theory of Possessive Individualism: Hobbes to Locke* (1962). A controversial, Marxist interpretation.

Sources

M. B. Hall, ed., *Nature and Nature's Laws: Documents of the Scientific Revolution* (1970). A good collection.

CHAPTER 38
The Enlightenment

FIGURE 38.1. "Madame Geoffrin's Salon," 1755   Meetings in aristocratic Parisian salons such as this were typical of the Enlightenment. Here thinkers, artists, musicians, writers, and aristocrats exchanged views and helped spread the philosophy of the Enlightenment. (Giraudon/Art Resource)

As a period of intellectual history, the eighteenth century is usually referred to as the Enlightenment, or the Age of Reason. The Enlightenment was initiated toward the end of the seventeenth century by a number of intellectuals who attempted to popularize the ideas of the Scientific Revolution. During the eighteenth century this popularization continued, and new attempts were made to apply the methods of natural sciences to human behavior and social institutions. Western thinkers were speculating on the broader meaning of science—its ethical, political, social, and economic implications. They subjected almost everything to the critical standard of reason. In doing so, Enlightenment thinkers rejected the assumptions of their medieval and Renaissance predecessors who looked to the Christian or classical past for guidance. Enlightenment thinkers argued for reform and change. They felt that people were ready to shrug off the shackles of tradition and custom and participate in the progress of civilization; to these optimistic intellectuals, people were ready to become enlightened.

The Enlightenment was limited in some respects. During the eighteenth century the Enlightenment was centered in western Europe. Moreover, Enlightenment thought spread primarily to only the elite of the urban aristocracy and middle classes. Nevertheless, the ideas and attitudes developed during the Enlightenment would come to dominate most parts of Western civilization over the next two centuries.

1. ENLIGHTENMENT CONCEPTS

Although Enlightenment thinkers differed widely among themselves, they shared a belief in certain broad concepts that together make up the philosophy of the Enlightenment. The three most important concepts were reason, nature, and change and progress.

Enlightenment thinkers argued that all assumptions should be subjected to critical and empirical reasoning. Traditional institutions or customs should not be accepted because they have been long-lasting but rather should be examined critically and held up to the standard of reason. True knowledge is gained empirically. All we know and all we can ever know is what we perceive through our senses and interpret with our reason. There are no such things as innate ideas or revealed truth.

Enlightenment thinkers believed that nature is ordered, functions reasonably, and constitutes a standard for judgment. Nature is governed by a few simple and unchangeable laws. Those who think they can change one of these laws—who think they can, by praying, for instance, bring down the rain on parched crops and perchance a neighbor's unroofed house—are dupes of their own egotism. Nature does not act capriciously. Proper empirical analysis will show that nature functions in line with the laws of reason. Nature is good and beautiful in its simplicity. Human beings have corrupted it with their complex political, social, and religious restrictions. A move to nature is a move toward wholesome vigor and freedom.

Most Enlightenment thinkers felt that change and progress work hand in hand as human beings work to perfect themselves and their society. Change should not be viewed with distrust as a deterioration from a previously superior, more perfect state of things. Change, when dictated by reason and when in line with nature, liberates individuals and should be pursued. Such change contributes to individual and social progress on earth. Human beings are naturally rational and good, but the proponents of mystic religions have distorted human thinking and prevented proper progress by preaching false doctrines of original sin and divine moral laws. Rid people's minds of these religious hindrances and they can and will build for themselves a more perfect society.

The concepts of reason, nature, and change and progress worked together in the minds of Enlightenment thinkers and generally formed a structure for their more specific ideas. Enlightenment thinkers used reason and nature to criticize institutions and customs of the past, which still dominated their eighteenth-century society. Reason and nature further guided these thinkers as they determined what changes should take place. They felt that as individuals and societies made appropriate changes, human life would become more informed by reason and more compatible with nature. They believed human beings were on the verge of enlightenment—of great progress—if people would simply open their eyes and become mature, reasoning adults. This progress would take the form of people leading increasingly happier, freer, more moral lives.

2. THE *PHILOSOPHES*

Enlightenment ideas were put forth by a variety of intellectuals who in France came to be known as the *philosophes*. *Philosophes* is French for philosophers, and in a sense these thinkers were rightly considered philosophers, for the questions they dealt with were philosophical: How do we discover truth? How should life be lived? What is the nature of God? But on the whole the term has a meaning different from the usual meaning of "philosopher." The *philosophes* were intellectuals, often not formally trained or associated with a university. They were usually more literary than scientific. They generally extended, applied, popularized, or propagandized ideas of others rather than originating those ideas themselves. The *philosophes* were more likely to write plays, satires, histories, novels, encyclopedia entries, and short pamphlets or simply participate in verbal exchanges at select gatherings than to write formal philosophical books.

It was the *philosophes* who developed the philosophy of the Enlightenment and spread it to much of the educated elite in western Europe (and the American colonies). Although the sources for their philosophy can be traced to the Scientific Revolution in general, the *philosophes* were most influenced by their understanding of Newton, Locke, and English institutions.

The *philosophes* saw Isaac Newton as the great synthesizer of the Scientific Revolution who rightly described the universe as ordered, mechanical, material, and only originally set into motion by God, who since then has remained relatively inactive. Newton's synthesis showed to the *philosophes* that reason and nature were compatible: Nature functioned logically and discernably, and what was natural was also reasonable. Newton exemplified the value of reasoning based on concrete experience. The *philosophes* felt that his empirical methodology was the correct path to discovering truth.

John Locke (1632–1704) agreed with Newton but went further. This English thinker would not exempt even the mind from the mechanical laws of the material universe. In his *Essay Concerning Human Understanding* (1690), Locke pictured the human brain at birth as a blank sheet of paper on which nothing would ever be written except by sense perception and reason. What human beings become depends on their experiences—on the information received through the senses. Schools and social institutions could therefore play a great role in molding the individual from childhood to adulthood. Human beings were thus by nature far more malleable than had been assumed. This empirical psychology of Locke rejected the notion that human beings were born with innate ideas or that revelation was a reliable source of truth. Locke also enunciated liberal and reformist political ideas in his *Second Treatise of Civil Government* (1690), which influenced the *philosophes*. On the whole Locke's empiricism, psychology, and politics were appealing to the *philosophes*.

England, not coincidentally the country of Newton and Locke, became an admired model for many of the *philosophes*. They tended to idealize it, but England did seem to allow greater individual freedom, tolerate religious differences, and evidence greater political reform than other countries, especially France. England seemed to have gone furthest in freeing itself from traditional institutions and accepting the new science of the seventeenth century. Moreover, England's approach seemed to work, for England was experiencing relative political stability and prosperity. The *philosophes* wanted to see in their own countries much of what England already seemed to have.

Many *philosophes* reflected the influence of Newton, Locke, and English institutions, but perhaps the most representative in his views was Voltaire (1694–1778) (see Figure 38.2). Of all the leading figures of the Enlightenment, he was the most influential. Voltaire, the son of a Paris lawyer, became the idol of the French intelligentsia while still in his early twenties. His versatile mind was sparkling; his wit was mordant. An outspoken critic, he soon ran afoul of both church and state authorities. First he was imprisoned in the Bastille; later he was exiled to England. There he

FIGURE 38.2 **Frederick the Great with Voltaire**
Voltaire, seated, talks with Frederick the Great.
This picture reveals the image of the great Enlightenment thinker at work with books, papers, and pen and with the international stature sufficient to gain the ear of enlightened despots such as Frederick. Yet Frederick's enlightenment may have been more form than substance. Bibliothèque Nationale, Paris)

encountered the ideas of Newton and Locke and came to admire English parliamentary government and tolerance. In *Letters on the English* (1733), *Elements of the Philosophy of Newton* (1738), and other writings, he popularized the ideas of Newton and Locke, extolled the virtues of English society, and indirectly criticized French society. Slipping back into France, he was hidden for a time and protected by a wealthy woman who became his mistress. Voltaire's facile mind and pen were never idle. He wrote poetry, drama, history, essays, letters, and scientific treatises—ninety volumes in all. The special targets of his cynical wit were the Catholic church and Christian institutions. Few people in history have dominated their age intellectually as did Voltaire.

The work that best summarizes the philosophy of the Enlightenment is the *Encyclopedia*. The *Encyclopedia* was a collaborative effort by many of the *philosophes* under the editorship of Denis Diderot (1713–1774) and Jean le Rond D'Alembert (1717–1783). This gigantic work undertook to explore the whole world of knowledge from the perspective of the *philosophes*. Its articles on subjects ranging from music to machinery expressed the critical, rationalistic, and empiricist views of the *philosophes* (see Figure 38.3). The practicality of science and knowledge in general was emphasized. One of the work's main messages was that almost anything could be discovered or understood or clarified through reason. An underlying current was criticism of the irrational and of whatever stood in the way of the Enlightenment, whether it was religious intolerance or traditional social institutions. The first volume appeared in 1751. Its threat to the status quo was recognized by governmental and Church authorities, who censored it, halted its publication, and harassed its editors. Thanks in great part to the persistence of Diderot, who fought the authorities and dealt with a difficult group of contributing authors, the project was completed with the publication of the final volume in 1772. The *Encyclopedia* sold well and played an important role in the penetration of Enlightenment ideas outside the major cities and courts.

By this time the Enlightenment was evolving to a different stage. The *philosophes* were becoming more quarrelsome among themselves. This argumentation reflected a greater acceptance of the fundamental philosophy of the Enlightenment, for the debates tended to center on how far Enlightenment concepts could be extended. Some *philosophes*, such as Baron d'Holbach (1723–1789), verged on atheism in attacks on organized religion. Others, such as Marie-Jean de Condorcet (1743–1794), were so optimistic that they almost made a religion out of progress itself. Enlightenment thinkers were also tending to specialize. Some laid the foundations for the development of the social sciences during the nineteenth century. For example, Cesare Beccaria (1738–1794) contributed works on modern criminology and penology, and Adam Smith (1723–1790) wrote what would turn into the fundamental text of classical economics. Finally, some Enlightenment thinkers took more challenging positions, often contradicting some of the ideas of the Enlightenment itself and providing a transition to the succeeding intellectual traditions. The most important example of these thinkers is Jean-Jacques Rousseau (1712–1778).

One of the most original thinkers and writers of all time, Rousseau crusaded for a return to nature—beautiful, pure, simple nature. The message struck home in a society weary of arbitrary and often corrupt governmental bureaucracy and an oppressively artificial and elaborate code of social etiquette. Rousseau was lionized. Great ladies, including the queen of France, began playing milkmaid. In his novel *La Nouvelle Heloise*, Rousseau extolled the beauties of free love and uninhibited emotion. In *Emile* he expounded the "natural" way of rearing and educating children. He would let children do what they like and teach them "practical" knowledge. Rousseau shared much with other *philosophes*, even contributing to the *Encyclopedia*, but after the 1750s he broke from them for personal as well as intellectual reasons. In *Origin of Inequality Among Men* (1753), Rousseau argued that civilization was not necessarily a progressive boon to humanity, that human beings had lost much since their exit from the state of nature. In *The Social Contract*, Rousseau became one of the few *philosophes* to make a fundamental contribution to political theory. Rousseau generally placed greater faith in emotion, feeling, and intuition than in reason. In this he was a forerunner of the romantic spirit and expounded its principles long before that movement reached its peak.

The *philosophes* had a self-conscious sense of a spirit of enlightenment. They felt that they were leading a mission of liberation, that by striking the match of reason the darkness of the past would be dispelled and humanity would quickly and easily liberate itself. By becoming thus enlightened, humanity could move from childhood to adulthood. They attacked war and the military values of the traditional aristocracy. They rejected artificial social distinctions. They lauded most forms of freedom, including freedom of the press, of speech, and of religious belief. They supported the application of science to economic activity, a view appealing to the middle class and liberal aristocracy. They believed that their eighteenth-century civilization was ready for enlightenment and the great progress that would result. Yet the optimism of most of the *philosophes* was not wild-eyed; indeed, there was an underlying current of pessimism in the works of thinkers such as Diderot, de Sade, Rousseau, and even Voltaire.

In characterizing the *philosophes*, historians have disagreed. Some view the *philosophes* as shallow, self-concerned dilettantes who had few deep or original ideas and who were afraid of real reform. Most historians, however, argue that the *philosophes* were thoughtful, sincere thinkers who performed an important service by laying the intellectual foundations for modern society.

FIGURE 38.3. **The Encyclopedia** This engraving from one of the many technical articles in the *Encyclopedia* shows workers preparing type for printing, with detail of materials used in the process. It reveals the optimistic faith in the ease and practicality of learning typical of Enlightenment thought. (French Embassy Press and Information Division)

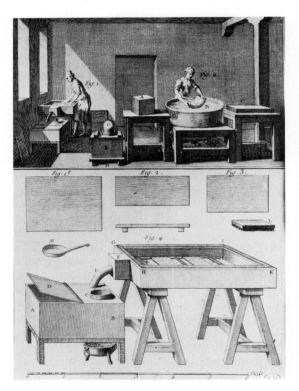

3. WOMEN AND THE SOCIAL CONTEXT

There were several centers of Enlightenment thought in the cities and courts of Europe, particularly western Europe, but the heart of the Enlightenment was in Paris. Several regular gatherings were held in the salons of wealthy Parisian patrons, usually women of the aristocracy or upper middle class such as Madame du Deffaud or Madame Geoffrin. There the *philosophes* met with each other and members of the international upper middle class and aristocratic elite. They debated the ideas of the Enlightenment in an environment lush with art, music, and wealth. These gatherings facilitated the spread of Enlightenment ideas among social and intellectual elites and added much to the social respectability of intellectuals.

As patrons and as intellectual contributors to these gatherings, women played an important role in the Enlightenment. Women such as Madame Geoffrin provided essential financial support to several *philosophes*, particularly for the *Encyclopedia*. Other women corresponded by letter with leading intellectual, political, and social figures throughout Europe, using letter writing as an art just as conversation was an art in the salons. The salons were open to women with the right intellectual or social qualifications. The *philosophes* tended to support improving the education and position of women. The Enlightenment emphasis on individualism theoretically and in the long run led toward accepting the idea of political and social equality between men and women. Nevertheless, it cannot be said that the *philosophes* advocated equal rights for women in a modern sense nor that they challenged fundamental assumptions about the subordinate public roles appropriate for women. One of the few people to argue for real change in the condition of women in the eighteenth century was Mary Wollstonecraft (1759–1797). In 1792 she published *Vindication of the Rights of Women*, but generally her plea for equal rights for all human beings fell on deaf ears.

Meetings in Paris salons were paralleled by smaller meetings in other French and foreign cities as well as by less organized meetings in coffeehouses and homes of the liberal aristocracy. Enlightenment ideas were read and discussed in local academies, Freemason lodges, societies, libraries, and clubs.

4. ENLIGHTENMENT AND RELIGION

The Enlightenment was profoundly secular in character, but religion played an important role. Very few Enlightenment thinkers were either atheists or traditional Christians. Most were skeptics, influenced by the arguments of Pierre Bayle (1647–1706). Many believed in some form of deism. They believed that this wonderful mechanism called the universe could not have come into being by accident. Some infinite Divine Being must have created it and set it in motion. However, the finite mind of human beings cannot comprehend the infinite. Therefore, God is unknowable. Furthermore, God, having set his perfect mechanical laws in motion, will never tamper with them nor interfere in human affairs. God is impersonal.

It is readily apparent that the beliefs of the *philosophes* were diametrically opposed to the doctrines of the Christian churches—Roman Catholic, Protestant, and Orthodox alike. Christian theologians argued that God remained active in the universe, that God's ways are revealed through religious literature and institutions, and that faith constitutes a valid alternative to reason. Enlightenment thinkers and Christian leaders were soon engaged in debate, both spending much time and effort attacking each other. In countries such as France and Italy, where clerics were strongly entrenched in government, they censored the writings of the *philosophes* and sought to interrupt their work. In the long run, however, the ideas of the Enlightenment spread, and the Church probably lost more than it gained by so ardently attacking the *philosophes* and their ideas.

5. POLITICAL AND ECONOMIC ASPECTS OF THE ENLIGHTENMENT

Enlightenment thinkers devoted much thought to matters of government. If human beings are by nature rational and good, then surely, if given the opportunity, they can devise for themselves efficient and benevolent political institutions. Corrupt tyrannies were no longer tolerable. Of the numerous "enlightened" thinkers in the field of political science, three stand out above the others in influence: Locke, Montesquieu, and Rousseau.

Locke's most eloquent plea was for the natural rights of human beings, which are life, liberty, and property. He theorizes, in his *Two Treatises of Civil Government*, that to safeguard these rights individuals voluntarily contracted to surrender a certain amount of their sovereignty to government. The powers of the government, however, whether it be monarchical or popular, are strictly limited. No government may violate the individual's right to life, liberty, and property. If it does, the people who set it up can and should overthrow it. These ideas were fundamental in the thinking of the makers of both the French and the American revolutions. Jefferson wrote many of Locke's ideas into the Declaration of Independence, frequently using his exact words. They likewise appear in the United States Constitution and in numerous French declarations of liberty.

Baron de Montesquieu (1689–1755) was less a theorizer than a discerning student of history and shrewd analyst of political systems. His masterpiece is *The Spirit of the Laws*. Although a great admirer of the English government after the Glorious Revolution, Montesquieu came to the conclusion that different types of government are best suited to various conditions. For instance, absolute monarchy is best for countries of vast area, limited monarchy for countries of moderate size like France, and republics for small states like Venice or ancient Athens. Not only did he approve of Locke's doctrine of limited sovereignty, but he specified how it can best be secured—by a separation of powers and a system of checks and balances. The powers and functions of government should be equally divided among king, lords, and commons, each one being checked by the other two. This theory was probably Montesquieu's greatest practical contribution to the science of government. The principle was incorporated into the United States Constitution—kings, lords, and commons becoming executive, judicial, and legislative branches of government.

The real father of the theory of modern democracy was not Locke nor Montesquieu, both of whom distrusted rule by the masses, but Rousseau. This morbid, erratic genius based the conclusions in his *Social Contract* and in his *Second Discourse* upon pure imagination. People in the state of noble savagery were free, equal, and happy. It was only when some began marking off plots of ground saying "this is mine" that inequality began. In order to restore their lost freedom and happiness, people entered into a compact, each with all the others, surrendering their individual liberty to the whole. Since sovereignty is indivisible, the general will is all-powerful. Although Rousseau never made it clear just how the general will would actually operate in practice, he apparently assumed that the individual would be free by virtue of being part of the general will. Rousseau had great influence on the leaders of the second and more radical phase of the French Revolution.

Some of the eighteenth-century planners of the better life through reason turned their thoughts to economics. Since the late fifteenth century, mercantilism had been the dominant economic theory and practice in western Europe. This system of regulated nationalistic economy reached its peak in the seventeenth century. Only the Dutch Netherlands held out for free trade. But if, according to the fundamental assumptions of the Enlightenment, the universe is run by a few simple mechanical laws, why should there not be a similar natural order in the field of economics? A group of French Physiocrats, led by Quesnay, personal physician to Louis XV, began to teach that economics has its own set of natural laws, that the most basic of these laws is that of supply and demand, and that these laws operate best when commerce is freed from government regulation. This doctrine came to be known as *laissez faire* (or free trade and enterprise).

The chief developer of the theory of laissez faire was Adam Smith, a Scottish professor of philosophy who associated with the Physiocrats while sojourning in France. His *Wealth of Nations*, published in 1776, has remained the bible of laissez-faire economics ever since. The ideas of the French Physiocrats and Adam Smith strongly influenced the leaders of the American and French revolutions.

6. ENLIGHTENED DESPOTISM

While critical and combative, the *philosophes* were not political or social revolutionaries. They hoped for rather painless change from above rather than a revolutionary transfer of power to the still unenlightened masses. Many followed Voltaire in believing that enlightened despotism was the form of government that offered the greatest chances for enactment of enlightened reforms. By the middle of the eighteenth century several monarchs found these views attractive, styled themselves as enlightened monarchs, and attempted to enact reforms that at least appeared to fit with Enlightenment thought. These monarchs have been distinguished from their predecessors and termed "enlightened despots." To what extent this is a valid characterization of their rule remains to be seen.

The most sensational of the enlightened despots was Frederick the Great of Prussia (1740–1786). Frederick had from boyhood loved music, poetry, and philosophy. At the end of the Seven Years' War (1756–1763), the second of his two wars of aggression, he settled down as a model enlightened despot and attempted to apply the laws of reason to statecraft. Frederick was an avid reader of the French philosophers. He even invited Voltaire to visit him at Potsdam, but Prussia was not big enough to hold two such egos at once. The two quarreled and, after several years, parted.

Frederick made much of religious toleration. However, he continued to penalize the Jews and never ceased to ridicule Christians of all denominations. He was a strong advocate of public education, although he spent very little on it in comparison with what he spent on his army. The centralized Prussian bureaucracy became the most efficient government in Europe. True to the prevailing thought of the Enlightenment, however, he had no faith in popular self-government. Nor did he make a move to free the serfs or to end the feudal system in Prussia. Probably the most lasting of Frederick's contributions to Prussia were his codification of the law and improvements in the administration of justice. In the field of economics, Frederick was a mercantilist, although he did share the Physiocrats' appreciation of the importance of agriculture.

The most sincere of all the enlightened despots was Joseph II of Austria (1780–1790). Unfortunately, he lacked the practical sagacity of Frederick the Great. His well-meaning but ill-conceived efforts to centralize the administration of the far-flung Hapsburg territories, to replace the numerous languages of his subjects with German, to secularize the strongly entrenched Roman Catholic church, and to free the serfs in a society still based on feudalism, all backfired.

Other monarchs, such as those of Sweden, Sardinia, Spain, and Portugal, attempted or enacted reforms that could be seen as enlightened. Even in Russia, Catherine the Great made apparent efforts at enlightened reforms, but ultimately she did not put most of those reforms into practice.

Significantly, France alone of the great powers on the Continent failed to produce an even faintly enlightened despot. Upon attaining the French throne in 1774, the well-meaning Louis XVI appointed the Physiocrat Turgot as minister of finances. Turgot, a friend of Voltaire, initiated a program of sweeping reforms that might have forestalled the French Revolution. However, within two years' time the powerfully entrenched vested interests persuaded the weak-willed king to dismiss him.

Whether there was a phenomenon of enlightened despotism occurring during the eighteenth century remains a debated question among historians. If there was, it was usually a matter more of form than content. Several eighteenth-century monarchs acted in certain enlightened ways, believed themselves to be enlightened, admired some of the *philosophes*, and were admired in return. Several supported culture, favored a less religious and more rational justification for their rule, and consulted with *philosophes*. Yet most of their "enlightenment" was superficial. Many of the reforms they made were simply an update in the long process of making the central government more effective and powerful. Few tried to enact fundamental social, political, or economic reforms dictated by Enlightenment thought, and even those who tried, such as Joseph II, generally failed to effect those reforms.

7. CONCLUSION

Enlightenment thinkers applied and popularized a secular, rational, reformist way of thinking that undermined the intellectual foundations of traditional society. These thinkers, probably unknowingly, laid the intellectual foundations for the rev-

olutions that swept Europe and America from the last quarter of the eighteenth century to the mid–nineteenth century. Moreover, their way of thinking and the ideas that arose from it would form the intellectual core of the liberal middle-class ideology that was ascendant during the nineteenth century and is still strong in the twentieth century.

SUGGESTED READING

General

C. Becker, *The Heavenly City of the Eighteenth-Century Philosophers* (1932). An influential, thought-provoking volume by a leading historian.

E. Cassirer, *The Philosophy of the Enlightenment* (1951). An important synthesis, but difficult.

P. Gay, *The Enlightenment: An Interpretation. Vol. I: The Rise of Modern Paganism. Vol. II: The Science of Freedom* (1969). Detailed treatment of a leading authority.

P. Hazard, *The European Mind, 1680–1715* (1963). Excellent on the early Enlightenment.

L. Krieger, *Kings and Philosophers, 1689–1789* (1970). A broad survey making connections between thought and politics.

H. Payne, *The Philosophes and the People* (1976). Focuses on the gap between the *philosophes* and the people.

The *Philosophes*

T. Bestermann, *Voltaire* (1969). A solid biography.

A. M. Wilson, *Diderot* (1972). An excellent biography.

Enlightened Despotism

J. Gagliardo, *Enlightened Despotism* (1967). A good introduction.

E. Wangermann, *The Austrian Achievement, 1700–1800* (1973). A good study of enlightened monarchs.

Sources

L. G. Crocker, ed., *The Age of Enlightenment* (1969). A good anthology.

P. Gay, ed., *The Enlightenment: A Comprehensive Anthology* (1973). A good selection of documents

RETROSPECT

The seventeenth and eighteenth centuries were the apogee of royal absolutism as a form of government in the Western world. The clearest example of royal absolutism arose in France, where under Henry IV, Richelieu, Mazarin, and Louis XIV, the Bourbon monarchy achieved a degree of control that was virtually complete and a position of dominance in Europe that has seldom been equaled. European history during the years 1661–1715 has been called the age of Louis XIV. Louis and his court were the envy of all other monarchs, who sought to emulate them. France possessed a military strength so great that the major states of

western and central Europe working in combination held France in check only with difficulty.

The most noteworthy exceptions to royal absolutism in western Europe were found in England and the Dutch Netherlands, where constitutionalism prevailed. In England royal absolutism had reached its peak during the sixteenth century under the vigorous and politically crafty Tudor rulers. The Stuart kings, who came to the throne in 1603 when Elizabeth I died childless, were full of fine absolutist theories but were unable to carry them out smoothly. They soon found themselves in a running fight, mostly over money matters and power, with Parliament, a stronghold of the landed and commercial interests. In a showdown—the Puritan Revolution—the parliamentary forces, under the able leadership of Oliver Cromwell, triumphed. Before the century had ended, one Stuart king had been executed, another invited to the throne on terms, and a third driven out of the country. During the course of the seventeenth and eighteenth centuries England's parliamentary and cabinet system gradually took shape. Constitutionalism had prevailed over royal absolutism. The landed and commercial interests now in control of the English government, however, were no less aggressive in foreign and colonial affairs than had been the royal monarchs.

The Dutch Netherlands, while somewhat unique, also developed a political system emphasizing constitutionalism rather than royal absolutism. Lacking the military resources and potential of their larger neighbors, France and England, the Dutch nevertheless achieved a phenomenal commercial and financial dominance in the Western world. Their economic exploits were accompanied by a preeminence in the fields of painting and philosophy. The Dutch lived under a republican form of government and enjoyed a degree of individual freedom that could not be matched in Europe.

Royal absolutism dominated political forms in central and eastern Europe during the seventeenth and eighteenth centuries. There the most important political developments were the rise of two military despotisms—Prussia and Russia. The Hohenzollerns of Prussia, consistently pursuing the policies of royal absolutism, militarism, and territorial aggrandizement, more than doubled their territory and population and challenged Austria for the leadership of the German-speaking world. Russia, under two strong absolutist monarchs, Peter the Great and Catherine the Great, decisively defeated Sweden and the Ottoman Turks and gained valuable territory facing the West. Poland, failing to develop a strong central government, disappeared from the map, carved up by Russia, Prussia, and Austria.

While Prussia, Russia, and Austria were struggling for the mastery of central and eastern Europe, the French, the English, and the Dutch were competing for dominance in North America and Asia. In this contest the English emerged victorious in North America and India, and the Dutch in the East Indies. The English found it relatively easy to drive the Indians out of eastern North America and colonize the continent with Europeans. In Asia the English and the Dutch defeated the natives but were unable to Europeanize these people who had such firmly established societies, cultures, and religions.

The economy and society—rural, based on agriculture, and with a vast mass of peasantry dominated by the privileged aristocracy—changed only slowly for most of the period. Gradually the central governments, the growing cities, and the middle classes altered life within the traditional village. The pace of social change quickened in the mid–eighteenth century as population grew, agriculture was revolutionized, and cottage industry spread. Religious affiliations changed little; established Catholic and Protestant churches remained committed to the hierarchical social order and the dominant political systems of their states. Even the numerous pietist and quietist religious sects that arose during this period passively accepted, for the most part, the political authority of the established and usually absolutist governments.

The baroque and classical styles, which prevailed in literature and the arts in western Europe throughout most of the seventeenth and eighteenth centuries, generally harmonized with and often exalted the absolutist monarchs and their courts. These styles stressed a combination of grandeur, richness, and order that appealed to monarchs and the privileged orders, who so often were the patrons of the arts.

The seventeenth and eighteenth centuries spawned two developments that would eventually undermine the intellectual foundations of the traditional Christian Western society: the Scientific Revolution and the Enlightenment. The Scientific Revolution challenged the traditional, theological, earth-centered conception of the universe and offered a new perception of the universe as infinite, moving, and lawful, with the earth merely one of many bodies. Truth would no longer be based on custom, faith, or authority but, rather, on rigorous reasoning founded on observed facts and mathematical laws. In the process of this Scientific Revolution, the foundations for the modern natural sciences were established. The Enlightenment popularized and extended the Scientific Revolution. The main Enlightenment thinkers—the *philosophes*—used reason to criticize traditional customs and institutions. They optimistically believed that people could easily become enlightened and thereby progress to a new level of maturity. Their ideas would play an important role in the revolutions of the late eighteenth and the nineteenth centuries and would form a basis for the liberal ideology that would rise to dominance during the nineteenth and twentieth centuries.

Yet even these intellectual developments properly belong to the seventeenth and eighteenth centuries. They stressed order and power, which were so important to the period. They reflected the dynamic between royal absolutism and constitutionalism—particularly in the Enlightenment admiration for English political institutions and enlightened despotism. They remained limited to a small elite, just as the glamour, affluence, and power of the period remained limited almost entirely to the royalty, the aristocracy, and the small upper middle class. The lower classes, whose labor and blood made so much regal and military splendor possible, received few benefits and were unaware of the fundamental intellectual developments that were occurring. From the late eighteenth century on, much would change.

PART NINE
THE AGE OF REVOLUTIONS, 1776–1850

The period between the last quarter of the eighteenth century and the middle of the nineteenth century was an era of revolution in the Western world, both in Europe and in America. The most dramatic and striking of the revolutions occurring during this period were political, starting with the American and French revolutions in the late eighteenth century and ending with the Revolutions of 1848 that swept the European continent. The more subtle but even more historically significant revolution of this period was economic: the Industrial Revolution. Starting in Great Britain toward the end of the eighteenth century, the Industrial Revolution spread to continental Europe and the United States during the first half of the nineteenth century and would eventually extend to most of the rest of the world.

Both the political and economic revolutions reflected stirrings of change already underway within the still fundamentally traditional society of the eighteenth century. The Enlightenment was propagating liberal ideas that had politically revolutionary implications. The growth of commerce and industry, particularly in certain parts of western Europe, was altering the old economy. The bourgeoisie was increasing in strength and numbers and was exerting pressure on the aristocracy. The peasantry, too, and even the urban workers were becoming restive.

When the privileged classes steadfastly refused to yield and traditional institutions proved unable to cope with demands for political change, a series of revolutionary upheavals ensued. The first occurred in America, where in 1776 the British colonies revolted and declared their independence as the United States. The American Revolution was followed by the French Revolution of 1789, which was of considerably greater significance, for it represented an almost complete overthrow of traditional institutions in a powerful country in the heart of Europe. During the succeeding two decades, elements of the French Revolution were spread throughout Europe by imitation and by the revolutionary and Napoleonic armies. After 1815 conservatives, representing the traditional forces of order, reasserted control and struggled with the revolutionary forces unleashed by the French Revolution. But the era of revolutions was not over. Uprisings, usually inspired by some of the same liberal goals as the French Revolution of 1789, occurred in several areas during the 1820s and 1830s. A culmination of many of these struggles came in 1848 when revolutions toppled governments almost everywhere.

The Industrial Revolution was only seemingly less of an upheaval than these political revolutions. As economic activity shifted from the farm to the factory, cities grew, classes changed, and ultimately society itself was transformed. By 1850 a new industrial society was firmly entrenched in Great Britain and was clearly establishing itself elsewhere.

Together the political and economic revolutions occurring between 1776 and 1850 transformed Western civilization. Indeed, so massive were the changes stemming from these revolutions that historians usually mark this period as the beginning of modern times.

CHAPTER 39
The American Revolution

FIGURE 39.1. The Constitutional Convention   This painting, by Junius Brutus Stearns, represents the Constitutional Convention in session in Philadelphia in 1787 with George Washington presiding. At times the proceedings of the Convention were less sedate and reflective than this scene portrays; nonetheless, it catches the sense of high purpose that the delegates believed they were serving in seeking to strengthen the new nation. (The Granger Collection)

The forces of change that were building up during the seventeenth and eighteenth centuries found early expression in a somewhat unexpected place—in the British colonies in North America. The American colonists waged a successful rebellion against Great Britain and established the new nation of the United States of America. The forces that produced the American Revolution and gave shape to the new nation reflected in important ways the ferment working everywhere in western Europe to threaten traditional society. Placed in a global setting, the American Revolution was a major event in shaping the modern world.

1. AMERICAN COLONIAL SOCIETY

The American Revolution was a complex movement, but behind it lay one fundamental fact: During the century and a half prior to 1776, American society had become different from British society in particular and European society in general. Its uniqueness was due chiefly to the fact that European immigrants and their offspring had to adapt traditional patterns of life in order to survive in a new environment. As a consequence, the colonists came to think of themselves as a separate people. This realization, coupled with Great Britain's efforts to bend colonial society to British purposes, led the colonials to act in the name of independence and nationhood.

By 1776 an obvious sign of the vitality of colonial society was its large population, which had reached about 2.5 million. During the eighteenth century population had grown faster in America than in Europe. The growth was in large part due to emigration from Europe and Africa (by 1776 blacks constituted 20 percent of the population). Americans were also reproducing more rapidly than Europeans, largely because of longer life expectancy and earlier marriage in a land where it was easier to establish a new household than it was in traditional European society.

The rapidly growing population had created a bustling, diverse economy in the American wilderness. Its backbone was agriculture, ranging from the small, independently owned family farms of New England and the Middle Atlantic colonies to the great plantations worked by slaves in the southern colonies. The American soil and climate permitted a variety of crops: grain, tobacco, cotton, rice, indigo, vegetables, fruits, livestock. After the first hard years the colonists were more than able to feed themselves; some of their crops, especially tobacco, found markets in Europe. And off to the west lay vast areas of rich, unexploited land to attract the growing population.

The colonists had not neglected commerce and industry. Colonial merchants, especially in New England and the Middle Atlantic colonies, did a thriving business within America, and some of them traded with Great Britain, the West Indies, and continental Europe. The bulk of the international trade involved colonial raw materials, which were exchanged for manufactured goods and slaves. By 1776 the colonists were producing considerable amounts of manufactured goods, sometimes in defiance of British mercantilist regulations. The colonists were by no means self-sufficient, but neither were they totally dependent on Great Britain and Europe. American entrepreneurs were increasingly intent on protecting their commercial and manufacturing interests and on minimizing external constraints.

By 1776 American society was becoming stratified into a class structure that bore an outward resemblance to the society of Great Britain. An aristocracy of wealth made up of merchants, plantation owners, and successful professionals dominated many aspects of life and grew increasingly conscious of its status. A large, enterprising group of independent farmers, shopkeepers, artisans, and modestly successful professionals ranked below the aristocrats. Still lower were numerous tenant farmers and laborers—a group that was increasing in size and economic hardship. Finally, there were black slaves, whose position as property gave them no status in society and whose lot was harsh in every respect. However, social stratification in America was not as rigidly defined nor as inflexible as was the class structure in Europe. The chief forces that sanctioned aristocratic status in Europe—birth, royal favor, tradition, unique life style—simply did not exist in America. Few European aristocrats migrated to America; the family trees of most American aristocrats had shallow roots. In America aristocratic status rested chiefly on wealth amassed in America through farming or commercial activity. It was possible for a capable, enterprising, and lucky individual of low status to advance to aristocratic status by amassing a fortune. The frontier also offered escape for those who resented aristocratic control. Colonial conditions thus loosened the bonds of aristocratic society and provided a measure of freedom for people of lesser status and means—except black slaves.

Early American society was dominated by males whose authority as heads of the basic social unit, the family, allowed them to dominate women and children. Marriages were usually arranged by families. Under the terms of English law, which prevailed everywhere in the colonies, a married woman was legally subject to her husband and barred from participation in almost all aspects of public life. In addition to the legal constraints on women, the social code stressed the virtue of submission by women to male authority. In the typical household on farms and in the cities, women were expected to carry out an array of tasks generally viewed as "women's work": preparing food, making clothing, tending animals, raising a garden, raising children. Particularly harsh was the treatment of slave women. Although slaves were permitted to maintain family units, traffic in slaves often disrupted these households. Slave women were frequently sexually abused by their masters. In the upper classes, women of wealthy families enjoyed considerable comfort and leisure but little independence. The cities offered some economic opportunity for single women and widows to lead a more independent life as nurses, teachers, or shopkeepers. But on the whole colonial women had almost no opportunity to assert their talents beyond the confines of the household.

Religious life in colonial America took unique forms. Generally, the founders of each colony attempted to define a single religious establishment for that colony, usually based on a European model. One such establishment was the Puritan order that emerged in New England. Based on the principles of local control of each congregation by those who believed themselves to be saved, simple ceremonies involving Scripture reading and preaching and austere moral codes, the Puritan congregations exercised a powerful influence on the manners and morals of New England society. However, the Puritans were never able to exclude from their society those who would not conform and eventually were forced to tolerate dissenters. Elsewhere an effort was made to implant Anglicanism as practiced in Great Britain. A variety of factors combined to make the Anglican church in America different from that in Great Britain. No Anglican bishoprics developed in America, and there was a shortage of educated clergymen trained to sustain the elaborate Anglican services. As a consequence, a hierarchically directed Anglican system based on uniform doctrines and rituals failed to develop. Local Anglican churches fell under the direction of local lay leaders, who tended to define religious practice as they saw fit. The Anglican establishment moved in the direction of a congregational system that allowed considerable room for local differences and thus toleration. To some extent the same fate befell the other highly structured religions established in colonial America, especially Lutheranism and Roman Catholicism. Each found it difficult to maintain uniformity and conformity to traditional practices. The common tendency was toward the acceptance of religious diversity and toleration.

Prior to 1776 the colonists distinguished themselves only modestly in cultural activities. They did establish lower schools and colleges in an attempt to prepare people for careers. Newspapers and book publishers appeared in many areas. The rudiments of a distinct architectural style emerged. But in the main American cultural life depended on western Europe. Perhaps the most notable cultural development was the ability of some colonists to keep abreast of Europe's chief intellectual and cultural movements, especially those associated with the Enlightenment and science.

Especially significant in setting the stage for the rebellion in America were the differences that emerged between the political system of Great Britain and that of its colonial subjects. In theory one system applied to both. The colonials recognized the British monarch as the head of state, but the colonials had no active role in the government presided over by the British ruler. Every colony developed its own local government. Each had a governor, usually appointed by the monarch, who represented the authority of the crown and who provided a channel through which the concerns of the colonists were conveyed to the British government. Each colony (except Pennsylvania) had a two-house legislature. The lower house was elected by property owners, and the upper house was appointed by the king or the colonial governor. The property qualifications were such that a much larger proportion of male colonials were eligible to vote than was the case in Britain; as a consequence, colonial legislatures reflected a broader spectrum of society than did the British Parliament. The powers of colonial legislatures were never clearly defined, but in general they had extensive authority to control local affairs and to levy taxes. The governors had nearly absolute power of veto over legislatures, but they were not usually in a position to exercise these powers because they depended on legislatures for their salaries and operating funds. The colonists developed a system of courts patterned after the British court system, and they enjoyed the legal rights of British subjects as incorporated in English common law. Although the Americans recognized that the British government had authority over them, the system of local government that developed in the colonies encouraged them to feel that they had a right to decide their own political destiny. One hundred fifty years of experience in self-government created a breach wider than the Atlantic between Great Britain and its American colonies.

Although by 1776 there were wide differences between American and British societies, these differences did not preordain an American effort to establish independence. Most colonists still felt that they were British and still were attached to a European tradition. What eventually aroused American resistance to British rule was a conviction that the British were denying them the right to sustain the tradition they shared. That perception drew much of its substance from the fact that American society had become different, causing the Americans to view tradition in a different way.

2. THE AMERICAN REVOLUTION: FROM SALUTARY NEGLECT TO WAR

The numerous forces working to create a unique society in America were little understood in Great Britain. In conformity with mercantilist thought, America was viewed as a source of scarce raw products and a market for manufactured goods. This view was legislated by the Navigation Acts of the mid–seventeenth century, which implied that Britain would act politically and economically to shape the colonial economy to serve its own interests. It was assumed that the colonists would benefit by conforming to British direction. However, until mid–eighteenth century Britain was lax in enforcing its mercantilist policies. During this interval American economic development took its own direction and shaped its own interests. And political evolution accustomed the Americans to asserting considerable control over their destiny.

With the end of the Seven Years' War in 1763, British policy began to change in the direction of tightening control over its colonial empire. The vast lands won from the French needed some kind of administration that would ensure their sensible utilization and deal with the Indian population whose frustrations were expressed with frightening emphasis by a general Indian uprising in 1763, led by the Ottawa chief, Pontiac. Great Britain was faced with a huge debt, incurred in part to save Americans from the French and the Indians; it was time for the colonials to share that burden. Britain's rapidly growing population and the increasing importance of manufacturing to its economy produced a need for imported foodstuffs and for larger markets for manufactured goods. All of these considerations prompted a series of acts, such as the Grenville (1764–1765) and the Townshend (1767), designed to increase revenues and tighten administration in America.

The colonists were hardly in a mood to bend before British interests after so long enjoying the "salutary neglect" of earlier years. They felt they had made sufficient contributions to the British victories in the wars of the first half of the eighteenth century to relieve them of further responsibility. They resented what they felt was treatment as inferiors by the British forces sent to drive the French and Indians out of land that belonged to the Americans. The American population was growing even faster than that of Great Britain, creating powerful pressures to expand the American economy and to move westward into the territories won from the French. The growing demand for manufactured goods created an unfavorable balance of trade, which increasingly made many Americans debtors to England. To correct this situation, the Americans needed to increase native manufacturing and expand markets in Europe, both of which ran counter to British mercantilist policy. A depression following the Seven Years' War sharpened the growing tension.

The Americans reacted to Britain's changing policy with fiery speeches, boycotts of British goods, protest meetings (such as the Stamp Act Congress of 1765), and occasional riots. They complained that they were being taxed without representation in Parliament and that their own legislatures, long the chief source of governing regulations, were being disregarded. Although British reaction to American resistance was inconsistent, its government pressed on in its effort to tighten its hold on America. It increased its military presence in America and ordered royal officials to seize American property in ways that paid little heed to British law. Between 1768 and 1774 sterner measures, such as the Tea Act, the "Intolerable Acts," and the Quebec Act, were imposed to bring the colonials under tighter control. Resistance in America spread, reflected by the meeting of the First Continental Congress in 1774. And it was fed by growing radicalism, which focused on British violation of fundamental rights as justification for independence and self-government.

In Great Britain a few leaders realized the danger, and some even sympathized with the principles upon which the protests of the colonists were based. But these forces could not muster enough parliamentary support for conciliatory actions aimed at reassuring that considerable segment of the colonial population still not ready to break with Britain or for a fundamental change of policy that would take into account the realities surrounding relationships with colonists whose interests no longer coincided with those of the mother country. The British leaders agreed on only one thing: that it was an act of rebellion and a perversion of the British constitution to claim

that British subjects had a right to disobey laws passed by Parliament, as indeed Americans were doing with increasing frequency. This attitude prompted an increase in British armed forces in America, an action that appeared to reinforce King George III's words: "Blows must decide whether they are to be subject to the Country or Independent."

Indeed, it came to blows. Armed hostilities opened in April 1775 when American militiamen challenged British forces in skirmishes at Lexington and Concord. In May 1775 the Second Continental Congress assembled. Led by men ready to break with Great Britain, the Congress took steps to organize the war and to appoint George Washington as commander of the American armies. The hour had come to settle long-debated issues on the field of battle.

When the war began, Britain seemed to enjoy overwhelming superiority. In fact, the British government took the rebellion lightly; one royal official characterized the rebels as a "rude rabble without a plan." But such a view proved erroneous. It did not take into account Britain's ineffective military leadership, the distance to the battle scene, and the determination of the rebels. For almost a year after the encounters at Lexington and Concord, the main British forces were pinned down in Boston by an American militia drawn chiefly from New England. The Second Continental Congress proceeded with plans for raising money, supplying a military force, and winning allies. A variety of actions were taken to transfer power from British officials into the hands of American authorities. Most significant of all, once the shooting started, opinion in America moved rapidly toward acceptance of the idea of independence.

Popular sentiment in favor of independence crystallized in 1776, when several colonies instructed their delegations to the Second Continental Congress to break with Britain. On July 4, 1776, Congress issued the Declaration of Independence, crafted chiefly by Thomas Jefferson. Its magnificent preamble, leaning heavily on the political philosophy of John Locke and European disciples of the Enlightenment, justified rebellion on the grounds of "self-evident" truths, especially natural rights and government by contract. The British government had violated these "inalienable" rights and thus had no claim to the allegiance of its subjects, who were entitled to form a new contract to ensure their rights. For many, the Declaration of Independence elevated the struggle above mere revolt; it became a struggle for an "enlightened" polity. The principles enunciated in the Declaration would inspire later generations to act in the name of rights so fundamental that they were beyond the authority of any government.

However, the Americans were far from united. Many—perhaps 20 percent—opposed independence and the war. Some of these loyalists—contemptuously dubbed "Tories"—fled to Canada and Great Britain; those who remained were a source of concern to American leaders and a target of British efforts to promote dissension. Many Americans were essentially neutral; only under duress did these neutrals contribute to the war effort. Some black slaves saw the war as an opportunity to shed their shackles and enjoy the liberty of which the patriots spoke so much. Loyalists and British tried to exploit this hope; the fear of slave revolts dampened enthusiasm for the war in the southern colonies. Even among the patriots there was perpetual disagreement on how to conduct the struggle for independence. The fact that the Americans could sustain their cause in the face of these divisions was remarkable. In part, success was due to the leadership provided by men like George Washington, John Adams, Thomas Jefferson, and Benjamin Franklin, all of whom demonstrated considerable talents for leading armies, organizing resources, rallying popular support, and negotiating with foreign powers.

The war itself unfolded indecisively during 1776 and 1777 (see Map 39.1). While there were victories and defeats on both sides, the British seemed to be gaining the upper hand, especially when they undertook a major campaign in the Hudson Valley aimed at isolating New England from the other colonies. However, that campaign ended in October 1777 with the surrender of a major British force at Saratoga. This victory not only raised flagging American spirits but also was decisive in persuading a hesitant France to commit itself to the American cause. In 1778 a formal alliance was concluded, and France began to supply needed money, ships, and troops. Subsequently, other European powers showed increasing friendliness toward America; Spain and the Dutch eventually declared war on Britain, and several other nations threatened to do likewise. Britain now had a world conflict on its hands; the pressure on America was considerably relieved.

After 1777 military activity spread over a large area. The British concentrated their main force in New York City, where it could be reinforced by sea. In a series of hotly contested engagements in New York, New Jersey, and eastern Pennsylvania the Americans managed to contain British forces and avoid a decisive defeat in the crucial Middle Atlantic area. The British undertook a major offensive in the South in 1780 and 1781. The campaign ended in a stunning defeat at Yorktown, Virginia, in October 1781. This was the last major battle of the war. By 1781 Britain was anxious to end a costly war that threatened its position around the world. Prolonged negotiations, involving not only Britain and America but also France and Spain, finally ended with the Treaty of Paris in 1783. In its essential provisions, Britain recognized American independence and ceded to the Americans all territories east of the Mississippi from Canada to Spanish Florida. The new nation had won a magnificent victory.

3. THE AMERICAN REVOLUTION AND THE DEMOCRATIZATION OF SOCIETY

The American Revolution was more than a successful war of independence carried out by determined colonial subjects against a somewhat inept mother country. Between 1775 and 1783 a variety of steps were taken within American society that resulted in a new political and social order unique in the contemporary world. The changes accompanying the Revolution did not uproot the old order entirely, but they did modify it in ways that reflected many of the ideas of the Enlightenment. The thrust toward restructuring society and government found its chief inspiration in the concept of republicanism. Rooted in a tradition that

Map 39.1 REVOLUTIONARY WAR CAMPAIGNS This map portrays at least in broad outline the central strategy involved in the revolutionary war. With their main strength concentrated in New York City, where they could be reinforced by sea, the British tried to cripple the Americans first by attempting to seize control of the Hudson Valley and then by an extended campaign to win the South. The Americans countered both of these moves successfully while still containing the main British forces in New York, New Jersey, and eastern Pennsylvania.

reached back to ancient Greece and Rome, republicanism visualized the ideal society as one composed of equals living in small communities under a government of limited power controlled by its constituents. In such a society, the natural virtue of people would constrain anyone from infringing on the rights of others and would allow all to pursue their individual interests. It was the success the Americans achieved in moving toward the republican ideal that caught the attention of a world standing on the brink of other, more drastic revolutions.

The first important efforts at reordering society on republican principles were made within the several states (as the colonies were called after July 4, 1776). New governments, based on British principles of government, colonial political experience, and theoretical concepts derived from Enlightenment thought, were formed in all the states. The framers of these governments tried to create a political order that would protect the people's liberties without becoming tyrannical. Nearly every state drew up a written constitution carefully defining the structure and functions of government. Elaborate bills of rights, stressing traditional British liberties, were included in the constitutions. Since sovereignty rested with the people, all official positions were filled by elections and the right to vote was extended. Two-house legislatures were established in most states, the lower houses being controlled by property-holding voters and the upper houses being selected by the lower chambers. Systems of representation were devised to ensure that each elected representative spoke for roughly the same number of voters. Legislatures were given wide-ranging powers that assured their control over public affairs. Especially significant were the powers granted to legislatures to control and check executive officials, who were universally suspected of being the chief instigators of tyranny. Independent judiciaries were almost universally adopted. The concept of separation of powers was thereby incorporated into the new state governments, signifying a strong conviction that the powers of government must be limited by constitutional safeguards. Taken as a whole, the state constitutions framed between 1776 and 1780 inaugurated a degree of popular control over government unknown in the contemporary world, although none of them was completely democratic.

The Revolution brought about changes in other areas of life as significant as those altering the political structure. Several states took steps to disestablish state-supported churches, to institute religious toleration, and in general to separate political and religious life. Many states passed new land laws that tended to make it easier to gain ownership of property. Especially significant was the abolition of primogeniture, which required that the eldest son receive all his father's land. Slavery was abolished in some northern states, in part at least because this institution seemed out of place in a society dedicated to the principles of the Declaration of Independence. Efforts were made to expand educational opportunities and to take more adequate care of society's unfortunates. In the name of republicanism people spurned the old social customs that called for deference to aristocrats and replaced them with behavior patterns that reflected greater egalitarianism. Even the lot of women improved somewhat. In writing to her husband, John, in 1776 Abigail Adams chided him to "remember the ladies" in his schemes to increase liberty in America. Women came to be credited with playing a major role in building the virtues on which a republican society must rest. And expanding opportunities for occupations outside the household began to emerge for women. All these liberalizing movements pointed toward an increasingly greater freedom in the future.

Quite accidentally, the Revolution had an important leveling effect in terms of the distribution of wealth. An inflation, caused by the efforts of the Americans to pay for the war with paper money, wiped out fortunes, aided debtors, and allowed new fortunes to be built. Many established merchants suffered heavy losses from the disturbance of foreign trade, but new opportunities in trade and industry emerged once America was free from the British commercial system. Small farmers flourished during the war, bolstered by easy money and high prices. Under these varied pressures, the prerevolutionary social order did not survive intact. Again, a greater degree of social equality and personal freedom emerged to characterize life in the new nation.

4. LAUNCHING THE NEW NATION

Once independence had been declared, American leaders were faced with creating a central government. In responding to that challenge, they were guided by the above-noted principles working to democratize society. Movement toward a national political system had to contend with republican distrust of large-scale government and with the existence of thirteen separate states long accustomed to independent action. But the realities of a war for survival, the dangers inherent in a world of large and ambitious nations, and the sense of a shared experience in creating a new society in the American wilderness gave irresistible force to a national government.

The first attempt at forming a national government was carried out by the Second Continental Congress. Dominated by men who had a deep distrust for strong government over which the populace had no control, the Congress shaped the Articles of Confederation, finally approved by all of the states in 1781. The articles established a loose union of thirteen nearly independent states headed by a central government that could not compel the states to do anything but could only encourage them to cooperate. The inadequacies of the confederation and the self-serving actions of state governments rather quickly generated sentiment in favor of a stronger central government. As a result, in May 1787 a convention was summoned to consider revising the Articles of Confederation.

The convention immediately decided to scrap the Articles and to write a new constitution (see Figure 39.1). Once this task was undertaken, the delegates found themselves in broad agreement on many crucial issues. They agreed that a republican form of government based on a written constitution enumerating the powers of the central government was necessary, that there must be popular control over the central government, that there must be separation of powers with built-in checks among the various branches of government, that the states must enjoy certain jurisdiction, and that the central government must have authority to deal independently with matters affecting national interests. Working from these premises, the delegates forged a constitution out-

FIGURE 39.2. **Congressional Debate**   This cartoon shows a "discussion" in the House of Representatives in 1798 between a Vermont Republican (with the tongs) and a Connecticut Federalist (with the cane). It reflects the intensity of party strife just prior to the key election of 1800. (New York Public Library Picture Collection)

lining the basic framework for a new government. A two-house legislature, an elected president, and a national judiciary were established. Each branch was assigned specific functions, and an elaborate system of internal checks was devised to constrain each branch from exercising too much power. The powers of the national government were specifically enumerated, while other powers were reserved to the states. However, specific provisions were made allowing the central government to coerce the states in those matters over which it had jurisdiction. This principle of federalism was a unique feature of the new government. A major roadblock centering on the fears of smaller states

was overcome by a compromise providing equal representation of each state in one branch of the legislature, the Senate, and representation in proportion to population in the other, the House of Representatives. To ensure a degree of flexibility, provisions were made for amending the constitution.

By 1789 a sufficient number of states had approved the new Constitution to allow the new government to begin operation with George Washington as president and with elected representatives who were committed to the Constitution (Federalists) in control of Congress. During the next decade the new government proved its worth. Congress enacted legislation that filled in vital details: a bill of rights, a federal court system, and administrative departments to assist the president in discharging his responsibilities. Taxes were levied and collected, public credit was established, and new states were added to the nation as a part of the process of utilizing the vast territory ceded by Britain in 1783. As president, Washington conducted himself in a way that gave the office dignity and allayed deep-seated fears of executive tyranny. Under the guidance of his cabinet, especially Alexander Hamilton as secretary of the treasury and Thomas Jefferson as secretary of state, policies were formulated that helped to restore prosperity and to steer the fledgling nation along a path of neutrality in the stormy international scene agitated by the French Revolution.

Despite the successes of the new government under Washington and his successor, John Adams, there was mounting discontent with the Federalists who dominated it (see Figure 39.2). This party made it increasingly clear, especially through the policies promoted by Alexander Hamilton, that it intended to make the central government as strong as possible and to bind the wealthy to the cause of strong central government by favoring their economic interests. This direction aroused opposition not only from those who felt their economic interests threatened but also from those philosophically suspicious of strong government, those committed to human equality, and those confident of the political wisdom of the common people—ideas powerfully reinforced by the French Revolution. This opposition began to rally around Thomas Jefferson to form a new party, called the Republicans (not to be confused with the present Republican party, founded in 1854). The emergence of political parties added an element to the new political system that the makers of the Constitution had not foreseen. In a close and bitter election in 1800, Jefferson and the Republicans won the presidency in what has been called "the Revolution of 1800." Perhaps it would be more accurate to say that this election completed the revolution begun twenty-five years earlier. It provided final proof of the workability of the new government by demonstrating that the voters controlled the state and that they did not have to rebel to force a government to be responsive to the wishes of a majority.

Between 1775 and 1800 the Americans had put on an impressive display for a changing world. By force of arms they had rid themselves of a political regime they perceived to be tyrannical. To replace it, they had fashioned, by a rational process, thirteen state governments and a national government capable of effective governance but restricted from abusing the rights of people. These governments proved sensitive to popular control and made the exercise of popular sovereignty a fact. Liberal, enlightened people everywhere saw their ideals become a reality in America. Here was inspiration and guidance for those elsewhere who aspired to change society. Many believed, as the German poet, Goethe put it, "America, thou hast it better/Than has our Continent, the old one." The age of revolutions had been launched in practice as well as in theory.

SUGGESTED READING

Colonial Society

Daniel J. Boorstin, *The Americans: The Colonial Experience* (1958). A challenging portrait.

James A. Henretta and Gregory H. Nobles, *Evolution and Revolution. American Society, 1600–1820* (1987). A stimulating treatment of many aspects of colonial society.

Edwin J. Perkins, *The Economy of Colonial America*, 2nd ed. (1988). A brief but effective description of colonial economy.

Gary B. Nash, *Red, White, and Black: The Peoples of Early America*, 2nd ed. (1982). An interesting study of race relations in colonial America.

C. Duncan Rice, *The Rise and Fall of Black Slavery* (1975). A fine study with an historiographical analysis.

Patricia U. Bonomi, *Under the Cope of Heaven: Religion, Society, and Politics in Colonial America* (1986). A broad survey stressing the vitality of colonial religious life.

Mary Beth Norton, *Liberty's Daughters: The Revolutionary*

Experience of American Women, 1750–1800 (1980). A fine study.

The Revolutionary Era

John C. Miller, *Origins of the American Revolution* (1959). A provocative exploration of the forces that produced the Revolution.

Marc Egnal, *A Mighty Empire. The Origins of the American Revolution* (1988). A challenging treatment stressing the role played by upper-class factions in the struggle against Great Britain.

Bernard Bailyn, *The Ideological Origins of the American Revolution* (1967). A brilliant study.

Edmund S. Morgan, *The Birth of the Republic, 1763–1789*, rev. ed. (1977). A brief account of major events.

Robert Middlekauff, *The Glorious Cause: The American Revolution, 1763–1789* (1982). A full narrative account.

Don Higginbotham, *The War of American Independence; Military Attitudes, Policies, and Practices, 1763–1789* (1971). A fine military history.

Merrill Jensen, *The American Revolution Within America* (1974). Stresses the impact of the Revolution on American society.

The New Nation

John C. Miller, *Toward a More Perfect Union: The American Republic, 1783–1815* (1970). A good narrative account.

Richard B. Morris, *The Forging of the Union, 1781–1789* (1987). A superb analysis of the path toward the Constitution.

Gordon S. Wood, *The Creation of the American Republic, 1776–1787* (1969). Especially good on the growth of republican thought.

Richard B. Bernstein with Kym S. Rice, *Are We to Be a Nation? The Making of the Constitution* (1987). An exciting account of the Constitutional Convention.

John C. Miller, *The Federalist Era, 1789–1802* (1960). An excellent study of the first years under the new Constitution.

CHAPTER 40
The French Revolution, 1789–1799

FIGURE 40.1. David, "The Tennis Court Oath," June 20, 1789 This painting by the sympathetic artist Jacques Louis David glorifies a crucial step in the French Revolution when the leaders of the newly formed National Assembly swear to draw up a constitution for France. In the center representatives of the three Estates—clergy, nobility, and commoners—join in a cooperative gesture. (French Embassy Press and Information Division)

In 1789 the French monarchy was brought to its knees by one of the greatest and most far-reaching upheavals in the history of Western civilization—the French Revolution. During the following ten years revolutionaries eliminated the centuries-old French monarchy, overturned the social system of France's old regime, and transformed France's religious institutions. Underlying these changes was the spirit of the Revolution, best summarized by its slogan: *Liberté, Égalité, Fraternité* ("Liberty, Equality, Fraternity").

The Revolution was so fundamental, so dynamic, and so threatening that it could not be contained within France. The news alone of what was happening in France spread fear among those hoping to maintain the status quo and stirred the hopes of those longing for change. Then by force of arms the French carried the ideas and institutions of the Revolution beyond France's borders. For France, and for much of Western civilization, the Revolution was a watershed that would mark the beginning of the modern world.

1. THE LAST DAYS OF THE OLD REGIME IN FRANCE

France at the succession of Louis XVI, though somewhat weakened by the defeats and failures of Louis XV, was still the richest and most influential nation in continental Europe. During the course of the eighteenth century, France's commerce and prosperity had steadily increased. Half of all the specie in Europe was to be found in France. The French enjoyed a relatively high standard of living. It is not, therefore, to desperation born of poverty that one must look as an explanation for the French Revolution but, rather, to frustration caused by existing institutions—social, religious, political, economic—that had failed to adjust to changing conditions.

French society on the eve of the French Revolution was divided into three distinct orders, or *estates*. The first estate was the clergy, numbering approximately one hundred thousand out of a total population of some 24 million. The Catholic church in France owned over 10 percent of the land—the best land—and from its lands and tithes and fees enjoyed an income probably half as large

as that of the government itself. It controlled all educational institutions and censored the press. It monopolized public worship and continued to harass all other religious groups at a time when the spirit of religious tolerance was rising throughout most of the Western world. The clergy itself was sharply divided. The upper clergy—the bishops and the abbots—were rich and powerful. They were drawn exclusively from the ranks of the aristocracy and were generally looked upon by most of the lower clergy and the common people as parasites. The lower clergy—the priests and the monks—came from the lower classes. The income of the priests was modest. They shared the lives of the people they served and were generally popular, but they had almost no influence on Church policy.

The second estate was the nobility, numbering approximately four hundred thousand. The nobility owned over 20 percent of the land of France but was exempt from all direct taxation. The richest of them lived at Versailles as absentee landlords, where they hunted, intrigued, made love, and read the books of the *philosophes* of the Enlightenment. They were reputed to possess the best manners and the worst morals of any class in Europe. The most haughty of the nobility—the most jealous of their rights—were the newcomers, the *noblesse de la robe* (nobility of the gown). They were former rich bourgeois who had purchased judgeships in one of the high law courts. They led the newly reassertive eighteenth-century French aristocracy that had, since the death of Louis XIV in 1715, recouped some of their power and influence at the expense of the king and the bourgeoisie. By the second half of the eighteenth century, almost all high governmental posts were held by the nobility. This nobility was emboldened to challenge the authority of the monarchy when it sought reform and to assert ancient rights and privileges that had fallen out of use against those below them.

The third estate was composed of commoners—the bourgeoisie, the proletariat, and the peasantry—and comprised about 96 percent of the total population. Of all the social and economic groups in France in 1789, the bourgeoisie were probably the most frustrated. They were business and professional people—the bankers, merchants, shopkeepers, and lawyers—who had grown into a middle class between the nobility and the peasantry. By the late eighteenth century France's upper bourgeoisie had gone as far as their wits and energy could take them. Some had become richer by far than most of the nobility—only to find the highest levels of government and society closed to them. Others, less wealthy but well educated and ambitious, resented the second-class status assigned to them by the nobility.

The urban populace was a mixture of groups—wage earners, servants of the rich, artisans, and the unemployed. There was enough distress among them to create tensions—tensions that would increase with the maladjustments caused by the Revolution. During the course of the eighteenth century, the price of bread had risen three times as fast as wages. Paris was the only city in France with an urban populace large enough to make its influence strongly felt. There, they included about three hundred thousand citizens (about half the total population of the city)—enough to play a significant role in a revolution.

At least 90 percent of the French people in 1789 were peasants, tillers of the soil. Although they were probably better off than most peasants elsewhere in Europe (they owned at least 30 percent of the land, and serfdom had virtually disappeared), they were on the whole discontented. Most peasant-owned land was subject to feudal dues. Probably a majority of the peasants owned no land at all but were sharecroppers who gave up 50 percent of their produce to the lord in addition to the feudal dues (the fees paid by the peasant for use of the lord's mill, oven, wine press, and breeding stock, death taxes, inheritance taxes, sale-of-property taxes). Not only were peasants forbidden to hunt; they could not even protect their crops from the lord's hunting parties—nor, for that matter, from the game itself. Although French peasants no longer had to donate their labor to the lord, they were still required to furnish so many days' labor for roads and public works. On them fell nearly all the direct taxes levied by the national government. Altogether, peasants gave up much of their income in taxes to their landlords, to the church, and to the state.

The life of the peasantry too had evolved only slowly since the Middle Ages. Peasants generally lived in little rural villages, the houses close together. The house usually consisted of one room, with a dirt floor, thatched roof, and neither chimney nor glass windows. The livestock were frequently under the same roof. The peasants' daily diet was made up almost entirely of dark bread and wine; meat was reserved for special occasions. Entertainment centered around the Church. On Sundays and holy days, of which there were many, their attire and attitudes were festive and gay. Ambitious young French peasants, unlike the peasants in most other parts of Europe, did have opportunities for advancement. Many engaged in cottage industry. A peasant could buy some land, become a priest or the lord's steward, a blacksmith or innkeeper, or seek a new life in the city. Only relatively few, of course, would succeed.

The government of France was arbitrary. Usually the king's decree was, in effect, law. The Estates General, the French counterpart of the British Parliament, had not met for nearly two centuries. Justice was capricious and corrupt. There were 237 different codes of law to confuse the litigants. There were no juries as in Great Britain. The king could arrest and imprison at will (although Louis XV and Louis XVI seldom did). The judges of the thirteen superior courts, called *parlements*, purchased or inherited their titles and were all members of the nobility. It was therefore impossible for commoners to obtain justice in a case against the nobility. The arbitrariness and inherent injustice of this system, which had long been taken for granted, clashed with the widely circulated ideas of the Enlightenment.

2. THE BREAKDOWN OF THE OLD REGIME

The breakdown of the Old Regime in France began in the field of finance. Louis XVI had inherited a large and constantly growing national debt. It was not excessive for a nation as rich as France; Great Britain and the Netherlands had higher per capita debts. But when combined with the exemption of the nobility and the clergy and much of the bourgeoisie from direct taxation and the extravagant cost of maintaining the military establishment and servicing the national debt (most of which had been incurred by past wars), it spelled eventual bankruptcy. Furthermore, France lacked an adequate banking system and was still burdened with the corrupt system of tax collection (called tax farming) that allowed much revenue to be diverted from the treasury into the pockets of private collectors.

Upon assuming the throne, Louis XVI appointed the Physiocrat Turgot, a friend of Voltaire, as minister of finance. Turgot initiated a series of sweeping reforms designed to clean up the mess. However, those with vested interests in the old system brought about his dismissal at the end of two years, and his reform measures were rescinded. A succession of ministers then tried all kinds of palliatives, such as borrowing, pump-priming expenditures, and better bookkeeping, but to no avail. By 1786 the debt was 3 billion livres,[1] and the annual deficit had reached 125 million. Bankers refused to lend the government more money. In a desperate effort to save his regime, Louis called an Assembly of Notables in 1787 and attempted to persuade the nobles and the clergy to consent to be taxed. But the privileged orders refused and demanded, instead, a meeting of the Estates General, thinking that they could control it and thereby assert their own interests. Pressured by a virtual revolt of his own nobility, the king gave in.

3. THE TRIUMPH OF THE THIRD ESTATE

During the early months of 1789 elections were held for members of the Estates General. All France was agog with excitement. Hundreds of pamphlets appeared, and there was widespread public debate. By tradition, each of the three es-

tates, the clergy, the nobility, and the commoners, elected their own representatives. All males who had reached the age of twenty-five and paid taxes were permitted to vote. Since the third estate, which included the bourgeoisie, the peasantry, and the urban populace, comprised more than nine-tenths of the total population, it was given as many seats as the other two combined. However, by tradition the three estates sat separately and each group had one vote.

By April 1789 the delegates began to arrive at Versailles. Goodwill prevailed. Violent revolution was far from anyone's mind. The delegates came armed only with *cahiers*, the lists of grievances that had been called for by the king. Of the six hundred representatives of the third estate, not one was a peasant. Except for a handful of liberal clergy and nobles who were elected to the third estate, they were all bourgeois. Nearly all the members of the third estate, as well as many members of the two privileged estates, were acquainted with the philosophy of the Enlightenment. They held inflated hopes of quickly solving long lists of problems that had been growing for years.

The first formal session was held on May 5. Immediately a sharp debate began over the method of voting. The two privileged estates demanded that, according to custom, the three estates meet separately and vote by order—that is, each estate cast one vote. This procedure would mean that all attacks on privilege and inequality would be defeated by a vote of two to one. The third estate demanded that the three estates meet jointly and that voting be by head. Thus all measures for fundamental reform would pass, for not only did the third estate have as many members as the other two combined, but a number of liberal clergy and noble men sympathized with the cause of reform. Both sides realized that the outcome of this issue would be decisive.

On June 17, after six weeks of fruitless haggling, the third estate, bolstered by the support of a few priests from the first estate, declared itself to be the National Assembly of France and invited the other two estates to join it in the enactment of legislation. Three days later, on June 20, when the members of the third estate arrived at their meeting hall, they found it locked. Adjourning to a

---

[1] The livre was technically worth about twenty cents, but its purchasing power in the eighteenth century was much greater than that of the late-twentieth-century American dollar.

nearby building used as an indoor tennis court, they took the "Tennis Court Oath," vowing never to disband until France had a constitution. It was the third estate's first act of defiance. On June 23 the king met with the three estates in a royal session at which he offered many liberal reforms but commanded the estates once and for all to meet separately and vote by order. The king, his ministers, and members of the first two estates filed out, but the representatives of the third estate defiantly remained seated. When the royal master of ceremonies returned to remind them of the king's orders, Mirabeau, a liberal noble man elected by the third estate, jumped to his feet and shouted, "Go and tell those who sent you that we are here by the will of the people and will not leave this place except at the point of the bayonet!" When the startled courtier repeated these words to his master, Louis XVI, with characteristic weakness, replied, "They mean to stay. Well damn it, let them stay." A few days later he reversed himself and ordered the three estates to meet jointly and vote by head. The third estate had thus won the first round.

The monarchy might have still been able to reassert control had not the new National Assembly received unexpected support from two sources: the Parisian populace and the French peasantry. Both had been suffering from unusually poor economic conditions initiated by poor harvests. Revolutionary events raised expectations in these hard times, making both groups unusually volatile. The first important disturbances came in Paris. In early July alarming news began to arrive that the king was calling the professional troops of the frontier garrison to Versailles. It appeared that he was at last preparing to use force. At this critical juncture, the Parisians countered the threat of force with force. On July 14 a riotous crowd searching for arms marched on and destroyed the Bastille, a gloomy old fortress prison in the working-class quarter that symbolized the arbitrary tyranny of the old regime (see Figure 40.2). (July 14 has long been celebrated as the French national holiday.) This show of force stayed the king's hand.

At the same time the forces of order were faced with uprisings in the countryside. During July and August peasants revolted against their lords throughout France, burning tax rolls, attacking manors, reoccupying enclosed lands, and generally rejecting the burdens of feudalism. These revolts were further inflamed by what has come to be known as the Great Fear—unfounded rumors that brigand bands, perhaps raised by nobles, were creating havoc everywhere. A panic swept the countryside. Many nobles fled from France (the *émigrés*). For all practical purposes, feudalism came to an end. The legal end of feudalism came on August 4 during a night session of the National Assembly when, in an effort to make the best of a bad situation, one noble man after another stood up and renounced his feudal rights and privileges.

These defeats suffered by the forces of order enabled the third estate in the National Assembly to take further actions. The most important of these actions occurred on August 26, when the National Assembly proclaimed the Declaration of Rights of Man and the Citizen. This document, which followed the English Bill of Rights by an even hundred years and preceded the American Bill of Rights by two years, was replete with the phrases of the philosophers of the Enlightenment. "Men are born and remain free and equal in rights." The natural rights were declared to be "liberty, property, security, and resistance to oppression." Liberty of opinion "even in religion," freedom of the press, and freedom from arbitrary arrest were all proclaimed.

The forces of privilege and reaction, however, still had to be brought to terms. The king not only refused to sign the August decrees but began once more to assemble troops around Versailles and Paris. In answer to this new threat of force, a huge mob of Parisian women on October 5 and 6 marched eleven miles out to Versailles, surrounded the palace, and with the help of the bourgeois National Guard, forced the king to accompany them to the city, where he became a virtual prisoner of the populace. As the carriage bearing the royal family rolled toward Paris, the surrounding crowd shouted jubilantly, "We have the baker, the baker's wife, and the little cook boy! Now we shall have bread!" A few days later the National Assembly moved its sessions to Paris, where it came increasingly under the influence of the radical populace of the great city. The third estate had triumphed.

FIGURE 40.2.   The Storming of the Bastille   The storming of the Bastille represented the first act of crowd violence of the French Revolution. Actually, the crowd of Parisians was merely looking for arms to defend itself against rumored attack by the forces of the king. However, the Bastille was believed to have held hundreds of political prisoners and was a symbol of all that was oppressive under the Old Regime. Its fall symbolized a direct blow for freedom and stayed the hand of the king, who was contemplating suppressing the defiant third estate. (Culver Pictures)

4. MAKING FRANCE A CONSTITUTIONAL MONARCHY

The National Assembly could now at last settle down to the task of transforming French institutions. During the next two years the Assembly passed a series of sweeping reforms that may be conveniently classified as follows.

Judicial

The *parlements*, and the manorial and ecclesiastical courts with their arbitrary procedures and overlapping jurisdictions, were swept away. An orderly system of lower and higher courts was established. The administration of justice was decentralized and democratized. Judges were to be elected for six-year terms. Torture was abolished. In criminai cases juries were to be used for the first time in French history.

Economic

In accordance with the doctrine of laissez faire, guilds, labor unions, and trading associations were abolished. All occupations were declared open to all classes. Feudal obligations, including labor on the public roads, had already come to an end on the night of August 4. Internal tolls and customs were abolished.

Financial

The complex and unequal taxes, direct and indirect, were swept away. They were replaced by a tax on land and a tax on the profits of trade and industry. Both were uniform and no one was exempt. Tax farming was at long last abolished. Expenditures were henceforth to be authorized only by the national legislature. To meet the pressing financial needs of the government, the National Assembly issued paper money called *assignats* to the value of 400 million livres. To back up this paper money, the property of the Roman Catholic church, valued at approximately that amount, was confiscated.

Religious

The seizure of its property was the first step toward the nationalization of the Church. Monasticism was abolished. The clergy was to be elected by the people (including non-Roman Catholics) and their salaries paid by the state. The bishops were reduced in number, wealth, and power. They were no longer to be invested by the pope. These measures were incorporated in the Civil Constitution of the Clergy, to which all members of the clergy were required to take an oath of allegiance in order to perform their functions and draw their salaries. The pope, whose control over the organization and the clergy of the French church would have been broken, declared the Civil Constitution of the Clergy to be founded upon heretical principles and ordered the clergy to refuse to take the oath of allegiance. A majority of the clergy, including nearly all the bishops, followed the pope's command. The defection of the "nonjuring clergy" and of thousands of their devoted parishioners was the first serious split in the ranks of the revolutionists.

Political

Under the new constitution, which was completed in 1791, judicial, legislative, and executive powers of the central government were separated. Law-making was given to the single-chamber Legislative Assembly of 745 members elected for two-year terms. Voting, however, was limited to males at least twenty-five years of age who paid taxes equivalent to three days' wages. It is estimated that some 4 million adult males ("active" citizens) could meet these qualifications and that some 2 million remained "passive" citizens. Actually to sit in the Legislative Assembly required the payment of taxes amounting to fifty-four livres. Only some seventy thousand Frenchmen could meet this qualification, and the weight of power fell to the bourgeoisie. The king was granted a suspensive veto over all but financial and constitutional measures, but three successive legislatures could pass a bill over the king's veto. The conduct of foreign relations was left in the hands of the king, but he could not declare war or make treaties without the consent of the Legislative Assembly. The king's expenditures were limited to a sum voted by the legislative body. France was greatly decentralized. For purposes of local government and administration, the country was divided into eighty-three departments, each of which was administered by a small elected assembly. The execution of the national laws was placed almost entirely in the hands of the local authorities.

In October 1791 the National Assembly, having completed its work, gave way to the Legislative Assembly, which had recently been elected under the new constitution. Within a brief span of two years and with very little bloodshed, France had been made over. The monarchy had been limited and made subject to a written constitution. The Roman Catholic church had been subordinated to the state. Feudalism had come to an end. Individual rights and liberties and legal equality had been defined and established.

5. FOREIGN WAR AND THE FAILURE OF THE MODERATE REGIME

The new government so optimistically launched lasted less than a year. The chief gainers in the French Revolution thus far had been the bourgeoisie and the peasants. The bourgeoisie had gained political control over the country and

WHERE HISTORIANS DISAGREE

The Origins of the French Revolution

No subject has provoked more historical research and debate than the French Revolution. The literature has become so extensive that several books have been written on the historiography itself.

Of all the aspects of the French Revolution, the most central and debated has been its origins. Why did it happen?

The most dominant interpretation of the twentieth century has viewed the Revolution as a struggle between rising and falling social classes. According to this view, which has a Marxist core, the Revolution was really a series of social revolutions. Most important was the revolution of the rising bourgeoisie, increasingly wealthy and numerous thanks to the growth of capitalism, commerce, and industry, but prevented from matching its economic dominance with social and political power. The bourgeoisie revolted against the assertive aristocracy, economically declining because of its ties to feudalism and agriculture but jealously fighting to retain its old social and political dominance. Adding to this fundamental struggle was the revolt of the urban proletariat at crucial points during the Revolution and the revolt of the peasants during the key months of summer 1789. Together, these revolts were too much for the monarchy, which along with the other institutions of the old feudal order were swept away and replaced by middle-class institutions. In each case, the social classes involved pursued their own interests. The base of this social revolution, which led to such sweeping political change, was the long-term shift from agriculture to industry and from feudalism to capitalism. Thus political change followed and was subordinate to socioeconomic change.

During the last twenty-five years, this dominant interpretation has come under increasing attack. Many historians now argue that the social conflict between the bourgeoisie and aristocracy has been exaggerated. They point out that the social backgrounds of those supporting or opposing the Revolution show no clear pattern, that the aristocracy lost less than assumed during the revolution, and that the rising industrial and commercial bourgeoisie were not the key supporters of the Revolution. New research seems to show that there was more mobility between the bourgeoisie and the aristocracy than previously known, that the aristocracy was more progressive and open to Enlightenment ideas than assumed, and that the aristocracy was not so firmly tied to the old economic order as argued. Apparently it was not the commercial and industrial middle class who were most important in pushing for revolution but, rather, lawyers and administrators—especially those who were young and most frustrated with the lack of social, economic, and political positions to match their talents and expectations.

Some of these revisionist historians place new stress on the political breakdown of the monarchy that began during the decades before 1789. According to this view, political conflict was shifting from the confined sphere of the central government, as had been the rule under royal absolutism, to the public sphere, as would be the rule under modern constitutional forms of government. As early as the 1750s and 1760s, the French monarchy was becoming unable to contain political debate. By the 1780s, the monarch's political authority was being undermined. Thus, political causes should not be subordinated to socioeconomic causes for the Revolution; political developments had a crucial force of their own.

A full explanation for the origins of the French Revolution must link social and political forces, which combined to bring down the monarchy and establish a new system. Exactly how those links are forged will remain of acute interest and debate among historians.

greater social mobility. Most adult male peasants, who constituted the bulk of the French male population, could now vote, and all of the peasantry was at least free from feudal obligations. To the many peasant landowners who owned their land before the Revolution were now added others who had seized the lands of émigré nobles or had purchased confiscated Church lands. Most of the bourgeoisie and the landowning peasants were satisfied and wished to see the Revolution stop where it was, lest they lose their sacred property and their political dominance.

However, other groups were quite dissatisfied. The royal family, the aristocracy, most of the clergy, and the army officers yearned for the restoration of their privileges. And many of Paris' urban populace, both men and women, wanted to see the Revolution continued in a more radical way. They had gained little except theoretical rights and legal equality. Owning no property, they could not vote. Yet they had supplied much of the physical force that had saved the third estate and made the moderate reforms possible.

Leadership for these disgruntled groups was found among radical members of the bourgeoisie, who came to favor overthrow of the monarchy and extension of the Revolution. These radicals, although a definite minority, were well organized and ably led. They came together in numerous clubs, which were formed to debate and plan political matters. The most important was the Jacobin Club. Although the Jacobins were and remained predominantly intellectual bourgeoisie and were moderate at first, they gradually became the most radical group in France. Three Jacobin leaders came to tower over all others. Jean Paul Marat, Swiss by birth, was an inordinately ambitious and frustrated physician and scientist turned popular journalist (see Color Plate 18). His was the gift of rabble-rousing journalism. He incessantly demanded the beheading of all those leaders who opposed the further extension of the Revolution. Georges Jacques Danton, a former lawyer in the king's council, was a thundering orator of great energy and ability. Maximilien de Robespierre was also a lawyer. This determined idealist was influenced by Rousseau and bent upon the creation of a virtuous republic.

Events soon played into the hands of the radicals. The kings of Austria and Prussia, fearful of the spread of revolutionary ideas to their own lands and urged on by the French émigrés, began to make threatening moves and to issue meddlesome warnings to the French revolutionaries. In France the reactionaries believed that a successful war would enhance the prestige and power of the throne and that a defeat would result in the restoration of the Old Regime. Most of the radicals believed that war would expose the inefficiency and disloyalty of the king and bring about his downfall. When, therefore, in April 1792 Louis XVI appeared before the Legislative Assembly to request a declaration of war against Austria and Prussia, only seven negative votes were cast. Thus lightly was begun a series of wars that was to last twenty-three years and embroil most of the Western world.

The French armies, almost leaderless since nearly all the high-ranking officers were members of the nobility and had either fled or been deposed, were badly defeated. As the Austrian and Prussian armies advanced toward Paris, there was panic in the city. The king, who had already forfeited his credibility when he attempted to flee the country in June 1791, was now rightly suspected of being in treasonable communication with the enemy. A huge Parisian crowd of men and women advanced on the king's palace. The royal family fled for its life to the Legislative Assembly. The interior of the palace was wrecked, and several hundred of the Swiss guards were slain. The Legislative Assembly suspended and imprisoned Louis XVI and called elections for a national convention to draw up a new constitution to take the place of the one that had just failed.

6. THE TRIUMPH OF THE RADICALS AND THE REIGN OF TERROR

The elections to the constitutional convention took place in an atmosphere of panic and violence. During the interim between the overthrow of the limited monarchy and the meeting of the convention, Danton assumed emergency leadership of the nation. Feverishly he superintended the gathering of recruits and rushed them to the front. As the recruits were preparing to leave Paris, rumors spread that their wives and children would be murdered by the reactionary clergy and nobles.

FIGURE 40.3. **Execution of Louis XVI** In January 1793, Louis XVI was executed by guillotine in a public square before troops and a large crowd of citizens. Here the scene is portrayed as a triumph of the Revolution. (The Bettmann Archive)

Violent elements began murdering members of the nonjuring clergy and reactionary nobles who were being held in the prisons of Paris. During the first three weeks of September 1792 more than a thousand such victims were massacred. In the elections of the National Convention, held amid this hysteria, the radicals won a sweeping victory. Most of the conservative elements fearfully stayed away from the polls.

In the National Convention a long-simmering struggle between different Jacobin factions came to a head. The Girondins, so called because many of their leaders came from the vicinity of Bordeaux in the department of the Gironde, had once been the dominant and most radical faction of the Legislative Assembly—the Left.[2] In the National Con-

vention the Girondins found themselves on the Right. The new Left was made up of the Jacobin followers of Marat, Danton, and Robespierre, mostly from the city of Paris. They came to be called the Mountain, since they occupied the highest seats in the convention hall. This radical convention, elected for the purpose of drawing up a new constitution, was to rule France for the next three years (1792–1795).

The first act of the National Convention was to declare France a republic. The next move was to dispose of the king. After a close trial he was found guilty of treasonable communication with the enemy and sent to the guillotine—an instrument adopted by the revolutionists for the more mechanical and humane beheading of the condemned (see Figure 40.3). The execution of Louis XVI, accompanied by proclamations of world revolution by the evangelical Jacobins, sent a shudder of horror through the royal courts of Europe. Furthermore, the hastily recruited French revolution-

[2] The present political connotation of the terms *right* and *left* derives from this period. In the revolutionary assemblies the conservatives sat quite by chance on the speaker's right, the liberals and radicals on his left.

ary armies, which had checked the Austrians and Prussians at Valmy in September 1792, had taken the offensive and overrun the Austrian Netherlands.

Austria and Prussia were now joined by Great Britain, the Dutch Netherlands, Spain, Portugal, Sardinia, and Naples in a great coalition bent upon the destruction of the French Revolution and the restoration of the Old Regime. The French armies were unable to stand up to such an array of armed might. But the defeats and invasions were not the worst disasters to confront the revolutionary government. The peasants of the Vendée region in western France, who had been stirred up by the nonjuring clergy, rebelled against the radical government. The rebellion spread until some sixty of the eighty-three departments were involved. Major provincial cities such as Bordeaux, Lyons, and Marseilles were in revolt. Toulon, the chief French naval base on the Mediterranean, invited in the British fleet. Inside the convention itself many of the moderate Girondins were sympathetic to the rebels.

Faced with what seemed to be inevitable disaster to their radical cause and indeed to the Revolution itself, the leaders of the Mountain decided on drastic action. For support they turned to the Paris Commune, as the city government was called, which was controlled by radicals, and the *sans-culottes*—the common laborers, small shopkeepers, and artisans who wore trousers rather than the aristocratic knee breeches (or *culottes*). The men and women of this urban populace had already played an important role in the Revolution by opposing the old forces of order and supporting leaders of the third estate at crucial times, such as in the storming of the Bastille. By 1793 they wanted to carry the Revolution further, and for the next two years their wishes and actions would have considerable weight in France. Economically, they favored price controls to keep the cost of bread down and other governmental intervention in the economy to narrow the gap between rich and poor; they envisioned a society of small shopkeepers, artisans, and small farmers as ideal. Politically, they were antimonarchical and strongly republican, indeed favoring as much direct democracy as possible. While leaders of the Mountain did not fully agree with the *sans-culottes*, they were willing to work with them. On June 2,

1793, the National Convention, now dominated by the Mountain and surrounded by a threatening Paris crowd urged on by *sans-culottes* leaders, voted the expulsion and arrest of twenty-nine Girondin leaders. Having thus silenced all opposition within the convention, the leaders of the Mountain and their followers inaugurated a "reign of terror" against their political enemies. Their goals were to unite France and to save and extend the Revolution.

The National Convention delegated unlimited powers to a Committee of Public Safety, composed of twelve men working in secret. The most influential member of this all-powerful committee was Robespierre. At its call was the Committee of General Security, a national police force. A Revolutionary Tribunal was set up to try, condemn, and execute suspects without the usual legal procedure and as quickly as possible. Members of the National Convention were sent out in pairs to carry the Terror to every nook and cranny of France. Although tens of thousands of persons, possibly half a million, were imprisoned during the Reign of Terror, only some twenty-five thousand are believed to have been executed. The drastic policy was remarkably successful. The disaffected elements were quickly silenced, and the rebellions quelled. The defense of the republic was entrusted to Lazare Carnot. A *levée en masse* was ordered. All men, women, and children were called to the colors. The able-bodied young men were rapidly trained and rushed to the front. Everyone else contributed to the war effort on the home front. This common activity for defense of country produced a high state of morale—the first mass national patriotism in history. Able new officers were found. The armies of the coalition were defeated on every front and hurled back beyond the frontiers.

While Robespierre and his associates were saving the Revolution, they were also busy extending it to more radical ground. Robespierre was determined to make France a utopian republic where virtue and fraternity would reign supreme. During the emergency of 1793 a maximum price was placed upon the necessities of life for the protection of the consumer, particularly the *sans-culottes*. Efforts were made to control inflation by forcing people to accept the badly inflated *assignats* at their face value. New measures made it easier for peasants to acquire land. The metric system was adopted; the Louvre Palace was turned into an art gallery; the national library and national archives were founded; a law (never implemented) provided for a comprehensive national system of public education. Women adopted the flowing robes and hair styles of ancient Greece. Silk knee breeches, the symbol of aristocracy, gave way to trousers. Titles of all kinds were discarded and "Citizen" and "Citizeness" substituted. Even the calendar was revolutionized. The months were made equal and named after the seasons. Weeks were made ten days long, with one day of rest (thereby eliminating Sunday, a day of traditional Christian importance). The Year I was dated from September 22, 1792, the date of the declaration of the republic.

Meanwhile, discontent with Robespierre and his policies was increasing. The defeat of the invading armies of the coalition and the suppression of the internal rebellion appeared to most people to remove the justification for the Terror, yet the Terror was intensified. Robespierre felt that the republic of virtue for which he yearned had eluded him. When Danton counseled moderation, Robespierre sent even him and his most prominent followers to the guillotine. No one, not even the members of the National Convention, felt safe any longer. Finally, in July 1794, the Convention found the courage and the leadership to overthrow Robespierre and send him to his own guillotine.

7. REACTION AND THE RISE OF NAPOLEON

Since Robespierre was overthrown on July 27, which was 9 Thermidor by the revolutionary calendar, the reaction that followed is known as the Thermidorian Reaction. The propertied bourgeoisie, who quickly gained control of things, had been frightened and angered by the restrictive measures of Robespierre's regime. All such measures still in force were repealed. The Terror was brought to an end, and the chief terrorists executed. Armed bands of bourgeois hirelings went around for some time beating or killing Jacobins. Many individuals, weary of discipline and restraints, reveled in an outburst of licentious living. In 1795 the National Convention finally got around to the task for which it had been elected three years earlier: the drawing up of a new constitution. The resulting constitution reflected conservative reaction. Only property owners could vote for members of the legislative bodies. Executive functions were placed in the hands of five directors, who were chosen for five-year terms by the two legislative bodies. In October 1795 the National Convention turned over its powers to the Directory, the name that was given to the new government.

The most significant development of the period of the Directory, 1795–1799, was the rise to power of Napoleon Bonaparte. The directors, though men of reasonable competence, were unable to restore peace and political and social tranquillity. Though peace had already been made with Spain and Prussia, war with Great Britain, Austria, and Sardinia dragged on. Government finances were chaotic, and brigandage was rife. More and more people longed for a strong man who could bring peace abroad and order at home. Napoleon proved to be the man, and the story of his rise to power will be told in the next chapter. When in November 1799 Napoleon overthrew the Directory and made himself dictator, the French Revolution had run full cycle from absolute Bourbon monarchy to absolute Napoleonic dictatorship.

SUGGESTED READING

General

C. Brinton, *The Anatomy of Revolution* (1956). Seeks to discover a common pattern in revolutions by comparing the English, American, French, and Russian revolutions. Fascinating.

F. Furet, *Interpreting the French Revolution* (1981). An influential new interpretation.

N. Hampson, *A Social History of the French Revolution* (1963). A well-written, detailed account.

R. R. Palmer, *The Age of the Democratic Revolution*, 2 vols. (1959, 1964). Places the French Revolution in a broader transatlantic context.

S. Schama. *Citizens: A Chronicle of the French Revolution.* (1989). A vivid, revisionary account.

The Old Regime and the First Phase of the Revolution

William Doyle, *Origins of the French Revolution* (1980). Surveys recent interpretations.

G. Lefèbvre, *The Coming of the French Revolution* (1947). By one of France's leading authorities, it covers the first phase of the Revolution.

Alexis de Tocqueville, *The Old Regime and the French Revolution* (1955). A classic analysis with useful insights.

M. Vovelle, *The Fall of the French Monarchy, 1787–1792* (1984). A new synthesis.

Second Phase

M. Lyons, *France Under the Directory* (1975). A good brief treatment.

R. R. Palmer, *Twelve Who Ruled: The Committee of Public Safety During the Terror* (1941). Best book on the Reign of Terror.

A. Soboul, *The Parisian Sans-Culottes and the French Revolution 1793–1794* (1964). The most highly respected analysis of the *sans-culottes*.

Sources

J. H. Steward, *A Documentary Survey of the French Revolution* (1951). Excellent, broad collection of documents.

CHAPTER 41
The Era of Napoleon, 1799–1815

FIGURE 41.1. David, "Napoleon's Coronation" This painting by David was intended to glorify Napoleon at the height of his powers. Having just crowned himself emperor with a laurel wreath (alluding back to Roman emperors) in an 1804 ceremony presided over by Pope Pius VII (on his right), Napoleon prepares to crown Josephine as empress. (Alinari/Art Resource)

No individual in modern times has enjoyed a more meteoric career than Napoleon Bonaparte, the modern counterpart of Alexander the Great and Julius Caesar. He was essentially a product of the Enlightenment and the French Revolution. He rose to power in France quickly, both undoing and securing changes initiated during the French Revolution. As he extended his rule throughout Europe by military conquest, he spread revolutionary forces of change to other lands.

1. NAPOLEON'S RISE TO POWER

Napoleon was born on the French island of Corsica in 1769. At the age of nine he was sent to a military school in France. An unusually self-reliant individual, he studied history, geography, and mathematics. At sixteen he received his commission as second lieutenant of artillery. During several years of boring garrison duty he stuffed his photographic mind with history, the classics, and the philosophy of the Enlightenment.

The French Revolution provided unprecedented opportunities for soldiers of talent to rise in the officer corps. Most of the prerevolutionary army officers were nobles and had fled the country or been deposed. Moreover, the expanded size of the army created new demand for skilled officers. Napoleon took advantage of his opportunities. In 1793 he gained attention in the recapture of Toulon. In 1795 Napoleon was again called upon, this time by the National Convention, which was threatened by a Parisian crowd. Using artillery— his famous "whiff of grapeshot"—Napoleon quickly dispersed the crowd and became the hero of the Convention. He used his new prominence to secure command of the French army still fighting in northern Italy. Napoleon's dynamism and skill quickly galvanized the lethargic French forces, who defeated the Austrians and Sardinians and forced them to sue for peace. He personally negotiated a favorable peace with Austria and sent back glowing reports of his exploits.

Napoleon then turned toward France's most formidable opponent, the British. The British navy was too powerful for France to dare an invasion of the British mainland. Napoleon concluded that an expedition to Egypt would be a telling blow to British commerce with its colonies and to the British Empire in general. Moreover, it might prove to be an unexpected thrust and thus an easy victory, something to contribute to Napoleon's image as a daring heroic conqueror. Militarily, the expedition was a failure; Admiral Nelson (1758–1805) decisively defeated the French fleet at the Battle of the Nile on August 1, 1798. Yet Napoleon avoided personal disaster by slipping back to France with a few chosen followers and cleverly managing the reports that arrived from Egypt.

Meanwhile, matters were turning worse for France's government, the Directory. The expedition to Egypt prompted Great Britian, Austria, and Russia to join in a second coalition against France. By 1799 French armies had suffered defeats and France was threatened with invasion. Internally, support for the Directory was weakening as the economic situation worsened and as political factions vied for power. One of the conservative factions, led by Abbé Siéyès (who was already one of the directors), concluded that the Revolution had gone too far. The members of this faction wanted to return to a more authoritarian form of government, which respected the changes initiated during the first, moderate phase of the Revolution in 1789. This situation provided Napoleon with another opportunity. Siéyès and others conspired with Napoleon to overthrow the Directory in a coup d'état. This coup occurred on 18 Brumaire (November 9, 1799). Napoleon was only thirty.

2. THE CONSULATE—PEACE AND REFORM, 1799–1804

Having seized power by conspiracy and force, Napoleon had a constitution drawn up to conceal what amounted to a military dictatorship under the cloak of parliamentary forms. He gave himself the title of First Consul with the power to appoint key civilian and military personnel, declare war and make treaties, and initiate all legislation through a hand-picked Council of State. Two other consuls without any significant powers served as camouflage. Two legislative bodies were selected from a iist of candidates elected by all adult French males. But since they could not propose new laws, their power was very limited. Thus the voters were led to believe that they were participating in the government, whereas in reality their voice was but faintly heard. Local government was again brought under the strict control of the central government by placing each of France's eighty-three departments under the control of a powerful agent of the central government called a *prefect*.

Napoleon lost no time in making a treaty (1800) with the United States, bringing to an end a two-year undeclared naval war that had grown out of French seizures of American vessels and the pro-British and anti-French policies of John Adams' administration. Slipping over the Alps with a French army, Napoleon crushed the Austrian army in northern Italy in the battle of Marengo, knocking Austria out of the Second Coalition. Tsar Paul of Russia was cajoled with flattery and promises into making peace. Even Great Britain was persuaded to sign the Peace of Amiens in 1802. Shortly thereafter Napoleon cut his losses in North America and sold Louisiana to the United States.

Napoleon next proceeded to gain social support for his rule and create new permanent institutions. He approved the end of feudal privileges and the transfers of property, thereby winning favor with the peasantry. By affirming property rights as inviolable and formal equality before the law for adult males, he gained support from the middle class. He also welcomed back all but the most reactionary émigrés, most of whom had been part of France's old aristocracy. He deterred opposing groups by creating a secret police force under Joseph Fouché and suppressing political organizations. For those who displayed loyalty and achieved the most, he created the prestigious Legion of Honor.

Some of these measures were institutionalized in Napoleon's most important reform, the creation of the Civil Code of 1804 (the Napoleonic Code), which would later be copied by many other nations. The Civil Code, along with other codes for criminal and commercial law, reduced to order the dozens of different legal codes in existence. Generally they affirmed the reforms sought in the beginning stages of the French Revolution while rejecting the more radical measures enacted after

1792. But for women, the code was a clear defeat. Rather than granting them legal or political equality, it gave authority over the family to men and left married women legally and economically dependent on their husbands.

Napoleon was keenly aware of the political and social importance of religion. "Always treat the pope," he counseled his diplomats, "as if he had 200,000 men." He himself was a deist and a cynical moral relativist, believing that God was "always on the side with the most cannon." One of his first steps was to make peace with the pope and end the ten-year struggle between the French revolutionary governments and the Roman Catholic church. After arduous negotiations, the First Consul and the pope signed the Concordat of 1801, which was to govern the relations between the French state and the Catholic church until the beginning of the twentieth century. The Catholic religion was declared to be the religion of the majority of the French people, but freedom for other religions was also to be protected. The state was to appoint the bishops, but only the pope could invest them in their offices. The bishops were to appoint and discipline the lower clergy, thus restoring the traditional episcopal principle of the church. The salaries of the clergy were to be paid by the state, and the clergy were to take an oath of allegiance to the state. The pope accepted the permanent loss of church property seized by the National Assembly. While the Catholic clergy was never pleased with the Concordat (indeed, Pope Pius VII eventually renounced it), it ended the religious cleavage that had harassed France since the early days of the revolution.

Napoleon initiated several other institutional reforms. He established the Bank of France to handle government funds and issue paper money. He brought order and efficiency to government finances. He created a long-lasting system of secondary schools tied to the University of France. He established several professional and technical schools.

The first five years of Napoleon's rule were spectacularly successful. Law and order at home and peace abroad had been attained. Financial stability, equal and efficient justice, religious tranquillity, and the foundations of an effective educational system had all been achieved. Public morale was high. However, Napoleon was not satisfied with his accomplishments. He yearned for more glory. In 1804 he crowned himself emperor of the French and sought further fields to conquer.

3. THE EMPIRE—WAR AND CONQUEST

Great Britain, France's inveterate foe, had become increasingly alarmed at Napoleon's growing strength. Napoleon had not only continued to build up his military forces but had also taken advantage of the Peace of Amiens to further his commercial and imperial schemes at Great Britain's expense. Before the end of 1803 the British government declared war and the next year joined with Austria and Russia to form a third coalition against France. This was what Napoleon expected and wanted. He soon appeared at the English Channel at the head of a force sufficient to conquer the British Isles, if only the twenty-four-mile water barrier could be crossed. In the Channel, however, lay the world's mightiest fleet, commanded by the greatest of all Britain's admirals, Lord Nelson. Meanwhile, he was watching the movements of the Austrians and Russians and readying his own army. When the time was ripe, he suddenly marched his army eastward, surrounded an exposed Austrian army at Ulm in southwest Germany, and forced it to surrender. But the day after Ulm, Nelson sighted the combined French and Spanish fleets off Cape Trafalgar on the southwest point of Spain and annihilated them (October 21, 1805). Although Nelson was killed early in the battle, his victory saved Great Britain from the menace of a Napoleonic invasion and limited the scope of the French emperor's conquests to the continent of Europe.

On land, however, Napoleon seemed invincible. Moving his army eastward from Ulm, he met and crushed the oncoming combined forces of Austria and Russia at Austerlitz. Austria immediately sued for peace, and the demoralized Russians retreated toward their home country. At this juncture Prussia declared war on Napoleon. The time was inopportune, and the Prussian army was no match for Napoleon. At Jena and Auerstädt

Napoleon overwhelmed and virtually destroyed the Prussian forces (1806). Two weeks later the French were in Berlin. Hearing that the Russian troops were re-forming in Poland, Napoleon moved eastward to meet them. After being held to a draw by the Russians in a blinding snowstorm at Eylau, he defeated them decisively a few months later in the great battle of Friedland (1807). Tsar Alexander I now sued for peace. Although the Treaties of Tilsit (July 1807) were technically between equals, they actually left Napoleon master of the European continent and Alexander I only a junior partner. Russia was given a free hand to deal with Turkey in eastern Europe but was not permitted to take Constantinople, the prize the Russians most desired. In return for a dominant hand in eastern Europe, Alexander promised to join Napoleon against Great Britain and to force Sweden to do so. Tilsit recognized the changes that Napoleon had already made in central and western Europe and left him free to make any others he wished.

Between 1806 and 1808 Napoleon remade the map of Europe. The puppet Duchy of Warsaw was created out of part of Prussia's (and later, part of Austria's) Polish territory. Prussia's territory west of the Elbe was made a part of the kingdom of Westphalia, over which Napoleon's youngest brother, Jerome, was made king. Prussia was thus virtually halved in size. The Holy Roman Empire was at long last abolished, and its hundreds of little principalities greatly consolidated. A strip of German territory along the North Sea was annexed outright to France. The rest of German territory west of the Elbe was brought into the Confederation of the Rhine, with Napoleon as protector. Napoleon's younger brother, Louis, was made king of Holland; but when Louis began to favor the interests of his Dutch subjects over those of the French Empire, Napoleon deposed him and annexed his territory to France. The Italian peninsula was brought under French dominance. The coastal areas along the northeastern Adriatic Sea were detached from Austria and annexed to France. In 1808 Napoleon overthrew the weak Spanish royal house and made his elder brother, Joseph, king of Spain. Shortly before, the Portuguese royal family had fled to Brazil at the approach of a French army. Denmark (including

Map 41.1 **EUROPE, 1810** This map shows the Napoleonic empire at its height. Generally, French revolutionary and Napoleonic institutions spread most in those areas closest to France and under its direct control. Napoleon's empire was weakened when he tried to extend his control to Europe's geographic extremes—Spain and Russia.

Norway) became Napoleon's most faithful ally.

Thus, by 1808, most of Europe was under French control or French influence (see Map 41.1). No other conqueror has so dominated Europe. In all those territories under direct French control, Napoleon's "enlightened" institutions and administrative efficiency were introduced. The rest of Europe, impressed with the effectiveness of the French revolutionary ideas and institutions, adopted many of them voluntarily.

4. DECLINE AND FALL OF THE EMPIRE

A number of factors contributed to the decline and fall of the Napoleonic empire. One of the most obvious was British sea power. Because of it, Great Britain alone of the European powers was able to withstand the Napoleonic military onslaught. After Trafalgar had dashed Napoleon's hopes of invading the British Isles, he sought the destruction of "perfidious Albion" by economic pressure. In order to wreck the economy of the "nation of shopkeepers," he attempted to blockade the entire continent of Europe against British shipping. All British goods were confiscated. French privateers were set upon British merchant ships. These measures, known as "the Continental System," did cause Great Britain distress. However, with control of the sea, Great Britain was able to apply a more effective counterblockade against the Napoleon-dominated Continent. The Continental System created ever-increasing resentment in France's satellite states against Napoleon's rule.

Another factor that undermined the Napoleonic empire was the rise of a national spirit among the subject peoples. The mass spirit of intense patriotism or nationalism, which had its origin in France during the *levée en masse* of 1793, spread to the rest of Europe in the wake of Napoleon's conquering armies. The first people to rebel openly against the French yoke were the proud Spaniards. Hardly had Napoleon's brother Joseph been placed on the Spanish throne when his unwilling subjects rose up and chased him out of Madrid. The superior French armies, even when led by Napoleon himself, were ineffective against the hit-and-run guerrilla tactics invented

by the Spaniards. The British government, observing Napoleon's predicament in Spain, sent an army under Arthur Wellesley, the future duke of Wellington, to exploit the situation. Spain became a running abscess that drained away much of Napoleon's military strength. Meanwhile, Prussia, after the humiliation of Jena, had begun a rejuvenation under the leadership of Baron von Stein. Partly in secret and partly in the open, the Prussians modernized their army and their civil institutions and prepared for the day of liberation. In 1809 Austria declared war on Napoleon in a premature effort to free itself from subservience to the French emperor. Although Austria was once more defeated, the heroic valor with which the Austrian armies fought served notice of the rising spirit of national pride and resistance. Napoleon could no longer enjoy the advantage of fighting with soldiers fired with the heady wine of nationalism against lethargic professional armies.

The beginning of the end was a disastrous campaign against Russia in 1812. With their own interests pulling them apart, the alliance between Alexander I and Napoleon became strained. Napoleon, against the advice of his closest associates, decided to invade Russia. Amassing an army of six hundred thousand, the mightiest army ever assembled up to that time, he plunged into the vastness of Russia. Many of his troops, however, were unwilling conscripts from the puppet states. The Russian army retreated into the interior of the huge country, following a scorched-earth policy and drawing Napoleon ever-farther from his base of supplies. Finally, after the bloody battle of Borodino about seventy-five miles from Moscow, Napoleon's hosts entered the city. But Alexander I refused to make peace. A fire destroyed much of Moscow, leaving the invaders without shelter in the face of approaching winter. Napoleon began his retreat too late. The Russian winter caught his forces burdened down with loot. Tens of thousands froze or starved. Russian Cossacks, riding out of the blizzards, cut down or captured other thousands. Of the six hundred thousand men who marched into Russia, no more than one hundred thousand returned.

Napoleon dashed back to France to raise fresh conscripts, but the flower of French manhood was gone. One nation after another rose up to join the

PLATE 18.   Jacques Louis David, *The Death of Marat*, 1793.   The French artist, David, was an active figure in the French Revolution. Here he shows the death of Marat, one of the chief leaders of the radical second phase of the Revolution. Marat was working in his bathtub when Charlotte Corday assassinated him. The subject matter and the political message is in sharp contrast to earlier eighteenth-century art that reflected aristocratic tastes. (Musées Royaux des Beaux-Arts de Belgique, Brussels)

PLATE 19. John Constable, *The White Horse*, 1819. Like many romantic painters, John Constable (1776–1837) was fascinated by nature. Here he depicts a rural scene that is naturalistic (a real scene the viewer might come across) and idyllic. The painting, with its vast living sky and detailed foliage, pulls the viewer into nature. The reality of this image of rural life in nature was already starting to disappear as commercial agriculture, industrialization, and urbanization spread throughout England. (Copyright The Frick Collection)

PLATE 20. Joseph Mallard William Turner, *The Fighting Temeraire*, 1839. Turner is considered the greatest of the English romantic painters. In paintings dominated by the light and color, he depicted heroic, tragic struggles mirrored by the overwhelming forces of nature. Here an antiquated battleship sails off into the eternity of the setting sun. The grand ship of the past is replaced by a modern steamship, the smoke from its stack merging into the clouds that frame the sun. (National Gallery, London: Art Resource)

PLATE 21. **Eugène Delacroix,** *Entrance of the Crusaders into Constantinople,* **1840.** Romantic painters such as Delacroix (1793–1863) often glorified the medieval past and the exotic. In this dramatic scene, Byzantine patricians humble themselves before the intruding Crusaders. The scene swirls with passion and color—a romantic vision of the past in sharp contrast to the reality of mid-nineteenth century France. (The Louvre, Paris)

PLATE 22. **Gustave Courbet,** *The Stone Breakers,* **1849.** Realism rejected almost all elements of the Romantic movement. Realistic artists such as Courbet (1819–1877) depicted the mundane, everyday life of workers. Here he portrays stone breakers as a passerby might see them. While there is dignity in their work, Courbet does not glorify them or nature. (Staatlichen Kunstsammlungen, Dresden)

PLATE 23.   Auguste Renoir, *Le Moulin de la Galette a Montmartre*, 1876.   Impressionist painters emphasized the appearance of things as one might see things at a glance. Using new techniques that emphasized applying dabs of colors to the canvas so the eye could mix them, these paintings had great immediacy. Here Renoir (1841–1919), a leading French impressionist most known for his fleshy, optimistic paintings, portrays a festive scene at a Parisian outdoor dance hall. Youthful middle- and working-class figures brim with health and pleasure in this artificial urban environment. (Musée d'Orsay, Paris: Scala/Art Resource)

PLATE 24. Paul Cézanne,
Mont Sainte-Victoire,
1902–1904. Cézanne
(1839–1906) had roots in
impressionism, but ulti-
mately rejected it. He tried
to display the essence
rather than the surface of
reality by emphasizing the
geometric principles of
form and an analytic un-
derstanding of color. This
landscape is one of a series
of paintings of Mont
Sainte-Victoire in southern
France. Both Cézanne and
van Gogh created founda-
tions for twentieth-century
painting. (Philadelphia Museum of Art, George W. Elkins
Collection)

**PLATE 25. Vincent Van
Gogh,** ***The Starry Night,***
1889. Like Cézanne, Van
Gogh (1853–1890) had
roots in impressionism, but
went beyond it. He was
able to express his own intense emotions in bold,
dynamic paintings. Here
he seems to have poured
himself into this scene he
painted toward the end of
his life while at a sanato-
rium in St.-Remy. The
scene swirls with color applied in distinct, broad
strokes. It is not a scene of
reality one might see, but
rather an expression of
feelings that mingles with
external reality. (Oil on canvas, 29 x 36¼". Collection,
The Museum of Modern Art,
New York. Acquired through
the Lillie P. Bliss Bequest.)

PLATE 26.   James Ensor, *Intrigue*, 1890.
During the late nineteenth century a sense
of dissatisfaction and a criticism of middle-class life grew. This is reflected in ex-
pressive paintings such as those by the
Belgian painter, James Ensor (1860–1949).
Here people are shown as indistinct from
the obnoxious masks they seem to wear.
(Royal Museum of Fine Arts, Antwerp)

**PLATE 27.   Edvard Munch, *The Scream*,
1893.**   Like Ensor, Edvard Munch (1863–
1944) expressed an undermining of middle-class life, but on a deeper, more individual level. In *The Scream*, a nightmare-
like fear is revealed, reflecting an anxiety
and a turning inward toward the unconscious that was growing in late-nineteenth
century intellectual and cultural circles.
Similarities to van Gogh's paintings can be
seen in how paint is used boldly to express emotion. (National Museum, Oslo)

PLATE 28.   Max Ernst, *Europe After the Rain*, 1940–1942.   Max Ernst (born in 1891) became a leader of the surrealists during the 1920s. He painted *Europe After the Rain* while hiding in Paris during World War II. The painting seems to represent the illogical horror and destruction of that era, and it stands as a perhaps prophetic warning to us all. (Wadsworth Atheneum, Hartford, Ella Gallup Sumner and Mary Catlin Sumner Collection)

PLATE 29.   Salvador Dali, *The Temptation of St. Anthony*, 1947.   Surrealism, a relatively popular style of twentieth-century painting, emphasizes the power of dreams and the unconscious. The aim is to depict an unfiltered psychic reality that visually may seem shocking and impossible. One of the most well known surrealists was Salvador Dali (1904–1989). Here the subject is apparently traditional (St. Anthony trying to fend off temptations), but the painting has the feeling and appearance of an improbable nightmare. (Musées Royaux des Beaux-Arts de Belgique, Brussels)

PLATE 30. Piet Mondrian, *Composition*, 1929. The twentieth-century trend away from art that represents external reality toward abstract art was carried to an extreme by the Dutch painter, Piet Mondrian (1872–1944). Here he uses only black, white, and the three primary colors to express his logical, harmonious vision. (National Museum, Belgrade: Scala/Art Resource)

PLATE 31. Fernand Leger, *The Great Constructors*, 1950. This painting by the French artist, Léger (1881–1955), reflects several trends in twentieth century art. Clearly this is an urban scene, showing construction workers and the steel frame of a skyscraper; yet the lines, proportions, and colors scarcely conform to reality. Elements of expressionism—the attempt to convey a feeling about man in this mechanical age—and abstract art—the concern with nonrepresentation lines and colors—abound in this work. (Musée de Biot, France: Josse/Art Resource)

WHERE HISTORIANS DISAGREE

Who Was Napoleon?

Few individuals in history have inspired such passionate debate as Napoleon. In part, this controversy is a result of his meteoric rise to the heights of power and his string of military conquests. And in part, it is a consequence of the charismatic quality of his leadership. He combined personal dynamism and charm, which created faith in masses of followers and enabled him to dominate many of those with whom he came into contact. The debate is also related to difficulties separating the myth of Napoleon from the reality of Napoleon. Finally, all sides of the debate can find some support in the varied, contradictory legacy of Napoleon's intentions and deeds. Therefore it is not surprising that historians have bitterly disagreed over how to characterize Napoleon.

Many historians argue that Napoleon was fundamentally a dictator. They point to the methods he used to acquire power—the fame associated with military prowess, the coup d'état, and the plebiscite that seemed to affirm democratically his power without offering a real choice—as methods typical of modern dictators. They also point to his actions after acquiring power—crowning himself emperor, eliminating freedom of speech and press, removing the substance from representative institutions, initiating a systematic crackdown on political opponents, and creating a secret police—as characteristic of military dictatorships.

Other historians, see him as a preserver of the Revolution. They stress his familiarity with Enlightenment ideas and his early support of the French Revolution. They point out that Napoleon did affirm the end of feudalism, the overthrow of the old aristocracy, the establishment of equality before the law for men, and the rights of property. They also argue that his most important service may have been in spreading the ideas and institutions of the Revolution beyond France's borders—in particular, the rejection of aristocratic privilege and the spread of the Napoleonic Code. In short, Napoleon affirmed the fundamental reforms of the early French Revolution, institutionalized them, and then helped spread them elsewhere in Europe.

Still other historians argue that Napoleon is best viewed as the last in a line of eighteenth-century enlightened despots. They point out that like other enlightened despots, such as Frederick the Great of Prussia and Joseph II of Austria, Napoleon was most interested in maximizing the political and military power of the state. Like them, he saw that to do so required centralizing and rationalizing the government, improving finances, codifying laws, and supporting the armed forces. He shared their tendency to make religious concerns secondary to political unity and to gain support through the creation of educational institutions. Thus from an eighteenth-century perspective, Napoleon is recognizable as an enlightened despot.

Many historians argue that individual leaders themselves, even as extraordinary as Napoleon, do not decisively affect history's mainstream. More important are the forces, circumstances, and people that surround them. Other historians maintain that individuals, above all rare charismatic leaders such as Napoleon, can have significant historical consequences.

Which of these interpretations best fits the historical record depends greatly on the perspective of the viewer and on what aspects of Napoleon's personality and rule are emphasized. At the same time, how much can be attributed to the actions of any historical figure must be kept in mind in deciding exactly who was Napoleon.

Russians in a war of liberation. At Leipzig in central Germany, in October 1813, Napoleon was at last decisively defeated. The next year the allies entered Paris and exiled Napoleon to the island of Elba, off the coast of Italy. When the allies began to squabble over the peace settlement, Napoleon escaped back to France and raised another army, but he was finaliy defeated in June 1815 by the duke of Wellington and the Prussians under Marshal Blücher at Waterloo in Belgium. This time he was imprisoned on the island of St. Helena in the South Atlantic, where six years later he died.

5. OVERSEAS EFFECTS: LATIN AMERICA

One vast area outside Europe upon which the impact of the revolution of Napoleon was strong and immediate was Latin America. During the eighteenth century, discontent with colonial rule had been steadily mounting in the Spanish and Portuguese colonial empires in North and South America. As in the thirteen English colonies in North America, resentment was directed primarily against economic and political restrictions. As the native-born "Creoles" had come to outnumber the Spanish- and Portuguese-born settlers, the ties of loyalty to the mother countries had become more and more tenuous. The liberal writings of the French and British philosophers of the Enlightenment were smuggled into Latin America and made their converts, particularly among young intellectuals. These liberal Latin Americans could not help being impressed by the successful revolt of the English colonies to the north and the setting up of a liberal New World republic. The French Revolution had an even more profound influence on them. When, therefore, Napoleon overthrew Ferdinand VII of Spain and placed his own brother, Joseph Bonaparte, on the Spanish throne, the sentiments of loyalty on the part of the colonies for the mother country, which were already weak, became confused.

By 1810 the colonies were in open revolt. As with the English colonists three decades earlier, the cause of the Latin American revolutionists seemed hopeless. In addition to the regular Spanish troops, they had to struggle against most of the wealthy Spanish settlers and the local Roman Catholic hierarchy. Eventually two brilliant young leaders, Simón Bolívar and José San Martín, emerged to overcome the seemingly impossible obstacles and to lead the South American revolutionists to success. By 1822 the independence of Spanish South America was won. In the same year the issue was decided in Spain's Central American colonies and in Mexico, which then included the southwest quarter of what is now the United States. In all the former Spanish colonies, republics were established, although a long period of troubled apprenticeship preceded the establishment of effective popular governments. Real stability has continued to be a problem for Central and South American nations.

In the huge Portuguese colony of Brazil, the independence movement was delayed by the flight of the Portuguese royal family to Brazil in 1807. However, the return of the king to Portugal six years after Napoleon's fall and the efforts of the Portuguese government to reimpose the colonial status on Brazil quickly fanned the embers of revolt into flame. In 1822 the Portuguese king's son, Pedro, whom he had left behind as regent, yielded to native pressure and declared himself king of independent Brazil. In all of free Latin America the Napoleonic Code was adopted as the basis of civil law, and the impact of the Enlightenment on political institutions was clearly visible.

6. SIGNIFICANCE OF THE FRENCH REVOLUTION AND NAPOLEON

The French Revolution and its Napoleonic sequel had a profound effect on the course of history. Like Pandora when she lifted the lid of that fateful box, they let loose forces and ideas that have influenced and shaken the world ever since, especially the revolutionary ideals of *Liberty, Equality, Fraternity*. Originally conceived in the eighteenth century by the philosophers of the Enlightenment, they were born materially in the American and French revolutions and spread by Napoleon.

In the era of the French Revolution, the ideal of *liberty* meant freedom from arbitrary authority— political, religious, economic, or social. It meant freedom of speech, press, conscience, assembly, person, and profession, and the sacredness of property. During the moderate first phase of the French Revolution, a great deal of progress toward these goals was made; in the tumultuous and bloody second phase, a good deal was lost. Under Napoleon's rule there was no political liberty. However, he claimed that the efficiency, prosperity, and honor of his regime more than made up for the lack of popular government, for which, he believed, the world was not yet ready.

Equality meant essentially equality under the law and equality of opportunity for gain and advancement. Generally, it did not apply to women, even though women played important roles during the Revolution and had hoped for gains that never came. It was only during the brief dominance of Robespierre that even partial social equality of all male citizens became a goal. Napoleon's law codes were a great boon to the more moderate kind of equality among men. The codes left women devoid of political rights and legally dependent on men.

Fraternity manifested itself in the mass movements (sometimes violent) for reform, in the comradeship in the conscripted armies, and above all in the new popular and dynamic spirit of nationalism. These forces, released by the American and French revolutions, spread first to the rest of Europe, then to Latin America, and eventually to the rest of the world. Much of the history of the world since the era of the French Revolution has revolved around these forces.

In another sense, the French Revolution and the Napoleonic era constituted a decisive political watershed marking the beginnings of modern times. The French Revolution opened the road to constitutional government and democratic institutions. Although there would be numerous reversals, constitutional governments and democratic institutions would generally flourish over the course of the succeeding two centuries and come to characterize politically modern times. The administrative bureaucracy and legal codes established during the Napoleonic era would be imitated and also come to characterize modern political systems.

Finally, the French Revolution and the Napoleonic era provided two images that would invite study and imitation throughout the nineteenth and twentieth centuries. The first image was that of the successful popular revolution. While the French Revolution was not the first revolution, it was the one that occurred in the heart of Western civilization and toppled not only the government but the major institutions of traditional society. This revolution would inspire revolutionaries and warn those representing the status quo for decades to come. The second image was that of Napoleon as a nationalistic, charismatic leader who could suddenly grasp power and exert his will with great effect. During the nineteenth and twentieth centuries, this powerful image would inspire individuals who envisioned themselves as potential Napoleons and people who yearned for easy, decisive solutions to deeply felt problems.

SUGGESTED READING

General

P. Geyl, *Napoleon, For and Against* (1949). Good study of changing interpretations of Napoleon.

J. C. Herold, *The Age of Napoleon* (1983). Entertaining, well-written survey.

R. Jones, *Napoleon. Man and Myth* (1977). A fine recent treatment.

G. Lefèbvre, *Napoleon*, 2 vols. (1969). Scholarly treatment by a leading authority.

F. Markham, *Napoleon* (1966). An excellent biography.

France

L. Bergeron, *France Under Napoleon* (1981). A good recent analysis.

R. B. Holtman, *The Napoleonic Revolution* (1967). Good on domestic policy and propaganda.

The Empire

D. Chandler, *The Campaigns of Napoleon* (1966). Focuses on military history.

O. Connelly, *Napoleon's Satellite Kingdoms* (1965). A good study of Napoleonic rule in Europe.

F. Markham, *Napoleon and the Awakening of Europe* (1965). A good study of Napoleon's influence outside of France.

W. S. Robertson, *The Rise of the Spanish-American Republics* (1965). Good brief account.

CHAPTER 42

Restoration and Reaction, 1815–1830

FIGURE 42.1. Cruikshank, "The Peterloo Massacre," 1819 This painting by George Cruikshank depicts the troops of the conservative British government breaking up a rally for liberal political reform, including demands for universal suffrage and religious freedoms. During the restoration, many European governments attempted to repress liberal movements. (The Mansell Collection)

The overthrow of Napoleon in 1815 brought to an end, in Europe at least, the heroic and tumultuous epoch that had begun in 1789 with the meeting of the Estates General. The intervening twenty-six years had been filled with great expectation, experimentation, turmoil, and war. Now there was disillusionment and weariness. The European royalty and aristocracy, at long last triumphant over revolutionary France, were determined to put an end not only to the Mirabeaus, Robespierres, and Napoleons but also to the ideas of the Enlightenment.

The returning holders of power—the monarchs, the aristocrats, the established Christian churches, and the elite of the governmental and military bureaucracies—generally subscribed to a conservatism that was dominant between 1815 and 1830 and that would remain a powerful force throughout the nineteenth century. Conservatives tended to believe that a hierarchical Christian society authoritatively guided by traditional monarchs, aristocrats, and clergy was time tested and best. Edmund Burke (1729–1797), Great Britain's most influential conservative thinker, and conservatives in general rejected the abstract rationalism of the Enlightenment and the reforms of the French Revolution. Any rapid change was suspect, and the attempt by the middle class to grasp political power was a presumptuous act by individuals who simply did not know how to rule. For conservatives the experience of the French Revolution was a lesson in what to avoid.

In order to achieve their conservative goals, to redraw territorial boundaries and to establish lasting stability in Europe, the leaders of the victorious powers gathered at the Austrian capital of Vienna in the autumn of 1814. To this conference also flocked representatives of every state in Europe, hundreds of dispossessed princes, agents of every conceivable interest, and adventurers.

1. THE CONGRESS OF VIENNA (1814–1815)

The Congress of Vienna was dominated by the four major victors over Napoleon (see Figure 42.2). Great Britain was represented by her able foreign minister, Lord Castlereagh. Prussia's mediocre king, Frederick William III, headed his own delegation, as did Russia's tsar, the idealistic young Alexander I. Austria's emperor, Francis I, played host to the assembled great. However, the real leader of the Austrian delegation—and, indeed, the dominant figure of the whole congress—was the Austrian chancellor, Prince Klemens von Metternich. As guiding principles on which to base their decisions, the conferees decided on "legitimacy" and "stability." By *legitimacy* they meant that in the redistribution of various territories, attention would be paid not to the desires or interests of the people concerned but to the claims of the victorious—the former and the future sovereigns. By *stability* they meant establishing and maintaining a balance of power within Europe, with particular focus on restraining France. Many of the decisions formalized at Vienna had already been made by the four major powers shortly before and after Napoleon's overthrow in April 1814 (see Map 42.1).

Thanks in no small measure to the presence of the clever and able Talleyrand, France, the cause of all the turmoil, got off lightly. Prussia would have severely punished and weakened France, but her three major colleagues were fearful of upsetting the balance of power. Already saddled with the restored Bourbons, France was merely reduced to almost the same boundaries it had had before the wars of the revolutionary era. The Congress of Vienna had originally imposed no indemnity on France. But because of Napoleon's return from Elba in the midst of the congress and his hundred-day fling that ended at Waterloo, the four great powers compelled France to cede the Saar Basin to Prussia, to pay an indemnity of 700 million francs, and to return the art treasures stolen by Napoleon from the various galleries of Europe. Allied forces were to occupy France until the indemnity was paid. To contain France within its frontiers and to discourage future French aggression, Prussia was given a sizable block of territory along the Rhine, the Austrian Netherlands (Belgium) was annexed to the Dutch Netherlands, and Piedmont was enlarged by the annexation of the city-state of Genoa.

The main powers, taking advantage of political changes that had occurred over the previous twenty-six years and trading among themselves,

FIGURE 42.2. Jean B. Isabey, "Congress of Vienna" The principle figures of the Congress of Vienna are portrayed by Jean Baptiste Isabey. From left to right: Metternich is standing before a chair, Castlereagh is sitting with crossed legs, and Talleyrand is sitting with his right arm on the table. (Culver Pictures)

received new territories. Great Britain gained several strategic islands and colonies, increasing her sea power and overseas dominance. Prussia added some areas in central Europe that made it more homogeneously German and Western. However, the Rhineland territory was not contiguous to the Prussian homeland—a situation that invited further aggression. Russia's acquisition of Polish territory made the great majority of the Polish-speaking people subjects of Russia and brought Russia farther into the heart of central Europe. Austria, in exchange for the Belgian Netherlands, took the two rich Italian provinces of Lombardy and Venetia. Its preeminence in Italy, together with the presidency over the German Confederation, made Austria the dominant power in central Europe. The Holy Roman Empire, which Napoleon had destroyed, was not restored, but in its place was erected the weak German Confedera-

tion under the permanent presidency of Austria. Napoleon's consolidation of the more than three hundred German states into thirty-nine was allowed to stand, bringing the German people that much more political unity.

The Congress of Vienna has been both admired and criticized by observers ever since 1815. Critics point out that the peoples and territories of Europe were moved about by the great powers at Vienna like pawns on a chessboard, in complete disregard for the wishes of the people or for the spirit of nationalism that was now an increasingly virile force. Instead of trying to deal constructively with the budding forces of liberalism and nationalism, the great powers tried to ignore or repress them. Admirers point out that the Vienna settlement was not vindictive toward France and did establish a reasonable balance of power, both of which contributed to a century of freedom from European-wide war. While one may not agree with the conservative goals of the conferees, a settlement was achieved at Vienna and at least temporarily maintained in succeeding years.

2. THE CONCERT OF EUROPE

Metternich and his colleagues, pleased with their work, set up machinery for perpetuating it. Conveniently at hand was the Holy Alliance, conceived by Alexander to establish and safeguard the principles of the Christian religion. Russia (Orthodox), Austria (Roman Catholic), and Prussia (Protestant), the three bastions of conservatism, were to form the nucleus of the alliance. All Christian states of Europe were invited to join, and only Great Britain and the Papal States did not. Metternich considered the Holy Alliance a "sonorous nothing" but saw in it an opportunity for influencing the tsar. Intended by Alexander I as a bulwark of Christianity, the Holy Alliance became a symbol of reaction and repression.

Much more earthly an agency for perpetuating the Vienna settlements was the Quadruple Alliance. This was a military alliance of Austria, Russia, Prussia, and Great Britain created in November 1815 for the purpose of guaranteeing for twenty years the territorial boundaries established by the Vienna settlement. Metternich was determined to make of the alliance an international military police force that would suppress any liberal or national movements. It was arranged that the four member powers should hold periodic congresses to carry out the purposes of the alliance.

The first congress was held at Aix-la-Chapelle in northwest Germany in 1818. The purpose was to arrange the withdrawal of occupation forces from French soil. Since France had demonstrated good behavior under the restored Bourbon king, Louis XVIII, it was not only freed of occupying forces but was admitted to the Quadruple Alliance. Congresses at Troppau in 1820 and at Laibach in 1821, both on Austrian soil, concerned themselves with an insurrection that had broken out in Naples against the tyrannical Bourbon king, Ferdinand I. An Austrian army was authorized to put down the insurrection and reestablish the

hated Ferdinand I on his throne. The Neapolitan liberal volunteers, no match for the Austrian regulars, were soon defeated and their leaders executed, imprisoned, or exiled. What turned out to be the last of the congresses met in 1822 at Verona to deal with a liberal revolt in Spain against the reactionary Ferdinand VII. With the sanction of the Congress of Verona a French army crossed the Pyrenees and easily put down the rebellion.

The first of the alliance powers to repudiate the Metternich system was Great Britain. At the Troppau congress, the British clearly indicated their opposition to interfering in the internal affairs of other states. When the Verona congress decided, over British protest, on intervention in Spain, Britain's representative withdrew from the congress.

The Metternich system soon received further blows, some from unexpected quarters. At the Congress of Verona, the like-minded Austrians, Russians, and Prussians had been alarmed not only by the rebellion in the Spanish homeland but also by the revolt of Spain's New World colonies. When the corrupt government of Ferdinand VII proved incapable of putting down the revolt, Alexander I, with Metternich's blessing, proposed to send a Russian fleet to help coerce the colonies. Great Britain, enjoying a lucrative trade with the rebellious colonies, did not wish to see them restored to Spanish dominion and commercial monopoly. The British minister, Canning, who had succeeded Castlereagh in 1822, proposed to the government of the United States that Great Britain and the United States issue a joint statement against interference by the "Holy Alliance" in the affairs of the Western Hemisphere. However, Secretary of State John Quincy Adams foresaw that the time might come when the United States would wish to invoke such a policy alone, perhaps even against Great Britain. In 1823, President Monroe announced what has come to be called the Monroe Doctrine: The United States would regard any interference on the part of European powers in the affairs of the Western Hemisphere as an "unfriendly act." The United States was at the time, of course, a new and relatively weak nation, but Canning's immediate support of the American policy killed any further thought of "Holy Alliance" intervention in the New World,

German Confederation Boundary

Kingdom of Prussia

Austrian Empire

Kingdom of Sardinia

Italian States
PIEDMONT
PAPAL STATES
KINGDOM OF TWO SICILIES
A PARMA
B MODENA
C LUCCA
D TUSCANY
E SAN MARINO

German States
PRUSSIA
1 HANOVER
2 OLDENBURG
3 MECKLENBURG-SCHWERIN
4 NASSAU
5 HESSE-CASSEL
6 HESSE
7 SAXONY
8 BADEN
9 WURTTEMBERG
10 BAVARIA AND PALATINATE

Map 42.1   EUROPE, 1815   As this map indicates, the settlement at the Congress of Vienna left France with its lands little changed from 1789, but now France was bordered by strengthened states: the Kingdom of the Netherlands, Prussia, and the Kingdom of Sardinia. The victorious powers gained territories, but a balance of power was maintained.

for Great Britain had unchallenged dominance of the seas. The Monroe Doctrine marked the beginning of active participation by the United States in affairs beyond its own immediate shores.

The next blow to Metternich's concert of Europe came when the Greeks turned against their Moslem Turkish overlords in the revolt of 1821–1829. The valiant efforts of the Greeks were not sufficient to resist the power of the Ottoman Empire. By 1827 they were on the point of being hopelessly crushed. However, the sympathies of the great powers were being aroused for the courageous Greeks. Russia, Great Britain, and France in particular displayed a growing concern over the events in Greece. Russia's Orthodox Christian religion was the same as that of the Greeks. Furthermore, the Russians had long desired Constantinople, which controlled Russia's natural strategic and commercial outlet to the Mediterranean. Great Britain was concerned over the possibility of Russia's dominance in the Near East. In addition, the ruling classes in Great Britain and France were steeped in the classical culture of ancient Greece. Lord Byron, the most popular literary figure in Europe, lost his life fighting as a volunteer for Greece. In 1827 these three powers, over Metternich's protest, intervened in the Greek revolt and defeated the Turks on land and sea. The Treaty of Adrianople in 1829 granted independence to most of the Greeks on the home peninsula and local autonomy to the Serbs and Rumanians. The successful revolt of the Greeks was a victory for the resurging revolutionary principles of liberalism and nationalism. The intervention of Russia, Great Britain, and France further weakened the already battered concert of Europe.

3. THE BOURBON RESTORATION IN FRANCE

When the victorious armies of the coalition powers entered France and deposed Napoleon in the spring of 1814, they brought "in their baggage" the members of the Bourbon royal family who had fled the Revolution. In their wake trooped the émigré nobility. A younger brother of the guillotined Louis XVI was placed on the throne as Louis XVIII. (The son of Louis XVI, who had died in prison in 1795, without having ruled, was considered to be Louis XVII.) The "restored" Bourbon king was now fifty-nine and too fat and gouty to walk unassisted. He had traveled much and unwillingly during the long, lean years of his exile. When Napoleon returned from Elba in 1815, Louis XVIII had to flee once more. After Waterloo he returned to his throne, which he considered "the most comfortable of armchairs," determined to do nothing that might force him to leave it again.

Upon assuming the throne, Louis XVIII issued a charter, or constitution, that retained Napoleon's administrative and legal system and civil and religious liberty. Lawmaking was placed in the hands of a two-chamber legislature. The upper house was made an aristocratic stronghold, and the lower house was elected by a highly restricted electorate. Only those who paid direct annual taxes of three hundred francs could vote; this limited the suffrage to about one hundred thousand out of a total population of nearly 30 million. The lower house could be prorogued, or dissolved, by the king. Since the king also appointed and controlled his own ministers and the host of civilian and military officials, carried on foreign relations, controlled the military forces, and enforced the laws, his power was only somewhat limited by the charter.

Louis XVIII set out to use his powers with moderation so that tranquillity might be restored. There were no wholesale punishments of revolutionary leaders. The peasant and bourgeois purchasers of church and noble lands were not dispossessed. However, most of the returned émigrés—largely from the highest ranks of the clergy and the nobility—were of a different spirit. They came back from their unhappy exile angry and vengeful, demanding their old privileges and indemnification for their lands. Their leader was the king's younger brother, the Comte d'Artois—a typical Bourbon who had "never learned anything and never forgotten anything." The reactionaries controlled both houses of the national legislature, since even in the lower elected house, suffrage restrictions heavily favored the aristocracy and the *nouveaux riches* bourgeoisie. Louis XVIII found it increasingly difficult to hold these fire-eating reactionaries in check. Shortly before he died in 1824, he warned his incorrigible brother of the danger to the Bourbon dynasty if he did not adopt a more moderate attitude.

Unfortunately, Charles X, as the Comte d'Artois now styled himself, was a stranger to moderation. He quickly aroused animosity against his regime to an explosive pitch. The Napoleonic generals who had brought so much glory to France were immediately retired from duty. An indemnity was voted the émigrés for their confiscated lands, the money to be raised by reducing the interest on government bonds from 5 percent to 3 percent. This angered the upper bourgeoisie, who were the chief bondholders. The peasants were alarmed by a proposed establishment of primogeniture, which seemed to endanger the principle of equality and the security of land titles. The Jesuits were brought back to France, and favors were bestowed on the Catholic church. Opposition mounted rapidly. By 1827 Charles X had lost his majority in both houses of the national legislature. Totally blind to the political realities of the day, he twice dissolved the lower chamber and attempted to force the election of a friendly majority by censoring the press and using official pressure on the electorate. The hostile majorities only increased in number. Finally in July 1830 the king in a set of ordinances dissolved the newly elected chamber, called for new elections, restricted the suffrage so drastically that only about twenty-five thousand very rich citizens could vote, and abolished completely the freedom of the press. These measures set off an uprising in Paris. The Parisian proletariat erected barricades in the streets that the disaffected rank and file of the army were "unable" to break. After three days of desultory fighting, the insurgents had the upper hand, and the last Bourbon king of France was on his way to exile in England.

4. RESTORATION AND REPRESSION IN THE GERMANIES

In central and eastern Europe, particularly in the Germanies, Italy, and Russia, the conservatives and the Metternich system were more secure. The Germanies in 1815 consisted of thirty-seven little states and two large ones—Prussia and Austria. In all of them the influence of Metternich was strong. The German Confederation was an improvement over the old Holy Roman Empire, which Napoleon had destroyed, only in the sense that Napoleon's consolidation of the more than three hundred states down to thirty-nine was allowed to stand. The Diet was only a gathering and debating place for the representatives of the rulers of the thirty-nine states. The confederation had no treasury and no army at its command. There was not even a flag to symbolize its German national character. Reactionary Austria enjoyed a permanent presidency over it.

The German nationalism and liberalism that existed in 1815 centered primarily in the little states, some of whose rulers defied Metternich by granting liberal constitutions. The national and liberal activities here were largely the work of university students and professors, who shortly after 1815 began to form *Burschenschaften*, or brotherhoods, for the purpose of promoting German nationalism, liberalism, and the Christian religion. In 1817 in commemoration of the three hundredth anniversary of Luther's publication of his Ninety-five Theses, the *Burschenschaften* staged a giant festival at Wartburg, where Luther had hidden and had begun his translation of the Bible. Although the festivities were primarily religious in character, enough enthusiasm for German nationalism and liberalism was displayed to fill Metternich with anxiety. The murder two years later of a reactionary propagandist by a fanatical student gave Metternich his opportunity to strike. Calling together the princes of the leading German states at Carlsbad, he joined them in drawing up a set of harsh decrees designed to crush the embryonic national and liberal movements. The *Burschenschaften* were outlawed. Strict censorship was established. Classrooms and libraries were supervised. Liberal students and professors were terrorized by spies and police. The Carlsbad Decrees succeeded in suppressing for a number of years this first outcropping of the revolutionary spirit in Germany since the overthrow of Napoleon.

In Prussia the militaristic, paternalistic, despotic Hohenzollerns reigned. Behind them stood the equally reactionary landed aristocracy, the *Junkers*. The Junkers served as officers in the Prussian army and filled the key posts in the civil service and administration. These military lords hated not only liberalism in any form but also German nationalism. They did not wish to see virile, martial Prussia contaminated by association with the lesser German states that were now infected with the French disease of liberalism. It was only in the economic field that German unity received any encouragement from Prussia. Because its territory was separated into two noncontiguous segments, Prussia in 1819 began making commercial treaties with its smaller German neighbors, providing for the free flow of trade among them. By 1834 nearly all the states of the German Confederation except Austria had joined the Prussian-sponsored *Zollverein* (customs union). Though it was not so intended, the *Zollverein* proved to be a forerunner of German political unity under Prussian leadership.

As was to be expected, conservatism reached its height in Austria. The spirit of the French Revolution and Napoleon, with the one exception of nationalism, had hardly touched the Hapsburg state and its feudal society. In addition to the natural conservatism of the Hapsburgs and their chief minister, Austria had a language problem that caused its rulers to fear liberalism and nationalism like the plague. Austria proper is German-speaking, but during the sixteenth, seventeenth, and eighteenth centuries the Hapsburgs had annexed territories inhabited by Hungarian (Magyar), Czech, Slovak, Ruthenian, Polish, Rumanian, Serb, Croat, and Slovene language groups. In 1815 two Italian-speaking provinces were added. Before 1789 these various language groups remained relatively quiet under their feudal lords, the Hapsburg dynasty, and the Roman Catholic church. In the wake of the French Revolution, they began to stir with national consciousness.

Metternich saw clearly that if this new force was not suppressed, the Hapsburg state would fall apart. Furthermore, nationalism unchecked would cause Austria to lose its dominance over Germany and Italy. The various German and Italian states would be drawn together into powerful national states from which Austria would be excluded, for most of the people in the Hapsburg state were neither German- nor Italian-speaking. When these facts are considered, it is not surpris-

ing that Austria in 1815 was the most reactionary state in Europe save Russia. In the Hapsburg provinces Metternich's police and spies were everywhere. Permission to enter or to leave the country was made very difficult, lest dangerous ideas be brought in from the West. Classrooms, libraries, bookstores, and organizations of all kinds were considered suspicious and closely supervised. Even music (in the country of Mozart and Beethoven) was censored for fear that musical notes would be used as a cryptic code for conveying revolutionary ideas. On the surface, these policies appeared for some time to succeed. Nevertheless, Metternich was aware that the Hapsburg state stood on shaky ground.

5. RESTORATION AND REPRESSION IN ITALY

Austria dominated Italy even more completely than Germany. Lombardy and Venetia were annexed outright. Modena, Parma, and Tuscany were ruled by Austrian princes. The Papal States and Naples were under Austria's protection and guidance in both domestic and foreign affairs. In all these states the deposed aristocracy and clericals trooped back, full of hatred for French institutions and for the Italian liberals who had cooperated with Napoleon (see Figure 42.3). Nearly all the Italian intelligentsia were soon in prison or in exile. In the Papal States the Inquisition and the Index were restored, and such Napoleonic innovations as street lighting were done away with. Of all the Italian states, only Piedmont in the extreme northwest was free of Austrian control, but even here the restored heads of the house of Savoy were so reactionary as to cause Metternich only joy.

6. CONSERVATISM IN GREAT BRITAIN

Although Great Britain had been for years a home of representative government, its government in 1815 was far from democratic. The suffrage was

FIGURE 42.3. **Repression in Italy** This illustration shows Italians being shot as suspected revolutionaries; it epitomizes the spirit of reaction and repression as the great powers of Europe tried to restore the old order and stifle the new currents of liberalism and nationalism. (Historical Pictures Service, Chicago)

so severely restricted by property qualifications that only about 5 percent of the adult males could vote. Furthermore, the industrial cities of the north, which had emerged since the last distribution of seats in Parliament, were not represented at all. Both houses of Parliament were therefore monopolized by the landed aristocracy. It must be remembered, however, that the cleavage between the middle class and the aristocracy was not so sharp in Great Britain as on the Continent. The law of primogeniture in Great Britain granted the eldest son the entire landed estate and permitted him alone to assume the title. The younger sons sought careers in the church, in the military, or in business. This process brought

about much intermingling between the upper and the middle classes. The long-sustained prosperity of British commerce had produced a merchant class wealthy enough to purchase respectability, lands, and sometimes titles. The aristocracy frequently invested in commercial enterprises and later in industry. These facts help to explain why the great political and social struggles in nineteenth-century Britain, though sometimes bitter, lacked the violence of those on the Continent.

A period of economic depression and unrest in Great Britain followed the ending of the Napoleonic wars in 1815. For twenty-two years, with only one brief interruption, Britain had been engaged in a desperate struggle with France, a struggle that was economic as well as military. Meanwhile, British industrial expansion had gone on apace. The war's end found British warehouses piled high with unsold goods. Thousands of returning veterans found no jobs. Strikes and riots, which had begun during Napoleon's blockade, increased. The conservative Tory party, which had seen the country through the war, was strongly entrenched in power. Both the Tories and the slightly more liberal Whigs were still badly frightened by the specter of French revolutionary Jacobinism. The government therefore took strong measures against the restless workers. The writs of habeas corpus were suspended. The climax came in 1819 when troops fired on a crowd that had assembled outside Manchester to listen to reform speeches. A number were killed and hundreds injured in this "Peterloo Massacre."

Within a few years, however, as the postwar crisis of depression and unrest eased, the Tory government yielded slightly to the pressure for reform. We have already seen how Foreign Secretary Canning by 1822 had deserted Metternich's reactionary concert of Europe and aided independence movements in Latin America and Greece. During the 1820s the navigation laws were somewhat relaxed and the tariff slightly lowered. The Combination Laws were partially repealed, permitting laborers to organize unions, though not to strike. The civil disabilities against nonconforming Protestants and Roman Catholics were removed, permitting them to participate in political life on an equal basis with Anglicans. These measures, however, welcome as they were, did not get at the fundamental issue: a broadening of popular participation in the government. The pressure for suffrage reform would continue to mount, particularly from the industrial bourgeoisie, which was rapidly gaining in wealth.

7. REACTION AND REPRESSION IN RUSSIA

Even Russia had not escaped the influence of the French Revolution and Napoleon. Russia had joined in the second, third, fourth, and fifth coalitions against France, had been invaded and ravaged as far as Moscow in 1812, and had played a major role in the wars of liberation against Napoleon in 1813–1814. Meanwhile, the young tsar, Alexander I, and many of his aristocratic young army officers had picked up romantic and liberal ideas from the West. But Russia was not yet ripe for Western liberalism. It was a vast agricultural nation with a feudal social structure and a very small urban bourgeoisie that could serve as a liberal base. The Orthodox Christian church, dominated by an upper clergy drawn from the aristocracy, was a handy governmental agency for controlling the masses. The unstable Alexander I soon fell under the influence of Metternich and of his own reactionary boyar magnates and repented of his liberalism.

There was no trace of romanticism whatever in Nicholas I, Alexander's younger brother, who succeeded him in 1825. Nicholas was a handsome, austere autocrat whose military career wedded him to the concepts of discipline and authority. A quixotic revolt by a group of young liberal officers on the occasion of his ascension to the throne and a full-scale revolt by his Polish subjects in 1831 further embittered him against liberalism in any form. Both revolts were crushed with an iron hand. For thirty years (1825–1855) Nicholas I ws to stand as the perfect symbol of absolute reaction and the armed guardian of the Metternich system. When at the end of the nineteenth century Russia did begin to yield to liberal and revolutionary forces, it was with disorder and violence.

8. CONSERVATISM AND THE CHALLENGE OF LIBERALISM

Between 1815 and 1830 the forces of conservatism were dominant. They acted both in reaction to the events of the French Revolution and the era of Napoleon and in accordance with their own ideology—a set of beliefs and policies in support of a traditional Christian, ranked, aristocratic society wedded to old institutions and suspicious of change. In the international field this conservatism was epitomized by Metternich's policies, the Holy Alliance, and the concert of Europe. In domestic politics, this conservatism was characterized by the restoration of power to the traditional monarchs and aristocrats, the renewed influence of

Christianity, and the suppression of liberal and nationalistic movements. Yet conservatives were faced with formidable opponents even during the early years after the fall of Napoleon. The struggle between conservatism and liberalism, which would last into the twentieth century, had just begun.

SUGGESTED READING

General

F. Artz, *Reaction and Revolution, 1814–1832* (1968). The standard survey of the period.

E. J. Hobsbawm, *The Age of Revolution, Europe 1789 to 1848* (1970). A good Marxist survey covering this period.

J. Weiss, *Conservatism in Europe, 1770–1945* (1977). A good analysis of conservatism in its broad context.

The Congress of Vienna

C. Brinton, *The Lives of Talleyrand* (1963). Sympathetic biography of one of the leading participants.

H. Kissinger, *A World Restored* (1964). An interesting, sympathetic interpretation.

H. Nicolson, *The Congress of Vienna: A Study in Allied Unity 1812–22* (1970). Excellent volume on the subject.

The Bourbon Restoration in France

A. Jardin and A. J. Tudesq, *Restoration and Reaction* (1984). Covers France well.

P. Mansel, *Louis XVIII* (1981). A good recent biography.

Reaction in Central Europe

T. Hamerow, *Restoration, Revolution, and Reaction: Economics and Politics in Germany, 1815–1871* (1958). A respected, difficult analysis encompassing the period.

A. J. P. Taylor, *The Hapsburg Monarchy, 1809–1918* (1965). Lively and scholarly.

Conservatism in Great Britain

N. Gash, *Aristocracy and People. Britain, 1815–1867* (1979). Balanced coverage.

Reaction and Repression in Russia

A. Palmer, *Alexander I: Tsar of War and Peace* (1974). A thorough biography.

A. Ulam, *Russia's Failed Revolutionaries* (1981). Contains a good analysis of the Decembrists.

CHAPTER 43

Liberalism and Revolution, 1830–1850

FIGURE 43.1 **The Reform Bill of 1832** This engraving from the April 15, 1832, issue of *Bell's Weekly Messenger* depicts the successful struggle to enact the liberal Reform Bill of 1832 in Great Britain. At the top, under the banner of reform, Whig leaders unite with the king to pass the bill. At the bottom, the British lion uses reform to defeat the fleeing Tories and the dragon representing the rotten-borough system. (The Mansell Collection)

During the Restoration years following the defeat of Napoleon, liberalism was suppressed by the conservatives who came back into power. Between 1830 and 1850 liberals gained a series of victories, often by way of revolutions or threatened revolutions, marking this period as a heyday for liberalism (see Map 43.1). By the early 1830s Greece, Belgium, and most of Spain's New World colonies had gained their freedom. The restored French Bourbons had been overthrown in a liberal revolt. In Great Britain the Reform Bill of 1832 marked a new liberal era. A new constitution in 1834 brought liberal institutions to Spain. Liberal revolts and movements had at least raised their heads in Poland, Italy, and parts of Germany. By 1850 liberal institutions had spread and revolutions, almost all of which included strong liberal elements, had occurred in nearly every country of continental Europe.

1. GENERAL NATURE OF NINETEENTH-CENTURY LIBERALISM

Liberalism is a difficult term to define. It has various shades and from time to time changes its complexion. During the nineteenth century, liberalism had developed into an ideology—a loose set of beliefs about the world and how it should be.

The roots of liberalism stretch back through the French Revolution and the Enlightenment to the seventeenth-century political thoughts of John Locke and others. At the base of liberalism was a belief in individualism. Liberals optimistically believed that individuals, unaided and free from outside forces or institutions, should pursue their own interests. Individuals deserved equality before the law and the right to embark on careers open to talent. Government should be constitutional and based on popular sovereignty. The people should be represented by an elected legislature, to whom government ministers were responsible. Government should be limited in its powers, with such individual freedoms as freedom of the press, of speech, and of assembly guaranteed. The role of the government should be that of a passive police officer, enforcing laws

and contracts. Government should interfere in economic life as little as possible, leaving that realm to private enterprise. Liberals were also anticlerical; that is, they opposed interference in government by organized religion. During the first half of the nineteenth century, liberals were usually nationalists, since nationalism at that time was primarily concerned with freeing peoples from alien rule and uniting them under one flag, and nationalism seemed consistent with popular sovereignty, constitutional government, and people's rights. Liberals, particularly during the first half of the nineteenth century, were not democrats; liberals wanted to limit the right to vote to those holding wealth and the educated. Only later in the nineteenth century did liberals begin to favor universal male suffrage.

Liberals typically came from the middle class—the commercial and industrial bourgeoisie, the professionals, and the intellectuals. Their chief opponents were the vested interests of traditional society—the aristocracy, the clergy, and the military—seeking to retain their favored positions. The peasantry was still generally conservative, strongly influenced by the clergy and sometimes by the aristocracy, and not very active in politics. Liberals were sometimes contemptuous of the propertyless masses below, forming alliances with them against conservatives only so far as necessary. Middle-class liberals' contempt for those below them was often a mask for fear; their contempt of the aristocrats above them was tinged with envy.

Liberals stood in contrast to conservatives. Liberals were optimistic about the individual; conservatives were pessimistic. Liberals had great faith in reason; conservatives argued that reason was too abstract. Liberals favored many of the ideas and reforms of the Enlightenment and French Revolution; conservatives attacked them. Liberals valued the individual over the society; conservatives felt the individual was secondary. For liberals the state was an agent of the people; for conservatives the state was a growing organism not to be tampered with.

After 1850 the nature of liberalism would change. The outcomes of the revolutions occurring between 1848 and 1850 were a blow to liberals. As commerce and industry spread, the bourgeoisie

Map 43.1   EUROPEAN REVOLTS, 1820–1831 AND 1848–1849   The first map indicates the location and dates of revolts, both major and minor, taking place between 1820 and 1831. The second map indicates the location of revolutions between 1848 and 1849. While the specifics of each outburst differed, most involved demands for liberal reform. Together, these maps reveal the geographical breadth of revolutionary activity during this period.

acquired wealth and power, and soon the vested interests of this class made it more hostile to rapid political and social changes. Its place in movements for political and social change was taken by the industrial working class, which was slowly becoming politically active. Groups deriving from the working classes, lower middle classes, and intelligentsia began to advocate greatly increased government intervention in economic affairs on behalf of the masses as well as the participation of the masses in political life. More progressive advocates of liberalism joined these groups in arguing for greater democratization of political life and government intervention in economic and social affairs. This, however, takes us beyond the primary concerns of this chapter. Liberalism flowered between 1830 and 1850, and this story needs to be told.

2. POLITICAL AND SOCIAL REFORM IN GREAT BRITAIN

During the 1820s Great Britain had already taken some moderate steps on the road to liberal reform (see pp. 541–542), but these steps did not go to the heart of the matter—broadening the franchise. Pressures mounted on the conservative Tories to effect electoral reform, but they were unwilling or unable to do it. Finally in 1830 the aristocratic but more liberal Whigs, long out of power, drove the Tory government from office.

The new prime minister, Earl Grey, immediately introduced and forced through Parliament the Reform Bill of 1832. This bill redistributed the seats of the House of Commons, taking away many from the "rotten boroughs" (once-important towns that had dwindled in population or had even disappeared) and giving them to the industrial cities of the north. The suffrage was extended to all those who owned or rented property with an annual value of ten pounds. It is estimated that the number of eligible voters was thereby increased from approximately four hundred and fifty thousand to eight hundred thousand out of a total population of some 16 million. Although on the surface the Reform Bill of 1832 appears innocuous, it represents a great turning point in British history. The long era of dominance of the conservative landed aristocracy was ending and that of more liberal property owners, including the commercial and industrial bourgeoisie, had begun. The supremacy of the House of Commons over the House of Lords, which had opposed the Reform Bill, was established. A new period of political and social reform had opened.

Both political parties recognized the new era. The Whig party, supported by the industrial bourgeoisie but containing a right wing of liberal aristocrats and left wing of intellectual radicals, changed its name to the Liberal party. For the next half century the Liberals were often in power, under the leadership of such personalities as Lord Grey, Lord John Russell, Viscount Palmerston, and eventually William E. Gladstone. The Tory party was still predominantly the party of the landed aristocracy, but it contained some bourgeois elements, and its more liberal wing, led first by Sir Robert Peel and later by Benjamin Disraeli, was now in ascendancy. The somewhat discredited "Tory" designation was changed to "Conservative."

Both parties, conscious of the rising importance of public opinion, supported a series of reforms. In 1833 slavery was abolished in the British Empire with compensation for slave owners. The Municipal Corporations Act applied the principles of the Reform Bill of 1832 to local government. The old penal code was reformed, reducing the number of capital offenses to three and generally softening the punishment of criminals. The penny post increased the circulation of mail and literature. Parliament granted small but gradually increasing subsidies to the schools, most of which were run by the Anglican church. Between 1833 and 1847 Parliament passed a series of laws that prohibited the employment in textile mills of children under nine and limited the hours of older children and of women to ten hours a day. The employment of women and children in underground mines was prohibited. In 1846 the Corn Laws (the import tariff on grain), long opposed by liberals and the object of a major reform movement, were repealed, reducing the price of bread.

These reforms were not the work of the masses but of wealthy middle-class and aristocratic liberals along with a few intellectual radicals. The only reform movement initiated by the laboring classes in this period was the Chartist movement (see Figure 43.2). The hard-pressed urban workers, bitterly aware that they had been bypassed by the

Reform Bill of 1832 and that they were not sharing in the unprecedented national prosperity, were dissatisfied with the reforms of the bourgeois liberals. In 1838 working-class leaders drew up a People's Charter, which demanded (1) universal male suffrage, (2) the secret ballot, (3) removal of property qualifications for members of Parliament, (4) pay for members of Parliament, (5) annual elections, and (6) equal electoral districts. The charter was twice presented to Parliament and twice summarily rejected. In 1848, the Chartists planned a huge petition and demonstration in London. The frightened government prepared to use force. However, only a few mild disorders followed the third rejection, and the movement came to an end. Nevertheless, the Chartist movement had its influence. The most immediate result of the movement was to make both political parties aware of the growing influence of the working classes and of the advisability of winning their favor. In the following decades, all the demands in the charter were enacted into law.

3. LIBERAL REVOLUTIONS IN BELGIUM AND FRANCE

The year 1830 was a bad one for conservatives in Belgium and France. The union forced upon Belgium and the Netherlands at Vienna had never been a happy one, and Belgian discontent with Dutch rule had been mounting for fifteen years. In addition to differences in language, the Belgians were Roman Catholic, whereas the Dutch were predominantly Calvinist. The Belgian economy was based on industry, the Dutch on commerce. Belgium, more populous than the Netherlands, was not given its fair share of representation in the government. When the halfhearted efforts of the Dutch failed to suppress the revolt, Austria and Russia threatened to intervene in the interests of legitimacy and tranquillity. They were deterred by British and French support of Belgian independence, which was therefore achieved. Belgium soon adopted a liberal constitution and would remain a liberal nation throughout the nineteenth century.

The July Revolution in France was an even more serious blow to conservatism. Liberals and the people of Paris had toppled the reactionary

FIGURE 43.2.   Chartist Print   This print shows Chartists in a powerful but peaceful procession in London. (The Mansell Collection)

regime of Charles X, the last of the Bourbons. There was strong sentiment to form a republic, but a coalition of liberal legislators and leaders of the wealthy bourgeoisie wanted only a constitutional monarchy. They set themselves up as a provisional government and named a new king: Louis Philippe (1830–1848), head of the house of Orléans and a cousin of the departed Bourbon.

Louis Philippe, recognizing that a new era had come to France, catered to the rich. He assumed the role of the Citizen King, casting aside the trappings of royalty and donning those of the Parisian upper middle class. His eighteen-year reign came to be called the bourgeois monarchy (see Figure 43.3). His twofold policy, from which he never veered, was order and prosperity at home and peace abroad. One of his first acts was to lower the taxpaying requirements for voting from three hundred francs to two hundred francs per year. This act raised the electorate from approximately

one hundred thousand to two hundred fifty thousand in a nation of some 32 million people and placed political control in the hands of the wealthy. Louis Philippe's chief minister during the 1840s was the historian François Guizot. He was a thoroughgoing liberal. He believed in government by the property-owning classes, particularly the bourgeoisie. He therefore opposed any further extension of the suffrage, even to members of the intelligentsia like himself.

Beneath the surface, problems simmered. The national prosperity was not shared by the working class, who suffered the usual hardships, insecurity, and maladjustments that accompanied the advent of industrialization. Slums mushroomed in Paris and the industrial cities of the northeast. Workers clamored for the right to vote and the right to organize unions but got neither. Poor harvests, financial crises, and growing unemployment in 1846 and 1847 heightened the frustration.

4. THE REVOLUTION OF 1848 IN FRANCE

The mounting discontent came to a climax in February 1848 when the government prohibited the holding of a reform banquet. Street brawling broke out in Paris. Louis Philippe attempted to quiet people by dismissing Guizot, but the appeasement failed. A shot fired during a brawl between a mob and the troops guarding the residence of Guizot unnerved the troops, who fired a murderous volley into the mob and set off a full-scale insurrection. Barricades flew up all over Paris, and when the disaffected national guardsmen began going over to the rebels, Louis Philippe followed Guizot into exile in Great Britain.

The working classes of Paris had triumphed, but only for a fleeting moment. A group of bourgeois liberals led by Alphonse de Lamartine hastily set up a provisional government that was republican in sentiment but in which the only prominent radical member was the socialist Louis Blanc. The provisional government immediately called for the election by universal male suffrage of an assembly to draw up a new constitution. Under the pressure of the Paris populace, the provisional government admitted the workingmen to the national guard, thereby arming them, and set up emergency-relief national workshops. The workshops, however, were a parody of those outlined by Louis Blanc, who cried that they were deliberately planned so as to ensure their failure. Workers of all kinds were assigned to hastily arranged projects, and when more workers enrolled than could be used, the surplus workers were paid almost as much to remain idle. Tens of thousands rushed to Paris to join the workshops. The resulting demoralization of labor and the cost to the taxpayers thoroughly frightened all property owners, the peasants as well as the bourgeoisie. The elections held in April 1848 resulted in an overwhelming victory for the conservative republicans and limited monarchists, in part thanks to the conservatism of the landowning peasants, who constituted the great majority of the French population. The socialists were crushed. Even in Paris, their only real stronghold, they won a mere handful of seats.

One of the first acts of the newly elected constitutional assembly was to abolish the national workshops. The workers were told either to join the army or to go look for work in the provinces. The desperate Paris working class resorted to arms and the barricades: "Better to die from bullets than from starvation!" For four days all-out war raged in the streets of Paris between the working class, armed with national guard rifles, and the regular army of the conservative constitutional assembly, using artillery in addition to small arms. When the last barricade had been destroyed, some fifteen hundred, mostly workingmen, had been killed. Several hundred were sent overseas to French colonial prisons. Louis Blanc fled to Great Britain. The bloody "June Days" widened the cleavage between radical urban Paris and conservative rural France—a cleavage that has long complicated France's public life.

The inexperienced constitutional assembly hurriedly drew up a constitution establishing the Second French Republic. (The First French Republic had been declared by the revolutionists in 1792 and had been overthrown by Napoleon in 1804.) Legislative power was given to a single-chamber legislature elected by universal male suffrage. All executive and administrative powers were placed in the hands of a president, also elected by universal male suffrage. The first presidential election, in December 1848, resulted in a sweeping victory for Louis Napoleon Bonaparte, nephew of Napoleon Bonaparte, as president. It took this ambitious and clever politician only three years to destroy the weak constitution and to take power in a coup d'état.

The Revolution of 1848 in France involved the first violent reaction of the urban working class against bourgeois liberalism. The working class was too small as yet to make any headway outside Paris. The revolution shattered against the solid mass of landowning peasantry allied with the propertied bourgeoisie. Its bloody suppression left a heritage of bitterness that would cloud the future of France.

5. THE REVOLUTION OF 1848 IN CENTRAL EUROPE

The February explosion in Paris set central Europe aflame with revolt (see Figure 43.4). However, the Revolution of 1848 in central Europe was a rising

FIGURE 43.3. **Daumier, "The Chamber of Deputies"** This print by the French artist Honoré Daumier presents a satirical view of the French Chamber of Deputies during Louis Philippe's July Monarchy. This governmental body, though clearly more liberal than its predecessor under Charles X, was dominated by the relatively wealthy, satisfied upper classes. (The Art Institute of Chicago)

of the intelligentsia and the middle classes with a little support from the working class. Furthermore, in 1848 the cause of liberalism in central Europe was entwined with that of nationalism. The two forces frequently conflicted with each other, nationalism proving to be the more virile of the two.

The most crucial center of revolution was Vienna. This beautiful metropolis was the seat of the Hapsburg government, which not only ruled over the various language groups of the Austrian Empire but also dominated both the German Confederation and Italy. When early in March 1848 news of the events in Paris arrived in Vienna, the long-repressed student liberals began rioting in the streets and clamoring for an end to the Metternich

system. As the uprising gained in momentum, Metternich was forced to flee for his life. The Hapsburg emperor, Ferdinand I, hastily abolished the repressive laws, ended serfdom, and promised constitutional representative government. However, he too was soon forced to flee his own capital. Meanwhile, the Magyars in Hungary, under the leadership of the eloquent Louis Kossuth, set up a liberal autonomous Hungary. The Czechs did the same in Bohemia and called for a Pan-Slavic congress to meet at Prague. In Austria's Italian provinces of Lombardy and Venetia the rebellious populace drove the Austrian garrisons into defensive fortresses and declared their independence. By June 1848 it appeared that the Hapsburg Empire would become liberalized, fall apart along

FIGURE 43.4. Revolution in Germany In central Europe in 1848, liberal sentiment emerged in the form of public demonstrations by the intelligentsia—particularly the university students. Here, in June of 1848, German students convene at Wartburg, the castle that had once served as a refuge for Martin Luther. (Copyright Staatsbibliothek, Berlin)

national (language group) lines, or both.

In Berlin, the capital of Prussia, the news from Paris and Vienna set liberals demonstrating in the streets. The vacillating Hohenzollern king, Frederick William IV, promised a liberal constitution and support for German national unity. As in Paris, an unauthorized volley into the mob set off bloody street fighting, which the king ended by making further concessions to the liberals. Hohenzollern Prussia, like Hapsburg Austria, appeared for the moment to be on the road to liberal government.

Meanwhile, in the rest of the German states a group of self-appointed liberals called for a pop-

ularly elected assembly to meet at Frankfurt to construct a liberal German nation. The two questions confronting the Frankfurt Assembly were whether the German-speaking portions of the multilingual Hapsburg Empire should be included in the projected German nation and who should head the new nation. Tied in with the Austrian question was that of religion. With Austria (and Bohemia, which was alleged to be predominantly German), the Roman Catholics would predominate, and without Austria and Bohemia, the Protestants. For eleven precious months these knotty problems were debated. Eventually Austria virtually excluded itself by refusing to consider coming into the new German nation without its non-German provinces. By a narrow margin it was decided to offer the emperorship to the king of Prussia. But now it was too late. The situation in Vienna and Berlin had drastically changed.

In Austria the inexperience and weakness of the liberals and the rivalries and conflicts among the various language groups played into the hands of the Hapsburgs. Skillfully playing off one group against another, the Austrian rulers beat down the liberal and national revolts one after the other. In Hungary they had the help of the reactionary Nicholas I of Russia, whose army crushed the rebels.

In Prussia, too, the liberals were weak and inexperienced. The unstable Frederick William IV, after his first uncertainty, gradually fell under the influence of his militaristic and reactionary Junker advisers. Further stiffened by the news from Vienna that the Hapsburgs had regained their autocratic position, he spurned the German crown offered him by the Frankfurt Assembly and replaced the constitution drawn up by Prussian liberals with one that was a travesty of liberalism.

The Hohenzollerns' rejection of the crown of a united liberal Germany blasted the hopes of the Frankfurt Assembly. When a few of the most determined attempted to continue their efforts, they were dispersed by Prussian troops.

6. REVOLUTION IN ITALY

On the Italian peninsula 1848 was a year of revolution. These revolts reflected an already long history of liberal and nationalistic movements in Italy. Soon after 1815 Italian nationalists began to form secret societies, called *Carbonari* (charcoal burners), which met at night around charcoal fires to plot freedom from Austrian and local tyranny and to plan for national unification. In 1821 revolts erupted in Naples, Sicily, and Piedmont, but all were short-lived. In the early 1830s a romantic young intellectual, Giuseppe Mazzini (1805–1872), organized the Young Italy society, which was dedicated to the task of achieving a free, united Italian nation. Although the first uprisings inspired by the Carbonari and Young Italy were crushed by Austrian arms, the Italian national movement, once aroused, could not so easily be suppressed.

In 1848 revolutions occurred in Sicily, Naples, Piedmont, and Tuscany. By 1849 republics had been established in Rome and Venice, and other Italian states had adopted liberal constitutions. Yet the time for the permanent overthrow of Austrian rule and the unification of Italy had not yet arrived. Austrian arms (and in Rome, French arms) prevailed. It would be another ten years before liberalism and nationalism, under the leadership of Piedmont, would gain a more lasting victory in Italy.

7. AN ASSESSMENT

The struggles between liberals and conservatives, which had resulted in several liberal victories since 1830, came to a climax with the revolutions of 1848. Economic turmoil, demands for liberal reform, nationalistic sentiments, and ineptitude by frightened governments combined to spell a series of stunning victories for revolutionaries in almost every major country in Europe. The major exceptions were England, which had compromised in response to demands for liberal reform, and Russia, which remained the bastion of reaction. Once in power, revolutionaries initiated major reforms, most of which fit well with the recognized canons of liberalism.

Nevertheless, the revolutionaries' victories were short-lived. By 1850 the conservative forces of order had regained control. Louis Napoleon, soon to be Napoleon III, sat as president in France. The Prussian king regained control over his lands and ended hopes for a liberal unified German nation. In Austria and Hungary the Hapsburgs were again in power, just as they were in their Italian lands. Liberalism and nationalism were not yet strong enough to form new, lasting governments in these areas.

Several factors account for the defeat of liberal and nationalist forces, though the situation differed in each case. First, the alliance between middle-class liberals, radicals, socialists, artisans, and workers was one of convenience. Once revolutionary forces were in power, the interests of the various groups were too divergent for the alliance to hold. This division was most clearly evident in France, where the frightened middle class and conservative peasantry broke with the Parisian working classes, as revealed by the outcome of the elections and the bloody June Days. Second, liberalism and nationalism were forces that worked together when out of power; once in power they often were at cross-purposes. This lack of harmony between liberalism and nationalism was particularly so in central Europe where the aspirations of German, Polish, Magyar, Croatian, Serbian, and other nationalities conflicted with efforts to form new governments with liberal institutions. Third, the strength of conservatism and the forces of order should not be underestimated. With industrialization only beginning in central Europe, the main source of liberal strength, the industrial middle class, and an important source of revolutionary urban discontent, the working class, were weak. Revolutionary liberal leaders were inexperienced, particularly in central Europe and Italy. Once the shock of initial defeat was over, experienced conservatives marshalled their resources, and forces of order overcame the now divided revolutionary forces.

The reestablished governments had learned lessons from 1848 and maintained themselves with new vigor. In a few cases liberal reforms initiated between 1848 and 1850 were retained, and in other cases those reforms in modified forms would be passed in succeeding years. But the great period of revolutionary liberalism ended in 1850.

SUGGESTED READING

General

W. L. Langer, *Political Upheaval, 1832–1852* (1969). Excellent survey of the period.

Liberalism

G. de Ruggiero, *History of European Liberalism* (1959). A classic study.

J. S. Schapiro, *Liberalism: Its Meaning and History* (1958). Good brief summary; includes readings.

Reform in Great Britain

D. Beales, *From Castlereagh to Gladstone, 1815–1885* (1969). A useful study of political history.

M. Brock, *The Great Reform Act* (1974). Solid, scholarly, respected.

D. Thompson, *The Chartists: Popular Politics in the Industrial Revolution* (1984). A thorough, recent study.

The Bourgeois Monarchy in France

D. Pinkney, *The French Revolution of 1830* (1972). Excellent study of the topic.

J. B. Wolf, *France, 1814–1919: The Rise of a Liberal Democratic Society.* (1963). Excellent survey.

Central Europe and Italy

I. Deak, *The Lawful Revolution: Louis Kossuth and the Hungarians, 1848–9* (1979). Excellent study of the individual and the revolution.

T. Hamerow, *Restoration, Revolution, Reaction 1815–1871* (1966). Highly respected analysis of Germany.

Gaetano Salvemini, *Mazzini* (1957). Excellent introduction to Mazzini's ideas.

The Revolutions of 1848

G. Duveau, *1848: The Making of a Revolution* (1967). Excellent study of the 1848 revolutions in France.

L. B. Namier, *1848: The Revolution of the Intellectuals* (1964). An eminent historian shows how nationalism wrecked the liberal movement.

P. Robertson, *The Revolutions of 1848: A Social History* (1960). Scholarly and lucid.

P. Stearns, *1848: The Revolutionary Tide in Europe* (1974). A good summary.

CHAPTER 44
The Industrial Revolution

FIGURE 44.1.   François Bonhomme, "Workshop with Mechanical Sieves," 1859   This realistic painting of a factory interior in France shows the mixture of raw material (zinc ore), machines, and division of labor that epitomized the Industrial Revolution. Men, women, and children work together in this dismal environment; but the men have the more skilled jobs (a foreman sits in the rear to the left), while the women and children are assigned to the less skilled jobs (sorting and splitting chunks of ore). (Conservatoire National des Arts et Métiers)

The term *Industrial Revolution* refers to the vast economic and social changes initiated in Great Britain during the last few decades of the eighteenth century and spreading to the Continent and other parts of the world during the nineteenth and twentieth centuries. It involved a shift from production by individuals alone or in small groups using hand tools powered by muscles, wind, and water to production by organized groups of people in factories using machinery powered by steam. These changes in the methods of production resulted in sustained economic growth. In the process of industrializing, nations experienced rapid population growth and a general shift from a rural society based on agriculture to an urban society based on manufacturing. Along with the French Revolution, the Industrial Revolution set in motion changes that would transform almost all aspects of life in the West during the nineteenth and twentieth centuries.

1. THE COURSE OF THE INDUSTRIAL REVOLUTION

The Industrial Revolution began in Great Britain for several reasons. Demand for the production of goods in Great Britain was growing rapidly during the eighteenth century, thanks to relatively widespread domestic prosperity, a growing population, and abundant markets within Britain's large colonial empire. Great Britain was well positioned to meet this growing demand for goods. It had an abundance of conveniently located raw materials, such as coal and iron. Investment capital amassed from merchants and landowners was available to enterprising entrepreneurs through family connections, partnership arrangements, and banks. Thanks to their leading role in the eighteenth-century agricultural revolution, Britain's farmers could more efficiently produce food for urban populations (see pp. 466–467). A large, mobile force of skilled and unskilled workers provided industrial entrepreneurs with a cheap supply of labor. Hindrances to commerce and industry so common in other countries were not present to the same degree in Great Britain. British transportation facilities were good, there were fewer governmental restrictions on commerce, and wealthy citizens did not disdain involvement in commerce and industry. Britain's government had been stable since 1689 and was strongly influenced by capitalistic landowners, merchants, and bankers.

British inventors and entrepreneurs responded to these conditions by developing new machines, sources of power, transportation facilities, and factories. These new developments increased production and trade tremendously and made Great Britain an early leader in the Industrial Revolution. By the middle of the nineteenth century, Great Britain was the first industrialized society. It was urbanized, covered with railway lines and canals, and dotted with factories. It produced far greater quantities of textiles, metals, and machines than any other country.

During the eighteenth century, nations on the Continent lacked this combination of circumstances so conducive to British industrialization. In addition, between 1789 and 1815 the Continent suffered from the economic, social, and political turmoil of the French revolutionary and Napoleonic periods. After 1815, and particularly after 1830, the Industrial Revolution spread, first to Belgium, shortly thereafter to France, parts of Germany, and the United States, and later to other areas of Europe. At first Continental entrepreneurs copied British inventions and imported skilled British laborers and technicians. Governments recognized the British lead and became more directly involved in promoting industrialization by supporting the construction of railways, subsidizing certain industries, and erecting protective tariffs for domestic industries. By the end of the nineteenth century, countries that once lagged far behind Great Britain were competing successfully for industrial markets.

2. TECHNOLOGY AND TRANSPORTATION

Probably the most dramatic change the Industrial Revolution brought about was the continual creation of new technology and transportation facilities (see Figure 44.2). A virtual explosion of inventions increased productivity and mechanized productions, above all in textiles, mining, and metallurgy. The steam engine provided a vast new

Figure 44.2. Railroad, Ship, and Factories This nineteenth-century print shows the outward signs of the Industrial Revolution: railroads, steamships on canals, and smoke-belching factories. (The Bettmann Archive)

source of reliable power. New roads, canals, and especially railroads provided regular, inexpensive means of transportation for people and materials.

The cotton textile industry was the first to become mechanized. In 1733 John Kay invented the flying shuttle, which doubled the speed at which cloth could be woven. In 1764 James Hargreaves hitched eight spindles to his wife's spinning wheel instead of one. The result was the far more efficient spinning jenny (named after his daughter Jenny). The number of spindles was soon multiplied. Five years later, Richard Arkwright patented the water frame, a system of rollers driven by water power, which spun a much finer and firmer thread than the jenny. In 1779 Samuel Crompton, combining the principles of the spinning jenny and the water frame, produced the hybrid spinning mule—a great improvement over both. In 1785 Edmund Cartwright invented the power loom.

The mechanization of both spinning and weaving greatly increased demand for cotton. In 1793 a young American, Eli Whitney, invented the cotton gin, which helped meet this demand. Removing the seeds from cotton fiber by hand was a tedious process; one person could separate only five or six pounds a day. Cotton was therefore grown only in small patches. Whitney's gin not only made possible an adequate supply of cotton for Britain's mills but also brought into existence the huge cotton plantations worked by black slaves in the American South.

Meanwhile, better sources of power were being developed. In 1769 James Watt significantly improved on earlier, inefficient steam engines and invented the first steam engine that could be used to drive machinery. The power that could be generated by the steam engine was almost unlimited.

Constant improvements were made in the mining of coal and the production of iron, crucial for heavy industrialization. As large quantities of relatively inexpensive coal and iron became available, still better machines were produced and a sufficient supply of fuel was available to drive them.

An integral part of the Industrial Revolution was the improvement of transportation and communications. Without both, sufficient quantities of raw materials to feed the hungry machines and adequate markets to absorb the finished products would not have been available. Moreover, the massive population shifts accompanying industrialization would have been much more difficult.

The last decades of the eighteenth century and the first decades of the nineteenth century were a time of road and canal building in Great Britain, France, and the United States. Around the turn of the century Thomas Telford and John McAdam in Great Britain pioneered in the construction of well-drained and surfaced roads. In Great Britain canals were particularly useful for transporting coal. In the United States completion of the Erie Canal in

1825 opened up the Great Lakes region to lucrative world communications and ensured the primacy of New York City as the chief port and metropolis of the United States.

A more dramatic revolution in transportation came with the application of the steam engine to locomotion. In 1807 Robert Fulton demonstrated the practicability of the steamship by steaming his *Clermont* the one hundred fifty miles up the Hudson from New York to Albany in thirty-two hours. In 1825 George Stephenson in Great Britain convincingly demonstrated the usefulness of the locomotive by hauling a train of thirty-four cars twenty-five miles at twelve miles an hour. By the middle of the nineteenth century, railway lines covered Great Britain and were spreading rapidly on the Continent and in North America. The railroad transported people and material, opened up areas to commerce and urban growth, constituted a major source of demand for industrial products such as coal and iron, and symbolized the spread of the new industrialized society.

3. THE FACTORY SYSTEM

Many of the components of the Industrial Revolution were brought together by the development of the factory system. Industrial capitalists invested considerable funds in machines, buildings, and raw materials. They trained workers to do specific jobs in conjunction with artificially powered machines, which increasingly determined the pace and nature of the work. Industrial capitalists organized the process of producing goods into a series of steps and specialized tasks. Their new factories pumped out unprecedented quantities of manufactured goods.

Before the factory system was instituted, goods were produced either by craft guilds or under the domestic, or "putting out," system. (See Chapter 36.) Under this system workers did as much or as little work as they wished without supervision. The operations were necessarily small in scale, much time was lost distributing the raw materials from cottage to cottage and collecting the finished products, and uniformity of quality was virtually impossible to attain.

The spread of the factory system spelled the end of the domestic system of manufacturing. The rise of the factory system resulted in a tremendous growth of productivity in manufacturing and a seemingly fantastic increase of manufactured goods. Artisans, although not immediately displaced, found it increasingly difficult to compete with factories that were producing similar products much more rapidly and inexpensively. As the factory system took hold, hastily and cheaply built living quarters for workers and their families were crowded around factories. This factory system was the origin of the modern mill town and industrial city. It also contributed to the dramatic urbanization of industrial societies in the nineteenth century and fundamental changes among social classes in these societies.

4. SOCIAL CHANGES

Population Growth and Urbanization

A large variety of far-reaching social changes are related to the Industrial Revolution. The broadest changes were demographic. Population increased dramatically. In Great Britain population grew from about 9 million in 1780 to almost 21 million in 1850. European population as a whole rose from about 188 million in 1800 to 266 million in 1850. The exact causes for this explosion of population are difficult to pinpoint, but it was probably a result of a declining death rate (thanks to a decline in epidemics and an increase of food supplies) and a rise in the birth rate (caused by an earlier departure from home, earlier marriage, and earlier child bearing in an increasingly mobile population).

A more direct result of industrialization was the shift of population from rural to urban areas and the growth in size and number of cities. In England and Wales in 1800 about 17 percent of the population lived in cities of over twenty thousand inhabitants. By 1850 the figure grew to about 35 percent. This pattern was being repeated in other areas of Europe as they industrialized. The consequences were all too apparent. Already overcrowded, devoid of mass transportation facilities, equipped at best with vastly inadequate sanitation facilities, the cities became more densely packed and unhealthy each year. At the same time, these cities exhibited a vibrancy and image of opportunities that continued to attract people. Often the alternatives available in the countryside were even less appealing hovels and rural slums.

Social Classes

Even before the Industrial Revolution, the French Revolution had already altered many people's perceptions of the social order. Industrialization added economic and social foundations to this new understanding of society. People viewed themselves less as part of a rigid, ranked, ordered society and more as part of a flexible society of a few classes with mobility between classes both possible and proper. Class membership was not a formal designation but a description of the amount of money, the type of work, the style of life, and the beliefs held by people. Nevertheless, this does not mean that society had in reality become egalitarian. As in centuries before, there remained sharp differences between different classes of people.

The two classes most firmly tied to traditional rural society, the aristocracy and the peasantry, were doomed by the Industrial Revolution. Over the nineteenth century they would decline in number, wealth, position, and influence. Yet the extent and speed of this decline should not be overestimated. It was not until the second half of the nineteenth century that urban dwellers outnumbered rural populations in even the most industrialized nations; in some countries, such as France, the small farm was more the rule than the exception. Moreover, the aristocracy remained influential even in industrializing nations, commanding considerable wealth and prestige. Aristocrats still dominated many localities, staffed upper levels of government, and controlled certain professions such as the diplomatic and military officer corps.

The middle classes as a whole and the industrial bourgeoisie in particular grew in numbers and profited from the Industrial Revolution. Those who benefited most were the large factory owners, bankers, and merchants, who amassed great fortunes and rose toward the top of society. The smaller factory owners, professionals, shopkeep-

ers, and "white-collar" workers who made up the various ranks of the middle class also benefited. They gained their wealth by mental rather than physical labor and by the investment or manipulation of capital. This middle class tended to favor liberal reforms and believe in certain values such as hard work, thrift, careers open to talent, and prudence. Over time they outdistanced their two main competitors: the aristocracy, which remained dependent on the traditional society and rural economy, and the artisans, who were increasingly unable to compete with factory production. Though still a minority (even in the largest cities such as Paris they constituted no more than 25 percent of the population), the middle classes gained in prestige, political power, and cultural influence thanks to their growing wealth and numbers. During the second half of the nineteenth century they would gain dominance over much of Western society.

The urban working classes changed, grew, and suffered during the Industrial Revolution. Many of these workers were domestics, and this class grew still larger as the middle classes gained the wealth to hire them. Artisans remained a large class throughout the nineteenth century. On the whole they commanded better pay than the less skilled factory workers, and wealthier purchasers demanded their products. However, new factories increasingly displaced the artisans, and they often reacted radically, sometimes violently, to the changes brought by industrialization. They tended to join radical political organizations, lead in union-organizing activities and strikes, and be the most active elements of violent and revolutionary protests. After mid-century, this class would decline in size.

The industrial proletariat was the newest class. Demand from new factories swelled the ranks of the factory workers. Large numbers of surplus agricultural workers and displaced artisans were absorbed into factory work along with part of the overall increase in population. It was this industrial proletariat that most visibly grew with industrialization and stood in most striking contrast to the industrial bourgeoisie.

Factory workers were ruthlessly exploited by factory owners, particularly during the early stages of the Industrial Revolution. Wages for a

FIGURE 44.3. **Child Labor** This woodcut, dated 1853, portrays the supervisor of an English cotton factory whipping a young boy. Incidents similar to this were not uncommon during the first phase of the Industrial Revolution. Such conditions spurred speculation on ways to control industrial capitalism. (New York Public Library)

work week of six or seven days at twelve to sixteen hours per day were kept to a subsistence level. Unmarried women and orphaned children were more cheaply and easily exploited than men and were thus employed in the new factories. Contracts were made with orphanages for the employment of the children. Young children were

marched off before daybreak to work all day in the factories. If they fell behind the pace set by the machines, they were beaten (see Figure 44.3). Sometimes they were chained to their machines.

After the first few decades of the Industrial Revolution, a pattern of hiring whole families to work in the new factories emerged. Although this system meant that the amount of wages necessary for subsistence was kept to a minimum, it at least allowed the working-class family to stay together. By the middle of the nineteenth century the practice of hiring families and children was declining, but life for the industrial working class remained oppressive. The factories and mines were dark, dirty, and dangerous. The dwellings of the workers were likely to be hovels clustered around smoky, noisy mills or mine entrances. The workers were frequently compelled to spend their wages at company stores, paying monopoly prices arbitrarily set by the owners. Work lost its dignity. The factory workers were disciplined to the clock and the machine. The dull, monotonous, robotlike repetition of a single operation on a machine brought the workers none of the satisfaction and pride of skilled craftsmanship.

Many historians and social scientists argue that statistics show that the early factory workers received higher wages and enjoyed a better standard of living than they had ever had as agricultural or urban workers. Clearly, industrial workers were reaping material benefits from the Industrial Revolution after 1850, but in the years before 1850 workers may have lost more than they gained. Certainly the life of the agricultural laborer or artisan should not be romanticized: The conditions of work and life among the agricultural and urban poor had always been hard. But industrial work involved vast changes that were extraordinarily painful. The longer hours, the greater insecurity, the limits on freedom, and the more frequent unemployment of the uprooted slum-dwelling factory worker of the early nineteenth century do not appear in statistics of wages and prices (see Figure 44.4). The overall picture of the industrial proletariat during the first half of the nineteenth century is dismal and can be justly characterized as a new kind of slavery—slavery to the machine and the machine owner.

One of the industrial proletariat's first reactions was violence. Throughout the winter of 1811 to 1812, when the pressure of the Napoleonic war and the blockade against British commerce was added to the maladjustments of the Industrial Revolution, a wave of personal violence and machine smashing swept throughout Great Britain (the Luddite riots). Parliament, composed entirely of members of the property-holding classes, quickly made industrial sabotage a capital offense and suppressed violence with a heavy hand. Several dozens of offenders were hanged. Sporadic outbreaks of violence, however, continued for several years. This story was repeated in other countries as the Industrial Revolution spread. In the United States in the middle decades of the nineteenth century, violence broke out among the Irish immigrants working in the anthracite coal mines of eastern Pennsylvania. The exploited miners formed secret terror societies called Molly Maguires. For a number of years they intimidated, even murdered, unpopular bosses and uncooperative nonmembers. They were eventually ferreted out by civil authorities and ruthlessly suppressed.

More peaceful efforts of the industrial proletariat to bring group pressure to bear on their employers by organizing unions also at first met with defeat. In 1799 and 1800 the British Parliament passed the Combination Acts, which outlawed all labor combinations organized for the purpose of securing better wages, hours, or working conditions. In 1824 trade unions were legalized in Great Britain, but their activities were still severely restricted. In other countries strikes and union activities were outlawed. In some cases, as in the United States, the owners themselves organized for the purpose of breaking up labor unions. Private detectives and police were set upon labor leaders, who were beaten, fired, and blacklisted. It was not until the second half of the

FIGURE 44.4. Doré, "A London Slum" This woodcut by Gustave Doré portrays the squalor of an overcrowded London slum in the early nineteenth century. (Prints Division, New York Pubic Library, Astor, Lenox, and Tilden Foundations)

nineteenth century that labor unions were able to make consistent headway in major struggles with employers.

Nevertheless, factory workers and other elements of the working classes managed to assert themselves in various ways even during the first half of the nineteenth century. Many local working-class organizations were established and survived. A few larger organizations, such as the Grand National Union in Britain, had at least temporary life. Strikes, whether legal or illegal, were numerous and widespread if not always well organized. There were even significant working-class political movements in this early period, the most important of which was Chartism in Great Britain. Chartism, organized by the London Working Men's Association, arose in the 1830s and 1840s. Chartists agitated for various political and economic reforms and at times seemed to be a powerful, organized, even revolutionary threat in England. Although the movement had broken up by mid-century without having achieved its goals, it did reveal some of the potential political strength of an organized working class.

Social Institutions

Industrialization had a strong impact on social institutions during the nineteenth century. Some of the most subtle but significant and long-lasting changes took place in the family, particularly the middle-class family.

During the nineteenth century, what many historians and sociologists call the "modern family" predominated in the West, particularly in western Europe and the United States, and above all within the middle classes. Compared with the family of early modern times, this modern family was more tied together by emotional bonds, more child-centered, and more private. Within the middle-class modern family, which increasingly served as an accepted standard for all families, there was a growing division of roles and labor between the sexes. Ideally the middle-class man was authoritative, competent, and controlled. His wife was supposed to be deferential, emotional, and even frail—almost on a pedestal as a showpiece of success and propriety. Men increasingly specialized in the competitive world of work outside the home, while women specialized in domestic management. Proper middle-class women were excluded from almost all paid occupations, with the exception of such jobs as governess or elementary-school teacher, directly connected to the domestic role. Home was idealized as a "haven in a heartless world" of ruthless industrial capitalism to which the husband returned after work. The wife was to provide the emotional support for the husband, who supplied the money to support the household. The wife was to make sure the house was clean, the meals were served. In addition to being in charge of any domestic servants (a requirement for any middle-class home), she was supposed to be the all-caring mother. Her children were at the center of the family, and their childhood was more extended than ever before.

Outside the middle class, patterns differed. In aristocratic families, the wider social and political connections remained important and still played a major role in the selection of marriage partners. In peasants' and artisans' families, the household economy was still a reality. In industrial working-class families, women were more likely wage laborers, though for less pay and in lower-status positions than men.

Many other social changes exacerbated by industrialization, such as poor housing, lack of public transportation, horrible sanitation, child labor, and periodic unemployment, did not go unnoticed. Demands for social reforms grew. The wealthier classes were most comfortable supporting charitable institutions and self-help organizations, which proliferated during the nineteenth century. But pressure increased for governmental intervention. Public health organizations, sanitary codes, and housing regulations spread after the 1830s and 1840s. Governments took on greater responsibility for primary and secondary education. By mid-century, governments in industrializing areas had passed several laws to restrict child labor and control a few of the worst social conditions accompanying industrialization. But many of these laws were not effectively enforced until the second half of the century. Moreover, it was not until after 1850 that governmental programs such as urban planning, public sanitation (sewers and piped water), and urban transportation (horse-drawn and electric streetcars) had a real impact.

5. NEW ECONOMIC AND SOCIAL THOUGHT

The Industrial Revolution and the social changes related to it, like the French Revolution, were accompanied by new theories and doctrines. The increasingly dominant set of ideas, values, and beliefs—or ideology—was liberalism. Most middle-class liberals applauded both the Industrial and French revolutions while rejecting some of their "excesses" (see Chapter 43). Economic liberalism was more directly related to the economic and social changes accompanying industrialization. Socialism was another newer and more critical line of thought. Like economic liberalism, socialism directly related to industrialization, but not from the perspective of the middle class. Over the course of the nineteenth century, socialist ideology would grow and become the main alternative to economic liberalism.

Economic Liberalism

The growing middle classes, who were prospering from the Industrial Revolution, found intellectual support and justification for their interests in the doctrine of economic liberalism. This doctrine has been best stated by the Scottish philosopher Adam Smith in his classic *Wealth of Nations* (1776). The essence of Smith's theory is that economics, like the physical world, has its own natural laws. The most basic of the economic laws is that of supply and demand. When left to operate alone, these laws will keep the economy in balance and, in the long run, work to the benefit of all. If the sanctity of property and contracts is respected, competition and free enterprise will provide incentive and keep prices down. Government regulations and collective bargaining only impede the workings of the natural laws of economics and destroy incentive. Government should therefore follow a policy of laissez faire, limiting its activities in the economic field to enforcement of order and of contracts, public education and health, national defense, and in rare instances the encouragement of necessary industries that private enterprise does not find profitable. Here was a theory ready-made for the industrial capitalists, who already held all the trump cards.

A strong boost was given to laissez-faire thinking by a young Anglican clergyman, Thomas Malthus, who in 1789 published his *Essay on Population*. Malthus argued that since population increases by a geometric ratio whereas the food supply increases only by an arithmetic ratio, it is a basic natural law that population will outstrip the food supply. This alleged law has two important implications. One is that nothing can be done to improve the lot of the masses. If their condition is temporarily bettered, they will immediately produce children in such numbers that the food supply will be outstripped and starvation will threaten all. Only poverty and privation hold them in check. The second implication is that the rich are not to blame for the misery of the poor; the poor are themselves responsible because of their incontinence. These ideas were so soothing to so many of the book-buying upper classes that Malthus quickly attained fame and wealth.

David Ricardo supplied further support for policies of economic liberalism. Having made a fortune in stock market speculation while still a young man, Ricardo purchased a seat in Parliament and spent the rest of his life thinking and writing on economics. In *The Principles of Political Economy and Taxation* (1817), he propounded the law of rent and the iron law of wages. Rent is determined by the difference in productivity of land. Take off all restrictions and subsidies, and the poorest land goes out of cultivation, reducing the rent on the more productive lands proportionately. He argued for this idea so forcefully that it played an important part in the repeal of England's Corn Laws, which had maintained the price of grain at an artificially high level. Lower grain prices meant lower bread prices, which enabled industrial capitalists to pay lower subsistence wages to their workers. More important in economic thinking was Ricardo's iron law of wages, according to which the natural wage is the subsistence level and the market wage tends to conform to it. Raise the market wage and the workers will multiply so rapidly that soon the law of supply and demand will bring the market wage down below the subsistence level. Then the workers will die off from malnutrition and disease and slow down their reproduction rate. Eventually, they will become so scarce as to be able to bid the market wage up above the natural wage. Always, though, the pull is toward the subsistence level. This theory again was music to the ears of the industrial capitalists.

These economic liberals, being some of the earliest thinkers to analyze the economics of industrial capitalism, are often called the classical economists. Their ideas were popularized in Great Britain and spread to the Continent. There they were modified and expounded by men such as Jean Baptiste Say and Frédéric Bastiat.

A related stream of economic liberalism was initiated by the British Utilitarian philosopher Jeremy Bentham as early as 1789, in his *Principles of Morals and Legislation.* Bentham was an eighteenth-century materialistic rationalist who lived on until 1832, bridging the eighteenth and nineteenth centuries with his life and thought. The Utilitarians believed that the useful is the good and that the chief purpose of government and society is to achieve "the greatest good to the greatest number." But since every individual is the best judge of his or her own best interests, the surest way to achieve general happiness is allow individuals to follow their own enlightened self-interest. Individualism, then, is the best safeguard of the general welfare. At the same time Bentham himself and several of his followers saw the necessity for the state to act for the common welfare. Utilitarians became active during the middle decades of the nineteenth century in promoting legislation and creating governmental bureaucracies to handle some of the economic abuses and social problems connected with the Industrial Revolution.

Over the nineteenth century, economic liberalism evolved as industrial capitalists proved unwilling to adhere to laissez faire when it did not suit their interests, as the economic and social inequities of industrialism became too abhorrent to humanitarian sensibilities, and as perceptive criticisms of economic liberalism became persuasive. The most influential thinker to lead in this evolution of economic liberalism was John Stuart Mill (1806–1873). Mill, a child prodigy, was brought up to be a good Benthamite. However, he was too sensitive and humanitarian to remain in the hard materialist camp of the Utilitarians. Moreover, living a generation after Smith, Malthus, Ricardo, and Bentham, he was able to see

some of the social effects of the Industrial Revolution. Although Mill in no way rejected private property and free enterprise, he believed that in the industrial age restrictions must be instituted by the state for the protection of the poor. Although production is bound by the laws of supply and demand, the distribution of goods is not. Public utilities such as railroads and gas and waterworks are natural monopolies and should be owned by the state. The state should provide free compulsory education for all and regulate child labor. He favored income and inheritance taxes as economic equalizers. Mill's chief work on economics, *Principles of Political Economy,* was published in 1848. Mill was also the first influential philosopher in modern times to advocate equal rights for women. His *Subjection of Women,* which appeared in 1869, came to be considered the classic statement on the subject of women's rights. In his later years he considered himself a moderate socialist. More than other nineteenth-century liberals, many of his views fit those of twentieth-century liberalism.

Utopian Socialism

During the first phase of the Industrial Revolution the economies of the industrialized countries belonged to the bourgeoisie in thought as well as in deed. The theories of the economic liberals enjoyed ascendancy. The hard-pressed proletariat, though increasingly disconcerted, did not formulate new economic theories. However, as early as the opening of the nineteenth century, a number of intellectuals from the upper classes began to question the fundamentals of the existing system, such as private property and private enterprise for profit. They stressed the need for economic planning and wanted to base society on cooperation and community rather than competitive individualism. The ideas of these intellectuals were speculative and had limited impact, particularly when compared with those of Marx and other hardheaded socialists of the later nineteenth century. A number of these early, speculative intellectuals came to be called Utopian Socialists.

One of the first Utopian Socialists was the French nobleman Henri de Saint-Simon (1760–1825). He and his followers believed that society should be reorganized on a "Christian" basis, that all should work, and that the inheritance of private property should be abolished. His ideal society would be run according to the formula "from each according to his capacity, to each according to his deserts." Saint-Simon would reward the superior artists, scientists, engineers, and business people according to their merits. But he laid down no plan of action for achieving his ideal society.

Charles Fourier (1772–1837), a Frenchman of middle-class origin, advocated doing away with economic competition, the source of so much evil. In his utopian society, agriculture and industry would be carried on by voluntary cooperatives whose members would pool their resources and live in communal apartment houses. Distribution of goods and profits would be based on a mathematical formula: workers, five-twelfths; capitalists, four-twelfths; management, three-twelfths. Although Fourier's elaborate plans included many impractical ideas, some of his ideas found their way into practice.

A step forward in socialist thinking was taken by Louis Blanc (1811–1882), another middle-class Frenchman. Louis Blanc would abolish the evils of selfish competitive capitalism by setting up a system of social workshops. The government would lend money to voluntary workers' cooperatives, which would establish and run the workshops. Distribution of the proceeds would be according to the formula, "from each according to his ability, to each according to his need," the formula later adopted by Karl Marx.

A different kind of Utopian was Robert Owen (1771–1858). Born in Wales, Owen quickly made an industrial fortune in Manchester and bought large cotton mills in New Lanark, Scotland. He set out early in the nineteenth century to make New Lanark a model socialist utopia. Wages were raised, hours shortened, working conditions improved, child labor abolished, educational and recreational facilities provided, sickness and old-age insurance established. Owen spent the rest of his life and fortune drawing plans for and setting up model socialistic communities. Several were established in America, notably New Harmony, Indiana. All were short-lived; nor was Owen's benevolent example followed by other industrialists.

The Utopian Socialists were all strongly influenced by the materialistic rationalism of the eighteenth-century Enlightenment. They recognized some of the deeper significance of the Industrial Revolution and the alternatives it presented. They attacked the unbridled pursuit of profits in an unregulated economy. They attempted to show how a well-organized community or state could eliminate the misery of industrial capitalism and create a society of happy people. They opposed existing organized religion, although Saint-Simon believed that his ideal society should be dominated by a new social Christianity—a brand of Christianity that had never yet been tried. Most of the Utopian Socialists had little influence on their own times. They did, however, start a trend of economic and social thought that was to become influential. During the second half of the nineteenth century a more virile type of socialism would arise. For the most part, this later socialism would be organized, revolutionary, and bear the stamp of Karl Marx.

Marxian Socialism

During the second half of the nineteenth century a stronger type of socialism was formed—a type whose foundations were established in the social and intellectual atmosphere of the 1840s. For the most part, this socialism would be organized, revolutionary, and bear the stamp of its founder, Karl Marx (1818–1883).

Marx was born into a German middle-class family. His father was a Jewish lawyer who had converted to Christianity. A brilliant student, Karl Marx attained his doctorate in philosophy and history, but he was denied an academic position because of his radical views. After embarking on a career in journalism, he was exiled from Germany and later from France because of his radical ideas. He spent the last thirty-four years of his life in London working on his ideas and trying to build organizations to put them into action. Marx collaborated with his friend Friedrich Engels, son of a wealthy German manufacturer, in writing the *Communist Manifesto* (1848). This work, along with the later *Das Kapital* (the first volume of which appeared in 1867), contains the fundamentals of Marxism. Marx built his ideology on a basis of

German philosophy (Hegelian idealism), French social thought (what he referred to as the Utopian Socialists), and British economics (particularly the economic liberalism of David Ricardo). The most salient points of Marx's ideology are summarized next.

Economic Interpretation of History Although people and history are complex, material economic considerations are most important. Economic interests and motivations underlie the most critical actions of human beings, just as the dominant characteristic of an historical epoch is its prevailing system of economic production. Societies are formed around the means of production, around the principal ways that human beings make a living. The political system, the religious system, and the cultural system that develop must conform to the necessities of the economic system and the social system, which form around the economic realities of life.

Class Struggle Societies are broadly divided into the haves and the have-nots. The haves are the owners of the means of economic production; the have-nots are the exploited laborers for these haves. The haves and have-nots are opposing classes with opposing interests. Above all, the haves are interested in maintaining a fundamental status quo, while the have-nots have much to gain from fundamental change. Thus, "the history of all hitherto existing society is the history of class struggles": in ancient times freeman versus slave; in medieval times landlord versus serf; in modern times capitalist versus proletariat. The bourgeoisie (the capitalists), having overcome the aristocracy (the feudal landlords) in a revolutionary struggle (such as the French Revolution), will in time be displaced by the proletariat (the industrial working class) in a new revolutionary struggle.

Surplus Value In the capitalistic industrial economy, the law of surplus value prevails. According to this law, the workers, who are paid only subsistence wages, create, by their work, value in excess of their wages. This excess, surplus value, is the illegitimate source of profit for the capitalist.

Inevitable Destruction of Capitalism Capitalists are locked into a competitive struggle with each other. This struggle forces them to continually introduce new, costly machines while keeping wages to a minimum. Larger factories must be built, fewer and fewer capitalists succeed in the competitive struggle, and greater and greater quantities of goods are produced in a system running out of control. Correspondingly, the capitalist system is characterized by alternating periods of prosperity and depression. Under capitalism, then, the law of surplus value plus the increasingly more frequent and deep periods of depression will finally produce such misery that the working class will revolt, seize the means of production from the capitalists, destroy the capitalist system, and ultimately establish a classless socialist society.

Internationalism Workers in all countries have more in common with each other than they have with capitalists of their own country. Therefore workers should unite across national boundaries in their struggle against the common enemy—the capitalist bourgeoisie.

When the *Communist Manifesto* first appeared in 1848, it had little impact on the already developing revolutionary events of that year. It reflected, however, the intellectual and social turmoil being produced by the Industrial Revolution. In the following decades, Marxian Socialism would grow to become a major theoretical and ideological force in the West (see Chapter 50).

6. THE ARRIVAL OF INDUSTRIAL SOCIETY

The industrialization of Western societies during the nineteenth century was of tremendous significance. Indeed, industrialization has become a measure of whether a society is considered "modern" or "traditional." Industrialization carried in its wake fundamental changes in literally all aspects of life, from the concrete reality of an individual's everyday life to the arrangement of classes in society. Conflict wrought by these changes was inevitable and widespread, whether in an intellectual realm, at the work site, or at the barricades. Generally, it was the industrial bourgeoisie that emerged victorious in these struggles, establishing its control over the economy and the government in the industrialized countries. It is the story of these struggles, combined with the political changes stemming from the French Revolution, that constitutes much of the meat of nineteenth-century history.

SUGGESTED READING

Economic Aspects

T. S. Ashton, *The Industrial Revolution, 1760–1830* (1968). An "optimistic" historian who plays down the horrors of the Industrial Revolution.

P. Deane, *The First Industrial Revolution* (1975). Balanced brief analysis.

D. S. Landes, *The Unbound Prometheus: Technological Change and Industrial Development in Western Europe from 1750 to the Present* (1969). Thorough, insightful description and analysis of the developing technology of the Industrial Revolution.

S. Pollard, *Peaceful Conquest: The Industrialization of Europe* (1981). Up-to-date general survey.

Social Changes

R. Bridenthal and C. Koonz, eds. *Becoming Visible: Women in European History* (1976). Contains chapters on the significance of the Industrial Revolution for women.

C. Morazé, *The Triumph of the Middle Classes* (1968). A sympathetic survey.

P. N. Stearns, *European Society in Upheaval* (1967). A general survey of social classes and social history during the nineteenth century.

P. Taylor, ed., *The Industrial Revolution: Triumph or Disaster?* (1970). Samples a variety of views on the benefits and burdens of industrialization.

E. P. Thompson, *The Making of the English Working Class* (1963). Challenging interpretation stressing the culture and activities of the working class.

L. Tilly and J. Scott, *Women, Work and Family* (1978). A highly respected work.

E. A. Wrigley, *Population and History* (1969). Introduction to demographic changes during the Industrial Revolution.

Economic and Social Thought

R. Heilbroner, *The Worldly Philosophers* (1972). A well-written history of economists and their ideas.

A. S. Lindemann, *A History of European Socialism* (1984). A good modern treatment.

D. McLellan, *Karl Marx: His Life and Thought* (1977). An excellent biography and introduction.

F. Manuel, *The Prophets of Paris* (1962). A study of the French Utopian Socialists.

CHAPTER 45

Romanticism in Philosophy, Literature, and the Arts

FIGURE 45.1. Schinkel, "Medieval Town on a River," 1815 This painting by the German romantic artist Karl Friedrich Schinkel contains many of the key elements of romanticism: glorification of nature, religious mysticism, adoration of the medieval, and concern with the emotional. With these characteristics, romanticism stood in contrast to many of the industrial, secular, and rationalistic trends of the period. (Neue Pinakothek, Munich)

Schools of thought and art do not fall neatly into chronological patterns. Nevertheless, one is frequently able to observe a prevailing style that characterizes the culture of a given era. Thus, although romanticism began in the eighteenth century, the prevailing style until the last years of that century was still classical. Similarly, although classicism continued on through the nineteenth century and into the present day, romanticism was the dominant spirit in the last years of the eighteenth century and the first half of the nineteenth century.

1. THE NATURE OF ROMANTICISM

The romantic spirit had many facets, but essentially it was a reaction against the rationalism and formalism of the classic spirit. Whereas classicism extolled reason and perfection of form, romanticism appealed to the emotions, to feeling, and to freedom and spontaneity of expression. Whereas the classicist was interested in the natural order and the laws of human beings and the universe, the romanticist loved to sing of woods and lakes and lovers' lanes and to dream of faraway or imaginary times and places.

Romanticism was associated with and was in part a product of the French Revolution and Napoleon. Many classicists had been interested in peacefully reforming society in accordance with the natural law. They did not anticipate the violent upheaval that came, although many of the radical revolutionary leaders and Napoleon believed themselves to be in the tradition of classical Greece and Rome. It was the romanticists, breaking sharply with past forms and traditions and with bold abandon trying the new, who reflected the revolutionary spirit. This does not mean that all romanticists were political radicals or even liberals. Some, like Shelley and Heine, were. Others, like Edmund Burke and Sir Walter Scott, were conservatives representing a reaction against the excesses of the revolution.

Nationalism was another facet of romanticism. Whether liberal or conservative, the romanticist was likely to be an ardent nationalist. The romantic poet Lord Byron lost his life fighting for Greek national independence against the Turks. The dreamer and orator Mazzini was called the soul of Italian nationalism. He spent most of his adult life in exile because of his labors for a free and united Italy. Herder, as early as the eighteenth century, had pleaded eloquently for a German national culture. The fraternity and the freedom so common to the national movements before 1850, no less than pride in real or imagined national achievements, gave outlet to the emotions of the romanticist.

Romanticism also represented a reaction against the rationalistic deism of the eighteenth century and a return to mystic religion. In literature and art, romantics stressed the emotion of Christianity and the presence of God in nature. Romantic theologians such as Friedrich Schleiermacher (1768–1834) emphasized that the important part of religion was emotional—the feeling of dependence on an infinite God—not religious dogma or institutions. The revival of religion as part of the romanticism of the early nineteenth century brought about a renewed interest in the Middle Ages. The classicists had drawn their inspiration from pagan Greece and Rome. Now in the early nineteenth century the Knights of the Round Table and Siegfried and Brünhild came back in style once more. No more perfect example of the romantic spirit can be cited than the novels and verse of Sir Walter Scott, whose subject matter was primarily medieval. Gothic architecture enjoyed a revival. The "Dark Ages" were transformed into the "Age of Faith."

Finally, the interest in the Middle Ages and in nationalism reflected another aspect of romanticism: its passionate concern with history. History, written by people such as Thomas B. Macauley (1800–1859) in Great Britain and Jules Michelet (1798–1874) in France, was literary, exciting, and dramatic—a story of heroic individuals, national struggles, and great accomplishments. It became a subject of great interest among scholars as well as the reading public.

2. THE PHILOSOPHY OF IDEALISM

Any discussion of romantic thought should begin with Rousseau (1712–1778), even though this French genius lived during the heyday of rationalistic classicism and before romanticism came into full flower. Rousseau, like most of his fellow philosophers of the Enlightenment such as Voltaire, Diderot, Montesquieu, was a deist, believing in the mechanical universe of natural laws. However, he differed sharply with them over the place of reason. Far from believing that a person can know only what is perceived through the five senses and interpreted by reason, Rousseau stressed feeling, instinct, and emotions. He also anticipated the romantic movement in his inordinate love of nature. He would stretch himself out on the ground, dig his fingers and toes into the dirt, kiss the earth, and weep for joy. This emotional genius was a true romanticist in his revolt against the rules of formal society. Free love, undisciplined childhood and education, the noble savage—all were features of Rousseau's revolt. His influence on later generations was enormous.

It seems a far cry from the rough genius of Rousseau to the exquisitely ordered thought of Immanuel Kant (1724–1804), but the German philosopher was admittedly indebted to Rousseau. Kant, who was partly of Scottish ancestry, was a native of Königsberg in East Prussia. A frail and insignificant-looking man who never traveled more than fifty miles from the place of his birth, he slowly developed into one of the most powerful and influential thinkers of modern times. He was often in difficulty with the Prussian government because of his liberal and unorthodox views. Kant started out as a scientist and always respected the methods of natural science. He was also steeped in the philosophy of the Enlightenment. However, he was not satisfied with the conclusions of the eighteenth-century materialistic rationalists. Eventually he thought on beyond them. Kant came to believe that there are in reality not one but two worlds—the physical realm and the spiritual realm, or the realm of ultimate reality. The first he called the realm of phenomena; the second the realm of noumena. In the physical realm of phenomena the approach to truth of Descartes, Locke, and Voltaire—sense perception and reason—suffices. But in the spiritual realm of noumena, these methods fail. Ultimate spiritual truth may be attained only by faith, conviction, and feeling. Truths in the realm of the noumena, such as the existence of God or the immortality of the soul or

the existence of good and evil, cannot be proved by reason. And yet we are justified in believing them because they reinforce our moral sense of right and wrong. His principal work, *Critique of Pure Reason*, was a metaphysical answer of the highest intellectual order to the philosophers of the Enlightenment. These ideas came to be called the philosophy of idealism. Kant and his early nineteenth-century followers represented a sharp reversal in the philosophical trend toward rationalism and materialism, which in a sense began in the thirteenth century with the efforts of Albertus Magnus and Thomas Aquinas to rationalize Christian doctrines.

The most influential of Kant's disciples was Georg Wilhelm Hegel (1770–1831). Hegel's chief interest was the philosophy of history. Like his master, he rejected the mechanistic amoral universe of the Enlightenment. He believed, rather, that a benevolent but impersonal God created and runs the universe, making human society better by a process of purposeful evolution. This evolution is achieved by a dialectical system of thesis, antithesis, and synthesis. Any given system or civilization (thesis) is challenged by its opposite (antithesis). From the struggle emerges a new system containing the best elements of both (synthesis). This synthesis then becomes a new thesis, which when it has served its purpose is challenged by a new antithesis, and so on. Hegel believed that every historical epoch is dominated by a *zeitgeist* (spirit of the time). The zeitgeist of the nineteenth century was German civilization, whose greatest contribution was freedom through disciplined order. Hegel exalted the state. Only in and through the state can the individual find meaning and be free. Hegel's influence on romanticism and on the early nineteenth century in general was substantial.

3. ROMANTIC LITERATURE

The spirit of romanticism can be made to come alive in no better way than by a study of the British romantic poets. A number of British writers began to break with classicism during the course of the eighteenth century. The best-known and probably the most representative of these writers was Robert Burns (1759–1796). Born in a humble clay cottage, the Scottish poet lived an undisciplined life as if he had been reared in accordance with Rousseau's *Emile*. Burns idealized nature and the rustic rural life with which he was intimately acquainted. In spontaneous verse written in his native Scottish dialect, he wrote an ode to a field mouse, "Wee, sleekit, cow'rin', tim'rous beastie," which he had turned up with his plow. In *The Cotter's Saturday Night* we are given a charming and sympathetic picture of village life among the poor of Scotland. "Auld Lang Syne" is sung with nostalgia every New Year's Eve by millions throughout the English-speaking world. *John Anderson My Jo*, a touching tribute to love in old age, could never have been written by Racine or Alexander Pope.

The romantic spirit, early reflected in the poetry of Robert Burns, reached maturity with William Wordsworth (1770–1850) and Samuel Taylor Coleridge (1772–1834). The two were warm friends. Both were closely associated with the beautiful lake country of northwest England, Wordsworth by birth and Coleridge by adoption. They took a trip to Germany together, where they fell under the influence of Kant. Both, as young men, were ardent social reformers. The two collaborated on *Lyrical Ballads*, which appeared in 1798. *Lyrical Ballads* contains some of the best work of these gifted poets, such as Wordsworth's *Tintern Abbey* (see Figure 45.2) and Coleridge's *Ancient Mariner*. Both men were masters of versification and poetic expression. They were also lovers and students of nature, and both of them, particularly Wordsworth, sensed a brooding, mystical presence of the divine. Wordsworth's *Intimations of Immortality* is sublime in its spiritual depth and insight. In their ardent love of nature, their introspective concern for the individual, their preoccupation with the spiritual rather than the material, and their greater attention to substance than to form, Wordsworth and Coleridge broke distinctly with the spirit of classicism.

Once the vogue of romanticism was dignified and popularized in Great Britain by Wordsworth and Coleridge, a host of romantic writers appeared. A younger trio of poetic geniuses of the highest order, Byron, Shelley, and Keats (all of whom lived briefly and died between the years 1788 and 1824), are well known and loved. All

FIGURE 45.2. J. M. W. Turner, "Tintern Abbey"
Tintern Abbey, a twelfth-century Gothic ruin in Wales, was the object of both literary and artistic romanticism. Here Turner, the leading English romantic artist, evokes the power of nature, religion, and the medieval past. (The British Museum)

three gave spontaneous and unrestrained vent to their emotions. Byron and Shelley combined an exquisite esthetic sense with irrepressible revolutionary zeal, defying the forms and customs of society. Keats was a gentler soul, who after a lifelong quest for the beautiful died at the age of twenty-five.

Meanwhile, Sir Walter Scott in novel and verse was devoting his longer life (1771–1832) to glorifying the Middle Ages and his native Scotland. Scott, unlike Byron and Shelley but like Wordsworth and Coleridge in their mature and mellow later years, was conservative in his attitude toward public affairs.

On the other side of the Atlantic, Longfellow,

Cooper, and Irving were founding an American national literature. In their subject matter, their style, and their attitudes, they reflected the European romantic spirit. Many other American writers in the early nineteenth century wrote in the romantic vein. Ralph Waldo Emerson (1803–1882) was considered a religious radical and skeptic in his day. He gave up his Puritan pastorate (by then Unitarian) at Boston's Old North Church because of his heterodoxy. However, in his essays and poems it was the romantic philosophy of Kantian idealism, not the rationalism of the Enlightenment, that he introduced into America. Edgar Allan Poe (1809–1849), short-story writer, literary critic, and romantic poet of a high order, was in a sense an American Shelley, though less ethereal and more morbid. Henry David Thoreau (1817–1862) took Rousseau's back-to-nature idea more seriously than did its author. Rousseau, for all his passion for nature, would never have withdrawn from society for two years to live by Walden Pond in introspective solitude. Emerson, Poe, and Thoreau were all individualists to the point of being mild social revolutionaries. Thoreau preached civil disobedience and allowed himself to be put in jail rather than pay taxes for what he considered to be unworthy causes. The sensitive Poe, enduring oblivion and poverty, turned to drink and an early grave. Emerson weathered a storm of hostility from organized religion and society for his nonconformist views.

Romanticism came to German literature in the latter half of the eighteenth century, partly under the influence of the early British romanticists and partly as a result of the conscious effort of the Germans, led by Herder, to free themselves from bondage to French classical culture. Foremost among all German writers is Johann Wolfgang von Goethe (1749–1832). Like Shakespeare, Leonardo da Vinci, and Beethoven, Goethe is a genius of such proportions that he cannot be confined to any single cultural school or movement. However, insofar as it is possible to classify him, he belongs more nearly to the romantic tradition than to any other, both in time and in spirit. His prodigious energies were devoted essentially to a lifelong (eighty-three years) search for the secrets of happiness and wisdom. His encyclopedic mind delved fruitfully into literature, philosophy, sci-

ence, and public affairs. His novels, lyrics, essays, scientific and philosophical treatises, and dramas fill one hundred thirty-two volumes. No writer except Shakespeare has had so many of his lyrics set to music. Goethe's masterpiece is *Faust*, a philosophical drama written in exquisite verse (see Figure 45.3). It is about a medieval scholar who, dissatisfied with the fruits of knowledge, sells his soul to the devil in return for earthly pleasure and wisdom. Goethe explores the depths of human experience and aspiration. *Faust* was sixty years in the making. In his medieval interests, his fresh emotional spontaneity, his love of nature and of individual personality, and his courageous, robust, pioneering spirit, Goethe was a romanticist.

Goethe's friend and protégé, Friedrich Schiller (1759–1805), was more popular in his own day than the master himself. Schiller drew heavily on the Middle Ages and on nationalism (when national aspirations were associated with freedom) for his dramas, histories, and lyrics. *William Tell*, a drama based upon the Swiss struggle for freedom from Hapsburg tyranny, is probably Schiller's best-known work. Neither Goethe nor Schiller can be considered a German nationalist in the narrow sense; both were universal in their interests and their appeal.

Heinrich Heine (1797–1856) was considered to be Goethe's successor as a writer of German lyrics, though not of Goethe's stature. Most of Heine's voluminous writing was in the field of romantic lyrical poetry. One of his most representative works was an ode to the Silesian weavers who rose up against the hardships caused by the Industrial Revolution, which was just coming to Germany, and were shot down by Prussian troops. Because of the hostility of the various German governments in the age of Metternich to his radical political ideas, Heine exiled himself from Germany. The last twenty-five years of his life were spent in Paris. Many of his later lyrics show a touch of the light gaiety of the French.

Literary romanticism flowered later in France than England or Germany. Francois René Chateaubriand (1768–1848), a disillusioned noble man who began writing during the reign of Napoleon I, was one of the first French writers of influence to react against the rationalism of the Enlightenment. His *Genius of Christianity* is a return to mystic

FIGURE 45.3. Delacroix, Scene from _"Faust"_
This lithograph by Delacroix depicting the devil on
the left and the scholar Faust on the right is an illustration for Goethe's masterpiece, _Faust._ (Prints Division, New York Public Library, Astor, Lenox, and Tilden
Foundations)

passion and idealism. Victor Hugo (1802–1885) in
his long and tumultuous life wrote a vast quantity
of exquisite lyrics, dramas, essays, and fiction in
the romantic tradition. His _Hunchback of Notre
Dame_ is medieval in setting. In _Les Misérables_ he
immortalizes and idealizes the masses of under-
privileged humanity, preaching redemption and
purification not by planned social reform but
through suffering. Jules Michelet crossed historical and literary lines in his seventeen-volume _His-
tory of France._ He tells the thrilling story of France's
long and glorious achievements, usually with
skillful historical craftsmanship and always with
matchless grace.

The first great figure in Russian literature was
the romantic poet Alexander Pushkin (1799–1837).
The chief inspiration for his great lyrics, dramas,
histories, novels, essays, and tales came from
French and British writers, particularly Byron. Because of his revolutionary radicalism (of the
French variety), he was for a while exiled by the
Russian government to southern Russia. Later he
became a Russian nationalist and took many of
his themes from Russian history. His tragic drama
Boris Godunov (patterned after Shakespeare) is considered to be his masterpiece.

4. THE ROMANTIC SPIRIT IN THE ARTS

Words fail to convey the messages and the meanings expressed in the visual and musical arts. This
is particularly true of art, whose appeal is primarily to the emotions.

The leading painters glorified nature, religion,
and nationalism (see Figure 45.1). John Constable
(1776–1837) in Great Britain, Camille Corot (1796–
1875) in France, and George Inness the elder
(1825–1894) in the United States painted landscapes fit to have illustrated the moods of Wordsworth or Thoreau (see Color Plate 19 and Figure
45.4). Their idealizations of nature and the rural
life would have delighted Rousseau and Burns. J.
M. W. Turner (1775–1851) in England caught the
romantic mood in his eerie, misty impressions of
seascapes and mythological subjects (see Color
Plate 20). Jean François Millet (1814–1875) idealized both the French rural life (_The Sower_ and _The_

religion. He also dreamed and wrote of glorified
Indians in far-away tropical America. At almost
the same time, Madame de Staël (1766–1817) analyzed and helped popularize romanticism. Alexander Dumas the elder (1802–1870) has continued
to delight young and old alike with his romantic
and melodramatic _Three Musketeers and Count of
Monte Cristo,_ painting the haunting afterglow of
medieval chivalry. George Sand (1804–1876), an
unconventional woman and gifted author, wrote
numerous popular novels filled with romantic

FIGURE 45.4. Millet, ''The Angelus'' The spirit of romanticism that dominated art during the first half of the nineteenth century was marked by a religious revival and by an admiration for the simple, rural life, which Millet effectively captures in painting. (Giraudon)

Gleaners) and mystic religion (*The Angelus*) (see Figure 45.4). His compatriot, Eugène Delacroix (1798–1863) depicted on canvas Byron's *Prisoner of Chillon*. On great murals in the Louvre, the library of the Chamber of Deputies, and the Hôtel de Ville he portrayed glorious scenes from history (see Color Plate 21).

The romantic movement was less pronounced in the field of architecture. Its chief manifestation was a revived interest in the Gothic style. The French, after several centuries of apathy if not scorn for anything associated with medievalism, suddenly showed a renewed interest in their magnificent Gothic monuments. The Houses of Parliament, constructed in London in the early nineteenth century when England was rapidly becoming industrialized, were built in the Gothic style.

The romantic spirit was caught and expressed by a host of great musicians. They went beyond the controlled classical music, trying to translate emotions into sound. First and foremost was Beethoven (1770–1827), who was not only one of the greatest of classic composers but also the first of the romanticists. His earlier work was in the spirit of his idol, Mozart. In maturity his originality overflowed the bounds of classic forms, becoming freer, more individualistic, and emotional. Beethoven lived through the upheavals of the French Revolution and Napoleon, and his keen interest in these dramatic events is reflected in his music. His Symphony No. 3 (*Eroica*) was dedicated to Napoleon, whom Beethoven at first regarded as the embodiment of the democratic ideals of the French Revolution. His Fifth and Seventh symphonies were inspired by the German nationalistic upsurge, which helped to overthrow Napoleon. Karl Maria von Weber (1786–1826), Franz Schubert (1797–1828), Felix Mendelssohn (1809–1847), and Robert Schumann (1810–1856) carried on in the spirit of the great Beethoven.

These gifted and youthful Germans expressed in their melodic music the same spontaneous and emotional spirit that their contemporaries Byron, Shelley, and Keats were expressing in English verse. A German by adoption was the colorful Hungarian-born Franz Liszt (1811–1886). Liszt is believed to be the greatest concert pianist of his time. His glamorous personality and sensational, emotional compositions greatly popularized romantic music. Although Liszt was an international figure, his Hungarian folk music was characteristic of the growing national sentiment of the time. He befriended the youthful Richard Wagner, who later married one of Liszt's illegitimate daughters.

The romantic spirit is nowhere better illustrated than in the work of the Polish-French pianist-composer, Frédéric Chopin (1810–1849). Chopin could express his sweet sorrows in lilting nocturnes, his sunny gaiety in bright waltzes and mazurkas, his national patriotism in stirring polonaises, or his deeper, dramatic moods in more formal ballades and concertos—all with equal skill and all in the romantic tradition. Meanwhile, other notable Frenchmen were writing romantic symphonies and operas. Gounod's *Faust* is an operatic version of Goethe's great theme. The haunting melodies of Bizet's (1838–1875) *Carmen* are widely known and sung. The greatest Italian romantic composer was Giuseppe Verdi (1813–1901). His operas *Aida, La Traviata, Il Trovatore,* and *Rigoletto* are still sung every season in opera houses all over the world. Verdi was Italy's national cultural hero during the long, uphill fight for freedom and unity.

Richard Wagner (1813–1883) brought to a dramatic climax the romantic era in music. Wagner's tempestuous life, like his music, illustrates and marks the transition from the romantic, moderately liberal and nationalistic early nineteenth century to the more violent and restless spirit of the late nineteenth and early twentieth centuries. In his youth Wagner was a radical and was exiled from Saxony in 1849 for his revolutionary activities. Later he became an extreme German nationalist—even a German "master racist" of the type that has brought so much violence to the twentieth-century world. His operas, though containing some of the world's greatest music, are also grandiloquent and often stridently nationalistic. *Tannhäuser, The Meistersingers, Siegfried, Götterdämmerung, Lohengrin,* and *Das Rheingold* are an important part of the opera repertory today.

Romanticism in the arts, as in literature and philosophy, reflected a new recognition that human beings are complex, emotional, and only sometimes rational creatures. In a civilization that was becoming more scientific, materialistic, industrial, and urban, romanticism was a counterweight for the human experience. Although new cultural trends such as realism would appear during the middle of the nineteenth century (see Color Plate 22), romanticism would remain a strong current in Western civilization well into the twentieth century.

SUGGESTED READING

General

K. Clark, *The Romantic Rebellion* (1973). Clearly written, useful.

M. LeBris, *Romantics and Romanticism* (1981). A well-illustrated recent survey of romanticism in its political context.

S. Prawer, ed., *The Romantic Period in Germany* (1970). A good collection of essays.

H. B. Schenk, *The Mind of the European Romantics* (1966). A solid survey.

J. L. Talmon, *Romanticism and Revolt: Europe, 1815–1848* (1967). Survey of romanticism in its broad historical context.

The Philosophy of Idealism

E. Cassirer, *Kant's Life and Thought* (1981). Excellent, though difficult.

R. Stromberg, *European Intellectual History Since 1789* (1975). Surveys the topic well.

C. Taylor, *Hegel* (1975). Excellent introduction.

Romantic Literature

M. H. Abrams, *Natural Supernaturalism: Tradition and Revolution in Romantic Literature* (1971). A good survey of romantic literature.

J. S. Allen, *Popular French Romanticism* (1981). Relates literary romanticism and popular culture.

Romanticism in the Arts

A. Hauser, *Social History of Art* (1958). Relates artistic trends to social developments.

H. W. Janson, *History of Art* (1977). The standard survey with a section on romanticism.

RETROSPECT

The era between 1776 and 1850 was a period of great—some historians think the greatest—political, economic, and social upheavals. Politically and socially, it was a time of high expectation and excitement. In a matter of weeks—and sometimes days—the kind of fundamental changes that usually require decades took place. Time-honored institutions, privileges, and customs toppled. Wealth, power, and rights were redistributed. Economically, changes came only somewhat slower but were even more fundamental. Goods and services were produced in different ways and in different places. Where people lived, how they made a living, and how they related to each other were changing in irreversible, revolutionary ways.

The New World was the stage for the first of these revolutions. The American Revolution was primarily a matter of the thirteen English colonies winning their independence from the mother country. As a result of the Revolution, loyalist lands were redistributed, and the royal governors and their aristocratic councils gave way to the more democratic legislatures. The Declaration of Independence and the new Constitution were filled with the ideas of the Enlightenment.

The changes brought about by the French Revolution were more dramatic and significant for Western civilization. French society on the eve of the Revolution was still essentially feudal, with its privileged clergy and nobility. Government was in the hands of a monarch. The Church was intolerant and oppressive. Within a few months of the outbreak of the Revolution in 1789, a series of sweeping reforms had occurred—the end of feudalism, the Declaration of the Rights of Man, and the drawing up of a liberal but moderate constitution.

But the nobility and the clergy were not willing to see their privileges so easily lost. Nor were the radical Jacobins convinced that the Revolution had gone far enough. They wished to see the principles of "Liberty, Equality, Fraternity" extended beyond France's borders. When Austria and Prussia intervened in behalf of the French royalty and nobility, the radicals deposed and beheaded Louis XVI. All the great powers of Europe except Russia formed a coalition for the purpose of ending this threat to the established order. The revolutionary radicals, now in control, inaugurated a Reign of Terror for the purpose of uniting and mobilizing the nation. It was remarkably successful; the internal enemies of the Revolution were terrorized into silence or support, and the foreign enemies were defeated and driven back beyond the frontiers. But no one seemed able to consummate the Revolution and restore peace. The radical Jacobins were overthrown by the bourgeois moderates, and the Terror ended; but the moderates, too, proved unable to bring peace at home and abroad.

In 1799 a coup d'état brought Napoleon Bonaparte to power. Over the next few years he instituted stabilizing reforms that affirmed some of the changes wrought by the French Revolution and destroyed others. His fifteen-year rule was marked by almost continual warfare.

At the Congress of Vienna in 1814–1815, the major powers structured a peace settlement in accordance with the principles of conservatism. In many ways the ensuing decades between 1815 and 1850 were a struggle between these forces of conservatism and the newer forces of liberalism. Despite various revolutionary rumblings, the forces of conservatism generally remained in control until 1830. After 1830 reform and revolution in the name of liberalism started to wrestle control from the conservatives, culminating in the great liberal and nationalistic revolutions of 1848. Yet this great defeat for the conservative forces of order was short-lived. By 1850 most were back in power again and the great period of liberal revolution was over.

Meanwhile another kind of revolution had been taking place in western Europe—the Indus-trial Revolution. By the end of the eighteenth century new factories, using new sources of power, new machines, and new methods of production, were sprouting up in Great Britain in great numbers. Great Britain's economy was experiencing unprecedented, sustained growth. The Industrial Revolution had begun. After 1815 it spread to western Europe and the United States. Great social changes followed in the wake of industrialization. Cities grew, the class structure changed, new social institutions developed, and even the function of the family and the role of women evolved. The first beneficiaries of the Industrial Revolution were the industrial bourgeoisie—the factory owners. Whether the industrial proletariat benefited is questionable. While their wages may have risen, they lost skills and security and became the virtual slaves of factory owners. These radical changes in production and distribution and the ensuing stresses prompted new economic and social thought—economic liberalism, Utopian Socialism, and Marxism.

Both an affirmation of and a reaction to the revolutionary spirit that engulfed the Western world between 1776 and 1850 was reflected in the romanticism that characterized the philosophy, literature, and arts of the period. For liberals romanticism affirmed the optimism, the individualism, and the heroism epitomized by the French Revolution, Napoleon, and the revolutions of the first half of the nineteenth century. For conservatives romanticism rejected the rationalism of the Enlightenment and affirmed the glories of the pre-revolutionary and preindustrial world where the mysteries of nature and religion dominated. Although romanticism would remain an influential and popular cultural style after mid-century, the ensuing period would be more accurately reflected by realism.

PART TEN

NATIONALISM AND INDUSTRIALIZATION, 1850–1914

Nationalism had been growing as a force since the beginning of the Age of Revolutions and had played a particularly important role in the Revolutions of 1848. Between 1850 and 1914 nationalism became a much more pervasive force in the West. During the 1850s and 1860s nationalistic unification movements led to the creation of two new nation-states in Europe: Italy and Germany. At that same time the forces favoring national unification defeated forces struggling for separation in the United States. In France, Great Britain, and elsewhere, the nation-state was greatly strengthened as more citizens acquired the right to vote and as central governments acquired more power and took on greater responsibilities. Nationalism supported and was used by both liberals and conservatives striving to promote their own interests and struggling in a competitive international arena. By the later decades of the nineteenth century nationalism had taken a more militant tone and had even spilled over into a new imperialism. National pride and prestige helped drive Western nations into a race for new colonies and imperial influence in the non-Western world.

Industrialization, like nationalism, had been a growing force during the Age of Revolutions. But in 1850 only England and a few areas in western Europe were industrialized. Between 1850 and 1914 several nations in western Europe, along with the United States, became mature industrial powers, and eastern Europe had begun to industrialize. During this period industrialization interacted with nationalism. Nationalistic pride demanded that a nation have a modern industrial economy (also important for a strong military), and the creation of a modern industrial economy seemed to require national unification. Moreover, nationalism and industrialization joined hands to justify, and even seemed to require, the great imperial expansion of the West between the 1880s and 1914.

The forces of nationalism and industrialization were reflected in the social, intellectual, and cultural developments of the period. A mature industrial society was an urban society, and during this period the urban working classes were growing in numbers and self-consciousness. They were forming their own labor organizations, acquiring their own ideologies, gaining the right to vote, and becoming more educated—all often despite the distrust and hostility of the dominant bourgeoisie. This industrial society also depended on and admired science. The spread of the natural and social sciences along with the growing power of nationalism challenged Christianity, which was wedded to traditional society. Thought, literature, and art were influenced by nationalism, industrialization, and science. Indeed, certain cultural developments of the Age of Nationalism and Industrialization foreshadowed the disillusioning period of war and upheaval following the outbreak of World War I in 1914.

CHAPTER 46
Nationalism and the Nation-State, 1850–1871

FIGURE 46.1. Garibaldi Landing in Sicily The period between 1850 and 1870 was marked by a strong growth of nationalism and the successful unification of Italy and Germany. Here the lifelong nationalist Garibaldi is heroically portrayed landing in Sicily in 1860 as part of the struggle for Italian unification. (Historical Pictures Service, Chicago)

By 1850 many of the liberal and nationalistic aspirations of revolutionaries were dashed as conservative, authoritarian rulers came to power. However, nationalism as a dynamic force remained powerful and would continue to increase in strength during the nineteenth and twentieth centuries. Between 1850 and 1871 almost all political leaders, whether liberal or conservative, recognized the strength of nationalism. Nationalism's political impact was manifested most dramatically in Louis Napoleon's rise to power in France and in the successful struggles for national unification in Italy and Germany. More broadly, nationalism played a crucial role in the growing authority of the nation-state. Increasingly, central governments had to justify and bolster their authority by reference to a nation of citizens rather than dynastic links to the past. The period from 1850 to 1871, then, marks the beginning of a time when nationalism grew from earlier roots to become a dominant force in Western political life, and when the nation-state took on new authority and new functions.

1. THE NATURE OF NATIONALISM

Nationalism may be defined as feelings of common cultural identity and loyalty to one's country. What are the essential factors that contribute to these feelings? What makes a person a German or a Pole, even when there is no German or Polish national state?

The most important factor is language. Language brings people together in understanding and separates them from those they cannot understand. Probably second in importance is a historical tradition of unity. The Belgians with their two languages and the Swiss with their three languages and two religions illustrate the importance of this factor. Religion can be a powerful factor, too, though not so important as language. The German Empire with its common language came and held together in spite of a serious religious cleavage, and the Austrian Empire fell apart along language lines in spite of a common religion and a long tradition of unity under the Hapsburgs.

Territorial compactness and natural boundaries frequently contribute to nationalism.

Until the French Revolution, national loyalty was chiefly centered on the ruling monarch or dynasty and was limited for the most part to the educated upper classes who participated in the government of the nation. The French Revolution gave birth to a new and more virile kind of nationalism. The establishment of equal rights and popular representative government, together with the abolition of old provincial boundary lines, brought the masses of people into direct partnership with the national government. Universal conscription into the revolutionary armies gave the people a sense of fraternity in a righteous cause—a crusade. Nationalism acquired attributes of a religion. Such mass dynamism helped make the revolutionary and Napoleonic armies irresistible.

Nationalism soon spread to the other peoples of Europe. In the decades following the Napoleonic era industrialization and policies toward industrialization were becoming connected with nationalism. The Revolutions of 1848 clearly demonstrated the revolutionary potential of nationalism. By mid-century nationalism had grown from its deeper roots to become entwined with the central political, economic, and social forces of modern times.

2. THE SECOND EMPIRE OF NAPOLEON III

In France, Louis Napoleon Bonaparte blended support from below, reform, and authoritarian nationalism in his Second Empire, which was established in 1852 and lasted until 1870. Louis Napoleon was originally elected president of France's Second Republic in 1848. He benefited from his illustrious name, his appeal to property owners longing for order, and his well-publicized promises to link democracy from below with reforming leadership from above. When the National Assembly refused to change the constitution so that he could run for a second term, he organized a coup d'état and seized power on December 2, 1851. Resistance was limited, though thousands were arrested and deported. He quickly granted

FIGURE 46.2. Rebuilding Paris Under Napoleon III   Under Napoleon III, numerous slums and old winding streets were torn down to make room for new, wide boulevards. The boulevards made it easier for authorities to maintain order and more difficult for revolutionaries to raise barricades. (The Mansell Collection)

universal male suffrage, and during the following year he held two plebiscites in which over 90 percent of the voters supported him and made him hereditary emperor—Napoleon III.

Under the new constitution, most power resided in the emperor. Although there was an elected legislative body, it could not initiate legislation or exert control over Napoleon III's ministers. The emperor controlled elections by manipulating the electoral machinery, exerting official pressure, and supporting official candidates. He kept the press under scrutiny. Thus politically the Second Empire was clearly authoritarian, at least during the 1850s.

It was also during the 1850s that Napoleon III enjoyed his greatest successes. Economically, France prospered, in part thanks to Napoleon III's policies. He encouraged industrialization and economic growth by promoting railroad construction, public works, and financial institutions. Two giant investment banking corporations, the Crédit Mobilier and the Crédit Foncier, mobilized huge amounts of capital for industry, railroads, and real estate. The Bank of France expanded until each of the country's eighty-six departments had at least one branch. George Haussmann, the prefect of Paris, had large parts of Paris torn down and rebuilt (see Figure 46.2). With a new sewer system, new parks, and new large boulevards, Paris took on an envied image that would last well into the twentieth century.

Napoleon III also encouraged educational and social reforms, thereby increasing his popularity among a variety of groups. Hospitals, nurseries, and homes for the aged were built. Government subsidies kept the price of bread low. A system of voluntary social insurance for workers was instituted. Cooperatives were encouraged, and labor unions with limited rights to strike were partially legalized for the first time.

The peak of France's revived national prestige was reached during the Crimean War (1854–1856). Like his uncle, the second Napoleon was not satisfied with spectacular domestic achievements. His opportunity for glory in foreign affairs came when Tsar Nicholas I of Russia attempted to dismember the Ottoman Empire, "the sick man of Europe," and to achieve Russia's historic goal: Constantinople and access to the world through the Turkish Straits. France did not relish the prospect of an ambitious new rival in the Mediterranean. (Great Britain, with its vast holdings and interests in the Near and Far East, was even more sensitive to this threat than was France.) A second source of Franco-Russian conflict arose when the tsar, as the great champion of Orthodox Christianity, attempted to gain a protectorate over all Christians in the Ottoman Empire and over the Christian holy places in the Turkish province of Palestine. Since the Crusades France had been the leading champion of Catholic interests in the Near East, including the Christian shrines in the Holy Land. And Napoleon III's strongest ally in France was the Catholic church.

In 1853 the Russian army and navy suddenly attacked the Turks. Early the next year Great Britain and France sent their naval and military forces into the Black Sea and laid siege to Russia's naval base, Sebastopol, on the Crimean Peninsula. Sardinia came into the war to gain the friendship of France and Great Britain. Austria maintained a hostile and Prussia a friendly neutrality toward Russia. The war was fought with gross inefficiency on both sides. The only real hero was the British nurse Florence Nightingale, whose efforts helped to inspire the creation of the International Red Cross a few years later (1864).

Nicholas I died in 1855, humiliated by the knowledge that his creaking military machine was going to fail. The Peace of Paris in 1856 prohibited Russia's naval forces on the Black Sea and maintained the integrity of the Ottoman Empire. The autonomy of Serbia and the Rumanian provinces of Moldavia and Wallachia under the suzerainty of Turkey was guaranteed by the great powers. The Catholics were left in control of their shrines in the Holy Land. Great Britain at long last agreed to neutral rights on the high seas.

The chief loser of the Crimean War was Russia, whose massive military no longer looked so formidable. But more broadly a loss was suffered by the already crumbling "concert of Europe," which no longer could wield significant influence on behalf of a conservative international status quo. An immediate beneficiary of the Crimean War was Napoleon III. He played host to the peace conference and, of course, made it into a colorful spectacle. French nationalism and international prestige rose to new heights.

By 1859 Napoleon III had obtained not only the loyalty of the great majority of his own people but also some hegemony in the affairs of the European continent. France was prosperous and powerful. Then things began to go wrong. The dynamic force of nationalism, which he understood and used so well in France, he greatly underestimated abroad. In his efforts to control the Italian and German national movements he failed dismally—in the latter case fatally.

The first serious blunder came in 1859, when he made war on Austria in behalf of Italian freedom. The defeat of Austria set off a frenzy of Italian nationalism that threatened to dispossess all the rulers of the local states of Italy, including the pope. This situation alarmed and angered the French Roman Catholics, who blamed Napoleon. But when the French emperor deserted the Italian nationalists in the midst of the campaign, with the agreed-upon job only half done, he further alienated the French liberals, who were already unsympathetic to him.

Napoleon's efforts to create an overseas empire brought France little immediate profits and much trouble. The most ambitious and disastrous was his attempted conquest and control of Mexico. In 1862 he joined with Great Britain and Spain and seized several Mexican ports, ostensibly to collect debts owed by the revolutionary Juárez government. As soon as the British and the Spaniards saw that Napoleon had more ambitious plans in mind, they withdrew. The French armies then marched on to Mexico City, drove the Juárez government into the hinterland, and set up a Hapsburg prince, Maximilian, as puppet emperor for France. The government of the United States protested vigorously in the name of the Monroe Doctrine, but embroiled in its own Civil War, it could do no more. As soon as the Civil War ended early in 1865, the American government dispatched victorious Union troops to the Mexican border. Napoleon III, now hard-pressed at home, agreed to withdraw his troops. No sooner had the last French soldiers left Mexico City in 1867 than the Juárez forces captured and shot the well-meaning puppet emperor Maximilian. The Mexican fiasco added to the growing unpopularity of Napoleon III with the French people.

On the Continent, Napoleon III was attempting to slow the rapid growth of Prussia and to offset it by annexing territories on the left bank of the Rhine. His failures in this area of foreign policy would eventually prove fatal to his regime.

Meanwhile, the booming prosperity subsided after 1860. The Cobden Treaty, which lowered tariffs between Great Britain and France, flooded France with cheap British manufactured goods with which the less advanced French industries could not compete. The French textile industry also suffered heavily as a result of the American Civil War, which cut off its cotton supply. Both the industrial bourgeoisie and proletariat were hard hit. Overexpansion and speculation began to take their toll.

The emperor attempted to allay the mounting discontent of liberals and workers. Beginning in 1859 he made one concession after another until by 1870 the Second Empire was, at least on paper, a limited constitutional monarchy with a liberal parliamentary government. But 1870 was too late. The showdown with Bismarck's rapidly forming German nation was at hand. The sick and discouraged Napoleon III blundered into a war with Germany for which his armies were woefully unprepared (see pp. 591–592). He was defeated and captured, and his government was overthrown.

3. CAVOUR AND THE MAKING OF ITALIAN UNITY

For centuries Italy had been politically divided into various city-states, kingdoms, and provinces. After 1815 nationalistic sentiments and movements stirred throughout Italy. By 1848 three different plans for uniting Italy into a sovereign state had been developed; each had its own following. One plan was to make Italy a liberal democratic republic. This was the plan of Giuseppe Mazzini, an inspiring speaker and writer but not a very practical organizer or man of action. His movement was called Young Italy. The second plan was to form an Italian confederacy under the leadership of the pope. The third plan was to make Italy a limited monarchy under the leadership of the house of Savoy, the ruling dynasty in Piedmont-Sardinia. During the Revolution of 1848, the first two plans were discredited. Mazzini's chaotic Roman Republic, which he set up after the rebellious populace had driven out the pope, outraged the Roman Catholic world and was overthrown by a French army of Louis Napoleon. After this experience the pope bitterly opposed the unification of Italy, fearing that it would mean the loss of his political control over the Papal States.

At the same time, the heroic role played by Piedmont-Sardinia in battling the Austrians against hopeless odds won for the house of Savoy the devotion and confidence of Italian nationalists. However, the powerful Austrians were still in Lombardy and Venezia, the unsympathetic pope still ruled the Papal States, and the rest of the Italian states were weak and divided. Despite the new prestige of Sardinia, therefore, the task of uniting Italy required the work of a great political leader. He soon appeared: Camillo Benso, Count di Cavour (1810–1861).

Cavour was born into a well-to-do noble family of Piedmont. By the 1840s he was a successful businessman and had become enamored with moderate liberal ideas. Shortly before the Revolution of 1848, he founded a newspaper called *Il Risorgimento (The Resurgence)*, which never ceased to preach Italian unity. In 1850 Cavour was made minister of commerce and agriculture, and two years later prime minister of Sardinia.

Cavour's goals were limited: to modernize economically Piedmont, to make Piedmont the center of the national unification movement, and to form a new Italian state as a constitutional monarchy rather than a democratic republic. To these ends, he worked to lower tariffs, build railroads, and balance Piedmont's budget. He supported the nationalistic Italian National Society, which worked toward national unification under Piedmont. Finally, he used diplomacy and Piedmont's relatively small army to gain international support and overcome the primary obstacle to unification—Austria.

Cavour sent Piedmont's army into the Crimean War in the hopes of winning French sympathy. The plan worked, and at the Paris Peace Conference in 1856, he was given an opportunity to state impressively to the world Italy's case against Austria. In 1858, Cavour and Napoleon met at Plombières, a French spa, and there Cavour persuaded him to fight Austria. Sardinia would provoke Austria into a declaration of war; France would help Sardinia drive the Austrians out of Lombardy and Venetia, which would then be annexed to the kingdom of Sardinia. In payment Sardinia would cede the two little French-speaking provinces of Savoy and Nice to France.

When everything was in readiness in April 1859, Cavour easily provoked unsuspecting Austria into a declaration of war. To Austria's surprise, French armies poured across the Alps to fight alongside the Sardinians. In the two bloody battles of Magenta and Solferino, the Austrians were defeated and driven out of Lombardy. But to the dismay of Cavour, Napoleon suddenly made a separate peace with Austria (the Agreement of Villafranca) on condition that Sardinia receive Lombardy but not Venetia. Napoleon appears to have been motivated by the surprising bloodiness of the battles, the threatening attitude of Prussia, and the anger of the French Roman Catholics, who feared that the wild outburst of nationalism all over Italy following the victories over Austria threatened the independence of the Papal States. News of Magenta and Solferino set all Italy aflame with nationalistic fervor. Early in 1860, under Cavour's supporters, Tuscany, Modena, Parma, and Romagna (the northernmost of the Papal States)

joined Piedmont, bringing together all of northern Italy except Venezia.

At this juncture, the rawboned Giuseppe Garibaldi, the most colorful of all the makers of the Italian nation, performed a daring exploit. With a thousand civilian warriors dressed in red shirts and slouch hats, he sailed aboard two little Piedmontese ships for southern Italy. His goal was the conquest of the Kingdom of Naples, the largest and most populous of the Italian states, with a regular army of 124,000 men and a sizable navy. Cavour officially condemned the seemingly foolhardy expedition of the thousand but secretly aided it. Garibaldi's exploits read like a fairy story. He conquered the large island of Sicily, crossed the Strait of Messina, and entered triumphantly into Naples. The opposing troops had little heart for their cause and deserted to Garibaldi by the thousands after his first victories. Moving northward in the direction of Rome, Garibaldi defeated the last Neapolitan forces.

Not wanting to lose control of the situation and fearful that the daring but undiplomatic Garibaldi would march on Rome and bring down French armies, Cavour sent troops southward and seized all the pope's remaining territory except Rome and the territory immediately surrounding it. When Victor Emmanuel at the head of his army approached the forces of Garibaldi, the gallant warrior and patriot submitted to his king and retired to the rocky island of Caprera (see Figure 46.3). The Kingdom of Italy was formally declared in March 1861, with Victor Emmanuel II as king and the liberal Sardinian Constitution of 1848 as the national charter. The red, white, and green Sardinian flag now flew over all of Italy from the Alps to Sicily except Venetia and Rome (see Map 46.1). Those two provinces were not joined to the Italian state until 1866 and 1870, respectively, when, as we shall soon see, first Austria and then France was defeated by Prussia.

Cavour did not live to enjoy the fruits of his labors. Less than three months after the birth of his beloved Italian nation, he was dead. Paunchy, with ill-fitting glasses and a myopic stare, he was anything but impressive in appearance. Neither was he an orator. "I cannot make a speech," he once truthfully said, "but I can make Italy."

Map 46.1   **THE UNIFICATION OF ITALY**   This map shows the various stages of Italian unification after 1859. Most of Italy was unified under the leadership of Piedmont by 1860. The new Italian nation took advantage of international affairs to gain other territories after 1860.

FIGURE 46.3. Victor Emmanuel and Garibaldi This English engraving portrays King Victor Emmanuel and the heroic Garibaldi shaking hands in 1860, culminating the unification of Italy. (Culver Pictures)

4. GERMAN UNIFICATION

During the decade of the 1850s both liberalism and nationalism began to make rapid headway in the German states. The area was industrialized rapidly. In Prussia the rise of a middle class, imbued with liberalism and German nationalism, challenged for the first time the dominance of the Junker aristocracy, who abhorred liberalism and whose national loyalty was limited to Prussia. The conversion of the Hohenzollerns and the Prussian Junkers to German nationalism was facilitated by the "Humiliation of Olmütz" in 1850. Shortly after the vacillating Frederick William IV had spurned the German national crown offered him by the Frankfurt Assembly in the spring of 1849, he attempted to reorganize the German Confederation under Prussian leadership. The Hapsburg government of Austria, now completely recovered from

its embarrassments of 1848–1849, mobilized its superior army and ordered him to cease. At the town of Olmütz in Austrian territory, the king of Prussia abjectly yielded. After this, the Hohenzollerns and more and more of the proud Junkers sought an opportunity to avenge the national insult to Prussia and replace Austria as leader of the Germanies (see Map 46.2).

In 1858 the unstable mind of Frederick William IV gave way, and his younger brother, who three years later became King William I, assumed leadership of the Prussian government as regent. Unlike his romantic and idealistic brother, William I was a militarist. His first move was to rejuvenate and greatly strengthen the Prussian military machine. The liberals, now strong in the Prussian Landtag, began to take alarm. Might not this all-powerful military machine be used to suppress liberalism? The liberals hoped that by holding up

Map 46.2 **THE UNIFICATION OF GERMANY** During the 1860s Prussia won its struggle with Austria for leadership in Germany. Through wars and diplomatic maneuvering, Bismarck welded numerous German states into a single nation by 1871.

the military budget they might bargain for a stronger role for the legislature in the Prussian government. After several years of haggling the liberals in 1862 finally defeated the military budget. Liberalism and nationalism had collided head-on. William I, unskilled in and unsympa-

thetic with parliamentary government, threatened to resign. As a last resort, he called to the chancellorship Otto Eduard Leopold von Bismarck (see Figure 46.4).

Bismarck would remain chancellor for the next twenty-eight years. He stamped his iron will and

FIGURE 46.4. Bismarck Otto von Bismarck had little faith in democratic processes for achieving purposes of state. Rather, he trusted "blood and iron." The German Empire bore in large measure the stamp of his personality and ideals. (The Granger Collection)

his domineering personality not only on Prussia and Germany but also to a considerable degree on the rest of Europe. Upon assuming the chancellorship of Prussia in 1862, Bismarck, with the backing of the king and army, defied the liberal opposition in the Landtag, violated the constitution, and collected illegally the funds necessary for the military program. "Not by speeches and majority resolutions," said Bismarck, "are the great questions of the time decided—that was the mistake of 1848 and 1849—but by blood and iron." He came to be known as the "Iron Chancellor." Prussian liberalism was crushed. Bismarck believed that military victories won on foreign soil would turn the Prussian liberals into fervent German nationalists. This prediction soon came true.

Bismarck lost little time in putting his new military machine to work. An opportunity soon presented itself in the form of a dispute with Denmark over the long-standing and complex Schleswig-Holstein question. Schleswig and Holstein were two little provinces lying between Prussia and Denmark. Their population was partly German speaking and partly Danish speaking. Since 1815 they had been ruled by the king of Denmark, though they had not been incorporated into Denmark. In 1863 the Danish king suddenly annexed Schleswig outright. Bismarck, seeing an opportunity to test the Prussian army, to annex some territory, and also to embroil Austria, declared war on Denmark (1864). Since Holstein was a member of the German Confederation, Austria also entered the war against Denmark lest the leadership of the confederation pass to Prussia. Denmark sued for peace and Bismarck made the peace settlement as complicated as possible. Schleswig and Holstein were to be ruled jointly by Prussia and Austria.

Bismarck soon used this unworkable arrangement to stir up trouble with Austria. His first task was to obtain the support or the neutrality of the other three continental powers, Italy, Russia, and France. Prussia had been the first great power to recognize the new Kingdom of Italy. Now, promising Venetia, Bismarck drew the new nation into an alliance against Austria. It was always a cardinal principle of Bismarck to maintain friendly relations with Russia (at Prussia's back door). When Russia's Polish subjects revolted once more in 1863, Prussia alone of the great powers supported Russia. Bismarck neutralized Napoleon III by personal persuasion and deception. By the spring of 1866, with everything in readiness, Bismarck created by threats and maneuvers a state of alarm in Austria, finally manipulating Austria into a declaration of war.

In the Austro-Prussian War most of the little German states supported Austria. Their military forces, however, were quickly crushed beneath the Prussian steamroller. Prussia's armies overwhelmed Austria, a nation twice the size and population of Prussia and long the dominant power in central Europe. Bismarck saw that Austria was now harmless to Prussia and would make a valuable ally or at least friend in Prussia's future wars. Restraining his king and his generals, he

FIGURE 46.5. **Victorious German Troops in Paris**   Victorious German troops march down the Champs-Elysées (with the Arc de Triomphe in the background) at the end of the Franco-Prussian War. (Historical Pictures Service, Chicago)

made the terms of the Treaty of Prague extremely lenient. Austria was to pay no indemnity and to accept the rearrangement of Germany by Prussia. Austria was also forced to cede Venetia to Italy as Italy's reward for fighting on the side of Prussia.

Following the victory over Austria, Bismarck reorganized Germany. Hanover, Nassau, Frankfurt, and Hesse-Cassel were annexed to Prussia outright, bridging the gap between Prussia's Rhine province and the main body. The remaining twenty-one states north of the Main River were bound to Prussia in a North German Confederation. The confederation was completely dominated by Prussia, which alone constituted four-fifths of its area and population. Prussia's king and prime minister were made president and

chancellor of the confederation, for which Bismarck drafted the constitution.

Its government was fundamentally autocratic, despite some democratic and liberal forms. The chief administrative officer was the chancellor (Bismarck), who was responsible only to the king of Prussia as president, by whom he was appointed. The legislative body was composed of the Bundesrat, whose members were really ambassadors of the twenty-two state governments, and the Reichstag, whose members were elected by universal male suffrage. All new laws required the approval of both bodies. The Reichstag had no control over the chancellor and his cabinet, as in Great Britain, and little control over the budget and the army and navy. If the Reichstag failed to vote a new budget, the old one automatically continued in force. This document later became the constitution of the German Empire.

Meanwhile, the former liberals in the Prussian Landtag, caught up in the nationalistic fervor following the victory over Austria, repented of their sins of having opposed Bismarck and voted him exoneration for having violated the constitution. The four predominantly Roman Catholic states south of the Main River (Bavaria, Würtemberg, Baden, and part of Hesse-Darmstadt) were left out of the North German Confederation at the insistence of Napoleon III and because Bismarck preferred to have them come in later by their own choice. Bismarck recognized that the reluctant German states could be brought into the fold if German nationalism could be rallied against a foreign threat. France, itself stirred by nationalistic ambitions, provided that threat.

Bismarck's opportunity to confront France came in 1870 when the Spanish crown was offered to a Hohenzollern prince. Bismarck persuaded the reluctant prince to accept the Spanish offer, and the French immediately took alarm at the prospect of being surrounding by Hohenzollerns. Heavy French pressure was exerted on Prussia, to which both the prince and King William I yielded. However, the French ministers were still not satisfied and demanded more. After a meeting at Ems between the French ambassador and the Prussian king, the chancellor saw an opportunity to provoke the French into war. Cleverly editing the Ems dispatch so as to make it appear that the French ambassador and the Prussian king had insulted each other, he published it to the world. The French government, walking into Bismarck's trap, declared war.

The prevailing world military opinion was that this time Prussia had overreached herself and that Bismarck's work would be undone. But as in the case of the Austro-Prussian War, the military might of Prussia was grossly underestimated. The four predominantly Catholic south German states, far from joining Catholic France as Napoleon III had hoped, threw in their lot with Protestant, German-speaking Prussia as Bismarck had anticipated.

The issue of the war was decided in a matter of weeks. Moltke's superior hosts moved into France. The French were overwhelmed. One French army was surrounded at the fortress city of Metz, where it surrendered three months later. Another French army under Marshal MacMahon and Emperor Napoleon III was surrounded at Sedan and surrendered on September 2. Napoleon III himself was one of the captives. When this news reached Paris two days later, the liberals overthrew the government of the Second Empire and declared the Third French Republic. Within a matter of weeks, Paris was surrounded by the Germans. For four months the great city held out; starvation forced it to surrender on January 28, 1871 (see Figure 46.5).

Bismarck forced stricken and helpless France to sign a treaty designed to cripple the nation beyond recovery. The Treaty of Frankfurt required France to pay an indemnity of 5 billion francs in gold. German troops would remain on French soil until this amount was paid in full (which Bismarck mistakenly hoped and expected would take a long time). The province of Alsace and the greater part of Lorraine were ceded to Germany. Since these provinces contained much of France's vital iron reserves, the seizure of Alsace and Lorraine long poisoned Franco-German relations.

On January 18, 1871, while the big German guns were still battering Paris, the heads of the twenty-five German states at war with France met on Bismarck's call at Versailles (behind the German lines) and in the Hall of Mirrors proclaimed Wilhelm I emperor of the German Empire. The constitution that Bismarck had drafted for the North German Confederation became the constitution of the German Empire. Bismarck, of course, became its chancellor, and he lived to rule over his creation for the next nineteen years. The German Empire had now replaced France as the dominant power on the European continent and became a new rival of Great Britain for world hegemony.

In Germany, as in Italy, nationalism had succeeded. In the decades after 1871 the two new nation-states would join the competition in international affairs. And nationalism was strengthening the political institutions of other nation-states, furthering a trend that had already become apparent in France during the 1850s and 1860s. Nationalism would also contribute to the new imperialism of the late nineteenth century, which in turn would further increase the power of the na-tion-state and eventually help spread nationalism to the non-Western world.

SUGGESTED READING

General

W. E. Mosse, *Liberal Europe, 1848–1875* (1974). A useful comparative history.

N. Rich, *The Age of Nationalism and Reform* (1976). A solid survey.

The Nature of Nationalism

B. Shafer, *Faces of Nationalism* (1972). A good summary.

A. Smith, *Theories of Nationalism* (1983). A comparative approach.

The Second Empire of Napoleon III

A. Plessis, *The Rise and Fall of the Second Empire* (1985). A recent account.

N. Rich, *Why the Crimean War? A Cautionary Tale* (1985). A concise political and diplomatic interpretation.

T. Zeldin, *France, 1848–1945,* 4 vols. (1973–1980). Sophisticated, insightful, and thorough.

Cavour and the Making of Italian Unity

D. Beales, *The Risorgimento and the Unification of Italy* (1982). Brief survey with accompanying documents.

R. Grew, *A Sterner Plan for Italian Unity* (1963). Excellent analysis of the movement for Italian unification.

D. M. Smith, *Cavour* (1985). A highly respected work.

D. M. Smith, *Italy: A Modern History* (1969). Scholarly survey covering the period.

German Unification

T. S. Hamerow, *The Social Foundations of German Unification, 1858–1871* (1972). Relates economic, social, and political factors behind German unification.

H. Holborn, *A History of Modern Germany,* 3 vols. (1959–1969). Detailed, scholarly survey.

M. Howard, *The Franco-Prussian War* (1969). Excellent analysis.

O. Pflanze, *Bismarck and the Development of Germany* (1963). An excellent political analysis covering Germany during this period.

CHAPTER 47

Politics in the Age of Progress, 1871–1914

KEEPING IT DOWN!

FIGURE 47.1. Bismarck and the Socialists The satirical illustration from the September 28, 1878, edition of the British magazine *Punch* shows the German chancellor Bismarck in military dress vainly struggling to keep down the Socialist "Jack in the Box." Although Bismarck banned the Social Democratic party in 1878, it would not die. In the years just prior to World War I it became Germany's largest single party. Other socialist parties grew throughout Europe during the same period. (*Punch*, September 28, 1878)

F rom the end of the Franco-Prussian War in 1871 until the outbreak of World War I in 1914, the West was free from major wars. Despite some changes and shaky beginnings, European nations survived the period with their governments intact. When the considerable economic expansion, cultural production, and imperial success are added to this political picture, the years between 1871 and 1914 could be viewed as a time of great progress for Europe.

Nevertheless, some disturbing trends were evident. The freedom from war was accompanied by a growing militarism in several nations and a new precarious complexity in international affairs. Moreover, governmental survival did not mean political peace; political unrest and even some revolutionary activity threatened many European nations. Imperial success was purchased at a price of heightened international rivalries. These disturbing trends would bear bitter fruit with the outbreak of World War I in 1914.

The strongest political forces of the period were the spread of democratic institutions and nationalism. Both forces had been underway since 1850. However, the spread of democratic institutions occurred quite unevenly. And nationalism, while it differed according to the conditions in each country, took on more conservative, aggressive, militaristic, and even racist overtones. The political developments between 1871 and 1914 can be well exposed by stressing the themes of democracy and nationalism and dividing our examination of European nations roughly between western and eastern Europe.

1. WESTERN EUROPE: THE SPREAD AND REFORM OF DEMOCRATIC INSTITUTIONS

Most western European countries had formed a national identity and initiated democratic reforms before the eastern European countries. Between 1871 and 1914 democratic institutions continued to spread in western Europe and, in general, encountered fewer problems than in eastern Europe.

Great Britain

During the second half of the nineteenth century Great Britain was in a strong position. The country had avoided the revolutionary turmoil that struck the European continent between 1848 and 1850, largely due to the government's ability to reform and adapt just enough to contain pressures for radical change. Liberalism seemed to be working well. The British economy was the most modern in the world, and the British people were relatively wealthy (although the condition of the working class was still unenviable). Yet Great Britain was not immune from the forces of nationalism that were growing everywhere in the West. In the decades following 1850 British nationalism grew, and liberal and conservative British politicians increasingly used it to gain support, increase the responsibilities of the national government, and justify foreign policy.

For most of the 1850s and 1860s liberals controlled the government. Lord Palmerston, a liberal Whig, was prime minister and leader of the Whigs for much of the period between 1855 and 1865. While modest domestic reforms to modernize government and increase allegiance of the people to the government were instituted under his ministry, he relied on nationalistic sentiment for support. He willingly paraded British naval might whenever possible and sympathetically supported movements for national liberation abroad. But he did not bend to those who demanded greater inclusion in the political system by increasing suffrage.

By 1865 William E. Gladstone had risen to leadership within the Whig party and was transforming it into the more modern Liberal party. In 1866 he and the Liberal prime minister, Lord Russell, introduced a suffrage reform bill. Although the bill was defeated and the Liberal ministry was forced to resign, the narrowness of the defeat plus the popular demand for suffrage reform convinced the rising young leader of the Conservatives, Benjamin Disraeli (1804–1881), that reform was inevitable. The shrewd Disraeli decided to seize credit for the inevitable by introducing his own reform bill. The result was the Reform Bill of 1867, which, as amended by the Liberals, doubled the electorate and gave the vote to males in the lower middle class and upper working class for the first time.

Gladstone's Reform Bill of 1884 enfranchised most of the rural males. After 1884 virtually every male householder or renter in Great Britain could vote. Restricted woman's suffrage would come in 1918 and full suffrage in 1928.

Several liberal reforms were enacted during the 1850s, 1860s, and 1870s, making government responsible for primary schools, requiring competitive examinations for civil service, and removing some religious restrictions on non-Anglicans. Yet until the end of the nineteenth century, both the Conservative and Liberal parties were still controlled by the aristocracy and the wealthy bourgeoisie. Although both parties were fairly benevolent toward the working classes, the large and discontented industrial proletariat wanted its fair share in the government. Between 1881 and 1906 its leaders turned to a program of moderate socialism, and with the aid of a number of intellectual radicals, notably George Bernard Shaw, H. G. Wells, and Sidney and Beatrice Webb, the Labour party was formed.

In 1906 the rejuvenated Liberal party came to power under the actual, if not official, leadership of the fiery young Welshman David Lloyd George, who also had the backing of the Labour party. Between 1906 and 1911 Lloyd George put through Parliament a revolutionary program of accident, sickness, old-age, and unemployment insurance. To meet this and other increased costs to the government, he forced through the reluctant House of Lords his famous budget of 1909, which shifted the "heaviest burden [of taxation] to the broadest backs." A steeply graduated income tax and high taxes on unearned income, inheritances, idle parks of the landed aristocracy, and mining royalties struck heavily at the rich. The Parliamentary Reform Act of 1911 stripped the House of Lords of most of its former power and made the popularly elected House of Commons supreme. In 1914 the long-festering Irish question was resolved by granting self-government to Ireland, although the outbreak of World War I in that year delayed its implementation. And conflict between Protestants and Catholics in northern Ireland promised to persist. However, by 1914 Great Britain was on the road to greater social, economic, and political democracy.

Between 1871 and 1914 Britain increased its imperial holdings (see Chapter 49) and joined other nations in a dangerous international rivalry that combined nationalism and militarism. In the face of Germany's swift rise to power and prestige, the British took renewed pride in their dominant navy and in their empire, which contained one-fourth of all the earth's territory and people. Many well-to-do Britishers thought themselves to be so superior to the other peoples in Europe that they became the most unpopular of all travelers on the Continent. To some observers, it appeared that Great Britain was as big a bully on the seas and overseas as Germany was on the continent of Europe.

France

With the end of the Second Empire of Napoleon III during the Franco-German War of 1870–1871, the Third French Republic was proclaimed. However, the first elections, held in February 1871 after the surrender of Paris, resulted in a sweeping victory for the monarchists. This somewhat surprising result may be explained by the fact that the republican leaders wanted to continue the hopeless war with Germany. The city of Paris, made up largely of the liberal bourgeoisie and the radical proletariat, was unwilling to submit to the domination of conservative rural France. It declared its independence from the rest of France and set up its own city government, or commune. The Paris Commune gained a reputation as an experiment in Marxian socialism. In reality the Commune was dominated by a mix of different socialistic and republican groups and was more radically democratic than anything else. Two months (April–May 1871) of fighting, culminating in a week of all-out warfare in the streets of Paris, were required for the rest of the French nation (with the regular army) to subdue the Paris Commune (see Figure 47.2). Some twenty thousand Parisians were executed after they had surrendered, and seventy-five hundred were deported. The fall of the Paris Commune ended a threat to the integrity of France, heartened conservatives, and created martyrs for socialism.

The royalists, though in the majority, were split into a Bourbon faction and an Orléanist fac-

FIGURE 47.2. Executions During the Paris Commune Bloodshed and bitter reprisals were common on both sides during the Paris Commune. Here, in 1871, Communards (including women) execute hostages in response to a previous execution of Communard leaders. (BBC Hulton/The Bettmann Archive)

tion, neither of which was willing to yield to the other. Meanwhile, as this stalemate dragged on for several years, the liberals grew in strength. Finally, in 1875, the frustrated and frightened monarchists consented (by a single vote) to the adoption of a republican constitution. The constitution provided for a Chamber of Deputies elected by universal male suffrage, a Senate elected by a complicated indirect method, and a rather powerless president to be elected by the two legislative bodies. Most of the executive functions of the republic were to be carried on by a cabinet of ministers dependent on the Chamber of Deputies. It was not until four years later, however, that the liberal republicans under the leadership of the eloquent Léon Gambetta gained actual control of the republic.

But the Third French Republic, so furtively born, was still not safe. Powerful groups were hostile to it. The chief of these were the various factions of monarchists (Bourbons, Orléanists, and Bonapartists), the professional military, the Roman Catholic hierarchy, and large numbers of peasant proprietors. In the late 1880s these factions rallied around a handsome man on horseback, General Boulanger, who became so popular that he might have overthrown the republic had he been bolder and more skillful or had the republican leaders been less courageous. As it turned out, when he was summoned to answer charges of treason against the republic, he fled the country and eventually committed suicide.

In the 1890s the antirepublican forces rallied again around a group of army officers who had falsely accused a Jewish army captain, Alfred Dreyfus, and sent him to prison on Devil's Island. This time the enemies of the republic were aided by a rising militant nationalism and anti-Semitism. It required twelve years for the republicans, inspired by the novelist Émile Zola, to get Dreyfus acquitted and the army officers who had imprisoned him punished. The Dreyfus case strengthened the republic and discredited its enemies.

Democratic government did not work as smoothly in France as in Great Britain. The tradition of extreme individualism, the animosity between clericalist and anticlericalist, the sharp cleavage between radical urban Paris and conservative rural France, lingering provincial loyalty, and a historic suspicion of strong government and high taxes—all contributed to the formation of a multiplicity of political parties. Thus the cabinet was forced to rely on the support of a precarious combination of parties (a *bloc*) in order to carry on the executive functions of government. In France the Chamber of Deputies could overthrow a cabinet without having to risk an immediate national election, as was the case in Great Britain. As a result, there was a rapid turnover of French ministries. During the forty-three years from 1871 to 1914, no fewer than fifty-one ministries attempted to govern France. Nevertheless, the French government was not as unstable as it might appear. The same groups of ministers often rotated in and out of office, sometimes simply exchanging one ministry for another. Moreover, the actual details of administration were carried on with relatively little interruption by a stable civil service, firmly built in the tradition of Richelieu and Napoleon I.

As the twentieth century opened, democratic government in France appeared to be firmly established and increasingly responsive to the will of the masses. Trade unions had been legalized, a modern system of public education that bolstered support for the republic was well established, and (in 1905) all formal ties between the state and the Catholic church were broken. Factory laws were giving the workers increased protection. Between 1905 and 1910, a limited program of unemployment, old-age, accident, and sickness insurance was inaugurated. This program of social legislation, however, was only a modest beginning; and the French masses, becoming more politically conscious and active, expressed their discontent in strikes and more votes for the Socialists.

France, like Great Britain, was subject to the growing nationalism of the period that was related to international rivalries, imperial expansion, and military buildup. The already strong French pride had only been intensified by France's defeat at the hands of Germany in 1870–1871. The statue dedicated to the city of Strasbourg in the Place de la Concorde in Paris was draped in perpetual mourning as a constant reminder of the day of revenge. France greatly speeded up its overseas empire building and increased the size of its armed forces until they were larger in proportion to the population than those of the German Empire. France sought and found military allies. When a general strike in 1910 threatened the nation's military security and war preparations, Aristide Briand, himself a radical and former Socialist, did not hesitate to use the armed forces to break it up.

Italy

Italy entered the 1870s in a much weaker position than France or Great Britain. Italy had only just become a nation-state, and even that status was weakened by strong regional differences—particularly between the more economically developed north and the poorer south. Italy's new government was liberal, but the right to vote was limited to the middle and upper classes, who constituted a small minority of the nation's population.

Between the 1870s and World War I Italian governments weathered various political crises that sometimes reached revolutionary proportions. The nation was painfully modernizing and entering into the international arena. Italian governments became involved in the shifting international alliances of the period and the nationalistic race for colonial possessions. Toward the end of the period there were signs that Italy would follow the democratic pattern set in other Western nations. Economic and social reforms to benefit the working classes were enacted under the government of Giovanni Giolitti, and in 1911 universal male suffrage was enacted.

Smaller Countries of Northern Europe

The people of the smaller countries of northern Europe also witnessed the triumph of democratic government during this period. Belgium adopted universal male suffrage in 1893. Here the weighted vote was established, men of wealth and education getting two or three additional votes. The Dutch Netherlands extended the suffrage in 1887 and again in 1896; in 1917 all adult men and women were given the right to vote. Norway adopted universal male suffrage in 1898, Sweden in 1909, and Denmark in 1914. In 1913 Norway became the first European country to grant the vote to women. In these five nations, the traditional respect for government and the relatively high degree of literacy made democracy a vigorous reality.

2. EASTERN EUROPE: CONSERVATISM, MILITARISM, AND NATIONALISM

The democratic trends characteristic of western Europe were also occurring in eastern Europe, but they were longer in arriving, less firmly established, and not as complete as in western Europe. Moreover, nationalism, which was a general phenomenon, took on more strident, aggressive tones in eastern Europe where national identity was less comfortably fixed. Most of eastern Europe remained in the control of conservative groups. The governments were autocratic in nature and more dependent on the military for support.

The German Empire Under Bismarck and Kaiser Wilhelm II

The center of these trends in eastern Europe was the German Empire. Its creation by the blood-and-iron method, its autocratic constitution (despite the establishment of universal male suffrage), and its strong-handed leadership, first by the Iron Chancellor and then by Kaiser Wilhelm II, guaranteed that the German Empire would be an enlarged Prussia. The German Empire possessed a powerful army, a large, energetic, and disciplined population, a rapidly growing industrial machine, a fervent and restless national spirit. Bismarck ruled over his creation as chancellor for almost twenty years.

His first concern after the defeat of France and the declaration of the empire in 1870–1871 was to complete the consolidation and nationalization of the German states and people. The law codes, the currencies, and the military forces of the twenty-five lesser states were brought into conformity with those of Prussia. Banking and railroads were placed under control of the national government. The empire's spawning industry was protected against British competition by a high tariff. The

French in Alsace-Lorraine, the Danes in Schleswig, and the more than 3 million Poles in the eastern districts were pressured to give up their language and traditions.

Two other groups in Germany excited Bismarck's suspicion and wrath: the Roman Catholics and the Socialists. Any German who had a foreign loyalty was intolerable to Bismarck. From 1872 to 1878, Bismarck waged a political power struggle with the Roman Catholics that came to be called the *Kulturkampf* (battle for civilization). The Jesuits were expelled, civil marriage was made compulsory, and all education, including that of Roman Catholic priests, was brought under state control and largely secularized. When the Roman Catholic clergy and most of the laity, which constituted approximately one-third of the total German population, resisted and rallied to the pope, hundreds of priests and six bishops were arrested. But it was all to no avail. The Roman Catholic Center party in the Reichstag became stronger, and by 1878 Bismarck wanted its support for what he considered to be a struggle of greater importance—that against the Socialists. In 1878 upon the accession of a more conciliatory pope, Leo XIII, Bismarck "went to Canossa" and had the most severe of the anti-Catholic legislation repealed.

In the same year he began a twelve-year crusade against the internationally minded Socialists. He outlawed their publications, their organizations, and their meetings, and set the German police force upon them. But he only drove them underground. Throughout the decade of the 1880s, Bismarck sought to undercut the Socialists' appeal to the working class by setting up a comprehensive system of social insurance. Accident, sickness, and old-age insurance was provided for the industrial proletariat, the funds being raised by compulsory contributions from the workers, the employers, and the state. Although Bismarck's motives were not benevolent or humanitarian, his measures gave impetus to a trend toward state responsibility for social security. Nevertheless, the Socialists were not appeased, and Bismarck continued to fight them as long as he remained chancellor.

Bismarck's foreign policy after 1871 was one of security and retrenchment. He knew that France would be unforgiving and revengeful, forever seeking an opportunity to regain Alsace and Lorraine. Of France alone he had little fear, but France in league with other powers, particularly Russia and Great Britain, would be formidable. Therefore, his consistent policy was to maintain a close military alliance with Austria-Hungary and cordial relations with Russia and Great Britain. In 1873 Bismarck formed the Three Emperor's League among Germany, Austria-Hungary, and Russia. When the interests of Austria-Hungary and Russia proved to be incompatible, this league was replaced in 1879–1882 by the Triple Alliance among Germany, Austria-Hungary, and Italy. A separate "reinsurance treaty" of friendship and neutrality was made with Russia. Of course, Bismarck did not depend wholly on diplomacy. Throughout this period, the German military machine was made even more powerful.

In 1888 Wilhelm II (1888–1918) became kaiser. Wilhelm II was twenty-nine years of age when he ascended the throne. He had been brought up in the army, which was his first love. Egotistical and bombastic by nature, he was a dabbler in theology, history, and the arts and gave advice and instructions freely to the leading figures in those fields. He was also an eloquent and willing speaker and had his generous and humanitarian moments.

The young kaiser's personality and policies soon clashed with those of Bismarck. In 1890, just two years after he became emperor, Wilhelm II accepted Bismarck's reluctant resignation as chancellor. The immediate cause of the break was a disagreement over the control of the ministry and the repeal of the anti-Socialist laws, which Bismarck wished to be continued. The real reason, however, was that there was simply not room enough in Germany for two such prima donnas.

Bismarck's foreign policy was quickly reversed. The reinsurance treaty with Russia was immediately allowed to lapse, as the kaiser assumed a keen interest in extending German hegemony over the Balkans and the Ottoman Empire, areas the Russians considered to be vital to their own interests and ambitions. In 1894 Russia formed an alliance with France, the very thing that Bismarck had work so hard to prevent. Wilhelm II also soon alienated Great Britain. His extension of German influence in the Near East, particularly his Berlin-to-Bagdad railroad project (see pp. 622–623), threatened an area in which Great Britain had many vital interests and through which ran its "lifeline" to India and the Far East. In China, too, German interests began to rival those of the British.

It was the kaiser's naval policy, however, that alarmed the British the most. Wilhelm was an ardent and lifelong navalist. "The waves beat powerfully at our national gates," he cried, "and call us as a great nation to maintain our place in the world. . . ." Germany's "place in the sun" was a favorite phrase of the Hohenzollern emperor. The Reichstag voted an enormous naval building program that was steadily increased until in 1908 it called for twenty-eight new battleships of the biggest and latest design. The purpose of this program was to give Germany a battle fleet so great that "a war against the mightiest naval power would endanger the supremacy of that power."

Great Britain, whose food supply as well as her empire depended on naval supremacy, took utmost alarm. Failing in efforts to reach an understanding with the kaiser's government, Britain launched a huge and costly naval building program of its own. In 1904 Britain joined France, and in 1907 Russia, in the Triple Entente, which was in reality a defensive military alliance. The interests and policies of Great Britain, France, and Russia had long been so discordant that nothing less than maximum alarm could have brought them together. Thus in seventeen years Wilhelm had undone Bismarck's work and brought about the "encirclement" of the fatherland by three of the world's greatest powers.

Germany's economic exploits under Bismarck and Wilhelm II were no less phenomenal than those in the military realm. In 1871 Great Britain was the world's leading nation in manufacturing and commerce; the Industrial Revolution was still in its early stages in Germany. By 1914 Germany was a close second to Great Britain in industry and commerce; in many areas, such as the production of steel and machinery, Germany had far outstripped Britain. In the up-and-coming chemical and electrical industries and in scientific agriculture and forestry, Germany was far in advance of all other nations. Germany was also first in the application of science to industry and in industrial and scientific research. By 1914 the German merchant marine had captured the lion's share of the lucrative transatlantic passenger traffic.

At a time when other industrial nations, particularly the United States, were beginning to restrict the giant monopolistic trusts, the German imperial government was encouraging and subsidizing its cartels in order that they might compete more effectively with foreign companies. More and more of the world's market was captured by German business. "Made in Germany" became a familiar mark from the Andean plateau to the Congo jungles. Germany's population, keeping pace with its economy, increased from 41 million in 1871 to 65 million in 1914. Meanwhile, heavy emigration (which had reached a peak in the 1880s of some two hundred fifty thousand a year, most of it to the United States) dwindled to a mere trickle. In 1914 the number of German emigrants was less than the number of workers coming into Germany from neighboring countries. Only the United States was keeping pace with Germany in overall economic advancement.

The industrialization of Germany, although accompanied by the growth of a large and prosperous bourgeoisie, did not produce a tide of liberalism as it had in the other Western industrialized nations. The middle classes allied themselves with the conservative government. Only the Social Democratic party (working class) and the small and weak Progressive party (intellectuals, professionals, and small-business people) advocated liberal or radical reforms. But even the Social Democratic party, by 1914 the largest party in the empire, was inundated by the flood of nationalism that welled up during the international crises that preceded World War I.

Russia

Until the 1850s, Russia had remained relatively untouched by the Industrial Revolution and liberalism. Russia's government was autocratic under the tsar, its society was still feudalistic with serfs bound to the land and their lords, and its large army enjoyed an aura of near invincibility. Russia had earned the reputation of being the most conservative and unreforming of the European powers. After the Crimean War of 1853–1856,

FIGURE 47.3. Red Sunday In January 1905 the tsar's guards shot down hundreds of peaceful demonstrators in front of the royal palace in St. Petersburg. This event, known as "Red Sunday," left a bitter memory with Russia's liberals and radicals. (The Granger Collection)

it was clear that things would have to change soon.

Russia's army was humiliated in the war. Its leaders quickly realized that Russia was being left behind by the other powers, that the country lacked the economic and social foundations for a modern war—the railroads, the armaments industry, and the social support. The new tsar, Alexander II (1855–1881), announced a series of reforms. The most important was the freeing of the serfs in 1861. While the measure put an end to that form of human bondage and did transfer land to the freed peasantry, it did not make the peasants fully independent and self-sufficient. In general they received only the poorest land, they remained burdened by payments owed to the state, and they were tied by collective ownership to their village commune (the *mir*). Other reforms made the local judicial system more independent, created elected local political institutions, encouraged primary and secondary education, relaxed censorship, and modernized the military. At the same time, the government initiated a program of railway construction, which stimulated related industries. In Russia's cities a still small middle and working class began to grow.

A strong wave of dissatisfaction arose during the later years of Alexander II's rule. The former serfs had been cruelly disappointed by the fruits of emancipation. Another revolt of Russia's Polish subjects in 1863 made Alexander II more reactionary. His failure to follow through with more sweeping reforms after the emancipation of the serfs disappointed liberals, populists, and others, who were mostly intellectual young aristocrats. In despair over the possibility of reforming the huge Russian Empire by orderly methods, these young intellectuals became radical. They set out to undermine Russia's society, government, and church in order to build a new and modern Russia from the ruins. When their efforts were spurned by the masses whom they were seeking to uplift, a more violent wing of the revolutionaries turned to terror and assassination to achieve their ends. Numerous bureaucrats and police officials were slain by terrorists, and Tsar Alexander II himself was killed by a bomb.

The new tsar, Alexander III (1881–1894), was a harsh, reactionary autocrat. Blaming his father's death on softness, he set out to exterminate all liberalism in Russia. The ruthless Plehve was made head of the secret police, and its agents were soon everywhere. Thousands of suspects were arrested. Some were shot or exiled to Siberia. Alexander initiated a sweeping reactionary program of Russianization. The censored press, the closely supervised schools, the secret police, and above all, the clergy of the Orthodox church became potent agencies for Russianization. Non-Orthodox religions were persecuted. Language minority groups—the Poles, the Baltic peoples, the Finns, and even the Ukrainians—were forced to use the Russian language. The Jews suffered the harshest persecution. They were subject to such abuse, including bloody pogroms, that more than a quarter million of them fled, mostly to the United States.

Alexander III was succeeded by Nicholas II (1894–1917), also reactionary but less effective. Although Nicholas attempted to continue the policies of his father, he was unable to make them

work. During the 1890s, Russia experienced a new surge of industrialization, stimulated by the aggressive policies of Sergei Witte, the finance minister, and the infusion of foreign capital into Russia. A larger industrial bourgeoisie and proletariat emerged and with them movements for liberal and radical reform. Of the various liberal and radical parties that emerged, the one of greatest significance for the future was the Social Democratic party. This was a Marxist party whose leadership was made up almost entirely of intellectual radicals. Their chief concern was for the industrial proletariat. In 1903 the Social Democrats split into a moderate, gradualist wing called the Mensheviks (minority) and a violent revolutionary wing called the Bolsheviks (majority). The Bolsheviks were led by the brilliant and dynamic Vladimir Lenin, who was living in exile in Switzerland.

Taking advantage of the embarrassment of the tsar's government because of Russia's defeat by Japan in 1904–1905 (see p. 621), the various liberal and radical groups clamored for reform. In July 1904 the hated Plehve was assassinated. In January 1905 hundreds of peaceful demonstrators were shot down in front of the royal palace in St. Petersburg by the tsar's guard. This bloody event, known as "Red Sunday," fanned the flames of discontent (see Figure 47.3). In October 1905 a general strike completely paralyzed the country for ten days. Nicholas II, yielding at last, issued a manifesto that promised civil liberties and a popularly elected Duma. However, before the Duma could be elected, the return of the Russian troops from the Far East and a huge loan from Russia's ally, France, strengthened the hand of the tsar. During the next two years he and his advisers succeeded in reducing the Duma to an undemocratically elected body that had little real control over the government. Nevertheless, a break had been made in Russia's autocratic system. Russia's rural society had broken from its feudal bonds, its economy was industrializing, and its political system included parliamentary institutions that promised to gain authority in the future.

National Movements in Southeast Europe

While nationalism between 1871 and 1914 was crushing minority language groups in the German

Map 47.1 **LANGUAGE GROUPS, AUSTRIA-HUNGARY** This map indicates the difficulties facing the Austro-Hungarian Empire in an age of growing nationalism. Satisfaction of demands for independence by the various ethnic or language groups would spell dismemberment of the empire.

and the Russian empires, it was pulling the Austrian and Ottoman empires apart along language lines. After Austria's defeat by Prussia in 1866, the dominant German minority in Austria felt obliged to take into partnership the aggressive and restless Magyars of Hungary. The *Ausgleich* (compromise) of 1867 set up the Dual Monarchy of Austria-Hungary. Each country had its own separate parliament. But the two were united under a common ruler, the head of the house of Hapsburg; common ministries of war, finance, and foreign affairs; and joint delegations from the two parliaments whose

duty was to coordinate policies wherever possible. This arrangement was essentially an alliance between the Germans of Austria and the Magyars of Hungary against the Slavic, Rumanian, and Italian language groups, which constituted a majority of the total population of the Dual Monarchy. In effect, the Germans said to the Magyars: "You take care of your subject language groups [mostly Slavs] and we will take care of ours" (see Map 47.1).

Austria followed a relatively moderate policy in dealing with its subject language groups. Cultural autonomy was granted, and the suffrage was gradually extended until in 1907 all adult males were given the vote. However, the subject peoples were more interested in nationalism than in democracy. The various language groups developed images of a glorious cultural and political past. The prosperous Czechs of Bohemia were especially adamant. The problem was confounded by the fact that many of the language groups had kinspeople outside the Dual Monarchy whom they wished to join and who deliberately stirred up their disloyalty. Such groups were the Italians, the Poles, the Ruthenians (Ukrainians), the Serbs, and the Rumanians. Parliamentary sessions in Austria frequently degenerated into shouting, inkstand-throwing melees among the various language groups. Moreover anti-Semitism was growing in Austria, a development not unrelated to these problems among different ethnic groups.

Hungary made no pretense of conciliation. The Magyar aristocracy ruled over the Slovak, Rumanian, Serb, and Croat minorities with an iron hand. The aristocracy also refused to permit its own Magyar masses to participate in the government. The nationalist discontent in Hungary was even greater than it was in Austria; the Yugo (southern) Slavs (Croats and Serbs) were particularly troublesome. This explosive nationalism threatened to blow the Austro-Hungarian monarchy apart and, because of the network of entangling alliances, to draw the other major powers into a world conflict.

The Balkan portion of the Ottoman Empire between 1871 and 1914 was a hornets' nest of nationalism (see Map 47.1). The hatred of the Christian Balkan language groups for their Moslem Turkish masters was equaled only by their distrust for each other. The once potent Ottoman Empire crumbled throughout the course of the nineteenth century, and one Balkan language group after another, now aflame with national pride and ambition, emerged as an independent nation. Meanwhile, all the great powers of Europe became involved in the strategic and troubled area of the Near East. Russia, Austria-Hungary, Great Britain, France, Germany, and Italy had important imperial, economic, and military interests in the Balkans. In addition, Russia and Austria-Hungary had serious nationalistic interests there. Russia considered itself the big brother and protector of the Slavic-speaking Serbs and Bulgarians. Austria-Hungary's large Rumanian and Yugoslav populations desired union with their free kinspeople in Rumania and Serbia. Between 1829 and 1913 first the Greeks, then the Serbs, Rumanians, and Bulgarians, and finally the Albanians gained their independence from the Ottoman Empire. In each case a major crisis occurred among the great powers. These Balkan crises became progressively more severe, until finally one crisis got out of control and exploded into World War I.

SUGGESTED READING

General

A. J. Mayer, *The Persistence of the Old Regime in Europe to the Great War* (1981). A controversial, recent interpretation.

N. Stone, *Europe Transformed, 1878–1919* (1984). Fine new survey.

A. J. P. Taylor, *The Struggle for Mastery in Europe, 1848–1918* (1971). A good, interpretive study of international politics.

Great Britain

M. Bentley, *Politics Without Democracy, 1815–1914* (1984). Fine political coverage.

D. Read, *England, 1868–1914. The Age of Urban Democracy* (1979). Related politics and socioeconomic developments.

France

D. Johnson, *France and the Dreyfus Affair* (1967). Excellent study.

J. M. Moyem and M. Rebérioux, *The Third Republic from Its Origins to the Great War, 1871–1914* (1984). A thorough synthesis.

R. L. Williams, *The French Revolution of 1870–1871* (1969). Excellent analysis of the Paris Commune.

Italy

J. A. Thayer, *Italy and the Great War: Politics and Culture, 1870–1915* (1964). A solid analysis of Italian political history.

D. M. Smith, *Italy: A Modern History* (1969). A good survey.

Germany

G. Craig, *Germany, 1866–1945* (1980). Particularly good on German political history during this period.

P. Pulzer, *The Rise of Political Anti-Semitism in Germany and Austria* (1964). A well-written analysis.

C. Schorsky, *German Social Democracy, 1905–1917* (1955). Excellent analysis of the Social Democrats.

H. U. Wehler, *The German Empire, 1871–1918* (1985). A recent interpretive study.

Russia

W. Blackwell, *The Industrialization of Russia* (1982). Good on this important topic.

A. B. Ulam, *Russia's Failed Revolutionaries* (1981). Good study of Russia's revolutionary groups prior to 1917.

H. Rogger, *Russia in the Age of Modernization and Revolution, 1881–1917* (1983). Excellent synthesis.

Southeast Europe

B. Jelavich, *History of the Balkans* (1983). A useful recent survey.

L. S. Stavrianos, *The Balkans, 1815–1914* (1963). Relates domestic and international developments.

CHAPTER 48

Democracy, Expansion, Civil War, and Reform in the United States, 1800–1920

FIGURE 48.1. Manifest Destiny This painting, "Manifest Destiny," by John Gast, reveals the idealized myth of westward expansion. Moving from the Atlantic coast cities of the East across the plains and mountains toward the Pacific, the goddess of Destiny carries a schoolbook in one hand and a telegraph wire in the other. Below her come white male hunters and settlers, pushing Indians and buffalo farther west in retreat. In her wake follows the railroad. (Library of Congress)

By the end of the eighteenth century the United States was experiencing many of the same trends and developments as other nations of Western civilization. As we saw in Chapter 39, the United States was influenced by Enlightenment ideas, experienced a revolution, and established liberal political institutions—a pattern familiar to France and some other European nations. With the exception of the black slaves, almost all citizens of the new nation were from European stock. Most people worked the land, but there were some growing cities and early industrial establishments—again a pattern not too different from many areas in Europe.

There were some important differences between the United States and other nations of Western civilization in 1800. It had only recently emerged from colonial status and remained separated from Europe by the Atlantic Ocean. Politically and socially, the United States did not carry a strong legacy of monarchical rule or aristocratic distinctions. There was a surplus of land, thanks to the willingness of American citizens to take from the Indians, and a supply of cheap, noncompetitive labor, thanks to slavery.

During the nineteenth century the United States again shared in trends sweeping through Western civilization while remaining strikingly distinct in some important ways. In this chapter we will emphasize the pattern of shared trends and distinctions as we trace major elements of United States history in rough chronological order. By the end of the second decade of the twentieth century, the United States will have reached a point where its development can be better viewed as integrated with that of other Western nations.

1. DEMOCRACY AND GEOGRAPHIC EXPANSION, 1800–1861

Democracy in the young American republic received a boost with the election of Thomas Jefferson as president in 1800. Jefferson represented the ideals of a nation of small farmers and the realities of a political democracy with a party system. The coming to power of this liberal theorist—the author of the Declaration of Independence—was a shock to the more elitist Federalists, who flour-ished under presidents Washington and Adams. The conservative Founding Fathers had felt that the capable elite should rule and that political parties, or "factions," would undermine the new political system. Although the rich and well-born raised a cry of anguish at the triumph of Jefferson, he was a moderate individual who in fact did little that was radical as president. Although he was supported in the election by the yeoman farmers, he was an elegant Virginian and a scholarly philosopher rather than a man of the masses.

The War of 1812 with Great Britain resulted in an upsurge of American nationalism, which helped mold America's evolving political institutions. A new crop of nationally minded statesmen appeared, the ablest of whom were Henry Clay, John C. Calhoun, and Daniel Webster. The war itself ended indecisively, yet the United States emerged with a stronger national economy and a greater sense of being a nation with its own character and institutions rather than a former British colony.

The War of 1812 also produced a hero, Andrew Jackson. His rise to the presidency signaled a new stage in the development of America's democratic institutions. Not only did it represent the rise of a common man to the presidency—he defeated formidable, established, sophisticated political giants—it also marked the rise of western frontier states to national political importance and the early development of modern, mass-based political parties. During the Jacksonian era, which extended some two decades after his election in 1828, democracy advanced as new states without property qualifications for voting were rapidly admitted to the Union and as the older states eliminated property qualifications from their voting requirements. Artisans and small farmers used the egalitarian rhetoric of the Jacksonian era to assert their own interests and power. Yet much of the so-called Jacksonian "revolution" was more superficial than substantial. American Indians and blacks fared worse during the Jacksonian era than before, and like Jefferson, Jackson as president did little that was radical.

Meanwhile, the United States was expanding (see Map 48.1). Between 1800 and 1861 the United States was the most rapidly growing nation in the world, both in area and in population. The pur-

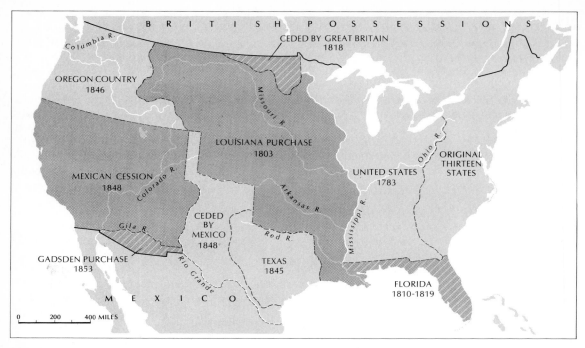

Map 48.1 **TERRITORIAL EXPANSION OF THE UNITED STATES, 1783–1853** Through a variety of means, including wars, purchases, treaties, and expropriation, the United States more than trebled its territory between 1800 and 1861. This territorial expansion kept land in surplus despite an unprecedented rate of population growth.

chase of the Louisiana Territory by Thomas Jefferson from Napoleon in 1803 for some $16 million doubled the original area of the United States. In 1819 Florida was purchased from Spain for $5 million. Texas, which was even bigger than now, was annexed in 1845. The next year the Oregon Country was annexed after the settlement of a longstanding dispute with Great Britain. The annexation of Texas resulted in a war with Mexico (1846–1848). After a quick and easy victory, the United States took a huge block of Mexican territory, comprising the present states of California, Arizona, New Mexico, Nevada, Utah, and parts of Colorado and Wyoming. This territory was enlarged to the south in 1853 by the Gadsden Purchase from Mexico ($10 million). These additions within a period of fifty years more then trebled the original territory of the young American nation. Yet the

cost was higher than the money paid for some of the territory. Indians had to be slaughtered and dispossessed. Wars of conquest had to be fought (Mexico), and other wars had to be risked (Great Britain). Westward expansion was not simply a sanitary, heroic struggle to a destined end.

The growth in population was keeping pace with the increase in area. Between 1800 and 1861 the population of the United States increased from approximately 5 million to 32 million. Adding to the high rate of natural increase was an ever-increasing tide of immigration from Europe. After 1840 the largest immigrant groups were the Irish, most of whom settled in the cities of the Northeast, and the Germans, most of whom pushed on to the fertile lands of the Middle West.

Between 1800 and 1861, then, American political institutions had evolved along democratic and nationalistic lines. Voting rights had been extended to essentially all adult, white males. Political power had been wrestled from the elite circles of the old colonial well-to-do. A modern political party system had been developed. Americans pridefully thought of themselves and their institutions as distinct within Western civilization. The United States had expanded westward to the Pacific Ocean. The western frontier itself was one of the greatest of nationalizing influences. To it came people from all the seaboard states and from abroad who looked to the national government for protection, for roads and canals, and for land titles. It was in this period that American culture began to free itself from strictly European influence. The American Indian was idealized by Henry Wadsworth Longfellow and James Fenimore Cooper. Washington Irving's pen made the legends of American colonial days enchanting. Gilbert Stuart and Charles Willson Peale made idealized portraits of American heroes. American schools and universities were teaching a particular American version of civilization and world affairs.

2. SLAVERY, CIVIL WAR, AND RECONSTRUCTION, 1861–1877

The central event for American history during the nineteenth century was the Civil War, which broke out in 1861 and lasted until 1865. The nature of the Civil War has been debated endlessly, but certain features stand out. The North was increasingly a growing, urban, industrial society based on free labor (see Figure 48.2). The South remained agricultural, dependent on large plantation crops such as cotton and based on slave labor (see Figure 48.3). The North was enjoying increasing influence over national policies and generally favored federal over state power. The South saw its influence over national policies slipping and increasingly favored states' rights over federal power. The North seemed to represent a modernizing, democratic, nationalistic society; the South a traditional, unegalitarian, regional society. In great part, the Civil War was a clash between these increasingly different societies with different interests. But the issue that provided much of the emotional energy to this clash and that prior to

1861 tied together the issues dividing North and South was black slavery.

The first boatload of blacks was brought to Virginia in 1619, one year before the Pilgrims landed at Plymouth Rock. Because of the tremendous amount of labor required to clear the American wilderness, the African slave trade flourished throughout the colonial period. By the time of the American Revolution, black slaves constituted approximately one-fifth of the total population of the thirteen colonies. Slavery was recognized and protected by the national constitution. Because of the climate and the diversified economy, however, slavery was proving to be unprofitable in the Northern states, and between 1777 and 1804 all the states north of Maryland passed emancipation laws. South of the Mason and Dixon line (the boundary between Maryland and Pennsylvania), where agriculture reigned supreme, slavery continued to be profitable and prevalent. But by 1789 many Americans, in the South as well as in the North, disliked the institution. After the Revolution scores of antislavery societies were founded. It appeared possible that slavery in America was on its way to an early and peaceful end.

Some unforeseen developments, however, changed the attitude of the South toward emancipation, and a sharp line was drawn between the North and South over the slavery issue. The first of these developments was Whitney's invention of the cotton gin in 1793. This machine made the raising of cotton so profitable that soon large cotton plantations worked by black slaves grew up throughout the South. The American South became the chief supplier of Britain's textile mills. By the mid–nineteenth century, the black slaves outnumbered the whites in South Carolina and Mississippi, and in the rest of the Deep South slaves were about equal in number to the whites. The Southern economy had become so wedded to cotton and to black slavery that the Southern antislavery movement had faltered, and the defense of slavery had gained momentum. Even more important than economic considerations in the development of proslavery sentiment in the South was the social problem. Black slaves were seen not only as the basis of wealth but also as the basis of power and status by Southern slaveholders. White slaveholders accepted as given the inferi-

ority of blacks. The Southern whites did not believe that they could absorb into their society or even live alongside so many free blacks under any circumstances.

The critical issue became the extension of slavery to the western territories. The population of the Northern states, with their growing industry, was rapidly outstripping that of the South. As the northwestern territories clamored for statehood without slavery, the Southerners took alarm. Already they were hopelessly outnumbered in the House of Representatives, whose membership is based on population. Their only security in the national government lay in the Senate, where each state has two members. The Southerners did everything in their power to slow down the settlement of the West and insisted that the admission of every free state must be accompanied by the admission of a slave state in order that equality in the Senate be maintained. But time and tide were on the side of the North. Geography, population, the growth of industrialization, and the march of liberalism in the Western world were irresistible.

In 1854 the Republican party was founded as a strictly Northern party committed to the restriction and, seemingly, ultimate extinction of slavery. In 1860, with Abraham Lincoln as its candidate, it won a sweeping victory over the Democrats, now split between North and South over the question of slavery. Rather than accept an inferior position in the nation and face the prospect of eventually having their power and status destroyed by some 4 million black slaves forcibly freed in their midst, eleven Southern states (about half the territory of

---

FIGURE 48.2.   A Northern Factory   (Top) This lithograph of the Stillman, Allen & Co. Novelty Iron Works of New York City shows the more industrial, urban nature of the North in the middle decades just prior to the Civil War. (Museum of the City of New York)

FIGURE 48.3.   A Southern Plantation   (Bottom) This picture, Charles Giroux's ''Cotton Plantation,'' shows the contrasting rural society with a large population of black slaves typical of the South. Courtesy, Museum of Fine Arts, Boston, M. and M. Karolik Collection)

the Union and a third of its population) seceded and set up an independent government.

The North had an overwhelming preponderance in population, wealth, industry, transportation, and naval power. But the South enjoyed brilliant military leadership and the further advantage of fighting on its own soil for what it believed to be the survival of white civilization. The war lasted four bloody years. For three of the four years it looked as if the Union could not be restored. But after numerous discordant elements in the North were brought together, Great Britain and France tactfully neutralized, and the winning commanders and strategy found, the Southern armies were finally crushed.

Slavery was abolished and the authority of the national government restored, never to be seriously threatened again. However, the war left a legacy of sectional bitterness. The conciliatory Lincoln was assassinated just five days after the war ended. The radical Republican congressional leaders, who now gained control of the government, treated the defeated and devastated South as a conquered province. They sought to achieve basic reforms and to ensure political and civil rights for the freed slaves. The effort ended by 1877 when the last federal troops were finally withdrawn from the South. Over the course of the next twenty years many of the gains made by blacks were lost. By this time a different dynamic was taking hold of American life and changing it in unprecedented ways: industrialization.

3. INDUSTRIALIZATION AND URBANIZATION, 1865–1901

Although the earliest factories were already present in the United States by the end of the eighteenth century, the growth of industrialization during the nineteenth century was at first quite slow. The French and British blockades during the Napoleonic wars and the War of 1812 with Britain cut the United States off from British manufacturers and caused much American commercial capital to be diverted to manufacturing. By the middle decades of the nineteenth century, industrialization was spreading, particularly in the Northeast. However, it was not until the years immediately

FIGURE 48.4. Cornelius Vanderbilt This cartoon attacks Cornelius Vanderbilt, who in the 1860s gained control over several railroads and amassed a great fortune. He is portrayed exercising monopolistic corporate power over the nation's railroads. (Culver Pictures)

connected with industrialization grew, fed both by migration from rural areas and massive immigration from Europe. The United States proved subject to the same problems that plagued other industrializing nations: poor working conditions, low pay, child labor, urban slums, inadequate sanitation, and few social services.

However, there were a few elements that seemed to characterize the United States' growing industrialization between 1865 and 1901. Above all, the degree to which business became concentrated in the hands of a few individuals and corporations was striking. Industrial capitalists such as Andrew Carnegie (steel), John D. Rockefeller (oil), Cornelius Vanderbilt (railroads), and J. P. Morgan (finance) amassed unbelievable fortunes and power (see Figure 48.4). The corporations they founded, such as U.S. Steel and Standard Oil, soon gained monopolistic control over vast resources.

More than in most other nations, in America governmental policies during this period favored business in general and these huge industrial firms in particular. Not surprisingly, then, in the United States the unionization of labor was relatively slow to emerge. In part this result was due to the continued abundance of cheap land and the influx of cheap mobile labor from Europe. But unionization was also deterred by the determined resistance of industrial capitalists backed by private and public police power, and by governmental policies and officials unsympathetic to unionization. Despite some earlier beginnings in various trades (such as the Knights of Labor), it was not until 1886 that Samuel Gompers, an immigrant from Great Britain, organized the American Federation of Labor—the first successful national labor organization in America.

By the end of the nineteenth century the United States not only was a major industrial power but also had outstripped the world in industrial production. The government and the economy of the country were still dominated by big-business interests that controlled the dominant "Old Guard" wing of the Republican party. Although the United States enjoyed enormous overall economic development, wealth was very unequally distributed, causing widespread discontent. Western and southern farmers had been

following the Civil War that the United States joined other Western nations as a leading industrial power.

In most ways industrialization in the United States proceeded much as it did in other Western countries. New machines and sources of power were applied to the manufacturing process. Large factories sprang up in the East and Midwest, turning raw materials into finished products in great quantities. Working-class and urban populations clamoring for public regulation of the railroads, on which they were dependent. Small business, labor, and consumers demanded protection against the monopolistic practices and prices of the great trusts and corporations, which were protected by a prohibitively high tariff. The United States government remained behind almost all other industrial nations in its willingness to deal with social abuses stemming from industrialization. Millions deplored the city slums, the corrupt spoils system in the civil service, and the squandering of natural resources by private interests. The forces of reform were growing and would break out in the two decades following the turn of the century.

4. REFORM AND PROGRESSIVISM, 1901–1920

The great reforms of the progressive era are usually dated from 1901, when Theodore Roosevelt assumed the presidency. Roosevelt firmly believed in the capitalistic system, but he was convinced that the time had come when the superiority of the government over private business must be asserted. After assuming the presidency in 1901 upon the assassination of McKinley, "T.R.," as he was popularly known, immediately launched a vigorous program of reform. The Interstate Commerce Act of 1887 and the Sherman Antitrust Act of 1890, which had lain dormant, were activated. Organized labor was given a little support in its unequal fight with organized capital. Pure food and drug acts were designed to restrict the corporations and safeguard the public health. More than 200 million acres of forest and mineral lands and water power sites were withheld from private exploitation. He strengthened the merit system in the federal civil service. Many of his reform efforts were blocked by Congress and the federal courts, which were still controlled by the Republican Old Guard.

In 1912 the Democrats, under the leadership of Woodrow Wilson (1856–1924), gained their first clear-cut victory since the Civil War. Wilson proved to be more liberal than Roosevelt. With the Democrats in control of both houses of Congress, Wilson's administration sharply lowered the tariff, passed the Clayton Antitrust Act (more specific than the Sherman Act), gave further encouragement to organized labor, and set up the Federal Reserve Banking System, which removed control of the nation's financial policies from the hands of private interests on Wall Street and placed them in the hands of the federal government.

The passage of the long-struggled-for women's suffrage in 1920 was the last reform of the progressive era. The return to power of the conservative Republicans under Warren Harding in 1920 brought to a close the progressive period. However, in those two decades American institutions and policies had adjusted to at least some of the social and economic realities of a modern democratic industrial society. At the same time the United States had joined other imperial powers with its acquisition of territories in Latin America, the Pacific, and Asia. Finally, the United States had become embroiled in World War I. From this point on, the United States would be too integrally connected to world-wide economic and political affairs to act in isolation.

SUGGESTED READING

General

R. Current et al., *American History: A Survey* (1987). A balanced, solid text.

Democracy and Geographic Expansion, 1800–1861

R. Billington, *Westward Expansion: A History of the American Frontier* (1974). An excellent survey.

J. Ellis, *After the Revolution: Profiles of Early American Culture* (1979). A useful survey of culture.

J. R. Howe, *From the Revolution Through the Age of Jackson: Innocence and Empire in the Young Republic* (1973). Good study of political development.

E. Spicer, *A Short History of the Indians of the United States* (1969). Useful introduction to the topic.

Slavery, Civil War, and Reconstruction, 1861–1877

M. Dillon, *The Abolitionists: The Growth of a Dissenting Minority* (1974). Concise summary.

E. D. Genovese, *Roll, Jordan, Roll: The World Slaves Made* (1974). A scholarly study of slave society.

J. H. Franklin, *Reconstruction After the Civil War* (1961). A classic study.

P. J. Parish, *The American Civil War* (1975). Includes chapters on the preceding and succeeding periods.

Industrialization and Urbanization, 1865–1901

D. J. Boorstin, *The Americans: The National Experience* (1965). Useful sections on the impact of modernization.

T. C. Cochran and W. Miller, *The Age of Enterprise* (1968). A broad, scholarly study covering the period.

E. C. Kirkland, *Industry Comes of Age: Business, Labor, and Public Policy 1860–1897* (1967). A good survey of industrialization.

Reform and Progressivism, 1901–1920

J. M. Cooper, Jr., *The Warrior and the Priest: Woodrow Wilson and Theodore Roosevelt* (1983). A comparative biography.

R. Hofstadter, *The Age of Reform: From Bryan to FDR* (1955). A classic.

A. Link and R. McCormick, *Progressivism* (1983). A succinct modern review.

S. M. Rothman, *Woman's Proper Place* (1978). Focuses on women's changing roles.

R. H. Wiebe, *The Search for Order, 1877–1920* (1968). Contains good material on reform and progressivism.

CHAPTER 49
Imperialism

FIGURE 49.1. Imperial Glory This picture of colonial troops parading in London in celebration of Queen Victoria's Diamond Jubilee in 1897 reveals some of the forces behind late-nineteenth-century imperialism: nationalistic pride, military power, social cohesion, and romantic sentiments. (Culver Pictures)

We have already seen that from the fifteenth to the eighteenth centuries the national monarchies of the West "discovered" and conquered most of the Western Hemisphere, the west coast of Africa, and southern Asia. Then from 1763 until 1871 there came a lull in expansion; Europe was busy with revolution, industrialization, and nation building. Imperial powers such as Spain, Portugal, and France lost many of their overseas holdings during this period, leaving Great Britain as the only Western nation with an extensive empire. Even some of Britain's holdings in North America had been lost during the American Revolution, and imperialism seemed incompatible with liberalism in the mid–nineteenth century. In the period from 1871 to 1914, however, a new burst of European expansion, the "new imperialism," brought practically all the remaining portions of the earth's surface under Western influence or domination.

1. CAUSES FOR THE NEW IMPERIALISM

One of the chief impulses behind the new imperialism was economic. The rapid expansion of industry in Europe and the United States created a demand for greater markets, new sources of raw materials, and investment outlets for surplus capital. Many people in Western nations pushed for imperial expansion, optimistically assuming that the new markets, the new sources of raw materials, and the new investment outlets could be found. These advocates of imperialism were primarily those most directly in a position to profit from it—certain financiers, merchants, shippers, settlers, and colonial officials as well as industrialists with specific economic interests in non-Western lands.

Probably a greater impulse to the new imperialism was nationalism. It flattered the national ego to see its colors spread over the map. It also provided military and naval bases and personnel for the hungry military machines that were an integral part of late-nineteenth-century nationalism. In Europe the conservative parties based on the landed aristocracy were even more imperialistic than the liberal parties based on industrial

and commercial interests. Most of the imperial governors, generals, and admirals came from the conservative aristocracy. National egotism also gave the citizens of the great Western powers a sense of mission; they were bringing the blessings of their civilization to backward peoples. Rudyard Kipling expressed the belief of many Westerners when he sang in rhyme of the "white man's burden" to hold in tutelage and to civilize the "lesser breeds" of the earth.

Another motivating factor in the new imperialism was the evangelizing zeal of the Christian religion. Christianity had long taken to heart the command, "Go ye into all the world and preach the gospel to every creature." At the very time that Christianty was wavering under attack in its homeland in the West, it was carrying on foreign missionary activity of unprecedented scope and intensity. More often than not, where the missionaries went, so went Western explorers, traders, troops, and officials.

In addition, political and diplomatic developments became intertwined after the 1880s to make colonial claims increasingly valuable assets. These claims could be used by Western nations to forge alliances or bargain with competitors in the growing international disputes of the period.

Finally, the processes involved in imperial expansion and the circumstances of the West help explain the new imperialism. Science and technology gave industrialized nations such a military advantage that they could easily conquer and control the nonindustrialized lands. Almost any penetration into such areas as Africa, southern Asia, or the Pacific quickly led to greater involvement and eventual control. Once missionaries or traders established their presence in a new area, home governments were called on to provide support, enforce contracts, or protect private interests. To provide that support and protection, they had to create new facilities in the new lands, thus increasing the Western presence. The governments soon requested the cooperation of the native political leaders, and when it was not forthcoming, they used force. Thus, initial contacts by Western explorers, missionaries, or traders blossomed into full imperial control by Western nations.

WHERE HISTORIANS DISAGREE

The New Imperialism

Scholars have debated the causes of the new imperialism almost since its appearance in the final decades of the nineteenth century. For years, there were two major competing interpretations for the causes of imperialism: The first focused on economic motivations, the second on nationalism.

The earliest explanations for the new imperialism were economic. In 1902 J. H. Hobson argued that imperialism was caused by industrial capitalism in general and influential financial capitalists in particular.

In 1916 Lenin, argued that capitalist competition produced monopolies that were being forced to look overseas for new areas to exploit. Many historians have favored related broad economic interpretations of imperialism. Their basic argument is that industrialization demanded ever-widening markets. As industrialization spread to several Western countries during the second half of the nineteenth century and as European markets were being limited by increasing tariffs, competition for markets intensified. At the same time the need for raw materials expanded, as did the search for new, profitable investment opportunities. These economic motives were translated into the new imperialism.

Opponents of economic interpretations for the new imperialism point out that the biggest markets, the largest sources of raw materials, and the most investment outlets for capital remained within Western civilization even during this period. Moreover, the imperializing Western nations did not necessarily profit economically from imperialism. Much of the territory seized between 1880 and 1914 had little economic value; some, in fact, was an economic liability. Many of these historians argue that the chief cause of the new imperialism was nationalism. They point out that the outbreak of the new imperialism occurred shortly after the unification of Italy and Germany and during a period in which nationalism was on the rise throughout Europe. This nationalism turned into a new competitive struggle for international prestige among Western nations that spilled over into non-Western areas after 1880. Imperial conquest became a measure of status, proof that a nation had become first rate. To be left behind in the imperial race was to be marked as a second-class nation. Thus economic motives were secondary; on the whole, imperialism was a nationalistic phenomenon.

Recently, several historians have pointed out that there is little evidence that European statesmen felt pressured to acquire colonies by wealthy capitalists or public patriotism during the crucial period of the 1880s and 1890s. Rather, the key to the new imperialism lay in political and diplomatic developments. In some cases, political problems within a territory only indirectly controlled by a European power pressured that power to annex the territory. This situation occurred in Egypt during the 1880s, when Great Britain took control and then expanded its interests to neighboring Sudan. In other cases, the new style of politics and diplomacy within Europe turned colonies into political assets that had to be acquired. Here Bismarck set a pattern of making claims to colonial territories and using those claims as bargaining chips against other powers. His tactics forced other nations to make their own claims, which led to the virtual partition of Africa.

Many historians take the middle road, arguing that the best way to explain the new imperialism is to include economic, nationalistic, and political-diplomatic factors. But here judgment is crucial, for historians must determine what elements of each argument are most valid and what weight should be given to them.

2. THE EXPLOITATION AND AWAKENING OF CHINA

One of the most important scenes of European imperialism during the nineteenth century was China. This huge and populous country was the seat of the oldest continuous civilization in the world. For some five thousand years China had been a vast melting pot, absorbing invading peoples and cultures and welding them into a tough but resilient civilization. The military conquerors were always themselves swallowed up or conquered by Chinese culture.

Over time, the Chinese chose to isolate themselves from the outside world. A great wall (never completed) originally constructed to defend China's northern border later symbolized its effort to retain the old and keep out the new. Although they admitted some European traders and Christian missionaries in the sixteenth and seventeenth centuries, they closed their doors rather tightly thereafter. By the nineteenth century their medieval society, under the corrupt and declining Manchu dynasty, constituted a power vacuum that tempted exploitation by the West.

The first Europeans to force themselves upon the Chinese were the British. Going to war in 1839, when Chinese officials interfered with their sale of opium in China, the British, with their modern weapons, easily defeated the Chinese. By the terms of the Treaty of Nanking (1842), the Chinese ceded Hong Kong to the British, opened many of their ports to foreign trade free of restricting tariffs, and granted the foreigners extraterritorial rights. This was the first of a series of unequal treaties and the signal for all the great Western powers to rush into China and seize what they could. In the ensuing scramble it was the rivalry among the great powers themselves rather than

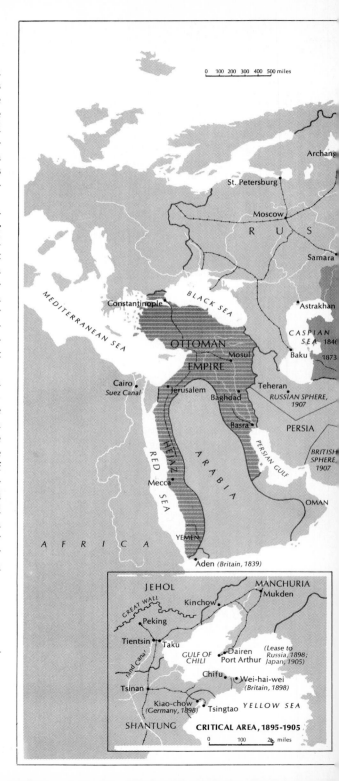

Map 49.1 **IMPERIALISM IN ASIA, 1840–1914** As this map indicates, almost all the Western powers participated in the imperial expansion into Asia. Once Japan westernized, it too joined the imperial race.

ARCTIC OCEAN

ALASKA
(Purchased by U.S.A.
from Russia, 1867)

BERING SEA

ALEUTIAN I. (U.S.A., 1867)

KAMCHATKA

Lena R.

•Yakutsk

S I B E R I A

SEA OF
OKHOTSK

SAKHALIN

KURILE I.
(Japan, 1875)

Ob R.

Yenisei R.

N E M P I R E

AMUR PROVINCE
1858

KARAFUTO
(Japan, 1905)

•Tobolsk

L. Baikal

Amur R.

•Khabarovsk

MARITIME
PROVINCE
(Russia, 1868)

•Omsk   •Tomsk

TRANS-SIBERIAN RAILROAD

Irkutsk   Chita

MANCHURIA

JAPANESE EMPIRE

•Urga

Harbin

Vladivostok
1860

SEA
OF
JAPAN

•Tokyo

L. Balkhash

OUTER MONGOLIA
(Autonomous, 1912 Russian Sphere)

INNER MONGOLIA

Mukden

KOREA
(Japan, 1905, 1910)

1854

JEHOL

864   •Tashkent 1860-65

SINKIANG

Peking•

Port Arthur
(Japan, 1905)

OKHARA 1876
1868   1895

Kashgar

Tientsin

Kiao-chow
(Germany, 1898)

PACIFIC OCEAN

bul

C H I N A

Huang Ho

Shanghai
(Britain, 1842)

RYUKYU I.

KASHMIR
1846

T I B E T

Nanking

Ningpo
1842

EAST
CHINA
SEA

PUNJAB

Hankow

Yangtse R.

MARIANA I.
(Germany, 1899)

Delhi•

HIMALAYAS
Lhasa•

Chungking•

Foochow

FORMOSA (Japan, 1895)

N Indus R.

NEPAL

BHUTAN

Amoy•

PESCADORES (Japan, 1895)

GUAM
(U.S.A., 1898)

Ganges R.

Brahmaputra R.

YÜNNAN

Canton
(Britain, 1842)

KWANGSI
(French Sphere)

Hong Kong (Britain, 1842)
Maçao (Portugal, 1557)

INDIA

Calcutta•

BURMA
(Britain, 1852, 1885)

Hanoi•

Kwang-chow
(Lease to France, 1898)

CAROLINE I.
(Germany, 1899)

rtugal)

B R I T I S H   I N D I A
1852

HAINAN

Manila•

PHILIPPINE I.
(U.S.A., 1898, 1899)

YAP

Bombay

Hyderabad•

Yanaon
(France)

Rangoon•

ANNAM

FRENCH
INDOCHINA
1884, 1907

Goa
(Portugal)

Madras•

BAY OF BENGAL

SIAM
1826

Mekong R.

SOUTH
CHINA
SEA

PALAU I.

Pondicherry
(France)

Bangkok•

NEW GUINEA

Karikal (France)

ANDAMAN I.
(Britain)

Saigon•

BRITISH
NORTH BORNEO
1888

KAISER WILHEMS
(Germany, 188

CEYLON

SARAWAK
1868

MALAY STATES
(Britain, 18 , 1824)

BORNEO

CELEBES

Singapore
(Britain, 1819)

SUMATRA

D U T C H   E A S T   I N D I E S

(Portugal, 1859)

INDIAN OCEAN

Batavia•

JAVA

TIMOR Darwin•

AUSTRALIA

Chinese resistance that saved China from complete loss of independence.

The British got the lion's share. In addition to Hong Kong and concessions in the Canton area of the southeast, they gained a virtual trading monopoly in the Yangtze Valley, which was the richest and most populous part of China. In the north they gained footholds in the capital city of Peking and its port city of Tientsin, in the Shantung Peninsula, and in Manchuria. They gained dominion over Tibet. In the 1880s they seized control of Burma, which owed a tenuous allegiance to China. The French took large areas in Southeast China and Hainan Island as their sphere. In the 1880s they completed the detachment of Indochina from Chinese sovereignty. The Russians took Manchuria as their sphere, annexed a large strip of China's northeast coast, including the port of Vladivostok, and became active in Korea. The Germans carved out for themselves much of the strategically located Shantung Peninsula and built a powerful naval base at Kiaochow. In 1894 the rejuvenated and modernized Japanese went to war with China. They easily defeated China and not only took away Formosa and Korea but also forced China to pay a huge indemnity. Even the United States got into the act. The United States had launched an imperialist program in the Far East in 1898 by seizing the Philippine Islands and Guam from Spain. Now, fearful for its growing trade with China, the United States attempted to gain a sphere of influence in Fukien Province and demanded an Open Door policy in China with equal trading opportunities for all.

Meanwhile, Chinese nationalism was being aroused by the Western and Japanese aggressions against the "Celestial Empire." In 1899–1900 a serious uprising against the foreign exploiters, known as the Boxer Rebellion, took place. Thousands of Chinese Christians and a number of foreigners were slain. This liberation movement was put down by British, French, German, Russian, Italian, Japanese, and American troops. The nationalist leaders were severely punished, and China was forced to pay the foreign governments a large indemnity.

A more far-reaching revolutionary movement, aimed not only at freeing China from foreign exploitation but also at modernizing and democra-

tizing its society and government, was being organized by Dr. Sun Yat-sen (1866–1925). Sun Yat-sen, the son of a poor Chinese farmer, studied in a British mission school in Hawaii, became a Christian, and later graduated from the British medical school at Hong Kong. Eloquent and dynamic, he organized his followers into the Kuomintang party, which was committed to a three-point program: (1) national independence, (2) democratic government, (3) social justice. In 1911 the reformers launched a revolution against the Manchu dynasty, declared a republic, and elected Sun Yat-sen as a provisional president. The revolution swept most of China. The Manchu officials in Peking, their power having evaporated, declared China a republic and abdicated in favor of General Yuan, organizer of the New Army of North China. Early in 1912 the idealistic Sun Yat-sen, in behalf of national unity, and fearful of rising anarchy and warlords within and the possibility of Japanese and Russian intervention from without, yielded to General Yuan. Yuan, however, soon proved to be more interested in power than in liberal reform. When the Kuomintang party won the elections of 1913, he suppressed the party and had its most promising young leader assassinated. Sun Yat-sen disassociated himself from Yuan's dictatorship and resumed his liberal activities in South China. When World War I opened a new era in 1914, China was torn with revolution and division.

3. THE EMERGENCE OF JAPAN

Japan's reaction to Western intrusion was quite different from that of China. The Japanese people inhabit four large islands and some three thousand small ones stretching along the eastern coast of Asia for a distance of about two thousand miles. Like China, Japan had admitted the sixteenth- and seventeenth-century European traders and Christian missionaries but had evicted them and closed its doors after observing what was happening everywhere in Asia where Europeans were admitted. At mid–nineteenth century the Japanese were living in isolation. Their stage of technical knowledge and their feudal society ruled over by

FIGURE 49.2. Japanese Silk Factory, 1905 By the early twentieth century Japan had successfully adopted Western industrial methods. In this 1905 photograph of a silk-weaving factory, supervising men are in formal Western attire and women work on the machines. (California Museum of Photography, University of California, Riverside)

military chieftains were quite similar to those of Europe five hundred years earlier.

In 1853, eleven years after the Treaty of Nanking opened up China, an American fleet commanded by Commodore Matthew C. Perry steamed into Tokyo Bay and so overawed the Japanese that they opened their ports to shipwrecked American sailors and to American trade. The alert Japanese were much impressed by the technological superiority of the Americans. In 1868, just fifteen years later, a group of forward-looking young Japanese overthrew the existing government and began reorganizing the Japanese government and society along modern Western lines. Taking what they considered to be the best from the various Western nations, they patterned their business methods after those of the United States,

their legal system after the French, and their navy after the British. But it was Bismarck's Germany that impressed the Japanese the most. They built a military machine and an authoritarian government and education system on the model of the German Empire.

In an incredibly short time Japan became a modern, industrialized, military, and, on the surface at least, a westernized power (see Figure 49.2). In 1894 Japan attacked China, defeated it with ease, and forced it to pay a large indemnity and to give up Korea (which Japan annexed in 1910) and the island of Formosa. In 1902 Great Britain became the first Western power to treat an Oriental nation as an equal by entering into a military alliance with Japan. Thus strengthened and reassured, Japan attacked Russia in 1904 and, to everyone's surprise, defeated Russia on land and at sea. As a reward, Japan took the southern half of Sakhalin Island and Russia's railroad and port concessions in southern Manchuria, thereby becoming the dominant power in that large and valuable section of China. By 1914 Japan was a first-rate westernized power—industrialized, militaristic, and imperialistic.

4. COMPETITION FOR THE STRATEGIC NEAR AND MIDDLE EAST

The term *Near East* usually refers to the area at the eastern end of the Mediterranean: Egypt, the old Ottoman Empire, and the Balkan peninsula. In the period 1871–1914, the term *Middle East* usually meant the area of the Persian Gulf, the territory northwest of India, and sometimes Tibet. (By the middle of the twentieth century the term *Middle East* was generally used to designate the whole area from and including Egypt and Turkey to the western borders of India.) Before the development of its oil resources after World War I, this area (with the exception of the Balkan peninsula) was relatively poor. It was inhabited chiefly by Moslems who were hostile to Europeans. The main importance of the area, therefore, was strategic. It is the land bridge between the world's two largest land masses—the continents of Eurasia and Africa. The opening in 1869 of the Suez Canal, which shortened the sailing distance between western Europe and the Far East by five thousand miles, doubled the strategic value of the Near and Middle East. Indeed, Suez quickly became probably the most vital single commercial and military focus point in the world.

The Suez Canal was built by a French company between 1859 and 1869. However, in 1875 Great Britain, taking advantage of the Egyptian government's financial distress, purchased the khedive's controlling portion of the canal stock. Seven years later, to quell an anti-European insurrection, the British occupied Egypt with their military forces. The French acquiesced in the establishment of Britain's control over Egypt and the Suez Canal in return for British support of French dominance in Morocco.

Serious competition for the British in the Near East soon came from an unexpected source. Wilhelm II, upon becoming kaiser of the German Empire in 1888, immediately began to show a keen interest in the Ottoman Empire. Sultan Abdul Hamid II (1876–1909) was such a cruel slaughterer of his Christian subjects that he was called in the Western world "Abdul the Damned." Nevertheless, Wilhelm II in 1889 paid Abdul Hamid a visit in Constantinople and declared himself to be the friend and benefactor not only of the Turks but also of all the Moslems. Friendship was followed by economic concessions and German investments in the Ottoman Empire. A second visit by the kaiser in 1898 led to a concession to Germany to build a railroad from the Bosporus to the Persian Gulf. This, with its European connection, was the famous Berlin-to-Bagdad railroad. The British took alarm. The Bagdad Railroad, with a fortified terminus on the Persian Gulf, would undercut Britain's longer water route to the East and threaten India, Britain's richest colonial prize. A projected branch running down through Syria and Palestine to Hedjaz would menace the Suez Canal itself.

Russia was equally concerned. Since the days of Ivan III in the fifteenth century, one of Russia's major ambitions has been to gain a warm water outlet to the world through the Turkish Straits at Constantinople. Russia had long looked to Constantinople as the seat and legitimate capital of its Orthodox religion and Byzantine culture. The decay of the Ottoman Empire in the nineteenth century encouraged Russia to try for Constantinople, and only the intervention of Great Britain and France in the Crimean War (1854–1856) prevented Russia from attaining its goal. In 1877–1878 Russia defeated Turkey and threatened to dominate the whole Balkan peninsula. This time Great Britain and Austria-Hungary forced Russia to submit to a general settlement by the European powers. At the Congress of Berlin, 1878, Russian ambitions in the Near East were once more thwarted. Bismarck's support of Austria-Hungary and Great Britain at the Congress of Berlin marked the beginning of German-Russian estrangement. Russia's defeat by Japan in 1904–1905 caused Russia to intensify its pressure toward the Middle and Near East. Russia's southward expansion so menaced India that Great Britain extended the northwest Indian frontier to the Khyber Pass and crossed over the Himalayas to checkmate Russian influence in Tibet, Afghanistan, and Persia.

The new German threat in the Near and Middle East, however, caused the British and the Russians to settle their long-standing differences. In 1907 they neutralized Tibet and Afghanistan and divided Persia into three spheres of influence—a Russian sphere in the north, a British sphere in the south, and an "independent" sphere in the center. Great Britain, Russia, and France, now diplomatic allies, prevented the sale of Bagdad Railroad bonds in their respective countries in an effort to embarrass the financing of the costly undertaking. Germany went right ahead, however, with the extension of its influence in the Balkans and the Ottoman Empire. In 1913 Germany dispatched a military mission to Constantinople to reorganize and instruct the Turkish army. The Ottoman Empire's friendship and eventual alliance with Germany was undoubtedly motivated by a greater fear of Russia. By 1914 the area of the Near and Middle East was a giant powder keg with fuses leading to St. Petersburg, Berlin, and London.

5. THE SCRAMBLE FOR AFRICA

At the opening of the nineteenth century, Africa was not the seat of ancient and highly developed civilizations, as was Asia. The brilliant civilizations of Egypt, Carthage, and Rome had long since disappeared. The Moslem religion still existed throughout North Africa, but the once vigorous Moslem civilization had declined. The Portuguese, Spanish, British, and French had trading posts along the gold, ivory, and slave coasts on the west. The Dutch and Portuguese had posts and settlements around the southern cape. But most of the huge continent still lay dark and mysterious.

By 1880 the African scene had still not changed very much. During the middle decades of the nineteenth century, the interior was explored for the first time, notably by David Livingstone, a Scottish missionary, and Henry Morton Stanley, a British journalist. The French had conquered Algeria and made it a part of France and had pushed up the Senegal River in the west. The British had taken the Cape Colony from the Dutch by the Treaty of Vienna in 1815, and the Dutch settlers had moved northward into the interior.

After 1880, however, the tempo of European activity changed drastically. The explorers' tales of strange wild animals and primitive peoples, of jungles, ivory, and gold, excited the imagination of western European adventurers and evangelical Christians. European politics, industrialism, and nationalism supplied much of the impetus. There took place such a mad scramble for Africa among the powers of western Europe that by 1914 the only independent areas left were Ethiopia in the east and Liberia in the west. Ethiopia, with French aid, had repulsed an invading Italian army, and Liberia had been sponsored by the United States as a hoped-for receptacle for liberated black slaves. The rest of the huge continent had been seized by France, Great Britain, Germany, Portugal, Belgium, Italy, and Spain (listed in the approximate order of size of territory held). (See Map 49.2.) The treatment of the natives was very similar to that accorded the New World Indians in the sixteenth and seventeenth centuries.

The seizure of so much territory did not occur, of course, without serious international incidents and crises. One such incident occurred at Fashoda in the Sudan in 1898. A French expedition under Major Marchand, bent on establishing an all-French axis across Africa from west to east, arrived at Fashoda and hoisted the French flag. The British, however, claimed the Sudan as an appendage of Egypt. Furthermore, they were interested in a Cape-to-Cairo railroad running through all British territory, even though they were already blocked by German East Africa. Lord Kitchener therefore hurried down from the north with a superior British force and compelled the French to withdraw.

In South Africa the British fought a major war with the Dutch settlers (1899–1902). When British settlers began to move into Cape Colony after the Congress of Vienna had ceded it to Great Britain in 1815, the Calvinist Dutch Boers (farmers) who had settled there in the seventeenth century trekked northward far into the interior. Eventually the British recognized the independence of the two Boer states, Transvaal and Orange Free State.

Map 49.2   IMPERIALISM IN AFRICA, 1914   This map indicates how the vast majority of Africa was carved up by European nations in the two decades of the 1880s and 1890s.

FIGURE 49.3. British in India
This photo of Indian servants catering to a British gentleman indicates the gulf between the British ruling class and the Indians they governed. It also reveals the appeal to Britishers of foreign service. (BBC Hulton/ The Bettmann Archive)

When, however, the richest gold mines in the world were discovered in the Transvaal in the 1880s, British immigrants (Uitlanders) flooded in. The unwelcome Uitlanders were badly treated by the Dutch Boers. The British empire builder Cecil Rhodes, with the support of powerful interests back home, was determined to brush aside the two little Boer republics. When the able Boer president, Paul Kruger, saw the British intent, he opened hostilities. What the world expected to be an easy victory for the British took three years of all-out military effort involving severe casualties and enormous costs. Britain's treatment of the defeated Boers, however, was lenient. They were taken into partnership in the Union of South Africa, and their war hero, General Botha, was elected the Union's first prime minister. During the course of the struggle, a telegram of congratulation from the German kaiser to President Kruger and the British seizure of a German ship attempting to violate the British blockade caused great tension between Great Britain and Germany. Only the superiority of the British navy, as the kaiser admitted, prevented him from going to war.

The British navy also proved decisive in two crises over Morocco. In 1905 France, with the approval of Great Britain, Italy, and Spain, began the conquest of Morocco. France claimed that it was necessary because of continual raids by wild Moroccan tribes on French Algeria. The German kaiser, seeing an opportunity to assert his own power and possibly to break up the Triple Entente, which France, Great Britain, and Russia were then forming, appeared at the Moroccan port of Tangier on a German warship and indicated his support of Moroccan independence. Great tension followed. At an international conference at Algeciras, France, supported by her own ally, Great Britain,

FIGURE 49.4. **Imperialism Satirized** This cartoon, which appeared in 1899, satirizes the attitudes of smug righteousness and superiority with which the Americans, the British, and the European nations extended their dominance over the rest of the world. The United States was dominant in the Western Hemisphere; the European imperialist powers in the Eastern Hemisphere. (New York Public Library Picture Collection)

and by Germany's ally, Italy, won a limited control over Morocco. Disorder continued, however, and in 1911 France sent a conquering army into Morocco, at which point Germany dispatched a cruiser to the Moroccan port of Agadir. Again tension mounted. In the face of Germany's threat to France, Britain's chancellor of the exchequer, Lloyd George, talked loudly of war. Again Germany backed down. Between Germany and Morocco stood the British navy. These two efforts of the kaiser to drive a wedge between the Entente powers had the effect of driving them closer together. Moreover, his own ally, Italy, had proved uncertain. These two crises growing out of imperialism hastened the coming of World War I.

6. THE BRITISH EMPIRE

Of all the European overseas empires, the British was by far the most successful. Indeed, it was the dazzling size and wealth of the British Empire that helped to excite the other European powers to greater imperialistic activity. By 1914 the British Empire included one-fourth of all the land and people of the earth.

Great Britain's commerce with its empire was enormous. In 1914 Britain's foreign investments, most of which were in the empire, totaled $20 billion—one-fourth of the total wealth of the homeland. (By comparison, France had $9 billion invested abroad; Germany, $6 billion. The United States was a debtor nation.) The empire, furthermore, provided lucrative and often glamorous careers for thousands of British governors, army and navy officers, diplomats, and civil servants of every description.

In the latter part of the nineteenth century, Great Britain adopted the policy of granting self-government to the English-speaking portions of its empire. Canada, which had gained self-government in 1849, was granted dominion status in 1867. With dominion status, the only remaining effective bond was allegiance to the British crown. The British governor-general was only a figurehead like the king at home. Australia was made a self-governing dominion in 1901, New Zealand in 1907, and the Union of South Africa in 1910. The policy was successful. All the dominions rallied to the mother country in both world wars.

Great Britain's richest imperial prize was India (see Figure 49.3). India's more than 300 million inhabitants accounted for at least three-fourths of the total population of the whole empire. India was nearly twenty times as large as Great Britain and more than seven times as populous. It was the mother country's best customer and supplied many minerals and raw materials. Until 1858 India was governed by the British East India Company, a private stock company. However, the great Sepoy Mutiny of 1857, the first large-scale uprising of the Indians against British rule, caused the British government to take over the government of India from the company. Between 1858 and 1914 Great Britain spent millions of dollars in India on railroads, industries, education, and public health. The enormous growth of India's population, which more than doubled during the period, is testimony to some improvement in the conditions of life under British rule. But the British took out of India more than they brought in, and they showed no inclination to grant self-government. Indian dissatisfaction with British rule mounted steadily. In the late nineteenth century, nationalism, which had provided so much aggressive energy for Europe, was coming to Asia—to India as well as to Japan and China. In 1885 the All Indian Congress party was formed for the purpose of achieving Indian independence. By 1914 it was becoming obvious that India would not remain a placid and profitable colony much longer.

7. THE LEGACY OF IMPERIALISM

The Western world's technology, its dynamic capitalism, and above all its aggressive nationalism had enabled it between 1880 and 1914 to subject most of the rest of the world to its domination (see Figure 49.4). In the process of dominating the non-Western world, Western nations not only exploited the natural and human resources of conquered lands but also profoundly undermined the cultures, societies, and political organizations of native peoples. Few in the West were able or willing to recognize how destructive this policy could be. By 1914 most people in the Western world had come to view imperialism as a normal and permanent state. In the course of the twentieth century, however, some of the very forces that accounted for the new imperialism would lead to its demise. The non-Western world was irreversibly changed by Western imperialism, but it would not remain under the thumb of Western nations for long.

SUGGESTED READING

General and Causes

D. K. Fieldhouse, *The Colonial Experience: A Comparative Study from the Eighteenth Century* (1982). A good introduction.

D. Headrick, *Tools of Empire* (1981). Examines what made imperial expansion relatively easy.

D. Mannoni, *Prospero and Caliban: The Psychology of Colonization* (1964). An excellent analysis from a psychological perspective.

T. Smith, *The Patterns of Imperialism* (1981). A good recent survey.

H. Wright, ed., *The "New Imperialism"* (1975). An anthology of different views.

The Exploitation and Awakening of China

J. K. Fairbank, *The United States and China* (1979). A scholarly, lucid history of China by a leading expert.

I. Hsu, *The Rise of Modern China* (1975). A useful survey.

The Emergence of Japan

J. W. Hall, *Japan, From Prehistory to Modern Times* (1970). A useful survey.

M. Hane, *Japan: A Historical Survey* (1972). Good on the nineteenth and twentieth centuries.

Competition for the Near and Middle East

S. N. Fisher, *The Middle East: A History,* 2nd ed. (1969). Reliable text.

The Scramble for Africa

J. Gallegher, R. Robinson, and A. Danny, *Africa and the Victorians: The Climax of Imperialism* (1961). A good, controversial analysis.

E. J. Murphy, *History of African Civilization* (1972). Solid on the nineteenth and twentieth centuries.

The British Empire

W. Baumgart, *Imperialism: The Idea and Reality of British and French Colonial Expansion* (1982). Up-to-date study.

B. Porter, *The Lion's Share, A Short History of British Imperialism, 1850–1970* (1975). A solid survey.

CHAPTER 50
Industrial Society, Social Classes, and Women

FIGURE 50.1. **The Urban Classes**
This French cartoon of 1845 shows a typical Parisian apartment house in which the various social classes lived in close proximity but different conditions. The bourgeoisie live on the first (American second) and second floors in wealth and prudent comfort. The lower classes, and aspiring artists, live on the bottom and upper floors in increasing poverty—thanks to their imprudence. (Bibliothèque Nationale, Paris)

Between 1850 and 1914 new areas in the West were industrializing, new industries were being developed, new methods of production were being used, and new business structures were emerging. The quantity and quality of industrial production underwent such a great change that historians have come to call these industrial developments the "second Industrial Revolution." During the same period social developments initiated during the earlier period of industrialization were maturing and evolving. Some, such as the rise of working-class organizations and ideologies, were directly connected to the industrial process. Others were more broadly based—the growth and movement of populations, the evolution of classes, and the developing experiences of women in an increasingly urbanized society. In short, mature, modern industrial economies and societies were becoming firmly established throughout the West.

1. THE SECOND INDUSTRIAL REVOLUTION

The first Industrial Revolution was initiated in Great Britain during the last decades of the eighteenth century. It spread to certain limited areas of western Europe and the United States during the first half of the nineteenth century. This early industrialization was based primarily on steam, iron, and textiles. During the 1850s and 1860s industrial production continued to expand, but mostly in the same areas and along the same lines as in earlier decades. In 1871, Great Britain was still the industrial leader, producing more industrial goods than the rest of the world combined. Besides Great Britain, only Belgium and parts of France, Germany, northern Italy, and the United States were industrially well developed.

The second Industrial Revolution was initiated in the last third of the nineteenth century. It was more widespread than the first Industrial Revolution and was based more on electricity, oil, steel, and chemicals. Great Britain, failing to invest sufficiently in new processes, falling behind in marketing techniques, and relying too heavily on old plants, lost its industrial leadership. Between 1871 and 1914, the United States and Germany sur-

passed Great Britain. By 1914 the Industrial Revolution had penetrated central and eastern Europe, Japan, Canada, Australia, and New Zealand; even India had a small textile industry. However, it was still in western Europe and the United States that most of the world's industry was to be found, and the greater part of Asia, Africa, and Latin America was still not industrialized. Moreover, it was in western Europe that both the prosperity and the uncertainties of economic life—exemplified by the industrial boom of 1850–1873 and the depression between 1873 and 1896—were experienced most.

New Products and Processes

Steel has been the mainstay of industry and transportation since the latter part of the nineteenth century. Until the mid–nineteenth century, steel was hard to make and very expensive. The discovery of the Bessemer process (1856) and the Thomas-Gilchrist process (1878) of removing impurities from molten iron greatly speeded up and cheapened the production of steel. In 1871 the total annual steel production in the entire world was approximately 1 million tons, of which about half was produced by Great Britain, a fourth by Germany, and an eighth by the United States. By 1914 the world's annual production had increased more than fiftyfold; the United States was producing approximately half the total, Germany a fourth, and Great Britain an eighth. Out of this steel were made tools and machines that constantly increased in numbers and efficiency. By 1914 in the industrialized countries, these increasingly automatic machines fabricated most metal, textile, leather, and wood products (see Figure 50.2).

The power to drive the steel machines was increasing in like proportion. In 1914 probably nine-tenths of the world's industrial power was still provided by the steam engine. Other and more efficient power generators, however, were rapidly coming to the fore. Between 1831 and 1882 the dynamo for generating electricity was developed by a number of inventors, the most important of whom were Michael Faraday (British), the Siemens brothers (German), and Thomas A. Edison (American). Sir Charles Parsons (British) pat-

FIGURE 50.2. Krupp Works Germany industrialized rapidly during the last quarter of the nineteenth century. This photo shows the armaments factory at the Krupp works in Essen, Germany. (Culver Pictures)

ented the steam turbine in 1884. The turbine proved to be so efficient that it was soon used to drive the largest ships and eventually to generate most of the world's electric power. In 1888 the electric motor was invented by Nikola Tesla, a naturalized American born in Croatia. The first practical internal-combustion engine was invented by Gottlieb Daimler (German) in 1886. One year later he put it to work in the first automobile. In 1892 the diesel engine, efficiently burning cheap crude oil, was invested by Rudolf Diesel (German). The invention of these two engines gave impetus to the oil industry.

In the last decades of the nineteenth century, pure science was playing an increasingly vital role in industry, and both science and industry were being applied to agriculture. Physics contributed most heavily to the rapidly growing electrical industry. Chemistry made possible such important industries as synthetic dyes, wood pulp, paper, plastics, synthetic fibers, photography, and motion pictures. The electrical and chemical industries were most highly developed in Germany. The mechanization of agriculture made its first big advances in the great grain-growing areas of the United States, Canada, and Australia, although western Europe was also steadily increasing its agricultural yields through the use of farm machinery and scientific farming techniques.

Transport and Communications

Between 1850 and 1914 a large part of humanity became mobile. Whereas before 1850 relatively few people had ever seen more of the world than could be seen on journeys by foot or on horseback, by 1914 millions of people were traveling considerable distances, often by rapid conveyance. Even in places such as China, Turkey, and Brazil, trains chugged along, hauling people for distances and at speeds unknown before.

This was the greatest era of railroad building in history. There had been a rather lively building of railroads before 1850 in western Europe and the United States. However, between 1850 and 1914 the world's railway system was fundamentally completed. There has been relatively little railroad building since.

At the same time, the steamship was making comparable progress, although it had stiff competition from the sailing ship until near the end of the nineteenth century. Steel hulls of great size, turbine engines, and screw propellers were too much for the beautiful sails. The opening of the Suez Canal in 1869 and the Panama Canal in 1914, together with the increase in the size and speed of ships, brought the world and its peoples, commodities, and markets much closer together.

During the last three decades of the nineteenth century, the humble bicycle became a common and important means of locomotion, especially in Europe. But the bicycle was not fast enough for the industrial age. When Gottlieb Daimler attached his little combustion engine to a wagon in 1887, the automobile was born. It quickly captured the imagination of daring pioneers. Daimler sold his patent to a French company, and until the end of the century the French led the field in automobile development and production. Leadership passed to America with the founding of the Ford Motor Company in 1903. Henry Ford, who started out as a bicycle mechanic, applied the assembly-line method of mass production to the new automobile industry. The rapid spread of the automobile created vast new industrial empires in oil, rubber, and concrete.

After the turn of the century the airplane was invented. The first successful heavier-than-air flying machine was flown by Wilbur and Orville Wright in 1903 over the sand dunes at Kitty Hawk, North Carolina. Aviation was still in its infancy in 1914, but already its tremendous future was obvious.

Communications were developing faster yet. In 1844 Samuel F. B. Morse sent a message by wire forty miles from Baltimore to Washington. The telegraph, transmitting messages instantaneously from one end of any length of wire to the other, caught on rapidly. In 1866 a telegraph cable was laid across the Atlantic, enabling news to travel from New York to London as quickly as from New York to Brooklyn. Ten years later Alexander Graham Bell, an American born in Scotland, invented the telephone, and in 1895 Guglielmo Marconi, an Italian, sent the first message by wireless telegraphy. Together with the revolution in transportation, these developments in communications accelerated the Industrial Revolution by greatly facilitating the large-scale mobilization of capital, raw materials, labor, and markets.

The Growth of Corporations and Monopolies

At the same time that industry was growing, individual companies were growing larger and combining to form monopolistic mergers or trusts. Such undertakings as railroads, shipping lines, and iron and steel mills were too large for all but a very few individuals to finance. As a rule, therefore, enterprises of this scope were carried on by joint stock companies. Entrepreneur capitalists would raise the necessary capital outlay by organizing a corporation and selling stock in it to other capitalists. All the industrialized countries encouraged the investment of capital in corporations by passing laws that limited the liability of stockholders to the amount of money invested (hence the "Ltd." usually seen after the name of a British corporation or combine). By 1914 most of the world's industry was controlled by large corporations and trusts. Although their stockholders were numbered by the thousands, they were really controlled by a relatively few banks and wealthy individuals. And between the owners of these corporations and the millions of workers, there lay a great gulf. The actual operation of the larger industries would be carried on by hired managers, who hired and fired and supervised the workers.

The giant corporations were ruthless in dealing with each other. In this era of unrestrained competition, the big and strong frequently destroyed the small and weak. The premium was on size and strength. The results were combines, mergers, and monopolistic trusts. The spectacular success of Rockefeller's Standard Oil Trust in the 1880s soon made it the model for many others, particularly in the United States, Germany, Japan, and to a lesser extent, Great Britain. The German monopolistic combinations such as the giant I. G. Farben Industries (chemicals and dyes) were called *cartels*. They received government encouragement and support, particularly in their operations abroad. In Japan three-quarters of the nation's industry was controlled by five giant family corporations.

2. THE RISE OF WORKING-CLASS ORGANIZATIONS AND IDEOLOGIES

Labor Unions and Cooperatives

Wherever industrialization occurred, distressed laborers almost immediately attempted to protect themselves by banding together. However, until the 1870s inexperience, poverty, hostile governments, and unfavorable public opinion effectively hindered their efforts. Anti–labor union laws were not fully repealed in Great Britain until 1875 and in France until 1884. In Germany Bismarck persecuted labor unions until his dismissal in 1890. Until the 1880s, the union movement in Europe was limited chiefly to skilled workers, organized by crafts, who were moderate in their aims and methods.

In the 1880s unionization spread rapidly to unskilled workers, cut across craft lines, and adopted socialistic programs (often Marxist) and more radical methods. In Great Britain the labor unions formed the national Trades Union Congress in 1868, and later they became identified with the

Labour party, which was founded between 1881 and 1906. In Germany the individual unions in 1890 formed a national organization that was frankly Marxist. In France in 1895 the various unions banded together in the giant CGT (Confédération Générale du Travail—General Confederation of Labor) with a radical program. By 1914 the working class in the industrialized countries was sufficiently large and organized (though only a minority was as yet unionized) to make itself a power to be reckoned with, both in the factories and mines and at the polls.

Meanwhile, a much bigger portion of the working class was participating in the milder cooperatives of various types. In 1910 in Great Britain membership in cooperative retail stores, fraternal insurance (friendly) societies, and credit associations is estimated to have been some 14 million, the great bulk of whom were wage earners. These organizations also provided muchneeded social fellowship for workers. In the 1880s Denmark became the home of the agricultural cooperative movement. By 1914 nearly all of Denmark's agricultural commodities were cooperatively produced and marketed, and the movement had spread to most of northern Europe, to Italy, and to the United States.

Socialism

During the second half of the nineteenth century socialism became a major ideological force within the working class and came to influence the society and politics of the West in important ways. The most prominent source of socialism was Karl Marx, who, along with Friedrich Engels, had already produced the *Communist Manifesto* in 1848. (See Chapter 44.) Marx argued that modern industrial society in the capitalist West was being split increasingly into two opposing classes: the capitalists (factory owners) and the workers. According to Marx, capitalism was doomed to be overthrown by a revolution of the working class and replaced by a socialist system.

Marx continued to write during the 1850s, 1860s, and 1870s, publishing his most important book, *Das Kapital*, in 1867. He played a key role in translating his ideas into actions by helping union organizers to form the International Working

Men's Association (the First International) in 1864. The association was an amalgam of non-Marxian socialists (such as followers of Louis-Auguste Blanqui and Pierre Joseph Proudhon), anarchists (such as Mikhail Bakunin), and Marxists, and it was divided at the start. Soon, however, Marx and his followers gained control. Although this organization proved to be fragile, falling apart in the 1870s after the Paris Commune, it helped spread Marx's socialism—particularly in Germany. The Second International was formed in 1889 and lasted until 1914. An international federation of socialist parties, it worked to spread socialism, maintain doctrinal purity, and develop socialist strategies.

After Marx's death in 1883, his followers split into various groups and often disagreed over the "correct" meaning of Marxism. The most important modification of Marxism was a moderate revisionism, led by the German socialist Eduard Bernstein (1850–1932). Bernstein argued that Marx had made some errors and that a revolution would not be necessary. He advocated cooperation with the capitalistic classes to obtain all the immediate benefits possible for labor and a gradual approach to socialism.

In Germany, where socialism had its greatest success before 1914, the Social Democratic party formally rejected Bernstein's moderate revisionism but in practice often tended to follow it after the 1890s. By 1914 the party was able to poll some 4.5 million votes and had become the largest party in Germany. The French Socialists were more radical than the Germans. In 1905 the orthodox and the revisionist wings of the French Socialists joined to form the United Socialist party under the leadership of the scholar-orator, Jean Jaurès. By 1914 they numbered 1.5 million voters and had 110 seats in the Chamber of Deputies. Contrary to the expectations of Marx, socialism in Great Britain was weak and mild. Among the earliest British Socialists were George Bernard Shaw, H. G. Wells, and Sidney and Beatrice Webb. These intellectual radicals formed the Fabian Society, which was committed to moderation and gradualism. The Labour party, founded between 1881 and 1906, was also mild and grew slowly before 1914. Neither the Fabian Society nor the Labour party could be called Marxist, although both were influenced by

Marx. In the United States, the socialist movement was relatively weak and (in retrospect) mild. The first prominent American Socialist, Eugene V. Debs, did manage to poll nearly a million votes for president in 1912 and again in 1920.

Anarchism

Anarchism was an extremely radical movement that has often been confused with Marxism. While both were anticapitalist and gained most of their support from the working classes, anarchists stressed much more the elimination of the state and any authority that impinges on human freedom. Anarchists optimistically believed that human beings, once freed from the corrupting institutions that oppressed them, would naturally cooperate with one another. Anarchism's two most influential leaders were the Russian activist Mikhail Bakunin (1814–1876) and the exiled Russian theoretician Prince Pëter Kropotkin (1842–1921). Anarchism became particularly influential in France, Spain, and Italy and among artists and intellectuals as well as members of the working classes. A relatively small wing of the anarchist movement turned to violent means to gain their ends. Among its victims were Tsar Alexander II of Russia in 1881, President Carnot of France in 1894, King Humbert of Italy in 1900, and President McKinley of the United States in 1901. This image of violence has tainted the general perception of anarchism ever since.

3. THE GROWTH AND MOVEMENT OF POPULATION

Since the eighteenth century, European population had been growing at a rapid pace. This growth continued as industrialization spread throughout Europe in the nineteenth century. Between 1850 and 1914 Europe's population expanded from 266 million to 450 million. However, there were important changes underlying this growth of population during the second half of the nineteenth century, particularly after 1870.

In many areas, particularly western Europe, increasing birth rates were no longer a prime generator of population growth; in fact, birth rates were declining. A trend starting in the middle class and spreading to the working classes of marrying later and intentionally having fewer children was limiting the size of families. Because parents could rely more on infants surviving into adulthood, there was less need to have so many children. Moreover, parents who wanted to ensure their own and their children's rising economic well-being and social position elected to have smaller families, which were less expensive and required less division of assets. Despite the declining birth rate, population grew, fueled by an even greater decline in the death rate. This decrease was caused by a combination of improved public sanitation, economic growth, and medical advances.

This European population was not only growing but also moving in vast numbers in two main ways: from Europe to overseas areas, particularly the United States, and from the countryside to the city.

The overseas migration of Europeans between 1850 and 1914 was phenomenal. Ever since the first settlements in the New World, there had been a sizable trickle of Europeans to the Americas. This trickle had become a flowing stream in the mid–nineteenth century. Great numbers of British, Irish, and then German immigrants landed in the United States during the 1840s, 1850s, and 1860s. After 1870 the stream of Europeans migrating overseas swelled into a rushing torrent as peoples from southern and eastern Europe joined the flow. In the brief span of forty-three years between 1871 and 1914, more than 30 million Europeans left their homelands and migrated to the New World or to the British dominion territories. The great bulk of them came to the United States.

Several factors help explain this massive movement of Europeans overseas. Perhaps the greatest impetus was the growth of population. The growing numbers led to increasing competition for land in rural areas and for living space and jobs in urban areas. As different areas of Europe underwent the economic and social transformations connected with industrialization, people were uprooted from traditional ways of life. When these upheavals were accompanied by political turmoil, many found additional reasons to migrate. As

these developments pushed Europeans from their homelands, opportunities in the New World, both real and imagined, pulled them across the Atlantic (see Figure 50.3). Land and economic opportunity seemed abundant in such places as the United States, Canada, Argentina, and Brazil. Improvements in transportation—railroads and steamships—made travel to these faraway places easier. This combination of push from Europe and pull from the New World induced millions of relatively poor, young, and often unmarried Europeans to migrate overseas. Although it is difficult to know how most of them experienced this change, clearly not all were satisfied. Approximately one-third of those migrating from Europe overseas eventually returned.

Europeans were moving from the countryside to the city at an even faster pace than they were moving overseas. In 1850, despite a long process of urbanization, in no country did those in cities outnumber rural inhabitants. This picture changed rapidly during the second half of the nineteenth century. By the turn of the century more than half the population in western Europe lived in urban areas. Agriculture had become an occupation for the minority in Great Britain, Belgium, the Netherlands, Germany, and France.

The movement to the city was brought about by the opportunities in industry and commerce, the growing attractiveness of urban life, and the application of mechanization and science to agriculture, which now required far fewer workers to produce greater yields. The social problems of the cities were being recognized and attacked. A public health movement to improve water supplies and public sanitation by introducing piped water and sewer systems was initiated in England during the 1840s. Urban areas in other countries followed England's lead in the succeeding decades. Urban life was altered by the introduction of mechanized, regular, and reliable means of public transportation, particularly electric streetcars in the 1890s. This development widened opportunities for better housing, since people no longer had to live so close to work. Central areas, which had housed people of all social classes together, were becoming dominated by public buildings, retail outlets, businesses, and theaters. Around the central areas new residential districts and suburbs

FIGURE 50.3. "Welcome to the Land of Freedom" In this romanticized painting a variety of emotions is displayed on the faces of immigrants as they pass the Statue of Liberty in New York Harbor on their way to a new life. Between 1871 and 1914, more than 30 million Europeans immigrated overseas, most of them to the United States. (The Granger Collection)

formed, often separated into working-class and middle-class sections. Some limited private and public programs were initiated to facilitate the construction of cheap housing.

Cities were thus becoming more attractive. Urban planning spread throughout Europe in the second half of the nineteenth century. The general pattern was initiated in Paris during the 1850s and 1860s, where the government tore down old, overcrowded, and almost inaccessible areas of the city and built large boulevards and parks and provided for more open spaces. Other cities such as Vienna and Cologne followed the example of Paris. Together the spread of sanitation facilities, public transportation, urban planning, and new

housing in Europe's cities was making life in urban areas relatively safe and appealing compared with life in the countryside.

4. SOCIAL CLASSES

The class divisions of industrial society continued to develop along the lines already established during the first half of the nineteenth century. The aristocracy continued to shrink in size and significance, yet it still retained some vestiges of wealth, prestige, and position. In part, it was supported by the increasingly conservative elite of the upper middle class. These families, who had gained great wealth from industry, commerce, and banking, mingled with the old aristocracy and copied much of its exclusive and expensive life style. Numerous servants, at least one country house surrounded by an estate, membership in exclusive clubs, extensive travel, major contributions to good causes, and support of culture were almost requirements for full membership in this elite, which constituted less than 5 percent of the population.

The bulk of the middle class, ranging from small factory owners, shopowners, schoolteachers, and professionals to clerks and minor officials, continued to benefit from industrial expansion and urbanization. During the second half of the nineteenth century, however, there were some important changes in the outlook and composition of this class. Before 1848, the middle class was often revolutionary and certainly at the forefront of progressive political change. After 1848, the middle class ceased to be revolutionary and more often fought to retain the status quo rather than promote progressive reform. For the most part, the middle class was gaining what it wanted and was achieving dominance in Western society. In composition, the middle class was not only growing (to some 20 percent of the population) but also adding new groups to its numbers. The two most important of these new groups were the professionals and the white-collar employees. The professionals included people such as engineers, chemists, accountants, and architects as well as public and private managers. These people utilized their education and expertise to fill specialized needs created by industrialization. In wealth, attitudes, and style of life they resembled the traditional middle-class entrepreneurs, merchants, and bankers they served. The white-collar employees were placed toward the bottom of the middle classes. They included the growing numbers of clerks, secretaries, bureaucrats, and salesmen who usually worked for large firms and earned little more than members of the skilled working class. But they self-consciously considered themselves apart from the working classes below them, ascribed to middle-class attitudes, and tried their best to follow a middle-class style of life—at least in appearances.

Generally members of the middle class copied as much of the envied life style of the wealthier upper middle class as they could. With care, most could afford one domestic, good food, a well-furnished apartment or house, schooling and perhaps music lessons for the children, attendance at cultural events, fashionable clothes, and travel.

In values and beliefs, middle-class people thought that they represented what was correct and best in Western society. They believed that prudence, control, rationality, and hard work were the keys to success. They respected traditional Christian morality, sexual purity, and marital fidelity, while they denounced drinking, crime, excesses, and even poverty as vices. They felt they should be able to live up to these standards, at least in appearances if not always in practice. Money remained an important consideration for marriage, but the union was supposed to be centered on sentiment. While this was the period of Victorian sexual propriety for the middle class, it now appears that there was increasing acceptance and expectation of sexual enjoyment within the marriage. Children were at the center of the family and fewer in number; they remained at home through the adolescent years and were more extensively educated.

The working classes—the wage laborers with little if any capital—were headed by an elite of workers whose skills as artisans, machinists, foremen, or specialists were in great demand. Often they struggled to distinguish themselves from the bulk of the working classes below them by adopting a stern, moralistic attitude, copying the appearance of the middle class, and striving to ensure that their children would maintain or surpass their own position in the social hierarchy. The bulk of the working classes were factory laborers, construction workers, transport workers, unskilled or semiskilled day workers, and domestics.

Clearly, the working classes were benefiting from industrialization during the second half of the nineteenth century. Real wages were on the rise, perhaps doubling in Great Britain between 1850 and 1914. The working classes engaged in the proliferating leisure-time activities, which included public drinking and socializing in cafes and pubs, watching organized sports such as soccer, boxing, and racing, and attending music halls, vaudeville theaters, and amusement parks. Nevertheless, the working class was still located toward the bottom of the social and economic scale, continually experiencing or being threatened by poverty, unemployment, poor housing, and insecurity. They may have been participating in an expanding industrial society, but that expansion did not benefit all equally. The gap between rich and poor remained wide; the upper 20 percent of the population usually received more national income than the combined total of the remaining 80 percent.

This society of the late nineteenth century and early twentieth centuries had acquired some permanence that reflected its mature industrial base. It was a society that was more affluent than ever but was still divided into classes of greatly differing status and wealth. Tensions ran through this society, as did great movements of people and ideas. Nevertheless, when the generations after World War I looked back to this society, it seemed enviable despite its faults.

5. WOMEN'S ROLES AND EXPERIENCES

It is difficult to summarize the situation of women between 1850 and 1914. Women's roles and experiences differed sharply according to class lines, and even within classes many of the relevant developments were contradictory. What generally unified women's experiences during this period, as before, was their legal inequality to men, their lack of political rights, their economic dependence and inferiority, and their social restrictions. In an age in which liberal values—stressing individualism, political rights, and equality before the law—were becoming firmly established, women were still relegated to a secondary position or actually excluded from most aspects of public life.

For middle-class women, the contradictions were greatest. The sexual division of labor, separating the woman's sphere from the man's sphere, was rigidified by the growing cult of domesticity. Accordingly, women were glorified as caring mothers, supportive wives, and religious beings. Their place was in the home, where they were in charge of the domestic scene. The wife was supposed to defer and cater to her husband and take

FIGURE 50.4. Emmeline Pankhurst Women led numerous demonstrations in their struggle to gain the vote, particularly in Great Britain. Here a policeman is arresting a leading suffragette, Emmeline Pankhurst. (Culver Pictures)

personal responsibility for nursing and rearing the children. The children's education and the religious well-being of the family was her realm. As domestic manager, she was supposed to have expertise as a consumer, and in turn she was the object of consumer advertising. She was also assumed to be interested in charity and willing to donate time for worthy causes. The middle-class wife was not expected to engage in paid occupations outside the home. The more successfully middle class the family was, the less likely it was that the wife engaged in paid work. Nevertheless, toward the end of the nineteenth century some professions such as schoolteaching, social work, and nursing were expanding and opening to even married middle-class women. Still, most of these occupations were associated with women's domestic roles, were relatively low paying, and were considered most appropriate for unmarried women.

Within the working class, middle-class views about the separate spheres of women and men and the particular domestic nature of women hovered and had some important effects, but the actual experience of women differed. In general working-class women were much more likely to work for wages than middle-class women. A common pattern was for young women to take jobs as domestics before they were married—often moving to cities for this purpose. In addition to the more traditional jobs for women in textiles, food processing, and retail outlets, some of the newer occupations in nursing and secretarial work were opening to women. When jobs were unavailable, prostitution (generally legal and regulated) remained at least a temporary alternative for some. After marriage, women were effectively excluded from several of the options they had when single. One of the main ways for working-class women to earn money was in "sweated industries," where they worked in small factories or at home, usually in textiles or decorating, and were paid by the piece. In all these occupations, women continued to be discriminated against; they received lower pay than men for the same work and were excluded from many jobs open to working-class men. Often middle-class notions of domesticity were used to justify the lower pay and status of women's work, employers arguing that women's primary role was not in paid labor. Women were the first to be affected by new legislation controlling the hours and conditions under which workers could be employed, although these laws were often poorly enforced.

During this period some organized efforts to challenge the role and status assigned to women arose. The strongest feminist movements arose in Great Britain and the United States, particularly movements to extend voting rights to women. In Great Britain organizations such as the National Union of Women's Suffrage Societies, led by Millicent Fawcett (1847–1929), and the more radical Women's Social and Political Union, led by Emmeline Pankhurst (1858–1928), petitioned, lobbied, and marched for the franchise (see Figure 50.4). Some women used more violent means to bring attention to their cause. But the government resisted and success was achieved only at the end of World War I.

In other countries, women's organizations argued for the right to vote and for changes in women's social and economic position, but these organizations were often splintered and rarely achieved their goals. Many continental feminist leaders such as Louise Michel in France, Clara Zetkin in Germany, and Anna Kuliscioff in Italy associated themselves with socialist or radical movements. Only in Norway did women gain the right to vote in national elections before World War I. However, the issues of feminism were now being raised publicly as never before and would become more powerful during the twentieth century.

SUGGESTED READING

General

E. J. Hobsbawm, *The Age of Capital* (1975). Examines middle-class life during the second half of the nineteenth century.

N. Stone, *Europe Transformed, 1878–1919* (1984). A broad survey.

E. R. Tannenbaum, *1900: The Generation Before the Great War* (1976). Good essays on social history.

The Second Industrial Revolution

A. S. Milward and S. B. Saul, *The Development of the Economies of Continental Europe, 1850–1914* (1977). A good treatment of the second Industrial Revolution.

D. S. Landes, *The Unbound Prometheus: Technological Change and Industrial Development in Western Europe from 1750 to the Present* (1969). Excellent survey emphasizing technological change.

S. Pollard, *Peaceful Conquest: The Industrialization of Europe* (1981). An up-to-date survey.

The Rise of Working-Class Organizations and Ideologies

L. R. Berlanstein, *The Working People of Paris, 1871–1914* (1985). A comprehensive study.

J. Joll, *The Anarchists* (1964). A good examination of anarchism and anarchists.

G. Lichtheim, *Marxism* (1971). Highly respected treatment.

W. Sewell, Jr., *Work and Revolution in France* (1980). Good treatment of French socialism.

E. Wilson, *To the Finland Station* (1953). Classic study of socialist leaders.

The Growth and Movement of Population

A. Briggs, *Victorian Cities* (1970). A good examination of Britain's industrial cities.

C. M. Cipolla, *The Economic History of World Population* (1962). A standard introduction.

J. Merriman, ed., *French Cities in the Nineteenth Century: Class, Power, and Urbanization* (1982). A good selection of recent essays.

Social Classes

J. Donzelot, *The Policing of Families* (1979). An important interpretation stressing governmental interference with family life.

P. Gay, *The Bourgeois Experience: Victoria to Freud,* 2 vols. (1984–1986). Excellent study of sexuality and the middle class.

P. N. Stearns, *European Society in Upheaval* (1967). Solid, if traditional, social history covering the period.

Women

M. Boxer and J. Quataert, eds., *Connecting Spheres: Women in the Western World, 1500 to Present* (1987). Fine chapters covering the period.

P. Branca, *Women in Europe Since 1750* (1978). A useful study.

R. Bridenthal and C. Koonz, *Becoming Visible: Women in European History* (1977). Contains good chapters covering the period.

M. Vicinus, *Suffer and Be Still: Women in the Victorian Age* (1972). Good essays on Victorian women.

CHAPTER 51
Science and the Challenge to Christianity

FIGURE 51.1. Eakins, "The Gross Clinic," 1875 This realistic painting by Thomas Eakins of an operation in progress conveys the sense of power of modern science and the optimism with which science was viewed in the nineteenth century. The lack of religious refernces in this medical scene indicates some of the potential challenge of secular science to Christianity. (Jefferson Medical College, Thomas Jefferson University, Philadelphia)

By the middle of the nineteenth century, science had gained much prestige. It was increasingly connected with the inventions and technology of industrialization, which provided wealth and power. It seemed to go hand in hand with the rationalism and prevailing bourgeois liberalism of the period. Over the course of the nineteenth century, people assumed that scientists had, or soon would have, a firm understanding of the physical world. They were optimistic that scientific methods would provide a similar understanding of human society. Although this sense of certainty and optimism would be somewhat undermined in the decades surrounding the turn of the century, the period between 1850 and 1914 must be considered one of great progress in the sciences.

At the same time Christianity faced serious and fundamental challenges. It was attacked from several quarters, but at the base of the many challenges were the successes and increasing prestige of science. Christian leaders often had difficulty adjusting their theology and institutions to the scientific, liberal, and secular assumptions of the period.

1. THE PHYSICAL, BIOLOGICAL, AND MEDICAL SCIENCES

The greatest advances in the field of the physical sciences in the nineteenth and early twentieth centuries centered on discovering the nature of matter, energy, and electricity. John Dalton (1766–1844), a gifted British scientist and teacher, started a fruitful line of inquiry by reviving the theory that all matter is composed of atoms. Dalton eventually concluded that what distinguishes the various chemical elements is the weight of the atoms of which each element is composed. Building on Dalton's theories, the Russian chemist Dmitri Mendeléev (1834–1907) in 1870 worked out a periodic chart showing the atomic weight of all the known elements and indicating by gaps in the chart that others remained to be discovered. Both Dalton and Mendeléev thought that the atom was an indivisible solid. But in the 1890s the British physicist Joseph Thomson (1856–1940) and the

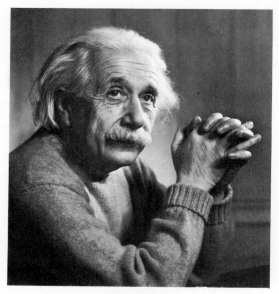

FIGURE 51.2. Einstein Albert Einstein (1879–1955) became one of the most recognized figures of the twentieth century. His theory of relativity, first proposed in 1905, undermined the concept of a stable material universe that Newton had so beautifully formalized early in the eighteenth century. (Karsh, Ottawa/Woodfin Camp & Associates)

Dutch physicist Hendrik Lorentz (1853–1928) independently discovered that atoms are composed of small particles, which Lorentz named electrons. Shortly thereafter another British physicist, Sir Ernest Rutherford (1871–1937), further developed Thomson's theories. Rutherford conceived of each atom as a miniature solar system, the nucleus being the sun, and the electrons the planets. Furthermore—and this was most startling—Thomson and Rutherford suggested that the protons and electrons might not be matter at all but merely positive and negative charges of electricity.

Meanwhile in the 1890s the German physicist Wilhelm von Roentgen (1845–1923) discovered X-rays, and the French physicist Pierre Curie (1859–1906) and his Polish wife Marie Curie (1867–1935) discovered radium and added to what was known about radioactivity.

During this same period, Albert Einstein (1879–

1955), a German physicist who later fled to America, was assailing time-honored concepts not only about the stability of matter but also about time, space, and motion (see Figure 51.2). Einstein derived a formula equating mass and energy: $E = mc^2$ (E = energy in ergs; m = mass in grams; c = speed of light in centimeters per second). According to this formula, the atomic energy in a lump of coal is some three billion times as great as the energy obtained by burning the coal—a truth that was proved several decades later with the development of the atomic bomb. In 1905 Einstein proposed his theory of relativity, which made time, space, and motion relative to each other and to the observer, not the absolutes they had always been conceived to be.

These stunning discoveries in physics and chemistry were triumphs, reflecting new sophistication in scientific theory and experimentation. But by the turn of the century a sense of uncertainty was creeping into elite scientific circles—a sense that the more we learn, the less solid and reliable the material world seems. This sense of uncertainty, particularly in physics, would spread in the early decades of the twentieth century.

The intellectual world was even more interested in and influenced by developments in the biological sciences. Evolution, like the atomic theory, had been suggested by the ancient Greeks and from time to time afterward. With the revival of scientific interests and attitudes in the seventeenth and eighteenth centuries, the thoughts of a number of scientists turned to the problem of the origin of the present world and its phenomena. By the mid–nineteenth century, the concept of a slow and gradual development of the earth's crust and its inhabitants was not at all uncommon among intellectuals. The time was ripe for a first-rate scientist to supply the evidence. That man was Charles Darwin (1809–1882).

Darwin was of a distinguished British family. His study of medicine at Edinburgh and theology at Cambridge failed to challenge him. The world of plants and, to a somewhat lesser extent, animals was his first love—or rather, his consuming passion. In spite of frail health, he turned his powers of observation and reflection to the amassing of biological knowledge. Gradually he devel-

oped his concept of evolution. Of great influence on his thinking was Malthus' *Essay on Population* (1798), which described the struggle of human beings for food and survival, and Sir Charles Lyell's *Principles of Geology* (1830–1833), which was the first truly scientific treatise on geology. Lyell demonstrated by the study of fossils the likelihood of a gradual evolution of the earth's crust and of plant and animal forms over eons of time. Darwin published *On the Origin of Species by Natural Selection* in 1859. In this historic work he described with an impressive array of factual data, convincing reasoning, and lucid prose, the long, slow evolution of present plant and animal species from simpler forms through a process of natural selection. In the struggle for survival in nature's jungle, the fittest survived. Those specimens that possessed the more useful characteristics—for instance, the horse with the longer legs—survived to produce more offspring and to transmit their superior qualities, both inherited and acquired, to future generations. Twelve years later (1871) in his *Descent of Man*, he undertook to show how humans evolved from more primitive species by the same process. Although Darwin's work leaves many fundamental questions unanswered, his main thesis quickly gained general acceptance in the scientific world.

Few books in history have had so much influence as *On the Origin of Species*. The industrial bourgeoisie seized upon Darwin's theory as an explanation and a justification of its own success. Rulers and dominant groups everywhere derived comfort from it. Philosophers, notably Herbert Spencer, undertook to broaden the principle of evolution to make it the key to all truth. Meanwhile, Darwin's brilliant work not only popularized but also significantly contributed to the advancement of the biological sciences.

Medical science lagged far behind the physical and biological sciences at the opening of the nineteenth century. The seventeenth- and eighteenth-century scientists had made great progress in discovering the secrets of the stars, of the elements, and of plants and animals, but where the ailments of the human body were concerned, they were still holding to theories of Galen, a Greek physician of the second century A.D. George Washington was bled to death in 1799 by a physician who was following the standard practice of the time.

Much groundwork had been laid, however, for medical progress. In the sixteenth century Vesalius made great advances in the study of human anatomy. In the seventeenth century Harvey discovered the circulatory system, and Leeuwenhoek and Malpighi were using the newly invented microscope to explore the structure of human tissue and to discover the existence of microbes. By the late eighteenth century the British physician Edward Jenner was successfully inoculating against smallpox, though he did not understand the secret of its success. During the 1840s anesthesia was discovered and used successfully. But the whole field of germ diseases and infections was still a mystery.

The secrets of bacteria, their nature and their control, were first explored by the French chemist Louis Pasteur (1822–1895). During the 1860s Pasteur, after intensive and imaginative research, discovered that fermentation is caused by airborne bacteria that could be destroyed by boiling (or by pasteurization). Later he discovered that many diseases of humans and animals are also caused by bacteria and that some of them can be prevented by vaccination. His spectacular services to French agriculture and to humankind made him the most honored man in France. Robert Koch (1843–1910), a country doctor in eastern Germany, hearing of Pasteur's first discoveries, picked up the trail and discovered the germs causing anthrax (a deadly disease of cattle), tuberculosis, sleeping sickness, and many other diseases. He became a professor at the University of Berlin and was awarded the Nobel Prize.

Also building on Pasteur's foundations was the renowned British surgeon Joseph Lister (1827–1912), who applied the new knowledge of bacteria to the use of antiseptics and disinfectants in surgery. His amazing success in controlling infection opened a new era in surgery, and Lister was raised to the peerage by the British government. The honors bestowed on Pasteur, Koch, and Lister, in contrast with the persecutions suffered by many of the sixteenth- and seventeenth-century scientists, are striking evidence of the triumph of science and the scientific spirit in the nineteenth century.

2. THE RISE OF SOCIAL SCIENCE

The spectacular successes of the natural sciences in the nineteenth century encouraged scholars to apply the techniques and principles of natural science to the study of the human mind and society. The result was the birth of modern psychology and sociology, both of which soon became popular.

Until the middle of the nineteenth century the mechanistic and associational approach to psychology stemming from the theories of John Locke (1632–1704) still prevailed. In the second half of the nineteenth century a number of psychologists began to systematically apply an empirical approach to the study of human behavior. One of the first to bring psychology into the laboratory was Wilhelm Wundt (1832–1920). In his famous laboratory at Leipzig he and his enthusiastic students tested human reactions and tried all sorts of carefully controlled and measured experiments on cats and dogs, assuming that the findings would also be applicable to human beings.

The Russian scientist Ivan Pavlov (1849–1936), pursuing Wundt's line of attack, excited the intellectual world with the discovery of the conditioned reflex. Pavlov showed meat to a hungry dog and the dog's mouth watered. Then Pavlov rang a bell while showing the meat. Eventually the dog's mouth watered when only the bell was rung. The implication was that many of our human responses are purely mechanical reflexes produced by stimuli of which we are often unaware.

Sigmund Freud (1856–1939) created the greatest stir of all in the rapidly growing field of psychology. Freud was a Viennese neurologist who became the father of psychoanalysis. Freud concluded that much of human behavior is irrational, unconscious, and instinctual. He argued that conflict is a basic condition of life, particularly conflict between our innate biological drives (such as sex or aggression) and our social selves. These conflicts are worked out on a mostly unconscious level and in stages during childhood. These conflicts invariably cause frustration. Freud believed that much neurosis and psychosis stemmed from the suppressed and frustrated drives of early life— frustrations that then festered in the subconscious. He concluded that the correct therapy for such neuroses was to make the sufferer conscious of the facts and circumstances of the original frustration. He stressed the interpretation of dreams as a key tool for revealing the unconscious. Freud and his followers developed psychoanalysis into an influential theory of human behavior, an insightful method of psychological investigation, and a useful therapy for certain problems.

During the second half of the nineteenth century sociology acquired status as a social science. This new discipline was founded and named by Auguste Comte (1798–1857), an eccentric Frenchman of great energy and imagination. The history of humankind, said Comte, can be divided into three epochs. The first was religious, when mystical or supernatural explanations were assigned to all phenomena. The second was metaphysical, when general laws and abstract principles were taken as explanatory principles. The third, which humankind was on the point of entering, was the specific or positive, when the truth would be discovered by the scientific gathering of factual data. Comte had utter scorn for the first and little respect for the second epochs. He believed that humans and society are as susceptible to scientific investigation as minerals, plants, and the lower animals. His religion was the worship of humanity, and he had great faith in its future. These ideas were called *positivism*. Comte's followers, eager and numerous, placed great faith in statistics. They amassed vast arrays of statistical data on every conceivable social problem.

Second only to Comte in importance in the founding and promotion of sociology was the Englishman Herbert Spencer (1820–1903). Spencer shared Comte's scorn for mystical religion and denied that morals should be based on religion. He also shared Comte's faith in the progress of humanity. In his ten-volume *System of Synthetic Philosophy,* Spencer undertook to synthesize all human and social phenomena into one grand evolutionary system.

People's interest in themselves and in human society, together with the scientific spirit of the times, guaranteed for the social sciences great popularity. Anthropologists and archaeologists dug feverishly into the physical and cultural past of the human race. Political scientists and economists tended to forsake theory for the statistical

and "practical." Strenuous efforts were made to make history a social science. Leopold von Ranke (1795–1886) strove to make history coldly scientific and morally neutral. History, he insisted, should be based on an exhaustive accumulation and analysis of documentary evidence. Ranke's historical attitude and methodology were imported from Germany into the United States. They became the standard in both countries.

Between 1850 and 1914 natural scientists appeared to be solving the last mysteries of the material universe. Medical scientists appeared to be banishing pain and disease from the earth. Social scientists were amassing voluminous knowledge about the human mind and social relationships. Science had become one of the mainstays for the widely popular belief in progress.

3. CHALLENGES TO CHRISTIANITY

The rapid growth of science was just one of several challenges faced by organized religion in the West. Christianity seemed to be threatened by most of the major forces of modernization.

Industrialization was in many ways inimical to Christian faith and practices. Industrialization contributed to the mass migration of people from farm to city and from country to country, tearing them loose from old social patterns and institutions, of which the church had long been one of the most important. Members of the flocks became separated from their pastors. Once in the active and exciting industrial cities, many of the newcomers seemed no longer to need the church for their social life and entertainment.

The liberal and radical political movements of the late nineteenth century were for the most part anticlerical. The established churches in Europe, particularly the Catholic church, had long been allied with the conservative aristocracy and royalty. Liberals, when they came to power, often attacked the powers, the privileges, and the property of the established church. France is a good example. After the revolutionary era had ended with the overthrow of Napoleon, the Catholic church made a comeback. It allied itself with the Bourbon regime and with Napoleon III's Second

Empire, and it opposed liberal movements, including the setting up of the Third French Republic. The liberal leaders of the Third Republic soon adopted anticlerical policies. During the 1880s the Ferry Laws loosened the hold of the Church on education by setting up a rival and favored system of public secular schools, in which the teaching of religion was banned. In 1901 the Associations Law virtually destroyed the Church's schools by outlawing the Catholic teaching orders or associations. In 1905 church and state were completely separated. In all the industrialized countries in this period, public secular education made great strides, usually under the sponsorship of liberal parties.

Another factor inimical to organized religion during the second half of the nineteenth century was the growth of nationalism, which afflicted all the great industrialized powers. International Catholicism and international Judaism were seen as competitors for nationalistic allegiance. Between 1872 and 1878 Bismarck waged *Kulturkampf* (battle for civilization) against the Catholic church in Germany (see p. 599). Bismarck regarded as intolerable the allegiance of millions of German citizens to a non-German pope and the formation of a Catholic political party in Germany. The anti-Semitism that arose in many countries at this time may be attributed in part to the resentment against the international character of Judaism and also to racism, which was often connected to strong nationalism. The Dreyfus case in France is an example (see p. 597). Bloody pogroms in Russia drove tens of thousands of Russian and Polish Jews to America. Many Jews themselves, after centuries of dispersion, became nationalistic and started a movement (Zionism) to set up a Jewish national state in Palestine.

In most of these challenges to Christianity, science—whether through use or abuse—was used to bolster or lend some credibility to the attack. During the twentieth century Christianity would learn to coexist with science, but in the nineteenth century the two were at odds with each other.

With the exception of the evolutionary hypothesis, the challenge to Christianity by natural science was more indirect than direct. The discovery of more and more of the secrets of the material world allowed people to attribute to natural causes many phenomena that previously had been attributed to divine intervention. Disease germs, for instance, now appeared to be doing things that had long been ascribed to God.

The greatest conflicts between natural science and the Christian religion to emerge in the nineteenth century grew out of Darwin's evolutionary hypothesis. The publication of *On the Origin of Species* in 1859 created an immediate religious storm. The proposal of a long, gradual, and seemingly mechanistic evolution of all present species from simpler forms appeared to contradict the account of divine creation given in the first chapter of Genesis. The whole process of evolution as suggested by Darwin appeared to leave God entirely out of the affairs of the universe. Any doubt concerning Darwin's place for human beings in his evolutionary hypothesis was removed twelve years later, when he published *The Descent of Man*. Human beings, like all other living things, evolved from more primitive species. According to Darwin's hypothesis, in the view of many readers, a human being seemed to be just another animal, albeit the highest.

Clerics raged against Darwin and his hypothesis. Efforts were made, sometimes successfully, to suppress the reading of Darwin's books and the teaching of the evolutionary hypothesis in the schools. Darwin was not lacking in champions able and willing to assail the forces of religion. Thomas Huxley (1825–1895), a biologist, surgeon in the British navy, and president of the Royal Society, popularized Darwin's work in dozens of vigorous and lucid books and pamphlets and heaped withering scorn upon the clergy. He called himself "Darwin's bull-dog." Herbert Spencer was carried away with Darwin's thesis and built a whole system of philosophy around the idea of evolution. Spencer considered evolution the key to all truth and all progress. Ernst Haeckel (1834–1919), a prolific German scientist and popularizer, made great claims for evolution and for science. He proclaimed that scientists would very soon be solving all the remaining mysteries of life and even creating life. The conflict between the evolutionists and the Christian clergy that raged in western Europe in the last four decades of the nineteenth century did not reach its climax in the United States until the 1920s.

The assault of social science upon Christianity was much more direct and severe than that of natural science. Anthropologists dug into the human race's distant past to unearth the primitive origins of its culture, of which religion is always an important part. Nearly all of them concluded that religion is based on primitive superstition. In 1890 Sir James Frazer (1854–1941) published *The Golden Bough*, a vast and fascinating history of early myths, superstitions, and cults from which he believed that modern religions, including Christianity, were derived.

Psychologists often viewed religion as a fantasy or illusion created by human beings. God served as a powerful parental figure to turn to when difficult problems drove human beings into a more childlike psychological state—someone who could be relied on to deal with a threatening world. Religion also provided psychological ecstasy as well as ways to enforce constraint and control.

But it was the sociologists who were the most persistently and pointedly hostile to religion. Supernatural religion had no place whatever in Comte's positivism, humanity itself being the object of worship. Through volume after volume of Herbert Spencer's sociological writings ran a vein of hostility to mystic religion in general and to Christianity in particular. Mechanical evolution became, for Spencer, the key to all social progress. Even morals evolved. Religious faith, said Spencer, retarded social progress and obscured human vision of the evolutionary social process.

Finally, the scientific spirit brought forth a number of biblical scholars who subjected the Bible to searching scrutiny and analysis—some for the purpose of establishing its exact meaning, and others for the purpose of detecting error or fraud. This type of scholarship is called "higher criticism."

The first prominent nineteenth-century "higher critic" of the Bible was David Strauss (1808–1874), a Lutheran theologian at the University of Tübingen in Germany. After long years of laborious work, Strauss brought out a *Life of Jesus* in two volumes that stripped Christ of his divinity and undertook to explain in natural terms the miracles and prophecies recorded in the New Testament. Strauss asserted that the New Testament was a very unreliable document, that the authorship of the four Gospels could not be proved, and that the four accounts of the life of Jesus were contradictory.

Much more popular and influential was the charming one-volume *La Vie de Jésus* by Ernest Renan (1823–1892), a French scholar and a Catholic. Renan pictured Christ in solely human and natural terms. Renan attributed Christ's belief in his own divinity to hallucinations. But it was these psychological aberrations that gave him his power and drive and much of his appeal. The work of Strauss, Renan, and the numerous other "higher critics" appeared to many to bring religion within the compass of onrushing science.

4. THE CHRISTIAN RESPONSE

The first reaction of Christianity to the new challenges was angry rejection of the new ideas and forces. In 1864 Pope Pius IX (1846–1878) issued a *Syllabus of Errors*, errors that Roman Catholics were to avoid. These errors, eighty in all, included separation of church and state, civil marriage, secular education, freedom of speech and press, religious toleration, liberty of conscience, liberalism, and materialism. In 1870 Pius IX called a Vatican council (the first general council since that at Trent in the sixteenth century), which pronounced the doctrine of papal infallibility. According to this doctrine, the pope, when speaking *ex cathedra* (that is, officially *from the chair* of St. Peter) on a matter of faith or morals, is not subject to error. This was the most authoritarian position that the Church and the pope had ever taken, and it came at a time when the intellectual, political, and religious trends seemed to be in the opposite direction. In the late nineteenth and early twentieth centuries, the Catholic hierarchy excommunicated numerous members and several priests who had compromised the official doctrines of the Church.

Many Protestants also rejected the new ideas and forces, particularly fundamentalist sects that interpreted the Bible literally. More established churches, such as the Anglicans in Great Britain and Lutherans in Germany, resisted but had to contend with undisciplined dissent within their

FIGURE 51.3. Pope Leo XIII Leo XIII (1878–1903) was the first pope to face up to issues raised by science and modernization. While clinging to the traditional doctrine of the Church, he accepted new scientific discoveries and supported some liberal reform movements. (UPI/Bettmann Newsphotos)

ranks and secular authorities that supported the new developments.

The second reaction of Christianity to the nineteenth-century challenges and assaults was to surrender to them. Many Christians, Catholics and Protestants alike, lost their faith and left their church. But many more who lost the traditional faith remained in their church and attempted to change its doctrines. They granted the claims of science and the "higher criticism," and they sympathized with the materialism, liberalism, and nationalism of the day. They continued to go to church, to sing the hymns, to say the prayers, and to recite the creeds, but they did not believe what they sang, said, and recited. They would reject the supernatural and deny the divinity of Christ. They would make the Bible a book of good literature and high ethical ideals; Christ, a great social reformer; and the church, an instrument for the promotion of good will, wholesome fellowship, racial tolerance, temperance, charity, patriotism, and so on. These Christians came to be called *modernists*. The Catholic church declared officially against modernism in 1907, and by 1914 it appeared to have either suppressed the modernists in its ranks or driven them under cover. In the various Protestant churches in Europe modernism competed with fundamentalism, both extreme and moderate, and by 1914 modernism had tended to gain the upper hand. In the United States modernism in the Protestant churches did not reach its peak until the 1920s and 1930s.

The third reaction of Christianity was moderate compromise: an acceptance of proved scientific facts and reasonable deductions therefrom together with attempts to harmonize the findings of science with the fundamentals of the Christian faith. This attitude involved interpreting certain passages in the Bible figuratively, particularly the first chapter of Genesis, and admitting to a few errors in various versions of the Bible. This harmonizing Christian reaction led to an increased awareness of the responsibility of the Christian churches to participate actively in the social and political problems of the day.

The Catholics were the first to reach this middle position. Leo XIII (see Figure 51.3), pope from 1878–1903, promoted the theology of Thomas Aquinas, which stressed the compatibility of faith and reason. He welcomed new scientific beliefs on condition that they be proved. He and his successors gradually took the position that natural science was not the province of the Church; that evolution could be taught in the Church's schools as a hypothesis; that the first chapter of Genesis should be taken figuratively; and that within these premises belief in evolution was a private and individual matter.

Leo XIII also faced up to some of the economic and social challenges of industrialization. In 1891, in the most famous of all his encyclicals, *Rerum Novarum* ("of new things"), he denounced materialism and Marxian socialism and proclaimed the sanctity of private property. He did, however, declare limits to the use of private property. Labor must not be treated as a commodity; workers must be paid a fair living wage and protected against too long hours, injury, and disease. Leo XIII advocated a wider distribution of property, labor unions for collective bargaining, and farming cooperatives. Roman Catholic labor unions were soon organized to challenge the socialist-dominated unions.

Christianity, so beset on its home grounds by challenges, assaults, and internal divisions during the late nineteenth century, was never more zealous in sending out missionaries to propagate the faith abroad. Roman Catholic, Protestant, and Eastern Orthodox missionaries vied with one another in Asia and Africa. By 1914 more than 40 million people outside Western Christendom professed the Christian faith. But since the Christian missionaries in Asia and Africa were often associated with Western imperialism and exploitation, they frequently aroused resentment. In 1914 Christianity in the West was still on the defensive.

SUGGESTED READING

General

O. Chadwick, *The Secularization of the European Mind in the Nineteenth Century* (1975). A useful, well-written study.

C. C. Gillispie, *The Edge of Objectivity* (1960). Good survey of modern science.

The Physical, Biological, and Medical Sciences

M. Ruse, *The Darwinian Revolution* (1979). An excellent introduction.

E. Mayr, *The Growth of Biological Thought* (1982). A good recent survey.

The Rise of Social Science

R. Aron, *Main Currents in Sociological Thought,* 2 vols. (1965, 1967). An excellent survey of the founders of modern sociology.

P. Gay, *Freud: A Life for Our Time* (1988). A well-regarded study.

Challenges to Christianity

J. L. Altholz, *The Churches in the Nineteenth Century* (1967). A solid survey.

H. Daniel-Rops, *A Fight for God* (1966). A good history of the Catholic church during the period.

J. McManners, *Church and State in France, 1870–1914* (1972). Solid and scholarly.

A. Vidler, *The Church in an Age of Revolution* (1961). A solid study of church and state during the period.

CHAPTER 52

Thought and Culture in an Age of Nationalism and Industrialization

FIGURE 52.1. Picasso, "Les Demoiselles d'Avignon," 1906–1907 Between 1850 and 1914 artistic styles evolved rapidly, moving from realism to the beginnings of modernism. Pablo Picasso (1881–1973) was one of the most influential artists during the latter part of this period and throughout the twentieth century. This painting reflects the sense of revolt, the rapidly changing values, and the tendency to turn inward that characterized many cultural products of the late nineteenth and early twentieth centuries. (Oil on canvas, 8' × 7'8". Collection, The Museum of Modern Art, New York. Acquired through the Lillie P. Bliss Bequest)

The nationalism of the increasingly powerful Western nation-states, the challenges to established religious and moral values, and the tensions of industrial society are reflected in the thought and art of the period between 1850 and 1914. There was no sudden or drastic break with the spirit of idealism and romanticism that prevailed in the thought and art of the Age of Revolutions, 1776–1850. Both idealism and romanticism continued throughout the nineteenth century and beyond. Nevertheless, after mid-century, realism tended to replace the romanticism of the early nineteenth century. As the bourgeoisie played a more dominant role in the culture of the period, artists, writers, and intellectuals became more of an *avant garde*—increasingly critical of bourgeois values and tastes. By the end of the nineteenth century and the beginning of the twentieth, these artists, writers, and intellectuals were injecting a theme of pessimism and painful introspection into Western culture.

The nationalism that was such an important component of political and social developments during the period was reflected in a growing body of thought. Nationalism was also one of the elements behind the spread of state-sponsored educational reforms, which led toward expanded literacy and the growth of popular journalism.

In literature a stream of realism and naturalism, characterized by an almost scientific examination of life, seemed to focus on individual and social failings. Art tended to slip away from the grasp of the ordinary viewer as photography displaced traditional representational art and impressionists applied a new understanding of the physical world and optics to their paintings. Post-impressionists veered into even more disturbing styles as art, like the new scientific disciplines, became more specialized.

1. POPULAR EDUCATION AND JOURNALISM

During this era of nationalism and spreading industrialization, and particularly after 1871, there were great advances in popular education. In 1871 northern Germany and Scandinavia were the only places in the world where practically everyone could read and write. In the United States most of the states had free public elementary schools, but a fifth of the total population was still illiterate. In Great Britain a third of the people were still illiterate, in France and Belgium a half, in Spain and Italy three-fourths, in Russia and the Balkans nine-tenths. Between 1868 and 1881 national systems of free and compulsory public education were established in nearly all the nations of western and central Europe and the United States. For the most part, the systems were as yet limited to elementary schools. Nevertheless, by 1914 illiteracy had practically ceased to exist in Scandinavia, Germany, Great Britain, and the Netherlands. The illiteracy rate was less than 10 percent in the United States, Canada, France, and Belgium. In Italy it had been reduced to 50 percent, in Spain, Russia, and the Balkans to a little more than 50 percent. Literacy, of course, is only the first step toward education.

The rise in literacy was reflected in a growth of popular journalism. In 1850 newspapers were relatively few, small, expensive, and written for a limited educated clientele. The London *Times*, probably the world's most influential newspaper, had a daily circulation of less than fifty thousand. During the second half of the nineteenth century, nationalism and industrialization were accompanied by a new kind of newspaper, one that was cheap, sensational, and popular in its appeal. One of the pioneer popular journalists was Joseph Pulitzer (1847–1911), a Hungarian immigrant to the United States. Pulitzer founded the St. Louis *Post Dispatch*. He bought and built up the New York *World* until it became the country's biggest newspaper. With screaming headlines, flag-waving patriotism, easy catchy style, sensational news, popular causes and features, and, above all, comics, he made a fortune and became influential in politics. In the 1890s William Randolph Hearst built a great newspaper empire patterned after Pulitzer's. In Great Britain Alfred Harmsworth founded the halfpenny popular *Daily Mail*, made a fortune, and then bought the London *Times*. Before the end of the century five newspapers—two in London, two in Paris, and one in Berlin—had a daily circulation of more than a million each. *Le Petit Journal* in Paris had a circulation of more than two and a quarter million. This type of newspaper not only catered to the masses but also became a powerful molder of public opinion. Hearst boasted, with a modicum of truth, that he manufactured the Spanish-American War. Since the popular newspapers made their money chiefly from advertising rather than from sales, they came increasingly to reflect the viewpoints of their chief advertisers, the great corporations. The big newspapers were themselves of course, big business. Although they catered to the masses, they generally did not represent the interests of the masses.

2. CURRENTS OF THOUGHT: NATIONALISM AND DISENCHANTMENT

During the nineteenth century a strong current of thought reflected and supported the growing nationalism of that era. German thinkers in particular contributed to the intellectual foundations of nationalism. In the first half of the century, Georg Wilhelm Hegel (1770–1831) was most influential. Among other things, he argued that individual freedom depends on ordered discipline under a strong state and that the zeitgeist (spirit of the time) of the nineteenth century was the spirit of German civilization.

Even more directly supportive of nationalism were the ideas of people such as Heinrich von Treitschke, probably the most influential German historian of the decades surrounding the turn of the century, who proclaimed that Germany's victory over France demonstrated the superiority of military autocracy over liberalism. Only strong states ought to exist. Dissident minorities, individualism, and parliamentary inefficiency must not be tolerated.

German thinkers were not the only ones to reflect the nationalism of the period in their ideas. The French historian Hippolyte Taine blamed France's defeat in 1870–1871 on the corrupting influence of liberalism born in the French Revolution and bred during the nineteenth century. He would take France back to the days of the Old Regime. In Great Britain, Thomas Carlyle in thunderous prose exalted heroes and hero worship, specifically the Prussian variety. Rudyard Kipling put his poetic gifts to use to sing of the glorious British Empire and the "white man's burden" of ruling and civilizing "backward" peoples.

The most extreme set of ideas underlying nationalism during the second half of the nineteenth century was racism. People of every nation began to think and talk of themselves as a distinct and superior breed. Language was more than ever confused with race. Thus one spoke of the various "races" in the Austro-Hungarian Empire. By far the most popular and serious of all the racial cults was the Aryan myth. The term *Aryan*, which was originally a linguistic term referring to the ancient Persians (Iranians) and later to all peoples speaking Indo-European languages, was now applied to the Germanic- or Teutonic-speaking peoples or to the Nordic (tall blond) type of northern European. After Germany's spectacular military triumphs and economic developments under Bismarck, the term *Aryan* came to be applied more specifically to Germans and to the energetic, aggressive, military qualities they were supposed to possess. Oddly, the two chief formulators of the Aryan myth were a Frenchman, Comte de Gobineau, and the renegade Englishman Houston Stewart Chamberlain, who left his homeland and became a German citizen. Their ideas, however, were taken much more seriously in Germany than in France or Great Britain. They argued that race was the key determinant of history. Chamberlain's racist ideas veered off into anti-Semitism, as did the ideas of other racist writers such as Richard Wagner. Wagner wrote violent propaganda tracts and composed grandiose operas stridently extolling the virtues of the early Nordic (German) supermen—Siegfried and the Nibelungs.

Although many philosophers of Social Darwinism and liberalism remained optimistic about the evolution of human beings and human society ever onward and upward, a new, strong strain of disenchantment surfaced in late-nineteenth-century philosophy. A forerunner of these pessimistic philosophers who were to have so much influence on the twentieth century was Arthur Schopenhauer (1788–1860). In *The World as Will and Idea*, published in 1819, forty years before *On the Origin of Species*, this German thinker set forth the idea that one force governs and motivates the whole world of animate life, and that force is will—the will to survive. The world, therefore, is a cruel and heartless place full of struggling and competing creatures, a place where the strong and fierce devour the weak and gentle. The only possible happiness to be found in it is by ascetic denial and withdrawal. They suffer least who participate least in the hard, competitive world.

This line of thinking (at least a variation of it) was carried to its ultimate by an admirer of Schopenhauer, Friedrich Nietzsche (1844–1900). Nietzsche was a disillusioned German theological student turned philosopher. He was a pain- and nerve-racked genius. Two of his most influential works are *Thus Spake Zarathustra* and *Beyond Good and Evil*. Like Schopenhauer, he believed that the greatest force in the animate world is will. However, this will is not only to survive but also, in the strong at least, to achieve power. "The will to power" was Nietzsche's key phrase. If a superior society is to emerge, it will have to come about through the efforts of strong and gifted individuals who will rise to power because of their superior strength, will, and intelligence. Anything that contributes to power is good, be it strength of will, boldness, cunning, or intelligence. Whatever leads to weakness is bad, be it gentleness, modesty, generosity, or compassion. The two greatest enemies of the good society are democracy and Christianity. Democracy is the rule of mediocre masses, cattle. But it was against Christianity that Nietzsche hurled his sharpest invective; he believed Christianity to be the greatest curse of Western civilization: a religion that extols the vices of slavery, such as meekness, compassion, sacrifice, and charity, to compensate for actual weakness. He went on to attack many other accepted foundations of nineteenth-century civilization, including liberalism, rationalism, and science. Although not a nationalist or racist himself, his ideas would later be used by others to support militant nationalism and even racism.

Less caustic and far more popular was the French philosopher Henri Bergson (1859–1941). Like Nietzsche he attacked bourgeois liberalism and extolled the instincts and the subjective will. His sense of the world as an evolving, vital, spontaneous place fit well with other trends in thought and the arts during the early decades of the twentieth century.

Also popular was the philosophy of pragmatism. The chief expounder of this school of thought, which has been so potent and widespread in the twentieth century, was William James (1842–1910), a professor of psychology and philosophy at Harvard University. Pragmatism reflected the uncertainties aroused by atomic physicists around the turn of the century. James rejected all absolutes of logic and religion. Truth is relative, depending on the individual and the circumstances. A thing is true if it works and is useful. We cannot know ultimate religious or moral truths, for instance, but if a particular religious faith gives an individual confidence and peace of mind, then it is practical and therefore true for that person. Thus spiritual, moral, and human values become as relative in the minds of William James and the pragmatists as the physical world in the mind of Albert Einstein.

3. REALISTIC LITERATURE

Much of the literature of the second half of the nineteenth century, like the philosophy, reflected the materialism, the cynicism, and the pessimism of the age. However, there was a strong carryover of romanticism beyond 1850 and into the twentieth century. The romantic Victorian poets Victor Hugo, Robert Browning, and Alfred Tennyson lived on until 1885, 1889, and 1892, respectively. Although Browning was a rugged and analytical realist when probing the depths of human psychology and emotions, he tended at times to be an idealist and an optimist, believing that "God's in his heaven, all's right with the world." And although in 1850 the young Tennyson in his *In Memoriam* revealed a religious skepticism bold for the time, in 1889 he hoped to see his "Pilot face to face" when he had "crossed the bar." Nevertheless, the prevailing and most significant trend in literature was realism. It was expressed most generally in the novel and drama rather than poetry. Realism tended to depict the seamy, sordid side of human nature and society. It villainized the *nouveau riche* industrial bourgeoisie and its religious and moral hypocrisy without idealizing the uprooted and distressed working class.

France took the lead in realistic literature. Balzac, who died in 1850, had foreshadowed realism. In his scores of novels and tales he subjected the dominant middle class to increasingly exact and severe scrutiny. The first French novelist to catch the full flavor of realism was Gustave Flaubert (1821–1880). His *Madame Bovary* related the illicit sex life of the wife of a small-town French physician in such full and unblushing detail that it scandalized a public not yet accustomed to such unrestrained "realism." *Madame Bovary* became a model to other novelists.

Émile Zola (1840–1902), though interested like Flaubert in individual personality, was more concerned with social problems, particularly those created by industrialization. Zola was a bold and radical republican who played a major role in finally securing justice for Dreyfus. In twenty penetrating but sometimes tedious novels he depicted and analyzed the problems of a changing society. His sympathy was with the industrial working class, but he suffered no illusions as to the natural goodness of people, including the distressed lower classes.

Charles Dickens (1812–1870) in Great Britain combined romanticism and realism. In his sentimentality, his moralizing, his optimism, and his spontaneous gush of words, he was a romantic. In his zeal for social reform, his pillorying of bourgeois arrogance and corrupt bourgeois institutions, and his graphic and often sordid detailing of the life of the urban working class, he was the first of the British realists. In *David Copperfield*, *Oliver Twist*, and *The Pickwick Papers*, three of the best-known of his numerous and lengthy novels, a galaxy of characters of the middle and lower walks of life in industrial Britain parade realistically before us.

Mary Ann Evans (1819–1880), writing under the pen name George Eliot, wrote popular novels depicting the realities of British social life. In *Middlemarch: A Study of Provincial Life,* she sensitively related psychological conflicts to the determining social realities that surround her characters.

Thomas Hardy (1840–1928), unlike Dickens, had a pessimistic view of the universe. His vivid characters—ordinary English countryside folk—struggle Darwin-like against fate, environment, and their own frail natures without any help from God or Hardy. *The Return of the Native, The Mayor of Casterbridge*, and *Tess of the D'Urbervilles* are some of the best examples in any language of the realistic novel.

Probably the most typical of all the British realists was George Bernard Shaw (1856–1950). Of Irish birth, Shaw early crossed over to London, where he long remained the gadfly of bourgeois society. In scores of urbane and sophisticated novels, essays, and plays, he charmingly but caustically taunted Christianity, capitalism, and democracy. Shaw was a cynic, a Socialist, and a stark materialist. He was the epitome of late-nineteenth-century and early-twentieth-century realism.

In the United States, the era of the realistic novel began with the works of Theodore Dreiser (1871–1945). Dreiser's novels depicted in hard, rough detail the life and the philosophy of the disenchanted and uprooted proletariat living in a materialistic, industrial world of changing values. His first novel, *Sister Carrie,* which appeared in 1900, was an American industrial version of *Madame Bovary* told with raw unrestraint. To escape poverty, Carrie became the mistress of a succession of men. The progressive degeneration of the characters constitutes the theme of the novel. Editors were so shocked at the frank and open presentation of lurid details that Dreiser had great difficulty getting the book published. The success of *Sister Carrie* was immediate, and other novels in a like vein followed.

One of the most influential of the realists was the Norwegian playwright Henrik Ibsen (1828–1906). A frustrated artist embittered by youthful poverty, Ibsen ridiculed bourgeois society in his popular dramas. In what is probably his best-known play, *A Doll's House,* one of his heroines rebels against the "doll's house" that her stodgy, hypocritical, middle-class husband created for her. In *An Enemy of the People,* Ibsen reveals the fickleness of the masses and their unfitness for democratic government. *Ghosts* deals with the social and personal problems of syphilis.

In Russia, Ivan Sergeyevich Turgenev (1818–1883) and Fyodor Dostoyevski (1821–1881) combined realism with romanticism in much the same manner as did Dickens in Great Britain. In his masterpiece, *Fathers and Sons,* Turgenev grapples

FIGURE 52.2. Claude Monet, "La Grenouillère," 1869 Monet was a leading French impressionist. His bold use of color, his emphasis on the play of light, and his focus on the appearance of things were typical of impressionistic painters. (The Metropolitan Museum of Art, Bequest of Mrs. H. O. Havemeyer, 1929. The Havemeyer Collection)

powerfully with the problems of the older conservative Russian generation versus the modern, sophisticated, and radical younger generation. Dostoyevski's two greatest novels are *Crime and Punishment* and *The Brothers Karamazov*. In them he delves psychologically and mystically into the problems of evil and purification through suffering. He was deeply religious, but not in any formal or orthodox sense. Leo Tolstoy (1828–1910) was more completely dedicated to realism and devoted his life and writing almost exclusively to social reform. His masterpiece is *War and Peace*. In this gigantic novel, scores of personalities along with more impersonal social forces so interlace with and influence each other that not even the strongest individual—not even Napoleon—can work his will alone. In his later years Tolstoy sought to combine Christianity with socialism, giving up his great inherited wealth to set a good example. Anton Chekhov (1860–1904) wrote polished but realistic and pessimistic plays about Russian life. Maxim Gorky (1868–1936), up from the proletarian ranks, analyzed the social problems of the Russian masses in his dramas and novels.

Realistic literature, with all its varieties, had many things in common. It reflected almost invariably the social dislocation brought about by the Industrial Revolution, particularly in its more advanced second phase. It reflected the materialism of an age of science and technology. It displayed over and over again the influence of Darwin and, later, of Freud. It was increasingly concerned with the disillusionment and cynicism brought about by changing religious and moral values.

4. IMPRESSIONIST AND MODERN PAINTING AND SCULPTURE

France, the birthplace of realistic literature, was also the chief seat of the impressionistic and modern painting and sculpture that predominated during the second half of the nineteenth century. Impressionism was a mild and sophisticated revolt against the artistic standards that had prevailed since the late fifteenth century. It reflected the intellectual challenge to traditional values and institutions that arose after mid-century. It took its chief inspiration from the seventeenth-century

FIGURE 52.3. Rodin, "Heroic Head" Auguste Rodin, "Heroic Head" (Pierre De Weissart), 1889, bronze. Rodin's powerful figures represent both a new departure in sculpture and a bridge from the nineteenth century to the twentieth. He brought the impressionistic spirit to his work, and he was a forerunner of much of the abstract and symbolist sculpture of the twentieth century. (Norweb Collection, The Cleveland Museum of Art)

Spanish painters Velázquez and El Greco, from Japanese art, which was rediscovered after 1853, and from new scientific knowledge concerning the nature of color and light. Impressionistic painting was informal, unposed, and random-angled. It sought to convey by studied casualness the impression of a view one gets at a glance. The chief founder of the impressionistic style of painting was the Frenchman Édouard Manet (1832–1883). Among his more illustrious disciples were

Claude Monet (1840–1926), Auguste Renoir (1841–1919), and Camille Pissarro (1830–1903) (see Color Plate 23 and Figure 52.2). These artists painted sunlit parks and landscapes, shimmering lakes and rivers, and subtle, sophisticated portraits. They omitted much detail, painting in only suggestive shapes, forms, and colors as first impressions, and leaving the rest to the imagination. Their work was sensuous, decorative, and mildly iconoclastic.

The breach that the impressionists made with long-established traditions was greatly widened near the end of the nineteenth century and early in the twentieth by more radical modern painters. The new trend was led by Paul Cézanne (1839–1906), a lifelong friend of Émile Zola (see Color Plate 24). Cézanne distorted freely in order to achieve a more powerful effect and applied thick paint to attain the appearance of solidity and roundness. Going far beyond Cézanne, the gifted but eccentric Frenchman Paul Gauguin (1848–1903) and Dutchman Vincent van Gogh (1853–1890) broke openly with artistic standards of the past. Gauguin was interested in painting not the literal document of his subject but only what the subject meant to him. He painted patterns formed in his mind by objects rather than the objects themselves, using violent reds, yellows, and greens. He finally became primitive, deserting Western civilization for the South Sea Islands. Gauguin's friend, van Gogh, would squeeze out paint directly from the tube on to the canvas to achieve striking effects (see Color Plate 25). Like Gauguin, van Gogh was an expressionist, freely distorting the images of nature to make them express his own feelings. Cézanne, Gauguin, and van Gogh were the forerunners of many iconoclastic schools, such as cubism and futurism, that marked twentieth-century painting.

Two of the most influential of the revolutionary modern painters were the Frenchman Henri Matisse (1869–1954) and the Spanish-born (French by adoption) Pablo Picasso (1881–1973), both of whom received their chief inspiration from Cézanne. In some of their work they carried distortion to great extremes. Matisse became enamored with primitive culture. Picasso's figures during one phase of his long career became geometric (hence cubism) and disjointed (see Figure 52.1).

He occasionally gave up color entirely for black and white.

It is characteristic of an age of intellectual revolt and changing values that the artists turn inward (see Color Plates 26 and 27). During the late nineteenth and early twentieth centuries, painting became highly individualistic. The artists tended to paint such objects as fruit, still life, and mandolins. Furthermore, they turned to figures on the periphery of a disintegrating society, such as prostitutes, solitary drinkers, blind beggars, and circus performers. The figures were separate from one another. This disjointedness and the symbols of science, machinery, and speed, which were so prominent in this painting, represented an age of intellectual revolt against traditional values, of materialistic science and technology, and of social tension. Unfortunately, much of this painting was so technical and highly specialized that it could be appreciated only by relatively few at a time when the many were seeking enlightenment.

The rapid growth of cities and of wealth during the second Industrial Revolution was responsible for the production of a large quantity of sculpture to decorate the new public buildings, squares, and parks. Most of it was patterned after the styles of the past, either classical or baroque, more often the latter. Probably the two sculptors of the period who most truly reflected the spirit of their own time and of future trends were Constantin Meunier (1831–1905) in Belgium and Auguste Rodin (1840–1917) in France. Meunier was the first great sculptor to recognize the importance of the industrial proletariat. Among his rugged and realistic statues are "The Hammersmith," "The Puddler," "The Mine Girl," and "The Old Mine Horse." Rodin introduced impressionism into sculpture (see Figure 52.3). His most famous statue, "The Thinker," illustrates not only impressionistic art but also the influence of the classical, Renaissance, baroque, and romantic styles. Rodin was the forerunner of much of the modern, abstract, and symbolist sculpture of the twentieth century.

5. FUNCTIONAL ARCHITECTURE

The architecture of the period 1850–1914, like the sculpture, combined the old with the new. The

Figure 52.4. Sullivan's Carson-Pirie-Scott Department Store The Carson-Pirie-Scott Department Store in Chicago was designed by the American architect Louis Henry Sullivan (1856–1924), who was the first to determine that function is the sole purpose of the style of a building. Sullivan designed the world's first steel-supported skyscraper. (Hedrich Blessing)

prevailing style in the numerous and increasingly large public buildings continued to be classical or baroque. Gothic architecture, which enjoyed a revival in the early part of the nineteenth century, was now limited primarily to university buildings and to churches. Even Byzantine, Moorish, and Oriental models appeared here and there throughout the West as the world was brought closer together by rapid communications.

The first great architect to develop a style appropriate to an age of steel, science, and speed was the American Louis Henry Sullivan (1856–

1924). Sullivan argued that "Form follows function." That is to say, the style of buildings should be determined by their intended use and by the materials used in their construction (see Figure 52.4). The architectural devices of the past had lost their utility, were purely decorative. And in fast-moving, crowded, and growing New York and Chicago, what sense did horizontal Greek or Moorish lines make? Sullivan designed the steel-supported skyscraper.

But Sullivan and his followers were not satisfied with the principle "Form follows function." They decided that function is the prime purpose of architecture. The application of this principle came to be known as "functional architecture." Structural steel, reinforced concrete, and glass brick made it possible for the functional architects to achieve unbroken horizontal lines impossible for the Greeks and towering heights combined with gracefulness and light that the medieval Gothic builders could not have contemplated. Furthermore, the spirit of intellectual revolt against the standards and values of the past gave the architects a freedom to experiment never before enjoyed. Finally, unprecedented wealth and technological advances provided them with the means to execute their ideas. Some of the massive utilitarian structures of this and later periods are creditable monuments to an age of materialism.

6. MUSIC OLD AND NEW

Of all the arts, music showed the least responsiveness to the economic and social trends between 1850 and 1914. Some of the greatest romantic composers lived well on into the second half of the nineteenth century. Wagner lived until 1883, Verdi until 1901. Their ranks were joined in the late nineteenth century by such great romanticists

as Camille Saint-Saëns (1835–1921) in France and Peter Tchaikovsky (1840–1893) in Russia. Nor was there any lessening in the spirit of nationalism in music, which was such an important ingredient of romanticism. Wagner's nationalism became more militant after 1870. Tchaikovsky combined Russian nationalism with his romanticism. More strictly nationalist in their themes and folk tunes were the Russian Nikolai Rimsky-Korsakov (1844–1908); the Czech Antonín Dvořák (1841–1904); the Norwegian Edvard Grieg (1843–1907); and the Finn Jean Sibelius (1865–1957).

Not only romanticism but also classicism was carried over into the late nineteenth century by the great German composer Johannes Brahms (1833–1897). Spending the last thirty-five years of his life in the Hapsburg capital of Vienna, Brahms became an ardent Hungarian nationalist without giving up loyalty to his native Germany. Probably more than any other musician, Brahms resembles Beethoven in style. Like Beethoven, he combined the classical spirit with the romantic.

The most important innovator in music of the period was the French composer Claude Debussy (1862–1918). Debussy was the father of impressionistic music. Experimenting with subtle and sophisticated dissonances, he was to music what Manet and Renoir were to painting. Meanwhile, in Germany Richard Strauss (1864–1949) was startling and scandalizing his pre–World War I audiences with his complex and sometimes harshly dissonant "realistic" tone poems. He is often said to have ushered in the "modern" period in music. In Russia, Igor Stravinsky (1882–1971) was beginning his long career of composing music that was still more iconoclastic and abstract. He is called the father of the expressionist school. Stravinsky, with his more violent and impetuous dissonances, bears somewhat the same relationship to Debussy as does Picasso to Monet in painting.

SUGGESTED READING

General

F. L. Baumer, *Modern European Thought* (1977). Good general introduction.

H. S. Hughes, *Consciousness and Society* (1956). A superb study of intellectual history during the period.

S. Kern, *The Culture of Time and Space, 1880–1918* (1983). An important, interpretive work.

G. Masur, *Prophets of Yesterday* (1961). A good examination of key intellectual figures.

C. E. Schorske, *Fin-de-Siècle Vienna: Politics and Culture* (1980). An excellent study of one of Europe's cultural centers.

R. Shattuck, *The Banquet Years* (1968). A well-written account of the social and cultural life of late-nineteenth-century Paris.

Popular Education and Journalism

C. M. Cipolla, *Literacy and Development in the West* (1969). Covers the rise in literacy during the period.

R. Williams, *The Long Revolution* (1961). A good study of literacy and popular literature in England.

Currents of Thought

W. Kaufmann, *Nietzsche: Philosopher, Psychologist, Antichrist* (1974). Highly respected analysis of Nietzsche and his thought.

K. Löwith, *From Hegel to Nietzsche: The Revolution in Nineteenth-Century Thought* (1964). A good analysis.

G. L. Mosse, *Toward the Final Solution: A History of European Racism* (1978). A useful introduction.

L. Poliakov, *The Aryan Myth: A History of Racist and Nationalist Ideas in Europe* (1971). An excellent introduction.

Realistic Literature

R. Pascal, *From Naturalism to Expressionism: German Literature and Society, 1880–1918* (1973). A good survey.

Art, Architecture, and Music

P. Collaer, *A History of Modern Music* (1961). Well-written survey.

G. H. Hamilton, *Painting and Sculpture in Europe, 1880–1940* (1967). A useful survey.

A. Hauser, *Social History of Art*, Vols. III and IV (1958). Connects art to social developments of the period.

H. R. Hitchcock, *Architecture: 19th and 20th Centuries* (1958). A good survey.

J. Rewald, *The History of Impressionism* (1961). A useful introduction.

RETROSPECT

Between 1850 and 1914 developments in Western civilization were dominated by the spread of nationalism and industrialization. Both had their roots in the preceding Age of Revolutions, but until the middle of the nineteenth century they were relatively limited in scope and intensity. During the second half of the century nationalism spread to new areas, achieved new successes, and took on a more pragmatic and aggressive quality. At the same time, industrialization matured in Western societies and spread eastward to Russia and westward to the United States.

Between 1850 and 1871 nationalism was used to strengthen the political institutions of the nation-state. The Second Empire of Napoleon III provides an outstanding example of nationalistic state building during this period. Domestically, Napoleon III involved the government in a series of new economic and social programs; in foreign affairs he intervened in areas stretching from Russia to Mexico. However, the fruits of nationalism were even more significant in Italy and Germany. First Italy, under the guidance of Piedmont and its prime minister Cavour, unified most of the diverse states of the Italian peninsula into a single nation in 1860. Then Prussia, under the leadership of Bismarck, used war and diplomacy to unify Germany into a powerful new nation in 1871.

Between 1871 and 1914 Europe was characterized politically by the spread of democratic institutions and the growth of a more militant nationalism. While the spread of democracy occurred in some form throughout Europe, it was more complete and more closely associated with liberalism in western Europe. In eastern Europe the spread of democracy was much less complete and, in some cases, more a matter of form than substance. There, governments such as those under Kaiser Wilhelm II in Germany, the tsars in Russia, and the emperor in Austria-Hungary tended to be conservative and authoritarian.

Meanwhile, in the United States many of the main developments occurring during the nineteenth century roughly paralleled European developments. Democratic institutions, along with a growing sense of nationalism, were spreading as the country expanded. At the same time that the Industrial Revolution was spreading from Great Britain to other areas of Europe, the United States was industrializing its economy—particularly after the Civil War in 1865. And like other Western governments, the American government attempted to adjust to the pressures of a mature industrial society by instituting political reforms toward the end of the nineteenth and the beginning of the twentieth centuries.

After 1880 nationalism and industrialization combined to thrust the leading nation-states of the West into a new imperial race. Within two decades the Western powers carved vast areas of Africa, Asia, and the Pacific into colonies and territories of imperial interest. As a result of this imperial expansion, non-Western societies were undermined and irreversibly changed, and Western powers became locked into added rivalries that would bear fruits of war in 1914.

Meanwhile the second Industrial Revolution was taking place in the West. Steel, chemicals, and electricity were replacing iron, textiles, and steam as the basis of new industrial development. Countries such as Germany and the United States successfully challenged the long leadership of Great Britain in industrial production. Industrial societies became much more urbanized and were dominated by the middle class, but the working classes were now rising to the fore with their own organizations and ideologies. Most significant was the rise of Marxian socialism, a powerful ideology that won many adherents and that was thrust into public life by socialist unions and socialist political parties.

Thought and culture between 1850 and 1914 reflected the influence of nationalism and industrialism. Both stressed secular beliefs and a certain pragmatic scientific approach. Both contributed to the growing problems facing Christianity during the period. The spread and the prestige of the natural and social sciences was particularly strong and was reflected in some of the literary and artistic trends of the period. Toward the end of the nineteenth century and the beginning of the twentieth century, however, a new strain of disillusionment, uncertainty, and even pessimism was appearing in philosophy, literature, art, and even science. This disturbing cultural trend foreshadowed the devastating turmoil of the decades following the outbreak of World War I in 1914.

PART ELEVEN

THE ERA OF THE TWO WORLD WARS, 1914–1945

Despite some growing social tensions, some expressions of uncertainty and doubt in intellectual circles, and some concern over deepening international rivalries and entanglements, in 1914 there was cause for the general sense of optimism that prevailed in Western civilization. Looking back over the previous century, one could see a long period of relative peace, political reform, economic growth, social adjustment, and cultural accomplishment. Western civilization seemed to have advanced greatly during the nineteenth century, and the twentieth century looked promising. Even the outbreak of war in August 1914 did not shatter this optimistic vision, for most anticipated a cleansing, short, painless, and victorious outcome. By the war's conclusion in 1918 reality had overwhelmed the early optimism. World War I initiated a new era of destruction, upheaval, and revolutionary change in the West.

But developments in the 1920s and 1930s were frightening to the liberal democratic powers who had won World War I at such a great cost. Revolutions in Russia had not only brought down the tsarist government but also had brought to power the Bolsheviks. The Bolsheviks, first under Lenin and then Stalin, transformed Russia into the Communist Soviet Union, which by the 1930s was a totalitarian nation pursuing policies in fundamental opposition to the principles of the liberal capitalistic West. Fascism arose in Europe, first in Italy under Mussolini and later in Nazi Germany under Hitler. Fascism directly and violently identified liberalism and democracy as enemies. Meanwhile, hopes for the spread of liberal democracy in southern Europe, eastern Europe, and Japan were dashed as these areas turned to authoritarian forms of government.

The democratic West reacted to these threats with disunity, confusion, and immobility. Nations such as Great Britain, France, and the United States had their own problems, heightened by the Great Depression of the 1930s. In the end Germany in Europe and Japan in the East were not to be restrained from their expansive goals. World War II broke out in 1939 and proved to be far more destructive than War I. At the war's conclusion in 1945, the aggressor states had been clearly defeated. Whether, and how, Western civilization would recover from this era of destruction remained to be seen.

CHAPTER 53
World War I, 1914–1918

FIGURE 53.1. Trench Warfare This photo of French troops on the western front in World War I illustrates the type of war it was: fought in deep trenches covered with barbed wire by foot soldiers wearing masks against poison gas. Despite the assumptions to the contrary by offense-minded generals, the advantage was with the defense. (Roger-Viollet)

The first blow that rocked the twentieth-century world was World War I. To most people, busy with their daily tasks, it seemed to be a sudden and unforeseen disaster. To statesmen and informed students of world affairs, it was the snapping of long-developing tensions.

1. ORIGINS OF THE WAR

World War I began as a showdown between two hostile alliances of European powers: the Triple Alliance, composed of Germany, Austria-Hungary, and Italy; and the Triple Entente, composed of Great Britain, France, and Russia. This system of alliances was begun by Bismarck shortly after the defeat of France and the creation of the German Empire in 1870–1871. In 1873, as a safeguard against a revengeful France, or indeed against any hostile combination against Germany, Bismarck formed the Three Emperors' League, composed of Germany, Austria-Hungary, and Russia. When the interests and ambitions of Austria-Hungary and Russia proved to be incompatible, Bismarck replaced Russia with Italy (1882) to form the Triple Alliance. However, as long as he remained at the head of the German government, he carefully nurtured cordial relations with Russia and also with Great Britain. This policy left France isolated.

Bismarck's diplomatic work was quickly undone by Kaiser Wilhelm II, who ascended the German imperial throne in 1888 and forced Bismarck's resignation two years later. Wilhelm II immediately dropped the friendship pact with Russia and began to antagonize Great Britain by his grandiose schemes in the Near and Far East and by his huge naval building program. France was now able to form an alliance with Russia (1894) and an entente (understanding) with Great Britain (1904). In 1907 the Triple Entente was formed after Great Britain and Russia had settled their long-standing differences in Asia. Growing fear of Germany helped reconcile the sharply divergent interests that had long existed among these three powers.

Suspicion and fear between the two power combinations mounted steadily. A ruinous armaments race ensued; the powers of the Triple Entente strove desperately to overcome Germany's long lead in land forces, while Germany sought to erase Great Britain's naval advantage. Rivalries and conflicts among the various members of the two alliances cropped up all over the world, threatening to embroil all the other members. In 1905–1906 and again in 1911 two such clashes occurred in Morocco between France and Germany. In both these crises, as we have seen (see pp. 625–626), Germany was forced to back down by the threat of the superior British navy. Two occurred in the Balkan peninsula between Russia and Austria-Hungary. In 1908 Austria-Hungary suddenly annexed two provinces, Bosnia and Herzegovina, which were inhabited by Serbs and Croats. Serbia had planned to annex these territories, peopled by its own linguistic king. Serbia appealed to its big Slavic brother, Russia. Russia threatened Austria-Hungary, whereupon Germany rattled its mighty sword and forced Russia to back down.

A second Balkan crisis occurred in 1912–1913. The various Balkan states defeated Turkey and then fought among themselves over the spoils. Victorious Serbia threatened to expand. Austria-Hungary not only thwarted Serbia's expansion to the Adriatic Sea but also threatened to annihilate Serbia. Again Serbia appealed to Russia and again Germany forced Russia to back down. Each of these crises brought the world close to war, increased international tension, and speeded up preparations for a final showdown.

It was in the Balkans that the fatal explosion finally occurred. Here the interests of Russia and Austria-Hungary clashed head-on. The Serbs, Bulgarians, Rumanians, and Greeks were religious (Orthodox) and cultural (Byzantine) kin of the Russians. The Serbs and Bulgarians were also linguistic (Slavic) kin of the Russians. Moreover, the Balkan peninsula was of great economic and strategic importance to Russia.

Austria-Hungary's interests in the Balkans were, perhaps, even more vital than those of Russia. The Dual Monarchy's chief interest in the area grew out of the polyglot nature of its empire. It was composed of numerous language groups, some of which, particularly the Serbs, Croats, Slovenes, and Rumanians, had linguistic kin in the Balkans. As the Ottoman Empire in the Balkan peninsula disintegrated in the nineteenth and early twentieth centuries, the various Balkan language groups emerged as independent nations.

Map 53.1   WORLD WAR I   This map indicates the surrounded position of the Central Powers and the areas of greatest fighting (and greatest destruction) during World War I.

These free peoples constituted a strong attraction for the members of their language groups in Austria-Hungary, who wished to break loose and join them. This was particularly true of Serbia, which attracted the Hapsburg's Yugoslav subjects (the Serbs, Croats, and Slovenes). But if the Yugoslavs should join Serbia, Austria-Hungary's other language minorities—Italians, Czechs, Slovaks,

Poles, Rumanians, and Ruthenians—would also demand their freedom from Austrian and Hungarian rule and the Dual Monarchy would fall apart. Austria-Hungary therefore felt it must control the Balkan peninsula in self-defense. It was also the only direction in which it could expand, particularly after its exclusion from Germany in 1866.

Overlying the clashing interests of Russia and Austria-Hungary in the Balkans were those of Germany and Great Britain. Germany felt it must maintain the integrity of the Dual Monarchy, which was its only effective and reliable ally. Then, too, Germany's own ambitions in the Balkans and the Near and Middle East were great. One of Kaiser Wilhelm II's chief imperial projects was the Berlin-to-Bagdad railroad (see p. 622), which would make German power dominant in the Ottoman Empire if not the whole Near and Middle East. This scheme gravely menaced Great Britain's own imperial lifeline running through the Suez as well as its immediate interests in the Near and Middle East. Germany's project threatened to blight permanently Russia's hopes of gaining an outlet through the Turkish Straits and to cut Russia off strategically from its allies. France and Italy had their own interests in the Balkans and in the Near and Middle East, although their primary concern was their commitments to their respective allies.

When, therefore, a third crisis occurred in the Balkans in the summer of 1914, all the great powers of Europe were automatically involved. The two Moroccan crises, the two Balkan crises, and the feverish armaments race had brought the tension in Europe to the breaking point. All that was needed was an incident.

2. THE FATAL EXPLOSION

The incident was the shooting at Sarajevo (in Bosnia) of the Austrian Archduke Francis Ferdinand by a Serb on June 28, 1914. The assassination was a deliberate plot involving numerous Serbian army officers. Francis Ferdinand, heir to the Austro-Hungarian throne, was singled out because the Serbs feared that his liberal policy toward the Yugoslavs in Austria-Hungary would allay their discontent, thereby lessening their desire to break away and join Serbia. After the assassination, the government of Austria-Hungary decided to crush Serbia and establish its own dominance in the Balkans once and for all. This tactic would require the backing of Germany, for clearly Russia would not stand aside and allow its Serbian kin and allies to be so treated or its own national interests to be thus violated. At a fateful conference in Berlin eight days after the shooting, the German government gave Austria-Hungary a "blank check." The Germans urged Austria-Hungary to act quickly while world opinion was still outraged by the assassination and promised support in any emergency.

Armed with Germany's blank check, Austria-Hungary presented Serbia with an impossible ultimatum. When Serbia failed to yield to all of its terms, Austria-Hungary declared war and invaded Serbia. Russia mobilized its forces against Austria-Hungary and Germany. Germany sent harsh ultimatums to Russia and to France. When Russia failed to reply and France gave an unsatisfactory reply, Germany declared war on Russia on August 1 and on France two days later. The next day, August 4, when German troops violated Belgian neutrality on their way to attack France, Great Britain declared war on Germany. Thus, by August 4, 1914, all the great powers of Europe except Italy were at war (see Map 53.1). Italy claimed that it was not obligated to aid its allies, Germany and Austria-Hungary, since they were the aggressors. The following year, after receiving promises from France and Great Britain that it would reap the spoils of victory, Italy entered the war on the side of the Entente powers. To the side of Germany and Austria-Hungary came Turkey and Bulgaria; these were referred to as the Central Powers. To the side of the Entente powers, who came to be called the Allies, eventually came much of the rest of the world—some thirty-two nations in all. This was truly a world war.

3. GERMANY'S NEAR TRIUMPH

In a long drawn-out war, the advantage would appear to lie with the Allies in view of their superior manpower and resources and their control of the seas. However, Germany had no intention of fighting a long war, and few world observers saw much possibility of the Allies preventing the superior German army from winning a quick and crushing victory on the mainland of Europe. The German high command had long anticipated the military situation that confronted it in August 1914 and had developed a plan of operation known as the Schlieffen plan. This plan called for a holding action against the slow-moving Russians while the main German forces thrust through neutral Belgium to quickly knock out France, which possessed the only army in the world that gave the Germans any real concern. Then the Germans would concentrate on and destroy Russia with relative ease. Great Britain, her allies gone, would sue for peace.

The Schlieffen plan nearly succeeded. Stubborn Belgian resistance held up the Germans long enough for the French to redeploy their forces to the north and for the British to throw their small army across the Channel. Nevertheless, the seemingly irresistible German juggernaut crunched ahead; four weeks after the beginning of hostilities, it was outside Paris ahead of schedule. At this juncture, the desperate French and British armies turned on the Germans and in the bloody seven-day Battle of the Marne not only defeated them but drove them back a few miles. Both sides extended their lines from the Swiss border to the North Sea and entrenched. The First Battle of the Marne was one of the decisive battles in history, for it forced on the Germans a long war of attrition that made possible their ultimate defeat.

An important factor in the German defeat at the Marne was the detachment at the critical moment of one hundred thousand of their best troops for use against the Russians, who had invaded Germany with unexpected speed. Generals von Hindenburg and Ludendorff, with several divisions, were hastily transferred from the western to the eastern front. Under their command the reinforced German armies trapped the Russians at Tannenberg and administered a crushing defeat that sent them reeling back into Russia. Meanwhile, the British navy swept the Germans from the surface of the seas and set up a blockade of Germany. However, the Germans quickly discovered Britain's Achilles' heel with a new weapon: the submarine.

In 1915 the Germans staged a holding operation in the west while they delivered a series of hammer blows on the Russians, driving deep into Russia and inflicting immense casualties. A major Anglo-French effort to come to the aid of the hard-pressed Russians by breaking through Turkish defenses at the Dardanelles was beaten back with heavy losses. In 1916 Germany returned to the assault in the west. In the nine-month Battle of Verdun, the French held the Germans back, but at an enormous cost in men and supplies. The four-month Battle of the Somme between the British and the Germans was even bloodier. Like Verdun, it ended in a stalemate. In the Battle of Jutland, the biggest naval battle in history up to that time, the British fleet thwarted the effort of the German fleet to break the blockade but suffered serious losses.

4. THE HOME FRONT

Most people expected the war to last a matter of weeks. But as the months dragged on and the toll of lives and material spent on the war rose, it became apparent that whole societies would have to be mobilized to support the war effort. World War I would be a total war that blurred distinctions between combatants and civilians, between the battle lines and the home front.

The most pressing need was to organize the economy to produce the materials consumed by modern warfare—most obviously the high quantities of bullets, shells, guns, and armaments of all types (see Figure 53.2). But a vast array of other materials were also necessary—everything from food and uniforms to trucks and railway cars. Over the long haul, war needs demanded both an advanced industrial capability and efficient organization of that industrial capability to produce what was needed and get it where it could be used. To varying degrees, the governments of the major powers, particularly Germany, Great Britain, and France, took control of their economies. Production, consumption, wages, and prices were determined by governmental agencies rather than the free marketplace.

**FIGURE 53.2.
Women War Workers** During World War I, the British created large armaments plants under the Ministry of Munitions. Under the wartime pressure, women replaced men in numerous occupations usually reserved for men. (Imperial War Museum, Great Britain)

The mobilization of resources included human resources. Not only were men drafted into the armed services, but women and men at the home front were often required to work in accord with priorities determined by the government. Labor unions were brought into partnerships with the government. Women's roles changed as they assumed jobs previously reserved for men. Class distinctions blurred as more and more members of society were included in the war effort.

Politically, governments became intolerant of dissent. Constitutional or democratic processes were often ignored in the name of authority and efficiency. Propaganda was used to create support for the government and hatred for the enemy.

Those nations less able to organize and maintain this vast effort—such as the Austro-Hungarian and Russian empires—faltered first. They lacked the strong industrial base and organizational strength of Germany, France, and Great Britain. But over time, even the strongest nations weakened under the strain. By 1917 the threat of mutiny by troops was accompanied by political

and social protests against the war. It had become clear that the war was to be won or lost on the home front as much as on the battle lines.

5. THE ENTRY OF THE UNITED STATES AND THE VICTORY OF THE ALLIES

By 1917 Germany and its allies, though beginning to show signs of strain, appeared to be close to victory. French morale dropped at the front and behind the lines; numerous units of the battered army mutinied. The Germans launched an unlimited submarine campaign against British shipping. The combined German and Austro-Hungarian forces administered a crushing defeat to Italy. In November 1917 Russia, suffering unbearable hardships at the front and behind the lines, succumbed to the Communist revolution and soon thereafter withdrew from the war. Although the harsh terms forced on helpless Russia by the Germans in the Treaty of Brest-Litovsk[1] showed the remaining Allies what they could expect from a victorious Germany and strengthened their will to fight to the finish, the Germans were now able for the first time in the war to concentrate their full strength on the weary French and British. The prospects for the Allies seemed dim. It was at this critical juncture that the United States entered the war.

When the war had begun in 1914, President Woodrow Wilson had admonished the American people to remain neutral in thought as well as in deed. However, from the beginning, the great majority of public opinion in the United States was that Germany and its allies were the aggressors. During the course of the war, the United States increasingly became economically tied to the Allied cause. The sinking of American ships by German submarines, however, provided the immediate impetus for the entry of the United States into the war. When the Germans first began large-scale sinkings of merchant and passenger ships in 1915, President Wilson had protested so vigorously that the Germans finally agreed to desist. Great Britain and France, it is true, had seized some American ships attempting to evade the blockade of Germany, but no lives had been lost and damages had been paid. Early in 1917 the German high command decided to launch an unlimited submarine campaign against enemy and neutral shipping alike. At about the same time, British intelligence turned over to the United States the Zimmermann note, in which Germany offered United States territory to Mexico as a reward for attacking the United States.

German leaders fully expected that these policies would bring the United States into the war, but they believed that Great Britain and France would be crushed before any appreciable American weight could be brought to bear in Europe. The American government immediately broke off diplomatic relations with Germany. After several American ships had been sunk, Congress, on April 6, at the request of President Wilson, declared war on the German imperial government.

Although a full year elapsed before American troops were able to play an important role at the front, the boost in Allied morale was immediate, and the Americans lost no time supplying financial, material, and naval aid. The total contribution of the United States to Allied victory was relatively small compared with that of France and Great Britain, but America's role, coming as it did when both sides were approaching exhaustion, was probably decisive. At the beginning of 1918 the race was between Germany and the United States. Germany transferred troops from the Russian front to overwhelm Great Britain and France before large numbers of American troops could arrive, while the United States strove to raise, train, and transport to France sufficient forces to stem the German tide. Again the advantage appeared to lie with Germany.

In March 1918 Field Marshall Ludendorff, now in command of the German armies, launched the first of a series of massive blows on the western front designed to end the war. The British and French were driven back with heavy losses. In desperation, they at long last agreed to a unified command under France's General Ferdinand Foch. The Americans, under General John J. Pershing, also accepted his command. By the middle of June, Ludendorff had launched four great drives, and the Allied lines had been battered so thin that when the climactic fifth drive began along the Marne River in mid-July 1918, Ludendorff wired the kaiser: "If the attack succeeds, the war will be over and we will have won it." When Foch heard the opening German barrage, he wired his government: "If the present German attack succeeds, the war is over and we have lost it." The Germans were stopped by a narrow margin. Foch, now receiving a swelling stream of fresh American troops and armaments, immediately ordered a counterattack. In the Allied counterattack, the tank, developed by the British, proved to be the breakthrough weapon. German strength and morale waned rapidly; the war was lost.

The first of the Central Powers to go out of the war was Bulgaria, which at the end of September 1918 surrendered to French, British, and Serbian forces operating from the Greek port of Salonika. A month later Turkey surrendered to British im-

---

[1] Russia was forced to give up territory containing one-third of its European population, three-fourths of its iron, and nine-tenths of its coal deposits, plus a heavy indemnity.

FIGURE 53.3.   The Big Four
The "Big Four" as they posed for newsreels at Versailles in 1919. Left to right, David Lloyd George, Vittorio Orlando, Georges Clemenceau, Woodrow Wilson. The biggest controversy that developed at the peace conference was between Clemenceau, who demanded a harsh treaty with Germany, and Wilson, who insisted upon a "just" treaty. (UPI/Bettmann Newsphotos)

perial forces in the Near East. Austria-Hungary, its various language groups in revolt, surrendered on November 3 to Italian, British, and French forces driving in from Italy. The following day a full-fledged mutiny that had been brewing for several days broke out in the German navy and quickly spread throughout Germany. Popular uprisings brought down the kaiser's government. On November 11 the German commanders, their armies hopelessly beaten and in full retreat from France and Belgium, accepted Foch's armistice terms, which amounted to outright surrender. However, the German commanders manipulated events so that most of Germany's population was unaware of the extent of Germany's military collapse (no foreign soldiers were yet on German soil), and a new civilian government of republicans and socialists had to accept responsibility for the surrender. This tactic set the stage for future charges that Germany had not really been beaten but had been "stabbed in the back" by the political forces that would rule Germany during the 1920s.

6. THE PEACE SETTLEMENT

The Allied statesmen who gathered in Paris in January 1919 to try to make a lasting peace were confronted with a formidable task. Hate and disillusionment poisoned the atmosphere. Although all thirty-two of the victorious Allies were represented at the Paris Peace Conference, the great decisions were really made by the leaders of France, Great Britain, and the United States (see Figure 53.3). The French delegation was headed by Premier Georges Clemenceau, the aged "Tiger of France." As host to the conference and the head of the nation that had done the most to defeat Germany and that had suffered greatly, he expected to dominate the decisions. Leading the British delegation was the eloquent and fiery "Little Welsh Attorney," Prime Minister David Lloyd George. As spokesman for the British Empire, which comprised one-fourth of all the land and people in the world, he also expected to dominate the conference. At the head of the American del-

NORTH CAPE

ARCTIC OCEAN

• Murmansk

Narvik •

Archang

ICELAND
(Denmark)

Reykjavik •

NORWAY

SWEDEN

FINLAND

L.

Areas Lost by Germany
Areas Lost by Russia
Areas Lost by Ottoman Empire
Austria–Hungary 1914

FAEROE I.
(Denmark)

L. Lado

Helsinki •

• Leningrad

Oslo •

Reval •

ESTONIA

0   100   200   300 miles

Stockholm •

Riga •

LATVIA

ORKNEY I.
SCAPA FLOW

NORTH

DENMARK

Copenhagen •

BALTIC SEA

LITHUANIA
Memel •

Kaunas •

WHITE

• Edinburgh

Vilna •

RUSSIAN

IRISH
FREE STATE

ULSTER

S.S.R.

GREAT BRITAIN

SEA

EAST
PRUSSIA

Dublin •

Liverpool •

Hamburg •

Danzig •

POLISH
CORRIDOR

POLAND

ATLANTIC

NETHERLANDS

Bremen •

Berlin •

Brest-
Litovsk

London •

Amsterdam •

GERMANY

Warsaw •

OCEAN

Rhine R.

WEIMAR REPUBLIC

Kiev •

Brussels •

RUHR

Weimar •

BELGIUM

Cologne •

Frankfurt •

Prague •

GALICIA

LUX

Paris •

SAAR

Metz •

Stuttgart •

CZECHOSLOVAKIA

U

Versailles •

ALSACE-
LORRAINE

Strasbourg •

Dniester R.

Munich •

Vienna •

Budapest •

BUKO-
VINA

BESSARABIA

FRANCE

SWITZERLAND

AUSTRIA

Geneva •

Locarno

HUNGARY

TRANSYLVANIA

Bordeaux •

Trent •

Trieste •

RUMANIA

Fiume •

Belgrade •

Bucharest

Bilbao •

YUGOSLAVIA

Danube R.

DOBR

Marseilles •

Florence •

ADRIATIC SEA

Zara
(Italy)

SERBIA

• Sofia

PORTUGAL

ITALY

BULGARIA

Lisbon •

Madrid •

Barcelona •

CORSICA
(France)

Rome •

ALBANIA

I.

SPAIN

Naples •

AEGEAN

BALEARIC I.
(Spain)

SARDINIA

Seville •

Cadiz •

Gibraltar (Britain)

• Smyrn

Tangier •

SPANISH
MOROCCO

Algiers •

SICILY

Athens •

GREECE

SEA

DODECA
(Italy)

MOROCCO
(France)

ALGERIA
(France)

TUNISIA
(France)

MALTA (Britain)

CRETE

MEDITERRANEAN SE

Map 53.2 **EUROPE, 1923** As a result of World War I the Austro-Hungarian and Ottoman empires were dismembered and both Germany and Russia suffered important losses of territory. However, the newly established states of eastern Europe were vulnerable and cut off from their strongest potential support: France and Great Britain.

egation was the idealistic President Woodrow Wilson.

A fundamental and bitter clash immediately developed between Clemenceau, who wanted a hard peace that would mutilate Germany and make it harmless in the future, and Wilson, who wanted a "just" peace free of vindictiveness of any kind. In the end Wilson received support from Lloyd George. Great Britain needed the trade of a recovered Germany and did not wish to see France become too dominant on the Continent. The Treaty of Versailles with Germany reflected Wilson's ideas in fundamental principles, though not in every detail.

Six months of hard work and bitter wrangling were required to draw up the treaty (see Map 53.2). Its most important terms were, in brief, as follows: Germany and its allies were forced to accept full responsibility for the war. Germany was compelled to give up all its overseas colonies and concessions. Alsace and Lorraine were returned to France. The Polish-speaking areas of eastern Germany were ceded to the resurrected Polish state. With one exception, wherever doubt existed as to the wishes of the people in the affected areas, plebiscites were held to determine their desires. The exception was the "Polish corridor," which was cut along the Vistula River to give Poland an outlet to the sea. Germany's army was cut down to one hundred thousand officers and men, who were to be long-term volunteers to prevent a rapid turnover of trained personnel. Germany's navy was reduced from the world's second greatest to six small battleships, six cruisers, and a larger number of auxiliary vessels. Germany was permitted no submarines, no military aviation, no poison gas (which it had introduced during the war), and no offensive weapons such as tanks and heavy artillery. Germany's Rhineland was to be permanently demilitarized, and its munitions industries were made subject to Allied inspection. Germany's general staff was to be dismantled and its top war leaders tried for violations of the rules and customs of war, and if found guilty, punished. (The kaiser fled to the Netherlands just before Germany collapsed, and the Netherlands refused to give him up.) Finally, Germany was held liable for an indemnity that in 1921 was set by an Allied reparations commission at approximately $33 billion. Wilson and Lloyd George believed these terms to be just. Clemenceau considered them to be suicidally lenient.

The treaties with Germany's allies were actually more severe than the Treaty of Versailles because the principle followed in territorial rearrangements was freedom or union of all national language groups, and Germany was more homogeneous linguistically than were its allies. The polyglot Austro-Hungarian Empire was split up along language lines. The Czechs and Slovaks were formed into the new state of Czechoslovakia, which unfortunately also included sizable German and other minorities. The Poles were joined to Poland, the Rumanians to Rumania, the Italians to Italy, and the Serbs, Croats, and Slovenes to Serbia, which now became Yugoslavia. Thus the Dual Monarchy was cut down from a nation of 50 million, second in area only to Russia among the nations of Europe, to an Austria of 6.5 million German-speaking Austrians and a Hungary of 8 million Magyars. Turkey was shorn of its far-flung non-Turkish territories. The new national boundaries, in spite of the painstaking care with which they were drawn, left many pockets of discontent to breed future conflicts.

Wilson placed his chief hopes for peace in an association of nations that would settle peaceably the tensions and conflicts that were certain to arise in the future. He insisted that its framework be incorporated in the treaty with Germany. The first twenty-six articles of the Treaty of Versailles therefore constitute the convenant of the League of Nations.

The League of Nations had no military forces at its command. Its only teeth, so to speak, were Article X and Article XVI. Article X stated that every member undertook to guarantee the territorial integrity of every other member. In other words, if one member was attacked, all the other members were morally obligated to come to its aid. However, there was no way to compel them to do so. Article XVI stated that if a nation went to war in violation of a decision of the League, all the members of the League were to boycott the aggressor. This weapon (economic sanctions) could have been a potent deterrent if faithfully applied.

In the last analysis, however, the success of the League of Nations depended primarily upon the support of the Big Three victorious democracies— the United States, Great Britain, and France. The refusal of the United States to join the League (see pp. 701–702) was a body blow. Great Britain and France immediately lost faith in it and began to pursue their traditional nationalistic aims. Moreover, a defensive alliance between France, Great Britain, and the United States, desperately wanted by France and agreed to at the conference, was not ratified by the governments of Great Britain or the United States. France felt betrayed and left alone to face a resentful Germany.

7. THE EFFECTS OF WORLD WAR I AND THE PEACE SETTLEMENT

World War I profoundly affected the West. Much of Europe was shattered by this war of unprecedented scope and destructiveness. Over 10 million people had been killed, some 3 million of them civilians. Even more died of diseases or hardships traceable to the war. Over 20 million had been wounded. The cream of a generation of Europe's future leaders had been lost, a reality that helps account for the poor quality of leadership during the 1920s and 1930s. The financial and material losses were incalculable. A tenth of the richest part of France had been laid waste. The most developed part of Russia was devastated. European nations were saddled with heavy debts. The German, Austro-Hungarian, Ottoman, and Russian empires had collapsed. The British and French empires were seriously weakened. The economic system of capitalism, based on a relative lack of governmental control over economic and social affairs, was undermined during the war as central governments mobilized and managed their na-

WHERE HISTORIANS DISAGREE

Causes for World War I

World War I shattered the world of 1914 and nearly destroyed a whole civilization. It is natural, then, that many historians and others should spend a great deal of time and thought trying to assess the causes and assign responsibility for such a disaster.

Initially, people had great difficulty distinguishing causes from responsibility. Most nations were allies or supporters of the victors, and they held Germany responsible for the war. To them, that was little different than concluding that Germany caused the war. This view was formalized in Article 231 of the Treaty of Versailles.

During the 1920s a reaction against this harsh judgment set in. Several historians offered "revised" analyses of responsibility for World War I. Harry Elmer Barnes concluded that primary blame did not rest with Germany but rather with Russia, France, and Serbia. Sidney Bradshaw Fay argued that World War I was a war that no one really wanted, and that if blame must be assigned, it should go to Russia, France, and England as much as anyone.

Responses to these "revisionist" judgments soon appeared. Since then the scholarly and ideological struggle has continued, some historians pointing to Germany, others to the Allies, and still others to Austria-Hungary.

In recent decades scholars have tended to avoid assigning responsibility or blame for the war and instead to focus on what were the crucial causes for the war.

Many historians point to the system of alliances developing in the decades prior to 1914. These alliances divided nations into hostile, distrustful camps. In this system of alliances the acts of one nation became tied to the acts of another. Increasingly, each nation lost its ability to be flexible. Thus, when a relatively local problem between Serbia and Austria-Hungary got out of control, other nations were sucked into a conflict they did not want by the terms of the alliances they had formed and feared to violate.

Other historians focus on nationalism as the real underlying cause for the war. They argue that it was nationalism that caused nations to view everything in terms of rivalry. It was nationalism that spurred the imperial struggle, the buildup of arms, the willingness to fight, the refusal to compromise, and the underestimation of war costs.

More recently, some historians have emphasized the social tensions of European nations as the more profound underlying cause for the war. They point to growing social unrest in almost all European nations and the revolutionary threat in some. These social tensions made governments and people unusually willing to go to war as a means for letting off social pressure and bringing internal unity in the face of an external threat. The near collapse of all opposition to war once war was declared (even among committed socialists) seems to support this view.

Finally, there are those, particularly Marxist scholars, who argue that World War I stemmed from economic rivalries. They emphasize that as industrial and financial capitalism developed, so did the international interests of influential economic groups. Economic rivalry led to imperial rivalry and eventually to military rivalry. It was these economic factors that set the stage for the particular events leading to the outbreak of World War I.

Ultimately, there are always individuals who make the decisions leading to war. The deeper question is what forces created the situation where such decisions occur and result in a major war such as World War I.

tions' economies as never before. Propaganda was unleashed on a massive scale and would thereafter become an important fixture of twentieth-century life.

The peace settlement negotiated in Paris left no one satisfied and many deeply resentful. Russia, which had suffered great losses, was not even invited to the conference. Germany, which would have to play an important role in postwar Europe, was not allowed to participate in the talks—rather, its representatives were presented with a treaty and offered little choice but to sign a humiliating and weakening settlement. The United States gov- ernment refused to sign the treaty. France's thirst for revenge was not satisfied and France soon felt isolated. The settlement left newly established na- tions in eastern Europe in a weak position. Cer- tainly, the task facing the negotiators was difficult and perhaps overwhelming. The passions and de- struction unleashed by the war may have been so great that no settlement would have been satis- factory. However, the Treaty of Versailles left a legacy of disappointment and resentment to be built upon during the two decades separating World Wars I and II.

SUGGESTED READING

Origins of World War I

F. Fischer, *Germany's Aims in the First World War* (1967). Controversial account stressing Germany's respon- sibility for the war.

L. Lafore, *The Long Fuse* (1971). A good analysis of the causes of the war.

J. Joll, *The Origins of the First World War* (1984). Excellent analysis.

The War

C. Falls, *The Great War* (1961). A brief narrative stressing military affairs.

A. Solzhenitsyn, *August 1914.* Inspired, detailed account of the Tannenberg campaign that virtually knocked Russia out of the war.

B. Tuchman, *The Guns of August* (1963). Well-written account of the immediate background and opening campaigns of World War I.

A. J. P. Taylor, *The First World War* (1963). A well-written account.

The Home Front

F. L. Carsten, *War Against War* (1982). A good study of radical movements in Great Britain and Germany.

G. D. Feldman, *Army, Industry, and Labor in Germany, 1914–1918.* Excellent analysis of the social effects of the war in Germany.

J. Williams, *The Home Fronts: Britain, France, and Germany, 1914–1918* (1972). A comparative study of the domes- tic impact of the war.

The Peace Settlement

A. Link, *Wilson, the Diplomatist: A Look at His Major For- eign Policies* (1965). By a foremost authority on Wil- son.

H. Nicolson, *Peacemaking 1919* (1965). Good examination of the Versailles process and settlement.

The Effects of World War I

R. Albrecht-Carrie, ed., *The Meaning of the First World War* (1965). Stress on international affairs.

P. Fussell, *The Great War and Modern Memory* (1975). Stresses the psychological significance of the war.

J. Roth, ed., *World War I* (1967). Excellent collection of essays analyzing the significance of the war.

Historical Fiction

E. Hemingway, *A Farewell to Arms.* Famous novel based on the author's experiences on the Italian front.

E. M. Remarque, *All Quiet on the Western Front.* Has brought home to millions the horrors of trench war- fare in World War I.

CHAPTER 54
Revolution and Communism in Russia

FIGURE 54.1.   Serov, "Lenin Proclaiming Soviet Power"   This painting shows Lenin, with Stalin and other Bolshevik leaders, proclaiming to the revolutionary forces the Bolsheviks' assumption of power in 1917. The style of the painting, social realism, is typical of Soviet art during the 1920s and 1930s. (Sovfoto)

World War I not only was militarily devastating for Russia but also was something that the centuries-old tsarist government could not survive. In March of 1917 the government of Nicholas II was swept from power by a revolution. This was the beginning of an extended period of revolutionary events in Russia that eventually resulted in the rise to power of the Bolsheviks, who in turn attempted to establish their vision of a Communist society in Russia. By the 1930s Russia was ruled by a totalitarian government that was effecting a massive economic, social, and cultural transformation of the nation and that was seen as a threat by most nations of the West.

1. THE RUSSIAN REVOLUTION OF 1917

Without the strain of World War I, revolution might not have occurred as it did and when it did in 1917, but that a revolution occurred in Russia should not be surprising. The violent Russian upheaval of 1917 was the result of maladjustments and discontent that had long been developing. Russia, except for a handful of intelligentsia, had been virtually bypassed by the great liberalizing movements, such as the Enlightenment and the French Revolution, that had influenced western Europe. The Industrial Revolution, which brought in its wake liberalism and radicalism, reached Russia only in the 1890s. While western and parts of central Europe and the United States were becoming politically, economically, and socially modernized, Russia remained a land of peasantry, feudal aristocracy, and tsarist autocracy. Many of the frustrated Russian intelligentsia in the latter half of the nineteenth century turned to revolutionary doctrines and even terrorism in an effort to effect rapid change. Others, including elements from the small but growing middle class, hoped for more moderate liberal reforms. But the tsarist government, particularly under Nicholas II (1894–1917), was generally reactionary and unbending.

The growing pressures for change exploded in the revolution of 1905. With little support and faced with dissension and revolt on all sides, Nicholas II was forced to grant some liberal reforms and promised to give the elected Duma some real powers. But as soon as the crisis passed, Nicholas II returned to old policies and rejected the substance of the liberal reforms.

The outbreak of the war in 1914 brought some temporary national unity as most factions rallied to the support of the nation. Soon, however, the strains of war proved too much for the inept Russian government. Russia suffered staggering losses at the hands of the German armies. Behind the lines the suffering of the civilian population, much of which could be attributed to the corrupt bureaucracy of the tsar, was acute. Members of the Duma and others increasingly demanded liberal reform, but the tsar and his ministers refused to share power. The disintegration of Russia's military forces was reflected in a disintegration of Russia's government. The tsar increasingly fell under the influence of his unbending wife, Alexandra. She in turn fell under the influence of Grigori Efimovich Rasputin (1871?–1916), an uneducated Siberian monk who claimed powers to heal the tsar's hemophilic son. Even the tsar's aristocratic supporters, a group of whom murdered Rasputin late in 1916, were demanding fundamental change.

In early March 1917, the dam broke. Demands for bread in Petrograd quickly turned into riots and strikes. The tsar's troops were unable to restore order, often refusing to fire on the rioters or actually joining them. On March 12 the Duma organized a Provisional Government and three days later Nicholas II resigned. The new Provisional Government was dominated by liberals and moderate socialists. The leading figures of this government were Pavel Milyukov and Prince Georgi Lvov, both relatively moderate liberals. The Provisional Government enacted into law civil liberties, religious freedom, equality before the law, union rights, and other typical liberal reforms. Its more moderate faction promised to turn Russia into a Western-style political democracy and enact fundamental social reforms; others demanded more radical change. However, in addition to its inexperience, its differing factions, and the pressures for change, the Provisional Government labored under two burdens. First, it had to share power with the newly organized soviets— political organizations of workers, soldiers, and radical intellectuals—particularly the powerful Petrograd Soviet. Second, it chose to continue the war that was draining Russia. Some of the crucial connections between these two burdens are indicated by the Petrograd Soviet's issuance of Order Number 1, which declared that military officers would be democratically elected by soldiers and military decisions would be democratically made. Order Number I contributed to the continuing disintegration of the Russian forces.

In May the liberal leaders of the Provisional Government resigned and the socialist Alexander Kerensky (1881–1970) became the leading figure in the government. By this time, however, the Bolshevik wing of the Marxist Social Democratic party was starting to play an important role in Russian affairs.

2. THE RISE OF THE BOLSHEVIKS

Marxism became influential among some intellectuals toward the end of the nineteenth century. In 1898 Russian Marxists formed the Social Democratic party, whose principal leaders were Gregory Plekhanov (1857–1918) and his disciple Vladimir Ilich Ulyanov (Lenin) (1870–1924). Repression by the tsar's government forced the Social Democrats into exile. At a London conference in 1903 the radical Bolshevik wing under Lenin split from the more moderate Mensheviks.

Until 1917, Lenin's Bolsheviks remained only a minor party. Its leaders were hunted down by the state police and shot, imprisoned, or exiled. For some seventeen years Lenin remained in exile in Switzerland, keeping his party alive and plotting for the eventual overthrow of the tsar's government. During that time Lenin developed theoretical and tactical principles for the successes the Bolsheviks would enjoy in 1917. Three of these principles were crucial. The first was that the party should not be open and democratic but rather should be an elite, highly trained, and constantly purged group of dedicated Marxist revolutionaries. The second was that the socialist revolution need not be a revolution of only the industrial working class; in Russia it could also be a dual revolution of workers and peasants—all part of an even broader socialist revolution that would

sweep other countries of Europe. The third was a continuing opposition to World War I.

Lenin and the Bolshevik's chance came in the months after the fall of the tsar's government in March 1917. In April 1917 the German government transported Lenin from his place of exile in Switzerland to the Russian border in an effort to increase the chaos and remove Russia from the war. Lenin refused to cooperate with the Provisional Government and instead unleashed a barrage of appealing slogans such as "peace to the army, land to the peasants, ownership of the factories to the workers." Meanwhile, the Socialist Kerensky came to power, but he was unable to extract Russia from the war. Bolshevik influence was growing, particularly among the Petrograd workers and soldiers. In July the Bolsheviks decided the time was ripe to seize power, but the effort failed. The Bolsheviks were not yet a dominant force, and the Kerensky government arrested many Bolsheviks and forced others, including Lenin, to flee to exile in Finland. The Kerensky government was further weakened by the failure of a new Russian offensive in the war and threatened coup d'état of General Kornilov. This threat led Kerensky to release the Bolsheviks and rely on the soviets to defend the capital in September. By October the Bolsheviks under the leadership of Lenin and the brilliant Leon Trotsky (1877–1940) gained control over the Petrograd and Moscow soviets. Lenin again judged the time was ripe for revolution, and this time he was right. On November 6 Trotsky conducted a well-organized revolution, seizing the crucial centers of power and arranging for the transfer of power to the soviets and Lenin. On November 7 the Bolshevik majority elected Lenin the head of the new government.

3. THE BOLSHEVIKS IN POWER, 1917–1927

The Bolsheviks immediately moved to fulfill their promises and consolidate their power. In place of the old tsarist hierarchy, a pyramid of people's councils, or soviets, was set up. These councils were elected by universal suffrage but were actually dominated by a relatively few Communist party members. When national elections failed to return a Bolshevik majority to a Constituent Assembly, Lenin had the Red Army disperse it. Capitalism was abolished. A barter system of exchange replaced money—the value of the ruble having been destroyed by inflation and devaluation. All industry and commerce were placed under the management of committees of workers responsible to party commissars. The land was nationalized and its management turned over to local peasant committees. They in turn distributed it to individual peasants to be worked by their own labor. All crop surpluses were turned over to the state. Church lands were expropriated by the state.

In order to free the new regime for the enormous task of refashioning Russian society, Lenin immediately opened peace negotiations with the Germans. The Germans, realizing Russia's helplessness (Russian troops were deserting in droves), demanded the harshest of terms. Lenin attempted to stall them off, but when the Germans threatened to march on Petrograd and Moscow, he was forced to sign the Treaty of Brest-Litovsk (March 1918). Russia lost Finland, Estonia, Latvia, Lithuania, the Ukraine, Bessarabia, its Polish provinces, and some of its Trans-Caucasian territory. These lands contained one-third of Russia's European population, three-fourths of its iron, and nine-tenths of its coal. In addition, Russia was compelled to pay a heavy indemnity.

But these hard terms were not the end, nor the worst, of Lenin's woes. Two years of bitter civil war followed the peace with Germany. The aristocracy, including most of the higher army officers, launched a counterrevolution against the Bolshevik regime. These "white" forces were aided by various other disaffected groups and by French, British, Polish, Japanese, Czech, and American troops. It was with the greatest of difficulty that the "red" armies, hastily organized by Trotsky, finally defeated the "whites." In doing so, the Bolsheviks regained the Ukraine. However, a large additional strip of territory was lost to Poland, thanks largely to French armed intervention on the side of the Poles.

Russia's war-torn economy was a shambles. The civil war compounded the destruction already suffered from World War I. Indeed, part of the reason for the Bolshevik victory in the civil war was their policy of "war communism," which succeeded in mobilizing Russia's economy and society for the war effort but also further disrupted normal economic activities. Lack of experience and some unpopular policies added to the economic difficulties. Often workers did not know how to run factories and trains. The distribution of goods was in inexperienced hands. When peasants saw that their surpluses would be seized by the government, they often resisted or refused to raise more than they needed for themselves. By 1921 some 30 million Russians were threatened with starvation, and in spite of considerable foreign relief, particularly from the United States, many did starve.

Lenin, a realist, saw the necessity for retreat. In 1921 he launched the NEP (New Economic Policy), which was a temporary compromise with capitalism. In order to provide incentive, industries employing fewer than twenty workers were permitted to operate under private ownership. These little industrial capitalists were called *nepmen*. Enterprising peasants, called *kulaks*, were permitted to own and rent land and hire laborers. Money and credit were restored. This small-scale capitalistic activity was closely supervised and regulated by the state. However, the NEP provided enough incentive to pull the Russian economy out of chaos. In 1923, just as the new policy was beginning to function, Lenin suffered a paralytic stroke and died the following year.

Lenin's death precipitated a power struggle among his chief associates (see Figure 54.2). Most assumed that his successor would be Leon Trotsky. He had been the chief organizer of the Red Army and had planned its victory over the Whites. A brilliant and eloquent Communist theorist, he was an apostle of world revolution. Trotsky, however, underestimated Joseph Stalin, executive secretary of the Communist party. This unobtrusive and taciturn man was an unscrupulous behind-the-scenes operator. Stalin was the son of poverty-stricken ex-serfs. Expelled from an Orthodox seminary because of his Marxist views and activities, he became a professional revolutionist and terrorist. (*Stalin* is a pseudonym meaning "man of steel.") He was repeatedly arrested and imprisoned and repeatedly escaped. World War I found him in exile in Siberia. Taking advantage of the

FIGURE 54.2.   Trotsky and Stalin   This rare photograph, taken in 1923 at a party meeting, shows the feud between Stalin (seated, at right) and Trotsky (standing, at left) that ended with Trotsky's murder in Mexico in 1940. As the brilliant, eloquent Trotsky speaks, the taciturn Stalin, son of ex-serfs, eyes him coldly. (UPI/ Bettmann Newsphotos)

amnesty granted to all political prisoners by the Kerensky regime in 1917, Stalin hastened to Petrograd, where he became a devoted associate of Lenin. He played a prominent role in the civil war against the Whites and became executive secretary of the Communist party. In this key position he made himself master of the all-important party machinery.

In this struggle for leadership, Trotsky took the position that all efforts must be made to bring the socialist revolution to other parts of Europe, and that without support from other more advanced socialist nations, socialism in Russia would fail. Trotsky also favored ending the NEP and immediately launching a policy of massive industrialization. Stalin took a more moderate stand, arguing that socialism in one country (Russia) was possible and therefore all efforts should be pointed toward securing what had already been gained in Russia. Trotsky was the more compelling speaker and accomplished theorist, but he also conveyed an element of arrogance. Stalin was more adept at political in-fighting. By conspiring with prominent groups of Bolsheviks and playing one faction against another, Stalin isolated Trotsky and had him expelled from the party and exiled from Russia. By the end of 1927 Stalin had maneuvered himself into a position of dominance over the Communist party and dictatorship over the Soviet Union.

4. THE FIVE-YEAR PLANS AND THE PURGES

In 1928 Stalin launched the first of a series of five-year plans (see Figure 54.3). They were units of planned economy with certain specific goals or objectives to be achieved every five years. They marked the end of the NEP, which had served its purpose of pulling the Communist economy through its first major crises. The objectives of the First Five-Year Plan were (1) the elimination of the last remnants of capitalism, (2) the industrialization of the Soviet Union, (3) the collectivization and mechanization of agriculture, and (4) national defense. However, underlying these objectives were even more fundamental goals: to transform the economy and society of the Soviet Union into a Communist economy and society, and to train and socialize Soviet citizens to be adaptive participants in this Communist system. Rarely has such an ambitious program been undertaken.

Achievement of the first goal meant the liquidation of the *nepmen* and the *kulaks*. When tens of thousands of the independent peasant-proprietor *kulaks* resisted, Stalin eliminated them. The consolidation of their farms into mechanized collectives and the organization of giant state farms went on apace. The state farms were huge outlays up to three hundred thousand acres in size run by party managers and hired laborers. Every effort was made to mechanize them. Vast tracts of land in southeast Russia and Siberia were brought under cultivation for the first time. The collective farms were of various types. In the most common type, independent farmers surrendered their lands and horses but retained their houses, gardens, cattle, pigs, and chickens for their own private use. The collective farm was run by elected managers who were instructed and supervised by party officials. Elimination of the tiny individual tracts, each one of which had been surrounded by ditches or hedgerows, made mechanization possible. A certain amount of the harvest was set aside for taxes, insurance, improvements, and feed. A large part had to be sold to the state at a fixed price. The rest was distributed to the peasant members in proportion to the amount of their original contribution to the collective in land and horses and to the amount and quality of their work. The mechanization of Russia's agriculture required the construction of huge quantities of tractors and farm machinery.

Since the Industrial Revolution was still in its infancy in Russia in 1928, industrialization meant building almost from the ground up and concentrating on producer rather than consumer goods. Western engineers and technicians were lured to Russia with high salaries. Capital was obtained by exporting scarce supplies of wheat, often at ruinously low prices. At the cost of much privation, enormous strides were made. Steel mills, power plants, foundries, mines, refineries, and railroads were built all over the Soviet Union. At Dnepropetrovsk on the Dnieper River, the world's largest dam and hydroelectric power plant were constructed. At the end of 1932 it was announced that all the goals of the First Five-Year Plan had been reached several months ahead of time.

During the 1930s the second and third five-year plans were launched. Generally the stress remained on the collectivization and mechanization of agriculture and on heavy industrialization. However, there was a new emphasis on the production of consumer goods to enable the masses to enjoy a slowly rising standard of living.

The results of the five-year plans are difficult to evaluate accurately. What might have happened if the policy choices had been different is unknown. The results in agriculture were most questionable. There was tremendous resistance to collectivization as well as mismanagement and drought. At times famine became a reality, as did a state of near civil war in the countryside. At one point Stalin admitted that problems with collectivization had claimed some 10 million human victims and brought about the destruction of half of

FIGURE 54.3. Stalin, "The Five-Year Plan in Four Years" In this 1930s Soviet propaganda poster, "The Five-Year Plan in Four Years," Stalin is portrayed leading industrial development against the reactionary forces of capitalism and religion. (The Fotomas Index, London)

the nation's draft and farm animals. Yet by 1939 over 90 percent of Soviet agriculture was collectivized and much of it was mechanized.

The results of the five-year plans in industry and defense were more gratifying and, in many ways, phenomenal. In 1928, at the beginning of the First Five-Year Plan, the Soviet Union was far behind other nations in industrial production. During the First Five-Year Plan industrial production doubled, a record equaled again in the Second Five-Year Plan. During this period the Soviet Union managed to achieve an unprecedented rate of growth in industrial output, but at great human cost. By 1941, when the Germans invaded the Soviet Union, it had become the fourth greatest industrial power in the world. In a number of categories it had surpassed both Great Britain and Germany and was second only to the United States. The Soviet Union could never have withstood the German assault had this not been true.

The 1930s were also the time of the Great Purges. In 1934 Sergei Kirov (1888–1934), a high Soviet official, was assassinated. It is unclear whether Stalin's enemies were responsible or whether Stalin himself ordered the assassination only to use it as an excuse to eliminate potential rivals. However, a long period of party purges,

arrests, trials, imprisonments, and executions soon followed. Eventually almost all the original Bolshevik leaders were removed from power and from the party, as were most of the Red Army's top officer corps. By the end of the Great Purges in 1939, hundreds of thousands—perhaps millions—of people had been affected. The government, the Communist party, and the military were now staffed by new, generally younger figures all beholden to Stalin.

Stalin's motives for the Great Purges are a matter of debate. Some argue that the purges were a manifestation of his paranoia; others argue that they were a logical step in the process of moving the Soviet Union from a revolution in 1917 to a totalitarian Communist state in the 1930s. In any case they did consolidate Stalin's power and eliminate all potential pockets of resistance to him.

5. TOTALITARIAN CONTROL

Between 1917 and 1939 the government effected totalitarian rule in the Soviet Union. The government was dominated by the Communist party and the party head served as virtual dictator. Not only did the party enjoy a monopoly over political affairs and the armed forces, but it also controlled to an unprecedented degree the economic, social, religious, and cultural life of the nation.

The Soviet Political System

On coming to power, the Bolsheviks divided the Russian Empire into eleven socialist republics—Russia proper and ten other language or dialect areas. In 1939–1940 five more were added from territories seized by Russia at the outbreak of World War II. The Soviet Union was in theory a union of autonomous republics. (U.S.S.R. stands for Union of Soviet Socialist Republics.) Actually, however, Russia itself constituted at least four-fifths of the total area and population and dominated the Union.

The Soviet system of government as originally set up consisted of a pyramid of elected councils—village, district, county, and provincial—culminating in the Union Congress of Soviets, which met once very two years and chose executive and administrative boards. Voting was by show of hands in mass meetings. The urban vote was given more than double the weight of the rural vote, since bolshevism's chief concern was the industrial proletariat. In 1936 Stalin promulgated a new constitution, which appeared to be more democratic. Voting was to be by secret ballot, the differential between the urban and the rural vote was abolished, and the members of the various soviets in the pyramid were to be elected directly by the local districts. The member republics in the Union were allegedly granted complete autonomy.

Only the Communist party was permitted to engage in organized political activity. It named the official candidates, made all political policies and platforms, and conducted all election promotion and propaganda. Opposition to the party's official candidates and program was considered to be disloyal and was ferreted out and crushed by the state police, both secret and regular. The all-powerful Communist party was organized on an authoritarian basis. The Politburo, sixteen men meeting in secret and responsible only to the secretariat of the party, made all decisions, which were transmitted without question down through the chain of command to the local cells. The real center of power in the Soviet system was the secretariat of the Communist party, and the first (or general) secretary of the party was the most powerful figure in the Soviet Union. Obedience to superiors was demanded of all party members. Party members were carefully selected and trained. As set up by Lenin, the total number was kept relatively small.

Soviet Culture and Society

In 1917 more than 60 percent of the Russian people were illiterate. It was Lenin's belief that a Communist state required an educated populace in order to succeed. Nearly all the top Bolsheviks themselves were educated—in fact, they would be considered members of the intelligentsia in almost any time or place. Little could be done in the educational field in the first turbulent years of the Communist regime, but education received major attention in Stalin's five-year plans. In 1928 the Communists launched a vast program of free compulsory secular education. The program covered all levels—elementary, secondary, and higher—for both the young and adults. It included a comprehensive system of technical and on-the-job training. Science and engineering were particularly stressed. Of course, Soviet education was interlarded with Communist propaganda, but its standards were high, and it turned out the trained people who were needed. In 1941 Stalin announced that illiteracy had been banished from Russia.

Advanced scholarship and the arts were not neglected in the Soviet Union. An extensive program of scholarships, prizes, and institutes was inaugurated for the purpose of encouraging and subsidizing superior talent. Soviet musicians, architects, painters, and dancers more than held their own in international competition. Yet the arts were subject to official Communist ideology. All liberal, bourgeois, or capitalistic literature (which was most of it) was heavily censored. Such world-renowned composers as Prokofiev and Shostakovich occasionally fell into official disfavor because of their modern "bourgeois" music. When some powerful commissar decided that the Mendelian law of genetics, which is generally accepted in the world of science, ran counter to the party line, Soviet geneticists were forced to disclaim it.

FIGURE 54.4. Women Workers and Architects Conferring The Soviet government promoted social realism to make art relevant to the working masses and carry explicit messages. Here the sun streams in on women workers and architects conferring over plans for a new factory. On the left, a bust of Stalin looks on. (Tass from Sovfoto)

Soviet society was made more egalitarian. Although the party, governmental, military, and cultural elite enjoyed some advantages, most class distinctions were eliminated. Women particularly benefited, because all formal discrimination against them was eliminated (see Figure 54.4). Indeed, Soviet women probably gained unparalleled economic equality with men. They received equal pay and were offered equal educational and professional opportunities. However, stronger patterns of discrimination within the household left Soviet women with some of the realities of inequality that generally prevailed elsewhere in the West.

In many ways Soviet society displayed the marks of totalitarian control. Most social organizations were saturated with official Communist ideology. The Communist party and the state took direct control when any social organization showed signs of gaining significant influence. Agents of the state, ranging from minor bureaucrats to members of the secret police, pervaded Soviet society. Terror, most evident during Stalin's Great Purges, was an ever-present weapon.

Religious Policy

The religious policy of the Bolsheviks, upon gaining power in Russia, was quite similar to that of the French revolutionists in 1789–1794. All church property was confiscated. The churches themselves were turned into museums or clubs of various kinds, although they were sometimes leased to religious congregations for purposes of worship. No religious instruction whatever was permitted in the schools, which were all public and secular. The churches were forbidden to give organized religious instruction and even to maintain seminaries for the training of their own clergy. At the same time, the schools were flooded with Communist propaganda.

The Communist leaders claimed that their harsh treatment of the churches was necessitated by the active opposition of the churches to the Communist government. They claimed that when they first came to power, they granted religious freedom for the first time in Russian history, but that the churches immediately used this freedom to advocate the overthrow of the very government that granted it. They further claimed that churches had always been the tools and agents of capitalistic governments and interests. Whatever truth there may be in these claims, it would appear that religion was perceived as a problem and danger to the Soviet regime.

6. THE SOVIET UNION AND THE WORLD

When the Bolsheviks first took over in 1917, they confidently expected some of the capitalistic governments in the war-weary world to collapse and follow Russia along the path to communism. To encourage them to do so and to avoid fulfillment of the harsh terms of the Treaty of Brest-Litovsk, the Communist leaders began an active campaign of revolutionary infiltration and subversion abroad, particularly in Germany. Although some headway was made in Germany, Bavaria falling under Communist control for a brief time, the only country to embrace communism was Hungary, where in 1919 Béla Kun set up a Communist dictatorship that lasted four months. To guide and aid the Communist parties in other countries in the common cause of world revolution, the Bolsheviks set up the Comintern (Communist International), with headquarters in Moscow.

The Western capitalistic powers were antagonistic to the Soviet Union. Thinking that the Bol-

shevik regime would soon collapse, France, Great Britain, Japan, and the United States landed troops on Russian soil in 1918 and aided the counterrevolutionary White forces. France helped the Poles to seize a large strip of Russian-speaking territory. Great Britain and France organized the anti-Soviet regimes in the countries of eastern Europe bordering the Soviet Union into a *cordon sanitaire* (health or quarantine belt). For several years, no Western power would recognize the Bolshevik regime. The Soviet Union was refused admission to the League of Nations until 1934, eight years after Germany had been admitted and one year after it had withdrawn under the guidance of Hitler. Even then the Western powers steadfastly refused to cooperate with the Soviet Union in any collective action against the rising Fascist menace.

Nonetheless, the failure of the Communist movements abroad and of the Bolsheviks' early efforts to communize Russia overnight caused the Soviet leaders to adopt a more conciliatory attitude toward the capitalistic powers. The NEP needed foreign commerce and foreign capital in order to function. The Soviet Union gained official recognition abroad. In 1922 Germany established official relations with the Soviet Union. Great Britain and France recognized the Soviet Union in 1924. The last capitalist state of the West to recognize the Soviet Union was the United States, which held off until 1933.

The five-year plans, which began in 1928, required much Western capital and technical assistance. Therefore, the next ten years represented the high tide of Soviet tractability toward the capitalistic Western democracies. Stalin, unlike Trotsky, was more interested in "socialism in one country" than in world revolution, which he believed would come later. The Comintern was allowed to languish. His foreign minister, Maxim Litvinov, became a respected and even popular figure in Geneva, Paris, London, and Washington. Of course, the Soviet Union's fear of the growing Nazi German menace after 1933 was a significant factor in its conciliatory attitude toward the capitalistic democracies. This honeymoon ended in 1938 with the Munich crisis (see p. 706). From that time, Stalin was apparently convinced that real cooperation with the Western democracies was impossible. The cooperation forced upon the Soviet Union and most of the capitalistic world by the menace of the Axis during World War II lasted only until victory was assured. Meanwhile, after Hitler came to power in 1933, the greatest threat to both the Soviet Union and the capitalistic democracies was Nazi Germany.

SUGGESTED READING

General

E. H. Carr, *A History of Soviet Russia*, 7 vols. (1951–1964). Scholarly and highly respected.

I. Deutscher, *Stalin: A Political Biography* (1967). Not only a scholarly biography of Stalin but also a good history of the whole Communist movement in Russia.

I. Deutscher, *Trotsky: 1879–1940*, 3 vols.: *The Prophet Armed* (1954); *The Prophet Unarmed* (1959); *The Prophet Outcast* (1963). A classic study of Trotsky.

The Russian Revolution and the Rise of the Bolsheviks

R. Daniels, *Red October* (1969). Well-written account of the Bolshevik revolution.

A. Ulam, *The Bolsheviks* (1968). A good introduction stressing Lenin's doctrines.

B. Wolfe, *Three Who Made a Revolution* (1955). Good study of Lenin, Trotsky, and Stalin; for the nonspecialist.

The Bolsheviks in Power, the Five-Year Plans, and the Purges

R. Conquest, *The Great Terror* (1968). Excellent study of Stalin's purges.

S. Fitzpatrick. *The Russian Revolution.* (1982). A brief, analytical treatment of the period.

G. Leggett, *The Cheka: Lenin's Secret Police* (1981). Good study of this topic.

J. P. Nettl, *The Soviet Achievement* (1967). Good analysis of economic development in the Soviet Union.

Totalitarian Control

S. Fitzpatrick, *Cultural Revolution in Russia, 1928–1931* (1978). A good analysis.

K. Geiger, *The Family in Soviet Russia* (1968). Well written.

R. Marshall, *Aspects of Religion in the Soviet Union, 1917–1967* (1971). A good book on this difficult subject.

R. Pipes, *The Formation of the Soviet Union* (1964). Stresses the problem of Soviet minorities.

The Soviet Union and the World

G. Kennan, *Russia and the West Under Lenin and Stalin*. By a former American ambassador to the Soviet Union; a harsh perspective.

A. Ulam, *Expansion and Coexistence: Soviet Foreign Policy* (1974). Scholarly, by a respected expert.

Historical Fiction

A. Koestler, *Darkness at Noon* (1956). Classic novel of bolshevism and the purges.

B. Pasternak, *Doctor Zhivago* (1974). Nobel Prize–winning novel depicting life in the Soviet Union by a man who experienced it.

A. Solzhenitsyn, *The Gulag Archipelago* (1974). Vivid account of terror.

CHAPTER 55
The Rise of Fascism and Authoritarianism

FIGURE 55.1. **Mussolini Addresses the Masses** This photo of Mussolini addressing a huge crowd in Rome after a victory of the Italian forces in Ethiopia shows some of the typical traits of fascism and authoritarianism during 1920s and 1930s: nationalism (the flag), militarism (the uniform), and mass politics (the cheering crowd). (UPI/ Bettmann Newsphotos)

During World War I many hoped that victory against the Central Powers would be a blow to authoritarianism and a triumph for liberal democracy. By the time of the Paris Peace Conference in 1919, a shadow was already being cast on these hopes by the triumph of the Bolsheviks in Russia. Nevertheless, the arrangements made at Paris seemed to establish parliamentary democracy in the states of eastern Europe and affirm it in western Europe. But in only a few years these optimistic hopes were dashed by the rise of authoritarian governments in southern, eastern, and central Europe and by the growth of authoritarian political movements within several Western democracies.

1. TOTALITARIANISM, FASCISM, AND AUTHORITARIANISM

The 1920s and 1930s witnessed a great growth of totalitarianism, fascism, and right-wing authoritarianism. Of these political systems, totalitarianism was the most revolutionary and rigorous. In a totalitarian system, a single political party with a revolutionary ideology controls the government. It appeals for active support from the masses and is dominated by a dictatorial leader. No opposition is tolerated. Propaganda, force, and terror are openly used to ensure control and further the goals of the government. Modern communications, technology, and organization are used to control the economic, social, religious, and cultural life of the nation as much as possible. The liberal ideology of limited government and individual rights is formally rejected in a totalitarian system.

As we have already seen in Chapter 54, totalitarianism had its beginnings in the Soviet Union under Lenin and came to full flower under Stalin during the 1930s. Since this totalitarianism was based on Communist ideology, it is often called totalitarianism of the Left. Totalitarianism arose in a mild form in Italy during the 1920s and in a virulent form in Germany during the 1930s. Since this totalitarianism was based on Fascist ideology, it is often called totalitarianism of the Right.

Both fascism and communism were ideologies—sets of ideas and values—that were gaining strength in the West throughout the 1920s and 1930s, but fascism proved to be the greater immediate threat to liberal democracy. Generally fascism was antiliberal, antidemocratic, anti-individualistic, and anti-Communist. It was ultranationalistic and militaristic. It was tied to somewhat mystical ideas of the all-powerful expansive state, of race, and of will. Fascism was initiated by Mussolini during the 1920s. During the 1920s and 1930s Fascist parties spread throughout Europe. The greatest triumph of fascism came with the rise to power of Hitler and nazism in Germany during the 1930s. Some other governments in southern, central, and eastern Europe were influenced by fascism and had some of its trappings, but for the most part they were right-wing authoritarian regimes.

Right-wing authoritarian regimes were less ideologically based than Fascist regimes, and they controlled life in their nations to a much lesser degree than totalitarian systems. Usually they amounted to a dictatorship backed by the military and conservative forces of the nation. They tended to be most concerned with preserving order and protecting the established status quo against perceived threats from liberal democracy, socialism, or communism.

Together totalitarianism, fascism, and right-wing authoritarianism posed a serious threat to the advocates of liberal democracy in the West. Indeed, the hoped for triumph of liberal democracy after World War I seemed to be turning into a triumph for its enemies—a triumph that would lead to growing conflict and a renewal of war in 1939. The story of the rise of fascism and authoritarianism begins with Italy, where Mussolini set up the first Fascist dictatorship.

2. MUSSOLINI CREATES THE FIRST FASCIST STATE

Italy emerged from World War I battered and humiliated. Although it was one of the victorious Allies, Italy's armies had made a poor showing, and Italy had realized few of the grandiose ambitions for which it had entered the war. In the Paris peace settlements Italy had been awarded the adjacent Italian-speaking areas of Austria-

Hungary but had been denied further acquisitions east of the Adriatic and in Asia and Africa, some of which it ardently desired. These frustrations were severe blows to Italian national pride.

Italy's weak economy emerged from the war acutely maladjusted. The national debt was huge and the treasury empty. The inflated currency, together with a shortage of goods, raised prices ruinously. Hundreds of thousands of demobilized veterans could find no jobs. In the summer of 1919, there was widespread disorder. Veterans began seizing and squatting on idle, and sometimes on cultivated, lands. Sit-down strikes developed in the factories. During the winter of 1920–1921, several hundred factories were seized by the workers, and Marxism seemed to be gaining strength. The Italian government, torn by factions, seemed too weak to prevent the disorder and protect private property. Although the strife diminished and the Marxist threat waned before the end of 1921, the landlords and the factory owners were thoroughly frightened. Many of them, and indeed many small-business and professional people, longed for vigorous leadership and a strong government. The vigorous leader who stepped forward was Benito Mussolini. The strong government was his Fascist dictatorship.

Mussolini was a dynamic organizer and leader. The son of a blacksmith, he became first a teacher and later a radical journalist and agitator. Before World War I he was a pacifistic socialist, but during the war he became a violent nationalist. After the war he began organizing unemployed veterans into a political action group with a socialistic and extremely nationalistic program. During the labor disturbances of 1919–1921, Mussolini stood aside until it became apparent that the radical workers' cause would lose; then he threw his support to the capitalists and the landlords. Crying that he was saving Italy from communism and waving the flag of nationalism, Mussolini organized his veterans into terror squads of black-shirted "Fascisti," who beat up the leaderless radical workers and their liberal supporters. He thereby gained the support of the frightened capitalists and landed aristocracy. By 1922 Mussolini's Fascist party was strong enough to "march on Rome" and seize control of the faction-paralyzed government. Appointed premier by the weak and distraught King Victor Emmanuel III, Mussolini acquired extraordinary powers. Between 1924 and 1926 Mussolini turned his premiership into a dictatorship. All opposition was silenced. Only the Fascist party could engage in organized political activity. The press and the schools were turned into propaganda agencies. The secret police were everywhere. Eventually, the Chamber of Deputies itself was replaced by Mussolini's handpicked Fascist political and economic councils.

Italy's economic life was strictly regimented but in such a way as to favor the capitalistic classes. Private property and profits were carefully protected. All labor unions were abolished except those controlled by the Fascist party. Strikes and lockouts were forbidden. Wages, working conditions, and labor-management disputes were settled by compulsory arbitration under party direction. An elaborate system of planned economy was set up to modernize, coordinate, and increase Italy's production of both industrial and agricultural goods. The very complicated economic and political machinery that Mussolini created for these purposes was called the corporate state. On the whole there was probably a small decline in per capita income under· Italian fascism despite some superficial gains. The budget was balanced and the currency was stabilized. But Italy's taxes were the highest in the world, and labor's share of economic production was small.

Fascism, however, was primarily political in character, not economic. The essence of its ideology was nationalism run wild. Although Italy never became such a full-blown, viciously anti-Semitic police state as Germany, Mussolini understood the dynamic, energizing quality of militant nationalism. His writings and speeches rang with such words as *will, discipline, sacrifice, decision,* and *conquest.* "The goal," he cried, "is always—Empire! To build a city, to found a colony, to establish an empire, these are the prodigies of the human spirit. . . . We must resolutely abandon the whole liberal phraseology and way of thinking. . . . Discipline. Discipline at home in order that we may present the granite block of a single national will. . . . War alone brings up the highest tension, all human energy and puts the stamp of nobility upon the people who have the courage to meet it." This grandiose vision was reflected in Fascist

FIGURE 55.2. Max Beck-mann, "The Night," 1918–1919 Beckmann, a German artist, reflects the sense of violence and disillusionment stemming from World War I in this scene of overwhelming, absurd torture. (Kunst-sammlung Nordrhein-Westfalen, Dusseldorf)

trappings and symbols, which were adopted from ancient Rome.

Fascism clashed head-on with Christianity both in spirit and in deeds. Nevertheless, Mussolini realized the advantage of coming to terms with the powerful Catholic church and made a treaty with Pope Pius XI—the Lateran Treaty of 1929. The pope recognized Mussolini's regime. [Since the pope had been despoiled of his territories (1860–1870), he had refused to recognize the Italian government.] In return, Mussolini paid him nearly $100 million in cash and government bonds from a hard-pressed national treasury and allowed the teaching of religion by Catholic clergy in the public schools. This seeming accord, however, was uneasy and quarrelsome from the start.

The building of a powerful army and navy and the recovery of Italy's national prestige were always uppermost in Mussolini's thoughts. Fascist Italy's militarism, self-assertiveness, and expansive ambitions played an important part in the breakdown of the peace settlement and the return to war. But before we examine these activities, we must examine the rise of fascism in Germany and authoritarianism elsewhere, all of which contributed to the outbreak of World War II.

3. THE WEIMAR REPUBLIC IN GERMANY

Germany emerged from World War I defeated, humiliated, and angry. As late as July 1918 the nation had seemed to be close to victory; four months later it had been forced to surrender, hopelessly beaten. Then Germany was compelled to sign a dictated peace treaty, the terms of which it considered unjust. The Weimar Republic (so-called from the city famous for Goethe and Schiller, where its constitution was drawn up), which the Germans set up in 1919, was structured to be a model liberal democracy. Politically divided and inexperienced, it inherited the taint of defeat from World War I and had to face tremendous postwar problems (see Figure 55.2).

Almost as soon as the Social Democrats, led by Friedrich Ebert, came to power, they were challenged, first by an uprising of radical Marxists (Spartacists), then by right-wing nationalists (under Wolfgang Kapp). Both of these challenges were met, but then economic problems threatened the new government. In the early 1920s inflation grew at an alarming rate. In January 1923, after the German government chose to default on its first payment of the huge reparations bill, French and Belgian troops occupied the Ruhr Valley, Germany's richest industrial area. The Germans fought back sullenly with passive resistance. The French countered by trying to stir up a secession movement from Germany in the Rhineland. Bloodshed between the occupying troops and the civilian population was frequent. Although the occupying forces were unable to collect any reparations, Germany's economy was paralyzed and a wild inflation swept the country. Thus more seeds of bitterness were sown.

In August 1923, Gustav Stresemann became head of the German government and offered conciliation. An international commission headed by Charles G. Dawes of the United States drew up a plan for the withdrawal of the occupying forces, for an international loan to Germany, and for the orderly payment of Germany's reparations installments. The German economy quickly recovered. From 1924 to 1929 Germany was the most prosperous nation in Europe and made its reparations payments as scheduled, mostly with loans from the United States. Under Stresemann's leadership Germany sought a *rapprochement* with its former enemies. In 1925 it signed the Treaty of Locarno with France, Great Britain, Italy, and Belgium, guaranteeing Germany's existing frontiers with France and Belgium. In 1926 Germany was admitted to the League of Nations, and Stresemann was elected president of the League. However, at home power was slipping from the moderate political parties toward the extremes, reflecting Germany's underlying economic and social maladjustments. One of the growing extremes was National Socialism, organized and led by Adolf Hitler.

4. THE RISE OF HITLER AND NATIONAL SOCIALISM

Adolf Hitler was the son of a middle-aged Austrian customs official and a young, sensitive, unhappily married mother. Of an artistic temperament, he went off to Vienna at an early age to seek an artist's career. Denied admission to the art academies for lack of training and too proud to work as a laborer, he lived for years in poverty and sometimes in squalor. He fed his ego with German master-race theories and filled his heart with hatred of the Jews. At the outbreak of World War I Hitler was in Munich, Germany, eking out a living at crude art work such as making posters. The ardent young German nationalist threw himself eagerly into the war, which he considered to be a righteous crusade for the beloved fatherland. Attaining the rank of corporal, he got his first taste for command. The experience of war—the sense of mission and unified struggle—would stay with Hitler and prove to be a source of appeal to many in future years. When the war ended, he was in a hospital, a victim of poison gas.

After the war Hitler frequented beer cellars, haranguing demobilized and unemployed troops and organizing them into violent political action groups. He soon discovered his magnetic powers of oratory and of leadership. The disgruntled and the disenchanted, particularly the frustrated university students and demobilized lesser army officers, began attaching themselves to Hitler in increasing numbers. He organized them into the National Socialist (Nazi) party. Among his most important early followers were Hermann Goering, who became second in command; Rudolph Hess, who became head of the political section of the party; and Paul Joseph Goebbels, who became the chief Nazi propagandist. As early as 1923 Hitler, in league with the popular war hero Field Marshal Ludendorff, made his first grab for power (the famous Beer Hall Putsch). It was premature, however, and Hitler was jailed for nearly a year. While in jail he wrote *Mein Kampf (My Struggle)*, which became the Nazi bible.

National Socialism, as outlined in *Mein Kampf*, was the German brand of fascism. In fact, the Nazis were heavily indebted to Mussolini for both ideology and methodology. At the center of its basic philosophy is the German master-race concept. The old Nordic myth of Gobineau and Chamberlain was revived. The terms *German, Nordic,* and *Aryan* were used interchangeably without regard to scientific fact. It was held that the Germans, the only pure representatives of the tall, blond Nordic "race," are superior to and destined to conquer and rule all other peoples. Militarism, indomitable will, pride, aggressiveness, and brute strength were held to be virtues; gentleness, peacefulness, tolerance, pity, and modesty, vices.

As a specific program of action, National Socialism was primarily concerned with foreign affairs. It called for repudiation of the Treaty of Versailles; all-out rearmament; the recovery of all territories, including colonies, lost at the end of World War I; and the annexation of all neighboring German-speaking territories such as Austria, the Netherlands, and most of Switzerland. Then the master race must have *Lebensraum* (living space), which was to be obtained by driving to the east (*Drang nach Osten*), particularly by conquering and enslaving the Soviet Union. There is little doubt that in the Nazi mind world domination was the ultimate goal.

The domestic program was vague and contradictory. Trusts and department stores were to be nationalized. Unearned income was to be abolished. Communism was to be destroyed and labor unions rigidly controlled. Finally, persecution of the Jews was part of the Nazi program. Over time, persecution escalated from legal discrimination, to economic exploitation, to violence, and finally, to literal extermination. The capitalistic classes never took the socialistic aspects of Hitler's program seriously. As in Italy, they looked to the Fascists to provide strong government, protect property, and control the working classes.

Hitler copied many of Mussolini's techniques. The rank and file of Nazi party members, wearing brown shirts, were organized along military lines as storm troopers. They marched, sang, and intimidated and beat up the opposition. An elite corps of black-shirted "SS" troops supervised and policed the brown shirts. Pagan symbolism, such as the swastika, was adopted. All party members swore unquestioning and undying allegiance to Hitler.

5. THE TRIUMPH OF HITLER

At first National Socialism grew slowly but steadily. National Socialism appealed particularly to youth, to displaced veterans, and to people from many classes who felt insecure and threatened by change. It promised much, seemed to provide membership in a movement with a clear cause and direction, and offered simple solutions to difficult problems. From 1925 to 1929, when Germany under Stresemann's leadership was the most prosperous nation in Europe and was being wooed by her former enemies, Nazi party membership grew from 27,000 to 178,000.

After the Great Depression of 1929, which struck Germany along with the rest of the capitalistic world, the Nazis gained rapidly. In the parliamentary elections of 1930 they obtained several million votes and increased their seats in the Reichstag from 12 to 107. They appealed to a broad spectrum of disaffected workers, members of the middle and lower middle classes, veterans, and particularly the young. They were now strong enough to disrupt the orderly functioning of parliamentary government, and President Hindenburg resorted to ruling by presidential decree. In the presidential election of 1932 Hitler ran as the Nazi candidate. The moderate and liberal parties, which in 1925 had feared and opposed Hindenburg, now persuaded him to run again as the only man who could stop Hitler (Hindenburg was now eighty-five years old). Hitler got enough votes to force a runoff election against the popular and venerable idol. In the runoff election Hindenburg was elected, but Hitler received more than 13 million votes. In parliamentary elections a few months later, the Nazis obtained 230 out of 608 seats in the Reichstag, the largest number ever held by any party under the Weimar Republic. Hindenburg now offered to make Hitler vice-chancellor, but Hitler, sensing complete dictatorship in the offing, refused.

Meanwhile, the Nazis, under Hitler's instructions, paralyzed Germany's political life with terror. When chaos threatened to play into the hands of the Communists, in January 1933, Hindenburg offered and Hitler accepted the chancellorship. Franz von Papen, head of the militaristic Nationalist party, was made vice-chancellor. It was the

FIGURE 55.3. **Adolf Hitler at Buckeberg**   Walking between two lines of Nazi banners, Adolf Hitler makes a carefully staged, dramatic entrance to a mass meeting at Buckeberg, Germany, in 1934. (Heinrich Hoffman, *Life Magazine* © 1945 Time, Inc.)

great industrialists who finally gave the Nazis the necessary support to come to power. Hitler, determined to have nothing less than complete dictatorship, immediately called for parliamentary elections. Now in official control of the state police and the agencies of information in addition to their own highly disciplined party machinery, the Nazis skillfully used every device of propaganda to frighten and confuse the people. Like the Fascists in Italy, they exaggerated and exploited the Communist threat. Five days before the elections, they made use of the burning of the Reichstag building, blaming the Communists. The elections themselves, however, were by secret ballot and were relatively free. The Communists polled 4.8 million votes, the Center (Roman Catholic) party 5.5 million, the Social Democrats (workers and small-business and professional people's party) 7.2 million, the Nazis 17 million, and von Papen's Nationalists 3 million. The Nazi and the Nationalist vote combined gave Hitler 52 percent of the seats in the Reichstag. A few days later, Hitler, wearing his Nazi party uniform, appeared before the newly elected Reichstag, from which the Communists were excluded, and demanded dictatorial powers for four years. They were granted with only 94 opposing (Social Democratic) votes. Long before the four years had expired, the moderate parties had been destroyed, and the Nazi dictatorship was complete (see Figure 55.3).

WHERE HISTORIANS DISAGREE

What Caused Nazism?

The rise of nazism in Germany was so dramatic and of such consequence that it demands explanation. Yet perhaps no other development has remained more difficult to explain.

Perhaps the simplest explanation for the rise of nazism focuses on the politics of Hitler's rise in the 1920s and 1930s—that the political parties of the Weimar Republic were disorganized, that political leaders were weak, that there was so much political struggle and intrigue going on that Hitler did not even need to seize power. This interpretation stresses the political failure of the Social Democrats and Communists to unify against the Nazi threat and the political blindness of those conservatives who offered him the chancellorship (even though they opposed him, believing that they could gain power themselves while controlling Hitler).

The economic interpretation, favored by many Marxists, holds that nazism was a logical consequence of the last, monopoly stage of capitalism—that large landowners and industrialists resorted to nazism in a period of economic crisis in order to prevent the collapse of capitalism and the spread of socialism. This interpretation stresses the growing strength of the Communist party and the restlessness of the working class. Thus Germany's real power holders tried to use Hitler and his nazism to control the threatening masses and maintain the endangered economic system that served the Junkers and industrialists.

A third interpretation holds that nazism was a logical continuation of German history itself. It stresses that the German people had long displayed tendencies favoring the authoritarianism, militarism, and racism that came to characterize nazism. This interpretation argues that in retrospect it is no surprise that Prussia had always been militaristic, that the liberal revolutions of 1848 failed in Germany, that Bismarck united the nation by blood and iron, that leading philosophers of racism were German, and that the democratic Weimar Republic was never very popular or effective.

More recently, psychosocial interpretations have been proposed to explain the rise of nazism in Germany. According to these interpretations, nazism both reflected and responded to the desires of certain large groups of Germans—people traumatized by the war such as the veterans and the young who suffered hunger and loss of their fathers, people disoriented by the political and economic upheavals immediately following the war, and people weakened and immobilized by the Great Depression. Nazism seemed to promise a sense of direction, action, purpose, power, and pride to these people.

An underlying controversy among historians is whether nazism should be viewed as an aberration of Western history. Many historians stress that nazism should be viewed as limited in time and place, that it was an unlikely product of circumstances. They stress the extraordinary character and role of Hitler, the peculiar circumstances of Germany after World War I, and the extreme qualities of nazism.

Others argue that there were many points of continuity between nazism and Western history. They stress the growth of fascism and totalitarianism in the West, the widespread nationalism and racism, and the general appeal of authoritarian practices in times of war or socioeconomic crises.

These and other interpretations are evolving as historians gain distance from the 1920s, 1930s, and 1940s. The topic remains controversial, and the debate over the causes of nazism are likely to continue for some time.

6. NAZI GERMANY

The Reichstag, having voted Hitler dictatorial powers, adjourned, to meet henceforth only on the call of the *Führer* (leader) for the purpose of voting approval of his acts. Hitler disbanded all political parties except the National Socialist party. Freedom of speech, press, and assembly was abolished. An elaborate and all-powerful secret police, the Gestapo, was established under the direction of Heinrich Himmler to spy out and destroy opposition. Hitler's most intense hatred was vented on the Jews, who were subjected to every conceivable humiliation. As fast as their services could be dispensed with, they were driven out of public and professional life. Eventually, the Nazis embarked on a program to exterminate all the Jews under their control. It is estimated that by the end of World War II the Nazis had murdered 6 million Jews out of a world total of 15 million.

The control and molding of thought always held high priority in Nazi activities. Indeed, this control appears to be an absolute necessity for any totalitarian dictatorship. Under the direction of Goebbels, minister of propaganda, the German press and radio spewed forth a constant stream of false or distorted information. To read or listen to foreign newspapers or broadcasts was made a crime. An incessant hate campaign was waged against the liberal democratic world. The schools were, of course, nazified. Only Nazi party members could be school administrators. Unsympathetic teachers were dismissed and punished. Members of Nazi youth organizations were set to spy on their teachers and parents. Textbooks were rewritten to conform to German master-race theories. The burning of liberal books, sometimes even those of Germany's greatest literary figures, such as Goethe and Schiller, became a national fad. The Nazi minister of education admitted that the sole function of education was the creation of Nazis. Hitler wrote in *Mein Kampf* that the German youth's "entire education and development has to be directed at giving him the conviction of being absolutely superior to the others . . . the belief in the invincibility of his entire nationality." The arts were nazified and only party members or sympathizers were permitted to publish, exhibit, or perform.

Since National Socialism was essentially an anti-Christian ideology, the Nazis realized the necessity of controlling the religious establishment. Much of the Lutheran church, which was the official state church and included more than half the German people in its membership, was brought under Nazi domination. Nazi officials attempted to turn it into a propaganda agency. The few Lutheran pastors, like Martin Niemöller, who resisted were thrown into concentration camps. The smaller Protestant denominations met the same fate. Hitler found it much more difficult to deal with the Catholic church, whose higher authority lay outside Germany. Although he soon signed a concordat with the pope, the terms proved to be unworkable. Catholic clergy, churches, and schools were subjected to constantly increasing pressures, indignities, and physical abuse.

The Nazis rejuvenated and regimented Germany's economic life. The property and the profits of the capitalistic classes were given special consideration. Labor unions were brought under Nazi control, and a system of enforced arbitration of disputes between labor and management was set up along the lines that Mussolini had established in Italy. Strikes and lockouts were forbidden. The entire German economy was forced into the overall pattern and policies of the Nazi government. The vast rearmament program gave employment to millions. Superhighways, airfields, hospitals, and apartment houses were built all over Germany. The most intricate financial trickery was resorted to, but the Nazis expected eventually to finance their huge undertakings out of the spoils of victorious war.

All other activities were subordinated to the prime purpose of making a military comeback. Shortly after assuming power, Hitler took Germany out of the League of Nations and out of the disarmament conference that was in progress in Geneva. Rearmament was pushed as rapidly as possible, and in 1935 Hitler openly repudiated the disarmament clauses of the Treaty of Versailles. In 1936 Hitler remilitarized the Rhineland and sent decisive aid to General Franco's Fascist rebels in Spain (see Chapter 56). The following year he made an alliance with Italy and Japan. This Berlin-Rome-Tokyo Axis was aimed specifically at the Soviet Union. More broadly, it was an aggressive antiliberal alliance for military expansion. Meanwhile, other events taking place elsewhere in Europe also threw liberal democracy into retreat.

7. AUTHORITARIAN REGIMES IN EASTERN AND SOUTHERN EUROPE

Beginning in the 1920s hopes for permanently establishing parliamentary regimes in eastern and southern Europe were dashed by the rise of right-wing authoritarian governments. Some of them had elements of Fascist ideology and policy, but most were dictatorships by royal or military figures and individuals backed by the military and conservative powers of the nation.

The rise of right-wing authoritarian regimes in eastern and southeastern Europe was initiated in Hungary under the regency of Admiral Miklós Horthy and the rule of Count Stephen Bethlen during the 1920s and General Julius Gömbös during the 1930s. In 1926 General Josef Pilsudaski set up a military dictatorship in Poland. In 1929 a royal dictatorship was established in Yugoslavia under King Alexander I; after his assassination in 1934 an authoritarian regime was set up under the regent Prince Paul. During the 1930s royal dictatorships were established in Rumania and Bulgaria. After 1934 Austria succumbed to authoritarian rule under Engelbert Dollfuss and then Kurt von Schuschnigg until its annexation by Hitler in 1938. In 1936 Greece's shaky parliamentary regime fell to the dictatorship of General Joannes Metaxas. Czechoslovakia was an exception. There parliamentary democracy survived until the nation fell to Hitler in 1938.

The Iberian peninsula, a scene of considerable turmoil, was an area where fascism became attractive to many. In Portugal authoritarianism and political instability was the rule rather than the exception during the 1920s and eventually led to the establishment of a strong dictatorship under Antonio de Oliveira Salazar in 1932. In Spain General Miguel Primo de Rivera ruled as de facto dictator between 1923 and 1930. After a democratic interlude between 1930 and 1936, the rise of the Fascist Falange and the revolt of Spanish generals led to a civil war and the triumph of General Francisco Franco as dictator in 1939.

Almost all these authoritarian regimes emphasized nationalism and militarism. They were bolstered by a fundamental fear of change, particularly the kind of change liberal democracy and socialism represented. Many regimes provided fertile grounds for the growth of Fascist organizations and the enactment of Fascist policies, but with the possible exception of Franco's Spain, these governments were not Fascist in the same sense as Italy under Mussolini and Germany under Hitler. This description of Europe's authoritarian regimes also describes Japan's government during the 1930s, which would become one of the Axis powers in 1937.

8. THE TRIUMPH OF AUTHORITARIANISM IN JAPAN

We have already observed (see p. 621) Japan's remarkable modernization and emergence as a great power between 1853 and 1914. Japan participated in World War I on the side of the Allies and received Germany's island possessions in the Pacific north of the equator as a reward. Japan in the early 1920s stood at the crossroads. It could use its great energies and skills either to develop Japanese institutions and raise the standard of living or to become a predatory military state.

Three divergent groups competed for the leadership of postwar Japan. The dominant group was made up of the great industrialists. Seventy-five percent of Japan's industry and capital was concentrated in the hands of five great families, called the *zaibatsu*. This handful of industrial giants had such a stranglehold on the Japanese economy that it was also able to control the highly restricted government. The *zaibatsu*, enjoying this economic and political monopoly, wished to see no fundamental change in Japan's undemocratic society; it advocated instead the peaceful economic penetration of Asia.

The liberals constituted the second group. This faction, with university professors and students providing much of the leadership, set out to broaden the suffrage, which was restricted to the well-to-do, to encourage the more effective unionization of labor, and to diminish the power of the military. Because of the political inexperience and

FIGURE 55.4. **Japan Invades China** Here Japanese soldiers are celebrating victory after a new assault on China in 1937. This photograph, showing armed Japanese troops on Chinese soil under the Japanese flag, symbolizes key elements of Japanese policy during the 1930s: nationalism, militarism, and expansionism. (Ullstein Bilderdienst, West Berlin)

the long tradition of passive submission to authority on the part of the Japanese masses, these were difficult undertakings. They were made more difficult by the activities of Marxists, who confused liberal reform movements and tainted them with the suspicion of treason. Nevertheless, Japan made encouraging progress toward liberal democracy. In 1925 the suffrage was broadened. Soon afterward, two liberal political parties appeared. The military budget was reduced. The prestige of the professional military declined to such an extent that many officers ceased wearing their uniforms in public.

The professional military, however, was determined to strengthen and exploit its own traditional power. In the late 1920s a group of restless and ambitious young army officers began to accuse their leaders of softness and plotted to seize control of both the armed forces and the government. When a coup planned for early 1931 was exposed and blocked, the conspirators decided on a bold move to throw the country into such hysteria and confusion that they could seize power. In October 1931 the Japanese army stationed in Manchuria made an unauthorized attack on the Chinese forces and began the conquest of all Manchuria. The next year Japanese forces attacked Shanghai, the chief port of China (see Figure 55.4). Once fighting with huge and potentially dangerous China began, war fever and patriotic hysteria swept Japan, just as the army plotters had foreseen. They now assassinated the premier and numerous other government officials and civilian leaders and cowed the rest into submission. Once in control, the military immediately turned to the destruction of the liberals. Liberal university professors were accused of disloyalty and silenced, dismissed, or imprisoned. The schools and the press and radio were made organs of propaganda. All democratic processes of government and civil rights were destroyed. The military and state police were given unlimited authority. The *zaibatsu* were corrupted and won over with lush military contracts.

Meanwhile, Japanese overran all Manchuria, which was made into a puppet state of Manchukuo. When the League of Nations declared Japan an aggressor and ordered its withdrawal from Manchuria, Japan defied the League and instead withdrew from the organization. In 1937 Japan joined the Berlin-Rome Axis. In the same year Japan began an all-out assault on China proper. By 1937, therefore, the Axis powers were on the march.

SUGGESTED READING

Totalitarianism, Fascism, and Authoritarianism

H. Arendt, *The Origins of Totalitarianism* (1951). A brilliant but difficult analysis.

F. L. Carsten, *The Rise of Fascism* (1982). Good, scholarly analysis.

E. Nolte, *The Three Faces of Fascism* (1963). A respected but difficult intellectual history of fascism in Italy, Germany, and France.

H. Rogger and E. Weber, *The European Right: A Historical Profile* (1965). Compares the rise of right-wing politics in various countries.

H. A. Turner, Jr., ed., *Reappraisals of Fascism* (1975). A good collection of articles.

Mussolini and Italian Fascism

A. Lyttleton, *The Seizure of Power: Fascism in Italy, 1919–1929* (1973). Excellent analysis of the rise of fascism in Italy.

D. M. Smith, *Mussolini's Roman Empire* (1976). Solid, informative account of Mussolini's rule.

E. R. Tannenbaum, *The Fascist Experience: Italian Society and Culture, 1922–1945* (1972). Fine examination of life in Fascist Italy.

The Weimar Republic

E. Eyck, *A History of the Weimar Republic*, 2 vols. (1963). Comprehensive.

P. Gay, *Weimar Culture: The Outsider as Insider* (1968). Excellent examination of Weimar Germany.

Hitler and Nazi Germany

K. D. Bracher, *The German Dictatorship* (1970). Excellent study of the Nazi state.

A. Bullock, *Hitler: A Study in Tyranny* (1971). Classic biography of Hitler.

D. Schoenbaum, *Hitler's Social Revolution: Class and Status in Nazi Germany, 1933–1939* (1966). Good study of social policies and social life in Germany.

J. Stephenson, *The Nazi Organization of Women* (1980). Useful study of women in Nazi Germany.

Authoritarian Regimes in Eastern and Southern Europe

C. A. Macartney and A. W. Palmer, *Independent Eastern Europe: A History* (1967). Good survey.

J. Rothschild, *East Central Europe Between the Two World Wars* (1973). Useful general account.

The Triumph of Authoritarianism in Japan

R. Benedict, *The Chrysanthemum and the Sword* (1967). Examines the role of the professional military in Japan.

E. O. Reischauer, *The Japanese* (1977). A highly respected survey.

CHAPTER 56
Paralysis of the Democratic West

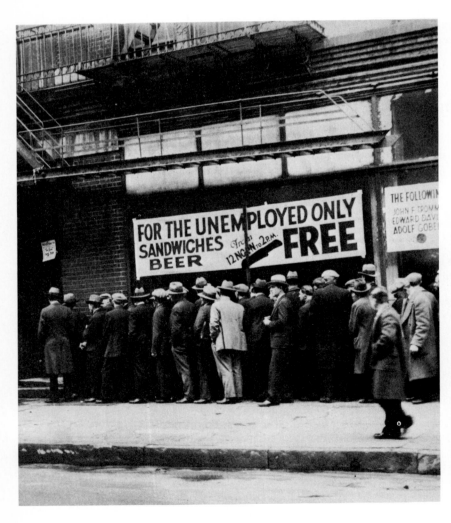

FIGURE 56.1. The Great Depression in New York Jobless and homeless men wait in line for a free meal in New York in 1930. These Depression breadlines are part of the reason for the seeming impotence of the democratic nations in the face of the growing Fascist menace. The Great Depression, which began in 1929, did not end unitl 1942, when World War II pumped billions of dollars into the American economy. (UPI/Bettmann Newsphotos)

The Western democracies emerged from World War I victorious. In many ways, each hoped to return to how things had been before the war, to quickly get back to "normal." But instead of the hoped-for smooth sailing, the Western democracies were faced with a series of challenges in the two decades following the war.

1. CHALLENGES OF THE 1920s AND 1930s

The first challenge was the immediate problem of postwar dislocation and recovery. The human, material, and economic losses were unprecedented and unequally borne—France and Belgium suffered most among the Western democracies. Soldiers had to be reintegrated into civilian life, economies had to be shifted from wartime production, and trade patterns had to be reestablished.

The second challenge was the roller-coaster ride of tension, optimism, and disillusionment that characterized international affairs in the 1920s and 1930s. The Treaty of Versailles left few happy and many resentful. The payment of reparations and wartime debts threatened the international order during the years immediately following the war. Then from 1925 to 1929, a period known as the Locarno Era, international tensions diminished and progress was made toward peace and disarmament. The Locarno Pact in 1925 (guaranteeing international boundaries in Europe), the admission of Germany to the League of Nations in 1926, the Kellogg-Briand Pact of 1928 (proclaiming a commitment to international friendship), and the earlier Washington Conference of 1921–1922 (limiting naval strength) seemed to establish a basis for optimism in international affairs. After 1930, however, this optimism gave way to disillusionment as discord, rearmament, and aggression marked international affairs.

The third challenge was the Great Depression. Economic depressions were not new to the West, but one of this magnitude and duration was unprecedented. In October 1929 the American stock market, bloated by speculation and borrowed money, crashed. Since the end of World War I, the international economic order had become dependent on the United States—particularly to keep up the flow of loans, debt payments, and trade. The financial crisis in America quickly spread to Europe. Stocks lost their value, banks failed, and confidence collapsed. This sudden financial crisis reflected the fragility of the postwar economic order, and between 1929 and 1933 economies almost everywhere were in a tailspin. World industrial production fell by more than 33 percent. Unemployment grew to massive proportions. Policies adopted to deal with the crisis probably made things worse—trade barriers rather than cooperation typified international economic policy, and cuts in spending instead of deficit spending marked domestic economic policy. Some countries started to recover after 1933, but in other cases the Great Depression extended until World War II.

The final challenge was the threat from the political extremes—communism on the left, fascism on the right. The most obvious threats were international, since communism was growing stronger in the Soviet Union and fascism was spreading in central and southern Europe. But the threats were internal as well, for both Communist and Fascist political organizations were growing within Western democracies—particularly during the 1930s.

The political and social development of each of the Western democracies greatly depended on how they met these four challenges. In retrospect it is easy to be harsh on the leaders of these societies, for in the end the world was immersed in another war even more destructive than World War I. However, these challenges were extraordinary and the leaders trying to deal with them often labored under overwhelming difficulties.

2. THE HARASSED BRITISH EMPIRE

At the end of World War I the British Empire still included one-fourth of all the land and people on the globe. Nevertheless, the British economy, empire, and world position were shaken beyond recovery. Britain's far-flung possessions in Asia and Africa were beginning to stir restlessly, as the spirit of nationalism, which long had provided the European world with so much of its expansive energy, spread eastward. Great Britain found it advisable to grant freedom to its already self-governing dominions, hoping to retain their loyalty. The Statute of Westminster in 1931 gave complete independence and equality with the mother country to Canada, Australia, New Zealand, the Union of South Africa, Newfoundland, and the Irish Free State (free since 1922). Great Britain could no longer count on their material support in world policies, nor could it count on its restless colonies. Furthermore, Britain was now clearly second to the United States as an industrial and financial power. (It would require many years, however, for the British to readjust their thinking to the reality of their country's reduced position.)

At home, postwar Britain was harassed with acute economic problems. National debt had quintupled during the war. Britain owed the United States a heavy war debt. German submarines had taken a toll of 9 million tons of British ships with their cargoes. British exports met sharply increased competition in the world markets, particularly from the United States. Rising protective tariffs all over the world hindered its commerce. Mines and industrial plants were antiquated and in disrepair. Returning servicemen found few jobs. Unemployment hovered around 3 million, a figure that came to be accepted as normal. Government support for the unemployed, sick, aged, and destitute increased Britain's financial problems.

These chronic economic ills were reflected in Great Britain's troubled postwar policies. In 1922 the Conservatives broke up Lloyd George's wartime coalition government of Liberals and Conservatives and won the ensuing parliamentary elections. They sought to restore classical nineteenth-century capitalism by means of rigid entrenchment of government spending, particularly for social services. This policy was so hard on the distressed masses that in 1924 a Labour-Liberal coalition headed by the Labour party leader, Ramsay MacDonald, ousted the Conservatives. The Labour party was now stronger than the Liberal party, and as times grew harder and feelings more bitter, the once great Liberal party was virtually crushed between the more extreme parties—Labour on the left and Conservative on the right.

But the majority of the British people were not yet ready to accept the mildly socialistic program that the Labour party advocated. MacDonald's ministry lasted less than a year. Dependent on the Liberals for his majority, he was forced to follow a moderate course. When he recognized the Soviet Union and made a commercial treaty with it, the Conservatives were able to capitalize on public suspicion and drive him from power. From 1925 to 1929 the Conservatives wrestled with rising discontent, strikes, and the steady growth of the Labour party. In 1929 a Labour victory, supported by the much dwindled Liberals, again brought Ramsay MacDonald to the head of the government. His moderation in the face of the deepening economic depression, however, caused the majority of his Labour followers to repudiate him two years later. But MacDonald was unwilling to give up the honors of office. In 1931 he therefore formed a national coalition of right-wing Labourites, Liberals, and Conservatives to deal with the mounting domestic and foreign crises. This national coalition was dominated by the Conservatives and MacDonald was really a captive of the Conservatives until he resigned in 1935. The Conservative-dominated coalition ruled Great Britain until the end of World War II. Although Great Britain was recovering from the Great Depression, the government was on the whole ineffective in dealing with social maladjustments at home and Fascist aggressions abroad. The Conservative prime ministers Stanley Baldwin and Neville Chamberlain, who followed Ramsay MacDonald as head of the national government, were unimaginative and unprepared for the challenges that would face them.

3. FRUSTRATED FRANCE

Although France enjoyed the advantage of being economically more self-sufficient than Great Britain, France had suffered greater wounds in World War I than had its island neighbor. Most of the fighting had taken place on French soil. A tenth—the most productive tenth—of its land area had been devastated. The retreating Germans had lain waste much of what had not been destroyed in battle. Orchards were chopped down, and mines were wrecked, many beyond repair. Even more tragic was the loss of life. France, with the lowest birth rate of any major nation in the world, suffered by far the heaviest casualties per capita of any of the combatants. Out of a population of less than 40 million, it suffered almost 1.4 million battle deaths and 1.7 million wounded. The civilian death rate from direct and indirect causes had also been high. France had fewer people in 1918 than in 1914, even after the return of Alsace and Lorraine.

Postwar France was confronted with a staggering job of economic reconstruction and an equally staggering war debt. To meet these obligations and to finance the reconstruction, the French government counted on German reparations, but little was forthcoming. Inflation became a chronic headache. A more basic and long-range problem was French industry, which was rapidly falling behind its competitors. The highly individualistic French had not gone in for large-scale corporate industry to the same extent as the Americans, British, and Germans. The little French family industries had difficulty competing with mass production. A like situation prevailed in French agriculture, most of which occurred on thousands of little family farms too tiny to use machinery profitably. Industrial and agricultural production per worker was lower in France than in most other major Western nations.

Considering the serious plight of France's postwar economy and the habitual disorderliness with which its multiparty democracy traditionally functioned, one is impressed by the remarkable stability of the French government during the decade of the 1920s. From 1919 to 1924, a bloc of conservative parties was in power. It followed an antilabor, probusiness policy. It also favored the Roman Catholic church and pressed hard for collection of German reparations. Meanwhile, discontent among the laboring classes was mounting. In 1924, the year of MacDonald's first Labour ministry in Great Britain, the parties of the Left under the leadership of Edouard Herriot were victorious. Like MacDonald, Herriot pursued a prolabor policy, advocating an increase in social services, and soft money. He was also conciliatory toward Russia and Germany. But, also like MacDonald, he lasted less than a year.

From 1926 to 1929, a strong right-of-center national bloc under the leadership of Raymond Poincaré was in power. Poincaré checked the inflation by rigid retrenchment. Upon his retirement in 1929, however, the increasing pressure of discontent threw the country into political turmoil. No leader or political combination seemed to be capable of dealing with the economic crisis brought on by the world depression, the growing menace of fascism, or the unrest in the French colonies. Ministry followed ministry in rapid succession. Scandals and riots occurred, and Fascist groups appeared. In 1936 the Popular Front, consisting of left-wing parties under the leadership of the mild Socialist Léon Blum, came to power (see Figure 56.2). The Blum ministry obtained a forty-hour week and two weeks' annual vacation with pay for the workers. It also nationalized the Bank of France and the great munitions industries. This was too much for the powerful propertied interests, who drove Blum from office the following year. But the conservative parties who regained control were unable to agree upon firm policies, domestic or foreign.

Thus France, like Great Britain, in the face of resurgent Nazi Germany, swashbuckling Mussolini, and militaristic Japan, could summon little strength or unity. The propertied classes were unwilling to share their wealth or privileges or to change their nineteenth-century practices. They feared and hated Léon Blum. The Great Depression persisted and fueled political turmoil. The army was basking in past glory. Seeking to maintain the status quo, the French were defenseminded. They constructed the Maginot line fortifications along the German border and formed defensive alliances with Poland, Czechoslovakia, Yugoslavia, and Rumania. These alliances were no stronger than the faith those small countries had in France's ability to defend them, which by the late 1930s was very little.

4. ISOLATIONISM, BOOM, AND BUST IN THE UNITED STATES

The United States emerged from World War I the world's richest nation. Although its entry into the war at its most critical phase was probably decisive in determining the outcome, the United States suffered far less war damage than any of the other major participants. President Wilson assumed a

FIGURE 56.2. **The Popular Front** In 1935 Socialists, Communists, and others on the French Left united for the first time as the Popular Front. In 1936 the Popular Front came to power under the leadership of the Socialist premier, Léon Blum. This photo shows Blum (on the left) and Maurice Thorez, secretary of the French Communist party, at a 1937 Bastille Day rally in Paris. (Photo Trends)

leading role in the making of the peace settlements and in the creation of the League of Nations.

When President Wilson returned from Paris in the summer of 1919 and sought to persuade his country to join the League of Nations, he faced a strong challenge from his political enemies, led by Henry Cabot Lodge. Wilson's opponents refused to accept the treaty, and particularly the League of Nations, as proposed by Wilson. Wilson, seeing the treaty and the League as a matter of principle, refused to compromise. In his struggle to rally support, Wilson suffered a paralytic stroke. Since he was unable thereafter to lead the fight for the treaty and was unwilling to give the leadership to others, his opponents easily defeated ratification in the Senate.

The League was not an issue in the presidential election of 1920. However, the victor, Warren G. Harding, announced that the League was now a dead issue. And during the cynical and disillu-sioned decade of the 1920s American public opinion became overwhelmingly isolationist. When during the international crises of the 1930s the League and the harassed British and French governments sought the support of the United States against the Fascist aggressors, they sought in vain.

The decade following World War I was a period of relative but uneven prosperity in the United States. The all-out war effort brought about a great expansion of American industry and unleashed huge quantities of money and credit. In 1914 the United States had been a debtor nation. It emerged from the war a creditor to most of Europe to the amount of $10 billion, a figure that doubled during the next ten years. Its chief economic competitors came out of the war battered and shaken. Production, profits, and purchasing power reached new heights. However, it was an uneven and unsound prosperity. Agriculture was de-pressed with surplus commodities and low prices, which meant low purchasing power for the farm population of the South and the Middle West. Nor did wages climb as rapidly as profits and prices in the industrial Northeast. These facts, plus increasing automation, meant growing unemployment and industrial surpluses. Labor unions declined in membership and bargaining power. Foreign markets were diminished by a policy of higher and higher tariffs designed to protect American industry from foreign competition. The government's philosophy of noninterference with free enterprise (except for tariffs) permitted unlimited speculation in the soaring stock market, often with other people's money and with unrestrained use of credit.

The stock market crashed in October 1929. Values tumbled. Thousands of banks and businesses failed. Millions were thrown out of work. The economic depression spread over the entire capitalistic world. For four years the Hoover administration, confident of the essential soundness of laissez-faire economy, refused to permit large-scale government relief measures, expecting and promising that the natural economic laws would soon bring back prosperity. But the depression only deepened.

In the presidential election of 1932 the Democratic candidate, Franklin D. Roosevelt, defeated Hoover, ending twelve years of Republican rule. The Roosevelt administration immediately launched a series of sweeping economic and social reforms that came to be called the New Deal. The New Deal was not a radical, new departure but, rather, a further advance along progressive lines established by Theodore Roosevelt and Woodrow Wilson and during World War I when the government engaged in economic planning and control. First, emergency measures were taken to relieve the suffering of the 12 million unemployed and their families. The chief of these was the setting up of the huge Works Progress Administration, which provided a large number of jobs. The Wagner Act strengthened the position of the labor unions by guaranteeing the right of collective bargaining. Old-age and unemployment insurance was inaugurated. For the desperate farmers, measures were passed that granted debt relief, commodity loans, price supports, and payments for acreage reduction. Deflation was checked by a de-

valuation of the dollar. Investments and deposits were protected by strict government supervision. Steps were taken to conserve the nation's natural resources against wasteful private exploitation. Gradually, some popular confidence was restored and the nation's economy began to recover. However, economic problems persisted and full recovery was not achieved until World War II, which forced the government to finance the war with greater deficit spending.

5. THE ROAD TO WAR

Early in the 1930s international affairs started slipping out of control. The League of Nations was challenged, rearmament spread, and aggression became the order of the day. Efforts to appease the aggressors and prevent the dreaded return to total war failed. By the end of the decade a new world war had broken out.

Breakdown of the League of Nations

The only international agency that existed for the maintenance of the peace was the League of Nations, which after the defection of the United States was largely dependent on Great Britain and France for support. For twelve years the League supervised the implementation of the peace treaties, administered relief to tens of thousands of war victims, promoted international good will, and settled numerous international disputes. None of these settlements, however, involved the disciplining of a major power, and thoughtful observers dreaded the time when the League would be called on to do so.

When in 1931 Japan began the conquest of Manchuria, China appealed to the League for protection. The League appointed a commission headed by Britain's Earl of Lytton to make an on-the-spot investigation. The Lytton Commission reported that Japan was guilty of aggression, having violated its solemn obligations both as a League member and as a signatory of the Kellogg-Briand Pact of Paris (1928), which outlawed war as an instrument of national policy. Forceful League action, however, would be largely dependent upon

Great Britain and France, who were unwilling to act without American support. President Hoover, reflecting the isolationist sentiment of American public opinion, would not consent to the use of force, the threat of force, or even economic pressure by the United States. The British and French governments, harassed by their own domestic economic and political problems and the rising menace of fascism in Europe, could not bring themselves to act alone. The League, without their backing, did nothing. It had failed its first major test and was on the way out as a potent force for peace. Japan's successful defiance of the League of Nations helped convince Mussolini and Hitler that they could safely launch aggressions of their own.

The deathblow was struck by Mussolini. Late in 1935 the Italian dictator invaded Ethiopia in East Africa. Ethiopia was a member of the League and appealed to it for protection. Great Britain, concerned for its numerous interests in the Near and Middle East and for its lifeline to the Far East, now became greatly agitated. Under the leadership of Great Britain and France, the League declared Mussolini to be the aggressor and invoked economic sanctions (Article XVI) against him. A list of commodities that League members were not to sell Mussolini was drawn up. However, the list did not include oil, and it soon became obvious that this was the commodity upon which the success of his aggression depended. But it quickly became apparent that, to be effective, an embargo on oil would require the cooperation of the United States. American exports of oil to Mussolini had trebled since the beginning of his campaign against Ethiopia. When the British and French governments requested the cooperation of the United States in withholding excess oil from Mussolini, Secretary of State Cordell Hull and President Roosevelt were sympathetic but were unable to get the oil companies to comply or to get Congress to force compliance. The press and public opinion were overwhelmingly isolationist, and Congress reflected that view. Mussolini got his oil. Britain and France, unwilling to resort to the only other means of stopping him, a shooting war, gave up the League struggle. Mussolini conquered Ethiopia. The League of Nations, for all practical purposes, was dead.

Appeasement

Since the triumph of the Nazis in 1933 Germany had been preparing for a military comeback. In March 1936 Hitler ordered his armed forces into the Rhineland, which, according to the Treaty of Versailles, was to be permanently demilitarized. France, recognizing this move as the gravest threat and challenge to itself, called for Great Britain's support. The British offered none. The French fretted and fumed but in the end did nothing. Hitler had won his gamble.

Fascism's next triumph was in Spain. Until 1931, it was dominated by the landed aristocracy, a few rich capitalists, aristocratic army officers, and the Catholic church. Most people were poor, landless peasants. Since the turn of the century and particularly since 1918, the pressure of discontent had been rising. In 1931 the king yielded, restored the constitution, and granted elections. The liberal and radical groups won such a sweeping victory that the king fled the country. The reformers then proceeded to make over the Spanish nation. They drew up a democratic constitution, granted local autonomy to Catalonia (the northeastern-most section of Spain, including Barcelona), began a sweeping program of public education, started to modernize the army by placing promotions on a merit basis, granted religious freedom, seized the lands and schools of the Catholic church, and planned to break up the great estates into peasant-owned farms.

There was much violence—riots and attacks on priests, nuns, and private property. After two years the conservative propertied interests, with the vigorous support of the pope, won the elections by a narrow margin and began to undo the reforms. Early in 1936, however, the liberal and radical parties won again and resumed their drastic reform program. The privileged classes were now desperate. In July 1936 a group of generals led by General Francisco Franco launched an armed rebellion against the government. Although the Rebels enjoyed the advantage of professional military leadership, the regular army, and most of the country's wealth, they were unable to make headway against the Loyalists, who enjoyed the support of the majority of the rank and file of the people.

FIGURE 56.3. The Munich Conference   The chief participants at the Munich Conference pose for the photographer in September 1938. Left to right: Chamberlain, Daladier, Hitler, and Mussolini. The sellout of Czechoslovakia and the Soviet Union at Munich by Chamberlain and Daladier, in an attempt to appease Hitler, destroyed any hope of maintaining a unified front in Europe against Nazi Germany. (UPI/ Bettmann Newsphotos)

The Spanish Civil War soon became a battlefield in the world struggle of fascism, liberalism, and communism. Hitler and Mussolini, seeing in it an opportunity to advance the cause of fascism, gain a like-minded ally and a strategic military position, and test their new weapons, sent abundant arms and troops to aid Franco. The Loyalists appealed to the democracies for aid but received none, although a few volunteers from the democracies fought as individuals in the Loyalist cause. The only nation that supported the Loyalists was the Soviet Union, but the amount of aid it could send was quite small and tainted the Loyalist cause with the suspicion of communism. After three years of slaughter, Franco and his German and Italian allies beat down the last organized Loyalist resistance. A dictatorship was established over Spain. Liberalism was shattered. The world prestige of Fascist Germany and Italy rose while that of the democracies declined further.

The year 1937 was the year of decision—the point of no return on the road to war. In that year the three great Fascist powers formed the Berlin-Rome-Tokyo Axis, which was aimed specifically at the Soviet Union but was in reality an alliance of these aggressor nations for expansion. In that year the military strength of the Axis powers—their war plants running day and night—forged ahead of that of the rest of the world. In that year the Nazis blueprinted their timetable of conquests, and Japan began its all-out assault on China.

Early in 1938 the Nazis' timetable began to function. In March they overran Austria without opposition, annexing the 6.5 million Austrians to the German Reich (Empire). Great Britain and France denounced this open aggression and violation of the Treaty of Versailles but did nothing.

Almost immediately Hitler turned his big propaganda guns on his next victim, Czechoslovakia. In constructing this little country out of Austro-Hungarian territory at the end of World War I, the Allied peacemakers had left 3.5 million German-speaking people on the Czech side of the border. Although these Sudeten Germans had never been a part of Germany and were separated from Germany by the Sudeten Mountain Wall, Hitler now claimed them. The Czech republic was allied with France and Russia, and in the coming war that Hitler was planning against those two countries, Czechoslovakia could be a threat to the German flank.

As early as May 1938 Hitler threatened Czechoslovakia. The Czechs, however, surprised him by rushing to their defenses. Hitler spent the next four months arousing his people to readiness for war and softening up the democracies by keeping them in a constant state of tension and alarm. This psychological warfare culminated in a giant Nazi rally at Nuremberg in mid-September. There Hitler screamed to his frenzied followers that if the Sudeten areas were not surrendered to him by October 1, he would march. With France and the Soviet Union standing firm in their alliance with Czechoslovakia, the world anxiously awaited the beginning of a major conflict that was likely to become World War II.

At this juncture, the British Prime Minister Neville Chamberlain took it upon himself to fly to Hitler's retreat at Berchtesgaden and plead for a compromise. The upshot was a conference at Munich on September 29, 1938 (see Figure 56.3). The participants were Hitler, Mussolini, Chamberlain, and Premier Edouard Daladier of France.

Chamberlain persuaded Daladier to yield to Hitler's demands for the Sudeten areas of Czechoslovakia. Czechoslovakia and the Soviet Union, France's allies, were not consulted. This was one of Hitler's greatest triumphs. By enticing Great Britain and France to abandon France's allies, Czechoslovakia and the Soviet Union, Hitler had driven a wedge between the Soviet Union and the Western democracies. The Soviet leaders never trusted the Western democracies again. Neither did many of the other countries that were watching to see where their greatest safety lay.

The Outbreak of War

Although the four participating powers at Munich had agreed to become joint protectors of what remained of Czechoslovakia, in March 1939 Hitler overran without warning the remainder of the stricken little republic. This crass act of betrayal opened the eyes even of Neville Chamberlain to the fact that Hitler could not be appeased. When Hitler threatened Poland, Great Britain and France decided to draw a line. In April 1939 they made a guarantee to Poland that they would come to its aid if it were attacked and resisted the attack. Hitler, however, was not deterred. He was demanding, among other things, the return to Germany of the Polish Corridor, which separated East Prussia from the rest of Germany, and the city of Danzig, which was governed by the League of Nations. But by now it was apparent to almost everybody that specific Nazi demands were tied to unlimited aggression. Throughout the summer of 1939 the Germans made feverish preparations for war and kept up a drumfire of vilification of Poland and the democracies. Meanwhile, both sides were bidding for the support of the Soviet Union. But after Munich, Stalin had no confidence in the integrity of the capitalistic democracies. He decided to try to make his own peace with Hitler.

On August 23, 1939, the world was stunned by the signing of a ten-year peace pact by Hitler and Stalin. In return for the Soviet Union's neutrality while Germany conquered Poland, Hitler gave Stalin a free hand to reannex the territories in eastern Europe, including eastern Poland, that Russia had lost at the end of World War I.

With the Soviet Union safely neutralized, Hitler readied the attack on Poland as quickly as possible. At the last moment the British government instructed its ambassador in Berlin to ask Hitler what concessions by Poland he would accept to refrain from war. Hitler informed the ambassador that he was not interested in concessions, that his army and his people were ready and eager for war, and that he could not disappoint them now.

The wires between Warsaw and Berlin were cut, lest the Poles make a last-minute peaceable surrender to Hitler's demands. At dawn on September 1 the Germans launched an all-out attack on Poland by land, sea, and air. Two days later Great Britain and France declared war on Germany, Hitler having ignored their ultimatum to desist. World War II had begun.

SUGGESTED READING

General

C. Kindleberger, *The World in Depression, 1929–1939* (1973). Excellent examination of the Great Depression.

R. J. Sontag, *A Broken World, 1919–1939* (1971). An excellent survey of the period.

E. Wiskeman, *Europe of the Dictators, 1919–1945* (1966). A good general examination of the period.

R. Wohl, *The Generation of 1914* (1979). A creative interpretation of the impact of World War I in the postwar years.

The Harassed British Empire

N. Branson and M. Heinemann, *Britain in the Nineteen Thirties* (1971). A social and economic perspective.

R. Graves and A. Hodge, *The Long Weekend: A Social History of Great Britain, 1918–1939* (1963). A vivid and witty picture of the British ruling classes between the wars.

J. Stevenson, *British Society 1914–1945* (1984). An important new analysis.

D. Thomson, *England in the Twentieth Century, 1914–1963* (1965). A good survey.

Frustrated France

J. Colton, *Léon Blum, Humanist in Politics* (1966). Excellent biography of Blum.

N. Greene, *From Versailles to Vichy: The Third Republic, 1919–1940* (1970). A good survey of France during the period.

Isolationism, Boom, and Bust in the United States

R. Dallek, *Franklin D. Roosevelt and American Foreign Policy, 1932–1945* (1971). Thorough and highly respected.

J. K. Galbraith, *The Great Crash, Nineteen Twenty-Nine* (1955). By a distinguished economist and lively writer.

G. Perrett, *America in the Twenties* (1982). A good general account.

The Road to War

G. A. Craig and F. Gilbert, eds., *The Diplomats, 1919–1939* (1965). Good collection of essays on international relations.

W. Neuman, *The Balance of Power in the Interwar Years, 1919–1939* (1968). A good study of international relations.

A. Rowse, *Appeasement* (1961). By a bitter eyewitness of British appeasement efforts.

H. Thomas, *The Spanish Civil War* (1961). A highly respected account.

CHAPTER 57
World War II, 1939–1945

FIGURE 57.1. A German Concentration Camp World War II was the most destructive war in history. Of particular brutality were the genocidal programs of Nazi Germany, which resulted in scenes like this one from the Landsberg concentration camp. (AP/Wide World Photos)

To much of the disillusioned and paralyzed democratic world, the outbreak of World War II seemed the beginning of the end of liberal Western civilization. For over two years these dire fears appeared to be justified. The seemingly invincible German and Japanese military machines swept on to victory after victory. Although liberal Western civilization would survive, World War II was by far the most destructive conflict in history. It served as a capstone to the period of unmatched death, loss, disruption, and terror begun by World War I.

1. TWO YEARS OF AXIS TRIUMPH

Striking without official warning at dawn, September 1, 1939, the German air force caught the Polish air force on its various airfields and destroyed it on the ground. Thereafter the German *Luftwaffe*, by ravaging Polish cities and communications centers and harassing troop movements, prevented the complete mobilization of the Polish army. Meanwhile, Nazi tanks and infantry poured into Poland from the north, west, and south. The Poles cried for help from France and Great Britain. The French and the British mobilized their armies along the German West Wall fortifications, and the British fleet blockaded Germany by sea. But that was all. The mechanized might of Nazi Germany overwhelmed Poland in a matter of days.

The Soviet Union, in accordance with its agreement with Hitler, proceeded to reannex territories in Poland and eastern Europe that it had lost at the end of World War I. Estonia, Latvia, and Lithuania were absorbed politically into the Soviet Union. In October 1939, the Soviet Union demanded three strategic little strips of Finnish territory. When the Finnish government refused, the Soviet Union attacked Finland and took these territories by force. In June 1940, while Hitler was busy in western Europe, the Soviet Union demanded and procured from Rumania the return of Bessarabia.

Early in April 1940 the Germans suddenly overran Denmark and Norway. The British fleet, attempting to intercept the invasion of Norway, was beaten off with heavy losses by the German air force. Denmark and Norway provided the Nazis with important food, timber, and mineral resources, sea and air bases, and a safe route for vital iron ore coming from Sweden.

On May 10, 1940, the German armies assaulted Luxembourg, the Netherlands, Belgium, and France. Luxembourg offered no resistance. The Netherlands fought heroically but was overwhelmed in six days. Trusting to the Maginot line to hold along the German border, the British army and a large part of the French army moved into Belgium to support the hard-pressed Belgian forces. In a surprise move through the Ardennes forest, powerful German mechanized forces on May 14 smashed through the French defenses at Sedan and drove quickly to the English Channel, cutting off the Belgian, British, and French armies in Belgium. Again the German "blitzkrieg"—a combination of highly coordinated air strikes and rapid deployment of tanks and motorized columns—proved overwhelming. Although some 300,000 British and a few French troops escaped by sea from Dunkirk, all the Belgian troops, the bulk of the French troops together with their weapons and supplies, and the British weapons and supplies were captured.

Only five more days of fighting, June 5–10, were required for the Germans to crush the remaining organized French resistance and turn the French retreat into a disorderly rout. On June 10 Paris was declared an open city (see Figure 57.2). And on that day Mussolini, thinking it safe, declared war on France and Great Britain. On June 16 Marshal Philippe Pétain became premier of France and the following day dispatched a surrender team to Hitler. On June 25 the "fighting" ceased. The collapse of the French military machine after five days of fighting was a colossal military debacle. Hitler forced a harsh treaty on the helpless French. The northern half of France and all the Atlantic coastal area were placed under German occupation. The unoccupied portion was compelled to disarm and cooperate with Germany. Some 2 million French prisoners were held as hostages to ensure French good behavior. In unoccupied France, Marshal Pétain and Pierre Laval set up a semi-Fascist regime, with headquarters at Vichy, and undertook to cooperate with Hitler.

Not all of the French accepted defeat. Many resisted the German army of occupation coura-

FIGURE 57.2. **Hitler at Eiffel Tower, Paris, June 1940**   The first year of World War II was marked by a series of stunning German victories. In June 1940, Hitler was in Paris. The Eiffel Tower, a symbol of French independence and power, is behind him. (Brown Brothers)

geously throughout the war, suffering heavy casualties in so doing. General Charles de Gaulle, having unsuccessfully attempted to warn his superiors of the unreadiness of the French army, escaped to Great Britain and declared himself leader of the Free French. With energy and skill he strove to rally the French both inside and outside the homeland to resist the Germans and the Vichy collaborators and to restore the dignity and honor of France.

The collapse of France left Great Britain to face the German fury alone. Hitler now demanded that Britain surrender or suffer annihilation. The situation was desperate. Nearly all Britain's land ar-

maments had been lost at Dunkirk. Against the nearly one hundred fifty battle-tried Nazi divisions, Britain had only one fully equipped division. And although Great Britain did have the English Channel and the world's greatest navy, the fighting around Norway had demonstrated that navies could no longer control narrow waters dominated by a hostile air force. Britain's chief weapon of defense was its relatively small but efficient air force. Not the least of its assets was Winston Churchill, who on May 10, 1940, had at last replaced Neville Chamberlain as prime minister. The dynamic and eloquent Churchill defied Hitler. ''We shall fight on the beaches; we shall fight on the landing grounds; we shall fight in the fields and in the streets; we shall fight in the hills; we shall never surrender."

Throughout the month of July 1940 Nazi invasion forces gathered along the French coast opposite Britain, twenty-four miles away. To make the crossing, however, absolute control of the air over the Channel was required. Early in August, therefore, swarms of German bombers and fighter escorts flew over the Channel, seeking to destroy the British air force and its landing fields. In the ensuing air battles, the British pilots in their swift Spitfires and heavily armed and manueverable Hurricanes knocked down German planes at the ratio of two or three to one. Nevertheless, by the end of August the British air forces were facing annihilation by sheer weight of numbers. At this critical juncture the Nazis suddenly shifted to massive daylight attacks on London, the world's largest city. The destruction and the suffering were immense, but the British defenses were improving, thanks to the use of radar, the total mobilization of the economy, the breaking of the German secret code (project Ultra), and the high morale of the people. The loss of German planes was so great that early in October the Nazis once more shifted their tactics to night attacks, which were more terrifying but less effective. Although the destructive air raids on Great Britain's cities, together with the even more menacing submarine attacks on British shipping, continued until the end of the war, the immediate threat of invasion had now passed (a winter crossing of the Channel would be too risky); the Battle of Britain had been won.

While the Battle of Britain was at its height, Mussolini set in operation his grandiose schemes for conquering an empire. Upon entering the war in June 1940 he had closed the Mediterranean to British shipping. In September his armies moved on Egypt and the Suez Canal from Libya to the west and from Ethiopia to the south. In October his armies attacked Greece from Albania. To meet this threat, Churchill made a daring and farsighted military move. Believing Suez to be the most strategic spot in the world in a global war, he sent half of Britain's scarce supply of tanks and artillery around Africa to Egypt while the Nazis stood poised across the Channel for the invasion of Great Britain. Mussolini's forces met disaster everywhere. The Greeks defeated them and drove them back into Albania. A squadron of British torpedo planes delivered a lethal blow to the Italian fleet at its base in southern Italy. During the winter of 1940–1941, the Fascist armies moving on Egypt were completely destroyed by light, mobile British forces; Mussolini's bubble had burst with a feeble plop; henceforth he was hardly more than a prisoner of the German forces that were sent to save him.

When in October 1940 it became evident that Great Britain could not be invaded that year, Hitler ordered his planners to complete blueprints for the earliest possible invasion of the Soviet Union. The conquest of the Soviet Union had always been uppermost in Hitler's thoughts, but he had hoped first to dispose of the French and British threat to his rear. The plans called for an assault date not later than May 15, 1941. But first the Balkan flank was to be secured. Hungary and Rumania yielded to Hitler's threats and joined the Axis Alliance in November 1940, Bulgaria, in March 1941. Immediately, Nazi forces poured into those countries. Yugoslavia and Greece, however, refused to yield, and the Germans attacked them in April 1941. Yugoslavia was overrun in eleven days, Greece in three weeks. British forces that Churchill had dispatched to Greece were driven out of the peninsula and also off the island of Crete. Suez now appeared to be doomed. It was open to attack from the north; to the west Germany's Afrika Korps, which had been sent to replace the defeated Italians, had driven the British back to the border of Egypt; pro-Nazi movements had broken out in Iraq, Iran, and French Syria. At this point, however, Hitler hurled his main forces against the Soviet Union, giving the British a breathing spell to recoup their strength in the Near and Middle East.

On June 22, 1941, the Germans launched against the Soviet Union the most massive assault in history. They were joined by the Hungarians, the Rumanians, and the Finns. Although Stalin was able to throw an equal number of divisions against the invaders, his troops were not so well trained or equipped. Hitler expected to crush Soviet resistance in six weeks; the top British and American military leaders were of the same opinion. The Russians fought with unexpected skill and determination, but the Nazi war machine crunched ever forward until by December 1 it was within sight of Moscow. Leningrad was surrounded, and Rostov, the gateway to the Caucasus oil fields, was captured. The richest and most productive part of the Soviet Union was in German hands. The Russians had suffered such staggering casualties that Hitler announced that the Soviet Union was destroyed and would never rise again. The Japanese, taking him at his word and thinking the golden hour had struck, attacked the United States on December 7, 1941. By that time, however, the Arctic winter and the Soviet counterattacks had forced the Germans to halt and in some places to retreat. The Soviet Union was still alive, and the United States was now in the war.

2. THE NAZI EMPIRE

By 1942 Hitler ruled most of continental Europe from the English Channel to Moscow. He had initiated his "New Order"—basically a program of racial imperialism—in the lands he controlled. The conquered peoples were used according to their ranking in Hitler's racial hierarchy. Those more directly related to the Nazi conception of the "Aryan race," such as the Scandinavians, the Anglo-Saxons, and the Dutch, were treated well and would supposedly be absorbed into the Nazi Empire as partners with the Germans. The "Latin races," such as the French, were considered clearly inferior but tolerable as supportive cogs in the New Order. Slavs were toward the bottom of Hitler's ranking; they were to be isolated, shoved aside, and treated like slaves. Large numbers of Russians, Poles, and others were removed from their lands and turned into slave laborers, more often than not perishing under the harsh conditions of their new existence.

Lowest on Hitler's scale were the Jews and such other groups as socialists, gypsies, intellectuals, Jehovah's Witnesses, and the mentally ill. These people were systematically hunted, rounded up, transported to concentration camps, and exterminated. This process was the "Final Solution of the Jewish Problem," and the SS, under Heinrich Himmler, was given the special duty of carrying it out. The quantity and quality of programmed inhumanity, torture, and death was so unprecedented that it could not be believed or understood. In the end some 6 million Jews were killed in that systematic, bureaucratized horror along with perhaps another 6 million victims of Nazi concentration camps.

This massive effort to racially reorganize Europe and perpetuate genocidal policies took priority over even the war effort—continuing until the last days of the war and using up needed troops and materials. Indeed, Nazi Germany itself was only partially organized for the military effort in the early years of the war, finally turning to full mobilization after 1942. Under the leadership of Albert Speer, German production multiplied in 1943 and 1944 despite Allied bombing.

The resources and treasures of conquered lands were taken or put under the control of the Nazis and used to further the Nazi war effort and implement the New Order. The Nazis attempted to gain the submission and cooperation of conquered peoples through the use of force and terror. While the Nazis always managed to find collaborators in occupied lands, they were never able to stamp out persistent resistance. Such resistance movements grew in France, Poland, Denmark, Greece, Yugoslavia—indeed, in almost every occupied territory. They established underground networks, provided intelligence for the Allied forces, conducted guerrilla actions, aided escaping prisoners or Jews, sabotaged military installations, and generally tied down Nazi forces that might have been used on the war fronts.

3. THE ENTRY OF THE UNITED STATES INTO THE WAR

The outbreak of the war in Europe caused hardly a ripple in the isolationist sentiment of the American public and of Congress. Most isolationists believed the French army and Maginot line and the British navy were capable of containing the Nazis.

But suddenly in May–June 1940, the picture drastically changed. The French army and Maginot line ceased to exist, and the British navy was in grave danger. Much of it would be used up in the defense of Britain in case of invasion. Roose-

FIGURE 57.3. Pearl Harbor On December 7, 1941, the Japanese attacked Pearl Harbor, Hawaii, and destroyed the Pacific fleet in the harbor and the air force on the ground. The attack brought the United States into the war. This photo shows the USS California as it went down. (UPI/Bettmann Newsphotos)

velt promptly came forward with a three-point program: (1) all-out rearmament, (2) bipartisanship in foreign affairs, (3) all aid short of war to those fighting the Axis (which at the moment meant Great Britain). There was little opposition to the first two points, and Roosevelt managed to overcome objections to aiding the British. American involvement grew from the supply of arms to the convoying of ships across the Atlantic by the American navy. Aid was extended to the Soviet Union, and in June 1941 Axis consulates were closed.

In August 1941 Roosevelt and Churchill had met at sea and drawn up the Atlantic Charter, a joint statement of ideals and war purposes. In it appeared such pregnant phrases as ". . . their

Sequence of German Expansion to 1942
1. Austria, Czechoslovakia, Poland, 1939
2. 1940, Denmark, Norway
3. 1940, Low Countries, France
4. 1940-1941, Balkans
5. 1942-1943, Russian Front
6. 1942, Vichy

Axis Powers, 1939

Axis Allies

Greater Germany, 1942

Areas of Axis Control, 1942

Neutral Countries

Areas Annexed by Russia, 1939-1940

Pre-1939 Political Boundaries

Map 57.1   EUROPE, 1942   This map shows the farthest extent of Axis power during World War II. By the end of the year German expansion had been stopped at Stalingrad in the East and Egypt in North Africa.

countries seek no aggrandizement, territorial or other; . . . they respect the right of all peoples to choose the form of government under which they will live; . . . after the final destruction of the Nazi tyranny, . . . the establishment of a wider and permanent system of general security. . . ." The Soviet Union subscribed to the Atlantic Charter shortly afterward. Thus, by October 1941 the United States was engaged in a shooting—but not yet official—war with Germany and was in a virtual alliance with Great Britain, one of the belligerents. The American people's eyes were on the Atlantic, where at any moment some new German act of aggression might make war official and total.

It was not in the Atlantic, however, but in the Pacific that the history-changing blow was struck; and not by Germany, but by Japan. Early in 1939 the Japanese, having conquered all the populous coastal areas of China and having driven Chiang Kai-shek's forces far into the Chinese interior, turned southward toward the territories of Southeast Asia and the Southwest Pacific. These territories, rich in rubber, tin, rice, copra, and oil, belonged (with the exception of independent Thailand) to France, the Netherlands, Great Britain, and the United States. Since the French, Dutch, and British had their hands full in Europe with the growing Nazi menace, President Roosevelt transferred the American fleet from the Atlantic to Pearl Harbor in Hawaii as a deterrent to further Japanese aggression. He also gave the Japanese the required six months' notice of the termination of the commercial treaty of 1911. These moves appear to have given the Japanese pause.

In 1940, however, after Hitler's conquest of France and the Netherlands and threatened conquest of Great Britain, the Japanese became much bolder. They took advantage of France's helplessness to occupy northern French Indochina and threatened the Dutch East Indies. But in the following year, 1941, when the Germans overran the Balkans and launched what promised to be a lethal attack on the Soviet Union, the Japanese leaders decided that the day of Axis world triumph was at hand.

Tensions rose between Japan and the United States. Finally on December 7, 1941, a large squadron of Japanese bombers and torpedo planes took off from carriers in a position north of Hawaii and caught by surprise the American fleet anchored in Pearl Harbor (see Figure 57.3). With little loss to themselves, the Japanese planes crippled the American navy in the Pacific and destroyed the air force in Hawaii on the ground. In rapid succession Japan and the United States declared war on each other and within four days the United States was at war with the other Axis powers.

4. CLIMAX AND TURNING POINT OF THE WAR, JUNE–AUGUST 1942

The entry of the United States, with its enormous resources and industrial potential, changed the whole complexion of the war. Together with the totally mobilized British economy and the massive economic and military resources of the Soviet Union, the long-term advantage was now clearly on the side of the Allies. However, many months would be required to mobilize America's resources, and the Axis was determined to win decisively before that mobilization could be achieved (see Map 57.1). To bring about Allied solidarity, Churchill hastened to Washington, where on January 1, 1942, he and Roosevelt launched the United Nations Alliance. Twenty-six nations, of which the United States, Great Britain, and the Soviet Union were the Big Three, promised to give their all to the common effort, to make no separate peace, and to abide by the principles of the Atlantic Charter. By the end of the war, the number of member nations had risen to forty-seven.

The now-global war was fought in three major theaters: (1) the Soviet Union, (2) the Mediterranean and western Europe, and (3) the Pacific. The Axis powers made their climactic bid for victory on all three fronts between June and August 1942. The biggest front in terms of numbers of troops, weapons, and casualties involved was that in the Soviet Union. Despite frightful losses, the Soviets had managed to keep their well-led army intact and to relocate or rebuild their wartime factories. The Soviet people were unified against the foreign aggressors in what they called the "Great Patriotic War of the Fatherland." The Germans, after having been stopped in December 1941 by the Russian winter and the counterattacks, resumed their forward thrust in June 1942, this time in the southern sector. Refreshed and reequipped, they seemed irresistible. By August they had reached the outskirts of Stalingrad on the Volga. Here Stalin ordered a stand: The battle of Stalingrad raged for six months. In February 1943, the Russians, having closed a pincer behind the Germans in Stalingrad, captured all who had not been killed of an army of almost three hundred thousand men. This action was the turning point; the Germans began a slow but general retreat.

The critical battle on the Mediterranean and western European front was fought in Egypt. General Rommel's tough Afrika Korps in its first drive on Suez in 1941 had been stopped and pushed back into Libya by the British. In June 1942 Rommel's forces, greatly strengthened, struck the British desert forces a shattering blow and chased them in near rout to El Alamein, only sixty-five miles from Alexandria. Suez seemed doomed, and the British fleet prepared to evacuate the Mediterranean before it could be bottled up. Churchill rushed to the scene and put in a team of winning commanders: Sir Harold Alexander in overall command and General Bernard Montgomery as field commander. In August Rommel's forces assaulted the British positions at El Alamein and were stopped. A race to build up men and supplies ensued; the British, with massive aid from the United States, won. Late in October 1942 Montgomery's superior Eighth Army attacked Rommel's forces and, after a desperate battle, drove them back across the desert in defeat. Suez and the Middle East were now saved from the Axis, and for the first time Great Britain and the United States were in a position to assume the offensive.

President Roosevelt had agreed with Churchill that first priority should be given to defeating Germany, which represented the gravest threat. Therefore the United States concentrated most of its efforts toward Europe, which made the war in the Pacific more difficult and predominantly naval in character.

Three days after Pearl Harbor, Japanese carrier-based torpedo planes struck the British Asiatic fleet a crippling blow in the Gulf of Siam. Now, with unchallenged mastery of the Pacific, the Japanese within the space of a few months were able to conquer with relative ease a vast area in the Southwest Pacific and Southeast Asia. The American islands of Wake, Guam, and the Philippines; British Hong Kong, Malaya, Singapore, and Burma; and the Dutch East Indies were overrun. In May 1942 Japanese naval forces were turned back by the Americans in the Battle of the Coral Sea, northeast of Australia. However, the main Japanese fleet was preparing a major thrust at Hawaii, which it could have taken easily immediately after Pearl Harbor. The United States navy, which had broken the Japanese code, massed for an all-out battle. Early in June 1942, just as the Stalingrad and El Alamein campaigns were beginning, the two powerful naval forces came within carrier plane range of each other off Midway Island, a thousand miles west of Hawaii. The climactic Battle of Midway was fought at long range entirely by aircraft and submarines. American planes sank all four of the Japanese carriers, while the Japanese were able to destroy only one of three American carriers. Pounded from the air and without air cover, the Japanese commander ordered a retreat, never to become so bold again. In August 1942 the Americans assumed the offensive by attacking Guadalcanal in the Solomon Islands northeast of Australia. By that time, it was evident that the tide was beginning to turn on all three fronts.

5. VICTORY

Although the greatest crises had passed by the end of 1942, two and a half more years of bloody fighting were required to subdue the Axis. In fact, the defeat of the Axis could not have been achieved at all without a high degree of cooperation among the Big Three allies. President Roosevelt, with his winsome personality, played an important part in maintaining mutual confidence and cooperation among the Allied powers, which were so divergent in their ideologies and specific interests. The chief planners of the coordinated global strategy were Churchill for Great Britain, Stalin for the Soviet Union, and Army Chief of Staff George Marshall for the United States.

INDIA

SINKIANG

TIBET

MONGOLIA

SOVIET UNION

**5. Soviet Union Enters the War
August 8, 1945**

ALASKA

CANADA

BAY OF
BENGAL

BURMA

C H I N A

Peking

MANCHUKUO

B E R I N G   S E A

Seattle

UNITED STATES

Chungking

Vladivostok

SAKHALIN

KARAFUTO

ATTU

ALEUTIANS

Dutch Harbor

San Francisco

THAI-
LAND

Canton
Hong Kong

Shanghai

INDO-
CHINA

FORMOSA

KOREA

Nagasaki

Hiroshima

JAPAN

Tokyo

KISKA

**2. Greatest Japanese Expansion,
June 1942**

OKINAWA

**6. Atomic Bombs Dropped on
Hiroshima and Nagasaki
August 1945
Japan Surrenders
September 2, 1945**

**1. Japan Attacks Pearl Harbor
December 7, 1941**

**4. U.S. Forces Reoccupy
the Philippines
October 1944**

Manila

PHILIPPINE I.

IWO JIMA

MIDWAY

HAWAIIAN I. (U.S.A.)

Pearl Harbor

Singapore

SUMATRA

LEYTE

MARIANA I.
SAIPAN
TINIAN

WAKE

P A C I F I C   O C E A N

BORNEO

YAP

GUAM

PALAU

CAROLINE I.

ENIWETOK

JAVA

CELEBES

TRUK

KWAJALEIN

MARSHALL I.

INDIAN OCEAN

Hollandia

HOWLAND I. (U.S.A.)

NEW
GUINEA

GILBERT I.

Port Moresby

SOLOMON I.

GUADALCANAL

**3. U.S. Forces Land on Guadalcanal
August 7, 1942**

CORAL SEA

NEW HEBRIDES
(Britain &
France)

TUTUILA (U.S.A.)

FIJI I. (Britain)

AUSTRALIA

Sydney

NEW
ZEALAND

Supply Lines

Allied Land or Naval Attacks

Allied Air Thrusts

Soviet Thrusts into Manchuria and Korea

Japanese Empire 1940

Occupied Areas, June 1942

At War Against Japan, August 7, 1945

Map 57.2   **THE PACIFIC WAR**   This map shows the farthest extent of Japanese expansion, attained in June 1942, and the course of the American counterattack across the Pacific islands toward the Japanese mainland between 1942 and 1945.

FIGURE 57.4. **Hiroshima After A-Bomb** This photo of Hiroshima, taken shortly after the first atom bomb was dropped, shows the incredible destructive power of atomic weapons. (Sygma)

The Russian Front

The Battle of Russia was the greatest and most destructive battle in history. Some 9 million men (five hundred divisions) were engaged. For two and a half years after Stalingrad, the Germans were slowly beaten back, doggedly contesting every foot of ground. At last, in April of 1945, the Russians entered Berlin. Along the fifteen hundred miles between Stalingrad and Berlin lay the wreckage of the greater part of Hitler's war machine. But the richest and most productive part of the Soviet Union lay devastated. At least twenty million Russians had been killed—possibly many more.

The Mediterranean and Western European Front

In November 1942, just as the Germans were beginning to retreat from El Alamein, a combined Anglo-American force under the command of General Dwight D. Eisenhower landed in French North Africa. Early in 1943, the converging forces of Eisenhower and Montgomery cornered the Afrika Korps in Tunisia, where it surrendered in May.

Meanwhile most of the threats from German submarines and planes were being eliminated, as the British and Americans gained in the air and seas. Massive bombing raids pounded Germany.

The distinction between strategic military targets and civilian populations blurred as Germany's cities were leveled.

In July 1943 the Anglo-Americans conquered the island of Sicily, which they used as a base for the invasion of southern Italy. Mussolini was forced to resign (July 25), and Italy surrendered. However, the peninsula was held by strong German forces. By the end of 1943, the Allies had reached Cassino Pass, about 75 miles south of Rome. At this point, the major objectives in the Mediterranean area had been achieved, and Eisenhower, along with most of his forces, was transferred to Great Britain to command the main Anglo-American thrust across the Channel.

This thrust came on June 6, 1944. Thanks in large measure to complete Allied mastery of the skies, successful landings were made on the Normandy coast. After a rapid buildup, the Anglo-Americans broke out of the beachhead and before the end of the year cleared practically all of France. Germany, meanwhile, was being pulverized from the air. Early in 1945 the American and British forces, now joined by French units, broke through the German West Wall, crossed the Rhine, and joined forces with the Russians on the Elbe. Germany surrendered on May 8, ending the war in Europe. Near the end, Hitler and several other top Nazis committed suicide, and Mussolini was shot by Italian partisans.

The Pacific Front

Early in 1943 American forces under the command of General Douglas MacArthur began with a strong naval escort an island-hopping campaign northwestward from their base in Australia (see Map 57.2). At the same time the main American fleet, under the command of Admiral Chester Nimitz, now definitely superior to the Japanese fleet, thrust westward from Hawaii toward Japan, capturing the numerous Japanese-held islands in its path. Although the islands, many of them covered by jungles, were bloodily defended, the American forces moved steadily toward Japan itself. In October 1944 the American forces made a bold landing on Leyte Island in the Philippines, which brought the Japanese fleet out for a last desperate effort. In the Battle of Leyte Gulf, the Japanese fleet was annihilated. Cut off, uncovered, and subjected to ceaseless air and sea attacks, Japan was doomed. After Germany surrendered in May 1945, American, British, and Russian troops that had been engaged in the European theater were rapidly deployed to the Far East. In mid-July the atomic bomb, which American and British scientists had been developing for several years, was successfully completed and tested. The United States wanted to avoid the heavy casualties that a direct assault on the Japanese home islands would cause. The United States thus decided to use the bomb to shock Japan into surrender, a decision that has remained controversial ever since that time. On August 6, 1945, the first atomic bomb to be used in warfare destroyed the Japanese city of Hiroshima (see Figure 57.4) and some eighty thousand of its inhabitants. Two days later, the Soviet Union declared war on Japan and began to overrun Manchuria and northern Korea. The next day, August 9, the second and last atomic bomb then in existence demolished the industrial city of Nagasaki. The Japanese surrendered five days later, August 14, 1945.

World War II had ended. Estimates of soldiers and civilians killed range from 30 million to 50 million; even more had suffered injuries from the war. Western society now faced an overwhelming task of recovery and reorganization.

SUGGESTED READING

General

M. Baumont, *The Origins of the Second World War* (1978). A solid, brief treatment.

B. Liddell Hart, *History of the Second World War* (1980). A good military history.

G. Wright, *The Ordeal of Total War, 1939–1945* (1968). Thoughtful analysis; goes far beyond the military aspects.

Two Years of Axis Triumph

W. Churchill, *Their Finest Hour* (1949). The second and best of Churchill's great six-volume history of the war. Covers the defeat of France and the Battle of Britain.

A. Clark, *Barbarossa* (1964). Good history of the war on the Russian front.

The Nazi Empire

N. Cohn, *Warrant for Genocide* (1966). An in-depth analysis.

A. Dallin, *German Rule in Russia, 1941–1945* (1957). A good analysis.

L. Dawidowicz, *The War Against the Jews, 1933–1945* (1976). A thorough study.

T. Des Pres, *The Survivors* (1976). A good analysis of life in Hitler's concentration camps.

J. Haestrup, *Europe Ablaze* (1978). Thorough study of the resistance movements.

E. Kogon, *The Theory and Practice of Hell* (1958). A classic study of the concentration camps.

The Entry of the United States

A. R. Buchanan, *The United States and World War II*, 2 vols. (1964). A good survey.

R. Devine, *Reluctant Belligerent: American Entry into World War II* (1969). Good brief study.

H. Feis, *The Road to Pearl Harbor: The Coming of the War Between the United States and Japan* (1967). A scholarly work.

Allied Victory

M. Sherwin, *A World Destroyed: The Atomic Bomb and the Grand Alliance* (1975). Analyzes the final years and the role of the atomic bomb.

J. Toland, *The Last Hundred Days* (1966). A fine account of the end.

RETROSPECT

A long period of relative peace, growing prosperity, and sense of progress ended in August 1914. World War I initiated a three-decade period in which Europe would be shattered politically, economically, and socially by war, revolution, and depression.

European nations were plunged into World War I by an entangling alliance system that enhanced nationalistic rivalries and by persisting domestic tensions that encouraged national governments searching for unity to adopt belligerent policies. The hoped-for short war turned into a nightmarish struggle between the Central Powers and the Allies. The destruction went beyond the massive human and material toll to the political entities themselves. The German, Austro-Hungarian, Russian, and Ottoman empires did not survive the war. The British and French empires were both weakened, as indeed were Britain and France themselves. Efforts to make a durable peace and to set up an international organization, the League of Nations, to keep the peace foundered on the rocks of national self-interest. Instead, the peace settlements left a legacy of resentment that would haunt the West during the following two decades.

The victors in World War I were the liberal-democratic nations, and it was hoped that this victory would be turned into a permanent gain for liberal democracy. The trend toward totalitarianism, fascism, and authoritarianism during the 1920s and 1930s dashed these hopes. The first blow to liberalism and capitalism came during the final stages of World War I when revolution brought a Communist regime to power in Russia. Lenin led the revolutionary Bolsheviks to victory in November 1917 and over the next few years extracted the Soviet Union from World War I, defeated rivals in a bloody civil war, and established the foundations for a totalitarian state. By the end of the 1920s Lenin's successor, Stalin, had initiated the five-year plans that would collectivize Soviet agriculture and industrialize the nation. His Great Purges in the 1930s eliminated all possible resistance, completing the transformation of the Soviet Union into a totalitarian state.

The next blow to liberalism came with the rise of fascism in Italy under Mussolini during the early 1920s. Over the next few years Mussolini took steps to turn his Fascist regime into a totalitarian state, but these steps were always incomplete. Full-blown totalitarian fascism was established during the 1930s in Nazi Germany under Hitler. Much more than the Italian variety, German fascism was tinged with violence and racism. Both regimes denounced liberal democracy and, indeed, most of the developments since the French Revolution that Western liberals had pointed to with pride. With their emphasis on nationalism, militarism, and expansion, these Fascist regimes represented a direct threat to peace and the democratic West.

Two more blows to liberalism seriously undermined the position of the democratic West. The first was the rise of authoritarian regimes in southern Europe, eastern Europe, and Japan—almost all replacing governments that had more liberal leanings. The second was the Great Depression, which encouraged authoritarian movements everywhere and caused the Western democracies to turn inward. Thus, during the 1930s, when the threat from Fascist and authoritarian nations was growing, the Western democracies were increasingly paralyzed by their own domestic problems.

Neither the foundering League of Nations nor a policy of appeasement could restrain Germany, Italy, and Japan from pursuing their policies of expansion. In 1939 World War II broke out. For over two years the Axis powers seemed unstoppable, gaining victory after victory. By the end of 1942, however, overexpansion by the Axis forces, the stiff resistance by Soviet troops, the heroic struggle by the British, and the entrance of the United States into the war had started to turn the tide. Almost three years of struggle on a worldwide basis were necessary to end the war in 1945. By that time the Nazis had carried out a policy of genocide and enslavement as part of Hitler's racist "New Order," and war had claimed some 40 million lives.

In 1945 Europe lay in ruin. World War I, the interlude of turmoil and depression during the 1920s and 1930s, and World War II had changed Western civilization in irreversible ways. Indeed, many questioned whether Europe, the heart of Western civilization for so long, could recover from the devastation.

PART TWELVE

GLOBAL INTERDEPENDENCE IN THE CONTEMPORARY WORLD, 1945–PRESENT

The year 1945 was a watershed between two different eras in several ways. First, when the last shots were fired, an end came not only to World War II, which had raged since 1939, but also to three decades of devastating turmoil in Europe that had begun with the outbreak of World War I in 1914. In the decades following 1945 the West would face problems, but not on the scale of the destructive wars, political upheavals, and economic fluctuations that dominated the 1914–1945 period. Indeed, for most of the period after 1945 the basic trend would be toward recovery, growth, and relative stability. Second, 1945 marked the last time when the bulk of power and leadership in Western civilization would be located in Western Europe. After 1945 the two new competing superpowers, the United States and the Soviet Union, would be the dominating nations in the West and, to a considerable extent, the world. Third, 1945 marked the beginning of the end of Western colonialism. Over the next two decades the imperial powers would lose colonies they had controlled since the end of the nineteenth century or even longer. As these former colonies became independent nations, they, along with other nations of the non-Western world, would become assertive in a world that could no longer ignore them. Finally, 1945 marked the beginning of an age of rapidly growing global interdependence. The West was increasingly becoming tied to the non-Western world by expanding communications, economic dependence, international organizations, systems of alliances, ideological competition, and cultural exchange. Western ideals, values, institutions, and problems were spreading to and interacting with those of the rest of the world. As we approach the present, it becomes increasingly difficult to make a firm demarcation between the Western and non-Western worlds. More than ever before, Western civilization must be studied within a global context.

CHAPTER 58

The Recovery of Europe and the Superpowers, 1945–Present

FIGURE 58.1. The Division Between East and West The post–World War II division between East and West in Europe is symbolized by the Berlin Wall and the Brandenburg Gate in Berlin blocked by barbed wire and troops in 1961. (AP/Wide World Photos)

In 1945 much of Europe was in ashes. Disorganization was the rule, and effective governments often were virtually nonexistent. Economic destruction was so great that the immediate problem was not so much how to rebuild factories and initiate economic growth but how to minimize the starvation that faced millions and create shelter for the dislocated. European nations would revive with amazing speed and go on to establish new patterns of relative political stability and economic growth. However, before that could happen, Europeans had to deal with the immediate problems of the settlement of World War II and the beginnings of the Cold War.

1. THE SETTLEMENT AND THE COLD WAR

In 1945 the leaders of the victorious nations were confronted with the tasks of making a lasting peace and restoring a shattered world. From the beginning these tasks were hampered by hostility between the United States and the Soviet Union. This hostility, which came to be called the "Cold War," pervaded and poisoned every area of postwar international relations. To understand the nature of the peace settlement and the origins of the Cold War, one must go back to the conferences held by the Allies during the war and to the legacy of assumptions held by participants in those conferences.

Legacy of Assumptions

Although Great Britain, the United States, and the Soviet Union were cooperating allies during most of World War II, they approached each other with differing perceptions and a history of distrust. Since the Communists came to power in Russia in 1917, leaders of the Soviet Union and the capitalist democracies had viewed each other as opponents. As ideologies, communism and capitalism had always been in direct opposition. As practiced in the Soviet Union under Lenin and Stalin, communism took a totalitarian form, in sharp contrast to the democracies of Great Britain and the United States. Specific developments between the Rus-

sian Revolution of 1917 and World War II added to the hostility between the Soviet Union and the capitalist democracies. During the Russian civil war, the Western nations had supported anti-Bolshevik forces with materials and some troops. The United States had not recognized the Bolshevik government until 1933. The Soviet Union had not even been invited to the Munich Conference of 1938. In viewing the rise of Fascist and authoritarian governments during the 1920s and 1930s, many in the Western democracies found consolation in the opposition of these governments to communism. The Western democracies failed to ally with the Soviet Union in the 1930s against the growing threat of Nazi Germany. In 1939 Stalin entered into an astonishing pact with Hitler, enabling Nazi forces to concentrate on Western Europe during the first years of World War II.

Hitler's invasion of the Soviet Union and the entry of the United States into the war united Great Britain, the United States, and the Soviet Union as allies more in opposition to Nazi Germany than in agreement over principles or goals. When concrete negotiations for war aims and terms of a settlement took place, the history of hostility, distrust, and fear between capitalist and Communist powers caused problems. These problems would increase after the war when the threat of Nazi Germany no longer held the Allies together.

The Conferences and the Settlement

The decisions that led to the peace settlements, that helped shape Europe in the immediate postwar years, and that laid the groundwork for the Cold War were made in a series of conferences held by the leaders of Great Britain, the United States, and the Soviet Union. The first conference took place in December 1943 at Teheran. There Stalin agreed to enter the war against Japan after the defeat of Germany, and Great Britain and the United States agreed to open a second front in France. The most crucial decision was to reject Churchill's plan to open a front in Eastern Europe, which would have given Great Britain and the United States more influence over developments there. With British and American forces concentrated in Western Europe, Eastern Europe was

FIGURE 58.2. **Allied Leaders at Yalta** With victory over the Axis in sight, the terms of the settlement were negotiated at the Yalta Conference, February 1945. Churchill, Roosevelt, and Stalin, representing the Big Three Allied powers, made a series of agreements concerning the major postwar problems. (UPI/ Bettmann Newsphotos)

open to the advancing Russian troops.

The next meeting of the three heads of state was in February 1945 at Yalta (see Figure 58.2). The four main areas of discussion were (1) the United Nations charter, (2) Germany, (3) Eastern Europe, and (4) the Far East. All quickly reached agreement on questions concerning the United Nations charter. They also agreed on most matters concerning Germany: complete denazification with severe punishment for the top Nazis; demilitarization; the division of the country into four occupation zones; and a long period of occupation by the Allies. There was no agreement on the stiff reparations demanded by Stalin. In the discussion

over Eastern Europe a sharp cleavage soon developed. Stalin argued that Eastern Europe, already behind Soviet lines, was vital to the Soviet Union's security. Russia had been invaded through these countries in both world wars and many of them had been Hitler's allies. Therefore, he asserted, the Soviet Union should maintain a measure of control over these countries. Roosevelt and Churchill insisted that these countries must be given complete independence. These disagreements were not resolved; they were papered over with a general agreement that elections would be held as soon as possible in the liberated states of Eastern Europe but that these states were to be friendly to the Soviet Union. In regard to the Far East, Stalin agreed to enter the war within three months after Germany's surrender in return for islands and port facilities that Japan had earlier taken from Russia and for increased Soviet influence in Korea.

The last meeting of the heads of state of Great Britain, the United States, and the Soviet Union took place in July 1945 at Potsdam. At this conference Clement Attlee had replaced Winston Churchill as British prime minister and Truman had replaced Roosevelt as the American president. Matters that had already been agreed on were affirmed in greater detail, but there was still no fundamental agreement over Eastern Europe. Despite a general accord to work out peace treaties with the various nations as soon as possible, treaties with Germany's allies were not signed until February 10, 1947, and a final treaty with Germany was never signed.

While the war ended in 1945 with a complete victory for the Allies, the basis for postwar problems was already present. The legacy of distrust and hostility between Communist Russia and the capitalist West was not eradicated by the temporary period of cooperation during the war years. Decisions and disagreements at the wartime conferences resulted in resentments and accusations on both sides, particularly over Eastern Europe. Faced with the reality of Eastern Europe's being behind Soviet lines, Great Britain and the United States were at a disadvantage. Europe, though struggling to recover, was already politically divided. Political divisions would merge into Cold War divisions in the years following 1945.

The Cold War

The Cold War was the struggle between the United States and the Soviet Union, each supported by its respective non-Communist and Communist allies, that colored international relations during the four decades following World War II (see Map 58.1). On the one side the Soviet Union strove to secure itself from external threats and to spread its version of communism to the border states and elsewhere in the world. On the other side the United States strove to contain Soviet influence and to counter Communist threats wherever they were perceived throughout the world. It was a war fought in almost all ways except open military conflict, and the threat of military force was always present. At times, the Cold War became violent, but the two superpowers never came together in direct armed combat.

The spirit of cooperation between the Western democracies and the Soviet Union was already being deflated by verbal salvos in 1945. Truman denounced the establishment of new governments through force, a clear attack on Soviet policies in Eastern Europe. In February 1946 Stalin described the Western democracies as enemies of communism. In March 1946 Churchill attacked Soviet actions in Eastern Europe and warned against Communist subversion. He described a Russian iron curtain "dividing a free and democratic West from an East under totalitarian rule."

These accusations focused mainly on developments in Eastern Europe. The United States and its allies felt that wartime agreements and a sense of justice should compel the Soviet Union to allow free elections in Eastern European states, all of which should be independent from Soviet control. The Soviet Union felt that these same wartime agreements and a higher sense of justice recognized the overriding need for the Soviet Union to make sure Eastern European states remained friendly and under Soviet influence. The United States became increasingly outraged when developments in Eastern Europe seemed to go Stalin's way. In 1945 the Soviets were already exerting control over the governments of Rumania and Poland, despite the protests of the British and Americans. By 1947 Soviet dominance in these two countries was solidified and spreading to other Eastern European countries. In 1948 Soviet threats forced non-Communist leaders out of the Czechoslovakian government, placing that country in Communist hands. By 1950 all the states of Eastern Europe were controlled by Communists and, with the exception of Yugoslavia under Tito, were dominated by the Soviet Union.

Struggles over Eastern Europe spread to Western Europe, where strong Communist parties in France and Italy pursued policies approved by Moscow. The United States and its allies feared these parties would subvert non-Communist gov-

Map 58.1 **EUROPE DURING THE COLD WAR** This map indicates the Cold War divisions in Europe during the 1950s. With some exceptions, nations in Western Europe joined NATO, a non-Communist military organization headed by the United States. Also with a few exceptions, nations in Eastern Europe joined the Warsaw Pact, a Communist military organization headed by the Soviet Union.

ernments and help spread Soviet control further south and west.

The verbal denunciations and discord over events in Europe were accompanied by a breakdown of cooperation between the United States and the Soviet Union. President Truman, who succeeded Roosevelt on April 12, 1945, was in favor of a tougher policy toward the Soviet Union. In May he cut off aid to the Soviet Union. When the possibility of international control of atomic weapons arose, the Americans and Russians could not agree. This led to the nuclear weapons race, which has flourished ever since.

The breakdown of cooperation was most striking in Germany. In accordance with the Potsdam agreements, most of Germany was divided into four occupation zones: American, Russian, British, and French. Berlin, which was in the Russian zone, was divided into four sectors and made the headquarters of a four-power coordinating commission. Sharp cleavages soon developed among the occupying powers, particularly between the United States and the Soviet Union. The Soviet Union, having suffered more at the hands of Germany during World Wars I and II than any other major nation, was determined to keep Germany permanently weak and as much as possible under Soviet domination. The United States, on the other hand, having little fear of Germany and seeing it as a valuable potential ally against the Soviet Union, soon set out to restore and rearm the nation. Matters came to a head in 1948–1949. In March 1948 the United States, having succeeded in merging the three Western zones and stepping up their economy to a level much higher than that agreed upon at Potsdam, announced plans for the creation of an independent West German state. To the Soviet leaders, this was the last straw. They attempted to dissuade the Western powers from going ahead with the project by blockading the three Western zones of Berlin in the hope of starving them out. For eleven months, from June 1948 to May 1949, the Soviets stopped all land traffic across their zone from the West to Berlin. The Western powers defeated the blockade through a giant airlift. The United States proceeded to set up the German Federal Republic, which began to function in September 1949. One month later the Soviet Union set up the German Democratic Republic in its zone.

Policies initiated in 1947 raised the Cold War to a higher level. The immediate occasion prompting the United States to inaugurate a new and harsher policy toward the Soviet Union was the situation in Greece and Turkey, both of which were under severe Soviet pressure. In February 1947 the British government, which had been supporting both Greece and Turkey with troops and money since the end of the war, announced that after March 31 it would be unable to continue to do so. On March 12, 1947, President Truman appeared before Congress and requested authorization to send American military and civilian personnel into Greece and Turkey. "I believe," he said, "that it must be the policy of the United States to support free peoples who are resisting attempted subjugation by armed minorities or by outside pressures." He asked for $400 million to implement the new program and warned that this was only a starter. Congress greeted this announcement with a standing ovation.

The new policy, which was soon called the Truman Doctrine, meant that the United States would draw a military ring around the Soviet Union and its satellites from Manchuria to Norway. It was the policy of military containment. All real diplomatic negotiations between the United States and the Soviet Union, of course, ceased immediately. The Soviet Union made no further pretense of withdrawing from the areas of Eastern Europe occupied by its troops; instead, the Soviet Union tightened the iron curtain that it had drawn around them.

In June 1947 Secretary of State General George Marshall supplemented the Truman Doctrine with the Marshall Plan. This plan was an offer of comprehensive economic aid to all European countries (except Fascist Spain) who would improve their economies, stabilize their currencies, and cooperate with each other in bringing about general economic recovery. All the countries of Europe except the Soviet Union and its satellites hastened to accept Marshall's terms and American aid. The Soviet Union regarded the Marshall Plan as an American scheme to shore up Europe's and its own tottering capitalism, to lure away the Soviet satellites, and to make the European countries economic dependencies of the United States. The Soviet Union therefore forbade the countries of Eastern Europe under its control or influence to participate. Congress voted $5.3 billion as the first of four installments totaling some $17 billion for Marshall Plan aid. In 1949 the United States took the initiative in organizing the North Atlantic Treaty Organization (NATO), which was a firm military alliance among the United States, Canada, and most of the nations of Western Europe against the Soviet Union (see p. 742 for details).

In the fall of 1947 the Soviet Union began a series of vigorous moves to counter the Truman Doctrine and the Marshall Plan. In September 1947 the Soviet Union set up the Communist Information Bureau, or Cominform, the better to coordinate policies of the Soviet Union, Poland, Hungary, Rumania, Bulgaria, Albania, Yugoslavia, and Czechoslovakia. This agency was in reality a restoration of the old Comintern, which was the Communist International working for world revolution. The following year the Cominform was supplemented by the Council for Economic Mutual Assistance, a Soviet Marshall Plan. At the same time the Soviet Union severely tightened its grip on its satellites. The local Communist parties were rigorously purged of moderates and national patriots. The Soviet Union strengthened military ties with its allies, eventually countering NATO with the establishment of the Warsaw Pact Organization in 1955.

By 1950 one stage of the Cold War was completed. Europe was clearly divided into a Communist camp in the East under the control of the Soviet Union and a non-Communist camp in the West under the leadership of the United States. The Cold War would continue in different ways and with varying intensity over the next four decades. Both sides were pitted against each other in a world-wide war of propaganda. Political struggles almost anywhere, whether purely internal matters or not, became potential fields for a victory or defeat in a Cold War competition. This competition expanded to the non-Western world and to a variety of fields not usually thought of as political, from the exploration of space to the Olympic games.

In 1950 the Korean War shifted the focus of the Cold War from Europe to the non-Western world. It also revealed how real the risk of military combat was in the struggle between Communist and non-Communist forces. In the mid-1950s there were some signs of a relaxation in the Cold War. Stalin died in 1953, and later that year an armistice was signed in Korea. The Soviet government made overtures to the United States to end the Cold War. In 1955 Soviet troops left Austria, which became an independent, neutral state. That same year a conference was held in Geneva between the leaders of Great Britain, France, the United States, and the Soviet Union. Little of substance was accomplished, but at least it symbolized an effort to solve problems peacefully. Talk of "peaceful coexistence" between the superpowers became popular and seemed confirmed when the two powers agreed to talks for a nuclear test ban treaty in 1958.

This apparent thaw in the Cold War was mitigated by some chilling developments. In the same year that Stalin died, John Foster Dulles became United States secretary of state in the new Eisenhower administration. It was his belief that all communism was a Moscow-directed conspiracy

bent upon world conquest. The time had come, he proclaimed, to pass over from containment to liberation. The United States tried to apply lessons learned in the struggles over Eastern Europe and Korea to Southeast Asia, where the French had lost to Communist-led insurgents in Vietnam. Efforts to hold a meeting between the American and Soviet heads of state in 1960 broke down amid Cold War accusations. In 1961 irritations over Germany were exacerbated by the construction of the Berlin Wall, sealing off democratic West Berlin from East Berlin and the rest of Communist East Germany. In 1962 the Cuban missile crisis, a Cold War confrontation over the placement of Russian missiles in Cuba, came close to erupting into a real war.

Nevertheless, the 1960s and most of the 1970s witnessed a general lessening of tensions in the Cold War. A nuclear test ban treaty between the two powers was signed in 1963, and strategic arms limitation talks were initiated in 1969. After 1969 relations between the United States and the Soviet Union were often described by the word *détente*, emphasizing cooperation rather than confrontation.

In the later 1970s and early 1980s events proved that the Cold War was not over. The increasing ties between Communist China and the United States were perceived as a threat by the Soviet Union. When Jimmy Carter became president in 1977, the Soviet leaders quickly took offense at his insistence on the granting of human rights throughout the world, including the Soviet Union, and they were uncomfortable with his more open style of diplomacy. A Soviet invasion of Afghanistan in 1979 led to the American boycott of the Olympic Games in 1980 and an embargo on grain shipments to the Soviet Union. The Reagan administration took a much tougher stand toward the Soviet Union and communism in general, reviving Cold War rhetoric and dramatically increasing arms production. In the 1980s the Polish crisis, American attempts to limit exportation of certain technology and materials by Western nations to the Soviet Union, the deployment of new American missiles in Europe, the American Strategic Defense Initiative, and the rejection of the 1979 Strategic Arms Limitation Treaty heightened tensions between the two powers. However, since 1985 the new arms limitations talks, the signing of an Intermediate-Range Nuclear Forces Treaty, a unilateral reduction of conventional forces in Eastern Europe, a more conciliatory foreign policy, a Soviet commitment in internal political and economic reforms, and the Soviet withdrawal from Afghanistan have contributed to improving relations between the United States and the Soviet Union.

2. REVIVAL OF A DIVIDED EUROPE AND THE WEST

Within the context of the Cold War struggle, Europe survived the difficult years immediately following World War II, recovered by the 1950s, and grew in new directions in the following decades. Yet there was a fundamental division between West and East in Europe, with Western Europe turning toward parliamentary democracy and support from the United States and Eastern Europe turning toward communism and support from the Soviet Union.

Western Europe

After World War II nations in Western Europe returned to liberal democratic forms of government. The political parties of the center generally came to power. On the Continent the Christian Democratic parties were particularly strong in France, West Germany, and Italy. They had ties to traditional prewar conservative parties but became more progressive after World War II. They stood for democracy, economic growth, moderate social reform, antifascism, and anticommunism. Their main competitors were a variety of moderate, democratic Socialist parties with ties to traditional prewar Socialist parties. With the exception of Great Britain, where the Labour party came to power in 1945, these Socialist parties usually found themselves in opposition rather than in power. Initially, Communist parties were also strong, but after 1947, when the Cold War heated up, these parties were systematically excluded from participation in national governments.

While the United States emerged from World War II economically strong, the postwar European governments were faced with the tremendous task of leading their countries to economic and social recovery. After the first few very difficult years, when hunger and dislocation were more a rule than an exception, Western Europe entered into a period of strong economic recovery lasting well into the 1960s. The economic recovery was fueled by money from the American Marshall Plan, pent-up demand since the beginning of the war for goods and services, cheap skilled labor, and a surprisingly strong birth rate. Different mixtures of national planning and free enterprise were used to direct the recovery. International cooperation, such as with the Organization of European Economic Cooperation (OEEC) and the European Coal and Steel Community, and the already high level of industrial and technological sophistication attained by Western Europeans, facilitated the recovery. Accompanying economic growth were government social policies providing for health care, unemployment relief, old-age benefits, and family support.

In the late 1960s and 1970s new problems appeared. The economic growth of the 1950s and early 1960s leveled off. Inflation became widespread, particularly after 1973, when oil prices started their dramatic rise. At the same time, growth rates started to decline and unemployment began to rise. This "stagflation"—economic stagnation coupled with sharp inflation—persisted into the 1980s. Partial recovery in the mid-1980s, led by the United States, was uneven and purchased at a high price. Governmental deficits and problems with trade balances became common in the West.

Social dissatisfaction was evidenced in a variety of movements, from the student protests of the late 1960s to the radical separatist movements of the 1970s and 1980s. While the period cannot be called one of political instability, voters often turned out incumbent parties in hopes that the opposition parties could solve problems. Socialist parties that came to power seemed to have as much trouble dealing with apparently intractable problems as their conservative counterparts.

These general trends and variations of them can best be understood by examining developments in some individual countries between 1945 and the present.

Great Britain

In Great Britain the Labour party swept to victory in elections held in July 1945, just as the war was coming to an end. Clement Attlee succeeded Churchill as prime minister. The problems confronting Britain and the Labour government were indeed formidable. More than half of Great Britain's merchant marine had been sunk; a third of its buildings had been destroyed or damaged; its foreign investments had been liquidated and used up; Great Britain owed the United States a huge debt; its empire was tottering. The Labour government strictly rationed the short supplies, raised taxes on the rich, and lowered taxes on the poor. It nationalized the Bank of England, the coal mines and the electrical and gas industries, inland transportation, and the steel industry. Altogether, some 20 percent of Britain's economy was socialized. A vast program of social security, public education, public housing, and national health insurance was launched. The dismantling of the British Empire was begun—India, the biggest of all of Britain's colonial prizes, was given its independence in 1947 (see Chapter 59). The six years of Labour rule were years of austerity for the middle and upper classes. However, the general morale of the people was high, and Britain recovered. By 1948 British production and exports were higher than before the war, and the masses of the people were enjoying more security, services, and material goods than ever before.

Unfortunately, Great Britain's economic condition was fundamentally unsound. The loss of its overseas investments and resources and of the income from most of its prewar shipping, together with the antiquated state of most of its mines and factories, left Britain far short of the funds needed for war repair, debt repayment, and social services. By 1949 the serious deficit in the balance of trade had become apparent, followed by a weakening of the pound and mounting inflation. Rising discontent enabled Churchill and the Conservatives to return to power in 1951. With the exception of denationalizing the steel and trucking industries, they tampered little with the Labour party's program, most of which the great majority of the British people now clearly favored.

But neither the Conservatives, who governed Britain from 1951 to 1964 and again from 1970 to 1974, nor the Labourites, who governed from 1964 to 1970 and again from 1974 to 1979, were able to strengthen Britain's deteriorating economy, which was not yet socialistic but was too restricted to allow free competitive capitalism to function as it had in the nineteenth century. Furthermore, it was difficult for many Britishers to adjust to their greatly diminished place in the world. Many could still remember the glamorous days when Britain ruled the seas and an empire over which the sun never set. But increasing numbers of the young and the poor knew and cared little about past glories. Lawlessness and violence escalated, reaching its peak of intensity in Ulster. There the Roman Catholic minority struggled fiercely to gain equality with the Protestant majority; many of the Roman Catholics demanded separation from Britain and union with Ireland. The Protestants fought equally fiercely to maintain their supremacy. Violence begat violence. Hundreds on both sides were killed and hopes for a harmonious society were destroyed for the foreseeable future.

Widespread dissatisfaction with the inability of the Labour party to discipline its own trade unions and to lessen the rate of inflation resulted in a sweeping victory for the Conservatives in 1979. Margaret Thatcher became Britain's first female prime minister. The coming into production of the North Sea oil discoveries of several years earlier promised to strengthen Britain's economy, which had been in decline since World War I. Nevertheless, during the early 1980s Britain's economy remained troubled. With unemployment at more than 12 percent year after year and economic growth modest, Britain was burdened with one of the poorest performing economies in Western Europe. Urban riots reflected growing dissatisfaction. Yet thanks to the nationalistic unity fostered by the brief Falklands War with Argentina in the spring of 1982, the divisions within the Labour party (which led to the creation of a new party, the Social Democrats), and a moderately improving economy, Thatcher's Conservatives managed to maintain control over the government in the elections of 1983 and 1987.

France

France emerged from the war not only ravaged but also, unlike Britain, defeated and demoralized. General Charles de Gaulle returned to France in 1944 with the American and British liberators, who gave official recognition to the government he set up in Paris. However, the first postwar elections, held in October 1945, resulted in a sweeping victory for the parties of the Left, with which the authoritarian de Gaulle could not cooperate. Early in 1946 he went into temporary retirement. The leftist coalition, suspicious of authority, drew up a constitution very similar to that of the Third Republic, with its weak executive. The one noteworthy advance made by the new constitution was the granting at long last of woman suffrage. The Fourth Republic, like the Third, was plagued by a multiplicity of parties and political instability.

Despite these difficulties the Fourth French Republic made some noteworthy changes in French economic and social life. Under the Monnet Plan, free enterprise was combined with economic planning. Major banking and insurance facilities, coal mines, and gas and electrical utilities were nationalized. Social services, somewhat less comprehensive than those of the British Labour government, were inaugurated. A strong if uneasy economic recovery was achieved. By 1958 the output of goods and services was far in excess of that before World War II. These accomplishments of the Fourth Republic, however, were offset by its unsuccessful effort to hold onto the French Empire. A costly attempt to put down a war for independence in Indochina, which had broken out in 1942, resulted in humiliating defeat for the French (see p. 752). In 1954 France was forced to grant independence to Indochina. An even costlier war to try to save Algeria, in 1954–1962, also ended in failure (see p. 757). Inability to solve the Algerian problem led to the mutiny of the French army in Algeria in May 1958, which brought down the government. Charles de Gaulle was recalled from his twelve-year retirement. The problems confronting him were formidable—a mutinous army, a disintegrating empire, a seemingly endless war in Algeria, a disgruntled working class, an inflated currency, governmental weakness amounting to anarchy, widespread cynicism.

De Gaulle was probably the only person in France who could have reestablished civilian control over the mutinous army, which he deftly proceeded to do. He drew up a new constitution that greatly strengthened the executive branch of the government, and in December 1958 he was elected by an overwhelming majority first president of this Fifth French Republic (see Figure 58.3). He immediately granted independence to all of France's colonies except Algeria with its large French population. Algerian independence was granted four years later. He undertook to strengthen France's capitalistic economy by means of an austerity program. In spite of widespread strikes and sabotage by the working classes, much of it Communist-inspired, France's economy was soon operating at its highest level in history, and the French masses were enjoying new prosperity.

In foreign affairs, de Gaulle set out to restore France's "greatness"—its prestige in world affairs and its hegemony in Western Europe. He also sought to make Western Europe a "third force" independent of both American and Soviet domination. To achieve these ends, he created at great cost an independent nuclear striking force, cultivated cordial relations with Germany, withdrew France's military forces from NATO because of its domination by the United States, and vetoed Great Britain's entry into the European Common Market because of its close ties to its Commonwealth associates and to the United States.

For eleven years these policies worked with remarkable success. France regained much of the stability and prestige it had lost in 1940. De Gaulle's strong role, of course, encountered much opposition, mostly from the extreme Right and the extreme Left. His position and that of France's economy were weakened by massive student and labor union strikes and riots in 1968. When, in early 1969, de Gaulle asked for a vote of confidence from the French people and lost by a narrow margin, he resigned.

During the early 1970s Gaullists remained in power under the more moderate leadership of Georges Pompidou. In 1974 the elegant, urbane Valéry Giscard d'Estaing, a moderate conservative, defeated his Communist- and Socialist-backed opponent by the narrowest of margins. Giscard d'Estaing represented France's techno-

**FIGURE 58.3.
Charles de Gaulle**
After the French army in Algeria revolted against the French government in 1958, de Gaulle was recalled by popular acclaim and given an overwhelming mandate to rewrite the constitution. With dispatch he set up the Fifth French Republic and was elected its first president. This photo shows de Gaulle on tour of the French provinces. (Henri Cartier-Bresson/Magnum)

cratic Right and pursued a policy of slow modernization and social conservatism. Stunning change came in the elections of 1981, which brought the Socialists, under the leadership of François Mitterand, into power. Immediately, policies stressing nationalization of industries and banks, shorter hours and increased pay for workers, and progressive social programs were enacted. Yet several years of persistent economic problems, particularly inflation and high unemployment, dampened the reforming zeal of the Socialists. In 1986 the Socialists lost their majority to conservatives, but in 1988 the popular Mitterand was reelected president.

West Germany

The German Federal Republic was formally established in September 1949. It was a liberal democratic government similar to the Weimar Republic. The Christian Democratic party, a slightly right-of-center party with Roman Catholic leanings, won the first election, and its leader, the elderly and pro-Western Dr. Konrad Adenauer, became the first chancellor. The Western powers replaced their military governors with civilian commissioners and relaxed their control over Germany.

West Germany's industrial economy recovered rapidly, in part thanks to American assistance in replacing wrecked industrial plants with the most modern equipment and to American military protection, which relieved West Germany of the enormous military costs that burdened the economies of the United States, Great Britain, and France. By 1957 West Germany had regained its former industrial supremacy in Western Europe.

In 1963 Konrad Adenauer finally stepped down (at eighty-seven) as chancellor of West Germany. His Christian Democratic successors vigorously pursued his policies of strengthening West Germany's military ties with the United States, demanding the reunification of Germany and the recovery of lost territories in Eastern Europe, and establishing a place in the family of nuclear nations.

In 1969 Willy Brandt, a Social Democrat, became chancellor and launched Germany on a new course. His government quickly signed a nuclear nonproliferation treaty that had been long pending and entered into bilateral talks with East Germany and the Soviet Union. In August 1970 Chancellor Brandt and the Soviet premier Kosygin signed a treaty renouncing force or the threat of force in international relations and accepting the existing boundary lines of Eastern Europe including the Oder-Neisse line between East Germany and Poland. An official accompanying letter specified that the treaty left open the possibility of the future reunion of the two Germanies. This possibly momentous treaty was accompanied by trade agreements that promised a greatly stepped-up commerce between West Germany and the Soviet Union. The Social Democrats instituted and implemented many social programs, such as a comprehensive system of national health insurance and government ownership of public utilities. In economic policy, the German Social Democrats, unlike the French and British Socialists who advocated government ownership or control, followed a policy of codetermination between labor and management—*mitbestimmung*. West Germany's industrial economy had become the most prosperous of the Western world.

Economic problems plaguing other Western nations finally caught up with West Germany in the 1980s. By 1982 West Germany was experiencing negative economic growth, inflation of about 5 percent, and unemployment of almost 7 percent. In October 1982 Helmut Schmidt and his Social Democratic party fell from power and were replaced by the more conservative Christian Democratic party, led by the new chancellor Helmut Kohl. The rise to power of Kohl and the Christian Democrats was affirmed by elections in 1983, which also witnessed the first substantial entry into national politics of the environmentalist Green party, and again in 1987. While Germany's economy has recovered, unemployment remains a persistent problem.

Southern Europe

Italy After the end of World War II, Italy abolished the monarchy and established itself as a republic. The Christian Democrats under the leadership of Alcide de Gasperi emerged as the dominant political party. The Italian Communist party also came out of World War II in a strong position, initially sharing power with the Christian Democrats in a coalition government. After 1947 the Communists, although continuing to command 25 to 35 percent of the vote and winning control of local elections throughout Italy, were excluded

from national governments. For the next three decades the Christian Democrats dominated Italian governments, although almost always in shaky alliances with other parties. Even though governments did not last long, the government bureaucracy was resistant to change and the same group of high governmental officials continued in office in succeeding governments.

Italy, and particularly northern Italy, enjoyed rapid economic growth and modernization in the 1950s and 1960s, for the first time becoming a leading industrial power in Europe. After the late 1960s Italy experienced greater economic, social, and political instability. Inflation became a perennial problem. Industrial growth slowed. The government, with its entrenched and sometimes corrupt bureaucracy, became less able to react to problems. In the mid-1970s voters turned increasingly to the Italian Communist party, which under Enrico Berlinguer was adopting more moderate policies. Radical groups, such as the Red Brigades, resorted to terrorism. By the 1980s the dominant Christian Democratic party was losing control of the government for the first time. In August 1983 Bentino Craxi was named the first Socialist premier in Italy and he managed to remain in power until 1987, but his coalition government was only moderately different from preceding governments. With inflation still a problem, unemployment averaging over 11 percent, and growth only moderate, prospects for governmental stability are dim.

Spain, Portugal, and Greece The three southern European nations of Spain, Portugal, and Greece did not enter the mainstream of European developments until the 1970s. Both Spain, under Francisco Franco, and Portugal, under Antonio Salazar, remained out of World War II and retained their prewar authoritarian governments. Compared with the economies of other nations of Western Europe, their economies were less modernized and their people had a lower standard of living. Major political change came for both in the mid-1970s. In Portugal in 1974 General Antonio de Spinola headed a revolt that removed Marcelo Caetono, Salazar's authoritarian successor, from power. A year later Portugal held its first elections, and the Socialists, led by Mario Soares, gained control of the government. Again in 1986 the Socialist Soares was elected to power, this time as president. Spain underwent similar changes after the death of Franco in 1975. With the support of King Juan Carlos, a democratic constitution was approved in 1976. In 1982 the Socialists, under the popular Felipe Gonzáles, were elected to power for the first time. Since then Spain has enjoyed relative political stability and, recently, significant economic growth.

Greece, which suffered greatly during World War II, emerged in chaos and civil war. The Greek Royalists, with the help of first the British and then the Americans, were victorious. Greece became politically stable and remained so until the mid-1960s, when threats from the Left and Right led to the fall of the monarchy and, in 1967, a coup by conservative army officers. Their strong, authoritarian grip on Greek life was broken in 1974 when a confrontation with Turkey in Cyprus proved too difficult to handle. Since 1975 Greece has been governed by democratic rule, culminating in the election of the Socialists under Andreas Papandreou in 1981.

All three countries have followed a similar pattern: They broke from authoritarian rule in the mid-1970s, established a democratic form of government, and eventually elected a Socialist government. All three governments have had to deal with economies less modern than those in Western Europe and with societies that have had a lower standard of living. Yet recent events are pulling these southern European countries into the mainstream of Western European affairs; in the 1980s all three gained membership in the Common Market.

The United States

Of the Western powers, only the United States emerged from World War II virtually unscathed materially. The war had forced billions of dollars into circulation, ended the long depression, and destroyed much of the nation's foreign competition. The end of the war found big business and a high-spending military machine in close alliance and firmly entrenched. For most of the three decades following 1945, the United States enjoyed great economic prosperity. The pinnacle of prosperity came in the early and mid-sixties. Under presidents Kennedy and Johnson, the government pursued liberal policies of social reform, which included attacks on poverty, new educational programs, low-income housing projects, and governmental support of medical services. These policies put the United States more in line with other Western nations that had already established these social and "welfare state" institutions. However, the expansion of new social programs and unquestioned prosperity would come to an end in the 1970s and 1980s with new economic and political problems. Indeed, underlying the prosperity and confidence of the decades after World War II were a series of problems, which often resulted in anxiety, unrest, fear, and violence.

The first problem for Americans was the Soviet Union and communism. From the very beginning of the postwar era, Americans feared the Soviet Union and communism. Many journalists, military leaders, politicians, and business and professional people exploited this fear. During the early 1950s Senator Joseph McCarthy of Wisconsin fanned this fear into hysteria. In the eyes of McCarthy and his millions of followers, the American government, defense industries, armed forces, and educational system were honeycombed with Communists and fellow travelers.

In 1957, just as McCarthyism was subsiding, the American people were shocked by the news that the Soviet Union had orbited a satellite—Sputnik. The implication was that the lean and eager Russians had forged ahead in nuclear weapons and delivery systems while the soft and contented Americans had slept. The United States had, of course, for some time been working on a satellite of its own and in 1958 successfully orbited one. In 1961 the Soviet Union and the United States sent men into space and began to race each other to the moon. This race was won by the United States in 1969 at a cost of some $40 billion.

Americans were strongly concerned over repeated Communist successes in Asia (see Chapter 59), and closer to home a Communist takeover in Cuba in 1959 caused grave anxiety. The Cuban rebel leader, Fidel Castro, overthrew an American-supported rightist dictatorship. In 1961 the American government encouraged and aided an unsuccessful attempt by Cuban refugees to overthrow the Castro regime and the following year, by heavy threats, forced the Soviet Union to dismantle the missile bases it had constructed in Cuba. This was the most frightening of all the confrontations between the two nuclear powers, both of which had the nuclear capacity to destroy all the people on the earth.

America's next problem was the long-festering failure to integrate its large black population. By 1945 the blacks numbered some 20 million—about a tenth of the total population—and although considerable advancement in material well-being and social equality had been made, the gains fell far short of the promise. The curve of expectation was rising faster than the curve of achievement. Black veterans returning from World War II were particularly frustrated. In 1954 the Supreme Court outlawed segregation in the public schools and later specified forced busing as a means of implementing the decision. In the following years the civil rights movement was born, as blacks struggled for greater equality within American society. White resistance varied in close proportion to the number of blacks in the affected population—resistance flared up first in the Deep South and later in the large industrial cities of the North. Federal troops and marshals were used to overcome white resistance in the South. Millions of whites in the large northern industrial cities fled to the suburbs, leaving many cities primarily black. In 1964 Congress passed civil rights acts that guaranteed voting rights and broadly outlawed racial discrimination. Nevertheless, this legislation did not end the turmoil that had been unleashed. Riots occurred in major cities during the 1960s, reaching a climax in 1968 following the murder of Dr. Martin Luther King, Jr., the most prominent of the black leaders.

During the 1970s and 1980s, the position of blacks in American society has evolved, but the record is mixed. On the one hand, the elevation of many blacks to positions of political leadership and the growing numbers of blacks in middle-class jobs and residential areas indicate important change. On the other hand, blacks remain overrepresented in the growing core of inner-city unemployed who live below the poverty line.

Violence was by no means limited to the blacks nor to the United States. During the decade of the 1960s, youth all over the world was in revolt. However, violence and the crime rate were higher in the United States than in any other country and were constantly increasing. President Kennedy was assassinated in 1963 and his brother Robert, a major candidate for the Democratic presidential nomination, in 1968. College and university students staged protests, which often turned violent. Among the factors contributing to this unrest were continued racial inequality, widespread poverty alongside great wealth, inflation, wasteful destruction of natural resources, and growing dissatisfaction with American involvement in the war in Vietnam (see pp. 753–754).

While some of these problems became less immediate in the 1970s, new problems arose. In 1974, confidence in the American political system was shaken by the Watergate scandal, which revealed widespread misconduct and crimes within the highest levels of President Nixon's administration. Numerous high officials in the Nixon administration were forced to resign and were convicted and imprisoned. In August 1974, after it had become obvious that the president would be impeached by the full House and convicted by the Senate, Nixon resigned. He was succeeded by Gerald Ford, the conservative Republican leader who granted Nixon full pardon for all crimes he "may have committed while in office."

At almost the same time, economic problems stemming from the cost of the Vietnam War, from an unfavorable balance of trade, from growing inflation, and from the fourfold increase of oil prices between 1973 and 1974 started catching up with the United States. The country was entering a new period of declining growth rates, increasing unemployment, and rising prices. In the world marketplace, it was losing its dominance.

In 1976 Ford was narrowly defeated by Jimmy Carter. The Carter administration was confronted by spiraling inflation, a threatened fuel shortage, a high rate of unemployment (particularly among blacks and youths), a sense of disillusionment over the Vietnam War and its end, and widespread distrust of government at all levels—difficult problems that were not solved. The Carter administration was further burdened with trying to free American hostages from a hostile Iran and a new rise of oil prices.

In 1980 Ronald Reagan and the Republican party were elected to power and initiated a series of conservative policies in an attempt to undo several of the liberal reforms of the previous decades: Defense spending increased; a harsher line was taken toward communism; American arms and forces were sent to several areas throughout the world; programs to protect the environment, the worker, and the unemployed were attacked; and tax reforms that benefited mainly the corporations, the wealthy, and the middle class were enacted. The recession that began in the late 1970s deepened, with unemployment figures higher than in any years since the Great Depression of the 1930s. After 1983 the economy was in recovery, but the relative prosperity was purchased by a series of huge governmental deficits. In 1988 George Bush was elected president, promising to maintain the conservative policies of the Reagan administration.

Eastern Europe and the Soviet Union

The Soviet Union and Eastern Europe participated in the general European recovery from World War II, but their recovery was slower, not nearly as spectacular as in Western Europe. The Soviet Union initially set the pattern of economic and political development, but over time the various nations within the Soviet sphere of dominance moved in their own directions. In the decades following the 1960s, economic problems appeared and persisted. Agricultural production became an almost yearly disappointment. High administrative costs, inflexibility to market demand, and lethargy in productivity plagued industry. The gap between the economies of Western and Eastern Europe seemed to be widening rather than narrowing. In recent years these economic problems and the Soviet Union's own efforts at political and economic reform have led to considerable unrest and demands for economic decentralization in Eastern Europe. There are signs that the Soviet Union and Eastern Europe are embarking on a series of major long-term reforms.

The Soviet Union The Soviet Union emerged victorious from World War II, but the social and economic costs had been high. Few changes from prewar policies were evident. Stalin continued to assert totalitarian rule with a tightly planned economy stressing heavy industrialization. Political dissent was not allowed, and purges removed those perceived as potential threats. Prisons and forced-labor camps remained a feature of Stalin's rule. Despite the heavy expenditures required to maintain the Red Army, the Soviet Union recovered.

The death of Stalin in 1953 led to a liberalization of policies within the Soviet Union. Initially, Malenkov and Khrushchev struggled for power, but by 1955 Khrushchev had emerged as Stalin's successor. The most dramatic indication of changes from the Stalin era came in a 1956 speech in which Khrushchev denounced the crimes of Stalin before startled Communist leaders in Moscow. Khrushchev removed many of the conservative Stalinists within the party hierarchy but avoided the use of harsh Stalinist purges. Controls over cultural life were slightly loosened, as evidenced by the publication of novels by Boris Pasternak. Economically, there was a new stress on consumer goods and an attempt was made to reform agricultural policy. He embarked on an ambitious foreign policy. But Khrushchev may have tried to do too much at once, for domestic and international difficulties began to undermine his position. The gravest problems occurred in foreign affairs. The Soviet Union became involved in a growing ideological dispute with the Chinese Communists, who were younger and more evangelical in the Marxist faith than the Russians (see p. 749). The split between the Soviet Union and China was intensified by boundary disputes. Then in 1962 Khrushchev blundered into a showdown with the United States by trying to set up Soviet nuclear missiles in Cuba and was forced to make a humiliating retreat.

In October 1964 Khrushchev was suddenly ousted from power by his colleagues in the party's Central Committee. Leonid Brezhnev replaced him as party secretary, eventually emerging as the actual head of government by the late 1960s. Brezhnev reversed some of the liberalization of the Khrushchev years but did not fully return to Stalinist policies or practices. The Brezhnev era was marked by relative stability within the Soviet Union, a stability that seemed to persist under

Andropov, his successor. The Soviet economy has continued to expand but unevenly and not as rapidly as expected—in part thanks to the drain of military and administrative expenditures. By the 1980s the Soviet Union was a world leader in the production of steel, oil, coal, and cotton, and its industry was being computerized. Soviet agriculture was less successful. Although mechanization constantly increased, periodic droughts, poor management, and lack of incentive forced the government to make repeated and expensive grain purchases from the United States and Canada. The standard of living rose, but it still trailed that of the West and even that of some of the satellite countries in Eastern Europe. Soviet citizens enjoyed free education and medical services and relative job security. The Soviet Union continued to assert itself internationally as a world power, as indicated by its involvement and intervention in Czechoslovakia in 1968, Africa in the 1970s, Afghanistan in 1979, and Poland during the 1980s.

After Brezhnev died in 1982, Yuri Andropov (1982–1984) and then Konstantin Chernenko (1984–1985) came to power, but they did little to change the policies of the Brezhnev era. However, in 1985 the relatively young fifty-four-year-old Mikhail Gorbachev rose to power and initiated a series of important reforms (*glasnost*—"openness"; *perestroika*—"restructuring") in both foreign and domestic policy, including remodeling of the political system, attacks on corruption within the bureaucracy, decentralization of economic policy, relaxation of controls over political and cultural dissent, and new efforts to relax international tensions and stimulate disarmament agreements. These reforms seem to be producing both resistance and change within the Soviet Union.

Eastern Europe The governments and economies of Eastern Europe were brought under Stalin's control and set up in imitation of the Soviet model during the late 1940s. Initially, the Soviet Union drained off economic resources from these countries to strengthen its own economy. Soon single-party "people's democracies" were established in Poland, East Germany, Czechoslovakia, Hungary, Rumania, Yugoslavia, and Albania. Each of these governments was dominated by the head of its Communist party, who usually ruled in Stalinist

pattern. Each developed a planned economy stressing industrialization and collectivization of agriculture, and generally a high rate of economic growth was achieved. Each was required to cooperate politically, economically, and militarily with the Soviet Union. All major policies were tightly coordinated to the wishes of Moscow. Contact with the West was strictly limited. The one exception was Yugoslavia, where in 1948 Tito managed to break from the rest of the Communist bloc and take an independent course. Tito initiated a more decentralized form of communism stressing increased local control and worker participation in management.

Nevertheless, Eastern Europe should not be thought of as a mere appendage to the Soviet Union, even during the Stalinist period. Each state had its own sense of nationalism, each had its own particular ethnic mix, and each had its own history. The Soviet Union has not found it easy to gain or maintain control.

The first stirrings of revolt from Soviet control followed Stalin's death. In 1953 East Berliners rose but were quickly crushed by force. Following Khrushchev's 1956 speech denouncing Stalin and some of his policies, Poland rose in revolt. A compromise that left Poland within the Soviet sphere of control avoided the use of Soviet troops in Poland. Poland would enjoy a mild liberalization of its intellectual life and some economic independence. Shortly thereafter, a more violent armed revolt took place in Hungary. This more challenging demand for independence was met by an invasion of troops and the ouster of the new government. Nevertheless, under the Moscow-approved but moderate Janos Kádár, Hungarians were allowed increased individual freedom and greater national self-determination.

These revolts revealed some of the discontent and hopes for greater independence within East European nations, but the Soviet response also indicated the allowable limits to any deviance from the Soviet line. National differences between the various East European states and the Soviet Union were recognized. Contact with the West would be allowed. Cultural activities might be less restricted than in the Soviet Union. But fundamental political, economic, and military cooperation with Moscow was not to be violated.

FIGURE 58.4. **Soviet Tanks in Prague** Efforts by Czechoslovakia to reform its socialist system and gain greater independence from Moscow were brought to an end in August 1968 by a Soviet invasion. Here Soviet tanks overwhelm any potential resistance in the streets of Prague. (Josef Koudelka/Magnum)

Since the late 1950s the various Eastern European nations have pursued separate courses within the limits set by the Soviet Union. East Germany, Hungary, and Rumania remained relatively tranquil during the 1960s, 1970s, and 1980s. East Germany has closely followed the Soviet line while developing its industrial capacity. Hungary has successfully managed to orient its economy toward consumer goods, due to a loosening of state control and the introduction of limited capitalistic practices at the local level. In 1989 Hungary took new steps toward substantial democratic reform. Rumania has taken a more politically independent and conservative course under the leadership of president Nicolae Ceauşescu.

Albania, Czechoslovakia, and Poland have proven to be more of a problem to Moscow. In 1961 Albania, under Enver Hoxha, broke from Moscow and took the side of the Chinese in the Sino-Soviet split. Since Albania was surrounded by the already independent Yugoslavia and Greece, there was little the Soviet Union could do. In 1968 the Dubĉek government in Czechoslovakia went too far in allowing intellectual freedom and some democratization. The Soviet Union mobilized the troops of the Warsaw Pact nations and occupied Czechoslovakia (see Figure 58.4). Dubĉek and his supporters were removed from power along with their liberalizing policies. In 1980 the Polish government began to have difficulty maintaining its control over the nation. Mainly protesting the continuing economic mismanagement and corruption within the government, Polish workers struck and organized a union, Solidarity, under the leadership of Lech Walesa. Solidarity became increasingly powerful and was succeeding in forcing the government to grant concessions. When the union seemed to go too far, pressure from Moscow and resistance from conservative elements in the Polish government stiffened. In December 1981 martial law was declared by the new leader of the Polish Communist party, General Wojciech Jaruzelski. After a series of governmental crackdowns, Solidarity was outlawed in October 1982. In 1983 martial law was lifted and the government, pressured in part by the Catholic church, made some minor conciliatory gestures. Yet the fundamental political and economic problems that led to the unrest still keep Poland in a state of tension, as revealed by new strikes, a renewal of Solidarity's activities in 1988, new agreements between Solidarity and the government, and elections in 1989 giving Solidarity even greater power.

When compared with the economies of nations in Western Europe, the economies of Eastern Europe seem deficient. This deficiency is particularly apparent in recent years as the gap between Western and Eastern Europe seems to have widened. In the late 1980s Eastern Europe has been marked by growing discontent, greater political instability, and new demands for decentralization of economic decision making (as in Western capitalistic countries). On the other hand the economies of Eastern Europe started from a lower base and had to overcome greater difficulties. On the whole these economies have been modernizing, and Eastern Europeans have been enjoying a rising standard of living. Basic social services are extensive. With the exception of the elite of the Communist party and certain professionals, the gap between rich and poor classes has been narrowed. In a variety of fields, outstanding cultural productions have been created. The Eastern European nations, while still under the shadow of the Soviet Union, are distinct states with their own pasts and futures.

3. INTEGRATION AND INTERNATIONAL ORGANIZATIONS

In the years following World War II it became evident that there were advantages to dealing with problems cooperatively and through international organizations. European nations had long suffered from competitive nationalistic rivalries. The world in 1945 was no longer a place where a country such as Great Britain or France was strong enough to get its way. The developing Cold War was forcing countries to take sides whether or not they wanted to. After the destruction of World War II and particularly under the new threat of atomic weapons, the international pursuit of peace seemed even more pressing.

During the 1940s and 1950s a number of cooperative and international organizations were formed. Some were military, such as NATO (an alliance of the United States, Canada, and non-Communist nations of Europe) and its counterpart, the Warsaw Pact (an alliance of the Soviet Union and the Communist nations it dominated in Eastern Europe). Others were economic, such as the Organization for European Economic Cooperation (for coordination among recipients of Marshall Plan funds) and the Council for Economic Mutual Assistance (the Soviet response to the Marshall Plan). The most important of these organizations were the efforts toward integration in Western Europe and in the United Nations.

European Integration

In 1949 several nations in Western Europe took an initial step toward political integration by setting up the Council of Europe. Many hoped that this organization would develop into a parliament of Europe with real political power. However, the major European nations have been unwilling to give the council significant power, and it remains an organization of potential rather than concrete importance.

Western Europe has been more successful in taking steps toward economic integration. In 1950 France and Germany created the French-German Coal and Steel Authority. In 1952 it was expanded into the European Coal and Steel Community with the addition of Italy, Belgium, Luxembourg, and the Netherlands. In 1957 these same six nations signed the Treaty of Rome establishing the European Economic Community (the Common Market). Its purpose was to eliminate tariff barriers, cut restrictions on the flow of labor and capital, and generally integrate the economies of the member nations. The organization was a surprising success in the 1960s, eliminating tariff and immigration barriers ahead of schedule while its member nations enjoyed relative prosperity. During the 1970s and 1980s other nations joined the Common Market: Great Britain, Ireland, and Denmark in 1973; Greece in 1981; Portugal and Spain in 1986. Although at times further steps toward integration have been slow and difficult, in 1986 the Common Market agreed to eliminate almost all economic barriers among member states in 1992. This agreement would create a single market of some 320 million people.

The United Nations

In 1945 the world's leaders set up the United Nations to provide for international cooperation and act as a watchdog over peace. Since then, it has done an enormous amount of work in economic, cultural, and humanitarian fields, most of which has not made headlines. It has assisted in arranging cease-fires in several conflicts between Israel and the Arab states and has helped stop wars between India and Pakistan, and the Netherlands and Indonesia. Under the leadership of the United States, it fought in the Korean War, 1950–1953 (see pp. 750–751). In recent years the United Nations has won prestige for its effective role in areas of conflict such as the Middle East (particularly in facilitating the cease-fire between Iran and Iraq in 1988), southern Africa, and the western Sahara. Yet from the beginning the United Nations has been hampered by the unwillingness of the major powers to submit to its authority, embodied formally in the right of the permanent members of the Security Council to veto any action involving the use of force or the threat of force. Often it has proven unable to prevent wars or assert its will over defiant nations. The United Nations reflects more than it controls the domestic and international problems of its member nations over the past forty years.

SUGGESTED READING

General

W. Laqueur, *Europe Since Hitler* (1982). A scholarly, respected survey.

J. R. Wegs, *Europe Since 1945* (1983). A concise, up-to-date survey.

The Settlement and the Cold War

L. Halle, *The Cold War as History* (1967). A balanced account.

A. Ulam, *The Rivals: America and Russia Since World War II* (1972). Broad analysis of the significance of the Cold War.

D. Yergin, *The Shattered Peace* (1977). A balanced, well-written study of the Cold War.

Revival of a Divided Europe and the West

R. Aron, *The Imperial Republic: The United States and the World, 1945–1973* (1974). A sophisticated analysis of American dominance.

T. Ash, *The Polish Revolution: Solidarity* (1984). A full account.

L. T. Caldwell and W. Diebold, Jr., *Soviet American Relations in the 1980s* (1980). A good study of present problems.

W. Connor, *Socialism, Politics and Equality: Hierarchy and Change in Eastern Europe and the USSR* (1979). A good recent account.

R. Dahrendorf, *Society and Democracy in Germany* (1971). A respected but difficult analysis of Germany.

A. W. De Porte, *Europe Between the Superpowers: The Enduring Balance* (1979). A good recent analysis of Europe in the context of the superpowers.

D. L. Hanley et al., eds., *France: Politics and Society Since 1945* (1979). A good collection of essays.

J. Hough and M. Fainsod, *How the Soviet Union Is Governed* (1978). A useful general study.

F. Fejto, *A History of the People's Democracies: Eastern Europe Since Stalin* (1971). A solid study emphasizing differences among Eastern European nations.

A. H. Halsey, *Change in British Society* (1981). A solid recent study.

W. Leonhard, *Three Faces of Communism* (1974). Analyzes the ideological divisions of the Communist world.

A. Marwick, *British Society Since 1945* (1982). A good survey.

R. Mayne, *The Recovery of Europe, 1945–1973* (1973). Emphasizes Europe's economic progress and economic integration.

Integration and International Organizations

R. Mowat, *Creating the European Community* (1973). A study of European integration.

C. Tugenhat, *Making Sense of Europe* (1986). A recent evaluation of the Common Market.

CHAPTER 59

Decolonization and the Non-Western World, 1945–Present

FIGURE 59.1. Victory Parade in China, 1970 An imposing ninety-foot statue of Chairman Mao Tse-tung towers over marchers celebrating the twenty-first anniversary of the Communist victory in China. The rise of China as a world power in recent decades exemplifies the growing importance of connections between the Western and non-Western worlds. (Sipahioglu/Sipa/Special Features)

The devastation of two world wars and the rising movements for independence with their colonies was too much for the European imperial powers to handle. Sometimes gracefully and sometimes only after protracted violence, Europe lost almost all her colonies in the two decades following World War II. As the formerly colonized peoples acquired their independence, they began to assert their power in many areas of the non-Western world. By the 1970s and 1980s it was becoming clear that neither Europe nor the superpowers could act without taking into account the concerns, power, and problems of the non-Western world.

1. JAPAN BETWEEN EAST AND WEST

Japan emerged from World War II defeated on sea and land, the shocked victim of history's first two atomic bombs used for military purposes. Since the United States had played by far the major role in the defeat of Japan, the United States refused to share the occupation and governing of the Japanese islands with its former allies. President Truman appointed General Douglas MacArthur supreme commander of the Allied powers in Japan and gave him absolute authority.

During the first year and a half of MacArthur's command, a democratic constitution similar to that of Great Britain was drawn up and put into effect. In the first elections under the new constitution, which gave women the right to vote and guaranteed civil liberties, the Social Democrats, who were somewhat similar to the British Labourites, won the largest number of seats in the national legislature. The activities of Japanese labor unions were encouraged, and they became effective for the first time. The five great families (the *zaibatsu*) who had monopolized Japan's industry and finance disbanded their great business combinations under pressure from the occupation authorities. Demilitarization was carried out and a number of top Japanese war leaders were tried and executed or imprisoned.

Of greatest significance was MacArthur's land-reform program. The great mass of Japanese farmers were poverty-stricken, landless sharecroppers,

giving up from 50 to 70 percent of their yield to absentee landlords. Laws sponsored by Mac-Arthur forced the landlords to sell to the government all land in excess of seven and a half acres (more in less fertile areas). The government, in turn, sold the land in plots of seven and a half acres to the tenant farmers, who were given thirty years to pay for them. By the end of 1946 Japan appeared to be on the way to becoming a liberal democracy.

Early in 1947, when the Cold War was being stepped up in intensity, General MacArthur suddenly reversed his liberal policy in Japan. He first cracked down on the newly formed labor unions. Industrial decentralization ceased, and land redistribution slowed down. Obviously, the United States was now interested in making Japan, like Germany, a link in the containment chain that it was forging around the Soviet Union. By 1949 the more conservative Liberal party, which later became the Liberal Democratic party, gained power and would hold it in elections through the following four decades.

In 1951 the United States drew up a formal treaty with Japan. The terms granted the United States military bases in Japan and a protectorate over the Ryukyu Islands (including Okinawa) and Japan's former mandated islands in the Pacific. (The United States gave up this protectorate in 1972.) Japan was to pay no indemnity and was to be free to rearm and to make its own alliances. Although forty-eight nations signed the treaty, India, Burma, the Soviet Union, and the Soviet satellites refused. China was not invited to sign.

During the 1950s and 1960s Japan made an astounding economic recovery that surpassed even that of West Germany. Like West Germany, Japan received massive American aid. In rebuilding its ruined industries, Japan adopted the most modern and scientific labor-saving devices (see Figure 59.2). It benefited from the rapid expansion of higher education and readily available, high-quality labor. By the mid-1960s Japan was the third greatest industrial power in the world, outranked only by the United States and the Soviet Union, and the Japanese people were enjoying a standard of living and social peace such as they had never known before. The Japanese, like the Germans, benefited greatly from American military protec-

FIGURE 59.2. Matsushita Electrical Industrial Company By the 1970s, Japan was a leading industrial power, particularly in electronics. Plants such as this Matsushita Electrical Industrial Company (producing VCRs) used technology and disciplined labor to manufacture products for the home and foreign markets. (Courtesy Matsushita)

tion, which relieved them of the enormous cost of maintaining a big military establishment. They also sold large quantities of industrial products, particularly electronics and automobiles, to the United States and bought relatively few American goods in return. Furthermore, the Japanese labor unions, like the German, but unlike the American, British, and French unions, have followed a policy of cooperation—codetermination—with their corporate managers.

Political stability and economic prosperity continued through the 1970s. In 1978 Japan signed a treaty of friendship and commerce with the People's Republic of China. During the 1980s Japan has managed to maintain a striking degree of economic health with a comparatively high growth rate and lower rates of unemployment and inflation than any industrial power of the West. But the Japanese economy would appear to be fragile. Japan has few natural resources. In an area smaller than California, of which only 14 percent is arable, live more than 100 million people. Any prolonged interruption of foreign trade would probably be calamitous, and new competition from other Asian nations such as Taiwan, South Korea, and Singapore may prove costly.

2. THE RISE OF COMMUNIST CHINA

Across the Sea of Japan a very different and even more exciting drama was being enacted in China. Here, a massive upheaval involving one-fourth of the world's population took place. Sun Yat-sen, after launching his revolution against both China's foreign exploiters and its own reactionary and conniving government (see pp. 696–697), died in 1925, in the midst of the struggle. His place at the head of the revolutionary Chinese government was taken by his young and vigorous supporter, General Chiang Kai-shek, who soon gained control of all China. Chiang Kai-shek, a professional soldier, was much more interested in making China a powerful and independent nation than in liberalizing its government and society. Under him, the revolutionary Kuomintang party, then dominant in China, swung definitely to the right. When the Chinese Nationalist armies were defeated by the Japanese in 1937–1938 and driven deep into the interior, Chiang Kai-shek and the Kuomintang party were cut off from the chief bases of their liberal support, which were the great coastal cities. Heavily dependent then on the warlords and landlords of the interior, they moved still further to the right.

Meanwhile, as China's Confucian civilization was crumbling faster than Sun Yat-sen's Western liberalism could replace it, another Western influence moved into the vacuum: Marxism. The hostility that the Western democracies showed to Sun Yat-sen's revolutionary liberal movement encouraged the Chinese Communists. In 1927 the Communists found an able leader in the scholarly and shrewd Mao Tse-tung (see Figure 59.3). This dedicated revolutionary from well-to-do peasant stock had risen to leadership by sheer force of intellect, personality, and energy. Chiang Kai-shek exerted every effort to crush the Chinese Communists—much more, in fact, than he spent to drive out the Japanese invaders. During the years 1939–1945, when the Kuomintang forces were inactive in Chungking and getting further and further out of touch with the Chinese masses, Mao Tse-tung's Communists were waging incessant guerrilla warfare against the Japanese and gaining a greater following among the Chinese people.

Following the surrender of Japan in August 1945, a bitter struggle for the control of China ensued between Chiang Kai-shek's Kuomintang forces, now known as the Chinese Nationalists, and the Chinese Communists. In this struggle the United States supported the Nationalists. However, the Communists won the support of ever-increasing numbers of the Chinese people. Morale in the long inactive and graft-ridden Nationalist armies was low, while that in the Communist armies, toughened by the continuous fighting against the Japanese, was high. Using Japanese weapons that had been left behind by the Russians, and American weapons and munitions that were surrendered by the Nationalists, the Communists began to gain the upper hand in 1947. During 1949 the victorious Communists swept over the entire Chinese mainland. Chiang Kai-shek, with a remnant of his Nationalist forces, mostly officers, fled to the island of Formosa (Taiwan), where after June 1950 they were protected by the United States navy. In 1949 Mao Tse-tung proclaimed the People's Republic of China and the following year formed an alliance with the Soviet Union. With Soviet aid, he began the enormous task of industrializing and communizing the world's most populous nation.

This formidable undertaking was interrupted shortly after it had begun by China's involvement in the Korean War, 1950–1953 (see the following section). When the United Nations forces, which were mostly American, defeated the North Korean Communists and approached the Manchurian border, the Chinese Communist armies crossed the Yalu River into Korea, drove the Americans back, and stalemated the war. This was a remarkable accomplishment for such an industrially backward country fighting against the world's greatest military power, and it cost the Chinese Communists nearly a million casualties.

In 1953 Mao Tse-tung launched his First Five-Year Plan, which was similar to Stalin's First Five-Year Plan twenty-five years earlier. The Chinese Communists, however, were starting from a much lower base than the Russians. Industry and agriculture were both collectivized. The emphasis was on building heavy industry. These were years of bleak austerity, but the Chinese masses had never known anything else. In 1957 the government announced that the First Five-Year Plan had been a great success. Most production quotas had been met or surpassed.

The following year it launched its Second Five-Year Plan. The vast new goals in industry and agriculture were to be achieved by communizing Chinese society more completely than had ever been attempted in the Soviet Union. The entire population was organized into strictly regimented communes; the ancient and sacred Chinese family structure was drastically altered. China's huge and rapidly growing population was set to building irrigation dams and ditches, steel mills, factories, railroads, schools, and hospitals, and in a frenzied hurry. This plan was called the "Great Leap Forward." But the plan was too ambitious. In 1959 a series of droughts and floods produced near-famine conditions in many areas. Overzealous local party officials provoked resentment and resistance among the harried populace. The realistic Red leaders slackened the pace and eased the regimentation.

The failure of the Great Leap Forward gave rise to ideological differences and set off a power struggle within the Communist party hierarchy. A

moderate group led by Liu Shaoqi, president of the republic and second in command to Party Chairman Mao Tse-tung, wished to slow down the pace of communization, produce more consumer goods, and encourage, at least temporarily, individual initiative. Mao took a different line. He believed many dangerous remnants of prerevolutionary capitalistic China and the newly bloated bureaucracy had to be destroyed. In 1966 he unleashed tens of thousands of Red Guards—fanatical Communist youths—upon the moderate element in what he called a "cultural revolution" and with the support of the regular army succeeded, after three years of turmoil, in crushing the moderates.

Of great concern to the Chinese Communists was their growing rift with the Soviet Union. In 1956 an ideological dispute had begun when Khrushchev denounced Stalin. Peking accused Moscow of becoming soft toward the capitalistic, imperialist West. In 1960 the Soviet Union began to withhold promised economic and technological aid from China. In 1964 Red China exploded its first nuclear device. This event, in addition to China's impressive military growth, appeared to give the Soviets grave concern. They moved many of their best mechanized divisions to the Far East, where in 1968 they clashed with Chinese units along the disputed border—the longest international border in the world. Both Red giants, fearful of each other, sought a détente with the United States.

In 1971 the United States government, shaken by its disastrous intervention in the Vietnam War (see pp. 753–754), began to face the changed realities in the Far East and to accept détente with both Red China and the Soviet Union. The United States ceased to block the admission of Red China to the United Nations, making it possible for the

FIGURE 59.3. Mao Tse-tung and Ho Chi Minh
These men were two of East Asia's most dynamic leaders since World War II. The North Vietnamese, though eager to get aid from China, were always suspicious and fearful of their big neighbor to the north. (Brian Brake/Rapho/Photo Researchers)

UN to admit the People's Republic of China (1971) and expel the Republic of China on Taiwan. Emissaries were exchanged between Peking and Washington. Only the continued American support of the Chinese Nationalist government on Taiwan (Chiang Kai-shek died in 1975) prevented the establishment of full diplomatic relations between the two great powers.

Mao Tse-tung died in 1976. The most influential and energetic leader in the new regime was Deputy Prime Minister Deng Xiaoping, who had been purged from the government by Mao. Late in 1978 Deng led a movement to diminish the image of Mao, reminiscent of Khrushchev's downgrading of Stalin in 1956. For the time being the fervor of permanent political revolution in Com-

Map 59.1 ASIA, 1989 Containing more than one-half of the world's population, Asia has been of growing concern to Western nations since 1945. Two wars (the Korean and the Vietnamese) have directly involved Western nations, while the economic might of Japan and the potential power of China are seen as threatening to many Western interests.

munist China had waned. Deng and his followers stressed rapid economic development, some economic decentralization, and opening more contacts with industrial powers. In the late 1970s and the 1980s these policies resulted in the treaty of friendship and commerce with Japan, improved relations with the United States, the quest for foreign loans, the opening of China to tourism and foreign investment, new economic growth, and greater economic freedom. However, in 1989 demands by students and workers for greater cultural and political freedom shook China, calling into question the stability of China's political system.

3. THE KOREAN WAR

The bitter Left-Right conflict among the Asiatic peoples and the global Cold War struggle between the United States and the Soviet Union merged in Korea to produce a shooting war of major proportions. In August 1945, in accordance with the Yalta Agreements, the forces of the Soviet Union overran Japanese-held Korea north of the thirty-eighth parallel, and the forces of the United States began to occupy Korea south of the thirty-eighth parallel. These moves were supposed to be for the purpose of setting up a free and united Korean nation. However, the Soviet Union immediately proceeded to set up a Communist dictatorship in North Korea under Kim Il-sung. The land was distributed to the peasants, and industry was nationalized. In South Korea the United States authorities sponsored a right-wing government under the leadership of the aged and reactionary Korean patriot Syngman Rhee. Late in 1948 the Soviet forces withdrew from North Korea, leaving behind an energetic Communist regime well armed with the latest Soviet weapons. Six months later the American forces withdrew from South Korea, leaving behind the Syngman Rhee landlord regime armed mostly with the weapons that had been captured from the Japanese. Both the North and South Korean governments talked loudly of conquering each other.

On June 25, 1950, North Korea suddenly attacked South Korea. The high-spirited and well-armed North Korean Communists easily defeated the South Koreans. The armies of Syngman Rhee, quer the world by military force and that there must not be another Munich. Secretary of State Dean Acheson persuaded the United Nations to take drastic action. Taking advantage of the absence of the Soviet Union's representative, the Security Council called upon the members of the United Nations to furnish military forces to repel the North Korean aggression and asked President Truman to name the commander of the United Nations forces. Truman named General MacArthur to command them. Truman also announced that he had already ordered American forces into the Korean War, that the American navy would protect Chiang Kai-shek's Chinese Nationalists on Taiwan against the Chinese Communists, and that American aid to the French fighting the native Communists in Indochina would be greatly increased.

The forces of the United Nations, mostly Americans, quickly defeated the North Koreans. By late November 1950, MacArthur's forces were approaching the Yalu River, which forms the Korean-Chinese border. At this point Red China entered the war and severely defeated MacArthur's forces, driving them in headlong retreat back down the peninsula. Eventually—January to March 1951—the battle line became stabilized roughly along the thirty-eighth parallel, where the war had started. Two years of negotiations brought an armistice in 1953. Total casualties— dead, wounded, and missing—are estimated to have been approximately a million and a half on each side, of which some 145,000 were Americans (including 54,000 dead) and 900,000 Chinese Communists. Most of the rest were Koreans. The war ended just about where it had started. However, Communist military aggression had been checked with severe punishment. The United Nations had functioned effectively and increased its prestige. Probably of equal significance is the fact that a revolutionary new Asiatic power, Red China, had fought the greatest Western power, the United States, to a standstill.

Since the end of the war, North and South Korea have gone their separate ways. North Korea has remained a tightly controlled Communist state under the long rule of Kim Il-sung. South Korea

FIGURE 59.4. **Nehru and Gandhi** Two great charismatic leaders of Asian independence, India's Jawaharlal Nehru and Mahatma Gandhi, are shown during a meeting of the All India Congress in Bombay in 1946. (UPI/Bettmann Newsphotos)

has remained under the control of right-wing authoritarian leaders, but its society is more open and more economically dynamic than that of the North. During the 1970s and 1980s it has become one of the most rapidly growing and industrializing economies in the world, and recently it has shown signs of broadening political participation.

4. THE REVOLT OF SOUTHERN ASIA

The end of World War II found the huge British, Dutch, and French empires in southern Asia aflame with the spirit of nationalism and revolt. Of the Western imperial powers, only the United States escaped direct embroilment in this revolt by granting independence to the Philippines in 1946.

In India, the world's second most populous country, the leader of the independence movement was Mohandas K. Gandhi (1869–1948), one of the most dynamic personalities of the twentieth century. This middle-class Hindu, educated in Great Britain, was a master of the psychology of the Indian masses. His chief tactics were passive resistance and civil disobedience. The British were unable to cope with him.

Indian nationalism reached its peak during World War II, but Churchill would not hear of Indian independence. "I did not become the king's first minister," said the doughty warrior, "in order to preside over the liquidation of the British Empire." The British Labour party, however, upon coming to power in 1945 immediately announced its determination to grant India independence. In 1947 independence was granted to India, containing some 350 million people, and Pakistan, with more than 70 million people.

Religious and national strife soon broke out between Hindu India and Moslem Pakistan. Gandhi tried to quell the strife, but he was assassinated in 1948 by a fanatical Hindu nationalist. Open war between the two states began in 1948 over possession of the disputed state of Kashmir. The United Nations was able to end the shooting but not the dispute.

One of Gandhi's most devoted followers, Jawaharlal Nehru, a charming, wealthy British-educated Hindu of the highest (Brahmin) caste, became the first prime minister of India (see Figure 59.4). The problems confronting him were staggering. Most of India's millions were poverty-stricken and illiterate. They spoke more than eight hundred languages and dialects (fewer than 50 percent spoke the official Hindi). Some 100 million Indians were of the untouchable class. Nehru inaugurated a liberal and mildly socialistic program somewhat similar to that of the British Labour government. For many observers, India would be watched as a test case. Could liberal democracy with a mixed capitalist-socialist economic policy do for the Indian people what Communism could do for the Chinese people in the way of modernization and material advancement? Not the least of Nehru's problems was avoiding embroilment in the Soviet-American Cold War. However, border clashes with Pakistan and with Red China frightened India into accepting military aid from both the United States and the Soviet Union.

Nehru's great charm and prestige kept India's restive millions fairly quiet. But when he died in 1964, his successors were confronted by rising discontent. In 1966 Nehru's daughter, Indira Gandhi, became prime minister. Many Indians felt that the economic and social reform program of the Nehrus was not drastic enough. In spite of sizable loans and much technical assistance from the United States, Great Britain, and the Soviet Union, India's standard of living was not keeping abreast of its ever-mounting population. In 1974, while millions of its people stood on the brink of starvation, India exploded its first nuclear device. In 1975 the opposition to Prime Minister Gandhi's administration became so disruptive that she invoked constitutional emergency decrees that amounted to dictatorship. Thousands of her most vocal opponents were imprisoned. But the opposition only increased. In 1977 Mrs. Gandhi granted national elections and was driven from power. However, her successors had little success in dealing with the overwhelming problems facing India. Indira Gandhi returned to power as prime minister in 1980, but she was assassinated by Sikh extremists in 1984 and has been succeeded by her son, Rajiv Gandhi. India still struggles with the problems of religious differences (particularly with the Sikhs of Punjab) and linguistic differences (as with the Tamils in the south) in a difficult environment of uneven economic development, overpopulation, and poverty.

Pakistan, divided into two states more than a thousand miles apart (see Map 59.1) and with a fragile constitutional government, soon became a military dictatorship closely aligned with the United States. In 1971 East Pakistan rebelled against the less populous but dominant West Pakistan and, with the help of India, gained its independence as the Republic of Bangladesh—but not before some 3 million of its helpless citizens had been slaughtered by the West Pakistani army. From 1977 to his death in 1988, Zia ul-Haq held power and remained an important if difficult ally of the United States.

The British Labour government also granted independence to Ceylon, Burma, and Malaya. This left only Hong Kong as a reminder of British imperialism in Asia.

The rich and populous Dutch East Indies declared independence at the end of World War II. The Dutch resisted fiercely for four years but yielded to pressure from the United Nations. In 1949 the Republic of Indonesia was recognized as an independent nation—a nation of approximately 125 million people, mostly Moslems, living on several thousand tropical islands rich in tin, rubber, oil, and many other valuable products.

Of all the European colonial regimes in Asia, that of the French in Indochina was probably the most predatory and the most hated. Immediately after the surrender of Japan in August 1945, the Indochinese nationalists, under the leadership of Ho Chi Minh, a Russian-trained Communist, proclaimed the independent "democratic" Republic of Vietnam. The returning French imperialists were fiercely resisted by the native Communist nationalists. Heavy fighting ensued, in which the French were aided by American Marshall Plan money. The majority of the Vietnamese people apparently preferred the Communists to the French, and the forces of Ho Chi Minh won victory after victory despite American aid to the French.

In 1954 the French government admitted defeat and ceded the northern half of Vietnam to the Communists. Although South Vietnam technically remained a part of the French Union, French influence quickly vanished. The United States, in accordance with its policy of military containment of communism—both Russian and Chinese—undertook to establish its power not only in South Vietnam but in Laos and Cambodia as well, which the French had also freed. Vigorous military and

FIGURE 59.5.   Vietnam, 1969   The intervention of the United States in Vietnam for the purpose of containing communism (Russian and Chinese, it was believed) resulted in greater bombing and destruction than in World War II. Millions of Vietnamese were killed, maimed, and made homeless. (Jones Griffiths/ Magnum)

financial aid was given to the conservative Ngo Dinh Diem regime in South Vietnam. Fearful of a Communist victory at the polls, American authorities refused to permit the holding of national elections, which had been promised by an international commission when the French withdrew. Diem became increasingly unpopular. Almost immediately, he was faced with a rebellion of his own people supported and soon led by the Communists in both South and North Vietnam. No amount of American aid seemed to be able to hold back the tide against the unpopular and faltering Diem regime. In 1963 Diem, having lost the confidence and support of his American protectors, was overthrown and assassinated by a group of his own officers, who set up a harsh military dictatorship of their own. Early in 1965 the Vietnam-

ese Communists, with significant material aid from both the Soviet Union and Red China, greatly stepped up their war against the American-supported but weakening South Vietnamese forces. The United States retaliated with heavy bombing of North Vietnam and increased its armed forces to over 500,000 troops. Vietnam was rapidly being devastated (see Figure 59.5).

Meanwhile, public opinion all over the world, including the United States, was becoming incensed at the wanton destruction. In 1968 a massive North Vietnamese surprise offensive convinced the American government that victory could not be won, and the United States began long, dreary peace talks with the North Vietnamese in Paris. In 1969 Ho Chi Minh died, but the war and new massive bombings (the United States dropped more explosives on Vietnam than were used by all combatants during World War II) dragged on until 1973, when peace agreements were finally signed and the United States withdrew its armed forces, leaving behind huge stores of war matériel for the South Vietnamese. The civil war in Vietnam, however, continued as both sides refused to abide by the terms of the peace agreements.

As in China and Korea, the graft-ridden armed forces of a corrupt government trying to maintain the old aristocratic society of a bygone era were no match for the high-spirited Communist forces. In 1975 the Communists swept to victory over all Vietnam and shortly thereafter over the rest of Indochina—Cambodia and Laos. Even then the violence did not end. In Cambodia the Communist Pol Pot regime devastated that society, resulting in the death of over a million people and ending in an invasion and occupation of Cambodia by Vietnam. Relations between Vietnam and China remain shaky, with violence having broken out along their border more than once during the past decade.

5. THE EMBATTLED MIDDLE EAST

One of the most explosive areas in the latter half of the twentieth-century world was the Middle East—that area between and including Egypt and Iran, where East meets West (see Map 59.2). In global terms it is probably the most strategic area in the world. It forms the bridge between the world's two greatest land masses, Eurasia and Africa; and through it pass the chief communication lines between the East and the West. The Middle East is the heart of the Moslem world, which stretches from Morocco to Indonesia and contains over 500 million followers of the Prophet. It is also the heart of the tumultuous Arab world. Moreover, the area contains more than half the world's known oil reserves.

During the early part of the century, while the great European powers competed for control of the Middle East, Arab nationalism was rising. This nationalism was vented first against the British, who were the dominant power in that area. As anti-British hostility mounted in the years between

the two world wars, Great Britain began to relax its control. By the end of World War II only Cyprus, Palestine, and the Suez Canal remained in Britain's possession, and the British were bidding strongly for Arab friendship. But continued British possession of the Suez Canal and the admission of tens of thousands of Jews into Palestine under the Balfour Declaration of 1917 proved to be effective barriers to Anglo-Arab accord.

Palestine was the ancient home of the Jews. However, in A.D. 70 they were dispersed by the government of the Roman Empire. In the seventh century the Moslem Arabs conquered Palestine and lived there until the twentieth century—thirteen hundred years. In the late nineteenth century, the Zionist movement began—a movement to restore Palestine as a national home for the Jews. During the anti-Semitic persecutions of the Hitler era, thousands of European Jewish refugees, many of them wealthy, poured into Palestine, buying up the land and dispossessing the Arabs. The whole Arab and Moslem world became incensed.

In 1948 the British Labour government turned Palestine over to the United Nations. The Jews immediately proclaimed the State of Israel and accepted the boundary lines that the United Nations had drawn to divide Palestine between the Jews and the Arabs. The Arab League refused to accept this arrangement and began hostilities with a view to eliminating the Jewish state. Tiny Israel, however, well armed and well financed, was more than a match for the Arabs. After a year of fighting, the United Nations succeeded in bringing about a truce. Israel had somewhat expanded its original borders, and it had expelled nearly half a million Arabs who had fought to destroy the State of Israel. Arab nationalism was thoroughly aroused, and border raids recurred as the Arabs armed for a renewal of the struggle. Israel, in the meantime, receiving financial aid from Jews abroad, prospered, built modern cities, introduced irrigation and scientific agriculture, and became a vigorous, democratic, cooperative Western society.

The Arabs found a vigorous leader when in 1952 a military coup in Egypt brought to power Gamel Abdul Nasser. Nasser set out to unite the Arab world and inflame it against the West. When

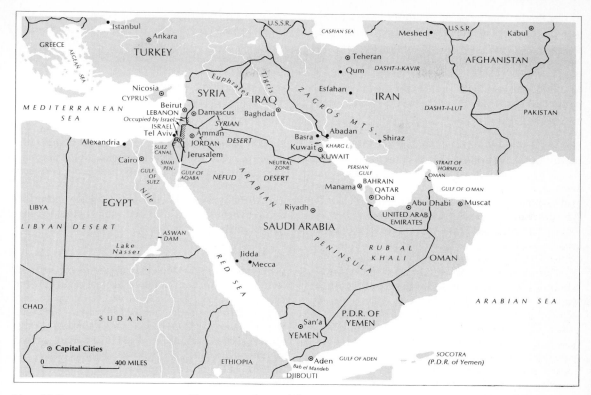

Map 59.2　**THE MIDDLE EAST, 1989**　Since 1945 the Middle East has been wracked by several outbreaks of war involving Israel and its neighbors. Cold war involvements, the growing strength of Arab nationalism, and OPEC control over oil production have made this part of the world of crucial concern to the West.

he threatened Israel, seized the Suez Canal, and aided France's rebellious subjects in North Africa, he was attacked by Israel, Great Britain, and France in 1956. He was saved only by the threatened intervention of the Soviet Union, which caused the United States to exert sufficient pressure on the three invading powers to force them to give up their assault. But nothing had been settled. Nasser continued to arouse Arab nationalism against Israel, and the Arab states received a swelling stream of arms from the Soviet Union.

In 1967 Nasser again brought on a showdown. He had prohibited the use of the Suez Canal by the Israelis since the 1956 war. When he blockaded Israel's only port on the Red Sea and Egyptian,

Syrian, and Jordanian armies massed along the Israeli borders, the Israelis suddenly attacked them and crushed them in six days' time. The Israelis then occupied Egyptian territory east of the Suez Canal, Syria's Golan Heights, and Jordanian territory west of the Jordan—territories that the Israelis claimed were necessary for their security.

The six-day 1967 war humiliated not only the Arab world but also the Soviet Union, who rushed billions of dollars' worth of arms, including deadly surface-to-air missiles (SAMs), together with thousands of military "advisers," to Egypt and Syria. Nasser died in 1970 and was succeeded as president of Egypt by Anwar Sadat.

As the Israelis were celebrating their Yom Kippur holidays in October 1973, Egypt and Syria, supported by the rest of the Arab states (except Morocco), suddenly attacked them. This time the Arabs, much better armed and trained than before, inflicted serious casualties on the Israelis and pushed them back on all fronts. Several weeks were required for the heavily outnumbered Israelis to recover from their initial shock, receive massive fresh supplies from the United States, and mount offensives of their own. They then crossed the Suez Canal, surrounded an entire Egyptian army, and began advancing on Cairo to the west and Damascus, the Syrian capital, to the east. At this juncture the Soviet Union threatened to intervene. The United States alerted its armed forces and forced the Israelis to halt their advance. The United Nations helped to arrange a cease-fire.

Ever since the 1967 war most of the world—much of it undoubtedly influenced by its hunger for Arab oil—has supported the Arab states in their demand for the return of all occupied territories. The Israelis, claiming these territories as necessary buffer zones and bargaining pawns, have refused to give them up without adequate guarantees of security, which under the circumstances are hard to envision. Only the United States and the Netherlands supported Israel.

The Arabs now made full use of their oil weapon; they quadrupled the price of their oil, curtailed production, and placed a complete embargo on its shipment to the United States and the Netherlands. These measures added greatly to the strain of inflation that had long gripped the capitalistic world. The poorer nations of Asia and Africa were particularly distressed.

In November 1977 Egypt's President Sadat surprised the world by going to Jerusalem and beginning negotiations with Israel's Premier Begin for a peace settlement. Sadat was denounced by all his Arab neighbors for breaking the solid Arab front against Israel. Negotiations soon broke down, however, over the disposition of the Palestinian West Bank, which the Israelis had seized during the 1967 war, and over the claims of the Palestinian refugees. Again the world was surprised when President Carter in September 1978 succeeded in bringing Sadat and Begin to his retreat at Camp David, Maryland, and persuading

them to sign the first draft of a peace treaty. Since 1978 the only major step that has been taken to lessen tensions in this area of the world has been the Israeli withdrawal from the Sinai, completed in 1982.

The Palestinian refugees were one of the most tumultuous elements in the whole Middle Eastern complex. Fleeing Palestine after the 1948 war, they first attempted to overthrow the government of Jordan. Failing there, they took refuge in Lebanon, which was too weak to expel them. Their numbers grew constantly until by 1975 there were between 2 million and 3 million of them. In that year they joined the Moslem Lebanese majority in attempting to overthrow the Christian-dominated government. In the civil war that followed, Beirut, the capital city and one of the most prosperous banking and commercial centers in the Middle East, was wrecked. Syria took advantage of the turmoil to move in and gain military control over most of the country. In 1982 Israel invaded Lebanon and occupied the southern half of the country. In vain, troops from Western nations, including Italy, France, Great Britain, and the United States, were stationed in Beirut by 1983, only to be withdrawn in 1984. Lebanon continues to be wracked by civil war and international animosities, and the Palestinian's struggles with Israel seem far from over. Under the leadership of the Palestine Liberation Organization and other radical groups, Palestinians have continued to resist Israeli troops from within Israeli-occupied territories and resort to guerrilla and terrorist tactics almost everywhere. Israel has responded with intransigence. Recently, however, the Palestine Liberation Organization, under the leadership of Yasir Arafat, has gained increased international stature. By admitting Israel's right to exist and rejecting terrorism, the Palestine Liberation Organization has convinced the United States to open negotiations with it for the first time.

The enormous oil wealth pouring into the Middle East accelerated the demands for change. Countries such as Saudi Arabia and Kuwait became suddenly wealthy, commanding strategic oil reserves and great financial muscle. But in other countries, problems arose. In 1978 Iran, second only to Saudi Arabia in the production of oil and precariously situated between the Soviet Union and the Persian Gulf, was the scene of massive uprisings. The Shah's government was strongly supported by the United States as a military strong point on the border of the Soviet Union. Though modernizing the country, the Shah's government was a military dictatorship. Now it was beset on the one hand by young liberals who wanted to democratize and further modernize Iran and on the other by the masses led by Islamic fundamentalists who rejected the West and secularism in favor of old Islamic values. Early in 1979 the Shah was forced to flee, and the reins of government were seized by the seventy-nine-year-old popular Moslem mystic Ayatollah Khomeini, who set up an Islamic republic (see Figure 59.6). The nationalistic Khomeini was strongly anti-American, anti-Soviet, and anti-Israeli. The violence and instability continued and indeed was increased in 1980 by the outbreak of a costly war between Iran and Iraq that lasted until 1988. The Soviet invasions of Afghanistan in 1979 and the Islamic resistance that followed indicate that the turmoil that has marked the Middle East has few boundaries. The Soviet withdrawal from Afghanistan initiated in 1988 offers some hope for greater peace in that country.

6. THE EMANCIPATION OF AFRICA

Africa was the last of the continents to rise against European imperialism, and the history of Africa since the end of World War II has been largely the story of emancipation from European domination (see Map 59.3). France and Great Britain, who held the most territory in Africa, were the first to begin to dismantle their vast empires there.

The end of World War II found France's huge North African empire seething with unrest. Its population, largely Moslem, was agitated by the rampaging Arab nationalism in the Middle East. France, in 1956, granted independence to Morocco and Tunisia. The problem of independence or autonomy for Algeria was much more complex because of the presence there of more than a million French settlers who feared reprisals from the 8 million Moslem Algerians. Efforts to hold back independence resulted in open revolt by Algerians that France could not handle and that helped bring de Gaulle back to power in France. Bowing to the

FIGURE 59.6. Khomeini In 1979 the Shiites' leader, Ayatollah Khomeini, gained power in Iran. As spiritual head of an Islamic fundamentalist movement, Khomeini commanded the passionate allegiance of masses of followers. (UPI/Bettmann Newsphotos)

force of Arab nationalism, in 1962 he granted Algeria independence. Meanwhile, he had granted independence to all the other French colonies, most of which were in Africa, and invited them to form a voluntary union with France. All but one, French Guinea, did so.

Great Britain's experiences in Africa following World War II were quite similar to those of France. All the native populations caught the spirit of na-

Tangier •

CANARY I.
(Spain)

MEDITERRANEAN SEA

MOROCCO
1956

TUNISIA
1956

Cairo •   *SUEZ CANAL*

ALGERIA
1962

LIBYA
1951

EGYPT
1922

• Aswan

RED SEA

MAURITANIA
1960

MALI
1960

Niger R.

NIGER
1960

CHAD
1960

SUDAN
1956

Nile R.

SENEGAL
Dakar • 1960

GAMBIA
1965

GUINEA–BISSAU
1974

GUINEA
1958

UPPER
VOLTA 1960

NIGERIA
1960

DJIBOUTI
1977

SIERRA LEONE
1961

IVORY
COAST
1960

GHANA
1957

ETHIOPIA
(Ancient)

LIBERIA
1847

TOGO 1960
BENIN 1960

CAMEROON
1960

CENTRAL
AFRICAN EMP. 1960

SOMALIA
1960

EQUATORIAL
GUINEA 1968
— Libreville

CONGO
1960

GABON
1960

Congo R.

UGANDA
1962

KENYA
1963

SÃO TOMÉ & PRINCIPE
1975

Brazzaville •
• Kinshasa
(Léopoldville)

ZAIRE
1960

RWANDA
1962

BURUNDI
1962

INDIAN

OCEAN

TANZANIA
1964

ATLANTIC

OCEAN

ANGOLA
1976

MALAWI
1964

ZAMBIA
1964

Zambezi R.

MOZAMBIQUE
1975

MADAGASCAR
1960

NAMIBIA

BOTSWANA
1966

ZIMBABWE
RHODESIA
1965

SWAZILAND 1968

REPUBLIC OF
SOUTH AFRICA
Cape Town • 1961

LESOTHO
1966

CAPE OF GOOD HOPE

0   500 miles

tionalism and turned in resentment against their white masters. Native terror bands, notably the Mau Mau in Kenya, made British life and property increasingly unsafe. In 1957 Great Britain granted independence to its Gold Coast colony, which became the Republic of Ghana. This proved to be the first step in the eventual freeing of Britain's remaining African colonies. During the next few years one after another of Britain's African territories was freed. By 1965 all of Britain's African empire had been dismantled.

In two of the former British African colonies sizable white minorities attempted to continue their domination over the black majorities and in so doing created tensions that became global in scope. In Rhodesia approximately a quarter million whites ruled 6 million blacks. When in 1965 the British government pressed the all-white government of Rhodesia to grant suffrage to blacks, that government declared its independence from Great Britain. Almost immediately the black majority demanded suffrage and civil equality; when it was refused, many of them resorted to guerrilla warfare, aided by neighboring black nations and by the Soviet Union. In 1979 the all-white government, under pressure from the United States, Great Britain, and the United Nations, formed a coalition with a group of moderate black leaders and granted universal suffrage. In the ensuing elections the coalition won a majority in parliament and named a black prime minister. However, the voting was so weighted and unfree that the black guerrillas continued their struggle for complete freedom and equality and an end to white privilege. In 1980 that freedom was gained. Zimbabwe acquired full independence from Great Britain, and Robert Mugabe, one of the principal black guerrilla leaders, was named prime minister.

South Africa was the scene of a bigger and potentially even more dangerous racial conflict.

Map 59.3 AFRICA, 1989 As this map indicates, the vast majority of African nations gained their independence during the 1950s and 1960s. Instability, often stemming from the legacy of Western colonialism, has plagued much of the continent.

The Dominion of South Africa had since 1931 (the Statute of Westminster) been completely free. There the prosperous white minority (4 million whites and 18 million blacks and other nonwhites) clung desperately to its superiority. In 1948 and thereafter, the white minority took severe measures to suppress the increasingly restless black majority and to enforce *apartheid* (racial segregation). When in 1961 several fellow members of the British Commonwealth censured South Africa because of its racial policies, South Africa withdrew from the Commonwealth, taking its large mandate, South-West Africa (Namibia), with it. Under pressure from the angry black majority and from the Organization of African Unity (set up in 1963 by the completely freed African nations), the United Nations, and world opinion, the all-white government of the Republic of South Africa from time to time made token concessions to *apartheid* but steadfastly refused to grant majority rule. During the 1970s and 1980s the situation became increasingly polarized and explosive. White South Africa now remains almost completely isolated in the world, censured because of its racism, a place where massive violence is expected to break out as peaceful alternatives for change are rejected.

The decision of the World War II allies to free oil-rich Moslem Libya from Italian control was consummated in 1951. In 1960 Italy granted independence to Somalia in East Africa, and Belgium gave up the Congo. Finally, Portugal freed her large African colonies in 1975, bringing to an end (with the exception of a few bits of territory here and there) the era of European domination of Africa that began in the fifteenth century.

The granting of independence, of course, did not bring peace and prosperity to the African people. The boundaries of the African states were drawn in many cases quite arbitrarily by nineteenth-century European imperialists sitting around plush green-topped tables in London or Brussels dividing up the spoils. In the Congo, for instance, tribal warfare flamed up immediately after independence. Russian and Chinese Communist agents moved in to exploit the chaos. UN Secretary-General Dag Hammarskjöld lost his life there in a plane accident while trying to mediate the differences. In Nigeria, the Ibos in the eastern region attempted to secede and set up the inde-

FIGURE 59.7. Ethiopian Refugee In recent decades, large areas of Africa have suffered from war, drought , and overpopulation. The results have been malnutrition, disease, starvation, and death. This photo of a starving child at a refugee camp in Ethiopia is all too common. (Michel Philippot/Sygma)

great wealth. Africa's rapidly growing population, dependent for the most part on agriculture, was faced with an increasing threat of hunger and starvation. An unprecedented drought in the huge sub-Sahara region of northern Africa during the late 1960s, the 1970s, and the 1980s brought death by starvation to tens of thousands (see Figure 59.7).

With the freeing of Africa, the expansion of the European world, which began in the fifteenth century, had after five hundred years been very definitely reversed. The non-Western world now challenged the West.

7. LATIN AMERICA

Finally, there remains to be examined a large and populous area of the world which is, in a sense, neither East nor West—Latin America (see Map 59.4). Just as Japan is a highly industrialized nation located in the East, Latin America is *in* but, in many respects, not *of* the West. Its religion and languages are, of course, Western. But the poverty and the illiteracy of the masses, the underdeveloped economy, and the unstable political institutions more closely resemble southern Asia and Africa than Western Europe and the United States.

At the end of World War II the governments of the twenty independent Latin American states were all republics in name. In reality, however, most of them were rightist dictatorships, representing the interests of the well-to-do bourgeoisie, the landowning classes, and the professional military. The Roman Catholic church, which during the nineteenth century had been one of the most powerful rightist forces, had during the twentieth century tended to become much more liberal. In some of the Latin American republics, notably

pendent Republic of Biafra. Thousands died in the futile struggle, and tens of thousands died by starvation. Since the newly freed African people were left without political experience and with few, if any, self-generated political institutions, instability, bloodshed, and rule by military strong men were often the result. Charismatic liberation leaders such as Kwame Nkrumah in Ghana and Jomo Kenyatta in Kenya (where a relatively stable parliamentary system was established) were more the exception than the rule.

Economically the European colonial powers did not leave African countries with a firm basis for balanced prosperity or self-sufficiency. In the early 1980s, Africa's economy was still primarily agricultural, despite a large development of oil and gas production in Libya, Algeria, and Nigeria and a beginning of industrialization (mostly foreign) in the Ivory Coast. Of course, gold and diamond mining in South Africa was still a source of

Map 59.4 LATIN AMERICA, 1989 With one of the world's highest population growth rates and seemingly unbridgeable gaps between the rich few and the poor masses, Latin America has become an area of great political, economic, and social instability. This instability has drawn Western powers, particularly the United States, into Latin American affairs.

UNITED STATES

Ciudad Juárez

Rio Grande

GULF OF MEXICO

MEXICO

Monterrey

Guadalajara

Mexico City

Veracruz

YUCATÁN PEN.

Havana

CUBA

Santiago de Cuba

BELIZE
Belmopan

JAMAICA   Kingston

GREATER ANTILLES

GUATEMALA
Guatemala
HONDURAS
EL SALVADOR   Tegucigalpa
San Salvador
Managua
NICARAGUA

CARIBBEAN SEA

LESSER ANTILLES

San José
COSTA RICA
PANAMA CANAL
PANAMA
Panamá

Barranquilla

Maracaibo

Caracas

Barquisimeto

LAKE MARACAIBO

COLOMBIA

Medellín

Bogotá

Cali

Orinoco R.

VENEZUELA

Georgetown
SURINAM
GUYANA   Paramaribo
FRENCH GUIANA
Cayenne

Quito
ECUADOR

Guayaquil

GALAPAGOS ISLANDS (ECUADOR)

A N D E S

Negro R.

Manaus

Amazon R.

MARAJÓ ISLAND

Belém

Fortaleza

SELVAS

Madeira R.

Xingu R.

Tocantins R.

PERU

Lima

Ucayali R.

B R A Z I L

São Francisco R.

Recife

LAKE TITICACA

Arequipa

BOLIVIA

La Paz

LAKE POOPÓ

Santa Cruz

Brasília

BRAZILIAN HIGHLANDS

Salvador

Belo Horizonte

Antofagasta

Paraguay R.

PARAGUAY

Paraná R.

São Paulo

Rio de Janeiro

Asunción

Santos

Curitiba

PACIFIC OCEAN

CHILE

Córdoba

Pôrto Alegre

Mendoza

Valparaíso
Santiago

Rosario

PAMPAS

URUGUAY

Montevideo

Río de la Plata

ATLANTIC OCEAN

A N D E S

ARGENTINA

Buenos Aires

Bahía Blanca

PATAGONIA

FALKLAND ISLANDS (ISLAS MALVINAS) (U.K.)

⊙ **Capital Cities**

0   500   1000 MILES

Magellan Strait

Punta Arenas

TIERRA DEL FUEGO

Cape Horn

HAITI

DOMINICAN REPUBLIC

VIRGIN ISLANDS (U.S.A., U.K.)

Port-au-Prince   Santo Domingo   San Juan

ANGUILLA (U.K.)

PUERTO RICO (U.S.A.)

ST. MARTIN (FR. & NETH.)

BARBUDA (U.K.)

ANTIGUA

ST. KITTS, NEVIS (U.K.)

MONTSERRAT (U.K.)

GUADELOUPE (FR.)

DOMINICA

CARIBBEAN SEA

MARTINIQUE (FR.)

NETHERLANDS

ST. LUCIA

ARUBA   CURAÇAO   ANTILLES

BARBADOS

BONAIRE

ST. VINCENT AND THE GRENADINES

GRENADA

COLOMBIA

TOBAGO

TRINIDAD & TOBAGO

VENEZUELA

Port-of-Spain

TRINIDAD

Chile, the Church was now actively engaged in liberal social and economic reform movements. Costa Rica was the most democratic of the republics. In Mexico a stable (though primarily a one-party) democratic regime had since 1934 been pursuing a liberal program of economic, social, and educational reforms.

Throughout most of Latin America the poor, illiterate, and ever more numerous masses became increasingly restive after World War II. Many of them turned to communism and were encouraged and supported by the Soviet Union. The United States, on the other hand, supported the rightist governments. In 1954 a military force armed by the United States invaded and overthrew the leftist government of Guatemala. Ten years later a rightist military takeover in Brazil was encouraged and applauded by the United States. In 1948 the twenty Latin American "republics" were persuaded to join the United States in an Organization of American States (OAS) for the purpose of resisting outside (Communist) interference. The Latin Americans were primarily interested in economic aid from the United States and were generally disappointed.

In Cuba the policy of the United States backfired. In 1959 the rightist dictator, Fulgencio Batista, long supported by the United States, was overthrown by the leftist revolutionary, Fidel Castro. Castro began a sweeping program of social and economic reforms including the seizure of property owned by citizens and corporations of the United States. Fumbling efforts of the United States to overthrow the Castro regime drove it into the arms of the Soviet Union. Cuba became a Communist beachhead in the Western Hemisphere.

In 1970 Chile became the first nation in the world to vote into power a Marxist regime. As a result of a split between the conservatives and the moderate liberals, Salvador Allende was elected president (with 36 percent of the vote) and immediately launched a Marxist program. All industrial properties, the biggest of which were owned by United States corporations, were nationalized. The government of the United States determined to destroy the Allende regime. In 1974 the American Central Intelligence Agency admitted that it had spent $11 million bribing Chilean legislators, stirring up labor strife, and supporting right-wing elements. In 1973 the Allende regime was overthrown by the professional military, which set up a rightist military dictatorship. Allende and thousands of his followers were executed.

In 1979 the Sandinistas, a leftist revolutionary force, overthrew the Somoza dictatorship in Nicaragua. During the 1980s, the new government pursued policies of radical social and economic reform, but it was weakened by pressure from the United States and the American-backed contra guerrillas. Although still fragile, this revolutionary regime—with support from Cuba and the Soviet Union—has managed to maintain control in Nicaragua.

In the 1980s Latin America, like much of the non-Western world, remains an area of sharp and dangerous contrasts. Rich natural resources are not being developed and used for the benefit of the rapidly increasing population, which for the most part is poor and illiterate. Increases in productivity seem more than matched by a rapid inflation of prices for goods and services. Great modern cities such as Mexico City and São Paulo, which rival New York and Chicago in size and modernity, stand surrounded by wretched hovels and an economically depressed countryside. Wealth is enjoyed by a small class of large landowners, industrialists, financiers, and governmental officials. The government of the United States supplies financial and technical assistance, but as in other parts of the world, it often supports rightist military regimes that are more interested in retaining their power than in aiding their people. Moreover a massive and mounting debt burden threatens relations with the United States and international financial stability. Even countries bolstered by income from oil production, such as Venezuela and Mexico, seem unable to keep their debts from growing to alarming proportions. Latin America thus remains an area of political instability and potential revolutionary activity, as revealed by the continuing guerrilla activity, coup d'états, mass demonstrations, and revolutions of recent years.

SUGGESTED READING

General

R. von Albertini, *Decolonization* (1971). A good survey.

G. Barraclough, *An Introduction to Contemporary History* (1975). An interpretive analysis of world history in an age of globalism.

C. E. Black, *The Dynamics of Modernization: A Study in Comparative History* (1966). Spans the Western and non-Western worlds.

A. Boyd, *An Atlas of World Affairs,* 7th ed. (1983). Useful, brief reference.

R. Critchfield, *Villages* (1980). Focuses on rural life in non-Western nations.

Asia and Africa

W. Brown, *The United States and India, Pakistan, and Bangladesh* (1972). An excellent brief survey.

F. Butterfield, *China, Alive in the Bitter Sea* (1982). Well-written observations by a journalist.

P. Caputo, *A Rumor of War* (1977). Fine book on the Vietnam War, by a Marine officer who served in Vietnam.

B. Davidson, *Let Freedom Come* (1978). Surveys modern Africa.

C. Fitzgerald, *The Birth of Communist China.* By a leading expert.

I. K. Y. Hsu, *China Without Mao: The Search for a New Order* (1982). A highly respected work.

E. Reischauer, *The Japanese* (1977). A brilliant and highly readable analysis.

The Middle East

W. Polk, *The Elusive Peace: The Middle East in the Twentieth Century* (1980). A fine survey.

J. Voll, *Islam: Continuity and Change in the Modern World* (1982). A brief survey.

Latin America

D. Collier, ed., *The New Authoritarianism in Latin America* (1979). Points to political problems in contemporary Latin America.

W. La Faber, *Inevitable Revolutions: The United States in Central America* (1984). A good background to this tension-filled area.

R. J. Shafer, *A History of Latin America* (1978). A useful survey.

CHAPTER 60

Culture and Society in the Twentieth Century

FIGURE 60.1 Don Eddy, "New Shoes for H," 1973–1974 This painting of a shoe store display in Manhattan reveals several trends of contemporary society and culture. The environment is one of urbanism and commercialism. The effect of the window panes is to show things from different perspectives and to distort. The style, photo-realism, combines technology and the newest painting techniques. (The Cleveland Museum of Art)

As we come closer to the present, it becomes more difficult to see and understand history. Current events—yesterday's headlines—may prove to be historically unimportant. Time must elapse before we can gain the perspective necessary to grasp their significance. This problem of perspective becomes magnified when the focus is not on dramatic political, military, or economic events but, rather, on the more subtle social and cultural developments of Western civilization. However, certain trends can be discerned.

Social, intellectual, and cultural trends have followed two broad patterns since World War I. Until 1945, there was a widespread sense of anxiety, disillusionment, and uncertainty in the West. In part, these feelings were an extension of a trend already developing in the two or three decades prior to World War I, but after World War I it was no longer confined to elite intellectual and cultural circles. It was also a reflection of the social turmoil and sense of decay that spread and deepened after 1914 in frightening ways. Much of the art, literature, philosophy, and even science of the 1920s and 1930s reflected this insecurity, this doubting of established values, this questioning of the future.

Since 1945, social, intellectual, and cultural trends have been marked by a complex mixture of continuity and change. There is still much of the disillusionment and anxiety that characterized the earlier decades of the twentieth century. At the same time, there has developed a new sense of experimentation and productivity, which reflects the lessening of social turmoil and a greater sense of stability compared with the difficult decades prior to World War II.

With these two broad patterns in mind, let us attempt to identify and explore some of the social, religious, intellectual, and cultural developments of Western civilization in the twentieth century.

1. WESTERN SOCIETY IN THE TWENTIETH CENTURY

Demographic and Social Changes

Population in the West has been growing since World War I but at varying rates. The broad pattern shows a slowing down of population growth as societies became more fully modernized, a pattern that has been evident in some countries since the end of the nineteenth century. During the 1940s and 1950s birth rates in most Western countries were relatively high (the "baby boom"), supporting an increase in the population. During the 1960s birth rates started to decline and reverse, to the point in the 1970s and 1980s where several countries have birth rates that are sufficient only to maintain the population or will result in a declining population. Some governments, such as France and East Germany, have begun to encourage larger families with financial aid. Changes in the makeup of the population are also evident. As a result of improved life expectancy, populations in the West have been growing older on the average, giving elderly groups more potential political power and making the social needs of the elderly more pressing.

Perhaps more important than population changes have been changes in where and how people live. Urbanization has increased in recent decades. Large cities have been swollen by migration from rural areas and immigration from southern areas. Northern European cities have absorbed large numbers of people from southern Italy, Greece, Turkey, and Africa, just as cities in North America have been expanded by people from Latin America and Asia. With the people came the traditional urban problems: congestion, overburdened transportation systems, insufficient social services, pollution, crime, and inadequate housing. At times the inner core of great cities has deteriorated and even suffered a decline in population, but this has usually been more than matched by the growth of surrounding suburbs. New shopping and industrial centers have grown up in the periphery of the older cities and even on the fringes of older suburbs. In reference to cities such as Paris, London, New York, and Moscow, it has become more accurate to include the metropolitan areas around them rather than merely the city itself.

In recent decades the most modern societies in the West have been termed "postindustrial," to emphasize the declining importance of traditional manufacturing industries and the growing importance of providing services—often through the use of high technology. The key figures in this postindustrial society are the financiers, technicians, managers, and professionals rather than the industrial entrepreneurs.

There have also been some broad shifts in the social classes that make up Western society. Generally, the shift has been away from rural classes to urban classes, away from traditional industrial jobs to service and white-collar jobs, and away from small firms toward corporate and governmental organizations. Class distinctions remain but are less clear than before. Society has become generally more mobile, both geographically and socially. While birth into wealth and position remains a great advantage, education or technical skill has increasingly become a relatively democratic avenue for social mobility.

In Western Europe and the United States the very wealthy have generally managed to retain their position at the top of society despite efforts in several countries to redistribute the wealth and lessen the gap between rich and poor. Most of the remnants of the traditional aristocracy have disappeared or merged with the wealthy upper middle class. While this elite class retains some protective barriers against intrusion from below and maintains itself through the aid of inheritance, it is increasingly being joined by a newer elite of corporate and governmental managers, successful professionals, and those with high scientific or technological expertise. These people tend to be highly educated, pragmatic, with a stake in the status quo, and yet always threatened by their younger, more recently educated competitors in the corporate or bureaucratic hierarchy.

Just below this upper middle class is the bulk of the middle class. Made up primarily of middle- and lower-level managers in corporate and governmental bureaucracies, those who hold salaried white-collar jobs in services, and professionals in a growing number of fields, this class has grown substantially. Entrance into this class is gained primarily through education, specialization, and technical expertise.

Since the end of World War II the industrial working class has generally seen an improvement in its standard of living and, at least until the 1960s, relative job security. Yet its ranks were thinning as the traditional industrial base eroded, forcing many to become service workers or enter the bottom level of white-collar employment. As economic problems became more acute in the 1970s and early 1980s, industrial workers faced unemployment matched only by pre–World War II statistics and declines in real income that had to be compensated for by more married women entering the paid work force. As they have grown more affluent, the distinction between them and the lower middle class has lessened: The incomes, diets, housing, leisure-time activities, and often even political affiliations of the two classes are becoming similar. Yet the working class has remained distinct in many ways; it has fewer opportunities for social mobility and greater frustrations at the workplace, as manifested by numerous strikes.

In many countries there remains a core of inner-city slum dwellers. They are usually without regular jobs, often marked by race or ethnic origin, and subject to the worst problems of urban life. In recent years there have been disturbing signs. This care of often homeless urban poor is growing.

The decline of rural populations has continued, with variations in each country. Generally agricultural productivity has been increasing, lessening the need for people on the farms. Many rural people have moved into the cities, leaving a small percentage of the population to grow food for the rest and for export. Those who adjusted to changing rural life—by mechanizing, enlarging their land holdings, joining cooperatives, and specializing—have enjoyed an uneven, but generally rising standard of living. But there remains a core of rural poor who have not adjusted to the agricultural changes since World War II or who have fallen victim to economic forces beyond their control. Rural life has also become less isolated with the spread of highways, cars, telephones, radio, and television.

In Eastern Europe social changes followed the model established in Russia since the revolution in 1917. The traditional landed aristocracy disappeared rapidly as their lands were taken away and redistributed or nationalized. Large collectivized farms arose. Eastern European states nationalized the factories, the banks, the commercial houses, and the large retail outlets of the middle class. The distinctions between urban classes were lessened as the state standardized basic housing, social ser-

FIGURE 60.2. Family Life
The changing roles of women and men within the family are reflected in this photo of domestic life. (Jim Harrison/Stock, Boston)

vices, consumption, and even leisure activities. Nevertheless, a new privileged order arose. High-level party and governmental leaders, certain professionals, and the cultural elite have enjoyed more access to consumer goods, improved housing, better educational opportunities, and greater political influence than the rest of the population. This social inequality within these Eastern European socialist societies has been a source of discontent and turmoil in recent years.

The Family

Since World War I, and in particular over the past few decades, the family in the West has become smaller, more mobile, and less stable. Although people still tend to marry within their social, religious, and ethnic groups and with an eye toward economic considerations, emotional attraction continues to grow as the primary consideration in mate selection. In the past two decades sexual fulfillment has been added as an increasingly important condition for marriage and its continuation. The development of new methods of contraception, particularly the contraceptive pill in the 1960s, and the accompanying acceptance of the idea of contraception (and, to a lesser extent, abortion) has given women and men greater sexual freedom and choice over marriage and childbearing. Since the baby boom of the immediate post–World War II years, married couples have fewer children on the average. The nuclear family—the couple and its children—has become more geographically mobile, and ties with extended family members such as grandparents, uncles, aunts, and cousins have become more distant. Other institutions, such as the school, the university, peer groups, family courts, family therapists, child psychologists, and day-care centers, have grown to take over functions that the family used to perform more exclusively.

The increase in premarital sex, cohabitation, gay life styles, divorce, and nontraditional family arrangements and a recent trend toward declining marriage rates and postponing marriage and childbearing have led many to question the viability of the modern family. The single-parent household and the childless household are gain-

FIGURE 60.3 French Women's Movement The women's movement since the 1960s has been international. Here French women demonstrate for equal pay with men for equal work. (Martine Franck/ Magnum)

ing acceptance. The rate of divorce has risen sharply since World War II, particularly since the 1960s. Yet the family is not disappearing, as some critics have argued. Rather its form and its functions are evolving, as are the roles that its members are expected to play, particularly women.

Women

Some of the most important social changes have involved the role of women within the family and in society as a whole. In both World War I and World War II women assumed jobs and responsibilities previously thought beyond their "legitimate sphere," but with the return of the soldiers those women were pressured to return to their more traditional domestic roles. However, the long-run trend in the twentieth century, and particularly since the 1950s, has been for women to enter the paid working force in a greater variety of jobs. In particular, married women have been moving out of their middle-class roles as housekeepers, child rearers, and supporters of their income-producing husbands. The female wage-earning work force is no longer dominated by the young and single, as it was earlier in the twentieth century. With a growing life expectancy (now over seventy-five years in most Western countries), a

relatively early age of marriage and childbearing, and an infusion of appliances to aid in housekeeping chores, more women have been turning to "second careers" at middle age, often involving a return to school to acquire new skills. Over 50 percent of all married women now work outside the home in the United States, a dramatic increase from pre–World War II levels and a pattern that has generally prevailed in the West. Women, married and unmarried, are moving into jobs that were once the almost exclusive domain of men, from the legal and medical professions to all varieties of blue-collar work. However, discrimination based on gender is far from over. Women remain underrepresented in most higher-paying, higher-status occupations and still earn only between 60 and 80 percent of men's salaries.

The women's liberation movement, gaining force since the 1960s, has made many women more conscious of their common concerns (see Figure 60.3). Generally, this movement demands that women no longer be oppressed or considered second-class citizens, whether it be in their political rights, the wages they earn, the positions they hold, or the attitudes they or their society share. This movement has struggled not only to open political, economic, and social life to all, regardless of sex, but also to change stereotypical portrayals of femininity and common assumptions about differences between the sexes that contribute to barriers facing women. These changes are of great potential significance to women and by necessity, to men (see Figure 60.2). As with most fundamental historical changes, they will take a long time to have full effect. The changes women are initiating will require numerous subtle changes in the way we raise our children and the messages our culture transmits about gender and sex roles.

Youth and Education

One of the institutions most affected by social changes, and in particular changes in the family, has been education. Schools have been expected to adapt to social and economic change and take up functions that were once handled by parents as part of child rearing. Schools are expected to assist children who have emotional, social, and family problems as well as purely academic problems.

With the growing demands for democratization of educational opportunities, universities have had to open their doors to more than the traditional elite. The number of students attending college and going on for advanced degrees has increased dramatically since World War II. Universities have had to change their curriculums to fit the new demands of a mobile society and a modern economy. The strains on universities were particularly great in the 1960s, when students in many Western nations combined discontent with the university with attitudes critical of the values and behavior of their parents' generation. Students attacked the lack of humaneness, the restrictive behavior and values, the social inequities, and the competitive impersonality of the traditional adult world of their parents represented by the large, bureaucratized, impersonal university. They criticized governmental policies and rallied around issues such as opposition to the Vietnam War and support for national liberation movements in the non-Western world. The numerous demonstrations and disruptions of university life often spread into the surrounding communities, involving clashes with police and other public authorities. The most dramatic confrontations took place in France in 1968, where a student revolt threatened to overturn the government, particularly when students gained the sympathetic but temporary support of workers. The government eventually retained control, but numerous reforms of universities in France and elsewhere were instituted in the late 1960s and early 1970s. Since then student activism has diminished. Students have veered away from the traditional liberal arts curriculum and have become more concerned with preparing for careers in an increasingly competitive economic environment. Programs and majors in fields such as business administration, computer science, and the professions have proliferated.

Social Welfare

After World War I and particularly after World War II, trends toward increased governmental responsibility for social welfare accelerated. Most countries increased their traditional social security benefits for unemployment, retirement, sickness, and old age. Government expenditures for education expanded. In some countries, particularly Great Britain, steps were taken to ensure that medical services were available to all. New governmental programs were established to provide family allowances, maternity grants, and low-income housing.

In general, governments were being held responsible for providing a floor of social and economic well-being below which their citizens should not be allowed to fall. The expanded role of the state in providing a large array of social services within an economic system that still remained substantially capitalistic has been termed the creation of the "welfare state." The degree of involvement varied in each country. Governments of Communist nations in Eastern Europe assumed the most control over social and economic matters, but the services they could provide were limited by the economic well-being of the nation. Among the nations of Western Europe the Scandinavian countries have generally gone the furthest in providing social services for its citizens. The United States, with its own particular problems and aversion to programs that hint of socialism, lags behind in governmental provision of social services.

Of course, these services come at a price. Taxes

FIGURE 60.4. Areas such as Africa and Latin America have gained increasing attention within the Catholic Church in recent decades. Here, in one of his many trips outside of Europe, John Paul II rides in a motorcade in Zaire. (UPI/Bettmann Newsphotos)

have risen to pay for them. Governmental bureaucracies have grown to administer them. Moreover, critics question the quality of some of the services provided, particularly medical services. Yet once established, such social programs are rarely reversed—although the Reagan administration in the United States during the 1980s made efforts to do just that.

However efforts by governments to promote social welfare have not brought to an end persisting social problems. In addition to poverty, the high rate of crime and the proliferation of drug abuse in recent decades, particularly in the United States, attests to the sense of alienation and dissatisfaction in many Western societies. In the 1980s the spread of AIDS challenges the ability of government and science to solve difficult new problems.

2. RELIGION AND THEOLOGY IN THE TWENTIETH CENTURY

Christianity remains an important religious force in Western civilization despite the secularization

that has taken place during the twentieth century. However, in the long run, Christian churches as institutions have continued to suffer a decline in influence in the West, particularly since World War II. Strenuous efforts were made to restore some of the lost unity of Christendom to enable the Christian church to face its problems with a united front. In 1948 leaders of hundreds of Protestant and Orthodox denominations met in Geneva and set up the World Council of Churches. The most spectacular step in this direction was taken by Pope John XXIII (1958–1963), who called the Second Vatican Council (1962–1965) in the spirit of Christian tolerance and unity. Although John XXIII died during the first year of the council and was succeeded by Paul VI (1963–1978), who was a less vigorous innovator, the Second Vatican Council introduced an ecumenical spirit into the Catholic church and showed a willingness to modernize the ritual and discipline that had been formalized by the Council of Trent in the sixteenth century. When Paul VI died in 1978, the College of Cardinals elected John Paul I, a man of great personal charm, who lived less than a month. The new pope, John Paul II, a Pole, was the first non-Italian pope since the early sixteenth century. Relatively young, forceful, and knowledgeable, John Paul II has traveled extensively, particularly to politically controversial areas such as Africa, Central America and Poland (see Figure 60.4). He has managed to convey an image of renewed dynamism and activism in the Catholic church. Nevertheless, he has been conservative in matters of faith and morals, refusing to liberalize Church policy toward theological doctrines, the priesthood, the family, and sex.

Theology in the Western world during the twentieth century for the most part reflected the materialism of the age and the influence of existentialist philosophy. Strong efforts were made to update Christian theology by making it a more secular philosophy. Paul Tillich (1886–1965), a German Protestant who spent his later years in the United States, conceived of God as "ultimate truth" and "inner reality." Such traditional terms as *original sin, salvation, forgiveness, immortality,* and *atonement* were useful symbols under his pen, actually referring to personal and social ethics. Harvey Cox (1929–) of Harvard University, in his widely read *The Secular City* (1965), defined Christianity as a continuing social revolution. During the decade of the 1960s the phrase "God is dead" enjoyed popularity among quite a number of divinity school teachers and students. The phrase apparently had a wide variety of meanings to its various users, including the belief that God is dead. Numerous religious cults sprang up, some of them quite wealthy and some violent, offering companionship and certainty to many of the lonely and the losers in this materialistic, competitive, and perplexing world.

On the other hand, a few powerful voices called for a return to an enlightened orthodox Christianity, notably the neo-Calvinists Karl Barth (1886–1968) in Switzerland and Reinhold Niebuhr (1892–1971) in the United States. God, they said, created the universe and runs it for his holy purpose, but selfish pride separates human beings from God. Only the Christian religion can remove that pride and bring men and women into God's purpose. Jacques Maritain (1882–1973) in France called for a return to the teachings of St. Thomas Aquinas. These learned theologians contributed dignity to the continuing claims of traditional Christianity.

3. TWENTIETH-CENTURY SCIENCE

After World War I, most scientific research was still carried out by individuals or small groups of scientists in a university setting. There was a sense of separation between theoretical and applied sciences, between research carried out by the best scientific minds and the later application of their discoveries by engineers or technicians. After World War II, that pattern would be modified by closer ties between science and technology and by a new infusion of funds for scientific research by government and big business (see Figure 60.5). Scientists tended to work in organized teams, in larger research laboratories with extremely expensive and sophisticated equipment, and with specific goals in mind. These trends are most clear in the physical sciences, particularly physics.

In the two decades after World War I, the main thrust in physics was to continue the probing of the atom, which was begun in the nineteenth century, to discover the truths concerning the nature of matter. The results tended to be disillusioning. Albert Einstein had undermined the Newtonian world of physical stability with his relativity theory (see p. 643). A more shattering blow was delivered by Max Planck (1858–1947). Although he published his quantum theory in 1900, its full impact was not realized until the decades following World War I. According to this theory, energy is not transmitted in a steady, measurable stream, as had long been supposed, but in little leaps or packets (quanta), and the behavior of subatomic particles is so irregular and complex that the ultimate secrets of nature can never be fathomed by objective observation. In 1919 Ernest Rutherford (1871–1937) opened the world of subatomic particles and the possibility of changing the structure of atoms by bombarding them with subatomic particles. The sense of relativity and uncertainty in physics was furthered by Werner Heisenberg (1901–1976), who in 1927 formulated the "principle of uncertainty." He argued that any model or measurement of atoms was inherently approximate and relative.

Since World War II, teams of physicists have used huge, powerful, expensive accelerators to explore the subatomic world to a far greater degree than was possible before the war. Astrophysicists

FIGURE 60.5 Moon Walk In July 1969, man walked on the moon. The United States' Apollo 11 moon mission is an example of the powerful combination of government and science. (NASA)

have combined new computer and radio telescope technology to expand our understanding of the universe. At the same time, many of these scientists have been employed by government and industry to create new, more destructive weapons of war or products, such as computer chips and superconductors, of economic importance to our consumer society.

The most exciting discoveries in the biological sciences were in the field of genetics. In 1953 the nature of the complicated DNA molecule, which controls the pattern of all living things, was discovered. It is assumed that by tampering with this molecule new forms of life may be created, and that given characteristics in all living things, including humans, can be controlled. Recent research with gene splitting and genetic engineering gives truth to this assumption.

The most beneficial discoveries in the field of biological science during the twentieth century

have been those that prevent and cure human ailments. Viruses were isolated and their role in the cause of many diseases, including infantile paralysis, influenza, and the common cold, was recognized. Vaccines were developed to combat successfully the infantile paralysis virus and a number of others—but the common cold still plagues most of humanity. During the late 1920s and the 1930s penicillin and sulfa drugs were discovered. These "miracle drugs" kill or control the bacteria causing many human infections. Since World War II, drugs have been found useful in treating mental illness, and artificial and transplanted kidneys and hearts have saved or lengthened many lives.

The chief drawback in the application of these wonderful discoveries has been their high and continually soaring cost and the shortage of trained personnel to administer them. Many nations, Great Britain and Sweden among the first, have recognized the enormous importance of public health by developing comprehensive programs of national health insurance. Communist regimes, of course, have always made the practice of medicine a public rather than a private matter.

The social sciences have continued to emphasize the application of the methods being used so successfully in the natural sciences—rigorous empirical research, inductive and deductive reasoning, conclusions couched in the value-free language of relativism and probabilities. In recent decades, three new approaches have been used in several of the social sciences. The first is an extension of previous methods—quantitative research aided by computers and newly developed statistical tools. Computers have enabled researchers to work with massive quantities of materials and factors. Statistical tools have sharpened the probability or predictability of their conclusions. The second is structuralism, which stresses the rules or the forms of behavior rather than the specific content. The third is relativism, which rejects universal values and assumes that societies and cultures should be viewed within their own time, place, and context.

Of all the social scientists, the sociologists and the anthropologists have been the most optimistic and energetic. Like all other social scientists, they attempted to apply the scientific method to the study of human behavior. Max Weber (1864–1920) of Germany set up ideal types or models as a method of scientifically analyzing various sociological problems—a method that has been widely used ever since. Emile Durkheim (1858–1917) established a sociological tradition emphasizing the use of statistics for analyzing social behavior. Karl Mannheim (1893–1947), a refugee from Nazi Germany to Great Britain, developed a sociology of knowledge. He argued that ideas are related to and influenced by social forces to a much greater degree than had been suspected. Anthropologists tended to move from their earlier measurements of skulls and other physical features to the concept that differing cultures are based essentially on differing ways of interpreting experience and adapting to the environment. Claude Lévi-Strauss, perhaps the most influential anthropologist in recent decades, used a structuralist perspective to analyze the forms and rules of culture.

Between World War I and the 1950s psychology continued to be strongly influenced by Freudian theory and practice, which emphasized the irrational, the unconscious, the sexual, and the aggressive elements in human thought and behavior. Behaviorism was also growing, and by the 1960s it overshadowed Freudianism. In the past two decades so many theories, approaches, therapies, and subdisciplines have proliferated within psychology that no single trend can be identified as dominant. Perhaps the most promising discoveries in recent years have been in physiological psychology. With so many people turning inward for answers and with secular explanations for human behavior deemed so important, psychology remains a field of growing influence.

Of all the social sciences, economics has taken most advantage of computer-aided quantitative research and sophisticated statistical tools. It is also the social science that most directly influences policy. Both governmental and private institutions rely on economists for the decisions they make. Underlying the quantitative research and statistical tools used by economists are more fundamental economic theories. Since the 1930s Keynesian economic thought has been most influential in countries with capitalistic or mixed economies. In 1936, in the midst of the Great Depression, John Maynard Keynes (1883–1946) published *The General Theory of Employment, Interest and Money,* advocating government regulation of the capitalistic system. He claimed that in times of recession the government should increase the supply of money in circulation by lowering interest rates and by deficit spending on public works. In times of inflationary boom it should restrict the money supply by raising interest rates and by other means. Liberals, not only in Keynes' native Britain but throughout the capitalistic world, accepted his theories, as indeed did many conservatives. But by the late 1970s and early 1980s it appeared that Keynesian theory could not account for many economic problems, particularly the combination of inflation and economic stagnation (with accompanying unemployment) that many termed "stagflation." Some theorists have called for greater governmental controls over wages and prices as well as general economic planning; others have attacked governmental involvement in the econ-

FIGURE 60.6. The development of tiny computer chips such as this has resulted in vast changes in science, business, and industry. (Charles Feil/Stock, Boston)

omy as doing more harm than good.

Probably the most important new tool for both the natural and social sciences is the computer (see Figure 60.6). The computer first became a tool of significance in the 1940s. By the 1950s and 1960s it was becoming linked with modern technology in a variety of ways, with strong impact on the sciences and in the economy. With developments in computer technology, particularly miniaturization, the use of computers proliferated in almost all fields of science during the 1970s and 1980s. Its ability to store and manipulate information has made the computer a necessity rather than a luxury for most scientists. Yet it is still no more than a tool: The scientist must feed the computer the right information, ask the useful questions, and interpret the answers.

4. TWENTIETH-CENTURY CULTURE

Philosophy

Philosophical thought in the twentieth century has been dominated by four trends, all of which can be traced back to the period just before World War I. The first was a wave of attacks on nineteenth-century optimism and rationalism that expanded the ideas set forth earlier by philosophers such as Friedrich Nietzsche in Germany and Henri Bergson in France (see p. 653). The most widely read of these post–World War I philosophers was Oswald Spengler. In his *Decline of the West* (1918), Spengler argued that the West was in decline, that World War I was the beginning of the end. This sense of decay and crisis appeared in many other works, most notably in José Ortega y Gasset's *Revolt of the Masses* (1930), which lamented the decline of liberal civilization and the rise of "mass man" in the West.

The second trend, which has clearly prevailed in Great Britain and the United States, is a combination of analytical philosophy and logical positivism. Analytical philosophy was first developed by Alfred North Whitehead (1861–1947) and Bertrand Russell (1872–1970) of Great Britain on the eve of World War I. The outstanding philosopher of logical positivism (or logical empiricism) was Ludwig Wittgenstein (1889–1951). Both analytical philosophy and logical positivism spurned any concept that could not be rationally and mathematically expressed. Under the influence of these doctrines, philosophy became highly technical, focusing on the exact meaning of words and logical relationships rather than the broad and ethical questions that traditionally concerned philosophers.

The third trend, which became more dominant on the European continent, is existentialism. Existentialism has its roots in the disenchantment of the late nineteenth century and the environment of anxiety resulting from the two world wars, the Great Depression, and the tensions of the Cold War. Existentialism drew heavily from Friedrich Nietzsche, who argued that there were no absolutes when he said "God is dead." Existential philosophy was also influenced by the mid-nineteenth-century Danish theologian, Søren Kierkegaard, who rejected systematized and institutionalized Christianity in favor of personal inspiration and individual commitment. In Germany during the 1920s Martin Heidegger and Carl Jaspers developed aspects of existentialist philosophy. Thereafter, the center of existentialist thought shifted to France. The most influential existentialist philosopher has been Jean-Paul Sartre (1905–1980). He argued that ultimately there is no meaning to existence and no final rights or wrongs. Individuals are born and simply exist. Individuals are free and responsible for the decisions and actions they take in life. Individuals must establish their own standards and their own rules, and each must take responsibility for living up to them. In the end, one simply dies.

The fourth trend, which has been a school of philosophy of varying strength, is Marxism (see pp. 565–566). Marxism has emphasized historical determinism, ethical relativism, and social meaning behind philosophical concepts. During the 1920s and 1930s, it grew in influence in several academic circles and disciplines. Since World War II its influence has waxed and waned, and its doctrines have been modified in several ways. But on the whole, it has remained influential as a philosophical and historical perspective in a variety of disciplines.

Literature

The literature of the twentieth century, like the philosophy, is essentially an outgrowth and continuation of the literature of the late nineteenth century. A number of the great realistic writers of the early twentieth century lived and wrote until the middle of the century. The realism that had shocked many Victorians was succeeded by the more starkly naked naturalism. The focus tended to shift to a more subjective point of view and to the feelings, uncertainties, and unconscious motives of individuals.

In English-speaking Europe, James Joyce (1882–1941), an Irish expatriate in Paris, Virginia Woolf (1882–1941), an English novelist and critic, and T. S. Eliot (1888–1965), an American expatriate in London, developed the stream-of-consciousness technique. They placed words and thoughts out of sequence, providing new insights into the psyche with dramatic effect. This method clearly reflected the introspection of Freudian psychology.

In Germany, Franz Kafka (1883–1924) depicted the alienation and frustrations of an intellectual in the World War I era. The haunting, ambiguous quality of his fiction symbolizes the uncertainties and fears of his age. Most of his work was published after his death, and he enjoyed wide popularity only after World War II. Hermann Hesse (1877–1962) also reflected the uncertainty and sense of alienation in Germany during the World War I era in his novels. His writings, particularly those stressing a youthful and psychologically insightful search for meaning in a life always threatened by despair, became particularly popular after World War II. Perhaps the towering figure of twentieth-century German literature was Thomas Mann (1875–1955). His style and content were more traditional than that of Kafka or Hesse, always stressing a reverence for human beings in the often distressing environment of Mann's lifetime.

In France, Marcel Proust (1871–1922) developed introspective writing to new depths in his influential *Remembrance of Things Past*. In seven volumes of exquisitely polished prose, he subjects to withering psychological analysis the remnants of French noble society and the vulgar social-

FIGURE 60.7 Picasso's "Guernica" This large mural in black and white by one of the greatest artists of the twentieth century captures some of the worst features of the century—war, terror, brutality, disjointedness, lack of direction, and despair. Guernica was a small Spanish town destroyed by the German air force during the Spanish Civil War. (Museo Nacional del Prado)

climbing *nouveau riche* bourgeoisie who were trying to imitate the nobility. During the 1940s and 1950s, Albert Camus (1913–1960) popularized existentialism in his novels and plays—stressing the plight of the individual seeking understanding and identity in an amoral and purposeless universe. During the 1960s writers such as Alain Robbe-Grillet and film directors such as François Truffaut and Jean-Luc Godard made France the center of the *nouvelle vague* (new wave) in literature and film, stressing experimentation and imaginative techniques.

In the Soviet Union, Boris Pasternak (1890–1960) wrote in the grand manner of Tolstoy and Dostoyevski. His most well-known novel is *Doctor Zhivago,* which traces life in Russia before, during, and after the Bolshevik Revolution in 1917. More recently, Alexander Solzhenitszen (1919–), living in the United States since his expulsion from the Soviet Union in 1974, has written novels critically depicting life in the Soviet Union during the Stalinist era.

In the United States Sinclair Lewis (1885–1951), much like Theodore Dreiser, ridiculed both the hypocritical and "puritanical" bourgeoisie and the stupid, vulgar masses. Babbitt, Elmer Gantry, and Arrowsmith, deflated heroes in Sinclair Lewis' novels by those titles, became stereotypes of typical Americans in the minds of thousands of untypical American readers of books. Eugene O'Neill (1888–1953) wrote plays in which the dramatic tension was maintained by psychological conflict (like those of Anton Chekhov—see p. 655) rather than development of plot and action. Ernest Hemingway (1898–1961) was an existentialist, entertaining his readers with his crisp and sophisticated prose. William Faulkner (1897–1962), with great depth and artistry, tore away the veil woven by civilization to conceal the violent and animallike nature of ordinary people. He extended the complex stream-of-consciousness technique.

The Fine Arts

The fine arts in the Western world in the twentieth century, like the philosophy and the literature, have proceeded generally along the guidelines laid down by the artists and writers of the late nineteenth century—disenchantment, rejection of tradition, search for new values, and experimentation. These characteristics have become intensified by the materialism and the uncertainties of the twentieth century.

Without a doubt, the most gifted and influential painter of the twentieth century was Pablo Picasso (1881–1973) (see Figure 60.7). A Spaniard, he emigrated to Paris as a young man. There he was influenced by the French postimpressionists (see pp. 656–657). In order to penetrate the surface and reveal the inner reality of things, Picasso would take his subjects apart—arms, heads, violin parts—and rearrange and distort them for maximum effect. Early in the century, at about the same time that young Whitehead and Russell were proclaiming their analytic philosophy based on mathematics, Picasso introduced cubism into the world of painting (see Figure 52.1). This technique was an effort, suggested by Cézanne, to demonstrate the solidity of the material universe by portraying the geometric composition of objects—spheres, cones, and cylinders. Cubism suggests the twentieth century's obsession with science.

Another prominent style of twentieth-century painting came to be called surrealism, whose chief proponents were Max Ernst (1891–1976) (see Color Plate 28), a German who later moved to the United States, and Salvador Dali (1904–1989) (see Color Plate 29), a Spaniard who lived many years in the United States. The surrealists, under the influence of Freud and his psychoanalytical techniques, attempted to express their imagination uncontrolled by reason and to suggest the activities of the subconscious mind, whether dreaming or awake. Picasso and Matisse (see p. 656), who were really laws unto themselves, painted many canvases in the surrealist style.

A third popular twentieth-century style of painting was expressionism, which had its origin in northern Europe, particularly Germany (see Figure 55.2). Its chief proponent was Vasili Kandinsky (1866–1944), a Russian who came to live in Germany. The expressionists, motivated by inner necessity, attempted to express freely their emotional reactions rather than the representation of the natural appearance of objects, resorting to abstraction and to violent distortion of color and form.

In recent decades, artistic styles such as pop art, op art, and photo-realism (see Figure 60.1) have continued to proliferate, often crossing boundaries between commercial and high art, between representational and abstract art (see Color Plate 30), and between traditional and nontraditional mediums (see Color Plate 31). All these styles reflect the artistic and the speculative mind of the Western world in the twentieth century—disenchantment, rejection of tradition, search for new values, and a turning inward for inspiration.

Twentieth-century architecture has been dominated by the functional style (see Figure 60.8), developed in Germany by Walter Gropius' Bauhaus school, in France by architects such as Le Corbusier, and in the United States by Louis Henry Sullivan (see p. 657). Sullivan's most illustrious student, and perhaps the most well-known architect of the twentieth century, was Frank Lloyd Wright (1869–1959). Like his teacher, Wright believed that function is the sole purpose of architecture. He further insisted that form should conform to the materials used and to the setting. He made brilliant use of the cantilever (a projecting member supported at only one end) to achieve striking horizontal lines and an unobstructed spaciousness. These effects were made possible by the tensile strength of steel. Wright combined artistic skill with a Shavian scorn for traditional values and institutions. The most spectacular monuments of functional architecture are, of course, the great bridges and skyscrapers, most of them in the United States.

Twentieth-century music, too, is for the most part a continuation and development of styles formulated during the period 1871–1914. Richard Strauss (1864–1949) and Igor Stravinsky (1882–1971), two of the originators of modern music, lived far into the twentieth century. During the course of the century, music in the Western world became increasingly dissonant, atonal, and experimental. These qualities probably found their ultimate composer in the Viennese Arnold Schoenberg (1874–1951), who abolished key, revolutionized the conception of melody, and replaced the seven-tone scale with one of twelve tones. Recent decades have witnessed the introduction of a universe of everyday and electronically produced sounds into music.

FIGURE 60.8   Pompidou Center of Art and Culture, Paris   The controversial Pompidou Center of Art and Culture, built in the center of Paris during the 1970s, carries the idea of functionalism in architecture to an aesthetic extreme. Structural and functional elements of the building show prominently on the outside, creating a vast open space on the inside. (Bernard Annebicque/Sygma)

Popular Culture

The twentieth century has witnessed an explosion of popular culture. Several developments account for the huge variety and availability of popular literature, art, and music. There has been a tremendous expansion of communications—from cheap newspapers and paperback novels to radio, cinema, and television. Numerous and large public facilities—from museums and concert halls to stadiums—have been built. The rising level of education has stimulated greater interest in cultural activities. Increasing affluence and leisure time among the urban classes has enabled more people to take advantage of cultural offerings.

The products of popular culture are usually distinct from those of elite culture, but there has been some blurring of the lines between the two in recent decades. In cinema, an almost endless stream of what critics consider undistinguished but popular films are produced year after year. Yet cinema is perhaps the most original art form produced during the twentieth century (see Figure 60.9). The works of filmmakers such as Ingmar Bergman in Sweden and Federico Fellini in Italy reveal the potential of cinema as a sophisticated, creative, artistic medium. In music there is much that distinguishes the dissonant, atonal music of Arnold Schoenberg from rock and roll performed

FIGURE 60.9 Fritz Lang's "Metropolis"   This eerie, futuristic scene from Fritz Lang's film "Metropolis" (1925) illustrates the overwhelming power of urban architecture and technology as well as the potential of the cinema as an artistic medium. (National Film Archive, London)

by groups such as the Beatles, but the distinction blurs with jazz, a development of America's black culture emphasizing sophisticated improvisation and rhythm. In art, most of the abstract or expressionistic paintings of the twentieth century remain outside popular tastes, but what was once elite art, such as the romantic or realistic paintings of the nineteenth century, or even avant-garde, such as impressionism, is now extremely popular.

5. PROBLEMS OF THE PRESENT AND FUTURE

Despite many real gains that have been made since the end of World War II, several persisting and growing problems in Western civilization contribute to a spreading sense of pessimism. Experience in the 1970s and 1980s shows us that eco-

FIGURE 60.10. Oil spills are one of the threats to the environment posed by modern industry. Here sea lions are trapped in oily waters off Alaska after a 1989 spill. (Reuters/Bettmann Newsphotos)

nomic growth can no longer be taken for granted; inflation, unemployment, and declining personal incomes for many have created social discontents that governments seem impotent to master. Moreover, the price we pay for economic growth and modernization seems to have been rising in recent years. Industrialization, urbanization, and affluence have strained our natural resources. Our air, our fresh water, and even our seas are becoming more polluted (see Figure 60.10). Depletion of the protective ozone layer and a heating up of the atmosphere threaten us. Our land is becoming blighted by concrete, tasteless commercial development, and poisonous wastes. The relentless march of technology with its accompanying urbanization has brought many creature comforts to the masses, but it has robbed millions of their manual skills and social contacts and lost people in the lonely crowd. At the higher levels of industry, corporate individuals have tended to lose their independence and individual identities. Government has expanded the social services it provides but that has not created a greater sense

of inclusion in modern society; rather, a sense of alienation seems to persist or even grow.

War, of course, has always brutalized those who are engaged in it, but the wars of the twentieth century have vastly exceeded those of the past in size and destructiveness. The threat of obliteration from nuclear war hangs over the post–World War II generations unabated as major powers refine their nuclear arsenals and other countries develop their own nuclear weapons. In other ways, violence seems to threaten us more than ever, whether it be from crime, terrorism, or potentially explosive smaller wars.

There is a growing awareness that the relatively affluent West can no longer ignore the non-Western areas of the world, with their pressing needs and growing demands. Clearly, the West must change its relationship to the non-Western world, but it is not clear how. There is a sense among many that the traditional values of the Western world are being eroded, but it is not clear what is replacing these values.

All these problems now weigh upon the West

and are not likely to go away in the foreseeable future. In some ways Western civilization and its institutions, which have been so long developing—the family, the governments, the courts of law, the churches, the traditions of social and moral behavior—are being severely tested. While problems of the present always seem more difficult than those of the past, the consequences of not dealing with today's problems are likely to be catastrophic. Whether and how Western civilization handles these challenges remains to be seen.

SUGGESTED READING

General

M. Crouzet, *The European Renaissance Since 1945* (1971). A balanced account emphasizing society and culture.

S. Hoffmann and P. Kitromilides, *Culture and Society in Contemporary Europe* (1981). Good collection of recent essays.

Western Society in the Twentieth Century

S. de Beauvoir, *The Second Sex* (1962). A classic, crucial analysis of women.

A. Cherlin, *Marriage, Divorce, Remarriage* (1981). Interpretive analysis of the American family.

E. Shorter, *The Making of the Modern Family* (1978). Well-written, controversial.

E. Wolf, *Europe and the People Without History* (1982). A provocative interdisciplinary analysis.

Religion and Theology in the Twentieth Century

S. P. Schilling, *Contemporary Continental Theologians* (1966). A good survey of modern theology.

Twentieth-Century Science

J. Ziman, *The Force of Knowledge: The Scientific Dimension of Society* (1976). Excellent analysis and bibliography.

J. Galbraith, *Age of Uncertainty* (1978). Writing lucidly for the nonspecialist, Galbraith argues for tight economic controls.

Twentieth-Century Culture

M. Biddiss, *Age of the Masses: Ideas and Society Since 1870* (1977). A fine intellectual history.

W. Barrett, *Irrational Man* (1958). A good treatment of existentialism.

M. Marrus, ed., *Emergence of Leisure* (1974). An important collection.

A. Neumeyer, *The Search for Meaning in Modern Art*. A useful guide for the nonspecialist.

J. Passmore, *A Hundred Years of Philosophy* (1968). A good, concise survey.

H. Read, *A Concise History of Modern Painting* (1974). Excellent brief survey.

E. Salzman, *Twentieth Century Music: An Introduction*. A good survey.

R. Stromberg, *After Everything: Western Intellectual History Since 1945* (1975). An interpretive, scholarly analysis.

R. Williams, *Communications* (1976). Analyzes the media.

Problems of the Present and Future

R. Heilbronner, *An Inquiry into the Human Prospect* (1980). Excellent analysis of our problems and our attitudes toward those problems.

C. Lasch, *Culture of Narcissism* (1978). A broad, controversial, insightful analysis of American life.

RETROSPECT

At the end of World War II devastation and disorganization were the rule rather than the exception. Most nations of Europe were so weakened that they had to rely on one of the two new superpowers that had emerged from World War II: the United States and the Soviet Union. Soon, even the unity of the victorious allies, which included the United States and the Soviet Union, proved too fragile to last. Deep-seated discord between these respective leaders of the non-Communist and Communist worlds broke out into the Cold War. Europe became divided into two camps—one of democratic capitalism (though often with elements of socialism mixed in) led by the United States, the other of communism modeled and led by the Soviet Union. This division of Europe and the broader Cold War struggle would dominate international policies for decades to come. Yet, despite the destruction of World War II, the emergence of the dominating superpowers, and the disunity brought about by the Cold War, European nations recovered, expanded their economies, and enjoyed relative political stability during the following decades. Problems in the 1970s and 1980s do not diminish from that record; rather, they indicate that Western civilization must face and deal with new and previously ignored difficulties. One way that nations have attempted to solve common problems has been through regional integration and internationalism, but the results have been mixed at best.

In the decades following World War II, France, England, Belgium, the Netherlands, and other Western nations lost most of their colonial empires. The new and old nations of the non-Western world struggled to get on their feet and assert themselves in an environment marked by Cold War rivalries, deep-rooted internal discord, and the disruption caused by the incomplete spread of Western values and institutions to their lands. In different ways, Japan and China emerged as leading economic and political powers in the Far East. The struggle between Hindu and Moslem in India, Pakistan, and Bangladesh and the wars in Southeast Asia made the British and French (and, later, American) withdrawals from southern Asia problematic. The Middle East has been marked by a series of wars and disruptions as well as the emergence of a new power bloc based on wealth from oil production. The long-lasting lack of peace between Israel and most of its neighbors, violence in divided Lebanon, and the war between Iran and Iraq suggest that this area of the world will remain explosive for the foreseeable future. Africans face tremendous difficulties in creating unity in nations artificially created by colonial powers and burdened by harsh economic conditions. The political instability of most African nations attests to these difficulties. Most Latin American nations have for decades been dominated by a wealthy elite and right-wing authoritarian governments (supported, and usually staffed, by the military). As the area's population grows, so does the contrast between the few haves and the mass of havenots. Revolutions, guerrilla activities, and political upheavals indicate that stability is likely to be the exception rather than the rule in Latin America.

The most significant social, intellectual, and cultural changes in Western civilization during the twentieth century are more difficult to pinpoint than the concrete political and economic developments. For the most part, the social, intellectual, and cultural developments have been a continuation of trends already underway by the end of the nineteenth century. Western society became more urbanized as it adjusted to the demands of continuing economic modernization. Women changed their roles and the perception of themselves, a reflection of some of the changes occurring within the basic unit of Western society: the family. Christian churches continued to have difficulty adjusting to a changing, secularizing, scientific world. Intellectual and cultural trends reflected the richness of Western life as well as the often discouraging problems encountered by the West since the end of the nineteenth century. New problems have been added to the persisting problems, testing the spirit and ability of Western civilization in disturbing ways.

INDEX

Page references in *italic* refer to illustrations, maps, and their captions.

Adbul Hamid II, 622

Absolutism, royal, age of, 417–496; challenge to, 429–440; decline of, 426; dominance of France, 419–428; Eastern Europe and the rise of Prussia and Russia, 441–451; Enlightenment, 486–494; overseas colonization and competition for empire, 452–463; religion, 424; Scientific Revolution, 477–485; society, faith, and culture, 464–485; Stuart, 430–432, 434, 435

Académie des Sciences, 479

Acceleration, Law of, 481

Acheson, Dean, 750

Act of Settlement, 436

Act of Uniformity, 434

Act of Union, 436

Action/reaction, law of, 481

Adams, Abigail, 506

Adams, John, 504, 506, 508

Adams, John Quincy, 536

Adenauer, Konrad, 735

Adrianople, 538; Treaty of, 523

Afghanistan, Soviet invasions and withdrawal, 731–732

Africa: emancipation of, 757–760; European penetration of, 455, 459–460; 1989, *758*; scramble for, 623–626

African Unity, Organization of, 759

Afrika Korps, 716, 718

Agriculture: collectivization of, 680–681; early American, 500; revolution in, 466–467, 556; Soviet, 680–681

Aida, 575

AIDS, 770

Aix-la-Chapelle: Congress of, 536; Treaty of, 444

Albania, 741

Albertus Magnus, 570

Alexander, Harold, 716

Alexander I, Tsar, 534, 536, 542

Alexander II, Tsar, 601–602

Alexander III, Tsar, 602

Alexandra, 676

Algebra, 484

Algeciras, international conference at, 625

Algeria, 625, 734, 757

Allende, Salvadore, 762

Amati family, 475

American Civil War, 585, 609–611

American Federation of Labor, 612

American Indians. *See* Native Americans

American Revolution, 499–509; causes and conduct of, 502–504; colonial society, 500–502; and democratization of society, 504–505; launching the new nation, 506–508

American States, Organization of (OAS), 762

Amiens, Peace of, 525, 526

Amsterdam, 439

Analytic geometry, discovery of, 484

Analytic philosophy, 774

Anarchism, 634

Anatomy, 483

Ancient Mariner (Coleridge), 571

Andropov, Yuri, 740

Anesthesia, discovery of, 644

Angelus, The, 575

Anglicanism, 430–431, 501

Anglo-Dutch alliance, 461; wars, 433, 435, 461

Anne, Queen, accession of, 437, 481

Anthrax, 644

Anthropology, 773

Anti-labor-union laws, 633

Anti-Semitism, 597, 602, 646, 652–653, 690–691, 694, 712

Antisepsis, 644

Apartheid, 759

Appeasement, 704–706

Aquinas, Thomas, 556, 570

Arab League, 754

Arafat, Yasir, 756

Architecture: functional, 657–658; nineteenth century, 657–658; seventeenth and eighteenth, 473–475, twentieth century, 777

Aristocracy; *see* Social Classes and Structure

Arizona, annexation of, 608

Arkwright, Richard, 557

Art: Dutch, 440; modern, 655–657, 682–683, 776–777; Romantic, 573–575; seventeenth and eighteenth century, 472–475

Artisans; *see* Social Classes and Structure

Aryan myth, 652, 690–691

Asbury, Francis, 451

Asia, 1989, 748

Asiento, 461

Assembly line method, 632

Assembly of Notables, 513

Assignats, 516, 520

Associations Law, 646

Astronomy, 479–481

Atlantic Charter, 713, 715

Atomic bomb, 718–719, 745

Atomic theory, 625

Attlee, Clement, 728, 733

Auerstdt, 526

Augsburg, League of, 426

Ausgleich (compromise) of 1867, 603

Austerlitz, Battle of, 526

Australia, 627, 700

Austria, 518, 521, 524, 529; authoritarianism in, 695; Concert of Europe, 536–538; Congress of Vienna, 534–536; conservatism in, 540; fall of Austro-Hungarian empire, 667, 672; German takeover of, 731; independence of, 731; Napoleonic wars, 526–528; and nineteenth century national movements, 603–604; revolution of 1848, 550–553; war with Prussia, 590–591; and World War I, 663–665, 667; *see also* Austro-Hungary, Hapsburgs

Austria-Hungary, 603–604, 663–667, 672

Austrian Succession, War of, 444, 462

Austro-Prussian War, 590–591

Authoritarian regimes, right-wing, 687; in Eastern and Southern Europe, 695; in Japan, 695–697

Axis powers, 694–695, 697; years of triumph for, 709–712

Aztecs, 455–456

Bach, Johann Sebastian, 475
Bacon, Francis, 482, 483
Bacteria, discovery of, 484
Bakunin, Mikhail, 634
Baldwin, Stanley, 700
Balfour Declaration, 754
Balkan peninsula and World War I,
    603–604, 663–665
Balzac, Honoré de, 654
Bangladesh, 752
Bank of Amsterdam, 439
Bank of France, 525
Banks, 439, 583
Barebones Parliament, 433–434
Barnes, Harry Elmer, 673
Baroque style, 470, 473, *474*, 495
Barth, Karl, 771
Bastiat, Frédéric, 564
Bastille, storming of, 514, *515*
Batista, Fulgencio, 762
Battle of Borodino, 528
Battle of Britain, 711
Battle of Concord, 503
Battle of Coral Sea, 716
Battle of El Alamein, 716
Battle of Friedland, 526
Battle of Jena, 526
Battle of Jutland, 666
Battle of Leipzig, 530
Battle of Lexington, 503
Battle of Leyte Gulf, 719
Battle of Liegnitz, 445
Battle of Magenta, 586
Battle of Marengo, 525
Battle of Marne, 666
Battle of Midway, 716
Battle of the Nile, 524
Battle of Plassey, 462
Battle of Russia, 718
Battle of Saratoga, 504
Battle of Somme, 666
Battle of Stalingrad, 716
Battle of Tannenberg, 666
Battle of Ulm, 526
Battle of Verdun, 666
Battle of Waterloo, 530, 534
Bauhaus school, 777
Beatles, the, 779
Beccaria, Cesare, 489
Beckmann, Max, *689*
Beethoven, Ludwig van, 575
Belgium, 548–549, 666, 709
Bell, Alexander Graham, 632
Bentham, Jeremy, 564

Bergman, Igmar, 778
Bergson, Henri, 653
Berlin airlift, 730
Berlin blockade, 730
Berlin-Rome-Tokyo Axis. *See* Axis
    powers
Berlin-to-Bagdad railroad, 600, 622,
    665
Berlin Wall, *725*, 731
Berlinguer, Enrico, 736
Bernstein, Eduard, 634
Bessemer process, 630
Bethlen, Stephen, 695
Beyond Good and Evil, 653
Biafra, 759–760
Bicycle, 632
Big Four, *669*
Bill of Rights: American, 508; En-
    glish, 435, 436
Bismarck, Otto Eduard Leopold,
    589–592; 599–601, 646, 663
Bizet, Alexandre, 575
Black slaves. *See* Slavery
Blanc, Louis, 550, 565
Blanqui, Louis-Auguste, 634
Blitzkrieg, 709
Blood, structure of, 484
Blücher, Marshal Gebhard von,
    530
Blum, Leon, 701, *702*
Boer War, 623, 625
Bohemian Brethren, 470
Bolivar, Simon, 530
Bolsheviks, 602; in power, 677–680;
    rise of, 677
Bombay, 455
Book of Common Prayer, 434
Boris Gudonov, 573
Borodino, Battle of, 528
Bossuet, Bishop, 422,424
Botha, General Louis, 625
Boulanger, George-Ernest Jean
    Marie, 597
Bourbon dynasty, 420, 494
Bourbon Restoration, 538
Bourgeois monarchy, 549
Bourgeoisie, French, 511–512; nine-
    teenth century middle class,
    637
Boxer Rebellion, 620
Boyle, Robert, 483, 484
Brahe, Tycho, 479–480
Brahmin caste, 457
Brahms, Johannes, 658

Bradenburg, 441–443; *see also* Prus-
    sia
Brandenburg Gate, *725*
Brandt, Willy, 735
Brazil, 530
Brest-Litovsk, Treaty of, 668, 678
Brezhnev, Leonid, 739–740
Briand, Aristide, 598
Britain. *See* Great Britain
Britain, Battle of, 711
British Empire, 626–627, 699–700
Brothers Karamazov, The, 655
Browning, Robert, 653
Broz, Joseph. *See* Tito
Bulgaria, 663, 668, 711
Burke, Edmund, 534, 569
Burns, Robert, 472
Burschenschaften, 539
Bush, George, 739
Byron, Lord George Gordon, 538,
    569, 571

Cabinet of ministers, English, 429,
    436–437
Caetono, Marcelo, 736
Cahiers, 513
Calculus, invention of, 481, 484
Calcutta, 455
Calhoun, John C., 607
California, annexation of, 608
Cambodia, 754
Camp David agreements, 756
Camus, Albert, 776
Canada, 462
Canning, George, 536, 542
Cape of Good Hope, 455
Carbonari, 553
Carlos, Juan, 737
Carlsbad Decrees, 539
Carlyle, Thomas, 652
Carmen (Bizet), 575
Carnegie, Andrew, 612
Carnot, Lazare, 520
Carson-Pirie-Scott Department
    Store, *657*
Cartels, 633
Carter, Jimmy, 738, 756
Cartesian dualism, 483
Cartwright, Edmund, 557
Caste system, 457
Castlereagh, Lord Robert Stewart,
    534
Castro, Fidel, 737, 762

Catherine the Great, 448–450, 493, 495
Catholicism. *See* Christianity; Papacy; Roman Catholic church
Cattle breeding, improved, 467
Cavaliers, 432
Cavour, Camillo Benso, Count di, 585–587
Central Europe, revolution of 1848, 550–553
Central Intelligence Agency, 762
Central powers, 665
Ceylon, 455
Cézanne, Paul, 656
Chamber of Deputies, *551*, 597
Chamberlain, Houston Stewart, 652, 690
Chamberlain, Neville, 700, 706, 710
Champlain, Samuel de, 420, 453
Charles I, King of England, 431–433
Charles II, King of England, 425, 434–435, 436, 479
Charles VI, Emperor, 444
Charles X, King of France, 538, 539
Charles XII, King of Sweden, 447, 450
Chartism, 548, 562
Chateaubriand, Francois-René, 572
Checks and balances, system of, 492
Chekhov, Anton, 655, 776
Chemistry, 483, 631
Chernenko, Konstantin, 740
Chiang Kai-shek, 715, 746–747
Chiaroscuro, 473
Child labor, 548, 560, 562
Children, 467–469, 635, 637, 765, 767–769
Chile, 762
China, 753; early European influence on, 459; exploitation and awakening of, 618–620; rise of Communist, 746–750; war with Japan, 696–697, 715
Chopin, Frederic, 575
Christian Democratic party: German, 735–736; Italian, 736
Christian IV of Denmark, 413
Christianity, 645–649; *see also* Papacy, Reformation, Roman Catholic church
Churchill, John, 437
Churchill, Winston, 711, 713, 715–716, 728, 733
Cinema, 778

Circulatory system, discovery of, 483
Citizen King, 459
City, movement to, 635–636
Civil Constitution of the Clergy, 516
Civil Rights Movement, 738
Civil War, American, 585, 609–611
Clarendon, Earl of, 434, 435
Clarendon Code, 434
Class. *See* Social class
Class struggle, 566
Classicism, 470, 495; in art, 472–473; in music, 475–476
Clay, Henry, 607
Clayton Antitrust Act, 613
Clemenceau, Premier Georges, 669
Clive, Robert, 462
Cobden Treaty, 585
Colbert, Jean Baptiste, 424, 455, 479
Cold War, 728–732
Coleridge, Samuel Taylor, 571
Colonial American society, 500–502
Colonialism. *See* Imperialism
Combination Acts, 542, 561
Cominform (Communist Information Bureau), 703
Comintern (Communist International), 684, 730
Committee of Public Safety, 520
Common Market, 734, 742–743
Commonwealth, 433
Communism, 699
Communist International, 684
Communist Manifesto, 565, 566, 633
Computers, 772, 774
Comte, Auguste, 645
Concert of Europe, 536–538, 584
Concord, Battle of, 503
Concordat of 1801, 525
Condé, 425, 426
Conditioned reflex, 644
Condorcet, Marquis de, 489
Confederation, Articles of, 506
Confederation of the Rhine, 526
Congo, 759
Congress of Vienna, 534–536, 623
Conquistadors, 456
Conservatism, militarism, and nationalism in Eastern Europe, 1871–1904, 599–604
Conservatism, nineteenth-century, 533–543, 599–604
Constable, John, 573

Constitution of the United States, 492, 506–508
Constitutional Convention, *499*
Constitutionalism, 417, 430–440, 494–495
Continental Congress, 503–504, 506
Continental System, 528
Contraception, 767
Conventicle Act, 434
Cooper, James Fenimore, 609
Cooperatives, 633
Copernicus, Nicolaus, 479–481, 485
Coral Sea, Battle of, 716
Cordon Sanitaire, 684
Corn Laws, 548, 563
Corneille, 471
Corot, Camille, 573
Corporate State, Italy, 688
Corporation Act, 434
Corporations and monopoly, growth of, 612–613, 632–633
Cottage industry, 467, *468*
Cotter's Saturday Night, The, 571
Cotton gin, 557, 609
Council for Economic Mutual Assistance, 730
Count of Monte Cristo, The (Dumas), 573
Court of High Commission, 431
Court of Star Chamber, 431
Cox, Harvey, 771
Craxi, Bentino, 736
Crédit Foncier, 583
Crédit Mobilier, 583
Crime and Punishment (Dostoyevski), 655
Crimean War, 584
Critique of Pure Reason (Kent), 570
Cromwell, Oliver, 432–434, 495
Cromwell, Richard, 434
Crop rotation, 466, 467
Cruikshank, George, *533*
Cuba, 731, 737, 738, 762
Cuban missile crisis, 731, 738
Cubism, 656, 777
Cultural revolution, 749
Culture and society, twentieth-century, 764–781; demographic and social changes, 765–766; family, 767; fine arts, 776–777; literature, 775–776; philosophy, 774–775; popular culture, 770–771; Science, 771–774; social welfare,

Culture and society (*continued*)
769–770; women, 768–769;
youth and education, 769
Curie, Marie, 642
Curie, Pierre, 642
Czechoslovakia, 706, 728, 741

Daily Mail, 651
Daimler, Gottlieb, 631
Daladier, Edouard, *705*, 706
d'Alembert, Jean le Rond, 489
Dali, Salvador, 777
Dalton, John, 642
Danton, Georges Jacques, 518, 519,
521
Danzig, 706
d'Artois, Comte. *See* Charles X
Darwin, Charles, 643, 646
Das Kapital (Marx), 565
Daumier, Honoré, *551*
David, Jacques Louis, *510*, 523
David Copperfield (Dickens), 654
Dawes, Charles G., 690
Debs, Eugene V., 634
Debussy, Claude, 658
Declaration of Independence, 492,
503
Declaration of Indulgence, 435
Declaration of Rights of Man, 514
Decolonization and non-Western
world, 744–763; Africa, 757–760;
Communist China, 746–750; Ja-
pan, 745–746; Korean War, 750–
751; Latin America, 760–762;
Middle East, 754–757; southern
Asia, 751–754
Deffaud, Madame du, 491
de Gaulle, Charles, 710, 734, *735*,
757
Deism, 491
Delacroix, Eugene, *573*, 574
Democratic institutions, spread and
reform of, in Western Europe,
1871–1914, 595–599
Democratic West, paralysis of, be-
tween World Wars, 698–707; ap-
peasement 704–706; breakdown
of League of Nations, 703–704;
British Empire, 699–700; chal-
lenge of 1920s and 1930s, 699;
France, 700–701; outbreak of
World War II, 706–707; United
States, 701–703
Demoiselles d'Avignon, Les, 650

Deng Xiaoping, 749–750
Denmark, 590, 598, 633, 709
Descartes, René, 439, 482–484
Descent of Man, The, 643
Despotism, enlightened, 493
Détente, 731
Devil's Island, 593
d'Holbach, Baron, 489
*Dialogue on the Two Chief Systems of
the World*, 481
Dickens, Charles, 654
Diderot, Denis, 489, 570
Diem, Ngo Dinh, 753
Diesel, Rudolf, 631
Diesel engine, 631
Diet, Polish, 449
Diplomatic Revolution, 444
Directory, French, 521
Discourse on Method, 483
Disenchantment, philosophy of, 652
Disraeli, Benjamin, 548, 595
DNA molecule discovered, 772
Doctor Zhivago (Pasternak), 776
Dollfuss, Engelbert, 695
Dominion status, 627
Don Giovanni (Mozart), 476
Doré, Gustave, *561*
Dostoevsky, Feodor, 654–655
Drama, French, 470–471
Dreiser, Theodore, 654, 776
Dreyfus Affair, 597, 646
Dual Monarch of Austria-Hungary,
603, 663
Dubĉêk, Alexander, 741
Dulles, John Foster, 731
Dumas, Alexander, 573
Dunkirk evacuation, 709
Durkheim, Emile, 773
Dutch East India Company, 438, 455
Dutch Netherlands. *See* Netherlands
Dutch War, 426
Dutch West India Company, 455
Dynamo, 630

Eakins, Thomas, *641*
East Germany. *See* German Demo-
cratic Republic
East Indies, 455, 458–459
Eastern and Southern Europe, au-
thoritarian regimes in, 695
Eastern Europe, conservatism, mili-
tarism, and nationalism, 599–
604; and the rise of Prussia and
Russia, 441–451; disappearance

of Poland and the decline of
Sweden and the Ottoman Empire, 448–451; early Hohenzollerns, 442–443; emergence of
Prussia, 444–445; Russia before
Peter the Great, 445–447; Russia
under Catherine the Great, 448;
Russia under Peter the Great,
447–448; since World War II,
738–742
Ebert, Friedrich, 690
Economic liberalism, doctrine of,
563–564
Economic life, early modern times,
424, 430, 438, 442, 460–461, 500;
nineteenth century, 556–558,
583, 600–601, 611–612, 630–633;
twentieth century, 666–667,
680–681, 688, 694, 700–703, 730,
732–743
Economic Mutual Assistance, Coun-
cil for, 730
Eddy, Don, *765*
Edict of Nantes, 410, 420, 421, 425,
442–443
Edison, Thomas A., 630
Education, modern, 651; nineteenth
century, 596, 598; twentieth
century, 682, 767–769
Egypt, 712, 754–756
Einstein, Albert, 642–643, 771
Eisenhower, Dwight D., 718
El Alamein, Battle of, 716
Elba, 530
Electric motor, 616
Electricity, nature of, 625
Elements of the Philosophy of Newton,
489
El Greco, 472, 473
Eliot, George (Mary Ann Evans),
654
Eliot, T. S., 775
Elizabeth, Russian Tsarina, 444
Elizabeth I, Queen of England,
430
Emerson, Ralph Waldo, 572
Emigrés, 514, 518
Emile, 490
Ems dispatch, 592
Enclosures, 467
Encyclopedia, 489–491
Energy, nature of, 642
Engels, Friedrich, 565, 633
England: challenge to absolutism,

430–437; civil war, Commonwealth, and Protectorate, 432–434; colonization in New World, 453; competition for overseas empire, 460–462; early Stuart absolutism, 430–437; Glorious Revolution, 435–437; overseas expansion in seventeenth and eighteenth centuries, 453, 455; restoration, 434–435; *see also* Great Britain
English East India Company, 455, 462
Enlightened despotism, 493
Enlightenment, 486–496; concepts, 487–488; enlightened despotism, 493; *philosophes*, 488–490; political and economic aspects, 491–492; and religion, 491; women and the social context, 490
Environmental concerns, 780
Erie Canal, 557–558
Ernst, Max, 764
Essay Concerning Human Understanding (Locke), 488
Essay on Population, 563, 643
Estates, 511–512
Estates General, 422, 512
Ethiopia, 704
Europe: Concert of, 536–538; conservatism, militarism, and nationalism in eastern, 599–604; 1810, 527; 1815, 537; 1923, 670–671; 1942, *714*; postwar recovery of, 725–743; spread and reform of democratic institutions in western, 595–599
European Coal and Steel Community, 742
European Economic Community (Common Market), 734, 742–743
European Integration, 742–743
Evans, Mary Ann. *See* Eliot, George
Evolution, theory of, 643, 646
Existentialism, 775
Expressionism, 777

Fabian Society, 634
Factory system, 558
Factory workers, exploitation of, 559–560
Falklands War, 733

Family: colonial American, 501; nineteenth century, 562, 634–639; seventeenth and eighteenth century, 467–469; twentieth century, 767–768
Far East, European penetration of, 455, 457–459
Faraday, Michael, 630
Farben, I. G., Industries, 633
Farms, collective, 680–681
Fascism, 687–695; causes of Nazism, 693; Mussolini, 687–689; Nazi Germany, 694–695; rise of Hitler and National Socialism, 690–691; triumph of Hitler, 691–692; Weimar Republic and rise of, 689–690
Fathers and Sons, 560
Faulkner, William, 776
Faust, 572, *573*
Fawcett, Millicent, 639
Fay, Sidney Bradshaw, 673
Federal court, system of, 508
Federal Reserve Banking System, 613
Federalism, 507
Federalists, 507–508, 607
Fellini, Federico, 777
Feminism, 639, 768–769
Femmes, Savants, Les, 471
Ferdinand, Archduke Francis, 665
Ferdinand I, King of Naples, 536, 551
Ferdinand VII, King of Spain, 530, 536
Ferry laws, 646
Fertilization of soil, 466
Fielding, Henry, 472
"Final Solution," 712
Five Mile Act, 434
Flaubert, Gustave, 654
Fleury, Cardinal, 426
Flying shuttle, 557
Foch, Ferdinand, 668
Ford, Gerald, 738
Ford, Henry, 632
Fort Duquesne, 462
Fourier, Charles, 565
Fourth French Republic, 734
Fox, George, 470
France: absolutism and religion, 424–425; Bourbon restoration, 538–539; Colbert and economy of, 424; competition for over-

seas empire, 460–462; decline of French absolutism, 426–428; decolonization of empire, 752, 757; democratic institutions in, 596–598; dominance of, 419–428; Enlightenment, 486–494; era of Napoleon, 523–532; Fifth Republic, 734–735; First Republic, 519, 550; Fourth Republic, 734; Franco-Prussian War, 592; French Revolution, 510–522; Louis XIV and his government, 422; Louis XIV's wars of aggression, 425–426; and new world, 453–454, 462; and paralysis of West, 700–701; postwar recovery, 734–735; revolution of 1848, 550; rise of, under Henry IV, Richelieu, and Mazarin, 420–422; second empire of Napoleon III, 582–585; Second Republic, 550; Third Republic, 595–598; twentieth century, 700–701, 734–735; Versailles, court of, 422–424; World War I, 661–674; World War II, 709–712, 719; *see also* French Revolution
Francis of Lorraine, Holy Roman Emperor, 444
Franco, Francisco, 694, 736–737
Franco-Prussian War, 592–593
Frankfurt Assembly, 552
Frankfurt, Treaty of, 592
Frazer, James, 647
Frederick I, King of Prussia, 443
Frederick II, the Great, of Prussia, 441, 444–445, 493
Frederick the Great with Voltaire, *489*
Frederick William, the Great Elector, 442–443
Frederick William I, King of Prussia, 443
Frederick William III, King of Prussia, 534
Frederick William IV, King of Prussia, 552, 587
French and Indian War, 462. *See also* Seven Years' War
French East India Company, 455
French-German Coal and Steel Authority, 742
French Republic, Second, 550, 582
French Revolution, 510–522; break-

French Revolution (*continued*)
down of Old Regime, 511–513;
constitutional monarchy, 515–
516; foreign war and failure of
moderate regime, 516, 518–519;
origins of, 517; reaction and the
rise of Napoleon, 521; triumph
of radicals and Reign of Terror,
518–521; triumph of Third Estate, 513–514
Freud, Sigmund, 644–645, 773
Friends, Society of, 470
Fronde, 422
Fulton, Robert, 558
Fur Trade, 454

Gadsden Purchase, 608
Gainsborough, Thomas, *464*, 473
Galilei, Galileo, 478, 481, 484
Gallican Liberties, 424
Gambetta, Léon, 596
Gandhi, Indira, 752
Gandhi, Mohandas K., 751
Gandhi, Rajiv, 752
Garibaldi, Giuseppe, 581, 586
Gasperi, Alcide de, 736
Gast, John, *606*
Gauguin, Paul, 656
General Confederation of Labor, 633
General Security, Committee of, 520
*General Theory of Employment, Interest
and Money, The*, 773
Généralitiés, 421
Genetics, 772
Geneva, Conference of 1955, 731
Genghis Khan, 445
Geocentric universe, 479
Geoffrin, Madame, 491
George I, King of England, 437
George II, King of England, 437
George III, King of England, 503
German Confederation, 535, 539,
589, 590
German Democratic Republic (East
Germany), established, 730,
740–741
German East Africa, 624
German Empire under Bismarck,
599–601
German Federal Republic, 730, 735–
736
German Unification, 587–592
Germany, 676, 678; appeasement of,

704–706; Berlin crisis, 729–730;
causes of Nazism, 693; German
Empire under Bismarck and
Kaiser Wilhelm II, 599–601;
Nazi, 695–696; restoration and
repression in, 539–540; revolu-
tion of 1848 in, 552–553; rise of
Hitler and National Socialism,
690–691; triumph of Hitler, 691–
692; Weimar Republic, 689–690;
West, 730, 735–736; World War
I, 660–674; World War II, 706–
707, 708–721; *see also* Holy Ro-
man Empire
Ghana, 459
Ghosts (Ibsen), 654
Gibraltar, 461
Giolitti, Giovanni, 598
Girondins, 519–520
Giroux, Charles, *611*
Giscard d'Estaing, Valery, 734–735
Gladstone, William E., 548, 595–596
Glastnost, 740
Gleaners, The, 573–574
Glorious Revolution of 1688, 426,
435–437
Gobineau, Comte de, 652, 690–691
Godard, Jean-Luc, 776
"God is Dead," 771, 775
Goebbels, Paul Joseph, 690, 694
Goering, Hermann, 680
Goethe, Johann Wolfgang von, 472,
572
Golan Heights, 755
Gold Coast, 759
Golden Bough, The (Frazer), 647
Golden Horde, 445
Gömbös, Julius, 695
Gompers, Samuel, 612
Gonzales, Felipe, 737
Gorbachev, Mikhail, 740
Gorky, Maxim, 655
Gotterdammerung (Wagner), 575
Gounod, Charles Francois, 575
Grand National Union, in Britain,
548, 562
Gravitation, laws of, 462
Great Britain: Act of Union, 436;
American Revolution, 499–509;
appeasement of Germany, 704–
706; British empire, 626–627,
699–700; competition for over-
seas empire, 461–462; conserva-

tism in, 540–542; decolonization
and, 751–752, 754, 759; imperialism, 618, 620, 622–627; industrial revolution, 556–558, 561–
564; Napoleonic wars, 524–530;
New World, 453–454; political
and social reform in, 547–548;
postwar conferences and settle-
ment, 726–728; spread and re-
form of democratic institutions,
595–596; twentieth-century,
699–700, 733; World War I, 662–
674; World War II, 706–721; *see
also* England
Great Depression, 691, 699, 703
Great Fear, 514
Great Leap Forward, 747
Great Purges, 680–681
Greece, modern, 538, 569, 711, 730,
736–737
Greek revolt, 538, 569
Grenouillere, La, 655
Grenville Act, 502
Grey, Earl, 547
Grieg, Edvard, 658
Gropius, Walter, 777
Gross Clinic, The, 641
Grotius, Hugo, 439
Guarneri family, 475
Guatemala, 762
Guernica, 776
Guizot, Francois, 549, 550
Gulliver's Travels (Swift), 472
Gustavus Adolphus, 450

Haeckel, Ernst, 646
Hals, Franz, 440, 473
Hamilton, Alexander, 508
Hammarskjöld, Dag, 759
Hammersmith, The, 657
Handel, George Frederick, 475–476
Hanoverians, 437
Hapsburgs, 540, 551; competition
with Prussia, 444–445
Harding, Warren G., 613, 702
Hardy, Thomas, 654
Hargreaves, James, 557
Harmsworth, Alfred, 651
Harvey, William, 483, 484
Hausaland, 459
Haussmann, Baron Georges-Eugen,
583

Hayden, Franz Joseph, 476
Health insurance, national, 773
Hearst, William Randolph, 652
Hegel, Georg Wilhelm, 570, 652
Heidegger, Martin, 775
Heine, Heinrich, 572
Heliocentric universe, 479
Henry IV, King of France, 420–421, 423, 494
Herder, Johann Gottfried von, 569, 572
Heroic Head, 656
Herriot, Edouard, 701
Hess, Rudolph, 690
Hesse, Hermann, 775
Himmler, Heinrich, 694, 712
Hindenburg, Paul von, 666, 691
Hinduism, 457
Hiroshima, destruction by atomic bomb, 718–719
History of France, 573
Hitler, Adolph, 687; appeasement policy toward, 704–706; extermination of Jews, 694, 712; and Nazi Germany, 694–695; rise of, 690–691; suicide of, 719; triumph of, 691, 692; and World War II, 709–719
Hobbes, Thomas, 484
Ho Chi Minh, 752, 753
Hohenzollerns, 442–445, 495
Holbach, Baron d', 489
Holocaust, 708, 712, 721
Holy Alliance, 536, 542
Holy Synod, 447
Hong Kong, ceded to Britain, 618
Hoover, Herbert, 703
Horthy, Miklos, 695
House of Commons, 420, 430, 437, 546
House of Lords, 433
Hoxha, Enver, 741
Hubertusburg, Peace of, 444
Hugo, Victor, 573, 653
Huguenots, 420, 421, 425, 443
Hull, Cordell, 704
Hunchback of Notre Dame (Hugo), 573
Hungary, 551, 695, 711, 730, 740; *see also* Austria-Hungary
Huss, John, 470
Huxley, Thomas, 646
Huygens, Christiaan, 484

Ibsen, Henrik, 654
Illiteracy, 651
Il Risorgimento (The Resurgence), 585
Il Trovatore, 575
Imperialism, 615–628; in Africa, 1914, *624*; in Asia, 1840–1914, *618–619*; British Empire, 626–627; causes for new, 616; competition for Near and Middle East, 622–623; disagreements among historians about, 617; emergence of Japan, 620–622; exploitation and awakening of China, 618–620; legacy of, 627; scramble for Africa, 623–626; United States, 613
Imperialism satirized, *626*
Impressionism, 655–656
In Memoriam, 653
Incas, 455–456
Independence, Declaration of, 492, 503
Independents, religious, 432–433, 434, 436
India, 455, 627; Anglo-French clashes in, 462; impact of Europeans on, 457–458; independence of, 733, 751–752; nineteenth century, 625–627
Indians. *See* Native Americans
Indochina, 734. *See also* Vietnam
Indonesia, 752
Indulgence, Declaration of, 435
Industrial bourgeoisie, 559
Industrial Revolution, 555–567; course of, 556; economic liberalism, 563–564; factory system, 558; German, 600–601; Marxian socialism, 565–566; new economic and social thought, 563–566; population growth and urbanization, 558–559; second, 630–633; social changes, 558–562; social classes, 559–562; social institutions, 562; Soviet Union, 602, 680–681; technology and transportation, 556–558; United States, 611–613; Utopian socialism, 564–566
Industrial society, social classes, and women, 629–639; growth and movement of population, 634–

636; second Industrial Revolution, 630–633; social classes, 636–638; women's roles and experiences, 638–639; working-class organizations and ideologies, 633–634
Inertia, 481
Infanticide, 403
Inness, George, 573
Intendants, 421, 422
Interdependence, global, 723–782
Intermediate-Range Nuclear Forces Treaty, 732
Internal-combustion engine, 631
Internationalism, 566
International organizations, 742–743
International Red Cross, 584
Interstate Commerce Act of 1887, 613
Intimations of Immortality (Wordworth), 571
Intolerable Acts, 503
Iran, 738, 756–757
Ireland, 433, 436, 596
Irish Free State, 700
Iron Chancellor. *See* Bismarck, Otto
Iron Curtain, 728
Iron Law of Wages, 563
Irving, Washington, 609
Isabey, Jean B., *535*
Isenheim Altarpiece, *367*
Isolationism in U.S., 700–701
Israel, 754–756
Italian Communist party, 736
Italian National Society, 586
Italy: alliance with Germany, 694; fascism in, 687–689; invasion of Ethiopia, 704; postwar, 736; restoration and repression in, 540; revolution of 1848, 553; unification of, 585–586; and World War I, 663, 665, 667; World War II, 711, 719; *see also* Mussolini, Benito
Ivan IV, Tsar (the Terrible), 445

Jackson, Andrew, 607
Jacobins, 518, 519
James, William, 653
James I, King of England, 430–431

James II, King of England, 435
Jamestown, 453
Jansen, Cornelius, 424
Jansenists, 424–425
Japan: attack on Pearl Harbor, 715;
    emergence of, 620–622; policy
    of isolationism, 459; postwar,
    745–746; triumph of authoritari-
    anism, 695–697; war with Rus-
    sia, 602, 621–622; and World
    War II, 712–719
Jaruzelski, Wojciech, 742
Jaspers, Karl, 775
Jaures, Jean, 634
Jefferson, Thomas, 492, 503, 504,
    508, 607
Jena, Battle of, 526
Jenner, Edward, 644
Jerusalem, 756
Jesuits, 424, 425
Jews, 597; Hitler's persecution of,
    691, 694, 712; and Zionism,
    754
John Anderson My Jo, 571
John Paul I, Pope, 770
John Paul II, Pope, 770–771
John XXIII, Pope, 771
Joseph II, Holy Roman Emperor,
    493
Journalism, 651–652
Joyce, James, 775
July (1830) Revolution, 548
June Days, 550
Junkers, 539–540, 587
Jutland, Battle of, 666

Kadar, Janos, 740
Kafka, Franz, 775
Kandinsky, Vasili, 777
Kant, Immanuel, 570
Kapital, Das (Marx), 565
Kapp, Wolfgang, 690
Karlowitz, Treaty of, 450–451
Kashmir, 751
Kaunitz, Count, 444
Kay, John, 557
Keats, John, 571
Kellogg-Briand Pact, 699, 703
Kennedy, John F., 738
Kennedy, Robert, 738
Kenya, 759
Kenyatta, Jomo, 760

Kepler, Johann, 480–481
Kerensky, Alexander, 677
Keynes, John Maynard, 773
Kiev, 445
Khomeini, Ayatollah, 757
Kierkegaard, Sören, 775
Kim Il-Sung, 750
King, Martin Luther, Jr., 738
King George's War, 462
King William's War, 461
Kipling, Rudyard, 616, 652
Kirov, Sergei, 681
Kitchener, Horatio Herbert, 623
Knights of Labor, 612
Koch, Robert, 644
Kohl, Helmut, 736
Korean War, 731, 747, 750–751
Kornilov, Lavr Georgyevich, 677
Kosciusko, Thaddeus, 450
Kossuth, Louis, 551
Kosygin, Aleksei Nicolayavich, 735
Kropotkin, Peter, 634
Krupp Works, *631*
Kulaks, 678, 680
Kuliscioff, Anna, 639
Kulturkampf, 599, 646
Kun, Bela, 684
Kuomintang party, 620, 746–747

Labor unions, 559–562, 612–613,
    633, 649
Labour party in Great Britain, 633–
    634, 700, 733
Laissez Faire, 492, 515, 563–564
Lamantine, Alphonse de, 550
Landsberg concentration camp, *708*
Lang, Fritz, 779
Language Groups, Austria-Hun-
    gary, *603*
Laos, 754
Lateran Treaty, 689
Latin America, 530, 760–761; 1989,
    761
La Traviata (Verdi), 575
Laud, William, 431
Laval, Pierre, 709
La Vie de Jésus, 647
Law, John, 426
Law of Rent, 563
Lawrence, Thomas, 473
League of Augsburg, 426; war of,
    461
League of Nations, 670–672, 684,

    690, 694, 697, 699, 702; break-
    down of, 703–704
Lebanon, 756
Lebensraum, 691
Le Corbusier (Charles-Edouard
    Jeanneret), 777
Leeuwenhoek, Antoni van, 484
Leibnitz, Wilhelm, 484
Leipzig, Battle of, 530
Le Nain, Louis, *466*
Lenin, Vladimir, 602, 675–678
Leo XIII, Pope, 599, 648
Letters on the English, 489
Levée en masse, 520, 528
Levellers, 432, 434
Leviathan, 484
Levi-Strauss, Claude, 773
Lexington, Battle of, 503
Leyte Gulf, Battle of, 719
Liberal party, 548
Liberalism and revolution, 1830–
    1850, 544–554; assessment of,
    553–554; liberal revolutions in
    Belgium and France, 548–549;
    nature of nineteenth-century
    liberalism, 545–546; political
    and social reform in Great Brit-
    ain, 547–548; revolution of 1848,
    550–553
Liberty, Equality, Fraternity, 511,
    530–531
Liberum veto, 449
Liegnitz, 445
Life of Jesus, 647
Lincoln, Abraham, 611
Lister, Joseph, 644
Liszt, Franz, 575
Literacy, 651
Literature: American, 609; realistic,
    653–655; romantic, 571–573; sev-
    enteenth and eighteenth cen-
    tury, 470–472; twentieth cen-
    tury, 775–776
Litvinov, Maxim, 684
Liu Shaoqui, 749
Livingstone, David, 623
Livonia, 447
Lloyd George, David, 596, 669, 672,
    700
Locarno Pact, 699
Locke, John, 436, 439, 484, 488,
    492
Locomotive, 558
Lodge, Henry Cabot, 702

Logarithms, 484
Logical Positivism, 775
Lohengrin, 575
London Slum, *561*
London Working Mens Association, 562
Long Parliament, 431, 433, 434
Longfellow, Henry Wadsworth, 609
Lorentz, Hendrik, 642
Lorrain, Claude, 473
Louis Philippe, King of France, 549, 550
Louis XIII, King of France, 420, 421
Louis XIV, King of France, 435, 436, 442–443, 453, 495; absolutism and religion, 424–425; age of, 417–428; court, 422–424; economy, 424; government, 422; wars of aggression, 425–426
Louis XV, King of France, 426, 492
Louis XVI, 493
Louis XVIII, 536
Louisburg, 462
Louisiana Territory, 453, 462; purchase of, 525
Louvois, Francois-Michel Le Tellier, 425
Luddite riots, 561
Ludendorff, Erich F., 666, 668, 690
Lully, 475
Lvov, Georgi, 676
Lyell, Charles, 643
Lyrical Ballads, 571
Lytton Commission, 703

McAdam, John, 557
MacArthur, Douglas, 719, 745, 750
McCarthy, Joseph (McCarthyism), 737
Macauley, Thomas, 569
MacDonald, Ramsay, 700
MacMahon, Marshal, 592
Madame Bovary (Flaubert), 654
Madras, 455, 462
Magenta, Battle of, 586
Magic Flute, The (Mozart), 476
Maginot line, 701, 709
Maintenon, Madame de, 424
Malacca, 455
Malenkov, Georgi, 739
Mali, 459
Malpighi, 644

Malthus, Thomas, 563
Manchu dynasty, 459
Manchurian incident, 696–454
Manet, Edouard, 656
Manhattan Island, Dutch colony, 454
Manifest Destiny, *607*
Mann, Thomas, 775
Mannheim, Karl, 773
Mao Tse-tung, 747, 749
Marat, Jean Paul, 518–519
March on Rome, 688
Marconi, Guglielmo, 632
Marengo, Battle of, 525
Maria Theresa, Archduchess of Austrian Hapsburg dominions, 444
Marie de Medicis, 420
Maritain, Jacques, 771
Marne, Battle of, 666
Marriage, early modern times, 468–469, 501; nineteenth century, 562; twentieth century, 767–768
Marriage of Figaro, The (Mozart), 476
Marshall, George, 730
Marshall Plan, 730, 732
Marx, Karl, 565–566, 633
Marxism, 565–566, 633–634, 775
Mary II, Queen of England, 435, 436
Mathematics, 481, 484
Matisse, Henri, 656, 777
Mau Mau in Kenya, 759
Maximilian, emperor of Mexico, 585
Mayas, 455–456
Mayor of Casterbridge, The (Hardy), 654
Mazarin, Jules, Cardinal, 421–424, 494
Mazzini, Giuseppe, 553, 569, 585
Medicine: eighteenth century, 465; nineteenth century, 643–644; twentieth century, 772–773
Medieval Town on a River, *568*
Medieval View of the Universe, *480*
Mein Kampf (My Struggle) (Hitler), 690
Meistersingers, The, 575
Mendeleev, Dmitri, 642
Mendelssohn, Felix, 475
Mensheviks, 677
Mercantilism, 424, 460, 461, 493
Messiah, The (Handel), 476
Metaxas, General Ioannis, 694

Methodism, 470
Metric System, 521
Metropolis, 779
Metternich, Klemens von, 534, 536, 538, 543, 551
Metternich System, 536
Meunier, Constanin, 657
Mexico, 585, 762
Michael Romanov, Tsar, 446
Michel, Louise, 639
Michelet, Jules, 569, 573
Microscope, 484
Middle class, 559, 637, 766; *see* Social Classes and Structure
Middle East, 622–623, 754–757; 1989, *755*
Midway, Battle of, 716
Mill, John Stuart, 564
Millet, Jean Francois, 573–574
Milton, John, 471
Milyukov, Pavel, 676
Mirabeau, 514
Mirs, 601
Misanthrope, Le, 471
Missionaries, nineteenth-century Christian, 649
Mississippi Bubble, 426
Mitterand, François, 735
Modernists, 648
Moguls, 457, 462
Molière, 471
Molly Maguires, 561
Moltke, Helmuth von, 592
Monet, Claude, *655*, 656
Mongols, 445
Monnet Plan, 734
Monroe Doctrine, 536
Montesquieu, Baron de, 492
Montgomery, Bernard, 716
Moon walk, *772*
Moravian Brethren, 470
Morgan, J. P., 612
Morocco, 625–626, 663, 757
Morse, Samuel F. B., 632
Moses, 359
Motion, three laws of, 480
Mountain, 519
Mozart, Wolfgang Amadeus, *475*, 476
Mugabe, Robert, 759
Munich Conference, 684–685, *705*, 706
Municipal Corporations Act, 548
Muscovy, 445

Music: classical, 475–476; modern, 658; opera, 475–476, 575; romantic, 575; twentieth century, 777–779
Mussolini, Benito, 687–690, 704–706; and World War II, 709, 711, 719

Nagasaki, 719
Nanking, Treaty of, 618, 621
Nantes, Edict of, 420, 421, 425, 442–443
Napier, John, 484
Napoleon Bonaparte, 521, 523–532; Consulate, 524–526; decline and fall of Empire, 526–528; effect on Latin America, 530; Empire, 526–528; evaluation of, 529; rise to power, 524; significance of Revolution and, 530–531
Napoleon, Louis. See Napoleon III
Napoleon III, 550, 553, 592; Second Empire of, 582–585
Napoleonic Code, 525
Nasser, Gamel Abdul, 754–755
National Assembly of France, 513–516
National Convention of France, 519–521
National movements in Southeast Europe, 602–604
National Socialism, 690–691, 694; causes of, 693; see also Nazi Germany
National Union of Women's Suffrage Societies, 639
National workshops, 550
Nationalism, philosophy of, 652–653
Nationalism and nation-state, 581–593; and imperialism, 616–617; Cavour and making of Italian unity, 585–586; German unification, 587–592; nature of, 582; Second Empire of Napoleon III, 582–585; United States, 607–609
Native Americans, 455–457, 495
Native terror bands, 759
NATO, 730, 742
Navigation Acts, 433, 461, 502
Nazi Germany, 694–695; concentra-

tion camps, 708, 712; empire of, 712; fall of, 719
Nazism, 690–691; causes, 693
Nehru, Jawaharlal, 751–752
Nelson, Lord, 526
NEP (New Economic Policy) 678–680
Nepmen, 678, 680
Netherlands: 709; art, 440; challenge to absolutism, 437–440, 494–495; competition for overseas empire, 454, 455, 460–462; Reformed Church, 438
Nevada, annexation of, 608
New Deal, 703
New Economic Policy (NEP), 678–680
New Harmony, Indiana, 565
New Imperialism, 615–628
New Lanark, 565
New Mexico, annexation of, 608
New Model Army, 432–434
New Order, Hitler's, 712
"New Shoes for H," 764
New World, the English, the French, and the Dutch, 453–454
New World Frontier, 454
New York City, chief port, 558
New Zealand, 627, 700
Newton, Isaac, 477, 478, 481, 484, 485, 488
Nicaragua, 762
Nicholas I, Tsar, 542, 553, 584
Nicholas II, Tsar, 602, 676
Niebuhr, Reinhold, 771
Niemöller, Martin, 694
Nietzsche, Friedrich, 653, 774
Nigeria, 759–760
Night, The, 689
Night Watch, 473
Nightingale, Florence, 584
Nimitz, Chester, 719
Nixon, Richard M., 738
Nkrumah, Kwame, 760
Nobility; see Social Classes and Structure
Noblesse de la robe, 511
Nonjuring clergy, 516
North Atlantic Treaty Organization (NATO), 730, 742
North German Confederation, 591

Norway, 598–599, 709
Notables, Assembly of, 513
Nouvelle, Vague, 776
Novum Organum, 482
Nuclear Test Ban Treaty, 731
Nuclear War, 780
Nuremberg, 442
Nystad, Treaty of, 447

"Ocean Devils," 459
OEEC (Organization of European Economic Cooperation), 732, 742–743
Oil Crisis, 756
Old Believers, 446
Oliver Twist (Dickens), 654
Olmutz, humiliation of, 587
On the Law of War and Peace (Grotius), 439
O'Neill, Eugene, 776
Open Door policy, 620
Opera, 475, 476, 575
Orange, House of, 438
Orange Free State, independence of, 623
Order Number I, 677
Oregon country, 608
Organization of American States (OAS), 762
Organization of European Economic Cooperation (OEEC), 732, 742–743
Origin of Inequality Among Men, 490
Origin of Species, The, 643, 646
Orlando, Vittorio, 669
Orleans, Duke of, 426
Ortega y Gasset, José, 775
Ottoman Empire, 450–451, nineteenth century, 584, 603–604, 622–623; twentieth century, 663–665
Overseas colonization and competition for empire, 452–463, 495; English, French, and Dutch in the New World, 453–454; European penetration of the Far East and Africa, 455; impact on the Far East, 457–459; impact on native Americans, 455–547; impact on sub-Saharan Africa,

459–460; struggle of overseas empire, 460–462

Overseas Migration, 1850–1914, 634–635

Overseas Possessions, 1763, *457*

Owen, Robert, 565

Pacific front, victory on, 719

Painting: Dutch, 440; seventeenth and eighteenth centuries, 472–473

Pakistan, 751, 752

Palestine Liberation Organization, 756

Palestinians, 754–756

Palmerston, Lord, 548

Panama Canal, 632

Pankhurst, Emmeline, *638*, 639

Papal infallibility, doctrine of, 647

Papandreou, Andreas, 737

Papen, Franz von, 691, 692

Paradise Lost (Milton), 471

Paris, Treaty of, 444, 462

Paris Commune, 596

Paris Peace Conference, 669–674; *see also* Versailles, Treaty of

Parlements, 426, 428, 512, 515

Parliament, English, 430–437, 495

Parliamentary Reform Act of 1911, 596

Parsons, Charles, 630–631

Pascal, Blaise, 425, 471

Pasternak, Boris, 776

Pasteur, Louis, 484

Patel, Pierre "the Elder," *419*

Paul VI, Pope, 770

Pavlov, Ivan, 644

Peace of Amiens, 525–526

Peace of Hubertusburg, 444

Peace of Paris, 1856, 584, 586

Peale, Charles Willson, 609

Pearl Harbor, *713*, 715

Peasants, and French Revolution, 512, 518, 520; nineteenth century, 559; seventeenth and eighteenth centuries, 465–466; *see* Social Classes and Structure

Peel, Robert, 548

Penal code, reform of, 548

Pendulum clock, 484

Penicillin, 772

Penny post, 548

People's Charter, 548

Perestroika, 740

Perry, Matthew C., 621

Pershing, John J., 668

Persia, 623

Petain, Philippe, 709

Peter I, the Great, Tsar of Russia, 447–448, 450, 495

Peter III, Tsar, 444, 448

Peterloo Massacre, *533*, 542

Petit Journal, Le, 651–652

Petition of Rights, 431

Petrograd, 676–677

Philippines, 719

Philosophes, 488–491, 493, 496

Philosophy: idealism, 569–570; nineteenth century, 652–653; *philosophes*, 488–490; twentieth century, 774–775

Physics: nineteenth and twentieth century, 641–642, 771–772; in Scientific Revolution, 478–483

Physiocrats, 492, 493

Picasso, Pablo, *650*, 656–657, *776*, 777

Pickwick Papers, The (Dickens), 654

Pietism, 469–470

Pilsudaski, Josef, 695

Pissarro, Camille, 656

Pitt, William, 462

Pius IX, Pope, 647

Planck, Max, 771

Planetary motion, three laws of, 480–481

Plantation system in New World, 453

Plehve, Vyacheslav K., 602

Plekhanov, Gregory, 677

Poe, Edgar Allan, 572

Poetry: romantic, 570–572; seventeenth and eighteenth century, 471–472

Poincaré, Raymond, 701

Poland, 442, 444, 448–450, 495, 695, 706–707, 740–742

Polish Corridor, 670, 706

Politburo, 682

Politics and the wars of religion, 405–415; *see also* Wars of Religion

Politiques, 420

Pompidou, Georges, 734

Pondicherry, 455, 462

Pope. *See* Papacy

Pope, Alexander, 471

Popular Front, 701, *702*

Population, early modern times, 465, 500; nineteenth century, 558–559, 608, 634–636; twentieth century, 672, 719, 765

Portugal, 438, 455, 460, 695, 727; since World War II, 736–737

Positivism, 645

Post Dispatch, St. Louis, 651

Postindustrial society, 766

Potato, 465, 466

Potsdam Conference, 728

Poussin, Nicolas, 472–473

Power loom, 557

Pragmatic Sanction, 444

Pragmatism, 653

Prague, Treaty of, 591

Prefect, 525

Presbyterianism, 431, 432, 433, 434, 436

Prime Minister, office of, 437

Primogeniture, 506, 541

Principia (The Mathematical Principles of Natural Knowledge), 481

Principles of Geology, 643

Principles of Morals and Legislation, 564

Principles of Political Economy and Taxation, The, 563

Prisoner of Chillon, The, 574

Progress, Politics in the age of, 1871–1914, 594–605

Progressivism, 613

Project Ultra, 711

Prokofiev, Serge, 682

Proletariat, industrial, 559–562

Protectorate, 434

Proudhon, Pierre Joseph, 634

Proust, Marcel, 775–776

Provincial Letters, 471

Prussia, 441; conservatism, 539–540, 553; growth of, 1614–1807, *443*, 495; revolution of, 1848, 553; rise of, 442–445

Psychoanalysis, 644–645

Psychology, 773

Ptolemy, 478–482

Public education, established, 651

Public Safety, Committee of, 520

Pugachev, 448
Pulitzer, Joseph, 651
Purcell, Henry, 475
Pure food and drug acts, 613
Puritans, 430–433, 495
Pushkin, Alexander, 573
"Putting-out" system, 467
Pythagoras, 479
Quadruple Alliance, 536
Quakers, 470
Quantum theory, 771
Quebec, 420, 453, 462
Quebec Act, 503
Queen Anne's War, 461
Quesnay, François, 492

Racine, Jean, 425, 471
Racism, 652–653, 690–691, 712
Radar, 711
Radioactivity, 642
Radium, discovery of, 642
Railroad building, era of, 632
Ranke, Leopold von, 645
Rasputin, Grigori Efimovich, 676
Razin, Stenka, 446
Reagan, Ronald, 731, 739
Red Brigade, 736
Red Guards, 749
Red Sunday, 602
Reform Bill of 1832, 544–545, 547–548
Reform Bill of 1867, 595
Reform Bill of 1884, 596
Reformed Church, Dutch, 438
Reign of Terror, 518–521
Relativity, theory of, 642–643, 771
Religion: absolutism and, 424; Enlightenment and, 491; French Revolution, 516; growth of pietism, 469–470; Hinduism, 457; nineteenth century, 525, 645, 649; twentieth century, 683–684, 694, 770–771; see also Christianity, Papacy, Roman Catholic church
Rembrandt, 439, 440, 473
Remembrance of Things Past, 775
Renan, Ernest, 647
Renoir, Auguste, 656
Rent, law of, 563
Republican party, 611, 613

Rerum Novarum, 648–649
Restoration and Reaction, 533–543; Bourbon restoration in France, 538–539; Concert of Europe, 536–538; Congress of Vienna, 534–536; conservatism in Great Britain, 540–543; in the Germanies, 539–540; in Italy, 540
Restoration of Stuarts, 434–435
Return of the Native, The (Hardy), 654
Revolutionary Tribunal, 520
Revolutionary War Campaigns, 505
Revolutions, age of, 497–577; 1848, 550–554; American, 499–509; era of Napoleon, 523–532; French, 510–522; Industrial, 555–567; Liberalism, 544–554; Restoration and reaction, 533–543
Reynolds, Joshua, 473
Rhee, Syngman, 750
Rhine, Confederation of, 526
Rhineland; occupied by Germany, 704
Rhodes, Cecil, 625
Rhodesia, independence from Great Britain, 759
Ricardo, David, 563
Richardson, Samuel, 472
Richelieu, Armand-Jean du Plessis, Cardinal, 410n., 420–424, 494
Rightist dictatorships, 760
Rights of Man and Citizen, Declaration of, 514
Rigoletto, 575
Rimsky-Korsakov, Nikolai, 658
Risorgimento, 585
Robbe-Grillet, Alain, 776
Robespierre, Maximilien de, 518–521, 531
Rockefeller, John D., 612, 633
Rococo, 470, 475
Rodin, Auguste, 656
Roentgen, Wilhelm von, 642
Roman Catholic Center, 599
Roman Catholic church: and Fascist Italy, 688; in Latin America, 760, 762; and Nazi Germany, 694; response to nineteenth century challenges, 647–649; Second Vatican Council, 770; see also Christianity, Papacy
Romanov, Tsar Michael, 446

Romanticism, 568–577; in arts, 573–757; in literature, 570–573; nature of, 569; philosophy of idealism, 569–570
Rome, Treaty of, 742
Rommel, Erwin Johannes, 716
Romney, George, 473
Roosevelt, Franklin D., 703, 704, 712–716
Roosevelt, Theodore, 613, 703
Rotten boroughs, 547
Roundheads, 432
Rousseau, Henri, 569–570
Rousseau, Jean-Jacques, 471, 472, 490, 492
Royal absolutism. See Absolutism, royal age of
Royal Society, 479
Rubens, Peter Paul, 472, 473
Rumania, 711, 728, 740
Rump Parliament, 433
Russell, Bertrand, 774
Russell, John, 548
Russia, 444, 448, 450; before Peter the Great, 445–447; growth in the West, 446; nineteenth century, 542, 584, 601–602; rise of, 380, 445–448, 451, 495; under Catherine the Great, 448; under Peter the Great, 447–448 ; see also Soviet Union
Russian Orthodox Church, 447
Russian Revolution and communism, 675–685; Bolsheviks in power, 677–680; five-year plans and purges, 680–681; revolution of 1917, 676–677; rise of Bolsheviks, 677; Soviet Union and the world, 684–685; totalitarian control, 681–684
Rutherford, Ernest, 642, 771

Sadat, Anwar, 755, 756
St. Helena, 530
St. Jerome in His Study, 454
St. Paul's, London, 475
St. Peter's Basilica, 474
St. Petersburg, 446
Saint-Saens, Camille, 658
Saint-Simon, Duke de, 471
Saint-Simon, Henri de, 564, 565
Salazar, Antonio, 736

Sand, George, 573
San Martin, José, 530
Sans-culottes, 520
Sans Souci Palace, 475
Sarajevo, 665
Saratoga, Battle of, 504
Sardinia, 585–586
Sartre, Jean-Paul, 775
Savoy, house of, 585
Say, J. B., 564
Scarlatti, Alessandro, 475
Schiller, Friedrich, 572
Schinkel, Karl Friedrich, *568*
Schleiermacher, Friedrich, 569
Schleswig-Holstein question, 590
Schlieffen, Alfred von, 666
Schmidt, Helmut, 736
Schoenberg, Arnold, 777
Scholasticism, 482, 483
Schönbrunn Palace, 456
Schopenhauer, Arthur, 652–653
Schubert, Franz, 575
Schumann, Robert, 575
Schuschnigg, Kurt von, 694
Science, challenges to Christianity,
    645–647; Christian response to,
    647–649; nineteenth and early
    twentieth century physical, bio-
    logical, and medical, 642–644;
    rise of social science, 644–645;
    scientific revolution, 477–485;
    twentieth century, 771–774
Scientific academies, 479
Scientific instruments, 484
Scientific methodology, 482–483
Scientific Revolution, 477–485, 495–
    496; astronomy and physics,
    479–481; causes and spread,
    478–479; scientific methodology,
    482–483
Scotland, 431, 434, 436
Scott, Sir Walter, 569, 571
Scripture, higher criticism of, 648
Sculpture, modern, 657
Sebastopol, 524
Second Coalition, 524
Second Discourse, 492
Second Five-Year Plan: China, 747;
    Soviet Union, 681
Second Treatise of Civil Government,
    488
Seed drill, 467
Sepoy Mutiny, 627

Serbia, 663–665
Settlement, Act of, 436
Seven Years' War (French and In-
    dian War in America), 444, 462,
    493
Sévigné, Marie de Rabutin-Chantal,
    471
Sex, *see* Family; Marriage
Shaw, George Bernard, 634, 654
Shelley, Percy Bysshe, 569, 571
Sheridan, Richard, 472
Sherman Antitrust Act of 1890, 613
Short Parliament, 431
Shostakovich, Dimitri, 682
Sibelius, Jan, 658
Siberia, Russia's conquest of, 445
Siegfried, 575
Siemens brothers, 630
Sièys, Abbé, 524
Silesia, 444
Silk culture, 420
Sino-Soviet Split, 739
Sister Carrie, 654
Six-Day War (1967), 755
Slavery: and American Civil War,
    609–611; impact on Africa, 459–
    460; plantation system and,
    453, 455, 609
Smith, Adam, 489, 492, 563
Soares, Mario, 736–737
Social change, early modern times,
    430, 466–467; nineteenth cen-
    tury, 558–562, 636–638; Soviet
    Union, 682–683; twentieth cen-
    tury, 712–713, 765–771
Social class, 559–562
Social classes and structure, early
    modern times, 442, 465–467;
    500–501; nineteenth century,
    511–512, 559–562, 636–638;
    twentieth century, 629, 636–637,
    683, 766
Social Contract, The (Rousseau), 490,
    492
Social Democratic party, German,
    599, 601, 634, 690, 692; Great
    Britain, 732
Social science, rise of, 644–645
Social welfare, nineteenth century,
    562, 583–584, 596, 598–599, 613,
    635–636; twentieth century,
    701–703, 732–742, 769–770
Socialism, 633–634; France, 634;

German, 599, 601, 634, 735–736;
    Marxian, 565–566; Russian, 677;
    Utopian, 564–565
Society, faith, and culture in the
    seventeenth and eighteenth
    centuries, 464–476; agricultural
    revolution, 466–467; cottage in-
    dustry, 467; family, 467–469;
    growth of pietism, 469–470; lit-
    erature, 470–472; music, 475–
    476; painting and architecture,
    472–475; population growth,
    465; rural life, 465–466; urban
    life, 417; women, 469
Society of Friends (Quakers), 399,
    470
Solferino, Battle of, 586
Solidarity, 741–742
Solzhenitszen, Alexander, 776
Somalia, independence to, 759
Somme, Battle of the, 666
Songhay, 459
Sophia Palaeologus, 445
South Africa, Union of, 627, 759
South-West Africa (Namibia), 759
Southern Asia, revolt of, 751–754
Southern Confederacy, 611
Southern Plantation, Northern Fac-
    tory, *611*
Soviet Union: Bolsheviks in power,
    1917–1927, 675, 677–680; Cold
    War, 728–732; culture and soci-
    ety, 682–683; five-year plans
    and purges, 680–681; peace pact
    with Germany, 706–707, 709;
    political system, 682; postwar
    peace settlements, 726–728; reli-
    gious policy, 683–684; revolu-
    tion and communism in Russia,
    675–685; rise of Bolsheviks, 677;
    Russian revolution of 1917,
    676–677; since World War II,
    739–740, totalitarian control,
    681–684; and the world, 684–
    685; and World War II, 709,
    711–712, 715–716, 718–719
Sower, The, 573
Spain, 545; civil war, 695, 704–705;
    death of Franco, 737; since
    World War II, 736–737; War of
    Spanish Succession, 426, 461
Spartacists, 690
Speer, Albert, 712

Spencer, Herbert, 645–647
Spener, Philipp, 470
Spengler, Oswald, 774
Spice Islands, 455
Spinning jenny, 557
Spinning mule, 557
Spinola, Antonio de, 736
Spinoza, Baruch, 439
Spirit of the Laws, The (Montes-
    queiu), 492
Sputnik, 737
Stadholder, Dutch, 437–438
Stael, Madame de, 573
Stalin, Joseph, 678–685, 706, 731,
    739; death of, 731; post-war set-
    tlement, 726–728; and World
    War II, 711, 716
Stalingrad, Battle of, 716
Stamp Act Congress, 503
Standard Oil Company, 612, 633
Stanley, Henry Morton, 623
Star Chamber, 431
States General, 438
Statue of Liberty, 636
Steam engine, 556–558, 630–631
Steamship, 558, 631
Stearns, Junius Brutus, 499
Stein, Baron von, 528
Stephenson, George, 558
Stock Market Crash, 702–703
Storming of Bastille, 514, 515
Stradivari, family, 475
Strategic Arms Limitation Treaty,
    731–732
Strategic Defense Initiative, 731
Strauss, David, 647
Strauss, Richard, 658, 777
Stravinsky, Igor, 658, 777
Stresemann, Gustav, 690
Stuart, Gilbert, 609
Stuart absolutism, 430–432, 494
Stuarts, restoration of the, 434–435
Subjection of Women, 564
Submarine, 667–668
Sub-Saharan Africa, European ex-
    pansion in, 459–460
Sudan, 623
Suez Canal, 622, 632, 755
Suffrage, nineteenth century, 547–
    548, 595–596, 598, 607; twen-
    tieth century, 609, 613, 639,
    695–696
Sulfa drugs, 772

Sullivan, Louis Henry, 657–658,
    777
Sully, Duke of, 420
Sun King. See Louis XIV
Sun Yat-sen, 620, 746
Superpowers, recovery of Europe
    and, 725–743
Surplus value, 566
Surrealism, 777
Swahili civilization, 459–460
Swastika, 691
Sweden, 414, 447, 450
Swedenborg, Emanuel, 470
Swift, Jonathan, 472
Syllabus of Errors, 647
Syndics of the Cloth Guild, 439, 473
System of Synthetic Philosophy, 645

Taine, Hippolyte, 652
Talleyrand (Charles-Maurice de Tal-
    leyrand-Perigord), 534
Tamerlane, 457
Tannenberg, Battle of, 666
Tannhäuser, 575
Tchaikovsky, Peter, 658
Tea Act, 503
Teheran Conference, 726
Telegraph, 632
Telescope, 484
Telford, Thomas, 557
Tennis Court Oath, 511, 514
Tennyson, Alfred Lord, 653
Tesla, Nikola, 631
Tess of the D'Urbervilles, 654
Test Act, 435
Texas, annexation of, 608
Textile industry, 467
Thatcher, Margaret, 733
Theology, 770–771
Thermidorian Reaction, 521
Thinker, The, 656, 657
Third Estate, 511–514
Third French Republic, 596–598
"Thirty Tyrants of France," 421
Thirty Years' War, 421, 422, 431, 465
Thomas Aquinas, 556, 570
Thomas-Gilchrist process, 630
Thoreau, Henry David, 572
Three Emperors' League, 600, 663
Three Musketeers, The, 573
Thus Spake Zarathustra, 653
Tillich, Paul, 771

Tilsit, Treaties of, 526
Time of Troubles (Russian), 445, 448
Times, London, 651
Tintern Abbey, 571
Tito, Marshal, 740
Tokugawa Shogun, 459
Toleration Act, 436
Tolstoy, Leo, 654–655
Tories, 435, 436, 542, 547, 548
Totalitarian system: fascism, author-
    itarianism, and, 686–697; in the
    Soviet Union, 681–684
Toulon, siege of, 524
Townshend, Charles, 467
Townshend Acts, 502
Trades Union Congress, 633
Treaties of Tilsit, 526
Treaty of Aix-la-Chapelle, 444
Treaty of Frankfurt, 592
Treaty of Nystad, 447
Treaty of Paris, 444, 462
Treaty of Prague, 591
Treaty of Utrecht, 426
Treaty of Versailles, 671–674, 691,
    694, 699
Treaty of Westphalia, 437
Treitschke, Heinrich von, 652
Trench Warfare, 662
Triennial Act, 434
Triple Alliance, 600, 663
Triple Entente, 600, 663, 665
Troppau, Congress of, 536
Trotsky, Leon, 677–680
Trovatore, Il, 575
Truman, Harry S., 728–730, 745
Truman Doctrine, 730
Tudors, 430
Tull, Jethro, 467
Tunisia, 757
Turenne, Vicomte de, 425, 426
Turgenev, Ivan Sergeyevich, 654–
    655
Turgot, Anne Robert Jacques, 493,
    513
Turkey, 665, 666, 668, 737
Turks. See Ottoman Turks
Turner, J. M. W., 571, 573
Turnip, 466, 467
Two Treatises on Civil Government
    (Locke), 436, 492

Uitlanders, 625
Ulm, Battle of, 526

Ulyanov, Vladimir Ilich. *See* Lenin, Vladimir
Uniformity, Act of, 434
Union, Act of, 436
Union Congress of Soviets, 682
Union of South Africa, 700
Unions, labor and trade, 561, 612, 667, 688, 694
United Kingdom. *See* Great Britain
United Nations, 727, 743
United Provinces of the Netherlands, 437, *438*, 439
United Socialist party, 634
United States, 492; American Revolution, 499–509; civil war, 609–611; Cold War, 728–732; colonial society, 500–502; constitution of, 507; democracy and geographical expansion, 606–609; industrialization and urbanization, 611–613; intervention in Latin America, 762; intervention in Russian civil war, 678; isolationism, boom and bust in, 701–703; Korean War, 731, 750–751; launching new nation, 506–508; Marshall Plan, 730, 732; occupation of Japan, 745; postwar settlement and Cold War, 726–732; reform and progressivism, 613; slavery, civil war, and reconstruction, 609–611; Territorial Expansion of, *608*; Vietnam War, 752–754; World War I, 667–669, 701–703; World War II, 712–719; since World War II, 737–739
Urban classes, *629*
Urbanization, early modern times, 467; in seventeenth and eighteenth centuries, 467; nineteenth century, 558–562, 611–613, 635–636; twentieth century, 765–766
Utilitarianism, 564
Utopian Socialism, 564–565
Utrecht, Treaty of, 426

Vanderbilt, Cornelius, 612
van Gogh, Vincent, 656
Vatican Council: First, 647; Second, 770

Vauban, Sébastien, 424
Velásquez, Diego, 472
Vendée, rebellion, 520
Verdi, Giuseppe, 575
Verdun, Battle of, 666
Vermeer, Jan, 440, 473
Verona, Congress of, 536
Versailles, 419, 422–424, 474; Treaty of, 671–674, 691, 694, 699
Vesalius, Andreas, 483
Victor Emmanuel II, 586, *587*
Victor Emmanuel III, 688
Vienna: Congress of, 534–536, 623; siege of, 379; Treaty of, 623
Vietnam, 752–754
Villafranca, Agreement of, 586
Vindication of the Rights of Women, 491
Voltaire, 488–489, 490, 493
von Moltke, Helmuth, 592
von Papen, Franz, 691, 692
von Schuschnigg, Kurt, 695
von Stein, Baron, 528

Wagner, Richard, 575, 652, 658
Walesa, Lech, 741
Wallachia, 584
Walpole, Robert, 429, 437
War and Peace (Tolstoy), 655
War Communism, 678
War of 1812, 528, 607
War of 1870 (Franco-Prussian War), 592–593
War of the Austrian Succession, 444, 462
War of Independence. *See* American Revolution
War of the League of Augsburg, 461
War of the Spanish Succession, 426, 461
Warsaw Pact, 731, 741
Washington, George, 503, 504, 507–508, 643–644
Washington Naval Conference, 699
Water frame, 557
Watergate, 738
Waterloo, Battle of, 530, 534
Watt, James, 557
Wealth of Nations (Smith), 563
Webb, Beatrice, 634
Webb, Sidney, 634
Weber, Karl Maria von, 575

Weber, Max, 773
Webster, Daniel, 607
Weimar Republic, 689–690
Welfare state, 769–770
Wellington, Duke of (Arthur Wellesley), 528
Wells, H. G., 634
Wesley, Charles, 470
Wesley, John, 470
West Indies: British capture of, 462; English colonies, 453; French colonies, 454
Westminister, Statue of, 700, 759
Westphalia, Treaty of, 437
Whigs, 435, 436, 437
Whitefield, George, 470
Whitehead, Alfred North, 774
Whitney, Eli, 557, 609
Wilhelm II, German Kaiser, 622, 663, 665; German Empire under Bismarck and, 599–602
William I, King of Prussia, 587, 589–590, 592
William III, King of England, 426, 435, 436, 461
William of Orange. *See* William III, King of England
William Tell, 572
Wilson, Woodrow, 613, 668, *669*, 672, 701–702
Wireless telegraphy, 632
Wittgenstein, Ludwig, 775
Wollstonecraft, Mary, 491
Women: colonial American, 501; early modern times, 468–469; Enlightenment, 491; French Revolution, 514, 518, 521; Napoleonic code, 525; nineteenth century, 562, 564, 633, 638–639; seventeenth and eighteenth centuries, 469; Soviet, 683; suffrage, 596, 599, 613, 638–639, 767–769; twentieth century, 667, 683, 745, 768–769
Women's Liberation Movement, 768–769
Woolf, Virginia, 775
Wordsworth, William, 571
Working class, industrial, 559–562
Workers (working class); *see* Social Classes and Structure
Working-class organizations and ideologies, rise of, 633–634

Workshop with Mechanical Slaves, 555

World as Will and Idea, The, 652–653

World Council of Churches, 770

World, New York, 651

World War I, 662–674; beginning of, 665; causes, 673; effects of, 672, 674; entry of United States and allied victory, 667–669; Germany's near triumph, 665–666; home front, 666–667; origins of, 663–665, 673; peace settlement, 669–672

World War II, 708–723; allied victory, 716–719; background, 703; climate and turning point, 715–

716; early Axis victories, 709–712; entry of United States, 712–715; Nazi empire, 712, outbreak of, 706–707; recovery from, 725–743

Wren, Christopher, 475

Wright, Frank Lloyd, 777

Wright, Wilbur and Orville, 632

Wundt, Wilhelm, 644

X-rays, discovery of, 642

Yalta Conference, 727–728

Yom Kippur War, 756

Yorktown, 504

Young Italy, 553, 585

Yuan Shih-kai, 620

Yugoslavia, 711, 740

Zaibatsu, 695, 697, 745

Zeitgeist, 570, 652

Zetkin, Clara, 639

Zia ul-Haq, 752

Zimbabwe, 759

Zimmermann note, 668

Zinzendorff, Nikolaus Ludwig von, 470

Zionism, 646, 754

Zola, Emile, 597, 654

Zollverein, 540